Green Constitutionalism

Serkan Koybasi

Green Constitutionalism

An Anti-capitalist Legal Framework to Tackle Climate Change

PETER LANG
Berlin · Bruxelles · Chennai · Lausanne · New York · Oxford

Bibliographic information published by the Deutsche Nationalbibliothek.
The German National Library lists this publication in the German National Bibliography; detailed bibliographic data is available on the Internet at http://dnb.d-nb.de.

Library of Congress Cataloging-in-Publication Data
Names: Koybasi, Serkan, 1980- editor.
Title: Green constitutionalism: an anti-capitalist legal framework to tackle climate change / Serkan Koybasi.
Description: New York: Peter Lang, 2026. | Includes bibliographical references. |
Identifiers: LCCN 2025023500 (print) | LCCN 2025023501 (ebook) | ISBN 9783631936634 (hardcover) | ISBN 9783631924679 (pdf) | ISBN 9783631937075 (epub)
Subjects: LCSH: Climatic changes--Law and legislation. | Sustainable development--Law and legislation. | Constitutional law. | Environmental law, International. | Fossil fuels. | Capitalism.
Classification: LCC K3585 .G74 2026 (print) | LCC K3585 (ebook) | DDC 344.04/6--dc23/eng/20250521
LC record available at https://lccn.loc.gov/2025023500
LC ebook record available at https://lccn.loc.gov/2025023501

Cover image: Burcu Başar
Cover design by Peter Lang Group AG

ISBN 978-3-631-93663-4 (Print)
ISBN 978-3-631-92467-9 (ePDF)
ISBN 978-3-631-93707-5 (ePUB)
DOI 10.3726/b22859

Published by Peter Lang GmbH, Berlin (Germany)

info@peterlang.com

This publication has been peer reviewed.

www.peterlang.com

Table of Contents

Preface

This book is the product of nearly six years of work. Published first in Fall 2023 in Turkish, you are reading the English version of the revised and updated second edition, which I translated myself. Most of this time was spent reading and thinking, and the last period was spent in intensive writing. As the title suggests, the book is a book of law (constitutionalism) written on a scientific subject (climate change). Moreover, the source of the problem it seeks to solve is economic (capitalism). While this is then necessarily a multidisciplinary study, climatology and economics are not my specialities. Although I have tried to overcome my deficiencies in these areas as much as possible, I may have made mistakes. If readers would like to correct me, contribute, or share any criticism, I would be happy to hear their thoughts. My email address is: <serkan.koybasi@bau.edu.tr>

Because of this multidisciplinary perspective, there are places where the book inevitably moves away from law. But I do not think this is wrong; on the contrary, I think it is the right thing to do. As you will read in the following pages of the book, the mechanistic approach, which is one of the main causes of the climate change problem, is quite common in the academic world. Today, academia is organised into relatively autonomous 'disciplines'. The reason for this is the dominant view that scientific problems require scientific specialisations. However, this has led to disciplines losing contact with each other. Lawyers do not know much about biology; biologists do not know much about sociology; sociologists do not know much about climatology. However, suppose we accept science as 'the endeavour to understand the functioning of the world'. In that case, we should take into account that the world is not a collection of independent parts and that everything is interconnected. Therefore, disciplines of science need to communicate and cooperate. Accordingly, I would like to point out that the multidisciplinary structure of this book is not only a necessity but also an aim to establish such cooperation.

The constitutionalism I refer to in the book is referred to by different words in different works. The more common terms are 'ecological constitutionalism' and 'environmental constitutionalism'. I have avoided using the word 'ecological' because I find it too far removed from the social sciences. I also did not use the term 'environmental' unless it is necessary because I find it too anthropocentric. Instead, I have chosen to use the word 'green' to qualify the constitutionalism I propose in the book. I accept that this word has a political aspect, which is one of the reasons I chose it: the issue is very closely related to politics. Climate change is not just a climatological problem; it is also an economic and political problem. In the same way, law is not a field that can be understood only through legal science, but a system of rules that should be considered together with its economic and political roots and effects. Therefore, the reason why I chose this word is to emphasise that a new constitutionalist approach to tackling climate change will inevitably have a political dimension. Moreover, 'green' is neither the monopoly of a political party nor of any other group.

Finally, there are three people I would like to thank. Renin Yaykın is the first among them. Throughout our friendship, which started in high school and deepened at university, she has been influential not only in my thoughts but also in the formation of my character with her knowledge, political views and freedom. She read the book manuscript with incredible care, corrected my mistakes, gave me ideas and sometimes criticised and questioned me, helping my thoughts to mature. When I was tired or unsure of myself, her emails and messages were my biggest source of motivation. She has contributed a lot to making this book more accurate and more consistent. I am very lucky to have a friend like her.

Second, I would like to thank Prof Jennifer Curtin for inviting me to the University of Auckland as a visiting researcher at the beginning of 2024.

Without the wonderful working environment, she offered me at the Public Policy Institute, this English version would not have been possible.

Finally, I would like to thank Colin Donovan, who has been by my side throughout this whole process and has always supported me. I look forward to being together in future adventures.

Serkan Koybasi
January 2025, Auckland

Abbreviations

ANC	African National Congress
BP	British/Beyond Petroleum
COP	Conference of Parties
ECHR	European Convention on Human Rights
ECtHR	European Court of Human Rights
EPA	Environmental Protection Agency
EU	European Union
FIE	Friends of the Irish Environment
FSC	Federal Supreme Court
GDP	Gross Domestic Product
GFCC	German Federal Constitutional Court
IACtHR	Inter-American Court of Human Rights
IEA	International Energy Agency
IPCC	Intergovernmental Panel on Climate Change
KSG	*KlimaSchutzGesetz* (Climate Protection Act)
NAFTA	North American Free Trade Agreement
NASA	National Aeronautics and Space Administration
NDC	Nationally Determined Contributions
ppm	Parts per million
UK	United Kingdom
UN	United Nations
UN IPBES	United Nations Intergovernmental Science-Policy Platform on Biodiversity and Ecosystem Services

UNFCCC	United Nations Framework Convention on Climate Change
USA	United States of America
WHO	World Health Organization
WTO	World Trade Organization

Introduction

In Davos, where she was invited to give a speech, Greta Thunberg responded to the wealthy businesspeople who praised her for giving them hope:

> I don't want your hope. I don't want you to be hopeful. I want you to panic. I want you to feel the fear I feel every day. And then I want you to act. I want you to act as you would in a crisis. I want you to act as if the house is on fire. Because it is.[1]

She is right. That is no longer a metaphor. The average global temperature continues to rise, and forest fires are spreading across almost every continent, some of them on a gigantic scale. July 2023 was the hottest month on record. Temperatures exceeded 40°C in France, Italy and Greece, and thousands of people were forced to evacuate due to wildfires on the island of Rhodes.[2] In Phoenix, USA, temperatures did not drop below 43°C for weeks.[3] According to the European Copernicus climate service, 2024 was the first year to pass the 1.5°C global warming limit.[4] In early 2025, dozens of people and animals died, and many neighbourhoods were reduced to ashes in Los Angeles in wildfires fuelled by drought and Santa Ana winds. A total of 150,000 people

---

1 'Address at World Economic Forum: Our House is on Fire – 25 January 2019', *Iowa State University – Archives of Women's Political Communication*.

2 Nadeem Badshah, 'July Was World's Hottest Month on Record, Climate Scientists Confirm', *The Guardian*, 8 August 2023.

3 Daniel Cusick, 'Phoenix Roast in Record Breaking 110-Plus-Degree Heat, With No End in Sight', *Scientific American*, 17 July 2023.

4 Mark Poynting – Erwan Rivault – Becky Dale, '2024 First Year to Pass 1.5C Global Warming Limit', *BBC*, 10 January 2025.

were evacuated from their homes. This important city of the global film industry was like the star of a monster movie, and the monster was climate change.[5] While some parts of the world are scorching hot, others are experiencing flash floods or more frequent and stronger hurricanes. The climate system that sustains life on Earth is in crisis. Understanding the causes of this crisis, preventing it, and strengthening social and ecological[6] resilience is the responsibility of individuals, companies, institutions and states. However, in many parts of our planet, these continue to make decisions and practices that trigger crises and increase their impact instead of stopping their climate-damaging actions.[7] They act as if climate change does not exist so the current order can continue.

Here is a huge contradiction: We live in a society where elites claim to rule in a 'rational' way, but humanity has never been confronted with such insane, such total irrationality, not even in the darkest periods of history.[8] It is a mistake to believe that the threats of global warming are hypothetical and will materialise in the very distant future. Climatic upheaval means that in less than a century, the earth's climate will change in a way that humanity has never experienced in the equivalent of the last 20,000 years. Some object to these scientific predictions that are not certain. Maybe not 100 per cent, but they are certain at least 90 per cent. Is it reasonable to drag our feet in the face of such a grave danger with a probability of occurrence ranging from 90 per cent to 100 per cent?[9]

The reason for this contradiction is actually understandable. Although climate change is now taken for granted by scientists and many people, it is difficult for managers and companies to accept that 'uncomfortable

5 Alexis Soloski, 'Los Angeles Is Starring in an All-Too-Real Disaster Story', *The New York Times*, 11 January 2025.

6 The term ecology, first used by the German biologist Ernst Haeckel in 1866, derives from the Greek words '*oikos*' meaning place/home and '*logos*' meaning science/word/discourse. See Ruşen Keleş – Can Hamamcı – Aykut Çoban, *Çevre Politikası*, 7th ed., İmge, Ankara, 2012, p. 46.

7 Burcu Meltem Arık, 'Bir Arada İyi Yaşamı Yeryüzüyle (Birlikte) Öğrenerek Örmek: Biyomimikri', *in* Didem Bayındır – Mine Yıldırım (ed.), *Ekoloji: Bir Arada Yaşamın Geleceği*, Tellekt, Istanbul, 2022, pp. 449–50.

8 Daniel Tanuro, *L'Impossible le Capitalism vert* (Turkish version), trans. Volkan Yalçıntoklu, Habitus, Istanbul, 2011, p. 148.

9 Tanuro, *L'Impossible le Capitalism vert*, p. 45.

information' because it involves various obligations for them.[10] If they fulfil these obligations, they will no longer be able to do what they have been doing: polluting the world and damaging the ecosystem without constraints. Therefore, they do not prefer this. At the point climate change is at today, it should no longer be up to their choice.

It is time to take drastic measures to prevent climate change. Because the ecological crisis we are in is worse than we usually think. We are not discussing a crisis that can be solved with partial measures while our lives go on as usual. What is happening is the simultaneous collapse of multiple interconnected systems on which human beings are fundamentally dependent.[11] If these partial measures have any function at all, they are cosmetics to conceal the depth of the ecological crisis. In so doing, they divert public attention and theoretical understanding away from an adequate understanding of the depth and scope of the necessary changes.[12] Climate change means global warming, loss of biodiversity, poisoning of the air, depletion of potable water, melting of glaciers and many other vital systems no longer functioning simultaneously.

Moreover, this problem does not occur slowly but rather rapidly. A common misconception about the climate crisis is that it is a future catastrophe. However, climate change is a disaster that is happening now, not in some imaginary future, and it will only get worse unless we do something about it. Therefore, the fight against the climate crisis is not for tomorrow but for the here and now.[13]

Recently, one of the most important symbols of global warming has been a polar bear on a melting piece of ice. This photo made it seem as if climate change was only happening in places 'far away' from us, such as the Arctic. However, climate change is happening everywhere simultaneously, and we

---

10 M. Thompson – S. Rayner, 'Cultural Discourses', *in* Rayner – Malone, *Human Choice and Climate Change*, 1998, pp. 265–344, cited in: Mike Hulme, *Why We Disagree about Climate Change: Understanding Controversy, Inaction and Opportunity* (Turkish version), trans. Merve Özenç, Alfa, Istanbul, 2016, p. 10 (foreword by Steve Rayner).

11 Jason Hickel, *Less is More: How Degrowth Will Save the World* (Kindle edition), Windmill Books, London, 2021, p. 3.

12 Murray Bookchin, *The Ecology of Freedom – The Emergence and Dissolution of Hierarchy* (Turkish version), trans. Mustafa Kemal Coşkun, Sümer Yayıncılık, Istanbul, 2013, p. 71.

13 Foti Benlisoy, 'İklim Krizi ve Yaklaşan İç Savaş', *in* Didem Bayındır – Mine Yıldırım (ed.), *Ekoloji: Bir Arada Yaşamın Geleceği*, Tellekt, Istanbul, 2022, p. 185.

know we do not have the technology to prevent it today,[14] and we are not sure that we will have it any time soon. Therefore, we cannot rely on this uncertainty to go about our daily lives.

It is time to accept a simple but essential truth: We live in a dying world.[15] Of course, death is not a foreign concept to us. History of bloodshed is indeed richer than it should be, with a record of horrific wars, unspeakable torture, massacres, and any conceivable violation of fundamental rights. Yet, climate change is different from everything seen before. It is the first time we are confronted with a threat to the disappearance of all organised human life in any recognisable or known form.[16] For this reason, climate change is a common problem that requires collective action on a scale that humanity has failed to take.[17] Unfortunately, the efforts made so far could not unite us around reason and logic.

Oxford University physics professor Raymond Pierrehumbert, lead author of the 2018 report of the United Nations (UN) Intergovernmental Panel on Climate Change (IPCC),[18] one of the most important of these efforts, begins his assessment of current conditions and options as follows: *Let's put this on the table openly as soon as possible. Regarding climate change, yes, it is time to panic. We are in big trouble.*[19] This warning comes from a physics professor, bearing in mind that scientists are cautious; they do not usually say things that would cause us to panic.

---

14 David Wallace-Wells, *The Uninhabitable Earth: A Story of the Future* (Turkish version), trans. Ebru Kılıç, Domingo, Istanbul, 2020, p. 3.

15 Hickel, *Less is More*, p. 18.

16 Noam Chomsky – Robert Pollin, *Climate Crisis and the Global Green New Deal* (Turkish version), trans. Onur Orhangazi, Ütopya, Ankara, 2021, p. 20.

17 Naomi Klein, *On Fire: The Burning Case for a Green New Deal* (Turkish version), trans. Elif Sema Mutlu, Doğan Kitap, Istanbul, 2021, p. 148.

18 The Panel is established to provide governments with the main data they will use in their policymaking processes on climate change, and its main task is to review and report on all published scientific sources in the field of climate change. It does not produce science itself. See Levent Kurnaz, *Son Buzul Erimeden: İklim Değişikliği Hakkında Merak Etiniz Her Şey*, 3rd ed., Doğan Kitap, Istanbul, 2022, p. 190.

19 Raymond Pierrehumbert, 'There is No Plan B for Dealing with the Climate Crisis', *Bulletin of the Atomic Scientists*, 75: 5, 2019, pp. 215–21, cited in: Chomsky – Pollin, *Climate Crisis ...*, p. 25.

There is also a political transformation due to climate change. The green politics of how to save the world as we know it is now ubiquitous. No longer just environmental movements disconnected from other struggles, but *all* political actors have to take a position on climate change. However, the issue has become part of a series of competing foci and is constantly being twisted and bent according to the different commitments attached to it. The result is a divergence of opinion bubbling beneath a superficial consensus. On the one hand, more and more people see climate change as a life-threatening development, but on the other, there is no consensus on the social forces driving this process – or the social changes needed to stop it. While there is broad consensus on the scientific side of the issue, politicians and voters are fragmented.[20] That makes it impossible to act together and make firm decisions. In the meantime, precious time is being lost.

Some political innovations have started to emerge. For example, some businesses have entered the carbon market.[21] Action groups have mobilised against aviation expansion and coal power plants. Millions of people have signed up to voluntary emission reductions. However, the Earth's temperature, sea level, and greenhouse gas[22] emissions are still rising[23] because these measures do not approach the problem from a holistic perspective and do not focus on the root of the problem. Climate change is not a problem that can be solved with one or two independent fixes to the current system. The problem lies within the system itself. In other words, the entire capitalist economic infrastructure and the legal superstructure that protects it need to be questioned.

Nevertheless, we all, especially lawyers, have been taught to avoid a systematic and historical analysis of capitalism. Moreover, we were taught to separate almost every crisis created by the system – economic inequalities, violence

---

20 Nancy Fraser, 'Climates of Capital' (Turkish version), trans. Deniz Keskin, *in* Didem Bayındır – Mine Yıldırım (ed.), *Ekoloji: Bir Arada Yaşamın Geleceği*, Tellekt, Istanbul, 2022, p. 49.

21 A mechanism adopted by the Kyoto Protocol that allows signatories to trade emissions in order to meet their carbon emission reduction targets. See 'The Carbon Market', *UNFCCC*.

22 The term 'greenhouse gas' is used for gases that cause human-induced climate change. These are carbon dioxide, methane, diazot monoxide, ozone and chlorofluorocarbon gases. See Kurnaz, *Son Buzul Erimeden*, p. 22.

23 Hulme, *Why We Disagree …*, p. 338.

against women, white supremacy, endless wars, ecological destruction – with sharp walls and not to look at the whole. Therefore, one of the most urgent tasks today is to use every means possible to show how inextricably linked the crises we are experiencing are and how they can only be overcome through an inclusive vision of social and economic transformation.[24] Taking this approach to climate change shows that neither scientists, politicians, nor lawyers alone can solve this problem. It is a problem that occurs everywhere and, in every system, and can only be solved through a multidisciplinary perspective and coordinated cooperation.

Climate change has usually been seen as an ecological crisis. Still, it is also an economic, societal, political, and public health crisis – a *generalised crisis* whose effects spill over into all areas, shaking confidence in established worldviews and ruling elites.[25] Everyone must seek solutions to this problem in their own sphere, but at the same time, these efforts must be managed harmoniously. That means – from a legal perspective – that the solution must be at the constitutional level. That is because a constitutional approach in line with scientific facts offers the only binding and fastest way to achieve a harmonised transformation of the entire legal system and, by extension, the political, economic and social structures. I call this approach to tackle climate change green constitutionalism.

According to available scientific data, human actions regarding climate are causing the biosphere to be transformed by humans. Therefore, in order to avert catastrophe, these human actions need to be channelled through political and legal institutions. Climate politics, therefore, constitutes the nexus of the Anthropocene[26] narrative and global constitutionalism – a growing field of research.[27] At this junction, green constitutionalism emerges as a legal approach that identifies the real problems at the root of climate

---

[24] Klein, *On Fire*, pp. 314–15.

[25] Fraser, 'Climates of Capital', p. 49.

[26] The word Anthropocene derives from the Greek words *anthropo*, meaning 'man', and *kainos*, meaning 'new', combined by biologist Eugene Stoermer and chemist Paul Crutzen to describe the period that began due to the noticeable impact of humankind on climate and ecosystems. See 'Anthropocene', *National Geographic*.

[27] Jordi Jaria-Manzano – Susana Borrás, 'Introduction to the Research Handbook on Global Climate Constitutionalism' *in* Jordi Jaria-Manzano – Susana Borrás (ed.), *Research Handbook on Global Climate Constitutionalism*, Edward Elgar, 2019, p. 2.

change and provides permanent solutions to these problems by using data and information from other fields of science.

The problem we are facing today is vital and huge. We can only overcome it through a transformation as great as it is. What we have learned from both the Great Depression and the post-World War II period is that transformative victories cannot be won simply by opposing the violation of our own rights. To win in a real crisis, we need an approach that is as forward-looking as it is bold, a plan for how to respond to the underlying causes of the crisis and what we can do to repair them. Moreover, this plan needs to be convincing, credible, and, above all, inclusive.[28] Green constitutionalism is, therefore, not only about examining the legal causes of climate change (Part I) but also about how to build a new constitutional order in harmony with nature (Part II).

The choice before us is between the continuation and eventual crush of the current unsustainable system, which is heading towards the self-destruction of humanity, or the development of a sustainable relationship with the Earth, which requires the creation of a new ecological civilisation. Humanity is facing the greatest challenge in its long history. It can only be overcome if we bring about a worldwide revolutionary transformation of social and ecological relations.[29] There is no time to waste. The struggle must and can be fought on all fronts.[30] This book aims to contribute on the constitutional law front to the efforts for the transformation we urgently need.

---

28 Klein, *On Fire*, pp. 280–1.

29 John Bellamy Foster, *Capitalism in the Anthropocene: Ecological Ruin or Ecological Revolution*, Monthly Review Press, New York, 2022, pp. 13–14.

30 Chomsky – Pollin, *Climate Crisis* …, p. 174.

The relationship between the current constitutional order and climate change

In the current era of climate change, constitutionalism should be taken out of the classical legal approach, where it is stuck between the modern concepts of nation and state, and be given a broader perspective. Thus, constitutionalism should be conceived in the context of protecting the fundamental values of the global community. This idea of a material constitution is closely related to its use by the courts as legal norms used to limit and control power. Accordingly, we should consider how certain legal norms can create material limits for climate change policies and how the consequences of decision-making processes in a global context can be taken under control by the courts.[31] Moreover, it should be possible that not only the norms written in constitutions but also some principles that are not written in constitutions could be recognised by the high courts on a constitutional or even supra-constitutional level against climate change.

From this perspective, the constitution moves out of its narrow meaning as a public law text emanating from state authority and at the top of the usual hierarchy and constitutes the essence of a changing social consensus that emerges in different texts and aims to build a legal framework for global governance.[32] Nevertheless, constitutional law is, of course, not just about the text of constitutions. It covers a broader field, encompassing all the regulations and principles necessary to limit power for a dignified and healthy life. In the context of climate change, constitutionalism is taking on

---

31 Jaria-Manzano – Borrás, 'Introduction to … ', p. 5.
32 Jaria-Manzano – Borrás, 'Introduction to … ', p. 7.

a new look that serves the purpose of identifying, limiting and sometimes preventing the root causes of the problem in order to sustain life on Earth.

The movement called constitutionalism emerged in the Age of Enlightenment. Its primary function was to replace the old traditions that had provided ample scope for arbitrary action by the powers that be. Written constitutions were used to limit absolutism and sometimes the despotism of monarchical powers. Constitutionalism is, therefore, historically about the limitation of power.[33] From this perspective, what is constitutional and what is not has always been a political issue. Moreover, what constitutes power and what constitutes the limits of that power have constantly changed throughout history. As an example of how old constitutionalism played a role against the rulers, in 1768, the Massachusetts House of Colonies declared the law passed by the London Parliament on the payment of taxes by the colonies in the Americas as 'unconstitutional' because it violated the 'natural constitutional right' to property.[34]

In this book, the term constitutionalism is used in this historical framework to limit power. But with one crucial difference. The power that the colonies tried to limit was the Kingdom of England. Similarly, the absolutism that the French bourgeois tried to limit in 1789 was their king's. In general, rights and freedoms are still used today as concepts that enable the limitation of state power. Today, however, another power is even above the state and has state organs and rulers in its employ: the capitalist economic order. This order has no clear ruler; the heads of many giant corporations rule it. It is such a power that is everywhere and in everything. There is nowhere else we can escape to. We cannot even imagine getting out of its order. In history, it has destroyed the alternatives it faced, and it is doing the same today. Capitalism has established both a physical hegemony in our lives and an intellectual hegemony in our minds.

Constitutionalism requires the limitation of such power for its very *raison d'être*. In addition, today, there is an even more important reason to limit the

---

33 Pierre Pactet, *Institutions Politiques – Droit Constitutionnel*, 16th ed., Armand Colin, Paris, 1997, p. 65.

34 İbrahim Ö. Kaboğlu, *Anayasa Hukuku Dersleri (Genel Esaslar)*, 16th ed. Legal, Istanbul, 2021, pp. 3–4. The United Kingdom's insistence on its position was one of the reasons why the colonies in America united and adopted the Declaration of Independence in 1776.

capitalist economic order: climate change. What I call 'green constitutionalism' in this book refers to the movement to limit this hegemonic system that confronts us with a global and vital threat. Just as the bourgeoisie used constitutionalism against the absolute power of the time, the king, in order to create its own survival space, we must today use constitutionalism against the hegemonic order established by the bourgeoisie in order to save humanity and the planet.

At the time of the formation of the modern state, kings saw themselves as the source of the law, with direct or indirect reference to Roman law, but they did not embrace the idea that they themselves were subject to the law. One of the meanings of the concept of 'absolutism' when it first emerged was that the king was *legibus solutus*: since the law was a product of the king's sovereign power, it could not subordinate or limit that power.[35] Today, we have moved beyond this idea. In fact, it is generally accepted that there cannot be a limitless constitutional body. Accordingly, all organs exercising sovereignty are constitutionally regulated and, therefore, limited.

However, there is one economic class that has not been limited and even constitutionally liberated in modern times. Its traces can be found at the deepest roots of the climate change problem: the bourgeoisie. The links between the emergence of this class, the founder of today's economic infrastructure, the architect of the modern constitutional and political structure, and the onset of climate change are today more visible than ever. The bourgeoisie, which limited the absolutism of kings by using constitutionalism in its favour, created the current constitutional order. Today, the constitutional state and the bourgeois state are identical.[36] However, the bourgeoisie, which argued that absolutism must be limited for rights and freedoms to emerge and survive and succeeded in putting this idea into practice, has turned itself into an absolute sovereign today. Just like the Roman kings, it thinks it cannot be limited. Indeed, in the current constitutional order, while all organs can be limited, those related to the economy can operate independently and autonomously, free from all restrictions. Even attempts to regulate them are met

---

35 Gianfranco Poggi, *The Development of the Modern State: A Sociological Introduction* (Turkish version), trans. Şule Kut – Binnaz Toprak, 4th ed., Istanbul Bilgi University Press, Istanbul, 2007, pp. 93–4.

36 Schmitt, *Théorie de la Constitution*, p. 263.

with great reaction. However, if we sincerely want to stop climate change, we must urgently consider and even succeed in using constitutionalism to limit today's absolute power, the bourgeoisie, and the capitalist infrastructure it has created. To do this, we must first get to the root of the problem and examine the emergence of the current constitutional order from a green perspective.

Historical analysis of the constitutional order from an ecological perspective

While the regulatory function of law in a society is easily recognised, it is often not recognised that it plays an equally important role in building and shaping society itself. Society can be seen as the collective creation of the individuals who build it. A society comes to life when a certain number of people conceive of a group identity for themselves and then begin to act on that belief. That is an ongoing process that takes place over generations and involves the development of theories, values, and systems.[37] In short, society creates law as much as law creates society.

After the late eighteenth-century revolutions, the codification of political institutions became an unrivalled concept of the material limitation of political power. The perception of the constitution as a contract played an essential role in this. In this context, not every constitutional text was recognised as legitimate. In order for a text to be recognised as a constitution, it was expected to have a particular content that protects the interests of the people who signed the social contract[38]. That paved the way for a less formal and more open concept of constitutional law and allowed for the definition of strategies for controlling the institutions and decisions that determine

37 Cormac Cullinan, *Wild Law: A Manifesto for Earth Justice* (Kindle edition), 2nd ed., Green Books, Totnes, 2011, p. 55.

38 Article 16 of the French Declaration of the Rights of Man and of the Citizen was the first and still remains being a guiding text in this regard: *In a society where rights are not guaranteed and there is no separation of powers, there is no Constitution.*

the status of members of society.[39] That fact opens today a critical door for community involvement in the context of climate change.

The actual cause of climate change and other environmental crises is not the action of human beings, the individuals who make up society, as the origin of the word 'Anthropocene' suggests. To say this is so is a fundamental strategy of the capital owners, who are mainly responsible for this problem. As the US philosopher and writer Jensen points out, the narrative that we can stop climate change through our individual actions is the result of a campaign of misdirection. Even a basic concept like 'carbon footprint', which has become very common in climate change debates, was actually promoted and popularised by *British Petroleum* (BP)[40] precisely because it reduces global warming to an individual issue (personal carbon footprint).[41] Even the most ecologically literate and ecologically sensitive people are now calculating their carbon footprints due to their actions and taking responsibility for them. Yet, it is estimated that if everyone in the United States followed all the recommendations in the movie *An Inconvenient Truth*,[42] total carbon emissions would only fall by 22 per cent, which is not enough for the solution. The reason for water scarcity is not the excessive water consumption by individuals since 90 per cent of water is used in agriculture and industry. Similarly, industrial agriculture, organisations, and governments consume the vast majority of energy. Further, the biggest producers of all kinds of waste are not us but capital. Changing light bulbs at home, recycling, or showering with less

39 Jaria-Manzano – Borrás, 'Introduction to … ', pp. 4–5.

40 In 2001, the company changed its name to 'Beyond Petroleum' as part of a rebranding and efforts to create the image of a company that treats the planet better. Nevertheless, it caused the worst pollution in Alaska in a pipeline accident in 2006 and the largest marine life annihilation in history with the explosion of the Deepwater Horizon oil platform in the Gulf of Mexico in 2010. It has tried to recover from the financial crisis by selling its solar and wind energy assets. See Scott Carpenter, 'After Abandoned "Beyond Petroleum" Re-Brand, BP's New Renewables Push Has Teeth', *Forbes*, 4 August 2020.

41 Benlisoy, 'İklim Krizi … ', p. 163.

42 In this 2006 documentary directed by Davis Guggenheim, former US Vice President Al Gore informs citizens about how to stop global warming and advises them on changes they can make in their personal lives. Although it does not address the important role of the capitalist economic system in global warming, it won Academy Awards for the Best Original Score and the Best Documentary.

water are planet-friendly behaviours and should be done, but they will not stop climate change. As long as the industrial-economic system continues, our world will continue to die.[43]

In other words, the answer to the question 'What can I do as an individual to stop climate change?' is 'nothing'. We cannot play a significant role in stabilising our planet's climate as single individuals or even as a crowd of individuals.[44] People of goodwill who think personal lifestyle changes will solve the current ecological crisis are doomed to be tragically disappointed. What is needed are fundamental structural changes.[45] We must, therefore, stop blaming individuals and their actions as the cause of climate change and target the root of the problem. The ecological problems we are experiencing today are rooted in conflicts between the economic order and ethnic, cultural, and gender-based conflicts.[46] Therefore, we must establish a new constitutional order that will eliminate these conflicts and reorganise rights and freedoms in an ecological framework. Only in this way will we be able to produce a permanent solution to the complex problem we face, not a superficial or temporary one.

Just as the past was not inevitable, predetermined, or scripted, the future is not predetermined by our present circumstances. However, to imagine a future that is not just a continuation of the patterns of the past, especially humanity's relationship with its natural environment, we must first understand the past and how we got here.[47] Once we understand this, we can see how complicated the problem is and where the solution lies.

---

[43] Derrick Jensen, 'Forget Shorter Showers', *Orion*, 7 July 2009.

[44] Klein, *On Fire*, p. 162.

[45] Murray Bookchin, *The Next Revolution: Popular Assemblies and the Promise of Direct Democracy* (Turkish version), trans. İbrahim Yıldız – Soner Torlak, Dipnot Yayınları, Ankara, 2015, p. 69.

[46] Murray Bookchin, *Social Ecology and Communalism* (Turkish version), trans. Fuat Dara Elhüseyni, Sümer Yayıncılık, Istanbul, 2013, p. 9.

[47] Robert B. Marks, *The Origins of the Modern World – A Global and Environmental Narrative from the Fifteenth to the Twenty-First Century* (Kindle Edition), 4th ed., Rowman & Littlefield, Lanham, 2020, p. 242.

1.1 Scientific and philosophical transformation before the capitalist period

Science is a constantly progressing phenomenon in a dialectical logic. Past knowledge leads to new knowledge, and new disciplines are added daily to old ones. The emergence of ecology as a separate discipline occurred in parallel with the visibility of the devastating damage caused by economic activities on the biosphere. In other words, ecology as a discipline cannot be dealt with independently from the history of capitalism and necessitates a political economy method.[48] For this reason, the origins of a problem such as climate change, which seems to fall under the science of ecology, should also be sought in the science of economics and, by extension, in the history of law.

For thousands of years, the human population on Earth has lived in nature and has been very attentive to the opportunities and limitations it sets for human actions.[49] These people saw themselves as part of nature. They were neither above nature nor below it but 'in' it.[50] This long period, once disparaged as 'prehistory',[51] accounts for 95 per cent of human history. Humans roamed the planet almost all this time, leaving no more remarkable trace behind than any other animal. That shows that the so-called 'history of civilisation' was an anomaly that brought us to the brink of a climate catastrophe rather than an inevitable upswing.[52]

Until the end of the Middle Ages, cultures worldwide closely observed nature and adapted their ways of living according to it.[53] Their observations were often expressed in religious or mythological language, and nature

---

48 Gözde Orhan, 'Modernizm ve Kapitalizm Sarmalında Ekoloji: Devlet, Sermaye, Sivil Toplum', *Praksis*, No. 25, 2011/1, p. 32.

49 Marks, *The Origins of* ..., p. 54.

50 Bookchin, *The Ecology of Freedom*, p. 74.

51 Approximately 70,000 years ago, before humans created complex structures called cultures. See Yuval Noah Harari, *Sapiens: A Brief History of Humankind* (Turkish version), 11th ed., Kolektif Kitap, Istanbul, 2016, p. 17.

52 Wallace-Wells, *The Uninhabitable Earth*, p. 219.

53 Harari traces the turning point when humans 'abandoned harmony with nature and ran towards greed and alienation' back much earlier, to the Agricultural Revolution 12,000 years ago. See Harari, *Sapiens*, p. 108. While this is a date that can be considered accurate for the beginning of human control over nature, our impact on it until the Middle Ages was not of a magnitude that would affect its cycles. Humans could only produce by following the rules of nature. Therefore, it did not affect sustainability.

and its laws were generally thought to originate from God or some other divine power. These beliefs created the law of the time and pointed to rules of behaviour that everyone was expected to follow. Law itself was a highly spiritual concept based on obligations and the role of the individual within a community in relation to the world that sustains life.[54] In the eyes of these societies, law is not a set of rules laid down by someone but by divine forces that set the conditions for living in harmony with nature. As a matter of fact, it was impossible for these societies, which have a close relationship with nature, to continue without obeying the rules of nature. Therefore, nature and law were intertwined.

Indeed, ancient societies' relationship with the land has always determined their identity, spiritual ecology, and identity.[55] In stark contrast to today's dominant Western worldview, which commodifies the land and determines its value through human use, in the eyes of many Indigenous peoples, their properly maintained relationship with the earth and the land has an intrinsic value, even if no one else places a value on it.[56] Indigenous societies have, therefore, seen value not in themselves but in the network of relationships in which they are embedded. The abandonment of this perspective is rooted in the West's political, technological, and economic developments.

In England, the monarchy and its barons were part of the same political and institutional resource extraction and appropriation system, albeit with sometimes violent tensions between them.[57] This union foreshadowed the basic institutional structure of today's economic, legal, and political globalisation. It was an alliance between those who controlled vast amounts of property and those with political power, based ideologically on a strict, zero-sum distinction between the public and the private, leaving no room for

54 Francis Oakley, *Natural Law, Laws of Nature, Natural Rights: Continuity and Discontinuity in the History of Ideas*, Continuum, New York, 2005, cited in: Fritjof Capra – Ugo Mattei, *The Ecology of Law* (Turkish version), trans. Ebru Kılıç, Koç University Press, Istanbul, 2017, p. 24.

55 James S. Y. Henderson, 'Empowering Treaty Federalism', Saskatchewan Law Review, Vol. 58, No. 2, p. 242, cited in: Lynda Collins, *The Ecological Constitution – Reframing Environmental Law*, Routledge, London & New York, 2021, p. 40.

56 Gordon Christie, 'A Colonial Reading of Recent Jurisprudence: Sparrow, Delgamuukw, and Haida Nation', *Windsor Yearbook of Access to Justice*, Vol. 23, Allard Faculty Publications, 2005, p. 50.

57 Capra – Mattei, *The Ecology of Law*, p. 91.

ordinary people. The social perspectives and structures primarily responsible for our inability to find sustainable solutions to climate change today were developed in the West between the late fifteenth and eighteenth centuries.[58]

Some important geographical and technological discoveries marked this period. Adam Smith, for example, cites 1492, when Columbus travelled to America, and 1498, when Vasco de Gama circumnavigated Africa on his way to India, as the most critical years in history. Marx likewise says that these two years are significant. Similarly, various twentieth-century scholars from the Marxist tradition consider these dates important because European colonisation, slavery, and the exploitation of colonies, which later emerged in North and South America and Asia, are the most powerful explanations for the rise of the West.[59]

These discoveries, which changed the centre of the world's wealth, were accompanied by different perspectives developed in science. In the sixteenth and seventeenth centuries, with the Scientific Revolution, in which the study of matter was advocated and the mechanistic science of Galileo, Descartes, and Newton came to the fore, the holistic and communal understanding of the universe and the planet that had been dominant since early times was abandoned.[60] The study of nature began to focus on singular phenomena rather than relationships. This transformation was in line with the rise of the bourgeois perspective, which emphasised individuals rather than society as a whole.

As Capra and Mattei point out, the concentration of capital, one of the results of the Scientific Revolution, brought with it the 'commodification' of land. The landowning class, which would later become the bourgeoisie, allied itself with government institutions to turn the land into its property and tried to break the resistance of people living in communities with subsistence agriculture and limited specialisation. The traditional production processes of these people were transformed into modern capitalist food production. The theory of unlimited property rights based on the ideology of liberty, progress, and productive labour developed by John Locke, together with the theory of unlimited state sovereignty developed by Thomas Hobbes,

---

[58] Capra – Mattei, *The Ecology of Law*, pp. 91–2.
[59] Marks, *The Origins of…*, p. 21.
[60] Capra – Mattei, *The Ecology of Law*, pp. 24–5.

contributed to the confiscation of peasants' land and the concentration of production in few hands.[61]

The leitmotif of Hobbes' theory is a state with a monopoly of legitimate violence. This state makes laws, rather than an ideal legal framework, in order to restrain the passions of the people, obeys these laws – as a rule – reflecting its own will, but more importantly, ensures that its subjects obey them under all circumstances. Nevertheless, it is a mighty political power that can abandon the law when necessary to preserve order. While criticising Hobbes' basic assumptions, Locke outlines both the principle of legality and the institutional features of the liberal rule of law, such as the supremacy of the legislature and separation of powers. Hobbes, who wrote Leviathan while the civil war in England was still raging, argues that all men can avoid the conflicts that plunge society into chaos by giving up their rights and submitting to a single supreme and indivisible will.

On the other hand, Locke wrote during the period of peace that followed the war, developing his theory, which was in line with the dominant doctrine of his time, that the state's primary duty was protecting property and liberty.[62] Although these seem to be opposing ideas, they converged in the bourgeoisie's power, creating the initial dynamic of today's ecological collapse through economic actors with unlimited freedom in a vigorous state order with a monopoly on violence. To better understand this dynamic, we need to take a closer look at this period from different angles.

1.1.1 The role of scientific developments in the West in changing the economic infrastructure

While climate change is a scientific reality, it is not a phenomenon independent of the legal order. On the contrary, it is a problem created by many structures intertwined with the legal order. Therefore, first of all, revealing the links between science and law is essential. It is generally accepted that the historical and conceptual links between science and legal theory began in Ancient Greece. From the beginning of Greek philosophy in the

---

61 Crawford Broug Macpherson, *The Political Theory of Possessive Individualism: Hobbes to Locke*, Clarendon Press, Oxford, 1962, cited in: Capra – Mattei, *The Ecology of Law*, p. 181.

62 Berke Özenç, *Hukuk Devleti: Kökenleri ve Küreselleşme Çağındaki İşlevi*, İletişim, Istanbul, 2014, pp. 184–6.

6th century BC, philosophers saw the world as a cosmos, a regular and harmonious structure, a living organism rather than a mechanical system. For them, all parts of nature had an inherent purpose. They all contributed to the harmonious functioning of the whole, and things naturally moved spontaneously towards their proper place in the universe.[63] This holistic view of the universe and nature was dominant for many years until the early Middle Ages. The human being as a concept was, of course, important, and it was the subject of philosophy and other sciences, but he did not occupy a position separate from and above the rest of nature.

By the Middle Ages, feudal rulers and their dependent village communities had developed elaborate legal rules regarding land over the centuries. These rules did not go beyond covering fairs and local markets based on the manor economy. These legal regulations were not flexible enough to derive the rules required by the new economy in the emerging cities with the increase in trade. The developing urban economy required a more complex division of labour, production requiring new skills and tools, new management of commercial transactions and commercial enterprises, and different legal arrangements.[64] In this period, which coincided with the rise of the myth of man's separation from the rest of the world in European history, nature was transformed from a nurturing mother into a machine in the eyes of the new merchant class.[65] The Western worldview, which, until the Middle Ages, had assumed that humans had to act in harmony with nature for production and survival, abandoned this view, placed humans in a unique position superior to nature, and pushed everything else down the hierarchy. This relatively recent acquisition of smugness and vain pride[66] has become dominant thinking, aided by technological advances.

While Galilei Galileo (1564–1642) developed ingenious experiments in Italy, Francis Bacon (1561–1626) formulated an explicit theory of the inductive procedure, introducing the empirical method of science in England. Accordingly, the emphasis was on conducting experiments, drawing conclusions from

---

63 Capra – Mattei, *The Ecology of Law*, p. 51. The explanation of a phenomena by its goals or purposes is called teleology. The term derives from the Greek word *télos*, meaning 'purpose'.

64 Poggi, *The Development of the Modern State*, p. 57.

65 Cullinan, *Wild Law*, p. 44.

66 Klein, *On Fire*, p. 80.

them, and then testing these conclusions with other experiments. Bacon strongly defended his new method and became an extremely influential figure. The 'Baconian spirit' radically changed the understanding of nature and the purpose of scientific enquiry.[67] In particular, arguing for a distinction between reason and revelation and pointing to the importance of experimentation to verify and falsify theories, Bacon argued that human societies could only progress if they stopped worshipping the 'idols of reason', which he claimed were useless, and instead adopted a scientific approach and used technology to 'subjugate' nature.[68] In his 1623 work *De Dignitate et Augmentis Scientiarum*,[69] Bacon briefly summarised this new system of values, emphasising that nature should be viewed as something to be 'pushed to its limits, shaped and renewed through art or as if by human hands'.[70] Bacon, today lauded in textbooks for his contribution to the scientific method, actually actively worked to destroy the idea of the living Earth and replace it with a new ethic that not only permitted but affirmed the exploitation of nature. To this end, he transformed the old theory of nurturing Mother Nature into what he called a 'common whore'.[71]

Bacon, who found nature to be untamed, disordered, wild, and chaotic and likened it to an animal that needed to be restrained, bound, and tamed, wrote that nature needed to be 'enslaved, squeezed, and kneaded like dough' by removing it from its natural state in order to serve human purposes.[72] Therefore, Francis Bacon ought to be considered the intellectual creator of the extractive economy of our time. His ideas, which envisioned that the land and the Earth should be completely knowable and controllable, were the impetus not only for the Scientific Revolution but also, and critically, for the colonial project, which sent its ships scouring the planet to drill and drill and transferred the wealth and secrets they discovered to their own countries.[73]

---

67 Capra – Mattei, *The Ecology of Law*, p. 58.
68 Cullinan, *Wild Law*, p. 45.
69 Dignity and Development of Sciences.
70 Klein, *On Fire*, p. 81.
71 Hickel, *Less is More*, p. 68.
72 Hickel, *Less is More*, p. 68.
73 Naomi Klein, *This Changes Everything: Capitalism vs. the Climate* (Turkish version), trans. Osman Akınhay, Agora Kitaplığı, Istanbul, 2015, pp. 241–2.

Another one of the initiators of the transition from an organic to a mechanistic worldview was René Descartes (1596–1650), a significant figure of the seventeenth century. Descartes is often referred to as the founder of modern philosophy, but he was also a brilliant mathematician and a very influential scientist. Descartes based his views on nature on a fundamental distinction: the realm of reason, the *res cogitans* (thinking being), and the realm of matter, the *res extensa* (being with extension). These were two independent, separate, and essentially different realms. For Descartes, the material universe was a machine, and it was nothing but a machine. Nature functioned according to the laws of mechanics, and everything living and non-living in the material world could be explained according to the order and motion of its parts.[74] At the heart of this thinking was the realisation that the domination of nature, as Bacon desired, could only be possible by purifying it of life. To do this, he returned to Plato's bifurcated world and developed a new approach. He argued that there was a fundamental dualism between mind and matter.[75]

Starting with the famous proposition *I think, therefore I am*, he constructed the idea that mind and matter are two completely separate and incompatible entities. In this view, humans were abstract rational minds somehow contained in a physical body, like a ghost in a machine.[76] For Descartes, of all other creatures, humans were unique in that they had intellects (or souls) that established their unique bond with God. Other creatures, by contrast, were nothing more than unthinking material. Plants and animals had no soul, will, inclination, or motivation. They were merely automata that, like a clock, worked according to predictable mechanical laws. To understand the mechanical nature of life, one had to go deeper and look at the parts, not the whole. What appeared to be life around us was, in fact, inert matter. In other words, an object.[77] In short, the idea of the separateness of human consciousness from the rest of the world, nourished by religious beliefs, led people to adopt a superior, arrogant, and domineering attitude towards nature and to see it as something that existed for the benefit of human beings – the idea of nature as a mother died.[78]

---

[74] Capra – Mattei, *The Ecology of Law*, p. 59.
[75] Hickel, *Less is More*, p. 69.
[76] Cullinan, *Wild Law*, p. 46.
[77] Hickel, *Less is More*, p. 69.
[78] Cullinan, *Wild Law*, p. 46.

Descartes' understanding of the complete separation of mind and matter, often referred to as 'Cartesian dualism', has profoundly influenced, and continues to influence, how we see the world and our place in it.[79] Descartes said that the purpose of science was to 'make us masters and owners of nature'. Four hundred years later, this ethic remains deeply embedded in our culture. We do not just see the living world as the other; we see it as an enemy to be fought and subjugated with the help of science and reason.[80] We kill animals that pose a danger to humans and poison the soil with herbicides and insecticides for more efficient agriculture.[81] We see nature outside the cities as 'wild' and are afraid to be alone in a forest or mountain. We do not recognise ourselves as a part of nature and perceive nature as something outside of us. This perception is based on the mechanistic approach that began with Descartes.

This philosophical transformation peaked in the seventeenth century with Isaac Newton (1642–1727). Thanks to Newton, the mechanistic work of his predecessors was synthesised, and the Scientific Revolution was completed.[82] Developing a complete mathematical formulation of the mechanistic view of nature and thus influencing not only his century but also those that would come after him, Newton presented a coherent mathematical theory of the world. A tremendous success in the eighteenth and nineteenth centuries, Newton's theory explained in minute detail the motion of planets, satellites, and comets, as well as tides and other gravitationally related phenomena. Newton's law of gravitation and its three central laws of motion were soon established as the correct theory of physical reality and were received with great enthusiasm by scientists and non-scientists alike. Newton's theory remained the unshakeable foundation of scientific thought well into the twentieth century.[83]

The idea that the universe was a gigantic mechanical system operating according to Newton's laws replaced the centuries-old notion that the universe

---

79 Cullinan, *Wild Law*, p. 46.

80 Hickel, *Less is More*, p. 79.

81 On the effects of herbicides and insecticides on nature and humans Rachel Carson's *Silent Spring* is considered a milestone. See Rachel Carson, *Silent Spring* (Kindle version), Tingle Books, Hapur, 2021.

82 Cullinan, *Wild Law*, p. 46.

83 Capra – Mattei, *The Ecology of Law*, p. 61.

was an ordered, harmonious, living whole. According to this new conception, the universe was made up of parts that could be separated, studied, quantified, and rearranged as needed. This new understanding of nature as a machine led to a shift away from ethical, religious, and ecological concerns over natural beings.[84] Indeed, this mechanistic view also seriously impacted the relationship between humans and nature and the laws humans make, so much so that this impact is still felt in the twenty-first century.[85] The contemporary fact that no entity other than human beings and human communities is recognised as a subject of rights at the constitutional level in our legal systems, that animals and natural beings are seen only as resources, and that a relationship of domination and ownership can be established over them through law are all reflections of this mechanistic approach. To better understand our current legal relationship with nature, it would be helpful to look at how the philosophical concepts underlying our current rules emerged and how they have functioned.

1.1.2 Philosophical concepts on which the bourgeoisie is founded

While the history of portraying society and nature as two separate, disconnected things is quite old, this narrative is also intensely embedded in capitalism's history. With the emergence of capitalism, man has constantly struggled with the nonhuman world and sought ways to separate himself from it. According to this modernist perspective, the 'wild' is undoubtedly the antithesis of the 'human'; it constitutes an obstacle to progress and civilisation and is therefore excluded.[86]

Indeed, the commodification of natural assets that began with the enclosure movements in England did not stop there. The change in question was not exactly a way of separating human beings from other life forms. In essence, nature was no longer to be conceived as a living and autonomous whole. In this sense, following the path of Locke and Hobbes, capitalism

---

84 Evrim Durmaz, *Doğanın Hakları: Çevre Hukukuna Alternatif Bir Kuram*, On İki Levha, Istanbul, 2023, p. 76.

85 Capra – Mattei, *The Ecology of Law*, p. 62.

86 Neil Smith, *Uneven Development: Nature, Capital, and the Production of Space*, Basil Blackwell, Oxford, 1991, p. 9, cited in: Gözde Orhan, 'Farklı Ölçeklerde Yerleşme, Tahribat ve Adalet Sorunları: Kent ve Kır Ekolojileri', *in* Didem Bayındır – Mine Yıldırım (ed.), *Ekoloji: Bir Arada Yaşamın Geleceği*, Tellekt, Istanbul, 2022, p. 383.

became one of the driving forces of the project of a world without an unappropriable outside.[87] However, this was not the case before. It is crucial to see how the pre-modernist holistic view of nature and the universe shifted to the current approach to understand the problems at the root of climate change.

The Renaissance, roughly defined as the period from the beginning of the fifteenth century to the end of the sixteenth century, symbolises the transition from the Middle Ages to the modern world in the history of Western thought. This period was marked by intense exploration of both ideas of Antiquity and new geographical regions of the world. The intellectual climate of the Renaissance 'gave birth a second time' to human beings by making them morally valuable and their abilities the primary concern. Thus, it shaped the philosophical and literary movement of humanism. Humanism meant a radical break with the teachings of the Middle Ages, which conceived of human nature from a religious perspective.[88] With humanism, the holistic view of Antiquity, which conceived of the Earth as a kosmos, the planet as God's generous gift to humanity, and a bountiful resource accessible to all, was replaced by an emphasis on the individual and human reason. That gave rise to the mechanistic view of rational natural law.[89] According to this view, rules no longer had to conform to or reflect nature. The best rules for individuals and societies had to be found by thinking within the framework of rationalism. Therefore, with the introduction of the human being as an essential actor, the law became something produced artificially rather than learnt from nature.

That may not be seen as a negative development per se. It could be argued that people's interest is in the health of nature, and therefore, people would not make decisions contrary to the rules of nature anyway. However, the development of the understanding of natural law paved the way for creating an unequal order in which the rules are not made collectively by everyone but where 'a group' of people make the rules on behalf of everyone else to protect and advance their own interests. Thus, the foundations were laid for an autonomous legal sphere that ordinary people could not change through

---

87 Achille Mbembe, *Brutalism* (Turkish version), trans. P. Burcu Yalım, İletişim, Istanbul, 2022, p. 40.

88 Capra – Mattei, *The Ecology of Law*, p. 55.

89 Paolo Grossi, *A History of European Law*, Blackwell-Wiley, Malden, Massachusetts, 2010, cited in: Capra – Mattei, *The Ecology of Law*, p. 65.

democratic means.[90] The 'thinkers' of natural law created a legal order in which they decided what was right and wrong, and others had to follow these rules.

In England, for example, social and economic transformation instrumentalised the understanding of natural law, leaving ordinary peasants landless and empowering industrialisation instead. Forcible enclosures led to the transformation of agricultural land into cattle pastures and the expansion of textile production, even in the absence of mechanisation. Land use and property changes were complemented in the sixteenth century by a series of essential moves towards nation-statehood and then by the scientific revolution in the following century. The scientific revolution brought with it a mechanistic view of nature.[91] This mechanistic perspective, which sharpened the distinctions inherited from Greek philosophy and Christianity, excluded nature from the world of meaning, eliminating the assumptions of intimacy between society and nature and creating a deep ontological vacuum. Through this objectification and externalisation by law and the state, nature emerged as the antithesis of humanity. Consequently, merchants saw this as a license to exploit nature.[92]

Thus, in the sixteenth and seventeenth centuries, the medieval worldview underwent radical changes. The idea of an organic, living, spiritual Earth was replaced by a view of it as a machine, and revolutionary changes in physics and astronomy strengthened this view. The Scientific Revolution marked the beginning of the modern era, also known as 'modernity'.[93] The organic philosophy of nature, whose goal since Antiquity had been to attain wisdom, understand and live in harmony with the natural order, was replaced by the metaphor of the world as a machine, and the goal of science became the pursuit of knowledge that could be used to dominate and control nature. The Earth would no longer be seen as a protective, nurturing mother but as a resource to be exploited without limits.[94]

---

90 Özenç, *Hukuk Devleti*, p. 62.

91 For Klein, there is nothing more anthropocentric than the Judeo-Christian exegesis that insists that God created the entire universe specifically to serve Adam's every need. Klein, *On Fire*, p. 172.

92 Fraser, 'Climates of Capital', pp. 69–70.

93 Capra – Mattei, *The Ecology of Law*, p. 57.

94 Capra – Mattei, *The Ecology of Law*, pp. 58–9.

Complementing humanist philosophy, Enlightenment thinkers put human beings at the centre of their philosophical thought systems.[95] They were not revolutionaries. They were dissident intellectuals who saw the upper classes as their sponsors.[96] In his *Lectures on Ethics*, Kant explicitly argued that our duties towards nature are indirect; indeed, they are towards other human beings. More generally, Kantian analysis strengthened the view that only humans can be worthy of moral concern. According to this view, only creatures capable of free and rational behaviour were moral beings.[97] The only creature capable of this was the human being. Therefore, he was the only one who mattered morally, and anyone could only have a legal responsibility towards him.[98]

In the eighteenth century, Enlightenment thinkers discredited animist ideas, claiming they were backward and unscientific. Seeing them as an obstacle to capitalist expansion, they eagerly eradicated these ideas.[99] That was done in the name of 'civilisation'. In their view, in order to be civilised and fully human, animist ideas had to be abandoned, and nature had to be seen as an object.[100] In this mindset, human progress was identified with controlling nature and putting it at the service of the market. Organic society's view of nature and treasure was utterly reversed. Nature was now the evil one, and the treasure the abundant one.[101] The human mind was considered unique, and there should be no room for 'wild' ideas in it. Humans were free to the extent that they could separate themselves from nature. In this approach, which claims to 'liberate' man from nature, found today in many different

---

95 Zeynep Özlem Üsküil Engin, *Ekolojik Kriz, Etik ve Hukuk*, Filiz Kitabevi, Istanbul, 2017, p. 3.

96 Chris Harman, *A People's History of the World – From the Stone Age to the New Millennium* (Turkish version), trans. Uygur Kocabaşoğlu, 3rd ed., Yordam Kitap, Istanbul, 2013, p. 243.

97 Joseph R. DesJardins, *Environmental Ethics: An Introduction to Environmental Philosophy* (Turkish version), trans. Ruşen Keleş, İmge, Ankara, 2006, p. 201.

98 The reason why I use the pronoun 'he' here is that all these theories were originally created with only men in mind, in a way that reflects the male-dominated mentality of the period.

99 Hickel, *Less is More*, p. 32.

100 Hickel, *Less is More*, p. 77.

101 Bookchin, *The Ecology of Freedom*, p. 252.

ideologies ranging from liberalism to Marxism, man is conceived as a creature who can solve the mysteries of nature with his rationality.

Due to this modern idea, nature was recognised as 'belonging' to humanity, and its primary purpose was to satisfy human needs. In traditional agricultural civilisations, everyday life experiences, albeit harsh and ugly, were used to connect human communities to the land and sustain a symbiotic relationship. With the rise of modernity, however, law and science have served to establish a contrast between humans and all other creatures and to 'liberate' humans from their ecological chains. Other creatures were thought to live in the 'natural state', but humans, with the social contract, had left the 'natural state' and had become 'civilised'. They no longer belonged to the same category as nature. Thanks to our science and technology, humans have supposedly figured nature out and started to play with it. Then, through legal institutions such as private property and sovereignty, we could transform the essence of nature into a commodity, a physical object that we could exploit or 'cure'.[102]

As a result, with the idea that nature was under control, it was assumed that every aspect of life could be controlled and put under human command. That is precisely what happened in modern societies.[103] However, at the point climate change has reached today, it has become clear that it is impossible for an element of a network that can exist depending on reciprocal relations, namely the human being, to free itself from this network and become its hierarchical superior. Therefore, it has become clear that the basic assumption on which modernity was founded was, in fact, a delusion.

In the mid-eighteenth century, the understanding of law that began to prevail throughout Europe, with some differences and peculiarities, began to take shape within the framework of market relations in accordance with this modern logic. According to this understanding, laws were defined not as a means to bring human beings to moral perfection but as a framework regulation that enabled autonomous individuals to implement their decisions without being subjected to any hindrance.[104] The 'autonomous individual'

---

[102] J. P. Dawson, *The Oracles of the Law*, University of Michigan, Ann Arbor, 1983, cited in: Capra – Mattei, *The Ecology of Law*, p. 26.

[103] Orhan, 'Modernizm ve ...', pp. 37–8.

[104] Mehmet Tevfik Özcan, *Modern Toplum ve Hukuk Devleti*, On İki Levha, İstanbul, 2008, p. 200, cited in: Özenç, *Hukuk Devleti*, p. 138.

here was obviously the trader who wanted to see neither internal nor external obstacles in his trade. He wanted both to protect himself and his wealth against the king and to be able to exploit everything wherever he went. Accordingly, he emphasised the concepts of equality against the social superiority of the king and other aristocrats, as well as the freedom to remove all obstacles to his trade.

In Western Europe and North America, where these ideas first emerged and took root, the tradition of reconciliation between human beings and nature began to come to an end at the beginning of the nineteenth century. This process was completed with twentieth-century capitalism,[105] and the subsequent period of neoliberalism witnessed the beginning of the destruction of nature. All this developed due to the understanding that humans are superior to nature and can use and control it as they wish. The human societies ruling the world today have, therefore, built their governments on a false understanding of the universe. The fundamental error was the idea that humans are separate from their environment and that even if the health of the Earth is deteriorating, our situation can improve. Today, our governance systems, legal philosophy, and laws still reflect and preserve this false idea of separation and independence.[106] One could even say that, as the result of this modern understanding, at the base of our legal systems lies the commodification of nature, in legal terms, property rights.

1.1.2.1 Property

Humanism, one of the fundamental philosophies of the Age of Enlightenment, presented individual reason as the foundation of modern society while transforming the organic community, the medieval form of organisation, into a symbol of collective oppression of the individual. It was denounced as a place where there was no law, only ignorance. Thus, modern legal institutions based on individual property rights replaced the medieval holistic view. The view of human development as a progressive transition from a brutal state of nature to a world where humans dominate nature and adapt it to their needs

---

[105] John Berger, *Why Look at Animals?* (Turkish version), trans. Cevap Çapan, DeliDolu Yayınları, İzmir, 2017, p. 18, cited in: Çiğdem Öztürk, 'Savaşın Yuttuğu Hayvanlar', *in* Didem Bayındır – Mine Yıldırım (ed.), *Ekoloji: Bir Arada Yaşamın Geleceği*, Tellekt, Istanbul, 2022, p. 291.

[106] Cullinan, *Wild Law*, p. 43.

has become dominant,[107] so much so that today, property is recognised as the fundamental principle of our governments and institutions.[108]

One of the most important reflections of our mistaken relationship with nature in our legal systems concerns the concept of property. Legal humanists laid the intellectual foundations for the seizure of the legitimate institutions of the people based on the commons[109] and their drastic transformation into private property legally concentrated in the hands of a few and eventually into capital. Private property, which initially functioned to establish individual ownership of land, became the most important legal concept that served to divide the whole into individualistic components. The sovereign state, which eventually came to be dominated by the bourgeoisie, was the mechanism to manage the relations between these parts.[110]

Western political theory today is shaped by the tension between two power sources. These are the state and private property.[111] Today's dominant understanding of property as a right protected by the state to enable short-term accumulation and resource extraction has become one of the natural building blocks of the existing legal order. This approach is responsible for the current crises that are erupting one after another, including climate change.[112]

The origins of the Western legal tradition do not generally go back to Ancient Greece but to Ancient Rome, where a professional legal tradition was born out of the process of resolving conflicts between equals.[113] It should not be forgotten that Roman law, which had the most advanced legal system of the pre-modern period, was based on regulations regarding property

---

107 Ugo Mattei, *Beni comuni: Un manifesto*, 9th ed., Laterza, Rome, 2011, cited in: Capra – Mattei, *The Ecology of Law*, pp. 78–9.

108 Pierre-Joseph Proudhon, *Qu'est-ce que la Propriété?* (Turkish version), trans. Devrim Çetinkasap, 12th ed., Türkiye İş Bankası Kültür Yayınları, Istanbul, June 2023, p. 15.

109 Forms of wealth that should be managed and shared by every member of a society. See Kohei Saito, *Slow Down: How Degrowth Communism Can Save The Earth* (Kindle edition), Weidenfeld & Nicolson, London, January 2024, p. 89.

110 Capra – Mattei, *The Ecology of Law*, p. 65.

111 Ellen Meiksins Wood, *Freedom and Property: A Social History of Western Political Thought from the Renaissance to Enlightenment* (Turkish version), trans. Oya Köymen, 2nd ed., Yordam Kitap, Istanbul, 2016, p. 23.

112 Capra – Mattei, *The Ecology of Law*, p. 31.

113 Alan Watson, *The Spirit of Roman Law*, University of Georgia Press, Athens, 1995, cited in: Capra – Mattei, *The Ecology of Law*, p. 66.

relations.[114] Indeed, private property is the basic building block of Roman legal organisation. Property is not a concept that emerged in Rome. However, the extraordinary contribution of Roman law to the Western legal tradition is that it developed a professional legal system capable of defining and enforcing in minute detail the interests related to private property that were already recognised elsewhere, including Ancient Greece.[115]

Transformation of commons into private property in Roman law

According to the distinction that emerged in Roman law throughout history and has influenced today's legal systems, 'things that belonged to no one' (*res nullius*) meant things that could be owned but were not yet owned by anyone and, therefore, could be freely occupied. In contrast, 'things belonging to everyone' (*res communis omnium*), such as air, sea, coasts, and rivers, were things that could not be owned by their very nature, in line with the principle of exclusion. Finally, public lands, squares, aqueducts, or sewers were 'things belonging to the city' (*res publicae*). However, these distinctions were not always clear and precise. A responsible administrator would work out which of these three categories something fell into on a case-by-case basis. This legal technique created a sense of unity among the Romans, as it was able to solve the problems of everyone in the vast territory of the Roman Empire so that property issues throughout the country could be resolved according to a pre-established rule rooted in individualised absolute property, which would ultimately lead to a similar solution.[116]

On the one hand, through a ruler or popular intervention, the law protected common property, such as a town square, the open sea, a river, or water in aqueducts. Thus, individuals could enjoy them, and no one was excluded from access. On the other hand, wild animals, fish, or forest products that belonged to no one could be appropriated through appropriation; in other words, 'whoever finds them owns them'.[117]

At the beginning of the 6th century, Emperor Justinian ordered the simplification, rationalisation, and rewriting of all laws in the Empire. *The Corpus*

---

114 Özenç, *Hukuk Devleti*, p. 128.

115 Alan Watson, *The Law of Property in the Later Roman Republic*, Clarendon Press, Oxford, 1968, cited in: Capra – Mattei, *The Ecology of Law*, p. 67.

116 Capra – Mattei, *The Ecology of Law*, p. 68.

117 Capra – Mattei, *The Ecology of Law*, pp. 94–5.

Iuris Civilis, also known as the 'Justinian Code', was completed in 534 AD. This text represents the first conscious attempt to create a corpus of law professionally organised around the powers and obligations of individual property owners empowered by the monarch's power. It also provided the conceptual framework for our current property-centred approach to law, a view that evolved over the following centuries. For this reason alone, Justinian's *Corpus Iuris* Civilis can be considered the most important legal work ever written and the foundational book of the Western legal tradition.[118]

The division of all nonhumans into three categories in Roman law benefited Roman property owners and, in later years, Roman consuls and emperors. They expanded their sphere of sovereignty by claiming their own lands and other assets previously held in common. To justify this occupation, jurists recognised these assets as *res nullius* (belonging to no one). The commons, which used to belong to and could be used by everyone, were suddenly seen as belonging to no one and were inaccessible to ordinary peasants. Therefore, since no one had private ownership over these things, they belonged to whoever got them first. With centralised authority and power applied to natural resources, natural assets were separated from the common wealth. Previously, this common wealth was governed by customs that protected access to it and laws that people agreed upon. Then, what was legally protected was that once someone has a claim to something, that person has the power to exclude others from access to it.[119] So, the commons decreased, and private property increased. Ordinary peasants were denied access to commons such as forests, pastures, or rivers, struggled to make a living, and were increasingly forced to work for wealthy property owners.

Even today, common assets are at the mercy of the government in power. They are seen as the state's property, not the people's property. As such, they can be freely sold and privatised without judicial review.[120] In other words, this dispossession movement inherited from Roman law continues in the twenty-first century with almost the same logic. Today, forests, our common

---

[118] Capra – Mattei, *The Ecology of Law*, p. 70.

[119] Ernst Levy, *West Roman Vulgar Law: The Law of Property*, Memoirs of the American Philosophical Society 29, American Philosophical Society, Philadelphia, 1951, cited in: Capra – Mattei, *The Ecology of Law*, p. 72.

[120] Ugo Mattei, *Beni comuni: Un manifesto*, 9th ed., Laterza, Rome, 2011, cited in: Capra – Mattei, *The Ecology of Law*, pp. 78–9.

assets, are given to companies for mining, dams are built in front of rivers, and our air is polluted by industrial production. Today, the dynamics of capital also envisage the transformation of everything owned in common into private property. That ultimately leads to the destruction of the environment.[121]

Enclosure as the origin of modern common law

A situation similar to developments in Roman law marked the origins of the common law tradition in England in the Middle Ages. The Magna Carta, signed in 1215, gave legal protection to the property rights of the barons vis-à-vis the king, while the Charter of the Forest, a continuation of the Magna Carta, was passed in 1217. This law, still considered valid today, established that the King owned the forests and protected ordinary people's rights to access them.[122] It also gave the people custody of common resources in English-speaking lands.[123]

However, this law, originally intended to protect the hunting grounds of the Norman conquerors rather than ecological concerns, was frequently circumvented by kings in times of economic hardship.[124] Over the following centuries, the law's influence gradually weakened. Enclosure, the largely private circumjacence of public property, legitimised by the power to extract and exploit natural resources and secured by the crime of trespass, became the best-known example of transforming public property into private property.[125] Thus, the real-life meaning of the Charter of the Forest disappeared, and public access to the commons became meaningless as common resources were diminishing daily. That was followed by the repression and intimidation of the villagers, whose living conditions worsened every day due to the decline in the commons and who, therefore, resisted the enclosure movement.

---

121 Michael Löwy, *Ecosocialism – A Radical Alternative to Capitalist Catastrophe* (Kindle edition), Haymarket Books, Chicago, 2015, Ecosocial Struggles of Indigenous Peoples (Loc. 833).

122 Peter Linebaugh, *The Magna Carta Manifesto: Liberties and Commons for All*, University of California Press, Berkeley, 2008, cited in: Capra – Mattei, *The Ecology of Law*, p. 73.

123 'The Charter of the Forest', *The Canadian Encyclopedia*.

124 Jean Gimpel, *La Révolution industrielle au Moyen Age* (Turkish version), trans. Nazım Özüaydın, 6th ed., TÜBİTAK, Ankara, 2004, p. 77.

125 Capra – Mattei, *The Ecology of Law*, p. 73.

It is often thought that capitalism emerged naturally with the collapse of feudalism, but in fact, such a transformation could not have been natural. That is because capitalism requires the material accumulation of elites. Someone has to be extremely rich so that they can make large-scale investments. However, Hickel argues that post-feudal conditions of egalitarianism, such as self-sufficiency, high wages, grassroots demand for democracy, and collective management of resources, made elite accumulation impossible. It was precisely these favourable conditions that the elites complained about. That is why they used violence to eliminate these conditions. The nobility, the Church, and the merchant townspeople united to carry out organised attacks to end the peasants' autonomy and lower wages. They did not do this by taking away the peasants' post-feudal freedoms again because they saw this as an impossible goal to achieve. Instead, they forced them off their land through violence and a continent-wide eviction campaign. Commons such as pastures, forests, and rivers, which were once collectively managed and sustained by rural society, were fenced off and made available to the elite. In short, they became private property.[126] This loss of the commons was nothing less than indirect violence against the peasants. Proudhon, too, argues that it should not be possible to claim property rights over land since recognising this right would mean giving up a natural right, such as the right to work, and, consequently, that would mean the abandonment of the title of being a human.[127]

Therefore, the rich and elite did not hesitate to use direct violence in the process. Thousands of rural communities were destroyed in the process of enclosure, harvests were ripped up and burned, and entire towns were levelled. Ordinary people lost access to land, forests, game, water, and fish – the resources they needed to survive.[128] Peasants opposing this situation revolted several times in many parts of Europe. In the largest of these, which took place in 1524, a text was prepared by blending local and regional demands. In this 12-point text, two of the most prominent demands were ending the occupation of common lands and stopping lords from preventing peasants

---

[126] Hickel, *Less is More*, pp. 45–6.
[127] Proudhon, *Qu'est-ce que la Propriété?*, p. 96.
[128] Hickel, *Less is More*, p. 46.

from hunting, fishing, and gathering trees.[129] However, these rebellions were violently suppressed, and hundreds of thousands of peasants were killed. Having overcome the most significant practical obstacle, the bourgeoisie gradually began to establish its own legal order, so much so that by the seventeenth century, the main characteristic of English constitutionalism was that it now considered liberty as dependent on the security of the right to private property.[130]

In the seventeenth and eighteenth centuries, notions of land improvement and scientific agriculture were invoked in the debates about the utility of enclosures. Agronomists, jurists, economists, engineers, and even philosopher John Locke (1632–1704) were busy turning a brutal class plunder of the poor into a narrative of progress and efficiency.[131] Locke, himself a landowner, acknowledged that enclosure was a theft from the commons and the ordinary people. However, he argued that this theft was morally justifiable because it enabled the transition to intensive commercial methods that increased agricultural output.[132] After two centuries of debate and theft, by the early nineteenth century, the commons, accessible to all and governed by ancient traditions, existed only in remote mountainous regions.[133]

There is no doubt that the usurpation of peasants' rights of access to land was not new or limited to England. Those in power in Rome also practiced the seizure of common assets used by the people. Nevertheless, the transformation of common land into private property in England, a process that began in the late fifteenth century and was completed in the early nineteenth, was unprecedented. Even customary rights, such as the right to collect what was left of the harvest and forest products or to use rivers and lakes, were abolished by law.[134] In the hands of the bourgeoisie, law had become a tool

---

129 Harman, *A People's History of the World*, pp. 189–90.

130 John Phillip Reid, *Constitutional History of American Revolution – The Authority of Rights*, University of Wisconsin Press, Wisconsin, 1986, pp. 31–2, cited in: Oya Boyar, *Anayasal Yoruma Giriş*, On İki Levha, Istanbul, 2021, p. 84.

131 Peter Linebaugh, *The Magna Carta Manifesto: Libertis and Commons for All*, University of California Press, Berkeley, 2008, cited in: Capra – Mattei, *The Ecology of Law*, p. 74.

132 Hickel, *Less is More*, p. 56.

133 Capra – Mattei, *The Ecology of Law*, p. 74.

134 Capra – Mattei, *The Ecology of Law*, p. 74.

for the seizure of the natural assets on which the lives of ordinary people depended. That was unprecedented in history, but it has persisted to this day.

This transformation of England's legal system and society then spread to the rest of the world through colonialism. Thus, the enclosure movement, which had reached its natural limits in England, moved to a stage where there were no borders. According to Klein, this idea of the inexhaustibility of nature's offerings is at the heart of all of the ideas and beliefs that underlie the foundations of today's Anglo-Saxon countries, ideas and beliefs that are deeply woven into their national histories. These new lands of immense natural wealth, which later became the United States, Canada, and Australia, appeared to the British colonial powers as vast lands with endless resources that could replace their homelands, where no nature to exploit left. Moreover, if the meadows in one part of these new lands were to dry up or become overcrowded, it would be easy to move the frontier further, designate new 'new worlds', and lay claim to those lands.[135] In the eyes of the colonial powers, the inhabitants of these new worlds were insignificant. They were not capable of having rights and freedoms and, therefore, as a part of nature, could be seized, exploited, enslaved, and killed without any fear of punishment. Their land was *res nullius*. It belonged to whoever seized it first. As the enclosure movement crossed the borders of England, the most fertile lands of the world became the property of the seizer, along with those who lived on them.

It can be said, therefore, that capitalism rose on the back of organised violence, mass impoverishment, and the systematic destruction of self-sufficient subsistence economies.[136] This transformation, which led to the rise of Western modernity, required the extraction, accumulation, and mobilisation of jaw-dropping amounts of natural and human resources. These resources later came to be known as 'capital'.[137] However, the acquisition and preservation of capital depended on the elevation of property to the status of a natural

---

[135] Klein, *On Fire*, pp. 36–7.

[136] Hickel, *Less is More*, p. 48.

[137] Karl Marx, *Capital: A Critique of Political Economy*, vol. 1, Penguin Classics, London, (1867) 1992, the so-called primitive accumulation theory is developed in vol. 1, part 8, chapter 26, cited in: Capra – Mattei, *The Ecology of Law*, p. 73.

right that could be abolished by neither kings nor commoners.[138] For this reason, it is of utmost importance to examine how the concept of property became a right as important and even sacred as the right to life and security.

The emergence of property as a natural right

The parallelism between the rise of liberalism, which the bourgeoisie defended with the aim of unlimited private property ownership, and the strengthening of property rights in Europe should not be considered surprising. Although liberalism is nowadays usually emphasised within the freedom of expression framework, it emerged from the freedom to own property. As a matter of fact, political philosopher Macpherson's criticism of the 'possessive' character of seventeenth-century individualism is directed against the type of individual, 'possessive individualism', which gains its freedom as a result of ownership and does not take sociality into consideration. This idea sees society as a structure composed of property owners and property relations as the determinant of the individual's freedom and self-realisation. In liberalism, even political society is constructed as a humanitarian mechanism for protecting property and maintaining a market society. In 'possessive individualism', individuals exist as much as they own, and the more they own, the more they realise their potential.[139] Therefore, if the condition of being human is to be free, it is no longer enough to separate oneself from nature; one must also acquire property.

William Blackstone (1723–80), professor of law at Oxford University, in his Commentaries on the Laws of England, defines private property as 'a solitary despotic sovereignty which one person claims and exercises over the external

---

[138] In Article 2 of the 1789 French Declaration of the Rights of Man and of the Citizen, property is considered one of the four natural and inalienable rights, along with life, liberty and resistance to oppression. Moreover, the last of the seventeen articles of the Declaration is devoted to the regulation of property as a sacred right.

[139] Crawford Broug Macpherson, *The Political Theory of Possessive Individualism: Hobbes to Locke*, Oxford University Press, Oxford, 2011 (1962), cited in: Didem Bayındır, '"Şimdinin Tarihini" Okumak', *in* Didem Bayındır – Mine Yıldırım (ed.), *Ekoloji: Bir Arada Yaşamın Geleceği*, Tellekt, Istanbul, 2022, p. 8. Cicero's *suum quidque cuiusque sit* (let each thing be to each one) opposes this view. According to Cicero, no one has rights beyond what he needs. Therefore, what belongs to a person is not what he can possess, but what he has the right to possess. See Proudhon, *Qu'est-ce que la Propriété?*, p. 57.

things of the world to the exclusion of the rights of any other individual in the universe'. That is probably the most accurate definition of natural law. This definition clearly reveals the property-oriented perspective in Western legal theory and shows how the model of individual dominance over nature was naturalised in his time.[140] At the same time, this definition is also important in that it reveals property as a positive phenomenon only for the rightful owner and as a limitation for everyone else. Indeed, the first and foremost function of the right to property used to be nothing more than the enclosure of communal areas, thus making them inaccessible to ordinary people.[141]

In the eighteenth century, the belief in a rational approach to human problems spread so rapidly among Europe's middle classes that it became known as the Enlightenment or the Age of Reason.[142] The philosopher John Locke was the dominant figure in this development, whose most essential writings were published at the end of the seventeenth century. Inspired by the main aspects of Newtonian mechanics, in which the relationships between different bodies are subject to immutable laws, Locke applied this approach to society. Perceiving society as a concept divided into individuals like atoms, he envisioned a society where the basic building blocks were individuals acquiring property. In other words, just as physicists reduced the properties of gases to the movement of their atoms or molecules, Locke reduced the phenomena observed in society to the behaviour of separate individuals.[143] In this way, he not only paved the way for unconstrained efforts by atomised individuals to achieve their freedom but also removed the source of a prosperous life from the relations with society and nature and linked it to individual success. Individuals were now responsible for their own lives, for better or worse. The sense of solidarity that had been dominant in societies up to that time

---

140 Capra – Mattei, *The Ecology of Law*, p. 84.

141 The 'No Entry' sign, for example, is still today a symbol of the sovereignty of owners over their property. Private land ownership denies many people access to and enjoyment of nature, it denies many people the right to produce healthy, safe food in their own areas using sustainable methods. Even animals are seen as objects of property, their sentient beings are ignored in the name of the food industry and production. See Capra – Mattei, *The Ecology of Law*, p. 139.

142 Knud Haakonssen, *Natural Law and Moral Philosophy: From Grotius to the Scotthish Enlightenment*, Cambridge University Press, Cambridge, 1996, cited in: Capra – Mattei, *The Ecology of Law*, p. 84.

143 Capra – Mattei, *The Ecology of Law*, p. 84.

was left behind. That, of course, on the one hand, led to destructive competition between individuals and, on the other, to the extreme acceleration of the appropriation and exploitation of natural assets for personal gain in order to get ahead in this competition. Enshrining individual rights for the first time in a constitutional amendment in the United States symbolised the pinnacle of the ideal of rational natural law, considering society as the sum of its individual components.[144] It is meaningful, of course, that this culmination first took place in a land that Europeans regarded as *res nullius* and subjected to rampant pillage and massacre for centuries. Moreover, the idea of an atomised and competitive society that prevailed when the United States was founded still dominates today.

Locke's ideas on property made him perhaps the most influential thinker on social and economic structure of any thinker in history. According to Locke, private property was inherent in the natural state of affairs and was, therefore, older than the social contract and civil society.[145] According to his labour theory, he assumed that if a person labours on natural resources, these resources become that person's property.[146] In his 1689 Second Treatise on Government, he wrote:

> I ask then, when did they begin to be his? [...] and it is plain, if the first gathering made them not his, nothing else could. That labour put a distinction between them and common: that added something to them more than nature, the common mother of all, had done; and so they became his private right.[147]

In Locke's view, which was also fuelled by Christianity,[148] wilderness was an asset given by God to all men for their use, waiting for someone with the power and will of initiative to come to it, work it, and in the process transform it into private personal good. In other words, nature outside of man was waiting

---

144 Capra – Mattei, *The Ecology of Law*, p. 97.

145 Jean Touchard, *Histoire des Idées Politiques* (Turkish version), trans. İsmail Yerguz, Islık Yayınları, Istanbul, 2015, p. 390.

146 Capra – Mattei, *The Ecology of Law*, p. 95.

147 John Locke, *Second Treatise on Government*, Project Gutenberg, 2005, Chapter V, Sec. 28.

148 By claiming that human beings are created in the image of God, Christianity not only creates a duality between man and nature but also claims that man's use of nature for his own purposes is actually God's will. See Lynn White Jr, 'The Historical Roots of Our Ecological Crisis', *Science*, Vol. 155, No. 3767, 10 March 1967, p. 1205.

for man to come and use it. It was almost as if this was a God-given task for human beings. With the influx of the bourgeoisie, which needed more capital to develop, large amounts of land with no owner became a productive and valuable commodity through the addition of human labour. The wilderness was now a potential resource that could be appropriated and used to create an individual good life. Once conquered, nature would become a source of wealth. The wilderness was merely an undeveloped mass of resources.[149]

Thus, in the process that began as the Enlightenment, nature was killed by the rationality of the bourgeoisie, transformed into 'something external and inferior, an object'.[150] Nature was no longer seen as a balanced system based on networks humans were a part of. There was no reciprocal relationship between man and nature; there was only a one-sided relationship of appropriation and utilisation. Based on an ontological contradiction between human beings and nature, the reason inherent in the capital system, without any historical context, reduced all human activity to a relationship of appropriation over nature. While nature was pushed down morally and legally, man was expressed as a reality outside and above nature.[151] Since man is superior and has been called by God to use nature, appropriating it has been accepted as a natural right of man, stemming from his being human.

This view was later supported by the famous thinker Hegel. In an effort to justify private property, Hegel, following in Locke's footsteps, wrote the following:

> A person has as his substantive end the right of putting his will into any and everything and thereby it his, because it has no such end in itself and derives its destiny and soul from his will. This is the absolute right of appropriation which man has over all 'things'.[152]

---

149 DesJardins, *Environmental Ethics*, pp. 306–7.

150 Max Horkheimer – Theodor Adorno, *Dialectics of Enlightenment*, trans. Oğuz Özügül, Kabalcı, Istanbul, 1995, p. 62, cited in: Ecehan Balta – Mustafa Bayram Mısır, 'Bir Politik Hareket Olarak Ekososyalizmin Ayırd Ediciliği ve Birleştiriciliği', *Praksis*, No. 25, 2011/11, p. 16.

151 Fevzi Özlüer, 'Ekososyalist Bir Kır Hareketine Doğru', *Ecotopianetwork*, 14 December 2009.

152 G. Hegel, *Hegel's Philosophy of Right 41*, transl. T. Knox, 1945, cited in: Christopher D. Stone, *Should Trees Have Standing? Law, Morality, and the Environment* (Kindle edition), 3rd ed., Oxford University Press, New York, 2010, p. 27.

'Absolute' here means that at the time, no one, including the king, could interfere with this right. Today, the fact that the right to property is still considered absolute puts it outside the reach of democratic bodies such as parliament, even on vital issues such as climate change. Whereas the right to property used to serve as a shield to prevent the bourgeoisie from being obstructed while the commons were being usurped, today, it does so while capitalism is driving the planet into the abyss. It is impossible to say that this is just or morally right. However, measures against criticism on this issue were taken from the very beginning.

In an effort to prove that the unlimited acquisition of wealth is not unjust or morally wrong, Locke addresses this situation in his theory of the social contract. In his description of the state of nature in which the limits to the acquisition of property are removed with the emergence of money, he identifies the common good of people, which is the purpose of political power, with prosperity. In other words, prosperity is the common good of people; therefore, the aim should be to increase prosperity. Prosperity, in turn, is possible through the increase in wealth. That requires peace and security. Since the increase in wealth requires the removal of the limits to greed, and at the same time, people must be able to acquire what they deserve safely, protecting private property becomes the raison d'être and purpose of political power.[153] In other words, political power, which is no longer defined by its acts but by its limits, has a new purpose compatible with this limit: protecting private property.[154] Indeed, according to Locke, 'the end of government is the preservation of property'.[155]

According to the public view, which Locke saw institutionalised in the English Act of Settlement in 1701, only three years before his death, the state and the property owner were sovereign in their respective spheres. However, the relationship between the sovereign state and the individual property owner was still controversial in legal and political texts. First, the French jurist Jean Bodin (1530–96) and later Thomas Hobbes (1588–1679) theorised state absolutism, giving ultimate power to the state. On the contrary, from

---

153 Leo Strauss, *Natural Right and History*, 5th ed., University of Chicago Press, 1965, pp. 244–6; cited in: Özenç, *Hukuk Devleti*, p. 189.

154 Özenç, *Hukuk Devleti*, p. 189.

155 Locke, *Second Treatise on Government*, Chapter XI, Sec. 138.

the perspective of the French Declaration of the Rights of Man and the Citizen of 1789, adopted by Locke and the American founders, property was a natural right based on natural law that existed before the state.[156] Therefore, it was natural for the state to protect this natural right that existed even before it. The state was sovereign but could not use this sovereignty to violate property rights.

From this perspective, one of the most fundamental functions of the property right was that even the king could not seize the property of his subjects in any way. Thus, through its function of preventing the primary source of oppression, the right to property acted as a shield, protecting other rights as well.[157] In other words, the relationship between private property and the state's sovereignty was frozen by the legal protection of private property against government confiscation. Government seizure of property was conditional. In this sense, ironically, the state's sovereignty was limited. It was permitted only under stringent public interest conditions, after payment of 'just compensation', defined as market value, within the framework of laws set by parliament, which was in the hands of the bourgeoisie.[158] However, it was also assumed that the government, in line with modern ideas of sovereignty, represented the common interest, that is, promoting prosperity. Therefore, the government could freely confiscate common assets and transfer them to private ownership to ensure their 'improvement'. In the United States, for example, the Home Rule Act provided for such a scheme with respect to all lands outside the thirteen initially established states.[159]

Thus, property and state sovereignty became the two organising principles of legal modernity.[160] With the support of these two pillars, the new order quickly took hold. The idea that land that was not privately owned belonged to no one instead of belonging to everyone was quickly established

---

156 Capra – Mattei, *The Ecology of Law*, p. 85.

157 John Phillip Reid, *Constitutional History of American Revolution – The Authority of Rights*, University of Wisconsin Press, Wisconsin, 1986, p. 28, cited in: Boyar, *Anayasal Yoruma Giriş*, p. 84.

158 J. W. Ely, *The Guardian of Every Other Right: A Constitutional History of Property Rights*, 3rd edition, Oxford University Press, Oxford, 2008, cited in: Capra – Mattei, *The Ecology of Law*, p. 97.

159 Capra – Mattei, *The Ecology of Law*, p. 97.

160 Capra – Mattei, *The Ecology of Law*, p. 11.

to justify the appropriation of land, enslaved people, and resources. In the eighteenth and nineteenth centuries, through this legal structure, defined and justified as natural law, cargo ships loaded with industrial products made in England travelled to the West African coast and received permission from local kings to enslave people in exchange. The same ships that sailed from Africa loaded with human cargo left their acquired human 'goods' in America. The minerals mined and agricultural products grown in the New World by enslaved people were transported to British ports on the same ships.[161] Thus, a triangle of exploitation was established between Britain, Africa, and America. The bourgeoisie was as responsible for this triangle as the rationalist Enlightenment thinkers who enabled it. As Harman's example aptly depicts, while philosophers talked about equal rights in the coffeehouses of Europe, the sweetened coffee they drank was produced by people who were loaded onto ships from West Africa at gunpoint, taken across the Atlantic Ocean in appalling conditions, sold at auctions, and then whipped for up to 18 hours a day until they died.[162]

It is evident that what Macpherson calls possessive individualism is not limited to the seventeenth century but extends to the present. As a matter of fact, capitalism both fed on this understanding of the individual and nurtured it. In fact, with neoliberalism, which crowned this relationship, the *laissez faire, laissez passer* motto of classical economics has been extended to *laissez mourir* since the last quarter of the twentieth century. That makes sense when one considers the fate of millions of enslaved people transported from Africa to the Americas, either while being transported on ships or later while working on plantations. That is a story in which those who owe their existence to their 'possessiveness' make it through, while those who cannot 'realise themselves' because they are not like that are left to die.[163]

It is well-known how cruelly the bourgeois economic order, which rises on the ideas of equality and freedom of all, has treated even human beings at its foundation and in its continuation. Given this situation, it was clear even then that the destructive impact on nature would be much more significant if the

---

[161] E. Galeano, *Open Veins of Latin America: Five Centuries of Pillage of a Continent*, Monthly Review Press, New York, 1973, cited in: Capra – Mattei, *The Ecology of Law*, p. 95.

[162] Harman, *A People's History of the World*, p. 248.

[163] Didem Bayındır, 'Reading the History of the Present', p. 9. (Emphasis is Bayındır's.)

understanding of property, which is shaped around the logic of ownership and use of natural assets as resources, were to be considered. When it comes to the natural environment, capitalism, unlike ancient societies, perceived it not as a source of joy or entertainment but as a means to its ultimate goals of profit and further capital accumulation.[164]

Moving the Nile perch out of its habitat, building in an unpolluted bay, digging for oil in Alaska, or applying fracking technology are all examples of the exercises of economic freedom protected by private property. According to bourgeois logic, these activities provide individuals with independence. As Capra and Mattei argue, in the classical capitalist conception, the state is the sole entity capable of regulating this freedom, dominating the zero-sum relationship between the two where increased state control results in reduced property freedom, and increased freedom leads to diminished state control; this relationship is viewed as a natural law. In the absence of legal constraints on a specific action, it is assumed that a rational individual is free to exploit resources. Additionally, these domains, considered mutually exclusive, are believed to be governed by the undeniable logic that a more robust market presence implies a weaker state, and a more robust state implies a weaker market.[165]

Moreover, neoliberalism has broken even this equation and placed the state at the disposal of the market. The bourgeois class now not only demands that the state not intervene with it and its rights and not exercise its sovereignty over private property rights; it also expects the state to use its sovereign powers to pave the way for more profits and, when it falls on hard times, to put it back on its feet through ordinary people's taxes. In the past, the bourgeoisie used to make the rules through parliaments and expected the executive to respect them. Still, now that it has also captured the executive, it has an unlimited capacity to govern. That, of course, paves the way for both the violation of the most fundamental rights of ordinary citizens and the unlimited exploitation of nature.

Strict protection of private property and no protection for the commons has become the norm in the capitalist world. As a sovereign power, the state

---

164 Paul M. Sweezy, 'Capitalism and the Environment', *Türkiye Monthly Review*, Issue 8, 2006, pp. 77–85, cited in: Balta – Mısır, 'Bir Politik … ', p. 19.

165 Capra – Mattei, *The Ecology of Law*, p. 27.

privatises the commons and freely transfers resources from the public to the private sector. However, it is only possible to do the opposite and transfer resources from the private sector back to the public sector within the framework of rules set by parliament and under the strict supervision of the judiciary. This process, therefore, leads to a continuous and practically irreversible flow of public resources towards private ownership.[166] Consequently, today's legal and economic situation is not very different from that of seventeenth-century England.

People, once interdependent, are now recognised by their individual property 'rights' that keep others away from them. The legacy of this move towards modernity today includes an unquestioning faith in the notion of individual human rights and a mechanistic, top-down rule of law. That paved the way for plunder and colonialism and the view of corporations as 'legal entities' constituting the building blocks of an atomised system.[167] Unlimited property rights, once belonging only to individuals, were extended to the emerging institution of corporation. The pressure on nature by corporatised people, combined with capitalist logic, has thus grown exponentially.

The new 'person' that comes into existence through the property: the corporation

Early modernity left one last legacy that is still enormously influential: the birth and development of the entrepreneurial company, which was given a 'legal personality' and legal rights.[168] Within liberal ideology, the legitimacy of granting legal personality to the joint economic ventures of individuals is very controversial and has its roots in pre-liberal, even anti-liberal, thought.[169] Today, it is essential to look at the history of corporations, and multinational corporations in particular, the leading cause of climate change emissions and ecological destruction, to understand the present and find solutions to the current crisis.

We generally believe that companies have existed from the very beginning, more or less in the form we see them today. However, in English law,

---

166 Capra – Mattei, *The Ecology of Law*, pp. 97–8.
167 Capra – Mattei, *The Ecology of Law*, p. 91. (Emphasis is Capra – Mattei's.)
168 Capra – Mattei, *The Ecology of Law*, p. 102.
169 Theodore J. Lowi, *End of Liberalism*, New York, 1969, p. 6, cited in: Poggi, *The Development of the Modern State*, p. 149.

corporations first emerged as 'non-profit institutions' intending to advance the interests of society as a whole. They included churches, schools, universities, and, at a broader level, municipalities, and what they could and could not do was tightly controlled initially.[170]

Towards the end of the sixteenth century in England, the Crown began to grant Royal Warrants to trade organisations to become corporates. One of these was granted to the East India Company[171] in 1600, allowing it to monopolise trade in India. Many Indian merchants felt that the Company would better defend their interests than the six kings who were at war with each other at the time, so they began to do business with this organisation, which came to the country with troops and arms.[172] At first, everything went as usual, but then the East India Company took some unprecedented actions: It created shares in itself and started trading them on its stock exchange to generate profits for its members. However, its bylaws did not permit this, so it was acting illegally. However, it increased its profits without facing any sanctions, and other companies followed suit.[173]

This *de facto* situation became permanent and normalised over the years and was transformed into a legal situation. The companies, initially strictly controlled by the Kingdom of England and the government, were authorised to determine their own objectives with the Joint Stock Companies Act of 1844.[174] Therefore, the British East India Company can be considered the ancestor of today's multinational corporations, both in terms of the way it paved the way for companies to be free from state control in terms of their objectives and to be legally protected in terms of setting profit as the primary goal and in terms of moving from country to country for the sake of more profit. Indeed, the company could do business wherever there were the best opportunities to increase its share value. Today's multinational corporations

---

170 Cullinan, *Wild Law*, p. 64.

171 The company that conquered India. Headquartered in Leadenhall Street, London, it ruled the Indian Empire for 100 years with an army of 350,000 men. The company's private army and India were only annexed to the United Kingdom in 1858. See Harari, *Sapiens*, p. 320.

172 Harman, *A People's History of the World*, pp. 347–8.

173 Cullinan, *Wild Law*, p. 65.

174 Cullinan, *Wild Law*, p. 65.

have followed in their footsteps, efficiently shuttling between regions where different methods prevail.

Nevertheless, there was as much fall as a rise in trade. Most investors were either part of or directly linked to the political elite and wanted high incomes to embark on these risky ventures. However, their personal wealth had to be protected by a mechanism known as limited liability, which separated their assets from those of the company's legal entity.[175] To this end, a law was passed in England in 1855,[176] limiting shareholders' liability for the company's debts to the amount they paid for their shares,[177] showing how faithfully the legislative organ of the state was working for the economic elite's benefit.

Other European countries followed this example. Geographical discoveries, the origin of European imperialism, were risky ventures. Many expeditions failed to return: Ships hit icebergs, sank in tropical storms, or fell into the hands of pirates. Europeans turned to limited liability joint stock companies to increase the number of potential investors and reduce risk. Rather than a single investor putting up all their money, joint stock companies raised money from a large number of investors, allowing them all to risk a small portion of their capital. So the risk was reduced, but there was no limit to the profits that could be made; even a small investment in the correct ship could make you a millionaire.[178] So, at this point, it is appropriate to emphasise the importance of the laws passed by parliaments in the growth of corporations. The growth of the bourgeoisie was made possible not by its struggle against the state but by its power, especially in parliaments, to join hands with the state. Property rights backed by the state made corporations the real owners of power.[179]

As Poggi emphasises, the control of the big business over the economic process, and thus over the entire social sphere, enabled them to influence the state itself, to persuade it to at least 'stay out of their business', and finally to put some of its governing powers at their disposal. In the twentieth century, capitalist business had great success with this strategy, expanding the sphere of

---

175 Tirthankar Roy, *The East India Company: The World's Most Powerful Corporation*, Penguin, London, 2021, cited in: Capra – Mattei, *The Ecology of Law*, p. 102.

176 *Act for Limiting the Liability of Members of Certain Joint Stock Companies*

177 Cullinan, *Wild Law*, p. 65.

178 Harari, *Sapiens*, p. 314.

179 Capra – Mattei, *The Ecology of Law*, p. 27.

the state's activity and changing the forms of its activity. It directed the state towards goals that would have been unacceptable in the nineteenth century. For example, states now allocate significant funds from public revenues to establish, strengthen, or modernise companies in advanced industries to be used according to the logic of profit. Indeed, profit is still a 'private' logic, regardless of the rules according to which companies operate and according to which funds are allocated. It should, therefore, not be possible for it to be publicly funded. However, especially after the occupation of state organs by the bourgeoisie, it has become commonplace for public resources, such as public land or, even more so, taxes collected from the population, to be used for private purposes. Moreover, the state's effort to expand and modernise the national education system, whatever its stated purpose is, has been reconfigured to provide the trained workforce and advanced scientific, technological, and managerial knowledge that the industry needs to operate and advance.[180]

In brief, corporations were created by the social and economic conditions of a certain period of history when the bourgeoisie became dominant. Inherent in these conditions is their greed. Accordingly, the laws governing corporations and their charters demand that they aggressively fight for control over the Earth's abundance and consume as much of it as possible without regard for the long-term damage to the Earth or its inhabitants.[181] Today, corporations are the most significant contributors to the destruction of ecosystems[182] and loss of biodiversity through deforestation, land grabbing, excavation, transportation and burning of fossil fuels, industrial agriculture, intensive livestock farming, industrial fishing, large-scale mining, and the appropriation of water and nature.[183] The aim of corporations to increase production indefinitely for the sake of profit leads to increased carbon emissions and the climate change we are experiencing today.

---

[180] Poggi, *The Development of the Modern State*, p. 152.

[181] Cullinan, *Wild Law*, p. 64.

[182] An ecosystem is defined as a relatively uniform and organised set of interrelationships that connect living things to each other and to their environment. See Keleş – Hamamcı – Çoban, *Çevre Politikası*, p. 48.

[183] David R. Boyd, *Report of the Special Rapporteur on the Issue of Human Rights Obligations Relating to the Enjoyment of a Safe, Clean, Healthy and Sustainable Environment*, UN General Assembly, UN DOC A/75/161, 15 July 2020, p. 20, § 75.

Ümit Şahin from Sabancı University's Istanbul Policy Center points out that the hegemony established by corporations has obstructed the structure of the discourse established while formulating climate policies as well as the scale of the transformation required to combat the climate crisis. Reducing greenhouse gas emissions from human activities forms the basis of policies against climate change. Still, a policy framework has been established as if reducing emissions is only related to demand and in the hands of consumers. The logic of such climate policies that remove the responsibility of companies is the assumption that if the demand for burning fossil fuels that cause greenhouse gas emissions decreases, the production of fossil fuels that cause emissions will also decrease. Consumers are, therefore, the ones who need to step up to the plate.[184] As can be seen, within this basic framework of climate policies, there are no obstacles to the extraction and sale of fossil fuels. Under the assumption that companies have the right to produce whatever they find profitable in a free-market economy, it is accepted that policies can only be made to reduce demand, not the supply of fossil fuels. However, it is states that allocate mining sites and oil wells to companies, grant exploration and drilling permits, distribute thermal power plant and pipeline licenses, plan, design, and operate them in some countries, and use them as a force in international relations. While this policy design severely limits the pace and scale of transformation, it continues to underpin the political discourse and feed the denial and delay in tackling the climate crisis.[185] This vicious circle reveals the extent to which today's states and corporations are intertwined and have even become one and the same thing. Therefore, the only solution in the context of climate change seems to be the effective involvement of

---

[184] In this framework, as Şahin points out in the same place, when a price is put on the carbon emitted, the fossil fuels used by companies and the products such as natural gas, electricity produced from coal, airline tickets, etc., which use fossil fuels in their production, will become more expensive as companies cannot stop making profit, which will affect rational consumer behaviour and direct them to products that use renewable resources. However, for this logic to work, the subsidies provided by the state for the production and use of fossil fuels in production must be removed. Otherwise, prices will not rise. Even if these subsidies are cut, states also need to support products produced using renewable energy. Otherwise, the demand for them will increase and their prices will rise. Consequently, the burden will again fall on consumers.

[185] Ümit Şahin, 'İklim Krizine Kavramsal Bir Giriş', *in* Didem Bayındır – Mine Yıldırım (ed.), *Ekoloji: Bir Arada Yaşamın Geleceği*, Tellekt, Istanbul, 2022, p. 38.

supreme courts in every country, as they are the only legal institutions with the authority to force both companies and state bodies with a green constitutionalist approach to reduce emissions and thus to take binding measures to protect the lives of humans and other natural beings. That is the subject of the second part of the book.

1.1.2.2 Equality

Equality has been present in political life since Antiquity. It is one of the concepts referred to first by those who talk about Athenian democracy. In Athens, equality and democracy were even used interchangeably since only a state in which the law was the same for all (*isonomia*) and participation in affairs (*isegoria*) and power (*isocratia*) was equal could be democratic.[186] The Athenians understood by equality that all free citizens[187] were on the same footing when participating in decision-making processes. In other words, no distinction could be made between individuals based on lineage, wealth, or profession while governing the city. After the collapse of Athenian democracy in the 3rd century BC, with democracy, the idea of equality also fell into a long silence.

As the bourgeoisie established and consolidated its power in the eighteenth century, one of the fundamental concepts on which it relied was equality, which it drew from Athens. From Locke's point of view, individuals continue to enjoy their natural liberty equally within the limits of the laws created by the legislature, the sovereign power of the civil society formed by the social contract. That represents an important step towards the rule of law that later became dominant in Anglo-Saxon legal orders. However, Locke's idea of equality does not include a political equality that grants everyone the right to participate in decisions. He states that the legislature, which is the supreme power, should be formed with the consent of the majority, and the majority should be determined *qualitatively*, not *quantitatively*. The right to rule is limited to the propertied class, which provides the material revenues and taxes on which power is based, and the majority he mentions is the majority of the members of the propertied class.[188] Therefore, equality,

---

[186] Touchard, *Histoire des Idées Politiques*, p. 35.
[187] In the Athenian democracy, only free Athenian men were considered citizens.
[188] Özenç, *Hukuk Devleti*, p. 190.

according to Locke's thought, is, in fact, equality only within the bourgeoisie. Thus, Locke, who used egalitarian and libertarian ideas as a basis for justifying social inequalities, added significant power to justify inequality, capitalism, and imperial expansion with his theory of property.[189]

Contrary to Locke, the thinker who defended equality in a way very close to its true meaning in Athens was Jean Jacques Rousseau (1712–78),[190] who radically opposed the bourgeoisised society in which he lived. Rousseau equated equality with freedom.[191] Rousseau argued that sovereignty, the supreme decision-making will, was equally distributed to all and thus opposed both aristocratic and bourgeois hierarchical societies. Ironically, this idea of Rousseau turned into a weapon used by the bourgeoisie against the aristocracy. In the 1789 French Revolution, the bourgeoisie embraced the discourse of equality and emphasised that careers should be open to talent. It demanded not privileges but equality and generality in access to state offices. Thus, for the first time in history, the French Revolution was a movement that opposed and destroyed privileges in the name of equality and freedom.[192]

On the other hand, the bourgeoisie did not care about the equality of the ordinary people, who became increasingly proletarianised by them. The primary function of the concept of equality for this new economic class was to eliminate the superiority of the aristocrats. In other words, behind the defence of equality by the bourgeoisie lay the destruction of the hierarchical superiority of the aristocracy, the rulers of the old order. With the discourse of equality as a natural right, the aristocracy lost its old privileged status based on lineage from the familial past, and the bourgeoisie, which had transformed from an ordinary group of people into an economic and social class by enriching itself through trade in the cities was elevated to its level.

The best example of this is the elections for the Parliament, which became a body exercising sovereignty after the French Revolution. The right to vote and be elected was conditional on property or education and was only granted to men.[193] Those who owned property or had the chance to be educated, leaving aside the aristocrats, were only those who had become rich by engaging in

---

189 Wood, *Freedom and Property*, pp. 14–15 (foreword by Oya Köymen).

190 Touchard, *Histoire des Idées Politiques*, p. 449.

191 Touchard, *Histoire des Idées Politiques*, p. 443.

192 Wood, *Freedom and Property*, p. 12 (foreword by Oya Köymen).

193 Poggi, *The Development of the Modern State*, pp. 144–5.

trade or came from a wealthy family and could go to school without having to work. Although the revolution had taken place and succeeded with the participation of the ordinary people and many social strata, in the new regime that followed, participation in government thus became a privilege reserved exclusively for the bourgeoisie. Although in the very first article of the Declaration of the Rights of Man and of the Citizen, issued immediately after the French Revolution, the principle of equality in all rights was declared to apply to all people throughout their lives, the people referred to here were in fact only the bourgeoisie.

Despite the explicit provision in the Declaration, parliamentarians in France and Britain resisted recognising universal suffrage for many years.[194] The exclusion of ordinary people from elections was because, in the nineteenth and early twentieth centuries, the most practical way to exclude groups whose interests conflicted with the maintenance and development of the capitalist system from the political sphere was to restrict the right to vote. Without the right to vote, these groups could only exercise other civic rights that had no direct political significance or resort to illegal forms of political opposition that police and other repression could suppress. Once interests at odds with the system had been 'filtered out' of the political process in this way, public institutions, especially Parliament, where only the bourgeois could elect and be elected, could reconcile other conflicting interests that arose within capitalist-bourgeois institutions and values.[195]

1.1.2.3 Freedom

If the first pillar of Athenian democracy was equality, the second pillar was freedom. To the Athenians, to be free meant not to be enslaved to anyone or anything.[196] In this framework, freedom in Ancient Greece was a right exercised collectively, not individually. Direct participation in decision-making processes, one of the elements characterising Athenian democracy, constituted the definition of freedom as it created a government without a ruler. For this reason, Athenians described their city as civilised due to the fact

---

[194] See Harman, *A People's History of the World*, pp. 376–7.

[195] T. Geiger, *Suggi sulla Società Industriale*, Turin, 1970, p. 613, 617 et seq., cited in: Poggi, *The Development of the Modern State*, p. 144.

[196] Touchard, *Histoire des Idées Politiques*, p. 38.

that they governed themselves without the need for a ruler and everyone else as barbarians because they were unable to establish an administration without a ruler.

With the Renaissance, the Athenian concept of freedom resurfaced. However, as with the concept of equality, in a pretty different way. What urban merchants understood from freedom in the context of John Locke's right to property was the unlimited acquisition of natural resources, production, and sale of these products. Such an environment could only be achieved by limiting the absolute power, namely the king, in line with the idea of constitutionalism. That required both the adoption of the principle of the supremacy of the rules established by parliaments and the transformation of the fundamental rights and freedoms, which stemmed from the theory of natural law and were written down in the French Declaration of the Rights of Man and the Citizen, into shields that could protect individuals even against the King.

Article 16 of the Declaration, which states that 'a society in which rights are not secured, and the separation of powers is not established has no constitution', clearly reveals the will to realise these two objectives simultaneously. With this article, the bourgeois class not only built a wall of protection against the king by stating that their rights could not be violated but also transferred the supreme rule-making power, which was formerly vested in the king in absolute form, to the Parliament, reducing the King to an executive body that had to obey these rules. What is remarkable here is that the conception of freedom in the immediate aftermath of the French Revolution, like equality, served the interests of the bourgeois class exclusively.

Indeed, by the end of the eighteenth century, freedom had a very different meaning than it does today. It did not mean that the powerless (especially blacks, Indigenous or women) could gain power and take over. It simply meant that the state could not confiscate the personal property of citizens and interfere in how they used it except in very exceptional circumstances.[197] Thus, in Locke's view, property and liberty were united[198] because property was the main and almost the only thing that liberty protected.

---

[197] Harari, *Sapiens*, p. 141.

[198] Touchard, *Histoire des Idées Politiques*, p. 443.

In conclusion, it is true that with the rise of the bourgeoisie, the concepts of equality and freedom came back to the agenda and even became the founding principles of the modern state. However, these concepts, which emerged in England in the seventeenth century and in France in the eighteenth, had a very different content from what we understand today. A society and legal order in which everyone is equal before the law and in which rights and freedoms apply to everyone was made possible not thanks to the bourgeoisie but to the struggle against it.

1.2 The connection between the development of capitalism and the modern state

We have chosen cancer as a model for our social system.[199]

We have a perception that the market economy has always existed throughout history. However, this is not true. Although 'markets' have been around for many years, the market economy *system* only came into our lives two centuries ago.[200] The word 'capitalism' entered the English language in the middle of the nineteenth century. Before that, starting in the fourteenth and fifteenth centuries, another word was used: *capital*, meaning 'head' or 'first' in Latin. Finally, in the eighteenth century, it acquired its current meaning as an economic category.[201] Capitalism is a system of power as well as an economic category. It involves the self-perpetuating domination of the capital-owning class over groups whose livelihood and social place depend on selling their labour.[202] Without understanding the connection between the capitalist infrastructure based on fossil fuels, which is the leading cause of climate change, and the modern state and legal system that has been formed in line

---

199 Bookchin, *The Next Revolution*, p. 12 (foreword by Ursula K. LeGuin).

200 Fotopoulos, Takis, *Towards an Inclusive Democracy – The Crisis of the Growth Economy and the Need for a New Liberatory Project*, Cassel, London & New York, 1997, p. 3. (Emphasis is Fotopoulos'.)

201 'Capital', 'Capitalism' and 'Capitalist', *Oxford English Dictionary: The Compact Edition*, vol. 1, Oxford University Press, Oxford, 1971, p. 334, cited in: Foster, *Capitalism in the Anthropocene*, p. 14.

202 Poggi, *The Development of the Modern State*, p. 144.

with the needs of today's bourgeoisie,[203] it is not easy to understand and solve the crisis we are in. Therefore, a closer look at the history and development of these interconnected concepts is helpful.

1.2.1 The emergence of the nation-state in line with the needs of the bourgeoisie

Until the late eighteenth century, the world's largest economies were in Asia, rich in natural resources and fertile land. Europeans had far less capital than the Chinese, Muslims, or Indians. However, the Asian empires were not trade-oriented. They were built by bureaucratic and military elites. Since they financed wars through taxes and looting, they did not have much need for banks or credit systems. Accordingly, they were indifferent to the interests of bankers and investors. In Europe, where the only natural resource was coal, not gold or silver, and not much else grew on the land, kings and generals inevitably had to adopt a commercial perspective. When technological development made it possible to build ships that could cross oceans and colonise, the money for this massive operation was found through bank loans rather than taxes collected from ordinary people. This process was led by capitalists who wanted maximum return on their investments. Moreover, merchant empires were much better at financing their conquests since no one wanted to pay taxes, and everyone was happy to invest.[204] That, of course, increased both the power and prestige of the merchants as the class that brought wealth to Europe and increased prosperity, both in the eyes of the public and at the state level.

The conquest of the world was essentially a business and not much different from the world of commerce today. For example, at the end of the fifteenth century, Christopher Columbus of Genoa sought investors for his voyage of discovery to find a trade route to East Asia, just as business people do today. That was not an easy task, as the voyage project was characterised

---

[203] Ellen Meiksins Wood argues against seeing the bourgeois and the capitalist as the same thing. While I partially agree with the author that the classical discourse that capitalism developed with the removal of barriers to urban trade is misleading on the grounds that there are qualitative differences between pre-capitalist trade and capitalist trade, this discussion is beyond the scope of this study. For more information on the subject, please refer to the author's book titled *Freedom and Property*.

[204] Harari, *Sapiens*, p. 313.

by uncertain outcomes and returns and required a significant investment. In the end, Spain's rulers were persuaded to finance the expedition. As we know today, this extremely risky investment gave the Spaniards enormous profits and power. Thus, the magic cycle of imperial capitalism was created: Credit financed discoveries, discoveries led to colonies, colonies led to profits, profits led to confidence, and confidence meant more credit.[205] The world's natural wealth began to flow to Europe, and global economic dominance began to shift. The geographical advantage of Asians was balanced by the commercial 'intelligence' of Europeans.

Both the internal dynamics of the production system in the cities – which was inevitably moving towards the capitalist mode of production – and the rapid commercialisation of the economy due to the influx of bullion to Europe from across the ocean played an essential role in the transition to absolute power structures.[206] It was inevitable that the change in the economic infrastructure with the strengthening of the merchant class would be reflected in the superstructural institutions. However, the dynamic that caused the transition from feudal structures to the modern state in Europe between the seventeenth and eighteenth centuries was influential in the system of states rather than individual states. Since the financing of explorations required large sums of money, small and weak governments either fell behind in the race and perished or had to merge to avoid falling behind. Thus, regional governments became more potent, and relatively few independent states emerged. Jean Bodin's (1530–96) concept of sovereignty, which he used to explain the reasons for the absolute decision-making power of the king with ideas typical of the Roman Empire,[207] paved the way for these new states to unite into nations and then engage in a power struggle in their relations with others.

At this point, it should be remembered that there was no concept of 'nation' in ancient societies. Individuals were loyal to their families, communities, or the region they lived in. For example, in Ancient Greece, what kept the Athenians together was their religious relationship with the city. They felt connected to the city, not to other Athenians. As another example, those

---

205 Harari, *Sapiens*, p. 313.
206 Poggi, *The Development of the Modern State*, p. 81.
207 Touchard, *Histoire des Idées Politiques*, p. 306.

who wanted to prevent the collapse of the Ottoman Empire in the nineteenth century tried to create a consciousness of 'Ottomanness' among its subjects. Young Ottomans, an underground organisation formed by young, well-educated civil and military officers who thought that only a 'modern state' could save the Empire from collapse, tried to instil a consciousness of an 'Ottoman nation' in people who lived for centuries under Ottoman rule felt attached to their religious communities. However, unlike in the West, this consciousness could not be created in the Ottoman Empire, where property rights were not secured, the bourgeoisie did not emerge, and the feudal economic infrastructure did not change. Thus, the country disintegrated at the end of the First World War. These examples reveal how the rise of capitalism and the concept of the nation-state are intertwined.

In the era of mechanised mass production, social control over the market had to be significantly reduced. Hence, there was a historical transformation in who held power. Before the marketisation process, power was often concentrated in one hand through political means (conquest, capture, plunder, slavery, religious power). The state's role was decisive in this process, while the market's was not. However, once the marketisation process began, power was captured primarily through economic means, and the state's role in this process became one of legitimising it.[208]

This new network of relations between larger political units ensured the control of the state's internal political order and the institutionalisation of governance in order to ensure the state's integrity, continuity, reliability, and efficiency. In addition, each state had to organise its form of government well so that the will of the centre could be transmitted promptly, equally, and reliably throughout the territories within the state's borders and to organise the society's resources when necessary.[209] Thus, the form of organisation we know today as the nation-state was shaped by the bourgeoisie's need to provide the financing it needed as it grew. In this process, the nation-state assumed two successive functions. First, in the mercantilist phase, the state provided the conditions for the nationalisation of the market by eliminating the economic independence of cities and towns. In the second stage, the

---

208 Fotopoulos, *Towards an Inclusive Democracy*, p. 9.
209 Poggi, *The Development of the Modern State*, pp. 79–80.

state assumed the role of preventing society from exerting effective control over the market.[210]

In this process, exploration and technological progress went hand in hand, feeding off each other. Just six years after the English explorer James Cook (1728–79) reached what is now Queensland in Australia in 1770, James Watt's (1736–1819) commercial steam engine was launched. The steam engine, which could run uninterruptedly thanks to the abundance of wood and coal in Europe, suddenly freed production from the constraints of nature. Thanks to this machine, energy became something that could be obtained independently of living beings or nature, sustained without interruption, and transported anywhere. The steam turbine had the advantage over wind, water, and animal power in that it only needed a fuel capable of generating high heat.[211] This multi-purpose machine paved the way for the industrial age.[212] The steam engine significantly accelerated the Industrial Revolution that began in England. In colonies such as the United States, it multiplied production by using a combination of slave labour and the almost ubiquitous coal that fuelled these commercial steam engines. In 1776, Adam Smith published *The Wealth of Nations*, a text that laid the foundations of modern capitalism, just as the American colonies were about to declare independence from Britain. Smith's economic liberalism, which believed in continuous economic development, asserted that national labour was the true wealth and extolled the benefits of competition and accumulation, assigned specific functions to the emerging new nation-state: Facilitating production, maintaining order and justice, and protecting property. Adam Smith's work thus changed not only the history of economics but also the history of politics.[213] In the space of just six years, colonialism, slavery, coal, and capitalism, closely intertwined, laid the foundations of the modern world.[214]

The first aim of the urban merchants in their political activities was the official recognition of their status as a privileged and legalised community.

---

210 Fotopoulos, *Towards an Inclusive Democracy*, pp. 10–11.

211 Roy Scranton, *Learning to Die in the Anthropocene: Reflections on the End of Civilization* (Turkish version), trans. Deniz Tordum, Edebi Şeyler, Istanbul, 2019, p. 27.

212 Timothy Morton, *Hyperobjects – Philosophy and Ecology after the End of the World* (Turkish version), trans. Bilge Demirtaş, Tellekt, Istanbul, 2020, p. 20.

213 Touchard, *Histoire des Idées Politiques*, p. 431.

214 Klein, *On Fire*, p. 232.

Thus, although they did not come from noble families, they also wanted to be distinguished from the rest of the population. In addition, they demanded the creation of broader frameworks to enforce the law and maintain order to secure and develop their commercial enterprises in cooperation with the monarch and feudal lords. For these groups, the monarch could ensure the establishment of a growing, standardised, and territorially encompassing framework for supporting and regulating urban economic activity. For the bourgeoisie, therefore, power was not yet a concept to be contained but to be patronised. Moreover, from the point of view of the emerging international legal system, the monarch was in a privileged position to assess the growing demands of the wealthy groups in the city and protect their interests in order to expand foreign markets, exploit transoceanic resources, or prevent foreign competition.[215] In other words, the king had to use his sovereignty to protect the bourgeoisie at home and to pave the way for exploration and colonisation abroad.

For this reason, Poggi argues that the fact that many Western countries experienced political revolutions during the transition to the modern bourgeois state should not lead us to exaggerate the 'interruption' between the system of absolute rule in the *ancien régime* and the subsequent system based on the separation of powers and the rule of law. In his view, two main reasons exist for the continuity between the systems before and after these revolutions. On the one hand, power relations between states had become even more critical as European countries raced for world markets and raw material resources. On the other hand, civil society itself was becoming increasingly complex and class conflicts were intensifying. Therefore, it was in the bourgeoisie's interest to preserve and even strengthen the potential power of the state.[216]

In conclusion, today's discourse that the bourgeoisie brought rights and freedoms to the people by fighting against absolute power does not reflect reality, at least during the nation-state's emergence. On the contrary, the bourgeoisie initially relied on powerful kings to secure and enrich itself by exploiting the world's natural resources.

---

[215] Poggi, *The Development of the Modern State*, p. 82.
[216] Poggi, *The Development of the Modern State*, pp. 104–5.

While capitalism and the modern state developed with a particular interaction and synchronicity, the condition of existence of this partnership was the political power's legitimate monopoly of violence and its relative autonomy from the economic ruling class.[217] At this point, rationalist natural law played an instrumental role in establishing the conditions for plunder.[218] Property and other related natural rights put forward by pro-bourgeois thinkers were realised through parliaments and formed the legal framework of the new state order. In this context, the 'sacred' and 'inalienable rights' of people emerged as a concept belonging to the citizens of a nation-state.[219] In other words, rights were granted to people only as citizens.[220] By the end of the eighteenth century, with the Industrial Revolution, the system had matured, Asian countries had ceased to be the centre of the economy, the new hegemonic power of the world economy was England, and the industrial age and unrestrained competitive capitalism had risen.[221] Of course, at the time, most people could not yet foresee that the constant increase in production and consumption and the unlimited growth dynamic that would result from the competition inherent in capitalism would lead to an ever-increasing need for energy, which in turn would have a devastating impact on natural resources and the climate. Despite realising it today, the concept of the nation-state continues to be ubiquitous, even though the market economy has transcended the borders of the nation-state and has become internationalised.[222]

1.2.2 The rise of capitalism as the dominant new economic system

As we have seen, capitalism is not a mode of production that has always existed in the world. Nor did it emerge peacefully and spontaneously through the

---

[217] Özenç, *Hukuk Devleti*, p. 177.

[218] Capra – Mattei, *The Ecology of Law*, p. 95.

[219] Giorgio Agamben, *Homo Sacer: Sovereign Power and Bare Life* (Turkish version), trans. İsmail Türkmen, Ayrıntı, Istanbul, 2001, p.167. At this point, Agamben rightly questions whether the terms 'human' and 'citizen' in the 1789 French Declaration of the Rights of the Man and of the Citizen refer to two autonomous entities, or whether instead they constitute a unitary system in which the second term always already includes the first.

[220] Agamben, *Homo Sacer*, p. 169.

[221] Foster, *Capitalism in the Anthropocene*, p. 15.

[222] Fotopoulos, *Towards an Inclusive Democracy*, p. 3.

gradual and peaceful expansion of the market. Capitalist production emerged due to a process of violence, brute force, and systematic dispossession in which the state and (international) law played a central role in enriching Western urban merchants with natural resources from the colonies.[223] The moment of this emergence in the West can be recognised as the Industrial Revolution. It spread around the world through colonialism, imperialism, and force.

Although capitalism as an economic category emerged at the height of the British Industrial Revolution in the mid-nineteenth century, Marx claimed that the capitalist period has been going on since the sixteenth century. That is because primitive forms of capitalism began to appear as early as the mid-fifteenth century with the beginning of the agricultural revolution.[224] The period between the sixteenth and the end of the eighteenth century, when the Dutch emerged as a hegemonic merchant power, is generally known as the phase of mercantilism and merchant capitalism. This period also coincided with the first colonisation of the world by European capitalist powers through the transatlantic slave trade and the genocide of Indigenous peoples in the Atlantic and the Dutch East Indies.[225]

The story of modern capitalism ironically began in Africa. European colonisers arrived in Africa in ships, enslaved the Indigenous people, and took their land. From the very beginning, this was a process that needed pseudo-scientific and theological theories that emphasised the superiority of the white race and Christians. Based on these theories, non-European peoples were treated as raw objects to be consumed and used. On the other hand, land, forests, rivers, and animals could be commodified and exploited without limits. The wisdom that humanity has accumulated over thousands of years on how to preserve and rehabilitate everything from forests to fish is being swept away in favour of a brand new idea that there are no limits to humanity's ability to dominate the natural world without the slightest concern for the consequences.[226] Thus, capital with the capacity to overuse

---

[223] Ntina Tzouvala, *Capitalism as Civilisation: A History of International Law*, Cambridge University Press, Cambridge, 2020, p. 24.

[224] Karl Marx, *Capital*, vol. 1, pp. 247, 875–6, cited in: Foster, *Capitalism in the Anthropocene*, p. 15.

[225] Fernand Braudel, *The Perspective of the World*, Harper and Row, New York, 1979, pp. 177–276, cited in: Foster, *Capitalism in the Anthropocene*, p. 15.

[226] Klein, *On Fire*, p. 36.

fossil fuels in production and consumption began accumulating, sparking the climate change we face today.

Before the Industrial Revolution, neither labour nor land were considered commodities.[227] However, the only way to ensure the continuity of production and profit in booming markets was to ensure an adequate supply of the production components. Therefore, production elements such as *labour, land*, and *money* had to enter the market as commodities. The only way to organise their supply in a commercial society was to ensure affordability. However, there was a problem: Neither labour nor land nor money had the empirical definition of a commodity as 'produced for sale'. Therefore, they were defined as commodities in a 'purely imaginary' way.[228] Thus, labour, land, and money became saleable assets, so much so that, unlike markets in history, the market economy emerged as a system that created markets for these three means of production.[229]

It was the enclosure movement that put this situation into practice. People who had no chance to live in the countryside after their lands were forcibly seized were forced to sell their labour in factories in the cities. Thus, the emergence of the capitalist mode of production was far from a smooth, natural, and spontaneous process with people 'discovering' the expected advantages of the free market. Instead, the whole process was dominated by state-imposed violence and law.[230] In other words, European capitalism emerged on the lands of colonised peoples, with goods produced by enslaved people and processed in factories populated by European peasants dispossessed by enclosure. It is a common mistake to perceive these as separate processes. In fact, they were all part of the same process and functioned within the same underlying capitalist logic.[231]

The bourgeoisie, having seized natural resources in its own country through enclosure and in other countries through colonialism, rapidly increased production by employing peasants and enslaved people in its

---

227 Fotopoulos, *Towards an Inclusive Democracy*, p. 8.

228 Karl Polanyi, *The Great Transformation: The Political and Economic Origins of Our Time* (Turkish version), 4th ed., trans. Ayşe Buğra, İletişim, İstanbul, 2005, pp. 122–3, cited in: Özenç, *Hukuk Devleti*, p. 130.

229 Fotopoulos, *Towards an Inclusive Democracy*, p. 10.

230 Tzouvala, *Capitalism as Civilization*, p. 24.

231 Hickel, *Less is More*, p. 53.

factories. In the hands of the bourgeois, the act of 'adding labour to nature', which lies at the core of Locke's theory of property rights, was transformed first into the commodification of land and human labour and then into the accumulation of a disproportionate share of the production. As a result, this disproportionate share of the social product was transformed into capital that could be reappropriated on the market. Thus, capitalist entrepreneurs, an increasingly important part of the European bourgeoisie throughout the history of absolute rule, redefined their social identity as a class. This phenomenon, which emerged as the capitalist mode of production began to take hold, was sometimes supported and accelerated by public policy.[232] Because the competition between states, which could no longer expand by taking territory from each other, turned into a race to increase the wealth within the country. The more capital could be accumulated within the borders, the more the country that strengthened its army and ensured the welfare of its people was ahead of the others. Thus, the race for economic growth began.

In this race, the king and the bourgeoisie were not rivals but allies. In order to protect the autonomous functioning of the market against any attack from a rival class, especially the working class, and to guarantee the bourgeoisie's seizure of formerly communal resources and their transfer to the personal control of individuals, an intermediary was needed to rule by coercion and force. At the same time, this agent had to rule from a single 'public' centre, structurally separate from and above all classes.[233] The best candidate for this intermediary was none other than the king at the head of the state with the monopoly of violence. Thus, at the stage of the establishment of the capitalist economic system, the government was not a body to be fought against but to be allied against other classes. Of course, the fact that the king was limited and even controlled through parliaments should not be overlooked. In fact, from this point of view, rather than an alliance between the king and the bourgeois class, it would be more accurate to talk about the bourgeoisie's use of the king as a tool to seize resources, suppress other classes that might resist it, and facilitate colonialism in other countries.

In conclusion, the processes of modernisation and capitalisation cannot be considered separately from each other. Capitalism indeed allows old forms

---

232 Poggi, *The Development of the Modern State*, p. 99.
233 Poggi, *The Development of the Modern State*, pp. 99–100.

of domination to continue in some geographies where it has a presence. However, the dynamics that have transformed modernisation practices for centuries are those inherent in capitalism. Therefore, if an 'enemy of nature' is to be sought in ecological debates, it is not modernism or its extensions but capitalism itself, which provides the material basis for all these superstructural processes.[234] In other words, the modern nation-state and the legal system that forms its framework were shaped in line with the needs of the bourgeois class, the founder of capitalism. If such a class had not emerged, such a transformation in social organisation and law would have been neither necessary nor possible.

Under capitalism, which spread across the world after Western colonialism and imperialism and has become the dominant economic model today, nature is simply seen as a ' gift' for capital. The vast majority of people are treated as exploitable and expendable masses who produce surplus value for their wealthy owners.[235] The result is a deadlock created by a system based on the simultaneous exploitation of humans and nature, a system that knows no boundaries, cares neither for the real needs of people, nor is sustainable in terms of natural resources. Based on fossil fuels from the beginning, this economic system has now reached its absolute limits in the Anthropocene.[236]

1.2.3 Social impact of the introduction of fossil fuels in production

The use of coal, and then oil, not only changed world economies but also rapidly added greenhouse gases[237] to the Earth's atmosphere. Therefore, critical issues in world history are how and why this transformation took place and what consequences it had.[238] We must examine when and why fossil fuels were needed to understand this transformation.

---

[234] Orhan, 'Modernizm ve …' p. 38.

[235] Karl Marx – Frederick Engels, *Collected Works*, Vol. 37, International Publishers, New York, 1975, pp. 732–3, cited in: Foster, *Capitalism in the Anthropocene*, p. 17.

[236] Foster, *Capitalism in the Anthropocene*, p. 17.

[237] Gases such as carbon dioxide, produced by burning coal, oil and natural gas, allow the sun's rays to reach the Earth while they remain in the atmosphere, but prevent them from being reflected back into space. This causes warming, just like in a greenhouse. This is why gases from fossil fuels are called greenhouse gases.

[238] Marks, *The Origins of …*, p. 109.

For thousands of years, agriculture provided not only food for all people but also raw materials for whatever was produced in that region. In China and India, it was silk and cotton; in Northwest Europe, it was wool. All raw materials came from farming. Fuel to process these materials and for heating came from forests. In this respect, the biological old order[239] was organic. Solar energy was used to grow crops for food, and the forests for fuel. Accordingly, the biological old order had limits to what humans could do since all human actions were essentially dependent on an annual input of renewable energy from the sun. What agriculture enabled humans to do was to capture natural processes and channel that energy to the human population. In the biological old order, agriculture was the first way for humans to change their environment and transform one type of ecosystem (e.g. forest or meadow) into another (e.g. field of rye, wheat or paddy, or fish pond) in a way that channelled food energy to humans more efficiently.[240]

In such an environment, for all its audacity, colonialism, and industrialisation, the dual project of the 1700s was still, in various aspects, subject to the constraints of nature. Ships could only sail when the wind was favourable, and the factories that transformed the raw materials into finished products worked with gigantic water mills. Water-powered factories had to be located in rural areas near fast-flowing water sources.[241] Thus, the biological old order set limits not only on the size of the human population but also on the economy's productivity. These limits disappeared in the nineteenth century.

As mentioned before, China, India, and the Middle East were the centres of the world economy for a long time, prospering through agriculture thanks to their fertile soils. From the early 1800s, Europe, a province that lagged behind these empires, was set apart from the rest of the world by the single word 'coal'[242] because from then on, people increasingly began to generate heat from coal, which was then captured and used to fuel the repetitive motion of steam-powered machines, which started to do the work that used to be

---

[239] The name Marks used to describe the period when everything depended on the annual energy flows of the sun and their capture by humans. See Marks, *The Origins of …*, p. 116.

[240] Marks, *The Origins of …*, p. 54.

[241] Klein, *That Changes Everything*, p. 242.

[242] Kenneth Pomeranz, *The Great Divergence*, cited in: Wallace-Wells, *The Uninhabitable Earth*, p. 178.

done by muscle power.[243] Thus, Europe, doomed to lose in the biological old order, gained a game-changing trump card when it began to use a mineral in the ground instead of the sun, its primary energy source until then.

Especially when there were no more trees to cut down in England, coal, which was plentiful everywhere, began to be mined more abundantly. Even in the thirteenth century, London's air polluted with coal smoke was the subject of complaints. As a result of investigations, coal burning was even banned in some lime quarries, and heavy sanctions were imposed on those who failed to comply.[244] In 1550, coal production in England was approximately 210 thousand tons. This figure reached 1.5 million tons in 1630.[245] Coal, used in small-scale production and inefficient steam engines, did not cause a revolutionary product increase at first, although it made things easier. However, in 1776, Scottish engineer James Watt succeeded in developing and producing an energy source that ended the dependence on nature for production. By adding a separate condenser, air machine, and rotary engine to an earlier model, Watt made the coal-fired steam engine enormously more powerful and adaptable than its predecessors. These new machines could be used in a wide range of applications, from ship transportation to industrial production.[246]

Initially, steam engines were only used to pump water out of the bottom of deep coal mines. Later, coal first replaced water and wind-powered machines.[247] Then, as their efficiency increased, they were connected to looms and gins. This new situation made it possible to produce cheap textiles in unprecedented quantities. By transporting Indian cotton to its own territory through the East India Company and undermining textile production there, England suddenly became the textile workshop of the world. In 1825, for the first time, the steam engine was connected to wagons full of coal, and the coal was transported to the nearest port, which was twenty kilometres away. In other words, thanks to a coal-powered machine, more coal started

---

[243] Marks, *The Origins of ...*, p. 109.

[244] Gimpel, *La Révolution industrielle au Moyen Age*, p. 80.

[245] Clive Ponting, *A New Green History of the World: The Environment and the Collapse of Great Civilizations* (Turkish version), trans. Ayşe Başcı-Sander, Sabancı University Press, Istanbul, 2000, p. 247.

[246] Klein, *That Changes Everything*, pp. 242–3.

[247] Kurnaz, *Son Buzul Erimeden*, p. 343.

to be delivered to production facilities in different locations. In 1830, the first commercial railroad line opened between Liverpool and Manchester. Just twenty years later, England had thousands of kilometres of rail network.[248]

Therefore, the fact that the Industrial Revolution took place in Britain is unsurprising, given its connection to coal. In 1800, 90 per cent of all coal mined globally came from Britain.[249] In the 1830s, coal began to replace water power as the primary energy source in manufacturing. Around 1850, 60 per cent of all carbon dioxide emissions from fossil fuels worldwide were produced in Britain.[250] Thus, the enormous increase in carbon dioxide emissions began with the Industrial Revolution.[251]

Coal-powered steam engines were a crucial milestone that brought humanity out of the biological old order and into an order that was no longer limited by the annual energy flows of the sun. In other words, using coal in efficient steam engines liberated humans from the confines of the biological old order and paved the way for the ever-increasing growth of the means of production and the number of people. The replacement of the wind, water, and animals that powered the means of production with energy generated from burning coal marked the beginning of the Industrial Revolution.[252] From this perspective, the Industrial Revolution was fundamentally a revolution in energy production.[253]

The transition from the muscular power utilising solar energy in plants, that is, the 'somatic energy regime' to the 'exosomatic energy regime' based on fossil fuels, is a phenomenon that changed the course of world history. In the 1800s, steam engines, which converted the chemical energy generated by burning coal into mechanical energy, provided 'the benefit of hundreds of millions of years of photosynthesis'.[254] Thus ended the 'solar energy era', also

---

248 Harari, *Sapiens*, p. 332.

249 Marks, *The Origins of* …, p. 126.

250 Chomsky – Pollin, *Climate Crisis* …, p. 85.

251 Saito, *Slow Down*, p. 1.

252 Marks, *The Origins of* …, p. 109.

253 Harari, *Sapiens*, p. 333.

254 John R. McNeill, *Something New under the Sun: An Environmental History of the Twentieth Century*, Allen Lane, London, 2000, pp. 10–13, cited in: Mustafa Emir Küçük – Onur İnal, 'Antroposentrizmin Ötesinde: Türkiye Modernleşme ve Kent Tarihinde Çalışan Hayvanlar', *in* Didem Bayındır – Mine Yıldırım (ed.), *Ekoloji: Bir Arada Yaşamın Geleceği*, Tellekt, Istanbul, 2022, p. 399.

called the biological old order, based on renewable resources, which began around 10,000 BC and lasted until the 1800s AD. In its place began the age of fossil fuels based on non-renewable resources, which is still ongoing today. This unprecedented transformation underpins the history of all relations between humans and the environment.[255]

The combination of these new machines and the new energy source has immeasurably increased the amount of things that can be produced. It also significantly reduced the time needed to move people and goods from one place to another.[256] Steam-powered machinery made it possible to move factories to the city, as production was no longer dependent on rivers. Thus, capital was able to exploit the masses of workers who had lost their land and living conditions due to enclosures and migrated to the city in search of work extremely cheaply.[257] All this led to an incredible increase in production and consumption. By the nineteenth century, coal had become the main form of energy and ushered in 'fossil capitalism', in other words, an industrial system based on fossil fuels as a source of energy alongside the exploitation of workers.[258]

The new socioeconomic accumulation regime of capital began to take shape in the early nineteenth century in Britain, which pioneered the historical transition to fossil energy. Coal, previously only burned locally to generate heat, was transformed into an internationally traded commodity. Energy reserves built up over hundreds of millions of years began to be extracted from confiscated lands, transported in vast quantities and far away, and consumed in very short periods to power mechanised industry. However, no thought was given to how these resources would be renewed or the resulting pollution. Once fossil energy sources became portable, capitalists no longer felt obliged to bow to the demands of rural workers. They moved production from the countryside to the city, where large masses of poor people needed work. In this way, they could easily use the proletarianised labour resources that had

---

255 Edmund Burke, 'The Big Story: Human History, Energy Regimes, and the Environment', *in* Edmund Burke III – Kenneth Pomeranz (ed.), University of California Press, Berkeley, 2009, p. 35, cited in: Küçük – İnal, 'Antroposentrizmin Ötesinde', pp. 399–400.

256 Harman, *A People's History of the World*, p. 313.

257 Saito, *Slow Down*, p. 154.

258 Andreas Malm, *Fossil Capital*, Verso, London, 2016, cited in: Foster, *Capitalism in the Anthropocene*, p. 16.

accumulated in a particular region, that is, workers who had less access to different livelihoods than their rural counterparts and were more amenable to the discipline of factory work.[259] Although coal, like water or air, was not free and required a certain amount of expenditure to extract and transport, this was insignificant compared to the gains from intensified exploitation.[260] In the end, Francis Bacon's dream has come true, and complete domination over nature and humans has been established.[261]

Meanwhile, coal production and consumption also increased in other countries for different reasons. In China, deforestation led to an increasing use of coal for cooking and heating. In Japan, restrictions on using wood as part of a policy of reforestation to replace forests that had been cut down in the past led citizens to use coal this time.[262]

The steam power derived from coal led to an Industrial Revolution in production and revolutionised transportation. Distances were shortened, time accelerated, and raw materials and manufactured goods could be quickly transported over vast distances. Thus, capital increased its turnover and profits exponentially. That also had devastating effects on agriculture. Due to the masses of workers accumulating in the cities, unsustainable, profit-oriented farming activities emerged in the countryside. This new order deepened what Marx called ' the metabolic rift' between the city and the countryside.[263] Accordingly, nutrients plundered from rural land did not return to their source but flowed as organic waste into urban sewers, which led to a steady de-qualification of the rural soil. Thus, in one fell swoop, the liberal-colonial regime both depleted agricultural land and polluted the cities.[264]

Another crucial invention that followed coal was the internal combustion engine, which transformed all transportation and transport in little more

---

[259] Andreas Malm, 'The Origins of Fossil Capital: From Water to Steam in the British Cotton Industry', *Historical Materialism*, 21(1), 2013, pp. 15–68, cited in: Fraser, 'Climates of Capital', pp. 70–1.

[260] Fraser, 'Climates of Capital', p. 71.

[261] Klein, *That Changes Everyting*, p. 245.

[262] Marks, *The Origins of …*, p. 126.

[263] Karl Marx's ideas on the impoverishment of the soil were influenced by his contemporary, the German chemist Justus von Liebig. See Saito, *Slow Down*, pp. 20–1.

[264] John Bellamy Foster, 'Marx's Theory of Metabolic Rift: Classical Foundations for Environmental Sociology', *American Journal of Sociology*', 105(2), 1999, pp. 366–405, cited in: Fraser, 'Climates of Capital', p. 71.

than a generation, turning oil into a political force. Oil had been known for millennia, used to keep roofs from leaking and to lubricate axes. Just a 100 years ago, however, no one thought of other uses for oil.[265] However, once the internal combustion engine was invented, it became clear that it could be used as an energy source in every field.

In particular, the Lockean concept of the atomised individual and the idea of individual freedom changed the balance in personal transportation. With the introduction of the car into daily life, public transportation vehicles such as trains became 'restricting freedom' as they moved in a certain order. Entire transportation networks, and of course cities, started to be designed for car owners who had the 'freedom' to go wherever they wanted, whenever they wanted. This understanding of individual freedom is at the root of the intensive use of cars, which today almost always clogs our cities and sometimes even the roads between cities, pollutes our air, and causes climate change with the greenhouse gases they emit.

The bottom line is that the modern world was built by fossil fuels and the extractivist mentality they represent. Since we are part of industrial or post-industrial societies today, we still live in a story written in coal.[266] The rise of capitalism was undoubtedly closely tied to burning fossil fuels to generate energy and power machinery. Thus, polluting the atmosphere with CO_2 emissions is also tied to the birth of industrial capitalism.[267]

The understanding that legally established the modern world, which is fundamentally dependent on fossil fuels, was heavily influenced by humanism, which enabled the bourgeoisie to stand on its own two feet. The ideas of humanist thinkers, which put human beings above everything else in nature and paved the way for the unlimited exploitation of natural beings and animals, were embodied in constitutional systems that enabled and even encouraged this through their rules. Let us now take a closer look at the emergence of these systems.

---

[265] Harari, *Sapiens*, p. 333.
[266] Klein, *That Changes Everything*, p. 250.
[267] Chomsky – Pollin, *Climate Crisis …*, p. 85.

1.2.4 Emergence of the anthropocentric constitutional system

The modern world as we know it, particularly the belief that humans are separate from nature, is a very recent phenomenon. If we place today's societies and beliefs in the context of human history over the last 2 million years and beyond, what is 'normal' instantly changes. Indeed, from a long-term perspective, a conception of law based on a worldview in harmony with the Earth's ecosystem is mainstream, with our societies today being the main exception.[268]

The ideas of holism and unity guided the thinking of jurists in the Antiquity and the Middle Ages. Holism, a view of reality in which religion, natural philosophy, politics, and law were understood as a whole with no points of convergence, had left its mark on fourteenth-century thought. Accordingly, jurists were knowledgeable and thoughtful not only in their own fields but also in religion, natural philosophy, and politics. One of the key intellectual strategies in the movement to privatise the commons was to eliminate this holistic perspective. Natural law had to be transformed from a system legitimised by God into a system legitimised only by human reason.[269] In this way, pro-bourgeois thinkers who claimed to have arrived at the rules of natural law through their rationality would be able to establish the foundations of the constitutional order with the principle of the rule of law.

In the sixteenth century, holism was still the dominant view of the late Spanish scholastics, the leading school of legal theory of the time.[270] In science, however, the mechanistic paradigm that had begun in the sixteenth century had consolidated its position. Galileo Galilei's emphasis on quantification, Francis Bacon's idea of man's dominance over nature, René Descartes' view that the material world was a machine separate from the mind, Isaac Newton's idea that there were objective, immutable 'laws of nature', and John Locke's rationalistic and atomistic view of society all fed each other and replaced the old holistic paradigm of the universe.[271] What remained was for the political and legal to follow this paradigm shift in science and transform accordingly.

---

[268] Cullinan, *Wild Law*, p. 158. Cullinan calls this legal theory '*Earth Jurisprudence*'.

[269] Capra – Mattei, *The Ecology of Law*, p. 81.

[270] Capra – Mattei, *The Ecology of Law*, p. 82.

[271] Capra – Mattei, *The Ecology of Law*, p. 23.

An already individualistic atomised society gradually emerged with the urban merchant class in the political structure. Secularisation in law followed it. The idea that the monarch, supported by the bourgeoisie for the sake of standardisation and stability, could make new laws by his own sovereign will and enforce them through his efficient and comprehensive court system was completely new. This idea transformed law from the framework of governance to its instrument. Through these new laws, the king began to shape relations in a general and abstract way and to impose their validity everywhere and always. In addition to these laws made by the king and enforced by his courts, it should not be forgotten that Roman law gained validity in many countries through the principles and rules of Justinian's *Corpus juris civilis*. Although this development did not coincide with the advent of absolutism geographically and chronologically, it coincided with the spirit of absolute rule and the advance of commercialisation and individualism in the socio-economic and cultural spheres.[272]

The mechanistic understanding of the world, controlled by humans for human benefit, saw nature as a vast collection of natural resources put there by God for human use. Gone were the majesty of the mountains and seas, the beauty of the grasslands and the birds and animals of the woods, and the sacredness and sublimity of nature as experienced in healing the loneliness of the human soul and the illnesses of the human body.[273] In other words, nature ceased to be something beautiful and precious in itself and became a resource in man's environment. In this sense, it is undoubted that recognising nature as an environment encircling man is an extension of the humanist perception of the world, which is closely related to Enlightenment thought[274].[275]

When we ceased to consider ourselves a part of nature and lead a life in harmony with the rules of nature, we put ourselves at the centre of the ecosystem and, thus, inevitably created a hierarchy. Both the concepts of 'nature' in an anthropocentric perspective and, obviously, 'environment' refer to something outside of human beings: A space that is not us (or that we

---

[272] Poggi, *The Development of the Modern State*, p. 93.
[273] Cullinan, *Wild Law*, p. 17 (foreword by Thomas Berry).
[274] Orhan, 'Modernizm ve … ', p. 34.
[275] Luc Ferry, *The New Ecological Order* (Turkish version), trans. Turhan Ilgaz, Yapı Kredi, Istanbul, 2000, p. 25, cited in: Orhan, 'Modernizm and … ', p. 33.

transcend) and that surrounds us.[276] That is because the concept of periphery necessarily entails the existence of a centre. Whatever we see at the centre becomes essential, and the periphery is only of secondary importance. That implies that what is less important can sometimes be sacrificed for what is more important.[277] Thus, the legal term 'environment' becomes a concept that places human beings and man-made institutions at the centre and places natural beings around and hierarchically below them.[278] This transformation of the environment into something that could be sacrificed (and thus profited from) was precisely why the bourgeois class promoted humanist thought.

Calling other beings 'environment' is meant to remind us that these things are not at the centre and to keep this idea alive, thus subordinating nature. Just as the 'periphery' is subject to the 'centre' in economic power relations, nature is subject to human beings. Nature, of which we used to be a part becomes the periphery. The periphery, therefore, cannot have a value in itself; it only gains meaning through the centre. Because without the centre, the periphery is also undefined.[279] From this perspective, human beings are placed at the centre, and their relationship with living and non-living beings other than themselves is emphasised.[280] This situation can be regarded as both a natural consequence and a means of commodification of natural assets. Since nature is distanced from human beings and is now pushed outside the moral community, we do not have direct responsibilities towards it. In this way, we can instrumentalise it for our ends. The further the moral distance, the easier it is to buy, sell, or dig it up. According to Serres, the word environment assumes that we are the navel of the universe, the masters and owners of nature and that we stand at the centre of the system of things that revolves around us. The term reflects our narcissism, which is placed at

---

276 Margaret Davis, *EcoLaw – Legality, Life, and the Normativity of Nature*, Routledge, Abingdon & New York, 2022, p. 39.

277 Üskül Engin, *Ekolojik Kriz, Etik ve Hukuk*, p. 3.

278 Durmaz, *Doğanın Hakları*, p. 27.

279 Orhan, 'Modernizm ve … ', pp. 33–4; Keleş – Hamamcı – Çoban, *Çevre Politikası*, p. 50.

280 Üskül Engin, *Ekolojik Kriz, Etik ve Hukuk*, p. 12.

the centre of the world, and humanism elevates us to the centre of things or their perfect completion.[281]

The French sociologist Bruno Latour states that one of the main characteristics of modernism is the separation of culture and nature.[282] Indeed, this concept of a 'separate nature' emerging from the Western Enlightenment led modern and rational societies to distance themselves from nature. In recent centuries, this concept has become permanent in the discourse of Western rationalist cultures. It can easily be said that the main reason for this permanence is the capitalisation process in Europe, which is why such an interpretation of the world is rarely found in traditional pre-modern or non-Western societies. In these societies, nature and culture are recognised as interconnected categories. There can be no nature unless it is interpreted by culture, and no culture unless there is nature.[283] In the West, however, culture is perceived as the opposite of the word nature. Nature is savage, and culture is civilisation. The roots of this dualism can be found in the same place, in Enlightenment thinkers and scientists.

In the seventeenth century, Descartes introduced the capacity to think as the distinguishing feature of the human being. His famous sentence, 'I think, therefore I am',[284] drew a thick line regarding who was morally and, thus, legally considerable. According to him, the condition for being morally considerable was to be conscious and able to think. Things that could not think – everything other than human beings – were unimportant; they were not part of the moral community. Although he did not deny that animals and plants were alive, Descartes argued that they were nothing more than machines, 'unthinking brute creatures'. In this Cartesian view, the issue of moral relevance was all about consciousness. Anything that was not conscious was a mere physical object that could be analysed and treated without regard to its well-being.[285] Accordingly, Descartes and his students nailed dogs to a board by their paws to study anatomy and dissected their hearts while still alive. Meanwhile, he recognised the screams of the animals as the sounds

---

[281] Michel Serres, *Le Contrat Naturel* (Turkish version), trans. Turhan Ilgaz, Yapı Kredi Yayınları, Istanbul, 1994, p. 47.

[282] Cited in: Hulme, *Why We Disagree …*, p. 41.

[283] Hulme, *Why We Disagree …*, p. 349.

[284] The original form is '*cogito ergo sum*'.

[285] DesJardins, *Environmental Ethics*, pp. 201–2.

of a machine as its parts were being separated.[286] According to the famous philosopher, they were unaware of anything, could not see, hear, smell, or taste, feel heat or cold, hunger or thirst, anger or rage, and of course, neither pleasure nor pain.[287] An animal could, therefore, have no moral standing.[288] Consequently, it was not possible for any legal responsibility to arise against them. Under this modern perspective, law became an order that protected not animals and other natural beings but human use of them.

Two thinkers who strengthened this anthropocentric approach in legal theory were Hugo Grotius (1583–1645) and Jean Domat (1625–96). The rationalist and mechanistic paradigm developed by these two seventeenth-century jurists applied the logic developed by Newton in the study of the universe to law. They saw reality as a whole composed of separate, identifiable components, property owners whose individual rights were protected by the state. This Cartesian tradition saw law as an 'objective ' structure separate from the individual subject.[289] In addition, law was detached from other disciplines and fragmented within itself, so much so that even different branches of law were absorbed into their own fields, and the ties between them and other branches of law were severed. With modernity, the structure of organic society and its law, in which everyone could do everything and progress in solidarity, disappeared, and a legal structure suitable for a mechanistic society was formed, in which everyone was perceived as a specific part of a machine. In this structure, constitutional rules ceased to be an element that 'effuse' from the relations among the members of society but took on a logic rationally determined by external elements. The external element here was usually the bourgeoisie, which had seized constituent power by force of arms or economic power.

One of the main features defining this modern constitutional structure is that it detaches the individuals from social relations, their living environment, and nature and reconstitutes them through relations defined through the

[286] Gary Francione, *Introduction to Animal Rights – Your Child or Your Dog?* (Turkish version), trans. Renan Akman – Elçin Gen, İletişim, Istanbul, 2008, pp. 50–1.

[287] Tom Regan, *The Case for Animal Rights*, University of California Press, California, 1983, p. 3.

[288] Gary Francione, *Animals as Persons – Essays on the Abolition of Animal Exploitation*, Columbia University Press, New York, 2008, p. 3.

[289] Capra – Mattei, *The Ecology of Law*, p. 23.

market process and embodied in forms such as law, money, and the state.[290] These relations are based on two organising principles: property rights, as advocated by John Locke, and state sovereignty, advocated by Thomas Hobbes.[291] In this new form of organisation, man against the state and nature against the bourgeoisie became defenceless. It is safe to say that the resulting Western philosophical tradition and the constitutional order that emerged from it are not sympathetic to the idea that there is a direct ethical responsibility towards the natural world. Indeed, it is now widely recognised that this order provides a justification for dominating and exploiting the natural world and that this is the cause of our present environmental situation.[292]

It should not be denied that the Judeo-Christian tradition also influences this modern scientific and technological approach to nature. This approach, based on biblical sources, is essentially anthropocentric. According to this view, humans have a privileged place among all creatures. Since human beings were created 'in the image and likeness of God', they have a moral and metaphysical uniqueness. Humans transcend nature and are separate from it. God has created a hierarchy in which God has commanded humans to dominate and rule over nature.[293] However, it should be noted that although this religious doctrine existed even before the capitalist economic system became dominant, it did not cause man to leave a distinct mark on nature. Of course, people still took advantage of nature, but not to the extent of exploitation. The balance was upset with the emergence of capitalism. Therefore, it can be said that this biblical discourse is not responsible for the ecological collapse we are experiencing today, but it served as a justification for those who were.

The mechanistic paradigm shift in science, combined with humanist philosophy, paved the way for establishing an anthropocentric constitutional system. The most adversely affected, of course, have been nonhuman natural beings. Animals, plants, and almost every other element of the planet have become legally the property of either humans or an artificial 'legal entity' such as a corporation, if not at that moment, then at any moment, for example, by

[290] F. Ercan, *Modernism, Capitalism and Underdevelopment*, Bağlam, İstanbul, 2003, p. 32, cited in: Orhan, Modernizm ve … ', p. 38.

[291] Capra – Mattei, *The Ecology of Law*, p. 23.

[292] DesJardins, *Environmental Ethics*, p. 203.

[293] White Jr, 'The Historical Roots…', p. 1205–6; Stone, *Should Trees Have Standing?*, p. 26.

being captured or killed. As the constitutional order became anthropocentric, it began to see living beings not as 'lives' but as 'things'. As long as this continues, it is impossible to accept that they can be the subjects of rights, for it is simply legally unthinkable for an object to have rights.[294] If something's legal status is that of a thing, it cannot be recognised as a subject of rights. It can only be the object of the rights of others legally recognised as subjects.

Contemporary Western philosophy and theology have adopted an anthropocentric view of the worthiness of moral concern. Human beings and only human beings are capable of moral concern.[295] All legally recognised rights are rights that can only be asserted in a court of law and can only be possessed by human beings or 'legal persons' such as corporations. What this means for our legal system, as Cullinan points out, is that billions of other species on the planet are extra-legal and should be treated accordingly. They are not part of the community or society that the legal system takes into account, and they have no inherent right to exist or to have a habitat in which to live. That may sound like an exaggeration, as most countries have laws protecting certain species or habitats, such as national parks. However, such laws do not give rights to nonhumans; they only limit human behaviour in some respects so that other people can continue to enjoy wild areas and animals.[296]

This situation is so internalised that it seems strange and incomprehensible from today's perspective that people were trying to develop an equal relationship with nonhuman things in ancient legal systems. The reason why the reality of this old legal understanding looks so distant for today's world is that modern humanism, which is embedded in the very essence of our legal systems, attributes a moral and legal personality to human beings and human beings alone.[297] However, as mentioned before, what prevailed throughout the long history of humanity was a more holistic legal order in which humans did not see themselves as superior to nature. The exception is the anthropocentric constitutional systems we have today. That is why the climate, which has been in balance for millennia depending on its dynamics, has provided an environment where humans could live. In the time of

---

[294] Cullinan, *Wild Law*, p. 63.

[295] DesJardins, *Environmental Ethics*, p. 215.

[296] Cullinan, *Wild Law*, p. 63.

[297] Luc Ferry, *The New Ecological Order* (Turkish version), trans. Turhan Ilgaz, Yapı Kredi, Istanbul, 2000, p. 17, cited in: Orhan, 'Modernizm ve … ', p. 38.

economic and legal structures that we built with the belief that we could overcome the laws of nature, we are struggling with one crisis after another. The roots of today's crises lie in the stories about human supremacy that we created and convinced ourselves about their reality. Ideas like 'progress', 'man is at the centre', or 'we are separate from nature' are just myths that the bourgeoisie created when they built their economic system. The problem is that they are all even more dangerous today because we have forgotten that they are myths.[298] While the Earth's ecosystem is on the brink of collapse, we must remember that they were created for specific self-interests in parallel with the relevant time's zeitgeist. It has been understood today that they also created an unnatural economic and legal order and paved the way for our planet's ecosystem to collapse. Once we correctly diagnose the problem, it will be easier to find the cure.

The legal theory of our current dominant cultures forms the intellectual underpinnings of a system that we have ordered for ourselves within the glasshouse of a human world that we have created by separating ourselves from the rest of nature. It is a legal system for a human society that is supposed to be separate from the rest of the universe. This system is based on various assumptions that we now know to be demonstrably false, such as the belief that the Earth is an unlimited resource waiting for us to use.[299]

We have become arrogantly confident that, thanks to our technologies, we can manage all the problems connected to our actions. We declared ourselves the centre of the world. In this understanding, the whole world existed for humans, and humans existed for themselves. After this stage, all that was needed was establishing a legal system that would allow the attack on nature. This legal basis was first expressed in the American Constitution, which elevated property-owning citizens beyond anything previously known in political history. The problem here was not that rights were granted to human beings but that no rights or protection were granted to any nonhuman being. From the very beginning, the American Constitution was a text designed solely for the advancement of man. The Bill of Rights, added as the first ten amendments, provided a detailed list of the rights of individual

---

298 Paul Kingsnorth – Dougald Hine, *Uncivilization – The Dark Mountain Manifesto*, The Dark Mountain Project.

299 Cullinan, *Wild Law*, p. 58.

persons. In the end, people became self-worthy both as individuals and as a political community. This act of self-worth was invented and sustained by the union of commercial and entrepreneurial forces through legal powers to continue the assault on nature.[300] Over time, this constitutional conception of the human as the centre, contrary to the order of nature, not only relegated everything else to the periphery but also rendered them legally insignificant and worthless, spread across the world.

Therefore, the foundations of our constitutions, the nation-states that were established by these constitutions, the rights and freedoms that belong only to human beings, the separation of powers that we pretend exist in these constitutions, and many other arrangements in our constitutional systems are based on false assumptions that we convinced ourselves were true. We thought that the society in the social contract was made up of only human beings, but it was not. Expanding capital and markets have destroyed subsistence economies in a balanced relationship with nature. In the framework of natural law theory, rationality was able to discover – somehow – only human rights in the world of ideas. Apparently, there were neither trees nor animals in the world of ideas. We thought we had divided sovereignty between the economic classes, and at first, we might have really done it. Still, then, we let the legislature determine both the executive and the judiciary. We failed to prevent the bourgeoisie from seizing all the powers. Unless we admit that we made mistakes in all this, we have no chance of correcting them and, thus, no chance of tackling climate change. So, we need to dig deeper into what went wrong in the creation of the modern state and question what we have been told is true for so many years.

1.2.5 The organic link between the bourgeoisie and the modern state

All production systems rest on a social infrastructure. It is difficult to produce without property rules to manage assets, a market to facilitate money and exchange, loan protocols to finance new projects, laws to secure the rights of shareholders, or a common language for communication. Production beyond a subsistence economy where everyone produces what they need requires

---

[300] Cullinan, *Wild Law*, p. 19 (foreword by Thomas Berry).

rules of organisation, that is, institutions such as laws and customs.[301] From this perspective, if science is one of the architects of the mechanistic modern worldview, one of its consequences is our current legal system. Modernity emerged first through the transformation in science and philosophy, and then, through the legal theory that allowed for it, it created the accumulative orientation of the Industrial Age from the seventeenth century onwards and the mentality of the extraction, appropriation, and utilisation of resources. The modern state and law developed, grew, and strengthened in accordance with these aims. All of these are the sources of today's global crisis.[302] Today, this mutuality is so advanced that distinguishing between private capital and a capitalist state is often impossible. That is because they both use the same behavioural patterns, and their economic policies are based on investment.[303] However, this has not always been the case, and we have never had a crisis of this scale before, so it is crucial to see the link between the modern state and climate change.

1.2.5.1 The construction of the modern state as a protective institution of the bourgeoisie

At the beginning of the sixteenth century, when the bourgeoisie was gaining strength and beginning to influence the economic system, there were about 80 million people in Europe. They were scattered among 500 states, statelets, and state-like organisations. Spain's attempt to establish an empire in all of Western Europe in an effort to create a larger market after its strengthening with the resources from the colonies in the Americas failed. The Thirty Years' War in the seventeenth century reduced the number of European states to the modern thirty or so.[304] After the Treaty of Westphalia in 1648, ending the war, a system of states emerged, organised differently in accordance with the new economic and political situation.[305] In other words, while putting

[301] Timothée Parrique, *Ralentir ou Périr: L'Économie de la Décroissance*, Seuil, Paris, 2022, p. 39.

[302] Capra – Mattei, *The Ecology of Law*, p. 23.

[303] Andreas Malm, *How to Blow Up a Pipeline: Learning to Fight in a World on Fire* (Turkish version), trans. Kurtay Kağan Işıtan, Ayrıntı, Istanbul, p. 37.

[304] Charles Tilly, *Coercion, Capital, and European States, A.D. 990–1990*, Basil Blackwell, London, 1990, pp. 38–43, cited in: Marks, *The Origins of the …*, p. 101.

[305] Marks, *The Origins of …*, p. 104.

an end to the Thirty Years' War, the Peace of Westphalia also organised the international legal order around a system of nation-states that were strictly independent of each other. This treaty thus defined what a 'sovereign' state was[306] and led to a new system of multiple states, each sovereign over its own territory, equal to each other and independent of any earthly authority. This new system was based on international law and a balance of power between states, not over them.[307]

However, the modern state was not an apparatus of government shaped by the bourgeoisie that was in line with its needs. It was a new power relationship that emerged through the interaction of new relations of production and political struggles.[308] Just as the heads of families were the owners of their lands in Rome, European states were now the owners of their own countries. Locke's theory of property and Hobbes' theory of the sovereign state became the two organising principles of legal modernity shortly before this political compromise, structuring the individual-centred view of law that is still valid today.[309] Therefore, it would be more accurate to say that the modern state is an artificially constructed structure rather than a spontaneously developed one. It is a 'made' reality.[310] It was not merely an organisation necessitated by circumstances; it grew on the theories of thinkers who provided the intellectual underpinnings of the bourgeoisie.

In addition, the French Revolution of 1789 and the spread of its ideas by Emperor Napoléon to other European countries in the early 1800s were particularly important for the emergence of the modern state. Some of the most prominent of these ideas can be cited as the right of the people to be politically active 'citizens' and not merely 'subjects' of the sovereign, administrative rules that applied to everyone, and direct contact between the state and the citizen.[311] However, it should be noted that 'active citizenship of the people' did not apply to everyone. After the French Revolution, only members of the bourgeoisie acquired the right to vote, be elected, and become active citizens. Of course, compared to the aristocracy, they were still considered

[306] Marks, *The Origins of …*, p. 101.
[307] Poggi, *The Development of the Modern State*, p. 110.
[308] Özenç, *Hukuk Devleti*, pp. 144–5.
[309] Capra – Mattei, *The Ecology of Law*, p. 85.
[310] Poggi, *The Development of the Modern State*, pp. 116–17.
[311] Marks, *The Origins of …*, p. 163.

'*Tiers-état*'[312] but it would not be correct to say that all sections of the people became active citizens by the Revolution. This privilege was granted only to the merchant class, who paid taxes to the nation in order to be worthy to assert the will of the nation.

In the field of law, two names in particular, the aforementioned Hugo Grotius and Jean Domat, came to the fore in the seventeenth century in the establishment of the modern state. Applying Newton's and Locke's ideas to law, these two thinkers saw reality as a community of separate, identifiable components, in other words, of free individual actors. They developed a worldview in which the sovereign state secured property and was an individual right to 'improve' nature, that is, to transform it into physical objects. Grotius and Domat, following Newton's mechanistic worldview, blended the right to property advocated by John Locke and the sovereignty of the state advocated by Thomas Hobbes and made them the two organising principles of legal modernity, also known to jurists as legal absolutism.[313] Thus, the function of the modern state was to give a new form to property relations, to establish and, when necessary, to protect the mechanisms that ensure the functioning of production relations and markets.[314]

As a result, after the seventeenth century, the state was no longer identical to society as in the ancient Greek *politea*.[315] The modern state took on a separate and autonomous structure from those within its borders. Its primary duty within the country was to protect the right to property by exercising its sovereign powers. This duty included protecting people's property as well as preventing attacks from other classes on the property-owning class, the bourgeoisie. Therefore, the state took on a structure that protected this separation, in other words, the relations of exploitation between the bourgeoisie

---

312 According to the social structure in France before the Revolution, there were three classes. The first was the aristocracy, including the king, the second was the clergy, and the third was the rest. While this mass, called the 'Tiers-état', or the third state, exhibited a more homogeneous structure at first, after the merchant class became richer and formed the bourgeoisie, it became divided and entered into a relationship of exploitation within itself. However, this was not reflected in the initial categorisation.

313 H. Berman, *Law and Revolution: The Formation of the Western Legal Tradition*, Harvard University Press, Cambridge, Massachusetts, 1985, cited in: Capra – Mattei, *The Ecology of Law*, p. 25.

314 Özenç, *Hukuk Devleti*, p. 145.

315 Poggi, *The Development of the Modern State*, p. 118.

and other classes, by preventing conflict between the classes. The external task of the modern state was to secure natural resources by using its sovereignty to protect the country's borders. One of these aims was to expand to find more resources for the national bourgeoisie, even though this was contrary to the new international order that emerged after the Treaty of Westphalia. Accordingly, the ideas of 'nation' and 'nationalism' were on the rise after the emergence of the modern state and industrial society.[316]

With the modern structure, the sovereign state and private property owners acted as two powerful allies in destroying the previous legal order based on social relations and human compliance with the ecological requirements of nature. The constitutional order was used as an instrument of human domination over nature. This order, which gave people rights and freedoms they could exercise over nature, gradually removed them from participating in the productive processes of nature and replaced the old organic wisdom and the corresponding organisational model typical of the Middle Ages.[317] It is often argued that the bourgeoisie, as a class, embarked on a radical revolt against absolutism to establish a free-market mechanism independent of the state. However, as shown, this is undoubtedly a too simplistic approach. On the contrary, the two formed strong alliances when necessary. Although the 'intervention in the market' of absolutist policies had adverse effects on the interests of the class in question, it can easily be argued that this was more than compensated for by domestic and foreign policies that favoured accumulation and maintained private ownership over a large part of the country's capital. In addition, the political demands of the bourgeoisie, roughly summarised as *laissez faire, laissez passer*, were, in fact, demands 'for' rather than 'against' the system of absolute rule, which later did its best to fulfil these demands.[318]

Therefore, the story that the bourgeoisie fought against strong powers 'in the name of rights and freedoms' and that this is how we got the democracies

---

[316] Marks, *The Origins of*…, p. 163. Marks argues that the emergence of the nation-state as the dominant political organization in Europe and the reasons for industrialisation occurred independently of each other. However, according to the author, once they were combined in the eighteenth century, a highly capable global power emerged. See Marks, *The Origins of*…, p. 29.

[317] J. P. Dawson, *The Oracles of the Law*, University of Michigan, Ann Arbor, 1983, cited in: Capra – Mattei, *The Ecology of Law*, p. 26.

[318] Poggi, *The Development of the Modern State*, p. 100.

we have today is a myth invented by this class. In the absence of a centralised and robust authority, the fragmented power structure did not allow for the establishment of general rules of law to regulate economic relations and social structure, nor for their enforcement through sanctions.[319] The bourgeoisie preferred a sovereign, unified, and powerful government with the capacity to enforce its rules to the letter in every part of the country. In this respect, the capitalist economy today is still deeply dependent on a range of political supports, such as repressive security forces to suppress tendencies that disagree with the system and maintain order, legal systems that guarantee private property and allow for the accumulation of capital, and a plethora of public assets that make it possible for private companies to operate at a profit. Without these political conditions, a capitalist economy cannot continue to exist.[320]

Due to this fact, the institutionalisation of absolute monarchies took place simultaneously with the development of capitalism. As a result of this interaction, the modern state became a fundamental institution that sustained the new relations of production.[321] As can be observed everywhere today, in most cases, individuals are exploited by the market, while the state, instead of defending individuals, protects markets against individuals with its army, police, and bureaucracy. Harari finds it incredible that this arrangement between the bourgeoisie and the state somehow works, even if not perfectly. After all, this deal has played havoc with generations of human social order. Millions of years of evolution have designed us all to think and live as members of a community. Yet, in two centuries, we have become alienated individuals. According to the historian, nothing better confirms the inconceivable power of culture.[322]

The constitutional and legal regulations that supported the process of capitalism's penetration into the social structure were enacted by monarchies that were increasingly dependent on the dynamic structure of these relations of production and the material resources they generated. These regulations, which reshaped property relations to serve the interests of the capitalist

---

319 Özenç, *Hukuk Devleti*, pp. 97–8.
320 Fraser, 'Climates of Capital', p. 60.
321 Özenç, *Hukuk Devleti*, p. 126.
322 Harari, *Sapiens*, p. 354.

class, forced ordinary people to work, and set the upper limit of wages, are remarkable for revealing how political power was instrumentalised in the hands of the bourgeoisie.[323] Through its constitutional order, the state has, on the one hand, proletarianised the people and, on the other hand, enabled capital to appropriate natural wealth for free or extremely cheaply. Ironically, it is the same public power that we turn to when ecological threats become so threatening that they can no longer be ignored. In other words, in modern capitalist societies, it is, ironically, the modern state's institutions that are entrusted with matters concerning ecosystems, such as growth, carbon emissions, or toxic waste.[324] Yet, the bourgeoisie and the modern state today are identical. Therefore, the remedy is sought within the very creator of the problem. That is why, even in a crisis as obvious and vital as climate change, and despite the fact that the solution is clearly known, efforts do not yield results. In fact, they should not be expected to. Currently, there is no counterforce to balance capitalism and prevent it from dragging us into the abyss. The bourgeoisie has captured all forces and has established its hegemony.

1.2.5.2 The *de facto* abolition of the separation of powers by the bourgeoisie

Today, the separation of powers is recognised as one of the fundamental principles of constitutionalism. In fact, since the French Revolution, it is considered that in a country where there is no separation of powers, there is no constitution.[325] In other words, although there is a constitutional booklet as a text, without constitutional checks and balances on power, that constitution has no real function. It is a sham constitution. The idea of the separation of powers that served before and immediately after the French Revolution, a vital function in balancing the absolute sovereignty of the king (the aristocracy) and thus in the emergence and protection of fundamental human (in fact, only European white male) rights and freedoms, unfortunately later turned into a veil that concealed the power of the bourgeoisie. Let us take a closer look at how this transformation took place.

---

[323] Özenç, *Hukuk Devleti*, p. 134.
[324] Fraser, 'Climates of Capital', pp. 61–2.
[325] Declaration of the Rights of the Man and of the Citizen, Art. 16.

The wars in Europe from the sixteenth century onwards affected the internal evolution of European states, strengthening some and weakening others. At that time, the rulers of European states were not rich, and wars were expensive. Basically, the first resource European rulers could turn to was taxation, but taxes were often met with resistance from landowners. They could impose them on the peasants working in their fields, but this risked revolt. Therefore, most European rulers had to negotiate with landowning elites to gain the right to impose and use taxes. That often resulted in creating representative assemblies to be consulted before imposing or raising taxes.[326]

The most obvious example of this process took place in England. Beginning in 1215 with the Magna Carta signed in Windsor by King John of England – nicknamed John Lackland since he was not expected to inherit significant lands – the process of limiting absolute power progressed with the transformation of the *Magnum Concilium* (Great Council), where landowners and the clergy negotiated with the King, into a locus of power. This Council became the Parliament of England in the thirteenth century after the urban merchants who had become wealthy through trade joined it. The merchants, first despised by the aristocrats and 'pushed' into the House of Commons, suddenly became rich and powerful thanks to the enclosures, plundering of nature and steam engines, and transformed into the bourgeois class. Then, as we know, in a long evolutionary process that spanned centuries and paralleled the establishment of the modern state, the House of Commons balanced the King (and the House of Lords, the assembly of the other aristocrats) and then reduced them to ineffective and symbolic forces. A political regime based on the supremacy of Parliament, identified with the House of Commons, emerged.

This process of forming the parliamentary system in England is the source of the principle of separation of powers, which is generally accepted to have been introduced by Montesquieu (1689–1755). However, when this French thinker wrote The Spirit of Laws,[327] in which he conceptualised this principle, the supremacy of the bourgeoisie had not yet been realised. A transition from monarchy to the parliamentary system had begun, and the king, lords, and commoners had just emerged as the governing bodies of the country's

---

[326] Marks, *The Origins of* ..., p. 103.
[327] Originally titled '*De l'Esprit des Lois*'.

governing bodies.[328] Thus, a balance and control between the classes had been established in the country's governance, and this balance had gained an appearance that could be called the separation of powers.[329] That was the model of a 'balanced' government in Britain, which Montesquieu would model his work after.[330]

As can be seen, when it was first introduced, the principle of separation of powers did not refer to the legislature, the executive, and the judiciary but to the balance between the king, the lords, and merchants (the bourgeoisie). Montesquieu referred to them as 'three powers' in the Spirit of Laws.[331] Indeed, in modern times, mixed government based on a class balance between the king, nobles, and commoners was first advocated in England in 1642 with the expectation that limiting power would benefit the government.[332]

However, a series of events in 1688–89, known as the Glorious Revolution, upset this balance. The Catholic King James II issued a Declaration of Indulgence suspending all religious penal laws, which aroused significant opposition, especially from the clergy. When James II insisted on his decision, many bishops and politicians prepared a letter inviting James's son-in-law, the Protestant William of the House of Orange, and his wife, Mary, to England. Arriving with an army of 15,000 men, William was welcomed enthusiastically by the majority of the people. Thereupon, James II, who had abdicated, was allowed to go to France. In 1689, even before William ascended to the throne, the Parliament convened and adopted the Bill of Rights, which included the rule that only Protestants could ascend to the throne from now on, as well as 'some ancient rights and liberties' known today as natural rights.[333] Thus, the

---

328 Maurice John Crawley Vile, *Constitutionalism and the Separation of Powers*, 2nd ed., Liberty Fund, Indianapolis, 1998, p. 59.

329 However, Montesquieu did not use the term 'separation of powers' anywhere in The Spirit of the Laws.

330 Wood, *Liberty and Property*, p. 201.

331 Vile, *Constitutionalism and the Separation of Powers*, p. 91.

332 Richard Bellamy, 'The Political Form of the Constitution: The Separation of Powers, Rights and Representative Democracy', *in* Richard Bellamy (ed.), *The Rule of Law and the Separation of Powers*, New York, 2016, p. 259, cited in: Aslan Delice, 'Karma Hükümetten Denetim ve Dengeye Kuvvetler Ayrılığı İlkesi', *Selçuk University Faculty of Law Review*, Vol. 30, No. 3, 2022, pp. 1667–704, 1681.

333 See House of Commons Information Office, *The Glorious Revolution*, Factsheet G4 – General Series, August 2010.

Parliament of England not only rose above the executive as a power that could determine who the King would be but also became a body that gave birth to its own rights and powers and, thus, determined the limits of other powers.

Almost immediately after these events, in 1714, the supremacy of Parliament in the country's governance was consolidated when George I, ruler of the Electorate of Hanover, became king, by some twist of fate, as the oldest Protestant heir to the throne. George, who had spent his entire life in what is now Germany, neither spoke English nor had any emotional ties to England. In fact, for a fifth of his reign, he was not even in England but Germany. To legalise his situation, Parliament unanimously amended the Act of Settlement in 1716, which prohibited the King of England from travelling abroad. Of course, part of the reason for this was that it was convenient for the King not to be in the country. In the King's absence, he was deputised by Robert Walpole, a member of Parliament. With the *de facto* rule of Walpole, today known as England's first prime minister, the transition to the modern parliamentary regime, in which a council of ministers led by a prime minister constitutes the executive branch, accelerated. The kings after George I could not reverse this trend.

A factor that not only accelerated this transition but also made it permanent was the emergence of political parties. After the start of elections for the House of Commons in England, the disciplined political parties that emerged spontaneously over time led to the merger of the parliamentary majority and the executive branch, rendering the principle of separation of powers ineffective and even meaningless. Due to the internal discipline of the political parties, parliamentarians, who came under the influence of the executive, had no free will. The party with the largest number of members in the House of Commons, which was determined by elections in which only bourgeois candidates were voted for by the same class members, constituted both the majority in the Parliament and the new executive organ independent from the King. That allowed the party leadership to control both the executive and the legislature. There was still a King, but he was relegated to a purely symbolic authority. Thus, in the parliamentary system based on political parties, which was already well established by the twentieth century, the strong ties between the ruling party and the parliamentary majority destroyed the idea of balance between these two powers. It even jeopardised the ability of the government to check its actions.[334] The bourgeois rulers began implementing their political agenda without fear of restraint or obstruction.

It would be a mistake to think that this situation exists only in parliamentary regimes, not regimes with a strict separation of powers. For, although the constitutional logic of the United States, which was founded by thirteen colonies that declared their independence from the United Kingdom, does not include the creation of a 'new king', it should not be forgotten that the President, who alone constitutes the executive branch, was initially chosen exclusively by men of white European origin. Therefore, although the executive branch in the United States did not emerge from a bourgeois legislature, it was still elected by the bourgeois from among themselves. Indeed, today, to become President of the United States, it is necessary to get the support of one of the two major capitalist political parties, the Republicans or the Democrats, and to spend millions of dollars on the election campaign, usually thanks to the support of wealthy donors.[335] Therefore, nothing has changed on the other side of the Atlantic either.

As an objection to this, one could argue that there are non-capitalist parties, even anti-capitalist parties, and parties that defend the rights of ordinary citizens and workers. That is true. However, I guess we can all see how difficult it is for these parties to come to power in a constitutional order built by the bourgeoisie. These parties face two major obstacles: First, even if I have a different programme for a different society based on a different relation of production, I still have to stay within the framework of the existing relations of production during the electoral campaigns and win the elections while stuck within this framework.[336] That requires me to either collect massive and regular dues and donations from the poor and proletarians who are my constituency – which is clearly a near-impossibility – or to find someone – if

---

334 Vile, *Constitutionalism and the Separation of Powers*, p. 255.

335 The latest example that comes to mind is, of course, billionaire Elon Musk, who donated millions of dollars to the campaign of Donald J. Trump, who won the 2024 elections.

336 According to the electoral laws in Türkiye, a political party need to be organised in half of the provinces just to participate in the elections. Being organised in a province also requires organising in one-third of the districts of that province. Just to achieve this, the party needs a vast budget even at the very beginning. So, the electoral system itself is designed to maintain the *status quo* and keep new, small, and leftist parties out of the system.

there really is such a person – who is wealthy but supports my economically egalitarian ideas. If I somehow overcome this hurdle, the second hurdle is that my sincerity as a political party in parliament, an organ of a bourgeois state organisation, will be questioned. Do I really want to overthrow this system, or have I become a part of it? If I am not a part of it, what am I doing there side by side with the establishment parties? Since this questioning will cause me to lose the support of other organised masses close to me and my voters, my chances of coming to power will approach zero.

As a result, when the idea of balancing the different interests of different social classes was substituted by the protection of the interests of the capitalist class, the principle of separation of powers, which replaced the mixed government that divided the state structure between king, lords, and commoners as in the old order, ceased to be a guarantee for the weak and powerless sections of society. All powers were put at the service of capital through the guardianship of freedom and property.[337]

At this point, the importance of written constitutions should be emphasised. In order to build a continuous and stable power structure as demanded by the bourgeoisie, constitutions were enacted as a result of the fact that it was not enough to regulate only private legal relations in a 'centralised' and 'planned' manner and that power relations had to be reorganised in a similar way. In other words, the bourgeoisie's supremacy in power was translated into written texts. What is new here is the 'conscious and planned organisation of the concrete structure of political unity through a written constitution'. In this way, the actions and transactions of the state are regulated for the future, conflicts are prevented, and a permanent and secure ground is created for the policies to be pursued.[338]

Özenç aptly identifies the system's main 'success' as its ability to largely exclude the lower classes from the upper echelons of this new administrative apparatus rather than placing a specific class (the bourgeoisie) directly in the administrative apparatus by openly discriminating against them in order not to contradict Enlightenment ideas of equality and freedom.[339]

---

[337] Delice, 'Karma Hükümetten … ', p. 1691.

[338] Hermann Heller, *Staatslehre*, 6th ed., Mahr, 1983, p. 153, cited in: Özenç, *State of Law*, p. 151, footnote 54.

[339] Özenç, *Hukuk Devleti*, p. 154.

However, as is well known, even if the people who hold office within each power are different, if these people represent the same class or interests, the limitations placed on the powers lose their meaning.[340] What is at stake in the modern state is the dependence of the state apparatus and its personnel, institutionally and personally, on capitalist relations of production – whose main objective is capital accumulation – for the existence and maintenance of their positions of power.[341] Despite this, we are told that, as a requirement of contemporary democracy, the powers are separate, separately elected, and mutually restraining, thus creating an environment in which our fundamental rights and freedoms can survive. If this were the case, shouldn't we have already been able to stop the bourgeois economic activities that are causing climate change, which is a direct threat to our right to life, by invoking one of these forces?[342]

Today, capital, embodied in the form of large multinational or national corporations, has taken a position above the state as a locus of power with all forces under control. The 'hand of the free market' manages the economy in a sphere separate from the state and beyond its intervention. The state institution, which has become dependent on the capitalist relation of production, does nothing but serve the interests of capital. Therefore, we are not living in a democracy with a separation of powers but in a period of 'dictatorship of international corporations'.[343] Furthermore, unfortunately, these corporations do not care about the damage caused to ordinary people and the ecosystem by climate change, which these corporations largely cause.

1.2.5.3 Eco-critical approach to the rule of law as an element of the modern state

One of the principles put forward as one of the conditions for democracy in the modern state is the rule of law. Classically, the rule of law is considered a limitation on state organs. According to this principle of restraint,

---

[340] Richard Bellamy, 'Introduction', *in* Richard Bellamy (ed.), *The Rule of Law and the Separation of Powers*, New York, 2016, p. XXXI, cited in: Delice, 'Karma Hükümetten …', p. 1688.

[341] Özenç, *Hukuk Devleti*, pp. 157–58.

[342] In the second part of the book, I address the intervention of the high courts in the system, which I see as the only solution to prevent climate change.

[343] Löwy, *Ecosocialism*, What Is Ecosocialism (Loc. 335).

the state can only treat its citizens in accordance with a pre-established rule.[344] However, there is no consensus on what this principle means. The lack of a single definition of the rule of law is linked to the concept of being a political ideal. That is because the political and social structures that have been advocated and idealised, both in theory and practice, have led to different definitions of the rule of law.[345]

A look at the modern constitutions of the bourgeois rule of law shows that they embody the constitutional ideals of individualism. These constitutions primarily include bourgeois freedoms such as personal liberty, private property, freedom of contract, freedom of trade, etc. In this view, the state is a servant of the society that strictly controls it.[346] However, a closer look reveals that the opposite is the case. During the mercantilist period, the first stage of the market economy, labour and land, which customs and traditions had previously controlled, were now controlled by laws and decrees.[347] Therefore, when we look at the concrete characteristics of a state of law, we see that they also concern other attributes of the state. According to Poggi, in a state of law, the integrity of the territory is the primary characteristic. Then comes the unity of the nation. Within this territory, the state has a single currency, a single ' national' language, which is often artificially subordinated to many local -and sometimes suppressed by force or gradually forgotten in the education system – languages and dialects, and, finally, a single legal system in which different legal traditions remain valid only for limited purposes and within peripheral regions.[348]

Although this emphasis is no longer entirely valid for countries that can be characterised as rule of law today, it is crucial in terms of showing how the concept is intertwined with the nation-state. That is because the principle of the rule of law is rooted in the fact that the rules set by the bourgeoisie both bind the king and apply uniformly throughout the country. This fact becomes more apparent when the rule of law is defined as the limitation of

---

344 R. Carré de Malberg, *Contribution à la Théorie Générale de l'État*, Volume 1, Recueil Sirey, Paris, 1920, p. 232.
345 Özenç, *Hukuk Devleti*, p. 15.
346 Schmitt, *Théorie de la Constitution*, p. 263.
347 Fotopoulos, *Towards an Inclusive Democracy*, p. 12.
348 Poggi, *The Development of the Modern State*, p. 114.

political power, in other words, the modern state, through law.[349] Political power, which was sovereign and therefore unlimited before the emergence of the modern state, turns into a limited power that has to govern in accordance with certain legal provisions with the adoption of the rule of law. Of course, knowing who creates the law at this point is vital and that is what we need to question regarding the subject of this book.

In Ancient Athens, where there was no distinction between ruler and ruled, the principle of the rule of law, an essential part of Plato and Aristotle's theories, was defined as the opposite of democracy because it was an idea about limiting the decision-making will of the Athenian people. Nevertheless, they found this situation positive, as they considered the rule of law as an ideal that would eliminate the weaknesses of democratic governance.[350] In the modern state, however, a particularly close relationship exists between the state and the law. Law is no longer perceived as the expression of legal principles that have been in force since ancient times, that have emerged spontaneously, that have been filtered through society, or that are based on the ecological balance of nature, and that have been reinforced in practice by a politically organised structure using the power of sanction. Modern law is a body of enacted laws. In other words, it is a law that is consciously made, often explicit, documented, and often validated by new decisions by an organ of the state exercising sovereignty.[351]

Considering the development of the modern state and how the principle of separation of powers has lost its function, it becomes clear that the will that consciously creates, documents, and validates the documents that constitute law, namely constitutions and laws, belongs to the bourgeoisie. That is also why the organisation of political power in the form of the rule of law took place almost simultaneously with the development of capitalist relations of production.[352] In the nineteenth century, when the bourgeoisie imposed the concept of the rule of law, it could not do so without establishing legal principles and norms against absolutism. It had to demand different political institutions, differently authorised but equally concrete, as opposed to public

349 Özenç, *Hukuk Devleti*, p. 16, 173.
350 Özenç, *Hukuk Devleti*, p. 17.
351 Poggi, *The Development of the Modern State*, p. 123.
352 Özenç, *Hukuk Devleti*, p. 18.

institutions that were concretely in force according to monarchical principles. Therefore, he was fighting not only for an abstract rule of law but also for the rights of 'popular representation', in other words, for the extension and expansion of parliamentary power and authority.[353] Of course, what should not be overlooked here is the fact that the parliament at that time had not yet developed the capacity to represent all social classes and was mainly in the hands of the bourgeoisie. Therefore, the bourgeoisie's struggle was one for a share of power by imposing its own rules on the monarchy.

As Özenç succinctly puts it, today, the rule of law, which is produced 'not by *the demos*, but by a class endowed with the privilege of exploiting *the demos (and nature)*' and which reflects the reason and virtue of this class, is placed at the foundation of the political system.[354] The material content of the theory of natural rights is reflected in the principle of the rule of law,[355] which is based on the freedom and equality of citizens.[356] However, freedom here means, first and foremost, the freedom of the bourgeoisie to exploit people and nature, and equality means, first and foremost, the absence of any other class that can exert pressure on the bourgeoisie. That is because capitalism needs a predictable legal order that prevents unexpected interventions by the state.[357] It realises this by imposing its rights arising from natural law on other state organs within the rule of law framework because, at the end of the day, the rule of law means that popular representation participates in, or eventually dominates, decision-making. In short, through the struggle for the rule of law, the bourgeoisie seeks to protect itself from attacks on its freedoms, especially its right to property.[358]

It must be acknowledged that the rights and freedoms that the bourgeois class has defined as law in line with its interests have been transferred beyond this class and extended to the entire society thanks to the struggles that expanded the scope of the principle of equality. Consequently, the rule

---

353 Schmitt, *Théorie de la Constitution*, p. 285.
354 Özenç, *Hukuk Devleti*, p. 54.
355 Özenç, *Hukuk Devleti*, p. 178.
356 Schmitt, *Théorie de la Constitution*, p. 292.
357 Max Weber, *On Law in Economy and Society*, trans. Edward Shils – Max Rheinstein, Harvard University Press, Cambridge and Massachusetts, 1966, pp. 266–76, cited in: Delice, 'Karma Hükümetten ... ', p. 1690.
358 Schmitt, *Théorie de la Constitution*, p. 286.

of law today also protects our rights and freedoms. That is an achievement, and it should not be lost. However, suppose our goal is to achieve something utterly contrary to the capitalist economic model, such as preventing climate change. In that case, it is evident that we need to be highly creative within the existing legal order. Unfortunately, it will not be easy to dismantle the bourgeois perspective that underpins the modern state system through the existing judiciary.

The concept of 'unity of state power', one of the characteristics of the rule of law, includes the idea that 'vertical' power-centred and power-activated relations exist only between the state and individuals in the modern state. Conversely, all relations are assumed to be 'horizontal', contractual, and force-free between individuals. The state should not interfere in these relations. However, capital ownership creates a *de facto* relationship of oppression between individuals of different classes. Moreover, it is a legally and politically protected instrument for its reproduction. The contradiction here is that the state, claiming to be the source of all power relations, in fact, acts as a guarantor of power relations that do not originate with it and are not under its control but arise from the concentration of capital in private hands.[359] That is because the basic structure of law, determined by parliaments dominated by the bourgeoisie, is shaped to permit and facilitate the exploitation of human beings and nature and to ensure that the state protects this hierarchical relationship.

Indeed, when we look at how the rule of law theory was put into practice in England, we see that the Glorious Revolution mentioned earlier, among other consequences, led to the establishment of the principle of 'rule of law' as a scientific fact. Common Law judges could serve for life. Thus, they were equipped to secure private property against any encroachment by the Kingdom. The Kingdom's encroachment on private property was limited 'by the law; ' the sovereign power had to respect both the Common Law and the contracts interpreted by the courts.[360] Subject only to (self-declared) law, the judges would hear conflicts of privilege between Parliament (representing

---

[359] H. Heller, *Staatslehre*, 3rd ed., Leiden, 1963, p. 109 et seq., cited in: Poggi, *The Development of the Modern State*, p. 116.

[360] J. Baker, *An Introduction to English Legal History*, 4th edition, Butterworth Lexis Nexis, London, 2002, cited in: Capra – Mattei, *The Ecology of Law*, p. 76.

private property) and the Crown (representing sovereignty),[361] and it was Parliament that decided the law to be applied in these conflicts.

Capra and Mattei explain clearly how the bourgeoisie built a system for its own interests within the rule of law framework. According to the authors, the Settlement Law completely excluded the commons and the political forces that represent them. It did not allow for serious judicial review of the enclosure process because ordinary people and peasants, who were not represented in Parliament, had no access to the court process. The courts of law were (and still are) ill-equipped to protect collective interests in general and the interests of the poor people in particular. Thus, this compromise, known as the rule of law, not only dispossessed the masses of peasants but also forced the dispossessed to work to serve a new mechanism by which property was concentrated. This mechanism was the manufacturing industry.[362] Therefore, the enclosure movement was not a 'usurpation' in the legal sense but a process in accordance with the law. One could even say that the bourgeoisie turned the law into a weapon against the peasants in order to take away the commons they used. Similar to the fact that we cannot find today a court to defend our rights violated due to climate change, the peasants had no institution to turn to.

The rule of law thus removed the commons from the sphere of interests protected by law. A few ancient collective rights disappeared entirely after the triumph of unrestricted modern private property. This significant change replaced a way of life, which was not easy at all but in which the peasant was one of the constituent parts of the ecological community, with another one that was perhaps more difficult than before, in which labour was exchanged for a wage. Before, the average person's life was not a unit of time quantified for sale on the market.[363] Yet, later, ordinary people whose living conditions in their villages were taken away from them came to the city and tried to find work in the factories and sell their labour. Thus, people also became part of the commodification process.

Meanwhile, in France, a powerful state was being built under the economic policies introduced at the end of the seventeenth century, known today as

---

[361] Capra – Mattei, *The Ecology of Law*, p. 76.
[362] Capra – Mattei, *The Ecology of Law*, p. 76.
[363] Capra – Mattei, *The Ecology of Law*, pp. 76–7.

mercantilism. According to mercantilist theory, the way for a state to gain an advantage over others was to ensure that the world's most valuable metals, especially silver (and later gold), came into the country in the highest possible quantity and stayed there. The reason for this was simple: Wars were expensive, weapons had to be bought, they were often manufactured outside the monarch's own country, and buying from a foreign country required large amounts of silver and gold. For a state to keep precious metals at home, it needed economic policies that prevented money from being spent on goods not used in war. Mercantilist thinking led states to adopt policies to ensure that raw materials were used and transformed into products within their borders rather than importing products. Although mercantilist policies thus led to the emergence of various new industries in European states, the aim was not industrialisation but keeping gold and silver within the country and preventing others from enriching themselves.[364] That created the logic of industrialisation and capital accumulation in the European states. The new task of parliaments was to change the rules or, if necessary, make new rules so that as much wealth as possible could accumulate in the country.

As an example of these mercantilist policies, in 1707, the British Parliament passed several laws restricting the import of Indian textiles made of cotton into England. However, limiting these imports was a blow to both the Indian producers and the ordinary people in England who could buy these textiles cheaply. However, British parliamentarians ignored this, intending to protect British manufacturers and develop a British cotton textile industry. Obviously, the Parliament was now entirely under the bourgeoisie's control and working in its interests. The merchants, who had initially challenged the aristocracy with the slogans of equality and liberty, began imposing prohibitions to increase their capital and prosperity. By the end of the eighteenth century, the government in England was ready to use state policies to support textile manufacturers and would later do the same for coal and iron producers.[365] As a result, the rule of law emerged as a mechanism to protect state sovereignty and private property, leaving very little space for ecological and social commons.

---

364 Marks, *The Origins of…*, pp. 105–6.
365 Marks, *The Origins of…*, p. 105.

In the case of the United States, its founders at the end of the eighteenth century had two main goals: a strong and effective government that concentrated administrative and military authority in its hands and a robust property rights system. These two goals were likely to give rise to some structural tensions, as there could be situations in which property rights advocates and a strong government would come into conflict. A system of checks and balances was therefore designed. This model included a complex federal structure and a system in which the Supreme Court had the final say. In the US, the right to property and the ideals of individual rights and freedom from government coercion that it was supposed to protect led to a veritable cult of the rule of law.[366] This legal superstructure is what we inherited from the founding fathers.

Capra and Mattei rightfully argue that today's dominant legal order serves the needs of capital accumulation. In order to do this, it has separated itself from politics and economics. In the political sphere, the modern legal order took the form of liberal constitutionalism with the expansion of the right to vote, and this political order dominates the world today. In the economic sphere, it has taken the form of a 'laissez faire' market capitalism that only the state can limit. The authors emphasise that in the Western understanding, social institutions artificially separate individuals from each other and their ecosystems. The theories of property (Locke) and sovereignty (Hobbes) are presented as ideologically opposed, but they are, in fact, consistent in their structure (concentration and individualisation of power and exclusion) and purpose (capitalisation of common assets).[367]

That is the law that we recognise as supreme today. The state, which we call the rule of law, is obliged to abide by and protect this law. Moreover, since the principle of the rule of law refers to rules above the state, the state organs have no choice but to implement them. These are written into constitutions and even recognised as supra-constitutional norms. Therefore, they have been elevated to a position beyond anyone's reach. It has almost turned into a *Grundnorm*.[368] That is because the current legal system is built within the

---

[366] Capra – Mattei, *The Ecology of Law*, p. 97.

[367] Capra – Mattei, *The Ecology of Law*, pp. 181–2.

[368] In line with the natural law perspective, rules that are considered to be even above constitutions. However, which rules constitute the *Grundnorm* is a matter of debate.

framework of the capitalist economic order and cannot be separated from it. However, suppose we believe that capitalism is the deepest underlying cause of climate change. In that case, we need to separate the law from it and create a new law that will regulate and, if necessary, prevent capitalist production, consumption and relations models. That is the subject of the second part. Let us first focus on a deeper understanding of the relationship between the two.

1.2.5.4 The symbiotic relationship between the capitalist economic order and the existing legal system

Admittedly, capitalism is one of the major forces behind the phenomenal rise of both science and empires.[369] So, it is true that, in general, capitalism has broadened our horizons, made our lives easier, and extended our lifespan. However, for nature, it means destruction, and for most people, it means overwork, accidents at work, depression, and suicide. Yet, all these things have been normalised. They are legitimised within the system because they result from activities that take place under the protection of the law. In line with Locke's idea of an atomised society, we tend to think that if someone fails at their job, goes into debt to the bank, is stuck in a job where they are overworked and underpaid, or becomes addicted to anti-depressants, it is the fault of that person, not the system. The primary reason why we think this way is our current legal system, which covers up the crimes of capitalism.

Legal systems before the emergence of the modern state were based on a distributive justice approach concerned with the whole. It prioritised the welfare of society, not the individual. Following the Treaty of Westphalia, this conception of justice was presented as a pre-legal idea belonging not to law but to politics or morality. Distributive justice was wholly excluded from legal science and abandoned for three centuries. During this period, a rationalised version of natural law, built around the individual, dominated Western legal and political thought. Absolute property rights, free from possible redistributive schemes and concerns for the commons, became the basis for the legal support of our current development model.[370] The law was

[369] Harari, *Sapiens*, p. 301. However, it should not be overlooked that socialist countries also enabled great leaps in technology and social welfare.

[370] Capra – Mattei, *The Ecology of Law*, pp. 87–8.

no longer concerned with society as a whole but with individuals and their rights and freedoms.

The modern state, fundamentally shaped by the free-market principles of capitalism, functioned through its administrative activities to favour and protect the class domination of the bourgeoisie over society. Protecting private property through constitutions and laws directed the activities of the security forces, the police, and the judiciary to favour the interests of the propertied classes.[371] At the constitutional level, everyone was equal, but if one was poor, they could not enjoy the property rights, nor indeed the rights to housing, travel, welfare, health, food, or self-improvement that flowed from it. However, this was their fault, not capitalism's. From this perspective, the most distinctive feature of modern law as a set of rules is that it reflects certain moral and cultural preferences of the bourgeoisie.[372]

The *sine qua non* condition of capitalism, which emerged with the development of the economic infrastructure of the bourgeoisie, is growth. Since growth increases resource consumption, nature is always increasingly damaged in this system. Therefore, in a capitalist state, it is almost impossible for regulations to protect nature, whether at the constitutional or legislative level, to be effective. In practice, they usually appear as anthropocentric 'environmental' regulations whose primary function is to prevent the violations of rights caused by economic activities from becoming blatantly visible. In this way, people focus on the prosperity of their share of production rather than the damage to the nature from which they are alienated. However, this does not change the reality we have to face: The spread of this economic system across the world through colonialism and imperialism has globalised the damage to nature and caused the climate change we face today. Accordingly, let us look at three reasons why the rule of law in a capitalist system cannot offer us solutions.

Growth as the fundamental rule of capitalism

For most of history, the economy has grown only in response to settling new lands and population growth. Production per capita has remained constant.

---

[371] Poggi, *The Development of the Modern State*, pp. 140–1.

[372] Jürgen Habermas, *Struckturwandel der Öffentlichkeit*, 5th ed., Neuwied, 1971, pp. 74–5, cited in: Poggi, *The Development of the Modern State*, p. 141.

That is because, in pre-modern times, people only produced what they could consume. There was no point in producing more; even if they did, it would spoil because it could not be consumed. Therefore, they worked as much as needed and spent time on other tasks or rested. Where profits were made from what was produced, the nobles of the Middle Ages spent it on competitions, banquets, palaces, wars, aid to the poor, and massive cathedrals. Few invested their profits in increasing the output of their farms, producing better wheat, or seeking new markets.[373]

What distinguishes capitalism from all other economic systems in history is that it reverses this logic and is organised around 'growth'. Capitalism is a system that constantly seeks to open new markets in order to accumulate capital and increase value. It is based on the exploitation of natural resources and human labour, and the cost resulting from this process is constantly externalised onto others. The essence of this economic order is never to stop growing in order to generate profit.[374] Today, especially after the collapse of real-life socialism, there is a high level of market and growth economy convergence in societies' economic and political institutions. A growth economy is defined as an economic organisation that aims at the objective or conscious maximisation of economic growth.[375] As is well known, economic growth refers to an increase in income through the production or provision of services, and the numerical unit of measurement is money.[376] Today, growth is recognised as the increase in the value-added produced by an economy, called gross domestic product (GDP), over a specific time.[377]

Since 1953, GDP has been the first-order measure in a complex System of National Accounts that sets international standards for measuring the economic performance of nations.[378] GDP is defined as the total market value of all goods and services in a country over a given period and is designed

---

[373] Harari, *Sapiens*, pp. 309–10.
[374] Saito, *Slow Down*, p. 72.
[375] Fotopoulos, *Towards an Inclusive Democracy*, p. 3.
[376] İzel Levi Coşkun, *Süreklilikten Sürdürülebilirliğe – Bir Kurumsal Sürdürülebilirlik Yolculuğu*, 3rd ed., Artisan, Istanbul, 2022, p. 39.
[377] Parrique, *Ralentir ou Périr*, p. 25.
[378] Tim Jackson, *Post Growth: Life after Capitalism* (Turkish version), trans. Akın Emre Pilgir, Ayrıntı, Istanbul, 2023, p. 21.

to measure a country's economic size.[379] The calculation of GDP takes into account the exchange value of goods and services, not their use value. Things that do not cause a monetary movement are worthless in this framework. For example, a mother taking care of her children, someone cooking for friends, or organising a meeting to discuss neighbourhood problems are not accounted for by GDP, even though they create social value.[380] Therefore, it can be recognised that it contains extremely important statistical limitations.[381]

The purpose of calculating and growing GDP was initially assigned specific functions. These included strengthening the American economy after the Great Depression, ending hunger and poverty, achieving full employment, and rebuilding Europe. Measuring GDP provided an understanding of how much progress was made in achieving these goals. However, by the end of the twentieth century, the criterion itself had become a goal: to grow for the sake of growing, without any other specific purpose.[382]

In the case of capital, the primary purpose of increasing production is not to meet people's needs or improve social outcomes; instead, it is to generate and accumulate an ever-increasing amount of profit. In other words, the purpose of growth is to grow again. That is the goal that trumps all others. Therefore, growth is the first commandment of capital, which Baudrillard describes as *a process of 'white magic' with numbers that conceals the black magic that causes a collective fascination*.[383] Growth within the system has a totalitarian logic: Every industry, every sector, and every national economy must always grow without an endpoint.[384] Growth is also a structural imperative under capitalism. If the economy does not grow, it stagnates, which is a bad scenario for both left- and, of course, right-wing politicians. These two sides of politics may have different ideas about distributing the benefits of growth, but they are united when it comes to growth itself. That is why growthism

379 Hulme, *Why We Disagree …*, p. 134.
380 Parrique, *Ralentir ou Périr*, p. 28.
381 Saito, *Slow Down*, p. 84.
382 Parrique, *Ralentir ou Périr*, p. 13.
383 Jean Baudrillard, *La Société de Consommation* (Turkish version), trans. Hazal Deliceçay – Ferda Keskin, 3rd ed., Ayrıntı, Istanbul, 2008, p. 38.
384 Hickel, *Less is More*, p. 19.

can be considered one of the most hegemonic ideologies in modern history.[385] At this point, it is worth taking a closer look at why this is so.

Economic growth is both a cause and a consequence of capitalism.[386] That is because the modern banking system, which forms the system's backbone, is based on credit. For the bank, a credit is a loan one gives today but expects to get back with interest. The borrower invests the money and promises to pay it back in full at a future date through production. The loan is granted if the future is secure and the project can earn more money than the amount lent.[387]

In the old days of subsistence and a closed economic system, there were neither lenders nor borrowers, as there could be no profitable investment, or even if there were, it would be pointless. However, with the development of technology and the flow of raw materials from new continents to Europe by ship, confidence in the growing economic pie led to a revolutionary change. In 1776, the Scottish economist Adam Smith (1723–90) published *The Wealth of Nations*. Smith made the following new claim, which has become commonplace for us today: If a landowner, weaver, or shoemaker makes more profit than is needed to feed his family, he uses this surplus to employ more workers and thus increase his profits even further. As his profits increase, he employs more workers. The increase in the profits of individual entrepreneurs is, therefore, the basis for the increase in the wealth and prosperity of the whole society.[388] So Smith was not only following Locke's lead in saying that people should selfishly and greedily increase their profits, but he was also justifying this by showing it as the path to the wealth and prosperity of society. In this sense, it was one of the most revolutionary ideas that transformed economic history.[389]

However, it was well known that Smith's theory did not correspond to reality. Even in Locke's time, although the commercialisation of agriculture increased the total product, the only 'improvement' was the growth of landowners' profits. For two centuries, ordinary people struggled with hunger

---

385 Hickel, *Less is More*, p. 22.

386 For the opposing view, see David Schweickart, 'Is Sustainable Capitalism an Oxymoron?', *Perspectives on Global Development and Technology*, Vol. 8, No. 2–3, 2009, pp. 557–78.

387 Harari, *Sapiens*, pp. 303–7.

388 Adam Smith, *An Inquiry into the Nature and Causes of the Wealth of Nations*, Liberty Classics, Indianapolis, 1979, pp. 86–7, § 18–20.

389 Harari, *Sapiens*, pp. 308–9.

while the product increased. It was the same in factories. No gains in worker productivity were returned to the workers, and wages continued to fall throughout the enclosure period.[390] The same is true today. The technological inventions that have emerged through capital investment are claimed to make our lives easier, yet despite our use of them, our working hours are increasing rather than decreasing. Even though technology advances, productivity does not lead to more quality time for ourselves but more production and corporate profits. That is because capitalism aims to maximise profit, not productivity. That is why companies almost invariably lay off workers, outsource production, or move factories to other countries rather than making environmentally meaningful improvements to their production methods.[391]

The modern capitalist economy is largely based on a modern ethic of reinvesting profits into production. The investment must ultimately yield more profit, which must be reinvested in production, which must yield more profit, and so on. This cycle goes on forever. Investments can be made in various ways: expanding the factory, doing scientific research, developing new products, etc. However, all these investments must ultimately increase production and generate greater profits. Because the first and most sacred commandment of the capitalist creed is this: The profits of production must be invested in increasing production.[392] That is why, contrary to Smith's example, profits do not usually translate into more jobs or greater social welfare. On the contrary, the owner of capital is always inclined to make his workers work harder, pay them less, and employ as few workers as possible in order to make more profit.

Despite this well-known fact, it is a fundamental doctrine of capitalism that economic growth is the best, or at least a means to the best, because justice, freedom, and even happiness depend on economic growth.[393] Growth is so deeply embedded in our economic and political system that the system cannot survive without growth. If growth stops, companies fail, governments struggle to finance social services, people lose jobs, poverty increases, and

---

390 Hickel, *Less is More*, p. 56.

391 Brian Tokar, *Toward Climate Justice: Perspectives on the Climate Crisis and Social Change* (Kindle edition), New Compass Press, Porsgrunn, 2014, A Utopian Movement? (Loc. 1505).

392 Harari, *Sapiens*, p. 309.

393 Harari, *Sapiens*, p. 311.

states become politically fragile. Under capitalism, growth is not just one of the attributes of human social organisation but a necessity to which everyone is subject. If the economy does not grow, everything starts to fall apart.[394]

According to economists, GDP under capitalism should grow by at least 2 per cent or 3 per cent yearly. Indeed, whereas around the year 1500, the average annual production per capita worldwide was 550 dollars, today, people produce an average of 12,000 dollars a year[395] despite massive population growth. In other words, the global economy has grown enormously over the centuries since capitalism emerged and established its hegemony. This growth has been made possible by an increase in production and consumption. That was enabled, as explained earlier,[396] by the introduction of fossil fuels into production processes. In this context, economic growth and fossil fuel consumption are deeply and inextricably linked.[397] However, as these have increased, the global economy has used more energy and resources and produced more waste. That is causing us to exceed the limits of what scientists calculate is a safe planet with devastating impacts on life.[398]

Reasons why environmental regulations in modern legal systems fail to protect nature

The fact that the modern state, which is the protector of an economic order based on a capitalist understanding of growth, also aims to protect nature means that it contradicts itself. The view of nature as a resource is inherent to the modern state. In other words, the raison d'être of this state structure is the unlimited commodification of natural assets, their use and consumption in production, and thus the continuation of growth by 'gaining' them for the economy. Therefore, it would be naïve, to say the least, to think that the modern state, whose primary goal is to protect and safeguard the capitalist economic order, would see nature as a subject of rights and restrict economic activities on it in a manner utterly contrary to this logic.[399] A state

394 Hickel, *Less is More*, p. 98.
395 Gross National Income Per Capita, Atlas Method (current US$), 2022.
396 See 1.2.3
397 Saito, *Slow Down*, p. 43.
398 Hickel, *Less is More*, p. 20.
399 The constitutions of Ecuador and Bolivia, which recognise nature as a subject of rights, will be discussed in detail in the second part of the study.

that is concerned with environmental problems such as global warming and pollution but at the same time wants to preserve and even advance the economic system as it is and is not interested in radical change can, at best, be characterised as 'environmentalist'.[400]

On the other hand, today's environmental law, inherited from modernity, is doomed to fail in protecting nature because it does not abolish the idea of unlimited exploitation of the planet based on the separation of man from nature and the supremacy of man.[401] It treats nature as a resource, a bundle of commodities to be used in our economy, rather than as an ecosystem with rights.[402] Environmental regulations in such a constitutional order do not touch the structural limits that leave the organisation of production processes to private companies. The system continues to make the necessary arrangements for capitalists to plunder natural resources. Most environmental protection regulations in such a system are either aimed at people's health and right to life or sham and changed when necessary, just like when a place that was once declared a national park because it was deemed to be very valuable was removed when it was discovered that there was a valuable mine there.[403]

Environmental regulations that fail to recognise nature as a valuable subject of rights in its own right and that fail to protect it holistically, not just regionally, will certainly not succeed in preventing today's climate change. To solve this crisis, we first need regulations that have the capacity to limit the economic activities of corporations that exploit nature without any respect

---

[400] Greg Garrard, *Ecocriticism* (Turkish version), trans. Ertuğrul Genç, Kolektif Kitap, Istanbul, 2016, p. 39.

[401] Teresa Vicente Giménez – Eduardo Salazar Ortuño, 'An Ecological Citizenship's Triumph: From the Popular Legislative Initiative to the Rights Granted for the Mar Menor', *in* Jenny García Ruales – Katarina Hovden – Helen Kopnina – Colin D. Robertson – Hendrik Schoukens, *Rights of Nature in Europe: Encounters and Visions*, Routledge, Abingdon & New York, 2024, p. 84.

[402] David R. Boyd, *The Rights of Nature: A Legal Revolution That Could Save The World* (Kindle edition), ECW Press, Toronto, 2017, p. 111.

[403] In any case, granting a place a status such as a national park is usually not meaningful considering the functioning of nature. Here again, traces of the mechanistic perspective inherited from Newton and Locke can be seen. Taking separate and distant areas under protection still disrupts the integrity of nature and interferes with its functioning. A protected area surrounded by cities and factories can no longer survive in its natural cycle.

for their support systems because it is them, not 'humanity' in general, that are causing global warming. Nor have corporations done it by mistake or out of sheer greed. The dynamic that determines their actions and leads to this result is the capitalist social structure itself.[404] Indeed, in the neoliberal era, environmental law has had to retreat in the face of the activities of corporations, the importance of natural assets has become secondary when it comes to private property rights, and the ' polluter pays for it' principle has become dysfunctional.[405] Therefore, hoping for environmental regulations that do not question this structure, unfortunately, means wasting even more of our precious time.

In addition, admittedly, environmental law has historically failed to recognise the contributions made by Indigenous peoples' legal systems.[406] On the contrary, Indigenous knowledge has often been made illegal and removed from the wider public view. So-called 'democratic' institutions have prevented Indigenous peoples from participating in decision-making processes, damaged their environment, and thus prevented the dissemination of knowledge about how to live in harmony with nature.[407] That has been done deliberately and intentionally in the name of the capitalist economic order and as a requirement of nature–culture dualism.

Consequently, today, we are at perhaps the lowest point in political history, not only for human rights but also for the conditions of animals and nature. Today's environmental legislation facilitates habitat fragmentation, pollution, deforestation, and destruction of natural areas by sectors such as construction, industry, transportation, etc., and many other economic activities that harm the ecosystem. For this reason, the current legislation can even be seen as a serious organised action that subverts the right of animals and nature to exist and results in species extinction.[408]

---

[404] Fraser, 'Climates of Capital', p. 58.

[405] Durmaz, *Doğanın Hakları*, p. XVI.

[406] Collins, *The Ecological Constitution*, p. 40.

[407] John Borrows, 'Living Between Water and Rocks: First Nations, Environmental Planning, and Democracy', *The University of Toronto Law Journal*, Vol. 47, No. 4, Fall 1997, p. 425, cited in: Collins, *The Ecological Constitution*, p. 40.

[408] Onur Akgül, 'Adil Dönüşüm: İklim Krizinden Sağ Çıkmanın Politikası', *in* Didem Bayındır – Mine Yıldırım (ed.), *Ekoloji: Bir Arada Yaşamanın Geleceği*, Tellekt, Istanbul, 2022, p. 100.

The spread of Western modernity and the creation of the international legal system

As mentioned earlier, the 'primitive' capital accumulation necessary for the beginning of the first capitalist social organisation was created not only by the enclosure of the commons but also by the transformation of the peasants living in a community in harmony with nature into quantified and alienated factory labour in the city. That created an accumulation of capital, and what accelerated it was the availability of various resources outside the country.[409] Other commercially colonised countries were subjected to external rule, and the self-regulating elements of the subsistence economy were dismantled.[410]

The Scientific Revolution and its discovery of universal 'laws of nature' left a legacy of tremendous technological progress in weaponry, naval engineering, and cartography. These made it possible to build ships that would not break apart in the rough waves of oceans and to discover new continents. Similarly, man-made laws of natural law were claimed to be universal, replacing rules derived from nature, and these laws became the common understanding of modernity. The essential point of view, given respectability by writers such as Niccolo Machiavelli (1469–1527), Jean Bodin, and Thomas Hobbes, and supported by the theology of Martin Luther (1483–1546), presupposed that potency creates rights concerning secular matters of sovereignty. Moreover, according to the mercantilist perspective, the wealth of sovereign nations could be measured by the size of the market they could create and control.[411] All this combined paved the way for Europeans to take over the world. The rest of the world became *res nullius* in the eyes of Europeans. That included other people. They were not considered human beings but a 'capturable' part of nature.

In the new modern legal order, time was freed from the cyclical movement of nature and began to flow linearly. Within the logic of 'progress', history was linear, and European civilisation was the most advanced in this sense. Anyone who looked back from the current point and was considered to be

---

[409] Ugo Mattei – Laura Nader, *Plunder: When the Rule of Law Is Illegal*, Blackwell, Malden, Massachusetts, 2003, cited in: Capra – Mattei, *The Ecology of Law*, p. 94.

[410] Joachim Radkau, *Nature and Power: A Global History of the Environmental* (Turkish version), trans. Nafiz Güder, Türkiye İş Bankası Kültür Yayınları, İstanbul, 2017, p. 257.

[411] Capra – Mattei, *The Ecology of Law*, p. 96.

behind was treated as a child, if not humiliated. In this respect, the European logic was discriminatory from the very beginning. The law of other societies was either disregarded as law or regarded as backwardness. The law in Europe, which had been transformed by the mechanistic understanding of science and the bourgeois economic order, became what it was supposed to be and the 'only' law.[412] According to this law, only citizens of modern states like their own could possess sacred and inalienable rights. As soon as rights ceased to be the rights of a citizen of a state, they became unprotected and lost their reality.[413] Accordingly, Europeans probably genuinely believed they were superior to the societies on the continents they reached. In any case, depriving them of their 'inherent' rights would not have been otherwise possible to turn them into commodities to be bought and sold because you could not promote the universal rights of 'all human beings' and enslave them at the same time. In order to enslave someone, one had first to deny their humanity and thus put a moral distance between them. In the eyes of Europeans, Africans and Native Americans were not human beings entitled to rights but part of nature and thus could be considered objects to be exploited.[414] In this framework, many cultures that saw nature not as a commodity to be owned or traded for profit but as a mother, a sister, or simply as the basis of existence were considered 'primitive' and 'uncivilised' for thinking differently from the Western anthropocentric understanding of nature. They have, therefore, been subjected to horrific interventions designed to transform and dispossess them.[415]

When the Indigenous peoples of the reached continents were not accepted as humans, their land became 'empty'. The idea of 'legal sovereignty over empty lands', which echoed Grotius' idea of the open sea,[416] provided the most substantial intellectual justification for exploiting the New World inhabited

---

412 Cemal Bâli Akal, *Hukuk Nedir?*, Dost, Ankara, 2017, p. 31.

413 Agamben, *Homo Sacer*, p. 167.

414 Hickel, *Less is More*, p. 76.

415 Carmen G. Gonzalez, 'Foreword: Deconstructing the Legal Architecture of the Anthropocene', *in* Usha Natarajan – Julia Dehm (ed.), *Locating Nature – Making and Unmaking International Law*, Cambridge University Press, Cambridge, 2022, p. xi.

416 According to this idea, which originated in Hugo Grotius's 1609 work *Mare Liberum* (Freedom of the Seas), the seas are international space and all states could freely use them for shipping trade.

by 'savages' who had no Christian God, rationality, or idea of property.[417] In various works, Grotius tried to find the foundations for a universally recognisable law of nations. He found it in the idea that 'all men and civilised states must accept certain fundamental rules', an indispensable rule of natural law. For him, these rules corresponded to the principles of human nature, constituting the common ground shared by all humans.[418] Accordingly, Europeans saw nature, which they reached through their voyages of discovery, as a vast and hostile desert, like the sea, and as an evil that had to be endured.[419]

In fact, questions existed about this point of view at the very beginning. In the sixteenth century, there was a deep academic debate among Spanish jurists about whether the invasion of South America was legitimate. However, a century later, during the colonisation of North America, there was no such debate.[420] That was because by then, Hobbes' and Locke's ideas on the social contract and European legal rationality had become the prevailing Western thought. In Europeans' eyes, it was a fundamental right to dominate nature and other people who were still in a 'state of nature' because they had not yet reached the stage of social contract. Both the exploitation of the land and the ownership of these people, whose subjectivity as human beings was denied, found a rational justification.[421] Consequently, during this period of colonisation, the peoples of what is now called the Global South[422] were routinely seen as nature: They were 'savages' and inferior to European men. That is why the Spanish word for the Indigenous peoples of the Americas was *naturales*.[423]

---

[417] Ugo Mattei – Laura Nader, *Plunder: When the Rule of Law is Illegal*, Blackwell, Malden, Massachusetts, 2008, cited in: Capra – Mattei, *The Ecology of Law*, p. 86.

[418] R. C. Van Caenegem, *An Historicak Introduction to Private Law* (Turkish version), trans. Ali Acar – Caner Birdal – İbrahim Doğan Takavut – O. Vahdet İşsevenler – Zeynep Arslan, Pinhan Yayıncılık, Istanbul, 2022, p. 172.

[419] John Fowles, *The Tree* (Turkish version), trans. Süha Sertabiboğlu, Ayrıntı, Istanbul, 2020, pp. 57–8.

[420] A. A. Cassi, *Ultramar: L'invenzione europea del Nuovo Mondo*, Laterza, Bari and Rome, 2007, cited in: Capra – Mattei, *The Ecology of Law*, p. 86.

[421] Capra – Mattei, *The Ecology of Law*, p. 86.

[422] According to the UN Conference on Trade and Development, the Global South roughly includes Africa, South America and the Caribbean, Asia excluding Israel, Japan and South Korea, and Oceania excluding Australia and New Zealand.

[423] Hickel, *Less is More*, p. 76.

Accordingly, the legal weapon of the British United East India Company, the first example of transnational capitalist formation, was natural law. Grotius, one of the company's well-paid advisers, used natural law in a highly creative way and, through his genius, transformed it into international law. In Grotius' view, the sea was a common good, which had to be open to all. Access to this asset was vital for a legal 'person' operating in international trade. The defence of access was based on a fundamental natural right, the right to exist. A legal 'person' could resist the violation of this fundamental right, even violently. Grotius defended his client's right to navigate the oceans based on this argument. Secondly, he justified that the company had the right to seize unused private property, even if it was located in a country under foreign rule, because individuals could own *res nullius* regardless of whose sovereignty they were under. This principle was particularly important for extracting and exploiting untouched minerals for Grotius and his company's clients.[424]

Following this logic, during the fifteenth and sixteenth centuries, Europeans circumnavigated Africa, discovered America, crossed the Pacific and Indian oceans, and created a network of colonies worldwide. In this way, they built the first truly global empires and the first global trade network. The logic of 'empty lands', combined with slavery, created a system of exploitation on an incredible scale. First, the society in the reached area was enslaved, and then they were forced to extract the minerals in their own lands, and the resulting wealth was sent to Europe. Since in places like the Americas, where both the top and bottom of the soil were very fertile, the population of the Indigenous people could not keep up with the pace of exploitation, enslaved people from Africa were brought there by ship. Thus, Europe's imperial expeditions changed world history: History was no longer the history of a series of disconnected peoples and cultures but a single, unified human society.[425]

In addition, Indigenous peoples in the colonised areas were forced to abandon animist ideas. The aim was to make the colonised as dualistic as the Europeans because 'civilisation' required it. So, not only the lands and bodies of Indigenous peoples were colonised, but also their minds. As Kenyan writer Ngũgĩ wa Thiongo underlines, colonialism imposed control

---

424 Capra – Mattei, *The Ecology of Law*, pp. 102–3.
425 Harari, *Sapiens*, p. 287.

over the social production of wealth through military occupation followed by political dictatorship. However, the most crucial sphere of domination was the intellectual universe of the colonised: The control, through culture, of how people perceived themselves and their relationship to the world.[426]

Between 1500 and 1800, most of the world's population, economic activity, and trade was in Asia. In 1775, Asia produced 80 per cent of all goods produced worldwide. The economies of India and China accounted for two-thirds of all world production. In contrast, Europe, together with Africa and the Americas, produced only one-fifth of the world's output.[427] However, within the European logic of colonialism, natural rights, which allowed them to do business without political obligations to other governments or societies, created a favourable playing field for private companies engaged in transnational activities from the very beginning.[428] European companies used their 'natural rights' to engage in all sorts of economic activities in these countries and remit the revenues to their nation-states in Europe. Thanks to mercantilist economic policies in the eighteenth century, industrialisation and capital accumulation advanced rapidly in Western Europe, especially Britain and France. Britain took over India's world leadership in textile production. Once it had done so, it began to advocate 'free trade' and abandoned mercantilist theory, practice, and tariffs on imports. In fact, at the height of its global power in the nineteenth century, 'free trade' became imperial Britain's ideological mantra.[429]

The centre of global economic power shifted to Europe between 1759 and 1850, when Europeans defeated Asian powers in a series of wars and conquered vast areas of Asia. By 1900, Europeans controlled most of the world's economy and territory.[430] Thus the rise of the West, which began in the eighteenth century, was completed in the nineteenth century. As the Industrial Revolution of the late eighteenth and early nineteenth centuries

---

426 Ngũgĩ wa Thiongo, *Decolonising the Mind: The Politics of Language in African Culture*, James Curry, London, 1986, cited in: Hickel, *Less is More*, p. 77.

427 Marks, *The Origins of …*, p. 93.

428 Noreena Hertz, *The Silent Takeover: Global Capitalism and the Death of Democracy*, Harper Business, New York, 2001, cited in: Capra – Mattei, *The Ecology of Law*, p. 103.

429 Marks, *The Origins of …*, p. 115.

430 David Christian, *Maps of Time: An Introduction to Big History*, University of California Press, Berkeley, 2004, p. 436, cited in: Harari, *Sapiens*, p. 278.

began, classical British political economists – Adam Smith, Thomas Malthus, David Ricardo, and their followers – added a new dimension to the story of the rise of the West: They characterised capitalist industrial development as 'progress', the West as 'progressive' and Asia (and indirectly Africa and Latin America) as 'backward' and 'despotic'. Although the idea of contrasting the West's virtues with the East's shortcomings can be traced back to Ancient Greece, eighteenth-century Europeans admired the wealth and rule of Asian countries, especially China. However, the pace of economic change in Europe increased in the nineteenth century. The synchronised decline of most Asian countries led European social theorists to think that the West was dynamic, forward-looking, progressive, and free, but Asia was stagnant, backward-looking, and despotic.[431] One could argue that this view is still quite widespread today.

Indeed, the 'civilisational standard', as Tzouvala calls it, still oscillates between two opposing positions today. On the one hand, there is a suspicion – if not hostility – about the inclusion of non-Western, non-white majority peoples in the realm of international law, and this stems from a deep-seated sense of cultural and racial inferiority; on the other hand, the inclusion of these communities in international law seems possible and desirable, but it is contingent on their undertaking certain reforms that guarantee their compliance with the requirements of capitalist modernity.[432] Thus, both a 'you are not me' and a 'you should be like me' approach are still very much dominant, reflecting the new economic global order and dualist culture that has emerged under the European umbrella.

---

[431] Marks, *The Origins of the …*, p. 19.
[432] Tzouvala, *Capitalism as Civilization*, p. 2.

The structural causes of the Anthropocene and the emergency it creates

> And yet now, almost half a century into the neoliberal revolution, much of our world is in ruins, or perhaps more accurately the ruination of the planet, which began with the capture of slaves and invasion of the 'new world', now is reaching its terrifying endgame.[433]

Theoprastus, a student of Aristotle in the 3rd century BC, is thought to have been the first to document how human activity was changing the local climate. Theoprastus observed that the draining of the marshes in Thessaly in Greece had cooled the climate, while the deforestation around Philippi had warmed it.[434] Indeed, human damage to nature can be capable of altering the microclimate. However, today, human activities are affecting the climate globally. Why is this happening right now, and who is responsible for it?

The roots of the climate crisis can be traced back to the central myths of civilisation on which the post-Enlightenment Western culture described previously is built. These myths are about humanity's duty to dominate a natural world that was once believed to be limitless and completely controllable. These are powerful cultural narratives that transcend geography and ideological divisions.[435] They spread around the world with colonialism and became the dominant worldview. Then, we realised that these self-made

---

433 Haiven, Max, 'Our Age of Uprisings: We Are a Remaking Itself', *ROAR*, Issue 11.

434 C. Glacken, *Thraces on a Rhodian Shore: Nature and Culture in Western Thought from Ancient Times to the End of Eighteenth Century*, University of California Press, Berkeley, 1967, pp. 129–30, cited in: Hulme, *Why We Disagree* ..., p. 62.

435 Klein, *That Changes Everything*, p. 227.

stories were causing a significant problem, and it was still not too late to fix it. In fact, quite early on, the first signals were being sent by scientists.

In 1824, Jean-Baptiste Joseph Fourier presented a paper on regulating planetary temperature to the Royal Academy of Sciences in Paris. In this paper, Fourier recognised that the atmosphere behaves asymmetrically in transferring incoming solar energy and outgoing terrestrial energy: The atmospheric gases were more opaque for the outflow of thermal energy than for the inflow of shortwave solar energy. This phenomenon was then called the 'greenhouse effect'.[436] Nearly seventy years later, in 1895, Swedish scientist Svante Arrhenius was the first to institutionalise this phenomenon, linking carbon dioxide levels to atmospheric temperature and suggesting widespread coal consumption could increase global temperatures.[437] Yet, it was not until 1957 that regular measurements of the amount of greenhouse gases in the atmosphere began to be made. Measurements were first taken at the South Pole, followed a year later by Mauna Loa in Hawaii. Today, these measurements continue routinely,[438] and the results are unfortunately not encouraging.

Charles David Keeling, working at Mauna Loa, developed a graph for measuring the level of carbon dioxide in the atmosphere. This graph, known as the 'Keeling curve', proved that the level of carbon dioxide in every million particles in the atmosphere was constantly increasing. Studies over the next thirty years confirmed this claim.[439] Because *we kept burning fossil fuels and carbon dioxide kept accumulating in the air. It's as simple as that.*[440]

The level of carbon dioxide in the atmosphere is a vital factor for all of us, as it was 280 parts per million[441] (ppm) during the centuries when favourable and stable atmospheric conditions prevailed, enabling the formation and maintenance of the form of organisation we call human civilisation.[442] This number should be somewhere between 300 and 350 at most, which is

---

[436] Hulme, *Why We Disagree …*, p. 67.
[437] Scranton, *Learning to Die*, p. 34.
[438] Hulme, *Why We Disagree …*, p. 79.
[439] Scranton, *Learning to Die*, p. 34.
[440] Ralph Keeling, *in* 'Atmosferde İklim Tarihinin En Yoğun Karbondioksiti Birikti: 415.5 ppm', *Yeşil Gazete*, 16 May 2019.
[441] The average number of CO_2 per million particles in the air.
[442] Marks, *The Origins of …*, p. 16.

considered the safe limit for the continuation of civilisation as we know it.[443] James Hansen, who headed NASA's Space Science Institute for many years, testified for the first time in the US Senate in 1988 that, according to his calculations, the Earth was warming due to an increase in carbon dioxide in the atmosphere and that *99 per cent of the time this warming is not a natural cycle, but is caused by the release of carbon dioxide and various gases into the atmosphere due to human activities*[444] and thus warned not only US senators but the whole world.

Precisely twenty years after this speech, in a 2008 study, James Hansen and his team concluded that the Earth's climate should have started to be affected by human activity 6,000–8,000 years ago. However, until the industrial age, this effect was quite insignificant. According to the study, it was only in the last quarter century that human-induced climate impact became dominant over naturally evolving impacts.[445] Therefore, it is essential to look at what happened in the last quarter century to find the causes of the acceleration of global warming.

The aftermath of World War II witnessed an incredible increase in production and consumption. That was due, on the one hand, to rebuilding destroyed countries and, on the other, to the competition between states caused by the Cold War. There was also a population explosion and various agricultural revolutions to produce the food needed to feed this population. Chief among these were mechanisation and the use of pesticides. Economic growth accelerated incredibly all over the world. In her 1962 book Silent Spring, Rachel Carson described this period as *dominated by industry, where there was almost no question of what was sacrificed to get a dollar.*[446]

Anthropogenic influence, shaped mainly by capitalism, became a major source of change in the Earth's ecosystem in the immediate aftermath of World War II. Thus, the previous Holocene epoch, which lasted 11,700 years

---

[443] James Hansen – Makiko Sato – Pushker Kharecha – David Beerling – Robert Berner – Valerie Masson-Delmotte – Mark Pagani – Maureen Raymo – Dana L. Royer – James C. Zachos, 'Target Atmospheric CO_2: Where Should Humanity Aim', *The Open Atmospheric Science Journal*, No. 2, 2008, p. 217.

[444] Philip Shabecoff, 'Global Warming Has Begun, Expert Tells Senate', *The New York Times*, 24 June 1988.

[445] Hansen et al., 'Target Atmospheric CO_2', p. 225.

[446] Carson, *Silent Spring*, p. 19.

and gave birth to civilisation, ended. The emergence of the Anthropocene coincided with a planetary disruption, as the human economic order, influenced by capitalism, has recklessly overstepped and continues to overstep the planet's boundaries.[447] The term Anthropocene was first coined in 2002 by atmospheric chemist Paul Crutzen. The beginning of the Anthropocene, which refers to humans becoming a force capable of altering the Earth's ecosystem formed during the Holocene through their actions, is considered by most geologists to be the industrialisation when we began to behave in ways that were out of sync with this ecosystem.[448] Although not officially recognised as a new era,[449] the Anthropocene is a term that accurately describes the fact that humanity as a whole has been living in a global environmental crisis since the end of the last century.[450] The use of the term has become more widespread as evidence grows that changes caused by global warming will affect the Earth's climate and biodiversity as well as its geological structure, and as climate disruptions become more visible and climate change becomes a popular topic.[451]

In geological history, the concept of the Anthropocene, which refers to how human society, through capitalism, has wreaked havoc on its planetary home, is not the result of a sudden epiphany. Instead, it should be seen as the product of a century-long debate about the growing human impact on the nature of the earth.[452] The primary function of a conceptualisation such as

---

[447] Foster, *Capitalism in the Anthropocene*, p. 13.

[448] Anthropocene Working Group, 'Results of Binding Vote by AWG, Released 21 May 2019'.

[449] The International Union of Geological Sciences, the organisation that determines and defines the names of epochs, reviewed the data on whether the Holocene Epoch has ended and the Anthropocene Epoch has begun, and after voting from 4 February to 4 March 2024, it rejected the proposal to recognise the Anthropocene as a new epoch by twelve votes to 4 (3 members did not vote). For the 20 March 2024 statement, see, IUGS, 'The Anthropocene'. However, the term Anthropocene continues to be frequently used in scientific studies.

[450] Jaria-Manzano – Borrás, 'Introduction to … ', p. 1. However, it is not any human behaviour that is actually degrading the ecosystem, but their behaviour within capitalist patterns of production and consumption. Therefore, although the Anthropocene is a good nomenclature, as will be discussed shortly, the 'Capitalocene' is an even better one for the current situation.

[451] Scranton, *Learning to Die*, p. 12.

[452] Foster, *Capitalism in the Anthropocene*, p. 19.

the Anthropocene is to indicate the stage reached in the history of human civilisations in controlling and dominating the forces of nature. Thus, it indicates that man is no longer a species that survives in nature but has become a dangerous being, a cosmic or tectonic force capable of changing the composition of the atmosphere, the topography, and the climate of the Earth, and thus the cause of one of the geological epochs.[453]

Urbanisation, erosion, global warming, sea level rise, sudden degradation of elements such as carbon, nitrogen, phosphorus, and various metals with new chemical compounds, acidification of the oceans, and the spread of dead zones are among the issues that the Anthropocene addresses as analytical categories. In addition, hunting, habitat loss, extinction of non-domestic animal populations and species, and rapid changes in the biosphere are among the questions and problems of the Anthropocene.[454] In addition, the Anthropocene, as a scientific term, identifies the extent of climate change and ecological collapse, but it is also a consequence of the economic and legal system. Therefore, it cannot be considered in isolation from these two. To understand the Anthropocene, we must consider it in terms of all social, economic, geographical, class, racial, ethnic, and gendered divisions.[455]

Today, the Earth has already warmed by 1.2°C compared to pre-industrial times, and – unless urgent and effective measures are taken – this figure is projected to rise to 1.5°C in the next twenty years.[456] Moreover, according to a critical study, even if we completely stop emitting carbon dioxide into the atmosphere, our planet will warm by 1.4°C more than today due to the greenhouse gases already emitted.[457] That is because we have long since exceeded the safe limit of 350 ppm. Currently,[458] the CO_2 rate in the atmosphere is

---

453 Şahin, 'İklim Krizine…', p. 19.
454 Deniz Gündoğan İbrişim, 'Ekolojinin Yazısı: Edebiyat', *in* Didem Bayındır – Mine Yıldırım (ed.), *Ekoloji: Bir Arada Yaşamın Geleceği*, Tellekt, Istanbul, 2022, p. 434, footnote 12.
455 Dipesh Chakrabarty, 'The Climate of History: Four Theses', *Critical Inquiry*, 35(2), 2009, pp. 198–9; cited in: Gündoğan İbrişim, 'Ekolojinin Yazısı: Edebiyat', p. 435, footnote 12.
456 'Climate Change Widespread, Rapid and Intensifying – IPCC', *IPCC*, 9 August 2021.
457 Hansen et al., 'Target Atmospheric CO_2', p. 221.
458 As of 12 December 2024.

425.9 ppm, increasing by almost three percentage points yearly.[459] Therefore, the 1.5°C warming limit envisaged in the Paris Agreement will probably have been exceeded around 2030. This level of warming will affect Earth's ecosystem in ways we cannot currently foresee. The Earth as we know it today will no longer exist in the coming decades. This is called the Anthropocene.

The biggest reason for this crisis is that our legal systems allow it. Even though everyone needs to do something about it immediately, perhaps lawyers have more of a duty than anyone else. To decipher these duties, first of all, the legal sources of the Anthropocene must be identified. We can envision and implement the proper treatment only when we diagnose the disease correctly.

2.1 Causes of climate change from a legal perspective

As mentioned earlier, the scientific revolution marked the beginning of an understanding of nature as a machine and the superiority of human reason over natural processes. In the following Industrial Revolution, technology developed rapidly, and production became incredibly efficient. The state-sponsored concentration of common assets into capital meant advances in industry, science, and the arts, the advancement of medicine, and, ultimately, more hygienic conditions for many people. However, the previous subsistence way of life in harmony with nature disappeared.[460] The increase in production and consumption led to an overuse of raw materials, so much so that nature was unable to compensate for the damage done to it. The economy has become increasingly dependent on fossil fuels, and the amount of carbon dioxide released into the atmosphere has left the ecosystem out of balance. All this, and the resulting crisis, has happened with the oversight, supervision, and even encouragement of the modern constitutional and legal system.

The economic and ecological crises are two sides of the same coin, linked on one side by capitalism's exploitation of workers and on the other by its usurpation of people and the earth.[461] This usurpation would not be possible

---

459 'Latest CO_2 Daily', *CO_2-Earth*. On this website, the average CO_2 content in the atmosphere can be monitored on a daily basis. The 'Environment' tab of The Guardian newspaper's website provides the same service.

460 Capra – Mattei, *The Ecology of Law*, p. 181.

461 Foster, *Capitalism in the Anthropocene*, p. 27.

if the law did not allow it. However, it could not be expected that it would not allow it because it was already designed to protect this mechanism of usurpation. In other words, our legal and political order perpetuates, protects, and legalises the continued destruction of the Earth, not by accident, but by design.[462]

Law has given humans and their representatives all the rights and privileges to use and exploit the Earth. For this, all the elements of the Earth and the creatures living on it have been reduced by law to the status of property. The grandiose constitutions of great societies form the dome of this self-interested human system and define it and its purposes. In an anthropocentric way, modern legal systems determine how we relate to this planet's other creatures and the Earth itself. It punishes and takes revenge on those who do not comply. In short, the law legalises the endless destruction of species and the deepest disrespect and exploitation of the Earth that keeps us alive.[463] It is impossible to say that our legal systems, serving such a purpose, are not responsible for climate change. Therefore, it must be recognised that today's legal structure does not have the capacity to stop this vital threat since it is one of its enablers.

It has been known since the first half of the nineteenth century that the atmosphere warms the Earth thanks to greenhouse gases, especially carbon dioxide, and since the early twentieth century, the climate would change if more fossil fuels were burned. It was also known before World War II that global temperatures were rising. However, only in the 1950s did it become clear that this would cause climate change and that it was a serious threat. It was only in the 1960s, thanks to Charles David Keeling, that it was definitively proven that the level of carbon dioxide in the atmosphere was rapidly increasing, as mentioned earlier.[464] We are talking about a consensus reached by scientists in the 1980s, which was formalised in the first IPCC report published in 1990. In other words, science has known for almost forty years that the climate is changing and that human activities are the leading cause.[465] Obviously, it is not possible for the law not to know what science already

---

[462] Cullinan, *Wild Law*, p. 62.
[463] Cullinan, *Wild Law*, p. 62.
[464] Spencer R. Weart, *The Discovery of Global Warming*, Harvard University Press, Massachusetts, 2003, cited in: Şahin, 'İklim Krizine … ', p. 21.
[465] Şahin, 'İklim Krizine … ', p. 21.

knows. Yet, because this knowledge contradicts the purposes that law serves, this fact has been ignored for all these years and treated as if it did not exist. Our legal systems, the guardians of the capitalist economic infrastructure, have neither made the necessary constitutional adjustments nor allowed a paradigm shift to take place as in science. Now, to stop climate change, we have to create a much more drastic transformation in a much shorter period of time. That can only be done by forcibly stopping the sources of emissions, namely capitalist production and consumption processes, through a legally binding method, which is constitutional law.

2.1.1 Capitalist economic infrastructure and the Anthropocene connection

The early capitalists not only had to find ways to persuade people to work for them but also had to change people's view of the living world. A new story about nature had to be written.[466] According to this story, the capitalist system has instilled in us a logic of competition, development, and unlimited growth. This economic order seeks unlimited profit by separating human beings from nature and establishing dominion over it. Water, land, the human genome, ancestral culture, biodiversity, justice, ethics, human rights, and even life itself have been turned into commodities. In this economic model that operates on the criteria of profit and growth, nature has been destroyed with a ruthless logic. On a historical scale, it is indisputable that none of the modes of production can hold a candle to capitalism in terms of nature's destruction.[467]

Under capitalism, nature has become a source of raw materials, and people have become consumers. People are valued not according to what they are but according to what they have.[468] Therefore, capitalism's relationship with nature and people is based on acquisition, extraction, commodification, and ever-increasing efficiency. Continuous 'progress' is the most important principle underlying this economic system.[469] Capitalism is a mode of production

---

[466] Hickel, *Less is More*, p. 62.
[467] Tanuro, *L'Impossible le Capitalism vert*, p. 177.
[468] Löwy, *Ecosocialism*, Ecosocial Struggles of Indigenous Peoples (Loc. 936).
[469] Hickel, *Less is More*, p. 66.

that recognises no inherent limits to its expansion, whether geographically, morally, or concerning human or nonhuman life.[470]

Accordingly, modern economics is the study of how people use and share resources. 'Resources' here refers to people's time and skills, natural resources such as land, air, water, and infrastructures, and how these resources are transformed into useful goods and services.[471] It is these patterns of production and consumption, human population growth, trade, technological innovations, and social values that underlie climate change. It is crucial to remember that, especially in the last fifty years, the human population has doubled, and the global economy has quadrupled. That has led to an explosion in the need for energy and raw materials.[472] Consequently, the damage to nature has increased, and the natural balance has worsened.

Humans' brutalisation of nature is closely related to their view of it as a mere 'factor of production'. In this sense, it is as absurd to think that capitalism should stop plundering natural assets as it is to think that it should stop exploiting labour power.[473] Because for capitalism, nature is a factor of production, just like human beings. According to classical economic theory, nature is limited and scarce, but it is a durable factor of production with no depreciation. This idea gives an important clue about the necessity of moving the nature–human relationship to the nature–capitalism relationship. For the sake of maximising profit, the rational man makes optimal use of nature, for which he pays no price for its depreciation. In doing so,[474] capitalism, which hides behind the paradigm of modernism, is a system that inherently and helplessly damages its own nest, and this situation is no longer localised but has expanded to the entire planet.[475]

Today, it is known that the unsatisfied greed for profit and the productivist and commercial logic of capitalist/industrial civilisation are leading us to an ecological catastrophe of incalculable scale. To say this is not to surrender to 'catastrophism' but merely to affirm that the dynamic of unlimited 'growth' driven by capitalist expansion threatens the natural foundations of human

---

470 Tzouvala, *Capitalism as Civilization*, p. 3.

471 Hulme, *Why We Disagree …*, p. 133.

472 Boyd, *Report of… (A/75/161)*, p. 7, § 16.

473 Tanuro, *L'Impossible le Capitalism vert*, p. 152.

474 Orhan, 'Modernizm ve … ', p. 36.

475 Foster, *Capitalism in the Anthropocene*, p. 13.

life on the planet.[476] For example, capitalist production has concentrated the population in large centres, giving the urban population an ever-increasing weight. In doing so, it has concentrated the historical mobilising force of society while simultaneously disrupting the circulation of matter between man and the land. In other words, it has disrupted the conditions necessary for the continued fertility of the soil by preventing the return to it of the items consumed by man as food and clothing. Thus, it simultaneously has destroyed the health of the urban labourer and the mental life of the rural labourer.[477] The water and air cycles of nature are similarly constantly disrupted by capitalism. That is because the rationality of the capitalist market, limited by the unpredictable calculation of profit and loss, is in inherent contradiction with ecological rationality, which takes into account the duration of natural cycles.[478] It is naturally and logically impossible for a global economic system in conflict with nature not to create crises.

Therefore, climate change is one of the global costs and products of the capital accumulation drive that flourished with the Industrial Revolution.[479] For this reason, societies organised in a capitalist manner harbour an ecological contradiction in their DNA. Fraser argues that they constantly produce ecosystemic weaknesses as part of their *modus operandi*. Even if these vulnerabilities are not always acute, sometimes not even visible, they accumulate over time until a certain critical threshold is reached and the damage is laid bare.[480] Löwy, too, says that ecological destruction, the result of the unsatisfied need to increase profits, is not something that capitalism causes by accident. According to the author, it is in the DNA of the system and cannot be corrected, no matter how much one wants to.[481] Hence, capitalist societies are like time bombs, ready to create recurrent environmental crises throughout their history. Unlike other societies, the ecological predicament of capitalist societies cannot be solved by increased knowledge or green goodwill movements. In addition to these, what is required is a profound

---

476 Löwy, *Ecosocialism*, What Is Ecosocialism (Loc. 134).
477 Karl Marx, *Capital*, Volume I, 2nd ed., trans. Alaattin Bilgi, Sol, Ankara, 1986, p. 516, cited in: Balta – Mısır, 'Bir Politik … ', p. 19.
478 Löwy, *Ecosocialism*, What Is Ecosocialism (Loc. 216).
479 Akgül, 'Adil Dönüşüm', p. 92.
480 Fraser, 'Climates of Capital', p. 58.
481 Löwy, *Ecosocialism*, The Belém Declaration (Loc. 1118).

structural transformation.[482] Consequently, the solution to the climate crisis cannot be found in a capitalist economic system and a modern state. A ' green capitalism' is not possible. The solution can only be found in a new model of economic system and state organised around green constitutionalism.

Based on the logic of the unlimited accumulation of goods, profits, and capital, conspicuous consumption, waste of resources, and the accelerated destruction of the environment, the present mode of production and consumption cannot spread across the entire planet without causing a major ecological crisis.[483] It can be safely said that capitalism is the number one social and historical driver of global warming. This claim is empirical; in other words, a cause-and-effect relationship. Contrary to the usual, vague references to 'anthropogenic climate change', the stick should not be pointed at 'humanity' in general but at the entrepreneurial class, which invented a production and transportation system based on fossil fuels, which releases incredible amounts of greenhouse gases into the atmosphere, and which is driven solely by the profit motive. Capitalism triggers global warming not by chance but because of how it exists.[484] It may not aim to do so directly, but it causes this result by its very existence.

In a nutshell, the climate is endangered by capitalism.[485] The ecological crisis we are facing today is a byproduct of this economic system, and, therefore, to overcome it, the primary reckoning must be with capitalism and its instruments.[486] Although the prevailing narrative about the Anthropocene claims otherwise, this crisis is not caused by ordinary people but by a particular economic system based on the principle of perpetual expansion, which works in favour of a small minority of disproportionately wealthy people.[487] In the age of disaster capitalism, the logic based on the accumulation of capital in the hands of a small minority that knows no limits but

[482] Fraser, 'Climates of Capital', pp. 53–4.
[483] Michael Löwy – Joel Kovel, 'Ecosocialist Manifesto', *Gray and Green*, Issue 1, 2005, pp. 37–41, cited in: Balta – Mısır, 'Bir Politik ... ', p. 20.
[484] Fraser, 'Climates of Capital', p. 52.
[485] Wallace-Wells, *The Uninhabitable Earth*, p. 178; Saito, *Slow Down*, p. 71.
[486] Balta – Mısır, 'Bir Politik ... ', p. 23.
[487] Jason W. Moore, *Capitalism in the Web of Life*, Verso, London, 2015, cited in: Jason Hickel, 'What Does Degrowth Mean? A Few Points of Clarification', *Globalizations*, Vol. 18, No. 7, 2021, p. 1105.

its own now threatens the world's very existence.[488] This threat stems from using fossil fuels over the past two centuries after the Industrial Revolution. In other words, the crisis is not caused by 'human activity' in general but by a specific form of this activity that is historically and socially determined. Ancient societies and contemporary communities using different modes of production cannot be blamed for global warming.[489]

From this perspective, the ecological crisis we are facing is not a continuation of the past but, on the contrary, a radical innovation. Unlike the one we live in now, no society in history has ever been driven by a greed for profit that encouraged the owners of capital to accumulate more and more and then to produce and sell more and more, constantly creating new needs. This so-called 'ecological crisis' is, in fact, a historical crisis of humanity's relationship with its environment. The root cause is the overproduction of goods, which has led to an increase in wealth and overconsumption at one pole and an increase in poverty and underconsumption at the other. Therefore, it is more appropriate to speak of capitalist climate change rather than an 'anthropic' change in the climate.[490]

With this in place, the root cause of the Anthropocene becomes clearer. As the scientific evidence shows, the last two centuries of capitalist development – and, in particular, the unprecedented levels of resource consumption over the last sixty years – have created conditions that endanger the lives of everyone.[491] Once it is seen that the rapid increase in industrialisation since the 1950s has led to a global upset of the balance, how we think about the solutions to this problem changes. It is called the Anthropocene because it is a human era; yet, it is not really about humans but about the dominance of a particular economic system.[492] Although the term Anthropocene is useful to refer to the impact of human activities on the Earth's ecosystem, the leading cause of the disruption of the ecological balance is not humanity but capitalism and the pursuit of unrestrained growth.[493] Therefore, calling the era the 'capitalocene' is more appropriate. This term was first proposed in a

---

488 Foster, *Capitalism in the Anthropocene*, p. 25.
489 Tanuro, *L'Impossible le Capitalism vert*, p. 53.
490 Tanuro, *L'Impossible le Capitalism vert*, p. 56.
491 Tokar, *Toward Climate Justice*, Projections and Realities (Loc. 483).
492 Hickel, *Less is More*, p. 39.
493 Parrique, *Ralentir ou Périr*, p. 11.

seminar in 2009 by Andreas Malm, a graduate student in Lund, Sweden.[494] It is an apt nomenclature as it draws attention to the primary perpetrator of climate change.

The term 'anthropic warming', which the IPCC also uses and by which blames 'humans' in general, diverts attention away from structural mechanisms and focuses instead on individual behaviour. It is as if to get out of the ecological crisis, we all need to act prudently in society, change our 'lifestyle', and assume personal responsibility. The problem with this discourse is that it places the struggle to rebalance the climate on individuals. Thus, economic classes, social inequalities, capitalist lobbies, and power centres are replaced by blaming individuals.[495] Individuals are encouraged to calculate their personal carbon footprint[496] and reduce it as much as possible. Those who do not do so feel social pressure and a guilty conscience. The real culprits, however, are the large multinational corporations that have condemned us to fossil capitalism and the politicians who protect and defend them.

Admittedly, fossil fuels, which contain more energy in a given volume than other sources, such as wood, have practical benefits. Unfortunately, burning this fossil biomass mined from deep in the Earth means spewing carbon into the air in quantities that green plants and oceans cannot absorb. Today, the world economy sends more than six gigatons of carbon[497] into the atmosphere every year through the use of fossil fuels. Add to that two gigatons from deforestation. That is twice the amount of carbon wells like forests and oceans can absorb.[498] This difference is accumulating in the atmosphere and causing our globe to warm.

The reason why capitalism has not stopped, despite its apparent relationship with global warming, is because, as Fraser makes clear, it is a relationship not only with labour but also with nature. What is at the centre of climate change

---

494 Donna Haraway, 'Anthropocene, Capitalocene, Plantationocene, Chthulusen: Making Kin', *Environmental Humanities*, Vol. 6, 2015, p. 163, footnote 6.

495 Tanuro, *L'Impossible le Capitalism vert*, p. 67.

496 It is now widely known that the concept of 'carbon footprint' was coined by BP (formerly *British Petroleum*, now *Beyond Petroleum*), one of the largest fossil fuel companies, to develop a social psychology that causes individuals to blame themselves for climate change. See Rebecca Solnit, 'Big Oil Coined 'Carbon Footprint' to Blame Us for Their Greed. Keep Them on the Hook', *The Guardian*, 23 August 2021.

497 Gigaton: One billion tons.

498 Tanuro, *L'Impossible le Capitalism vert*, pp. 34–5.

is an economic system that consumes more and more biophysical wealth in order to accumulate ever more 'value', all the while denying ecological 'externalities'. According to the author, another thing that has accumulated in the meantime, and not coincidentally, is the growing eco-destruction because the economy of capitalism, which is systemically conditioned to arbitrarily use nature without limit in an unrestrained, unregulated manner, is always on the verge of destabilising its own ecological conditions of possibility.[499] Therefore, the logic of profit and continuous growth inherent in capitalism magnifies the destruction of nature and leaves us with a sense of helplessness on a planet whose ecology is about to collapse. If there is a remedy, it lies in questioning the logic of growth.

2.1.1.1 The impact of growth logic on climate change

Humans have been living on Earth for thousands of years, but the amount of carbon dioxide in the atmosphere rose to a dangerous level only a few centuries ago. As described earlier, this breakthrough was caused by the capitalist system, it's absurd and irrational logic of unlimited expansion and accumulation of capital, unlike any other economic system, and its obsessive drive to increase material production in the pursuit of profit.[500] A close examination of this trajectory shows that it was inevitable from the very beginning that it would lead us to climate change.

At the beginning of the Industrial Revolution, in 1800, the global economy was roughly three times larger than it had been 300 years earlier. After that, growth accelerated and only grew thrice between 1800 and 1900. In the twenty-first century, the world economy is fourteen times larger than in 1900. Most of this happened after the end of World War II.[501] The imperative to grow within the capitalist economic system has led to an incredible increase in GDP since the end of the War in 1945. From an ecological perspective, this is also when everything started going wrong.[502] This period, which environmental historians call the Great Acceleration, saw an increase in economic activity affecting the world to the point where the planet's limits were exceeded or

---

[499] Fraser, 'Climates of Capital', p. 56.
[500] Löwy, *Ecosocialism*, Ecology and Advertising (Loc. 620).
[501] Marks, *The Origins of …*, p. 223.
[502] Hickel, *Less is More*, p. 98.

threatened to be exceeded.[503] The Anthropocene can, therefore, be considered to have its roots in the post-World War II period[504] because the essential principle of this period, which followed the victory of the countries known today as the Global North, was highly globalised monopoly capitalism.[505] Afterward, the logic of growth spread rapidly all over the world.

The development model pursued in the years following World War II focused on the goal of economic growth. According to the basic logic of this model, poverty and inequality would be reduced by raising global living standards. That would be possible through an increase in production and consumption. Therefore, GDP growth and national income per capita started to be considered success criteria,[506] and the political process in Western countries began to revolve around how to increase industrial development, prosperity, and similar concepts. That was a question to which all parties, rich and poor, left and right, sought answers because the problem of how to increase the national product was ultimately seen as a 'technical' rather than a political issue.[507] As a result, economics became a supra-political endeavour; capitalism created an intellectual hegemony in which no alternative to growth was possible.

Economic growth is a pretty crude indicator of our species' relationship with its environment because everything seen as 'economic' comes from the transformation of nature. Mining, manufacturing, and farming are processes of transforming a piece of nature into something humans can use or consume. The more we increase economic growth, the more we change nature. That is why, after World War II, when consumerism, productionism,

---

503 Will Steffen, 'Mid-20th Century "Great Acceleration"' *in* Jan Zalasiewicz – Colin N. Waters – Mark Williams – Colin P. Summerhayes (ed.), *The Anthropocene as a Geological Time Unit*, Harvard University Press, Cambridge, 2014; Ian Angus, *Facing the Anthropocene*, Monthly Review Press, New York, 1990, cited in: Foster, *Capitalism in the Anthropocene*, p. 18.

504 According to the UN Conference on Trade and Development, the term Global North roughly encompasses the countries of North America, Europe, Israel, Japan, South Korea, Australia and New Zealand.

505 Foster, *Capitalism in the Anthropocene*, p. 18.

506 Hulme, *Why We Disagree …*, p. 265.

507 Poggi, *The Development of the Modern State*, p. 163.

and developmentalism combined to push economic growth even further,[508] our impact on nature increased.

As mentioned earlier, it is now well known that fossil fuels are causing climate change. However, there is a deeper mechanism at work here that we often ignore. The first question to ask is why we need to use so much fossil fuel. The short answer is that growth requires energy. Throughout the entire history of capitalism, growth has always led to increased energy needs.[509] In fact, ordinary citizens aim for growth not so that an abstract number (namely, GDP) increases but so that they can consume or do more things, reflecting the current capitalist understanding of prosperity. That inevitably requires the use of more materials and energy. Thus, when economists and politicians advocate and desire growth, they are, in fact, advocating and desiring an increase in materials and energy, even if they do not explicitly state this. That is why Fraser says that the obsession with GDP is just a fetish hiding the reality that if GDP growth were not accompanied by material growth, people would not aim for such growth.[510]

For GDP to increase, more and more things with market value must be bought and sold. Some essential things that cannot be bought and sold are not included in GDP's calculation and thus become irrelevant in the eyes of companies, governments, and eventually society. In contrast, highly negative things with market value are taken into account. The GDP calculation shows no difference between \$100 worth of tear gas and \$100 worth of education because the ecological and social production costs are not considered. Indeed, a tree has to be cut down to be counted in GDP. The tree's creation by the biosphere or its myriad beneficial services during its life, such as producing oxygen, sequestering carbon dioxide, purifying the air, stabilising the soil, or preserving biodiversity, are irrelevant to GDP.[511]

Similarly, GDP increases if we increase the hours worked daily and postpone the retirement age. If the number of hospitalisations due to pollution increases, GDP increases. Yet, GDP says nothing about the loss of forests, home to wildlife and a sink for emissions. Nor does it say anything about the

---

508 Marks, *The Origins of ...*, p. 223.
509 Hickel, *Less is More*, p. 103.
510 Hickel, 'What Does Degrowth Mean?', p. 150.
511 Parrique, *Ralentir ou Périr*, p. 31.

damage done to the human body and psyche by overwork and pollution.[512] Therefore, what seems wrong to us today, such as the cutting down of forests, the poisoning of the soil, the increase in carbon emissions, or the psychological deterioration of people due to the pressure of work, is purposely not prevented by bourgeois law, which is tasked with protecting capitalism. All this is condoned because these are only the external effects of GDP growth.

Once the focus is on GDP growth, not only are the things that GDP can measure supported, but also the unlimited increase of those things, regardless of their costs.[513] Thus, the rush to constantly grow GDP also creates an unnecessary culture of production and consumption. A significant proportion of what is produced and consumed in the current global capitalist economy is wasteful, especially much of what high-income people consume. These products, produced for the sake of producing and consumed for the sake of consuming, do not actually fulfil any individual or social need. Examples range from SUVs used in the city to unhealthy sweets, from summer houses that remain empty for 11 months of a year to Pilates balls that are never looked at again after two uses. This cycle of production and consumption not only causes people to work more to buy unnecessary goods but also increases the damage to the environment.

The GDP calculation also does not consider how the costs and benefits of such an expanding economy are distributed across social classes. As is well known, these costs often fall on the poorest, who cannot afford to spend money on more than the bare necessities, while the benefits accrue to the richest. GDP also fails to account for unpaid labour, much of which women perform. GDP per capita also tells us nothing about the distribution of income and wealth.[514] Today, it is known that the extremely rich in the top 1 per cent benefit the most from growth. The poor share very little. That increases inequality between social classes every day. However, GDP is not concerned with this. Similarly, GDP does not consider whether one produces their own food, cleans their house, or cares for their ageing parents. However, if one pays a company to do all these, GDP considers that.[515]

---

[512] Hickel, *Less is More*, p. 91.

[513] Hickel, *Less is More*, p. 92.

[514] Chomsky – Pollin, *Climate Crisis …*, pp. 144–5.

[515] Hickel, *Less is More*, p. 91.

Since the second half of the twentieth century, the changing social perception that the planet's resources are not infinite has led to an increase in criticism of economic growth.[516] The first important text on the impossibility of attempting unlimited economic growth on a planet that would one day come to an end was the report Limits to Growth,[517] published by the Club of Rome in 1972. This reality, which had escaped the notice of classical economists until then, was laid out in this report published by brilliant economists who came together to make predictions about the future of the global economy,[518] and this has subsequently been confirmed by countless studies.

Some economists have argued that there is no direct relationship between carbon emissions and growth and that the two can be separated. According to this theory, called decoupling, environmental damage tends to decline in countries that reach a certain level of economic prosperity and wealth. This claim, represented by the Environmental Kuznets Curve, suggests that the negative impacts of economic activities on nature and people during a country's early development period decline after a certain level of GDP is reached. However, a large body of research now shows that even if some pollutants, such as sulphur dioxide, have declined in rich countries due to better regulation, there has been no similar reduction in carbon dioxide

---

516 Schmelzer, Matthias – Vetter, Andrea – Vansintjan, Aaron, *The Future is Degrowth: A Guide to a World Beyond Capitalism*, Verso, London and New York, 2022 p. 11.

517 Donella H. Meadows – Dennis L. Meadows – Jørgen Randers – William W. Behrens III, *Limits to Degrowth – A Report for the Club of Rome's Project on the Predicament of Mankind*, Universe Books, New York, 1972.

518 Serge Latouche, *Vers une Société d'Abondance frugale* (Turkish version), trans. Tahir Karakaş, İletişim, İstanbul, 2018, p. 11 (foreword by Tahir Karakaş). The report's call for 'zero growth' drew the reaction of non-industrialised countries that had just entered the development process at the time. These countries described the position of the environmentalist movement developing in the West, which suggested that the Earth, whose ecological balance had been disrupted by rapid industrialisation, could become balanced and liveable if all countries gave up their growth economies, as a new injustice of the West. For them, this meant the perpetuation of the underdevelopment of non-industrialised countries. See Hakan Reyhan, *Ekolojik Emperyalizm: Gıdaya Tahakkümün Biyopolitiği*, Alter, Ankara, 2012, pp. 139–40.

emissions, material use, or other global ecological damage,[519] which are the main source of climate change.

However, politicians and economists are still obsessed with the idea of growth.[520] That is because the word 'growth' has become a propaganda term. What is hidden behind this word is the increasing accumulation of the elite, the commodification of the commons, and the appropriation of human labour and natural resources. This process, which is generally destructive for people and ecology, has been marketed. For this reason, growth sounds natural and positive. People can be persuaded of this idea – which they might disagree with if confronted with it in any other way – and of the policies leading to its further increase. So, one could say that growth has become the ideology of capitalism and the fundamental principle of its cultural hegemony.[521]

This ideology of 'constant progress and growth' inherent in capitalism is supported by law. Yet, the natural global network is not linear at all and contains uncountable feedback loops that allow the planet to balance and regulate itself. In contrast, our current economic system is fuelled by greed for profit and a legal structure that knows no boundaries and is underpinned by ideas such as the freedom to accumulate individual property.[522] That is one of the reasons why stopping carbon dioxide emissions within existing legal systems is impossible. Plans to decarbonise the world are utterly incompatible with global capitalism. For capitalism to attract investment, it needs to generate income, and for income to generate growth. Because global economic growth, or even basic economic stability, depends on cheap and efficient energy.[523] The source of this energy is, of course, nature. That is why Cullinan argues that 'development' should often be translated as 'development destruction'

---

519 Kallis, Giorgos – Hickel, Jason – O'Neill, Daniel W. – Jackson, Tim – Victor, Peter A. – Raworth, Kate – Schor, Juliet B. – Steinberger, Julia K. – Ürge-Vorsatz, Diana, 'Post-growth: The Science of Wellbeing within Planetary Boundaries', *Lancet Planet Health*, No. 9, 2025, p. e64.

520 Capra – Mattei, *The Ecology of Law*, p. 100.

521 Hickel, 'What Does Degrowth Mean?', p. 1107.

522 Capra – Mattei, *The Ecology of Law*, p. 185.

523 Scranton, *Learning to Die*, p. 36.

since human development in the industrial sense is also the destruction of the natural world.[524]

As can be seen, due to its logic of growth, the relationship between capitalism and nature is essentially contradictory and crisis-prone. On the one hand, the economic system fundamentally depends on nature, which it sees as a resource for production inputs and a repository for waste. On the other hand, capitalist society makes a sharp distinction between these two 'spheres': It constructs the economy as the sphere of creative human action that produces value while positioning 'nature' as a 'field of things' devoid of value, infinitely self-renewing and generally ready to be processed and used for commodity production.[525] Briefly, capitalism is both in need of nature and constantly harming it. It is almost a love-hate relationship.

Fraser says this contradiction, deeply rooted in the system's structure, can be summarised in four words: dependence, separation, denial, and destabilisation. According to the author, capitalist societies make the economy dependent on nature but simultaneously ontologically separate them. This order programmes the economy to deny the costs of ecological regeneration that it causes, which continue to rise exponentially, destabilising ecosystems and periodically shaking the shambolic structure of capitalist society. Capitalism, which both needs nature and uses it as a garbage dump, is, in his words, a cannibal that consumes its vital organs like a snake eating its own tail.[526]

In the capitalist economic system, the pressure to increase profit and production has an impact on social and individual morality. In the rush for growth, governments and corporations are indifferent to every obstacle in their path. When growth is itself a value not limited by any moral value, it leads us to disaster. Indeed, under early capitalism, the managers of slave-trading companies did not hesitate to kill millions of people with a recklessness tinged with greed.[527] Today, similarly, the owners of oil companies know that their activities violate the most basic rights of an even larger number of people and even drive entire ecosystems to mass extinction, and for the sake of growth, this is ignored by both societies and the law. Therefore, despite the

---

[524] Cullinan, *Wild Law*, p. 18 (foreword by Thomas Berry).
[525] Fraser, 'Climates of Capital', p. 55.
[526] Fraser, 'Climates of Capital', pp. 56–7.
[527] Harari, *Sapiens*, p. 326.

existential threat we face, we should not expect any state today to willingly sacrifice economic growth to reduce carbon emissions, especially not in a system where economic power is the most significant source of status. Roger Pielke Jr, calling this the 'iron law' of climate policy, rightly argues that every time economic growth and emission reduction policies collide, economic growth wins.[528] Still, while growth wins, our planet loses. Our only home in the entire universe is slipping away. We must prevent our legal systems from allowing this to happen.

Just as slavery was outlawed when the idea of the universality of equality and other human rights became widespread, similarly, capitalism needs to be reined in to tackle climate change within the social dimension of the right to life. The constitutional limitation of growth is one way to achieve this goal and should be seriously considered.

2.1.1.2 Neoliberalism as an even more ecocidal form of capitalism

Although it has been scientifically known for many years that the climate is changing due to capitalist relations of production and consumption and that this poses a threat to life, the trend has not been in the form of limiting these relations and growth but in the opposite direction.

According to classical theory, capitalists argue that capital should be able to influence politics as it wishes, but politics should not be allowed to influence capital. Indeed, constitutional principles and legal regulations have so far been determined accordingly. If states intervene in the functioning of the market, it is recognised that political interests will lead to malinvestment and, ultimately, lower growth. According to this view, the wisest economic policy is to keep politics out of the economy, lower taxes, and minimise government intervention, allowing market forces to take their course. In such an environment, individual investors will put their money where they can make the most profit. The more profit they make, the more the country's GDP grows. However, markets alone cannot protect themselves against fraud, theft, and violence. Therefore, the state is obliged to establish legal sanctions against fraud on the one hand and systems to enforce the law through security

[528] Roger Pielke Jr, *The Climate Fix: What Scientists and Politicians Won't Tell You About Global Warming*, Basic Books, New York, 2010, p. 46, cited in: Scranton, *Learning to Die*, p. 37, footnote 7.

forces, courts, and prisons on the other.[529] All these are modern reflections of the search for a minimal state, following Locke and Smith, where the state only protects property rights and provides security.

However, as Özenç points out, the process of depoliticisation of economic decisions also involves some other profound contradictions. States' political power is embodied in regulations and practices related to privatisation, deregulation, and especially the flexibilisation of labour markets. Apart from this, state interventions in the face of the bankruptcy of large companies, which are deemed detrimental to the whole or the healthy functioning of capitalist relations of production, are noteworthy.[530] That shows that the state is not outside the economic functioning but rather an instrument of this functioning. The state is almost an officer of the economy and is identified with it.

As a result of the modern state's identification with the economy, the state is largely at the service of the industrial-economic process. As the state's economic obligations increase, its capacity for self-determination weakens. It can now only make decisions in the interests of capitalism. To put it more directly, the state's decisions are, in fact, shaped by capitalists. The state does regulate and supervise, but not as a 'third party' holding power over equal parties. Instead, it performs functions that complement the industrial-economic process. It is the industrial-economic process itself, not the state, that decides which aspects of the economic process to support and control.[531]

At the top of this process, which has become authoritative in political decision-making, is the oligarchy of capital owners who own the lion's share of the world's energy production. They dominate society using a technocratic ruling class of business executives and politicians and organise elections broadcast through the mass media, competing for control among themselves and gaining public consent for their rule. So, the elections are, in fact, between members of this top decision-making oligarchy. However, since people are led to believe that this is a democratic contest, the system also gains legitimacy through elections. Systematic restrictions block the few activists who try to

---

529 Harari, *Sapiens*, pp. 323–4.

530 Özenç, *Hukuk Devleti*, p. 282.

531 E.-W. Böckenförde, 'Die Bedeutung der Unterschiedung von Staat und Geselschaft im demokratischen Sozialstaat der Gegenwart', *Rechtsfragen der Gegenwart*, Stuttgart, 1972, p. 11 et seq., cited in: Poggi, *The Development of the Modern State*, p. 153.

make change.[532] They are usually marginalised[533] and portrayed as obstacles to 'economic development', often as pawns or even agents of 'foreign powers'. Thus, defending nature and trying to harm the state are equated in the eyes of society.[534]

If capitalism is the root cause of the climate crisis, neoliberalism is the driving force accelerating it. Neoliberalism is a variant of classical liberalism. Classical liberalism is based on the idea that everyone should be given maximum freedom to pursue their own interests within market arrangements. Neoliberalism differs from its basic premise that the free market will produce social outcomes superior to state interventions. The neoliberal discourse emphasises globalisation, freedom from state oppression, and freedom. The aim of eroding the nation-state's power through this discourse is to concentrate power in the hands of corporations. Power does not devolve to the people or pass to communities at the grassroots level. State institutions are transformed from protectors of people's health and rights to protectors of the property and rights of multinational corporations.[535] So what happens in practice under neoliberalism is not only that states allow giant corporations to pursue profits with the utmost freedom. In addition, whenever the profits of corporations are threatened, the state is expected to step in to rescue them.[536]

Neoliberalism is rooted in the growth principle of capitalism. At a certain point, in order to restore profits and keep capitalism alive, governments abandoned social goals and focused on improving conditions for capital accumulation. States adopted the interests of capital, and the distinction between growth and capital accumulation almost disappeared, so much so that states'

---

532 Scranton, *Learning to Die*, p. 53.

533 There are of course countless examples of this happening all over the world, but if one is looking for a crystallised example, there is probably no better one than Turkish President Erdoğan's declaration of ordinary villagers in Akbelen, Muğla, who want nothing more than to protect their habitat and livelihoods as 'marginal'. See 'Erdoğan İklim Sözlerinden Çark Etti: Türkiye'nin Kömür Gerçekleri', *Yeşil Gazete*, 8 August 2023.

534 In fact, from a theoretical point of view, when one considers how the modern state and neoliberal capitalism are intertwined, one has to admit that there is a grain of truth in this discourse.

535 Vandana Shiva, *Earth Democracy: Justice, Sustainability, and Peace* (Turkish version), trans. Ali K. Saysel – Elçin Gen – Onur Günay, BGST Yayınları, Istanbul, 2010, p. 126.

536 Chomsky – Pollin, *Climate Crisis …*, p. 40.

primary goal has been to remove all obstacles to profit by cheapening people and nature for the sake of growth.[537] Whatever government comes to power today finds itself under pressure to limit workers' rights, abolish environmental protection, open up public spaces for construction, and privatise public services. All these are imposed on them as conditions for growth.[538] At the political level, this new era has three pillars: (1) the privatisation of the public sphere, (2) the relaxation of rules in areas where large corporations operate, and (3) the reduction of tax liabilities of large corporations, made possible by cuts in public spending. Much has been written about the real social costs of these policies worldwide. However, less has been said about how market fundamentalism systematically sabotages our collective search for solutions to climate change.[539]

While there is some truth in the fact that global warming is often perceived as a kind of moral and economic debt that has accumulated since the beginning of the Industrial Revolution and is now due for repayment, more than half of the carbon released into the atmosphere by the burning of fossil fuels has been emitted in the last thirty years alone.[540] Therefore, at the very crossroads where we should have chosen to take the necessary measures to solve this problem and prevent the further burning of fossil fuels, in the very years when it was scientifically proven with scientific certainty that global warming was causing the gigantic threat of climate change, neoliberalism steered us in the opposite direction.

Human actions in the neoliberal order have not only caused global warming and biodiversity loss through greenhouse gas emissions but have also affected natural processes in other ways. Humans have excavated the Earth's surface to extract the coal, copper, gold, bauxite, and other natural resources beneath it. In addition, the habitats of wild animals were occupied for industrial livestock farming and food. Agricultural land now makes up 20 per cent of the Earth's land mass. Humans have also captured water for agriculture, energy, and daily use. Today, with dams built on almost every river, humans

---

[537] Hickel, *Less is More*, p. 94.
[538] Hickel, *Less is More*, p. 96.
[539] Klein, *That Changes Everything*, pp. 28–9.
[540] Wallace-Wells, *The Uninhabitable Earth*, p. 4.

control half of all fresh water on Earth.[541] All this means that we are leaving no habitat for other species.

The neoliberal economic structure culturally constructed by pro-bourgeoisie thinkers and the state mechanism that has become an officer of it has led to ecological and social destruction, the devastating effects of which are seen everywhere. Just as this destructive culture, which constitutes a historical exception in our relationship with nature, was created at a particular stage in history, it can be dismantled in the future and replaced by an economic infrastructure and political organisation in harmony with nature. That may seem impossible to imagine right now, but when we realise that the reason why it seems so is the capitalist hegemony created in our minds, we will have taken the first step in the search for a solution.

Today, it has become clear that the bourgeois discourse of rights and freedoms, which is based on property, is actually used as a cover for the unlimited exploitation of people and nature. Thanks to this discourse, the bourgeoisie, which first provided itself with legal protection and established a balance against the king's sovereignty, has now taken over all state organs and even the state itself, with the ambition given by its affirmed greed. Of course, it could not be expected that this would not be reflected in the social and political structure. Capitalism's ideological hegemony is such that it makes us insensitive to a collapse that is happening right in front of our eyes. Societies do not know how to get out of their fossil fuel-dependent lifestyles, so they act as if everything is fine. Meanwhile, scientists trying to warn us of the coming catastrophe suffer from Cassandra syndrome. We are all caught in a trap set by big business. It is a trap of a social and political structure dependent on fossil fuels. Getting out of this trap is not easy, but it is possible. What we need to do first to get out of it is to analyse more deeply the social and political structure it created.

2.1.2 Social and political structure based on fossil fuels

The Industrial Revolution enabled humans to break free from the confines of the old biological order and to develop entirely new economies and new forms of organisation of human life based on stored mineral energy sources, especially coal and oil. The way of life we have today was made possible by

---

541 Marks, *The Origins of ...*, p. 227.

the increase in material production created by the Industrial Revolution.[542] With the use of fossil fuels in production, the average standard of living and abundance increased unimaginably. However, this transition also radically altered the physical systems that regulate life. We have profoundly shaken the climate, biosphere, and geological structure by pulling millions of tons of carbon from the ground and mixing it into the air.[543]

The Earth is 4.5 billion, and Homo Sapiens is 300,000 years old approximately. On the other hand, the industrial order is only about 200 years old, but it has already left an unprecedented imprint on the world. It is generally accepted that this has brought us into the Anthropocene, where human actions have significantly impacted the environment. The relationship between humans and the global environment has changed. We live in a time when human actions are overpowering the forces of nature.[544]

The Earth's ecosystem is constantly trying to balance itself. When the concentration of carbon dioxide in the atmosphere increases for any reason, for example, as has happened before in history,[545] if the sun's influence naturally increases, which warms the ocean waters and accelerates gas evacuation, green plants grow faster to absorb the carbon and to some extent prevent overheating.[546] Thus, gas exchange between reservoirs remains balanced during regular periods, and the earth's temperature remains relatively constant. That has been the case ever since green plants covered the earth's surface and organised the atmosphere's composition in a way that approximates

---

542 Marks, *The Origins of …*, p. 137.

543 Scranton, *Learning to Die*, p. 28.

544 Marks, *The Origins of …*, p. 137.

545 According to calculations, such a period occurred in the Northern Hemisphere between 900 and 1300. During this period, called the *Medieval Warm Period*, temperatures in the Northern Hemisphere were 1°C above average as a result of increased solar activity. This increased food production in Europe, forest levels rose in the Alps, the population doubled, and new cities were founded. The Vikings' conquest of Greenland also coincides with this period. See Don. J. Easterbrook, 'Geologic Evidence of Recurring Climate Cycles and Their Implications for the Cause of Global Climate Changes – The Past is the Key for the Future', *in Evidence-Based Climate Science*, Elsevier, 2011, 5.1.1.6 The Medieval Warm Period (900 AD to 1300 AD).

546 Prior, Stephen A. – Runion, G. Brett – Marble, S. Christopher – Rogers, Hugo H. – Gilliam, Charles H. – Torbert, H. Allen, 'A Review of Elevated Atmospheric CO_2 Effects on Plant Growth and Water Relations: Implications for Horticulture', *Horticulture Science*, Vol. 46(2) February 2011, p. 160.

today's composition. However, extending the curves of atmospheric carbon concentration through the ages to the present day shows that the last two centuries have seen a significant and sudden rise. Today, the amount of carbon dioxide and methane in the air is about twice as high as during the interglacial periods over 800,000 years.[547] At the same time, methane levels have risen from 770 parts per billion to 1,900 parts per billion, a concentration not seen for at least 800,000 years.[548] For this reason, Tanuro says the term 'climate change' is the wrong choice, as it implies a gradual increasing change occurring steadily throughout the earth's long history. In his view, 'climatic upheaval' is more appropriate to describe our current situation.[549]

For the first time in 2007, the IPCC also acknowledged human influence on climate, stating that *it is undisputed that the climate system is warming* and that the increase in global temperature cannot be explained without reference to the human-induced increase in carbon dioxide and other 'greenhouse gases'.[550] This acknowledgement by this cautious and conservative body of the UN, whose reports are based on a review of almost all studies on global warming published worldwide, was an official recognition that our fossil fuel-based social structure is the leading cause of current climate change.

After the 2008 economic collapse, historians who had studied the links between fossil fuels and capitalism and economists who challenged established traditions began to argue that the rapid economic growth that began so suddenly in the eighteenth century was not the result of innovation or free trade dynamics, but was in fact entirely due to our discovery of fossil fuels and their raw power. This view, which was in the minority then, made a powerful argument that we now understand to have gotten to the heart of the matter.[551] The growth in economic volume with the introduction of fossil fuels in manufacturing has changed and continues to change our view of the world and our daily lives. Our notions of work, family, city, time, culture, and values are changing due to the industrial mode of production. Although the way this change has occurred varies from country to country, there are

547 Rebecca Lindsey, 'Climate Change: Atmospheric Carbon Dioxide', *Climate.gov*, 12 May 2023.
548 For current data, see 'Climate Indicators Explorer', *US Environmental Protection Agency*.
549 Tanuro, *L'Impossible le Capitalism vert*, pp. 30–3.
550 Tokar, *Toward Climate Justice*, Projections and Realities (Loc. 366).
551 Wallace-Wells, *The Uninhabitable Earth*, p. 126.

remarkable similarities between them. In Marks' words, where there used to be fields and farms, there are now factories; where there used to be seasons and annual festivals to mark time, there are now clocks; large families have been replaced by small ones; stability has been replaced by change. Social and economic change has not only stayed in the industrial centres of Europe and North America but has spread to the rest of the world, which has joined the global system by supplying workers and raw materials for industrial production. Industrial production ultimately led to the accumulation of additional capital for investment and the accumulation and concentration of wealth in the hands of elites.[552]

Thus, the most incredible legacy of liberal-colonial capitalism was not environmentalism but the energy transformation that 'liberated' the fossilised carbon reserves that had been safely under the Earth's crust for thousands of years, thereby changing social and political structures worldwide. In the last century, the United States took Britain's throne and built a whole new industrial organisation around the internal combustion engine and refined petroleum, which produced enormous carbon emissions. The result was the age of the automobile,[553] which catalysed the construction of highways, gave birth to suburbanisation, spewed carbon dioxide, and reshaped geopolitical balances. Thus, thanks to the United States, the 'carbon democracy' powered by coal gave way to a democracy fuelled by oil.[554]

The industries developed over the last century have dramatically changed ordinary people's lives. From private cars to computers, airplanes to washing machines, genetically modified foods to artificial intelligence, scientific progress has transformed life across the globe. These inventions have created a consumption pattern dependent on energy from the widespread burning of cheap fossil fuels.[555] No matter how activist and committed we are today, we cannot live a life free of fossil fuels. For our work or to be with our family

---

552 Marks, *The Origins of…*, p. 158.

553 For an excellent book that shows very clearly how ecologically destructive and how inefficient as a means of transportation the automobile is, see Peter Freund – George Martin, *The Ecology of the Automobile* (Turkish version), trans. Gürol Koca, Ayrıntı Yayınları, 1996.

554 Timothy Mitchell, 'Carbon Democracy', *Economy and Society*, 38(3) 2009, pp. 399–432, cited in: Fraser, 'Climates of Capital', pp. 74–5.

555 Marks, *The Origins of…*, pp. 175–6.

and loved ones, or at least to be able to see them, we have to use a fossil fuel-powered device somehow. Even someone who wants to live without work and away from everyone else, entirely on renewable energy, is bound to contribute to carbon emissions at some stage. Fossil fuels are all around us. For companies, of course, this is a very positive situation. The upside of selling the natural resources on which entire economies are built – and so far managing to block policies that would provide real alternatives – is that most people, like it or not, will continue to have to buy their product.[556] Indeed, fossil fuels are such products that we buy them willingly or unwillingly, and sometimes even unknowingly. Because they are at every stage of our daily lives, and we are forced to consume fossil fuels if we want to continue living.

This global fossil fuel infrastructure was built over the last 250 years. To tackle climate change, we must completely dismantle it in just thirty years and replace it with an energy infrastructure based on renewable sources.[557] The climate crisis makes a change in the status quo both urgent and inevitable.[558] That is not easy, however, because the giant fossil fuel companies, which have become incredibly wealthy and powerful while dragging us into this catastrophe, are resisting this transformation to the end and using highly immoral methods.

Take Canada as an example. In this country, big companies have no legal obligation to disclose how much they spend on lobbying. Of course, this is a problem in itself, that there is a legal provision that frees big corporations – oil companies being the most prominent among them – from having to disclose how much they spend on manipulating public perception, but it actually sums up the role of the state and the legal system vis-à-vis capitalism quite well. In Canada, however, the law requires large corporations to keep an official record of the number of times they meet with public officials. As Klein transmits, a 2012 report found that between 2008 and 2012, federal government officials met 536 times with the Canadian Association of Petroleum Producers and 279 times with TransCanada, the company behind the Keystone XL pipeline.

---

[556] Klein, *That Changes Everything*, pp. 215–16.

[557] Hickel, *Less is More*, p. 135.

[558] Julia Dehm, *Reconsidering REDD+ – Authority, Power and Law in the Green Economy*, Cambridge University Press, Cambridge, 2021, p. 1.

In contrast, the Climate Action Network, the country's largest coalition working on emissions reductions, had only six meetings with government officials over the same period. In the United Kingdom, the picture is similar. In David Cameron's first year in office, the energy industry had eleven times more meetings with the Department of Energy and Climate Change than green groups. A total of fifty employees of some oil companies were even given two-year secondments by the government to work on energy issues within ministries.[559] These numbers clearly show how intertwined the fossil fuel industry and political structures are. These two groups both depend on and feed off each other. Even in the midst of climate change, states still rely on the continuation and expansion of fossil fuel companies and make regulations in their interests.

Millions of people around the world are concerned about global warming today and believe that something must be done urgently. However, these people lack the tools, the power, or the conceptual framework to plan to protect themselves from the great dangers ahead, let alone to make things right. While brilliant, hardworking, thoughtful people are trying to do something through carbon pricing markets, protests, and political systems like the UN that do not work, people in the Global North continue to live unsustainable lives based on easy consumption – driving cars and flying planes, leaving the lights on and using heaters and air conditioners, consuming meat and charging unnecessary electronics[560] because they have been accustomed to it and made to believe that it is normal not to think about the externalities of this economic system. Under the legitimising influence of the law, they either do not question their consumer society or do not like the responsibilities they face when they do. Most of these people are probably aware of climate change and do not deny it. However, they assume that natural disasters related to global warming are just events that are reported in the news and always happen 'elsewhere'. As one disaster survivor interviewed[561] after the floods in Western Germany in mid-summer 2021, which killed hundreds of people,

---

[559] Daniel Cayley-Daoust – Richard Girard, 'Big Oil's Oily Grasp: The Making of Canada as a Petro-State and How Oil Money is Corrupting Canadian Politics', *Polaris Institute*, December 2012, p. 3, cited in: Klein, *That Changes Everything*, pp. 213–14.

[560] Scarton, *Learning to Die*, p. 60.

[561] Jon Henley, 'Death Toll Exceeds 180 as Germany and Belgium Hit by Devastating Floods', *The Guardian*, 18 July 2021.

put it: *We always thought it would happen elsewhere.* It is true that climate change is affecting the Global South more, but rich countries will not escape it either. This time, we are really in the same boat. Our very existence is at stake globally unless we abandon our current lifestyles and take real action.

2.2 The global existential threat posed by climate change

Man can hardly even recognize the devils of his own creation.[562]

Until recently, the warming of the Earth's climate was seen by most people as more of an esoteric scientific concern, which will be seen sometime in the future and affect some remote ecosystems uninhabited by humans. That is why the most iconic symbol of climate activism in the run-up to the United Nations (UN) 15th Conference of Parties[563] in Copenhagen in 2009 was a polar bear struggling to stay afloat on melting Arctic ice.[564] Glaciers were melting due to global warming. Polar bears had to be saved.[565]

Climate change does not simply mean a warmer planet. The ruptures in the world system, the ecological crisis, and the ongoing climate catastrophe are processes that will cause major upheavals in today's power relations and upend the foundations of current political and social debates. The new era we enter with Anthropocene capitalism will be unstable and uncertain.[566] Saying this is not a prophecy of doom. The facts need to be laid bare so that

562 Albert Schweitzer, cited in: Carson, *Silent Spring*, p. 12.

563 An annual conference held to monitor the implementation of the UN Framework Convention on Climate Change.

564 Tokar, *Toward Climate Justice*, Global Warming and the Struggle for Justice (Loc. 224).

565 The fact that the polar bear has been chosen as the symbol of the problem from among hundreds of other animals that have already been extinct or are threatened with extinction is, in fact, again rooted in an anthropocentric point of view. We perceive the polar bear and especially its cubs as white, fluffy and playful, in short, a cute animal. The fact that such an animal is under threat creates a feeling of pity in us, not a desire to fight for rights. This in itself is a supremacist perspective. Plus, it poses no threat to us and thus takes the problem of global warming out of the human world. A similar situation is found in the choice of the Panda as the logo of the World Wildlife Fund for Nature (WWF), a famous and prosperous environmental protection organisation.

566 Benlisoy, 'İklim Krizi ...', p. 185.

we know what we are up against and can determine the measures we must take accordingly.

Since the beginning of civilised society, humans have struggled with major crises. From famines and natural disasters to slavery and wars, we have faced many serious challenges and deadly threats. Still, climate change is arguably the greatest existential crisis we have ever faced. Greenhouse gas emissions from burning oil, coal, and natural gas, primarily to create energy, are raising average temperatures in all regions of the planet. The consequences of a warmer planet include extreme heat, heavy rainfall, drought, sea level rise, and biodiversity loss, with consequent impacts on health, livelihoods, food security, water resources, and human security.[567] We face a multi-dimensional, multi-layered, and complex problem that spans chemistry, biology, economics, law, and many other fields. We created this intricate problem, so we must find the solution now.

The reports of the IPCC, a science-policy organisation established within the UN within the climate change framework, represent the latest scientific consensus in climate science, not only in terms of physical sciences and their impacts but also for greenhouse gas mitigation, that is, related energy and economic policies. In its 6th Assessment Report published in 2021–22, the IPCC, whose reports are considered relatively conservative due to their consensus-based structure, has now definitively accepted that climate change results from human activities. However, while scientific certainty about the cause of the current climate crisis is getting stronger, uncertainty about how much the average temperature will increase is also increasing because it will be determined by what we continue to do and what we change. According to the same report, under different scenarios, it is possible to keep the global temperature rise below 1.5°C before the end of the century or to warm the Earth by up to 4.5°C. It is all about economics, lifestyle, and global politics.[568] In other words, while there are a few things that science does not know about how the climate system will respond to all the carbon we are putting into the air, the uncertainty about what will happen is not due to ignorance on the part of science, but mainly due to the unanswered question of how we will respond to this knowledge. In other words, the uncertainty is created by

[567] Chomsky – Pollin, *Climate Crisis …*, pp. 13–14.
[568] Şahin, 'İklim Krizine …', pp. 26–7.

the fact that we have not answered the question of how much more carbon we will emit, and this is a question for the humanities, not for natural scientists.[569] If we ignore this question or answer it with 'we will just carry on as we are', our very existence will soon be jeopardised as the ecosystem collapses.

2.2.1 The threat of the sixth major extinction

Disaster is not our destiny (unless we choose it).[570]

We generally see humans as a technologically advanced, highly intelligent, and hardworking species. This is a consequence of humanistic thinking that has dominated our thinking for many years. However, when we look at climate change, this crisis suggests not technological ingenuity but another environment created first by ignorance, then by sloth, then by indifference. Our civilisation is now acting like someone who has locked himself in a room or garage and is trying to commit suicide with gas.[571] Suicide can be seen as a right to one's own body, but the problem is that we are dragging all other species and the Earth's ecosystem with us. According to palaeontologists, the biosphere has experienced five waves of mass extinctions in its long history. We are about to cause a sixth with our economic and constitutional system.

Mass extinction is defined as an event that wipes out 'a significant proportion of living things on Earth in a geologically short period of time' or as a rapid and 'significant loss of biodiversity' on a 'global scale'.[572] Over the past 2 billion years, first, complex unicellular organisms and then multicellular organisms have evolved in cycles of sudden increase and mass extinction. As environmental and climatic conditions changed, genes passed down from generation to generation, and species and ecosystems emerged, evolved, and disappeared.[573]

There have been periods before when the climate has changed rapidly due to changes in the amount of carbon dioxide in the atmosphere. All of these

---

569 Wallace-Wells, *The Uninhabitable Earth*, pp. 47–8.

570 Kate Marvel, climatologist at Columbia University and the Goddard Institute for Space Studies at NASA, cited in: Klein, *On Fire*, p. 57.

571 Wallace-Wells, *The Uninhabitable Earth*, pp. 245–6.

572 Elizabeth Kolbert, *Sixth Extinction: An Unnatural History* (Turkish version), trans. Nalan Tümay, 7th ed., Okuyan Us, Istanbul, 2022, p. 32.

573 Scarton, *Learning to Die*, p. 100.

have been catastrophic for some living things. What matters for nature is not how hot it gets but how long it takes for the temperature to change.[574] There is today little doubt that the last great extinction occurred 65 million years ago when an asteroid hit the Earth. Living things in the area where this asteroid struck probably died immediately, but creatures outside this region died over the following years. Over time, the dust clouds caused a global cooling of the climate and a wave of extinction that wiped out even the dinosaurs.

Analysis of fossils from the geologic layers before and after this catastrophe reveals that 70 per cent of the world's plant and animal species went extinct. The extinction wave we are experiencing today is much more significant and faster than it was 65 million years ago.[575] From a different perspective, it is exciting that what has happened only five times in the last 500 million years is happening right now for the sixth time before our eyes. Yet, the bigger, darker, and far more consequential part of this story is that we are not just witnessing one of the events that will largely end life on Earth but that we also caused it[576] and will suffer the consequences.

Only in recent years has the urgency of the situation been fully realised. Today, we have definitive indicators of the crisis. The shocking conclusion is that our relentless consumption of all the fossil fuels on Earth threatens not only the survival of a million other species on the planet but also humanity's own existence. Moreover, the time we have left is probably less than we think.[577] The extinction of other species has already begun. We are now within the sixth extinction. The question is whether we can survive this biodiversity loss with as little damage as possible and without upsetting the ecosystem's balance.

Between 1970 and 2018 alone, the number of wild animals declined by 69 per cent.[578] The rate of species extinction is hundreds of times faster than the average for the last 10 million years, and 1 million more species are

---

[574] Kurnaz, *Son Buzul Erimeden*, pp. 125–6.

[575] Tanuro, *L'Impossible le Capitalism vert*, p. 44.

[576] Kolbert, *Sixth Extinction*, p. 23.

[577] James Hansen, *Storms of My Grandchildren: The Truth about the Coming Climate Catastrophe and Our Last Chances to Save Humanity*, Bloomsbury USA, 2009; cited in: Löwy, *Ecosocialism*, Preface: Before the Flood: The Political Challenge (Loc. 27).

[578] WWF, *Living Planet Report 2022 – Building a Nature Positive Society*, R. E. A. Almond – M. Grooten – D. Juffe Bignoli – T. Petersen (ed.), Gland, Switzerland, 2022, p. 4.

endangered.[579] Species extinction and biodiversity loss are probably the most important human impacts on nature. Soil, air, and water pollution can, in principle, be reduced and reversed, and even the challenges of global warming caused by greenhouse gas emissions can be tackled somehow. Still, once a species is gone, it is lost forever.[580]

Species loss is closely linked to the changes we have made to the Earth. Nearly three-quarters of the planet's entire land surface has been altered by humans. Two-thirds of the world's oceans are subject to devastating impacts, including acidification, oxygen deficiency, and glacier loss. Over half of the world's available freshwater resources are dedicated to human use, and 85 per cent of wetlands have been destroyed. Since 1990, 420 million hectares of forests have been destroyed for other land uses.[581] This is equivalent to half of the United States.

We altered 22 per cent of the Earth's landmass between 1992 and 2015 alone.[582] Humans and domesticated animals now account for 96 per cent of the world's mammals by weight; only 4 per cent remain in the wild.[583] With our exponentially growing population and exploitative lifestyles, we have overwhelmed all other species, forcing them to retreat to the brink of extinction.[584] That is why scientists believe that humans are driving the sixth extinction in the history of life on Earth.[585]

We are facing the collapse of the energy networks on which the global economy depends, the collapse of transportation and agriculture, the death

---

579 IPBES, *Report of the Plenary of the Intergovernmental Science-Policy Platform on Biodiversity and Ecosystem Services on the work of its seventh session*, Sandra Díaz – Josef Settele – Eduardo Brondízio et al, 2019, IPBES/7/10/Add.1, pp. 3–4.

580 Marks, *The Origins of …*, p. 43.

581 IPBES/7/10/Add.1, pp. 3–4.

582 Jakub Nowosad et al., 'The Global Assessment and Mapping of Changes in Mesoscale Landscapes: 1992–2015', *International Journal of Applied Earth Observation and Geoinformation*, October 2018, cited in: Wallace-Wells, *The Uninhabitable Earth*, p. 170.

583 Yinon M. Bar-On et al., 'The Biomass Distribution on Earth', *Proceedings of the National Academy of the Sciences*, June 2018, cited in: Wallace-Wells, *The Uninhabitable Earth*, p. 170.

584 Wallace-Wells, *The Uninhabitable Earth*, p. 170.

585 Gerardo Ceballos – Paul R. Ehrlich – Peter H. Raven, 'Vertebrates on the Brinks as Indicators of Biological Annihilation and the Sixth Mass Extinction', *Proceedings of the National Academy of Sciences*, Vol. 17, No. 24, 16 June 2020, cited in Boyd, *Report of … (A/75/161)*, p. 6, § 14.

of most of the living things in the biosphere, and perhaps the extinction of humanity. Even if humanity somehow survives the coming period, because of what we have done so far, the world we will live in will be nothing like the world we have lived in for 200,000 years.[586] In order for this change to happen as little as possible, we need to listen to the scientists we have ignored so far and transform our economic and legal systems accordingly.

We have known for a long time that we are completely disrupting the Earth's ecosystem and that things are going badly. Swedish physicist Svante August Arrhenius (1859–1927) was the first scientist to hypothesise that using fossil fuels would lead to climate change.[587] Two American oceanographers, Roger Revelle and Hans Suess, first warned of the risk of global warming in 1957. The Mauna Loa Observatory in Hawaii also announced the rapid accumulation of greenhouse gases in the atmosphere soon after its establishment in 1958. However, it took twenty years for the United Nations to organise a world conference on climate (Geneva 1979) and thirty years for the UN IPCC to be established.[588]

In 1992, the Union of Concerned Scientists published an article titled A Warning to Humanity from the World's Scientists, signed by some 1,700 scientists, stating:

> Human beings and the natural world are on a collision course. Human activities inflict harsh and often irreversible damage on the environment and on critical resources. If not checked, many of our current practices put at serious risk the future that we wish for human society and the plant and animal kingdoms, and may so alter the living world that it will be unable to sustain life in the manner that we know. Fundamental changes are urgent if we are to avoid the collision our present course will bring about.[589]

Following this introduction, the report described which ecological problems were caused by which human activities. Since 1992, the fundamental changes recommended in the report have not been made, and precious time has been lost.

---

[586] Scranton, *Learning to Die*, p. 13.
[587] Tanuro, *L'Impossible le Capitalism vert*, p. 37.
[588] Tanuro, *L'Impossible le Capitalism vert*, p. 25.
[589] Union of Concerned Scientists, 'World Scientists' Warning to Humanity', 1992.

Twenty-five years after this warning, a second one was issued. This time, the report, signed by more than 15,000 scientists, took stock of the last twenty-five years and showed that the situation had worsened on all the issues mentioned in the previous warning, except for the closure of the hole in the ozone layer.[590] As this second report points out, the problems have accumulated for years. With each passing year, they become more precise and more alarming. Yet, somehow, we have not changed our ways. The last half-century has been one of inaction.[591]

At a time when even ordinary people are feeling climate change, the Paris Agreement signed in 2015 set a target of limiting global warming to 2°C and pursuing efforts to limit it to 1.5°C increase compared to pre-industrial times.[592] States have made various promises to meet these targets. However, according to calculations, even if the signatory states keep their promises, the planet will warm by 3°C. The IPCC report predicts that even with a warming range of only 1–2°C, the planet's critical limits, the 'tipping points',[593] could be exceeded. If one or more of these are exceeded, it is calculated that the ecosystem could collapse rapidly with a domino effect.[594] The Panel's Sixth Assessment Report points out that climate collapse is accelerating sharply, that many impacts will be more severe than predicted, and that there is little chance of avoiding the worst damage.[595]

As it turns out, even scientists, usually known for lacking strong language, have now moved beyond this. As Hickel reports, Robert Watson, former

---

590 William J. Ripple – Christopher Wolf – Thomas M. Newsome – Mauro Galetti – Mohammed Alamgir – Eileen Crist – Mahmoud I. Mahmoud – William F. Laurance et al., 'World scientists' warning to humanity: A second notice', *BioScience*, 67(12) 2017, pp. 1026–8, cited in: Emrah Çoraman, 'Altıncı Büyük Yok Oluşu Durdurmak', *in* Didem Bayındır – Mine Yıldırım (ed.), *Ekoloji: Bir Arada Yaşamın Geleceği*, Tellekt, Istanbul, 2022, p. 227.

591 Hickel, *Less is More*, p. 18.

592 Hulme claims that the 2°C global temperature increase limit is a European Union project and a political decision rather than a scientific one. However, he does not provide any basis for this claim. See Hulme, *Why We Disagree ...*, pp. 120–3.

593 The original name is '*tipping points*'.

594 Timothy M. Lenton – Johan Rockström – Owen Gaffney – Stefan Rahmstorf – Katherine Richardson – Will Steffen – Hans Joachim Schellnuber, 'Climate Tipping Points Too Risky to Bet Against', *Nature*, 575(7784), 2020, pp. 592–5.

595 Fiona Harvey, 'IPCC issues "bleakest warning yet" on impacts of climate breakdown', *The Guardian*, 28 February 2022.

President of the United Nations Intergovernmental Science-Policy Platform on Biodiversity and Ecosystem Services (IPBES),[596] called the UN's climate change report 'alarming' and said, *The health of the ecosystems on which we and other species depend is deteriorating faster than ever before.* [...] *We are destroying the foundations of our economies, livelihoods, food security, health, and quality of life worldwide.* IPBES Secretary General Anne Larigauderie puts the problem more clearly: *We are systemically destroying all non-human species.*[597] At this point, given that humans can only exist in mutual relations with nature and all other living beings, it must be accepted that we are actually preparing our own demise.

It is no exaggeration to say we are heading towards a planetary catastrophe. Of course, the Earth will continue to revolve around the Sun even without us. Some forms of life will probably survive. Maybe even some of humanity will survive this crisis. However, as Barrau aptly asks, what will this planet look like without much of its biodiversity, without billions of humans and animals, without the delicate balance achieved through a very slow and complex evolutionary process? Will it still be 'the Earth'?[598] If we still want to live on this Earth, we must take urgent and radical measures. If even a COVID-19 pandemic can force governments to take such measures on rights that are considered fundamental, such as travel, property, and trade, why should not climate change, which threatens to destroy the planet's life-support systems, have the same result?[599] What we have to do is take measures to eliminate the sources of climate change regardless of the costs of these measures and whether we like it or not.

One of the reasons for the increase in the rate of greenhouse gases in the atmosphere that cause global warming is the destruction of forests. The decline of forests, one of the most critical elements in the carbon cycle, means the removal of the stores where carbon is stored as organic matter. The storage can be partially and temporarily extended, for example, in the form of wood products, but carbon dioxide is released once these products are burned. Forest stores of carbon do not only consist of tree trunks anyway.

---

596 Intergovernmental Science-Policy Platform on Biodiversity and Ecosystem Services, working under the auspices of the UN.

597 Cited in: Hickel, *Less is More*, p. 9

598 Aurélien Barrau, *Le Plus Grand Défi de l'Histoire de l'Humanité – Face à la Catastrophe Ecologique et Sociale*, Michel Lafon, Neuilly-sur-Seine, 2019, p. 90.

599 Malm, *How to Blow* ..., p. 10.

Stumps, roots, and humus[600] stockpile massive amounts of organic matter. Yet, stumps are burned, roots rot, and areas cleared for agriculture or converted to grassland lose a significant portion of their humus.[601]

The other and more important reason for the increase in carbon in the atmosphere is, as has been repeated many times above, the burning of fossil resources, namely coal, oil, and natural gas. These fuels are called 'fossil' because they are formed from the remains of ancient plants and animals that lived millions of years ago, essentially fossilised over time through a process of decomposition under high heat and pressure, similar to how other organic materials from fossils are buried underground. As previously reported, the use of fossil fuels began with coal for heating and power generation and increased rapidly with the transition to an oil-based economic model. The society of consumption[602] that has grown following fossil fuels, especially in the last century, is dragging the world ecosystem towards a collapse. As the world economy grows, the space left to nature shrinks.[603] This is why, due to the magnitude and speed of the biodiversity loss that is taking place today, many researchers agree that we are now entering a period of great extinction.[604]

We are not at the beginning of the so-called 'sixth great extinction' but in the middle. This intensity and speed of species extinction has probably not been seen since the extinction of the dinosaurs.[605] Everywhere, ecosystems are changing due to climate change. In some regions, especially in the Arctic and around Ecuador, the limits of adaptation have been exceeded, and ecosystems will no longer be able to regenerate naturally. Species are already becoming extinct due to global warming.[606] Research shows that nearly a million more

---

600 Substance formed by the decomposition of plant and animal organic residues by microorganisms in the soil.

601 Tanuro, *L'Impossible le Capitalism vert*, p. 34.

602 This term became generally used after Jean Baudrillard's *La Société de Consommation*.

603 Çoraman, 'Altıncı Büyük … ', p. 208.

604 Anthony D. Barnosky et al., 'Has the Earth's sixth mass extinction already arrived?', *Nature*, 471(7336), 2011.

605 Benlisoy, 'İklim Krizi … ', p. 168; Çoraman, 'Altıncı Büyük … ', p. 208.

606 Daniel Tanuro, 'Impacts of warming faster and more severe than expected says IPCC', *International View Point*, 3 March 2022.

species are threatened with extinction.[607] In an environment where so many species are disappearing, humans who evolved based on these species cannot be expected to survive. For this reason, Scranton argues that our most fundamental issue in the Anthropocene should be learning to die. We need to learn to die not as individuals but as a civilisation,[608] which means that our civilisation will be severely damaged by climate change. It is time to prepare ourselves for the impact.

Indeed, the IPCC's Sixth Assessment Report states that drought and heat waves are already killing trees and coral, that rising sea levels are forcing people in vulnerable areas to flee their homes, and that extreme weather events increase the likelihood of violent conflicts. The report also points out that if warming is not stopped soon and continues, half of terrestrial species will become extinct, malnutrition will become widespread in many parts of the world, and extreme weather events will increase.[609] As a matter of fact, July 2023 was the hottest month on record. Portugal, Greece, and Canada experienced endless forest fires. In China and South Korea, dozens of people lost their lives in floods. In August of the same year, a tropical storm[610] hit the US state of California for the first time in eighty-four years. In the first six months of 2024, 2,500 people lost their lives in just four natural disasters,[611] which are scientifically proven to have increased in strength due to the harmful effects of greenhouse gases in the atmosphere. The authorities estimated the total economic loss to be $41 billion during this period.[612]

Counting natural disasters across the globe in this way can sometimes be called disaster-mongering. However, revealing the extent of climate change and disaster-mongering are different. If one inflates a balloon too much, it

---

[607] IPBES, *Global assessment report on biodiversity and ecosystem services of the Intergovernmental Science-Policy Platform on Biodiversity and Ecosystem Services*, 2019, E. S. Brondizio, J. Settele, S. Díaz, and H. T. Ngo (ed.), IPBES secretariat, Bonn, Germany.

[608] Scranton, *Learning to Die*, p. 15. For a critique of this idea, see Malm, *How to Blow …*, pp. 148–54.

[609] Kieran Mulvaney, 'Climate change already worse than expected, says new UN report', *National Geographic*, 28 February 2022.

[610] Storm Hilary.

[611] Floods and landslides in Brazil, South and Southwest Asia and East Africa, and heat waves in Asia.

[612] Christian Aid, *Climate Breakdown 2024 – 6 Months of Climate Chaos Since COP 28*, June 2024.

will burst. If one throws a stone at a window, it will break. If one jumps off the roof, they will hit the ground and probably die. These are scientific facts. If saying these things are going to happen is not disaster-mongering, neither should predicting the disasters climate change will cause. It is scientifically proven that the ecosystem that sustains us is collapsing today. However, obsessing about this collapse can prevent us from considering other options. As McKibben points out, in such a situation, one is either covering their ears with their fingers or oiling their rifles in the basement. There is no room for creative thought. For the theologians of collapse, collapse is as automatic and against our will as it is for growth advocates.[613] Still, climate change is neither automatic nor against our will. We are indeed causing the problem, but this means that the solution is also in our hands.

If one is driving a car towards a cliff and speeds up, they are likely to die. Taking their foot off the accelerator would make them slightly more likely to live. If one really wants to live, they need to apply the brakes. So, the alternative to greasing the rifles is to summon the will to stop and even reverse the Anthropocene. It is still not too late, but time is running out fast. Biodiversity and ecosystem loss can be slowed, halted, and even reversed if action is taken urgently and simultaneously regarding climate change's direct and indirect causes.[614]

2.2.2 Impacts of climate change on people

Climate, unlike weather, is not something that can be directly experienced through our senses but is more abstractly constructed. How we think about climate depends on the region and time zone in which we live. Climate has very different physical and cultural meanings for someone living in the Amazon and the Sahara Desert.[615] Therefore, their understanding of climate change and the impact they experience due to it are also different.

Climate change is undoubtedly an environmental issue, but it is also a threat that has implications for every aspect of governance and public life, from finance and planning to agriculture, health, employment, and

---

613 Bill McKibben, *Eaarth: Making a Life on a Tough New Planet* (Turkish version), trans. Emel Anıl, Türkiye İş Bankası Kültür Yayınları, Istanbul, 2011, p. 99.

614 IPBES/7/10/Add. 1, p. 8, § C4.

615 Hulme, *Why We Disagree …*, p. 30.

transportation.[616] Timothy Morton calls this kind of threat a 'hyperobject'. He argues that hyperobjects cause us to think about our place on Earth and in the universe. According to the author, hyperobjects' most fundamental issue is that they may impose something on us that affects some fundamental ideas about what it means to exist and what the Earth and society are.[617] Yet, at the same time, the threat is so complex and extensive that it is difficult for us to perceive it. Since we cannot fully perceive it, we cannot think about how to act against it. That leads to inertia.

Our civilisation flourished during the Holocene, the most stable climatic era of the last 650,000 years.[618] Carbon-fuelled industrial capitalism has brought it to a close.[619] By the end of the twenty-first century's first decade, disturbing changes in the weather and the seasons we were once accustomed to are now impossible to ignore. At first, the changes were not immediately noticeable. Spring started a week or two earlier than usual, and autumn a little later. Unseasonably warm weather appeared sporadically throughout the year, while cold spells became more sudden, severe, and relatively short-lived. Rainfall has increased noticeably in some areas and decreased significantly in others. It was fast and intense when it rained, often causing devastating floods.[620] At first, these seemed like exceptions that we did not pay much attention to. Today, however, we know that these are the first signs of an imbalance that is increasing in frequency.

Climate change is already hitting humans so hard that we no longer need to look elsewhere, to threatened species or endangered ecosystems like the Arctic, to see the climate's terrible aggression. However, we continue to look at them and are saddened by the stories of polar bears trapped where they are and coral reefs struggling to survive. When it comes to climate narratives, we tend to like stories starring animals that remain silent when we do not speak

---

616 UNEP, *Global Environment Outlook – 4*, 2007, p. xviii.

617 Morton, *Hyperobjects*, p. 32.

618 David Archer, *The Long Thaw: How Humans Are Changing the Next 100,000 Years of Earth's Climate*, Princeton University Press, Princeton, 2009, p. 95, cited in: Scranton, *Learning to Die*, p. 31.

619 Scranton, *Learning to Die*, p. 31.

620 Tokar, *Toward Climate Justice*, Global Warming and the Struggle for Justice (Loc. 244).

for them, that die at our hands,[621] half of which will be extinct by 2100.[622] We act as if we live in a different ecosystem from them. We still suffer from the symptoms of Enlightenment dualism. Yet, this way of life and the order we live in is neither unshakeable nor permanent. We believe that we can live forever in the way we live today, and we demonstrate this belief through our actions worldwide. We continue to use gasoline, pollute the seas, exterminate living things, and release carbon into the atmosphere.[623] Our governments compete to give incentives to oil companies and permissions to dig to mining companies while forests are turned into industrial farmland and rivers are dammed.

After all, from the Arctic to the tropics, the reality of global climate disruption has become a part of most people's lives that cannot be ignored today. Extreme floods, droughts, and forest fires have increased systemically on all continents. Indigenous peoples in the Arctic are losing their frozen lands, while the peoples of small island states in the Pacific Ocean are being forced to abandon their habitats as rising sea levels encroach on their agricultural lands. In 2013, the strongest typhoon ever recorded devastated several islands in the Philippines.[624] In many parts of Africa and South Asia, agricultural crop losses due to drought or floods are increasing in frequency. In politically unstable Somalia, years of unrelenting drought have forced hundreds of thousands of people to flee the country or join anti-government guerrillas as the only source of income left.[625] In May 2024, floods inundated the Brazilian city of Rio Grande de Sul for days, killing thirteen people, affecting 2 million people, and forcing more than 620,000 to flee their homes.[626]

In June and July 2021, a heatwave hit the West Coast of the United States and Canada, breaking all-time temperature records. In Canada, known for its cold climate, the highest temperature ever was measured as 49.6°C.[627] According to

---

621 Wallace-Wells, *The Uninhabitable Earth*, p. 165.

622 Edward O. Willson, 'The 8 Million Species We Don't Know', *The New York Times*, 3 March 2018.

623 Scranton, *Learning to Die*, p. 17.

624 '2013 State of the Climate: Record-Breaking Super Typhoon Haiyan', *Climate.gov*, 13 July 2014.

625 Justin Rowlatt, 'Climate Change is Turbo-Charging Somalia's Problems – But There's Still Hope', *BBC*, 18 September 2024.

626 'Brazil, Rio Grande de Sul – Floods – Emergence Appeal No: MDRBR011', *ReliefWeb*, 13 May 2024.

627 In the province of British Columbia.

some scientists, the probability of this event, which should occur once in 1,000 years, has increased 150 times due to climate change.[628] In April 2022, India and Pakistan were hit by a heatwave that brought record-high temperatures. India's northwestern and central regions experienced the hottest April since measurements were taken 122 years ago. In New Delhi, the capital, temperatures hovered above 40°C for seven consecutive days. In the Sindh region of southeastern Pakistan, the temperature was measured at 47°C. Experts say that 1 billion people living in this region will be exposed to more frequent and stronger heat waves due to climate change.[629] In May and June of the same year, Spain and France experienced back-to-back similar heat waves. At the beginning of June, the temperature in Paris had already exceeded 35°C.[630] On 16 August 2023, Türkiye's temperature record was broken in Eskişehir. The air temperature was measured at 49.5°C.[631] Scientists say that these records and sudden and unexpected weather events will continue. Even due to the emissions we have realised so far, severe climatic impacts that will last for centuries await us. Therefore, we urgently need to stop the activities that cause global warming and reduce carbon dioxide emissions rapidly. However, we know that even if we stop carbon dioxide emissions immediately, the situation will worsen for a while due to the greenhouse gases already accumulated in the atmosphere. So, we need to mobilise policies to adapt to this new situation as quickly as possible.

It is a pointless endeavour to treat the human and ecological consequences of global warming in isolation from each other. To make this distinction is to cut corners, which weakens the awareness that humans are part of the biosphere.[632] As will be seen later in the study,[633] the consequences of the ecological crisis fall disproportionately on the countries and communities that have caused it the least and have the least capacity to mitigate the damage. However, no country, no matter how rich, can protect itself from the effects of this crisis. The countries of the Global North are already experiencing the devastating impacts

---

628 'Western North American extreme heat virtually impossible without human-caused climate change', *World Weather Attribution*, 7 July 2021.

629 Rhea Mogul – Esha Mitra – Manveena Suri – Sophia Saifi, 'India and Pakistan Heatwave is 'testing the limits of human survivability' experts say', *CNN*, 2 May 2022.

630 Jon Henley, 'Spain and southern France hit by second extreme heat event this year', *The Guardian*, 13 June 2022.

631 'Bakan Özhaseki: Türkiye'nin Yeni Sıcaklık Rekoru 49.5°C ile Eskişehir'de Kırıldı', *Yeşil Gazete*, 16 August 2023.

632 Tanuro, *L'Impossible le Capitalism vert*, p. 45.

633 See 4.4.2

of climate change as well. Moreover, allowing the consequences to fall on the most vulnerable countries leads to more conflicts, food insecurity, climate migration with forced displacement, and the emergence of zoonotic disease.[634] These are not only regional but also global issues affecting all countries and communities. As we have seen with the COVID-19 pandemic, we are only as strong as our weakest link globally.[635] This is why measures to address climate change must be designed locally and regionally but with a global perspective.

As changes in the Earth's ecosystem have reached a level that has negative consequences for human societies, the international community has belatedly begun to recognise that the belief that we can exploit nature without sanction is false. The ecosystems that humans interact with are connected through a 'feedback loop', not like a river of interests flowing one way from Nature to humans. More and more people understand that climate change is not a problem but a symptom of the systemic failures underlying the dominant form of human civilisation, that is, capitalism and its superstructure, the nation-state model. However, few governments seem to realise that symptoms cannot be eliminated without first tackling these underlying problems. We need to start by rethinking our species' role on this planet and how we should regulate our behaviour accordingly.[636]

Much of the landscapes we have believed for centuries to be intact and will remain so, on which we walk, build houses and highways, and send our children to school and adulthood, thinking they will be safe, will be hit by climate change.[637] *The 2014 Climate Change Adaptation Roadmap* published by the US Department of Defense includes the following warnings:

> Rising global temperatures, changing precipitation patterns, rising sea levels, and severe climate events will increase global instability, hunger, poverty, and conflict. These events will lead to food and drink shortages, epidemics, migration, natural resource conflicts, and the destruction of regions around the world by natural disasters.[638]

---

[634] Diseases that can be naturally transmitted from vertebrate animals to humans.

[635] 'Call for Emergency Action to Limit Global Temperature Increases, Restore Biodiversity, and Protect Health', *The BMJ*, 2021: 374. (Editorial published in numerous international journals on 6 September 2021)

[636] Cullinan, *Wild Law*, p. 39.

[637] Wallace-Wells, *The Uninhabitable Earth*, p. 23.

[638] Scranton, *Learning to Die*, p. 9. The original of the report is not accessible online as of 16 December 2024.

After ten years, we can see that these predictions are coming true. However, instead of trying to reorganise our economy and our law, we continue to pretend that nothing is happening and continue to invest in fossil fuels and permanently damage the environment.

James Hansen, who was the first person to warn the US Congress about climate change when he worked at NASA in 1988, wrote in 2012 about Canada's plan to produce fossil fuels from tar sands, warning that if it went ahead, our children would face an out-of-control climate and the consequences would be 'apocalyptic'.[639] Canada currently produces 3 million barrels of oil daily from tar sands and is the world's fourth-largest oil producer.[640] So, today's children are likely to face a genuinely out-of-control climate.

That is not just happening in Canada. Only ten days after the release of the final part of the IPCC's Sixth Assessment Report, which highlights the existential dangers of climate change and calls for an immediate end to the use of fossil fuels, seven new oil and gas projects were approved around the world.[641] The world's largest fossil fuel companies, including Shell, Exxon, and Gazprom, will spend €857 billion on new oil and gas fields by 2030. This figure is expected to reach €1.4 trillion in 2040.[642] In BP's 2023 budget, investment in fossil fuels is set to be twice as much as in renewable energy systems.[643]

Continuing our economic activities as usual has so far done nothing but push the ecosystem further out of control. As long as we maintain our current economic and legal order, global warming will continue to increase, shaping everything we do on the planet, from agriculture to human migration, from business to mental health. It will change not only our relationship with nature but also our relationship with politics and history, and a whole new system of knowledge as total as 'modernity' will emerge.[644] Andreas Malm summarises this trend as follows:

---

[639] James Hansen, 'Game Over for the Climate', *The New York Times*, 9 May 2012.

[640] Nicholas Kusnetz, 'Canada's Tar Sands: Destruction So Vast and Deep It Challenges the Existence of Land and People', *Inside Climate News*, 21 November 2021.

[641] Giulia Carbonaro, 'Seven new oil and gas projects approved since IPCC report called for an end to fossil fuels', *Euronews*, 15 April 2022.

[642] Rosie Frost, 'Fossil fuel firms set to spend more than €800 bn on new oil and gas fields by 2030', *Euronews*, 13 April 2023.

[643] Alex Lawson, 'BP criticised over plan to spend billions more on fossil fuels than green energy', *The Guardian*, 27 December 2022.

[644] Wallace-Wells, *The Uninhabitable Earth*, p. 170.

> There can be only one accurate description of the situation: Out of control. The classes ruling this planet are bent on burning what remains of it as fast as physically possible, and nothing – nothing – has yet reined them into even the slightest degree.[645]

An out-of-control climate change has little to do with a particular place or the spatial scale we are used to. The climate crisis is a reality where everything is about everything, and everywhere is about everywhere.[646] The impact of climate change will eventually appear not only in places 'far away from us' but also where we are. If a heat wave or an unexpectedly heavy rainfall does not knock on our door, a humanitarian crisis will. That is because extreme climate and weather events will lead to increased numbers of displaced people, damage to food supply chains and livelihoods, forced migration, and increased risk of conflict.[647] At this point, we need to take a closer look at some of the situations that human civilisation has to face due to climate change. In this way, perhaps we can approach these problems not with classical constitutionalism with the nation-state at its centre but with a global perspective and find lasting solutions that 'leave no one behind'.

2.2.1.1 Climate migrations

Climate change has consequences that affect everyone around the world. Some of these people will be forced to migrate due to worsening living conditions, loss of livelihood opportunities, or conflicts. By 2050, most of the people who will be forced to migrate due to sea level rise alone live in countries of the Global South with inadequate infrastructure and insufficient budgets for adaptation. Per-country estimates suggest that 10 million Chinese, 30 million Indians, 15–20 million Bangladeshis, 10–14 million Egyptians, and up to 10 million inhabitants of large deltas such as the Niger will migrate. A tragic future awaits the million or so inhabitants of small island states such as Tuvalu and the Maldives, which are likely to disappear in the next

645 Andreas Malm, 'Introduction – No Shortage on Targets', *in* Jessie Kindig (ed.), *Property Will Cost Us the Earth Direct Action – The Future of the Global Climate Movement*, Verso, London, 2022, p. 27.

646 Şahin, 'İklim Krizine …', p. 29.

647 Sanem Özer, 'İklim Değişikliği ve Çatışmalar', *Doğu Batı*, No. 95, November-December-January 2020–21, p. 57.

fifty years. In addition, around 50 million more people worldwide will be forced to leave their lands, which will become uninhabitable as the waters rise.[648] This migration may be within their homelands, but it will often be a cross-border migration, especially for island peoples who have lost their entire territories and those fleeing conflicts.

Island states in the Pacific Ocean are among the most vulnerable to climate change, particularly rising sea levels and increased hurricanes. Small island developing states are particularly vulnerable to biodiversity loss as they are more susceptible to the combined impact of land conversion, overuse, climate change, pollution, and invasive species in their limited areas.[649] In addition to being forced to flee their homes due to rising sea levels, residents of island states are also struggling to access clean drinking water. Drinking water quality on these islands is declining, and the taste is becoming bitter as seawater increasingly seeps into springs. Except for Papua New Guinea, all countries in the region are highly threatened, especially along the coastlines where populations are concentrated. Even in Papua New Guinea, the southern coast and low-altitude islands are vulnerable, and some citizens have already moved to safer new settlements on the islands of Carteret and Bougainville.[650]

However, not all countries are as prepared and successful as Papua New Guinea. For example, the Indigenous people living on Panama's Gardi Sugdub island, which is in danger of sinking due to climate change, have been waiting to be evacuated since 2010. Plans to transfer people who have no adequate living space due to rising sea levels to a designated area on the mainland[651] have not yet been implemented. In a report prepared by Human Rights Watch, it was revealed that this situation violates the rights of the Indigenous people living in Gardi Sugdub.[652]

---

[648] M. Parry – N. Arnell – T. McMichael – R. Nicholls – P. Martens – S. Kovats – M. Livermore – C. Rosenzweig – A. Iglesias – G. Fischer, 'Viewpoint: Millions at risk: Defining critical climate change threats and targets', *Global Environmental Change*, 11, 2001, pp. 181–3, cited in: Tanuro, *L'Impossible le Capitalism vert*, p. 40.

[649] Boyd, *Report of… (A/75/161)*, p. 15, § 60.

[650] Asian Development Bank, *Addressing Climate Change and Migration in Asia and the Pacific – Final Report*', 2012, p. 35, § 160.

[651] Linda Pressly, 'The Island People With a Climate Change Escape Plan', *BBC*, 21 September 2017.

[652] See Human Rights Watch, *'The Sea Is Eating The Land Below Our Homes:' Indigenous Community Facing Lack of Space and Rising Seas Plans Relocation*, 2023.

International climate migration is already underway in Oceania. Migration from island states in the Pacific Ocean to New Zealand has quadrupled in recent years.[653] New Zealand has yet to accept the moral, legal, and political responsibility for carbon emissions, even though the country's Ministry of Foreign Affairs and Trade has published two reports showing climate change will devastate island states.[654] This Global North country has made no promises to accept migrants from Pacific islands due to the negative consequences of climate change.[655] As an example of this denial policy, the New Zealand Immigration and Protection Tribunal recently rejected a Kiribati citizen's application to immigrate to New Zealand because of the negative impacts of climate change on his country. This case demonstrated once again how international law is failing to protect applicants regarding climate change and hold countries that are contributing significantly to climate change by emitting greenhouse gases heavily accountable.[656]

In a policy paper, even the World Bank has called on Australia and New Zealand to be open to migration from Pacific island states. In order to strengthen the economies of the struggling island states and prevent future mass migration, this bastion of the global capitalist economic order has asked the two countries to grant work and permanent residence permits to people from Tuvalu and Kiribati as a climate change adaptation measure.[657] However, neither country has yet responded positively to this request.

Of course, climate migration will not be limited to Oceania. In every corner of the world, people living in rural areas and engaged in animal husbandry and agriculture are increasingly under pressure to lose their livelihoods and migrate due to climate change. A report by the UK-based Environmental Justice Foundation found that 10 million people in Africa alone have already

---

653 Tokar, *Toward Climate Justice*, Who Is Affected by Global Warming (Loc. 341).

654 Andreas Neef – Lucy Benge, 'Shifting Responsibility and Denying Justice: New Zealand's Contentious Approach to Pacific Climate Mobilities', *Regional Environmental Change*, Vol. 22, paper no. 94, 2022, p. 6.

655 Richard Bedford – Charlotte Bedford, 'International Migration and Climate Change: A Post-Copenhagen Perspective on Options for Kiribati and Tuvalu', *in* Bruce Burson, *Climate Change and Migration – South Pacific Perspectives*, Institute for Policy Studies, 2010, p. 91.

656 Neef – Benge, 'Shifting Responsibility … ', p. 1.

657 Ben Doherty – Eleanor Ainge Roy, 'World Bank: Let Climate-Threatened Pacific Islanders Migrate to Australia or NZ', *The Guardian*, 8 May 2017.

been displaced or forced to migrate due to environmental degradation and desertification.[658] In areas where these people are migrating, the potential for conflict between locals and newcomers is increasing, especially as population pressure on limited resources such as land, food, and water increases.[659] The study by Rafael Reuveny of Indiana University examined thirty-eight cases of people forced to migrate for environmental (drought, floods, storms, soil degradation, pollution) or other reasons in the seventy years prior to 2007. In half of these cases, violent conflicts broke out between the migrant community and those in the destination. According to Reuveny, people who are most dependent on their environment for survival, especially in regions with scarce arable land and freshwater, are often forced to migrate when conditions change rapidly and unplanned.[660] Therefore, millions of people are caught between two fires due to climate change: starvation and death or migration and conflict.

2.2.1.2 Violence

It is important to remember that most resources needed to satisfy people's primary needs cannot be produced; they can only be taken from nature. Humans cannot even create a simple resource like water, without which we cannot live or grow food. Therefore, the view of natural assets as resources and their control and accumulation for future consumption was a key element of political tension in the past and remains so today.[661]

Written history records that sudden environmental changes threaten the prosperity of societies and states. The relationship between past civilisations and climate has been decisive in influencing the rise and fall of many long-established cultures.[662] Using archaeological findings and regional paleoclimate data, studies linking abrupt climate changes in the past to social instability,

---

658 Tokar, *Toward Climate Justice*, Who Is Affected by Global Warming? (Loc. 360).

659 Özer, 'İklim Değişikliği … ', p. 64.

660 Rafael Reuveny, 'Climate Change-Induced Migration and Violent Conflict', *Political Geography*, Vol. 26, No. 6, August 2007, pp. 656–73, cited in: Tokar, *Toward Climate Justice*, Projections and Realities (Loc. 451).

661 Capra – Mattei, *The Ecology of Law*, p. 73.

662 Özer, 'İklim Değişikliği … ', p. 48. For civilizations that collapsed due to climate change, see Özer, 'İklim Değişikliği … ', pp. 49–52.

conflict, and eventual collapse also shed light on the relationship between climate change and current and potential conflicts.[663]

The results of these studies clearly show that there is a close relationship between climate and the rise and fall of civilisations. Many civilisations that prospered and grew thanks to the climate in a certain region had to collapse due to changes in climate.[664] Our current civilisation is not exempt from this equation. According to James Lovelock, the future of all civilisations today depends on the rebalancing of the climate. Since our human structures and institutions are in such a complex relationship with the climate of the twentieth century, any deviation from the optimum climate will be catastrophic. According to the honourable English scientist, we are using the Earth so badly for our own benefit that we are on the way to return it to the temperature of 55 million years ago. If that happens, we and the generation after us will all perish.[665] Scranton takes a more pessimistic view, arguing that the drift has already happened and the extinction process has already begun. In his view, if we as humanity are to survive the Anthropocene, we will have to learn from now on how to live through the collapse of our civilisation, including change, danger, conflict, and strife. We have to learn to accept and adapt.[666] Unlike Stranton, some scientists say we still have a short time to turn things around. Still, we have not yet done what we need to do in that short time, and it does not look like we will. That increases the risk of conflict in many countries around the world, among other consequences of climate change.

Many of the world's poorest countries and societies face a two-headed problem: climate change and violent conflicts due to the high risk that climate change will increase the likelihood of violent conflict. In forty-six countries, home to 2.7 billion people, the consequences of climate change interacting with economic, social, and political problems are projected to create a higher risk of violent conflict.[667] As a result, these societies will become poorer and

---

663 Özer, 'İklim Değişikliği … ', p. 68.

664 Hulme, *Why We Disagree …*, pp. 53–7.

665 James Lovelock, *The Revenge of Gaia: Earth's Climate Crisis & The Fate of Humanity*, Hachette UK, London, August 2007, p. 1.

666 Scranton, *Learning to Die*, pp. 16–17. In his book, Scranton presents violence as a viable solution to various problems in the history. See Scranton, *Learning to Die*, p. 68.

667 Dan Smith – Janani Vivekananda, *A Climate of Conflict: The Links Between Climate Change, Peace and War*, International Alert, November 2007, p. 3.

less resilient to the consequences of climate change. Climate change creates a multiplier effect in troubled regions, exacerbating and magnifying already existing problems.

In addition, environmental problems themselves can also be the cause of violence because the limited resources that people are dependent on are shrinking every day, and competition for them, exacerbated by climate migration, is increasing. In some cases, population growth can lead to deforestation in order to clear more agricultural land, resulting in desertification and loss of biodiversity, disrupting the livelihoods and food chain needed by the local population. That, in turn, can lead to increased polarisation between ethnic groups and/or host communities and outsiders and violent conflict resolution.[668] This so-called ecological violence feeds into the security and development debate. The violence that will emerge as a result of climate change will primarily stem from the struggle for survival in an environment teetering on the brink of collapse.[669] Indeed, research has shown that deviations from normal rainfall and temperate temperatures often systematically increase conflict significantly.[670]

Therefore, it can be easily predicted that regional stability will be jeopardised by conflicts in places where the impacts of climate change are more severe. In addition, the following can be listed as potential social threats posed by climate change: The loss of material welfare that populations will experience due to climate change, especially in Global South states, could undermine the stability and legitimacy of governments. Loss of livelihoods could weaken states economically and militarily. Increasing inequality among people, diseases, and loss of individual and collective livelihoods could undermine domestic stability and the state's authority, paving the way for conflicts. Climate change could increase the cost of public services that states provide, leading to budget losses and limiting the opportunities and freedoms that states provide their citizens.[671]

Indeed, the US-based CNA, a research organisation working in the field of security, concludes in its report that climate change-related problems will

---

668 Özer, 'İklim Değişikliği … ', pp. 58–9.
669 Özer, 'İklim Değişikliği … ', p. 53.
670 Solomon Hsiang – Marshall Burke – Edward Miguel, 'Quantifying the Influence of Climate on Human Conflict', *Science* 341, 1235367, p. 1212.
671 Özer, 'İklim Değişikliği … ', p. 54.

cause political instability in countries where governments do not have the capacity to meet social demands. Noting that climate change will be a threat multiplier for instability, especially in fragile regions of the world, CNA states that some states in Asia, Africa, and the Middle East may lose their basic qualities.[672] Therefore, some states face the threat of losing their statehood due to climate change and becoming failed states.

Syria is a substantial example of this situation. The price fluctuations caused by President Bashar al-Assad's neoliberal policies after 2005 triggered a wave of migration from rural areas to the cities since the agricultural sector was the most affected by these policies.[673] Moreover, Syria, which receives about a quarter of the world's average rainfall, was experiencing various problems in managing water resources before 2011. In particular, local governments disregarded the illegal use of groundwater, which worsened the situation of the agricultural sector.[674] Under these conditions, a civil war broke out, triggered by the drought that began in the winter of 2006–7 and lasted for three years, bringing agriculture to the brink of collapse in the region. The southern border town of Daraa was severely affected by the worst drought on record. Unsurprisingly, the uprising began in 2011 there, when many farmers had already been forced to flee. While the drought was not the only factor that triggered the uprising, it is today generally accepted that the resulting internal displacement of large numbers of Syrian citizens contributed to the escalation of the conflict.[675] Indeed, a scientific study published in 2015 confirmed this argument. According to the study, the drought deepened the existing water and agricultural security crisis, leading to a drastic reduction in harvests and the death of livestock. As a result, around 1.5 million people have migrated from rural to peri-urban areas. Rapidly growing slums, overpopulation, poor infrastructure, unemployment, and the Assad regime's reckless policies in the face

---

672 CNA, *National Security and the Threat of Climate Change*, 2007, p. 6.

673 Efe Can Gürcan, 'Guerre et Crise Agraire en Syrie: Revisiter le Conflit Syrien au Prisme de la Justice Écologique', *Possibles*, Vol. 41, No. 2, Spring 2017, p. 68.

674 Tuğba Evrim Maden, 'Syria's Civil War and Changing Water Security', *ORSAM*, 27 November 2014.

675 Klein, *On Fire*, p. 195.

of crime created the causes of the growing rebellion.[676] As of December 2024, Assad had fled the country and sought refuge in Russia, and a group with Islamic extremist roots, considered a terrorist organisation by many countries, has taken power. The Israeli army has advanced to near Damascus. The future of the country is being drawn through national and international negotiations. Hence, the Syrian case can easily be recognised as a clear indication that even in our modern societies, climate change and violations of ecological justice have the capacity to lead to a war that affects the whole world.[677]

Some countries most vulnerable to the impacts of climate change are already in conflict zones. Countries such as Yemen, Mali, Afghanistan, the Democratic Republic of Congo, and Somalia are all struggling with conflicts. These countries, ravaged by years of armed violence, are less resilient to global challenges such as climate change than countries in the Global North. Years of conflict have weakened their adaptive capacity to cope with climate change. Even though climate change does not directly lead to armed conflicts, at least yet, as the Syria case shows, it exacerbates the social, economic, and environmental conditions underpinning conflict and increases the risk of conflict.[678] As another example, the violence and civil war in Darfur in Western Sudan are claimed to have been triggered by changes in the climate in recent years. According to Walker and King, Darfur is a dramatic example of how the slightest change in climate can have dramatic and frightening human consequences.[679] Similarly, drought is drying up wells and killing livestock in East Africa, triggering ethnic conflicts between tribes in the region.[680]

It is not difficult to foresee that not only drought but also rising sea levels and other climate change-related developments will lead to similar consequences. As the ecological crisis worsens, the world will face more ecological violence. Unfortunately, that will lead to further human rights violations that are already ongoing.

---

676 Colin P. Kelley – Shahrzad Mohtadi – Mark A. Cane – Richard Seager – Yochanan Kushnir, 'Climate Change in the Fertile Crescent and Implications of the Recent Syrian Drought', *PNAS*, Vol. 112, No. 11, 17 March 2015, pp. 3241–2.

677 Gürcan, 'Guerre et Crise Agraire … ', p. 71.

678 Özer, 'İklim Değişikliği … ', p. 63.

679 G. Walker – D. King, *The Hot Topic: How to Tackle Climate Change and Still Keep the Lights on?*, Bloomsbury Publishing, London, 2008, p. 48, cited in: Hulme, *Why We Disagree …*, p. 46.

680 Tokar, *Toward Climate Justice*, Who Is Affected by Global Warming? (Loc. 354).

2.2.1.3 Human rights violations

Climate change is already having a negative impact on many human rights. Given that the world's population will exceed 9 billion by 2050 if economic growth and high energy and resource use in wealthy countries continue, the global climate crisis will deepen and have an incredibly devastating impact on human rights unless urgent and radical measures are taken.[681] Therefore, there is a logical justification for including climate-related articles even in constitutions written from an anthropocentric perspective whose primary objective is to protect human rights, not the natural balance,[682] because it is impossible to protect human rights without protecting the climate. Enjoying even the most fundamental human rights and freedoms in a collapsed ecosystem will not be possible.

In this regard, the view of the Lahore High Court of Pakistan can be considered instructive. In a 2015 judgement on a lawsuit filed by a farmer affected by climate change due to the state's failure to implement climate policies, the court ruled that the state's failure to implement the climate change framework policy[683] violated the constitutional articles on the right to life and human dignity of citizens. The following important paragraph written by Judge Sayed Mansoor Ali Shah in the judgement summarises in a very striking way how climate and human rights protection are intertwined:

> Climate Change is a defining challenge of our time and has led to dramatic alterations in our planet's climate system. For Pakistan, these climatic variations have primarily resulted in heavy floods and droughts, raising serious concerns regarding water and food security. On a legal and constitutional plane, this is (a) clarion call for the protection of fundamental rights of the citizens of Pakistan, in particular, the vulnerable and weak segments of the society who are unable to approach this Court.[684]

Not only in Pakistan but all over the world, climate change threatens people's most fundamental rights. Obviously, foremost among these is the right to life. In a 2018 general comment on the right to life, the UN Human Rights

---

[681] David R. Boyd, *Report of the Special Rapporteur on the Issue of Human Rights Obligations Relating to the Enjoyment of a Safe, Clean, Healthy and Sustainable Environment*, UN General Assembly, UN DOC A/74/161, 15 July 2019, p. 4, § 3.

[682] Collins, *The Ecological Constitution*, p. 106.

[683] *Ashgar Leghari v. Federation of Pakistan*, W.P. No. 25501/201.

[684] *Ashgar Leghari v. Federation of Pakistan*, § 6.

Committee stated: *Environmental degradation, climate change, and unsustainable development constitute one of the most pressing and serious threats to the ability of present and future generations to enjoy the right to life.*[685] Indeed, the devastation caused by global climate change to ecosystems, natural life cycles, and the artificial environment and infrastructure seriously affects human life and safe access to vital needs. On the one hand, an increasing number of extreme weather events claim the lives of hundreds of thousands of people around the world every year. On the other hand, climatic disasters cause humanity to face a serious risk of food and water shortages. Thus, climate change directly and indirectly interferes with the right to life.[686] As Boyd points out in his report for the UN, both the damage to the ecosystem and the decline in biodiversity result in the violation of the right to life of many people.[687]

Another right fundamentally affected by climate change is the right to health. A healthy ecosystem acts as a buffer against epidemics. Environmental changes, such as deforestation, lead to diseases in wildlife, domestic animals, and humans.[688] The UN World Health Organization (WHO) describes climate change as humanity's most significant health challenge. Noting that climate change is already causing deaths and illnesses through extreme weather events such as heat waves, storms, and floods, WHO states that disruption of food systems, zoonotic diseases, food, water, and vector-borne infections and mental health problems are other causes of disease due to global warming.[689] Another impact of climate change on the right to health is related to access to health services. Even in developed countries, climate change-related disasters have a negative impact on the capacity to benefit in a timely and equitable manner from the goods, services, and conditions that make health possible. Due to these direct and indirect impacts on human health, climate change puts the right to health at serious risk.[690]

These are not the only fundamental rights and freedoms violated due to global warming. However, it is impossible to address them in detail here. Last

---

685 Human Rights Committee, *General Comment No. 36*, p. 13, § 62.

686 Seda Yurtcanlı Duymaz, 'Bir İnsan Hakları Sorunu Olarak İklim Değişikliği', *Journal of Constitutional Law*, Vol. 8, No. 16, 2019, p. 494.

687 Boyd, *Report of … (A/75/161)*, p. 11, § 37.

688 Boyd, *Report of … (A/75/161)*, p. 12, § 40.

689 'Climate Change and Health', *UN World Health Organization*, 30 October 2021.

690 Yurtcanlı Duymaz, 'Bir İnsan Hakları … ', p. 495.

but not least, it is necessary to mention the right to water and food because of its direct relationship with climate change. A large portion of natural freshwater is used in industry and industrial agriculture. Considering that clean water is a limited and rapidly becoming inadequate resource, it becomes clear that water has a crucial meaning for capital accumulation.[691] The right to access sufficient clean water is at risk in regions where water is polluted, poisoned, and overused.[692] For a person's right to water not to be violated, they must have access to 20 litres of clean water per day. However, climate change is causing both quantitative and qualitative degradation of water.[693] According to UN statistics for 2022, 2 billion people worldwide do not have access to clean drinking water, and almost half of the world's population suffers from water scarcity for half of the year. Moreover, this situation will worsen soon due to melting glaciers and rising sea levels caused by climate change.[694]

Global climate change also violates the right to food, which is essential for people to live healthy lives, as it causes drought and desertification, loss of biodiversity, depletion of water resources that enable agricultural activities, and salinisation of fertile soils.[695] Biodiversity, which has been largely lost in recent decades, protects the right to food by increasing the resilience of agricultural systems. It is also vital as it reduces the negative impacts on the environment during food production.[696] On the other hand, industrial food production and climate change go into a cycle that negatively affects each other. As is well known, there has been an explosion in food production in recent years to feed the growing human population. However, this has put incredible pressure on ecosystems and biodiversity. Degraded ecosystems are losing their ability to produce clean water, protect against disasters such as floods, and provide homes for species such as pollinators and soil organisms.[697] That means subsistence farmers can no longer get yields from the land, and more people become dependent on industrial food production companies.

---

691 Gaye Yılmaz, *Suyun Metalaştırılması: Kıtlığın Nedeni Kıtlığa Çare Olabilir mi?*, Evrensel Basım Yayın, Istanbul, 2013, p. 69.
692 Boyd, *Report of… (A/75/161)*, p. 13, § 47.
693 Yurtcanlı Duymaz, 'Bir İnsan Hakları … ', p. 496.
694 'Water: At the Center of Climate Crisis', *UN*.
695 Yurtcanlı Duymaz, 'Bir İnsan Hakları … ', pp. 496–7.
696 Boyd, *Report of… (A/75/161)*, p. 12, § 43.
697 Boyd, *Report of… (A/75/161)*, p. 12, § 45.

Thus, millions of people who cannot afford to buy food, which has become a commodity, are condemned to starvation. For example, in 2023, Ethiopia's number of people needing aid reached 6 million due to drought. A total of 1,400 people were found to have died of starvation sometime after the UN World Food Program stopped its aid to the country due to cases of theft.[698]

As it is clearly seen, the situation is bleak. The globe is warming, the climate is changing, and the ecosystem is collapsing. This is not just a problem of degraded nature or depleted animals. People are also suffering greatly, being forced to migrate and losing their lives due to climate change. These are not tomorrow's problems; they are happening right now. The biggest culprit is an economic system dependent on fossil fuels that came into our lives only 250 years ago, namely capitalism. So, the solution is simple. If we want to prevent climate change and avoid extinction, we need to limit it and, if possible, replace it with another economic system. However, the solution is also challenging because we do not know how to change an economic system that is embedded in every aspect and moment of our lives. Yet, there is one thing we do know: We have to somehow achieve it in the short time scientists say is left.

I suggest doing it through supreme courts since there is no time left for a grassroots democratic movement to mature. As the highest institutions of legal systems, they have the power to bind both state organs and individuals at the constitutional level. By ruling at the constitutional level, these courts can limit the climate change-causing workings of the capitalist economic order and ensure the protection of the ecosystem, natural assets, and people's fundamental rights. Just as the bourgeoisie once used constitutionalism to limit the absolute sovereignty of the king and create a free trading space for itself, today, we need to create a new wave of constitutionalism through legal mechanisms to limit capitalist hegemony and create a surviving space for ourselves and the Earth. I call this wave green constitutionalism.

---

[698] Girmay Gebru – Mercy Juma, 'Ethiopia's Tigray Crisis: Deaths From Starvation After Aid Halted – Official', *BBC*, 18 August 2023.

Establishing a new green constitutional order

The old is dying, and the new cannot be born;
in this intermediate period,
a wide range of terrible symptoms appear.[699]

Law has two classical functions, which appear opposite but complement each other. On the one hand, law 'exudes' from the relations between individuals in society. In other words, the rules of law are, in fact, the result of the relations we establish with each other. On the other hand, it defines our relations, thus structuring society. These legally defined relations organise society and determine, for example, how power is exercised among us. Legal rules are also used to guide and control the actions of individuals within society, for example, by prohibiting certain behaviours and punishing those who do not comply with them.[700] In short, both society shapes law, and law shapes society.

Therefore, as Indigenous peoples already know, it is our 'laws' and practices that make us who we are as a society and as individuals.[701] However, as a social system of human beings and an essential element of governance, law is also a meaningful tool used to shape people's behaviour for a particular purpose.[702]

---

699 Antonio Gramsci (while serving time in Mussolini's prison), cited in: Chomsky – Pollin, *Climate Crisis …*, p. 179.

700 Cullinan, *Wild Law*, p. 57.

701 Cullinan, *Wild Law*, p. 175.

702 G. Hadfield – B. Weingast, 'What is Law: A Coordination Model of the Characteristics of a Legal Order', *Journal of Legal Analysis*, 4(2), 2012, p. 473, cited in: Louis J. Kotzé – Rakhyun E. Kim, 'Towards Planetary Nexus Governance in the Anthropocene: En Earth System Law Perspective', *Global Policy*, No. 13 (Suppl. 3), 2022, p. 89.

The continuity of society lies in the harmony of its members' behaviour. Today's climate change encourages us to emphasise this society-shaping aspect of law. In doing so, however, we should go beyond the classical definition and look for legal harmony not only between us but also between humans and the rest of nature.

There is a powerful logical justification for the necessity to change the existing governance systems in most countries, as well as the international legal and political order: The world's ecosystem is collapsing rapidly. The current social, political, and economic emergency is an opportunity for transformation. The status quo is highly unstable, and change is necessary. On the bright side, this means we are in a good place to start building a better world.[703] As shown in the first part, the apparent economic success of today's dominant cultures is based on the consumption and expenditure of the Earth's natural 'resources' and growing inequality between humans and between humans and other members of the ecosystem.[704] If we consider the Earth a society with all the living and non-living things that inhabit it – and we should – it is evident that we have lost harmony. The main reason for this is the economic and legal order that puts a single element within this society, the human being, at the centre and puts everything else at its service. A just and sustainable society is built on equal and reciprocal relationships. So, a social order like ours, based on an unjust hierarchy, would eventually collapse.

Therefore, a different perspective is needed in the relationship between law and ecology today. Instead of closed normative legal debates on climate change, there is a need for an interdisciplinary perspective more intertwined with natural and economic sciences and their development. In other words, the relationship between ecology and law needs to be addressed from a completely different paradigm.[705] Establishing a new legal order designed by utilising natural and economic sciences compatible with the ecosystem is imperative. We must develop a constitutionalism that recognises and respects nature and limits or prohibits certain human activities within this framework. That is not social engineering; on the contrary, it is an effort to re-evaluate

---

[703] Natalie Bennett, *Change Everything*, Unbound, London, 2024, p. 20.

[704] Cullinan, *Wild Law*, p. 169.

[705] Sezgin Seymen Çebi, 'Ekoloji, İdeoloji, Özneleşme ve Hukuk', *Doğu Batı*, No. 95, November-December-January 2020–21, p. 27.

legal systems that are more compatible with human nature. Remember that the capitalist economic order and modernity have artificially shaped us and forced us into a form of relations that is not in accordance with our nature. That is an effort to overcome capitalism and reconnect with nature.

Even if we find the processes we are causing inconceivably large and complex, we should take comfort in knowing that global warming is ultimately a human invention. Yes, we should feel guilty, but on the bright side, we should also realise that we are still at the helm. No matter how out of control the climate system may seem, with powerful typhoons, unprecedented famines, heat waves, refugee crises, and climate conflicts, we are the ones who are doing it all.[706] So, it is up to us to stop doing them, take responsibility for our actions, and correct our mistakes. Even if we can no longer bring things back, we can prevent them from worsening.

There is always good in every bad. This crisis could potentially force us out of a destructive global capitalism in which only 1 per cent of society is fabulously wealthy while the rest scrape the crumbs. The reality is so urgent and the outlook so desperate that we can demand nothing less than a radically new ecological, social, and political structure. We need a movement that looks beyond the status quo, realises the transformative potential of an ecological and justice-centred structure, and sheds light on the imperative to create an entirely different kind of world.[707] Furthermore, because of the urgency of the situation, this transformative movement must emerge immediately.

Law can and should lead the way. A revolution towards a network society is only possible if legal institutions encourage individuals to behave in ecologically sustainable ways. In order to reproduce relations, this new institutional framework must avoid the concentration of power and spread it across the ecological community. It must reject the selfish accumulation and exploitation of resources that belong to everyone.[708] For civilisation to survive, jurists must lead a legal revolution away from mechanistic law based on capitalist owners and state sovereignty and towards a law based on social and natural relations and community ownership. For such a revolution to take place,

---

706 Wallace-Wells, *The Uninhabitable Earth*, p. 34.

707 Tokar, *Toward Climate Justice*, How Much Warming Can We Tolerate (Loc. 527 and 539).

708 Capra – Mattei, *The Ecology of Law*, p. 161.

a dialogue between law and ecology is needed.[709] However, this dialogue must yield results as soon as possible to prevent further climate change deepening. Therefore, it is vital that the high courts urgently step in and re-establish the links between the constitutional system and the ecosystem. In addition to scientific data, social support should provide a technical and democratic basis for their decisions.

The ultimate goal of green constitutionalism is to build a new form of organisation for people in this direction. This organisation should take into account not only people but also the networks of the ecosystem that sustain us. This understanding, which can be regarded as a constitutional reflection of what Cullinan calls 'Earth governance', aims to regulate human behaviour in accordance with the Earth's ecosystem. In this way, we will expand our understanding of governance and democracy to include not only human beings but also all living and non-living beings on Earth.[710]

Earth governance is based on the recognition that humans cannot continue to exist in the long term if they do not regulate their behaviour in a way that prioritises the well-being of the Earth. Governing for the Earth by prioritising not just one element within the system but the system's health holistically also means governing for humans since our own well-being is provided by this system as well, of which we are all a part. From this perspective, it is easy to see that Earth governance's long-term and holistic approach is much more beneficial for humanity than current governance systems based on short-term political goals and advantages.[711]

A grassroots demand for transformation is already emerging. Communities living in harmony with nature, Indigenous people, youth, nature and human rights activists, scientists, and many civil society organisations are working for the immediate implementation of actions to prevent and mitigate the crises caused by global climate change. They are demanding the downsizing of sectors that cause ecological destruction and inequalities, the abandonment of private property, the common use of goods, the protection and increase of the commons, an end to food

---

709 Capra – Mattei, *The Ecology of Law*, p. 199.
710 Cullinan, *Wild Law*, p. 116.
711 Cullinan, *Wild Law*, p. 118.

waste, the protection of natural areas and species, solidarity, and eco-social justice. However, these alone are unlikely to change economic and legal structures, at least in the short term. We know that the bourgeois class, the creator of capitalism and the prime suspect in the current climate crisis, will continue to ignore these demands. Moreover, we also realise with pain that our leaders in the service of the bourgeoisie do not look out for us, and no one even cares about our survival.[712]

Taking this grassroots demand for survival into account, the supreme courts, which should remember that their primary task is to create a habitat for rights and freedoms by limiting the powers that be, should first limit the ecosystem-damaging actions of the bourgeoisie and our leaders within a green constitutionalist logic, and then lead the way in abandoning our current anthropocentric legal order and establishing a nature-centred[713] legal order. In this part, I will address the fundamental philosophical and constitutional principles on which this transition should be based.

---

[712] Sally Weintrobe, 'The Difficult Problem of Anxiety in Thinking About Climate Change', in Sally Weintrobe (ed.), *Engaging with Climate Change*, Routledge, 2013, p. 43, cited in: Klein, *That Changes Everything*, p. 16.

[713] According to Aykut Çoban, putting eco/nature-centredness in opposition to anthropocentredness means perpetuating the nature-human dualism. The author argues that 'decentred thinking' can open a wider window of discussion, because placing humans or nature at the centre opens space for 'othering' the other, which prevents the root problems from being seen. See Aykut Çoban, *Çevre Politikası: Ekolojik Sorunlar ve Kuram*, İmge, Ankara, 2020, p. 293, cited in: Arık, 'Bir Arada … ', p. 461. In this study, a 'nature-centric' approach is proposed as an alternative to the anthropocentric approach of the current social and legal structure. In my opinion, this term does not create a human-nature dichotomy or marginalise the other, since the human being is a component of nature, not a separate creature from it. When I say 'nature', I do not mean 'the space outside of human beings' in the Western humanist sense, or 'first nature' in Bookchin's view, but the totality of networks that include human beings and sustain life. Therefore, for me, 'nature-centredness' is a decentred perspective that represents this totality of networks. The function of the word 'centre' used in the term is to emphasise the need to design social, economic and legal structures around this whole of networks.

Transition from a human-centred legal order to a nature-centred legal order

At a time when climate disruption, biodiversity collapse, widespread pollution, and epidemics are intertwined, the need to rewrite the basic rules of law governing human societies has become even more evident.[714] That, of course, is not an easy task. It will be difficult to abandon a legal order that we have accepted as accurate for centuries, that we were born into, and that we have probably even benefited from personally, and to accept a new one that we have to learn all over again, where we consume less, where we do not exploit animals and nature as much as we would like. Moreover, we do not know where to start. However, we must remember that no paradigm shift in history has been easy.

For example, Darwin's findings on evolution required such a radical transformation of the then-dominant worldview that it was almost impossible for people to accept. It required a complete paradigm shift to acknowledge that humans were not created by God but evolved from nonhuman creatures. A similar situation is occurring today.[715] However endeavouring this transformation may be, it is both a necessity to stop the collapse of the ecosystem and the responsibility of all those who demand a more just world. The report prepared by the UN IPBES emphasises this responsibility by stating that 'the goals of conservation, sustainable use of nature and achieving sustainability …

---

714 Collins, *The Ecological Constitution*, p. IX (foreword by David R. Boyd).

715 Hickel, *Less is More*, p. 124.

can only be achieved through transformative changes in economic, social, political and technological factors'.[716]

As we know from our relationships with other people, it is okay to give and take a little bit; it is even tolerable to take without giving for a while. In the long run, however, balance is essential. If one party starts taking too much to the detriment of the other party's essential quality, the relationship becomes dysfunctional and abusive.[717] Our relationship with nature and the ecosystem has long since taken on this abusive nature. We thought that we could always take from nature without giving it anything. We have developed rules, paved the way for companies, and created a law within this logic. That results from the dualism developed in Western philosophy and culture based on the human-nature disconnection. In this way, we have destabilised both our societies and the ecosystem.

As Cullinan points out, our current legal theory recognises, to some extent, that a balance between people's rights is crucial. Indeed, the word 'justice' is generally understood to encompass this phenomenon. Many jurists and political scientists also think linking rights and responsibilities in governance systems is essential. Accordingly, the greater the rights and privileges, the greater the responsibilities they entail. Still, while we recognise that we have responsibilities towards humans, we do not want to see that even though we have achieved great power over other species and the Earth, we may have great responsibilities corresponding to that.[718]

Today, we have a choice between the Earth's health and capitalism's profit motive. One must be abandoned, and history shows us that the vast majority of decision-makers would choose capitalism. Therefore, we are right to doubt that the establishment will take the necessary measures to save us from ecological catastrophe.[719] The solution will not come from politicians in bed with fossil fuel companies. Either a global grassroots movement must change the political landscape worldwide – a well-intentioned but unfortunately unlikely prospect – or the high courts, recalling their responsibility to protect the right to life, must put an end to politicians' callousness. Ideally,

---

716 IPBES/7/10/Add.1, p. 6.
717 Cullinan, *Wild Law*, p. 106.
718 Cullinan, *Wild Law*, p. 116.
719 Löwy, *Ecosocialism*, The Belém Declaration (Loc. 1134).

these two movements, one from the grassroots and one from the top, should work together.

That our legal systems are dangerously malfunctioning for nonhuman members of the Earth's ecosystem is obvious, but that they are also endangering us is something fewer people realise. Unless we fail to recognise and stop our actions that threaten the health of the whole of which we are part, these actions will continue to escalate. Therefore, the choice we have to make is simple: Either we suffer catastrophic consequences sooner or later (along with the rest of the ecosystem) or make fundamental changes in how we govern ourselves.[720] Our current leaders and the corporations at the system's centre are right to dislike this idea. However, legally preventing them from standing in the way of this change is now imperative for both the ecosystem and our own survival.

The mechanistic approach persisted with resistance in law-making because it provided invaluable services to nineteenth-century capitalism. In this way, the legal system was reduced to a compromise between private property and state sovereignty. Rather than ensuring the continuation of social order within a particular understanding of justice, it became a powerful tool used to oppress nature and society.[721] The shortsighted and anthropocentric laws we accept without question have often led to erroneous outcomes and prevented healthy relationships between humans and the rest of nature.[722] By denying that animals and natural beings are subjects of rights, our legal systems have infused an artificial idea of superiority into us and blinded us to the holistic nature of the ecosystem as a web of networks.

Moreover, bourgeois law has failed to achieve full equality even among people. Our legal systems, which see nature as a resource and property as the freedom to occupy these unclaimed resources, have supported a global capitalist economic system, threatening and destroying local communities around the world. Following ill-conceived biotechnology, it has attempted to turn diversity into monoculture, ecology into engineering, and life itself

---

720 Cullinan, *Wild Law*, p. 74.
721 Capra – Mattei, *The Ecology of Law*, p. 117.
722 Cullinan, *Wild Law*, p. 27.

into a commodity, violating not only nature's right to life but also the human right to life.[723]

We must acknowledge that the state and the market are not natural but cultural products and that they came into existence and function thanks to our positive law. They did not exist before; they appeared at a particular time in history to serve the interests of the lawmakers of that time. Therefore, they can be erased from the history stage through law if we so choose. If used properly, this mutable quality of law can pave a path away from destruction and towards productive, ecologically sustainable human endeavours.[724]

We need legal structures and political institutions that recognise that the way to the future is not through reckless industrial growth but through the living Earth to which we owe our existence and which is the only force that will keep us alive in the coming decades.[725] We need a perspective that defeats an economy based on individualism by placing law at the level of social networks and ecological communities.[726] We must reconnect people and the ecosphere, leaving humanist dualism behind, and move from an anthropocentric system of values to a nature-centred system of values. One of the best ways to begin this transition is to start a process that systematically identifies, modifies, and replaces the current legal doctrines and theories that prevent people from playing a responsible role in the Earth's ecosystem.[727] Green constitutionalism should be considered as part of this process.

3.1 Leaving the bourgeois legal order behind

As I tried to show in the book's first part, those of us living in capitalist societies have been taught to believe that there is a fundamental distinction between human society and the rest of the world. According to this doctrine, humans are separate from and superior to 'nature' and are the subjects of rights through their spirit, reason, and will, while nature is an inert and mechanistic object. This way of perceiving the world is known as dualism. We inherited this idea from a long list of thinkers, from Plato to Descartes,

[723] Capra – Mattei, *The Ecology of Law*, pp. 132–3.
[724] Capra – Mattei, *The Ecology of Law*, pp. 29–30.
[725] Cullinan, *Wild Law*, p. 22 (foreword by Thomas Berry).
[726] Capra – Mattei, *The Ecology of Law*, p. 146.
[727] Cullinan, *Wild Law*, p. 164.

who argued that we can rightfully exploit and control nature. Before that, we did not consider man superior and separate from nature. Therefore, those who paved the way to capitalism in the sixteenth century had first to eliminate other, more holistic views of the world and persuade or force people to become dualists.[728] Otherwise, the present economic and legal system could not have been established.

The mechanistic worldview of modernity is still widely embraced by lawyers and jurists and still influential among business and political leaders. These lawyers and leaders recklessly pursue the illusion of perpetual economic growth on a finite planet, encouraging overconsumption through a disposable economy that creates waste and pollution, depletes the earth's natural resources, and consumes excessive energy and resources.[729] Lawyers who continue to believe that the environment can be protected and sustainability achieved without questioning this dualistic logic at the root of our current problems are trapping themselves in an outdated view and making a false promise.[730]

What needs to be done today to stop climate change is to start rebuilding our relationship with nature from the ground up. That requires dismantling the system of dominant powers that claim to monopolise nature and rebuilding it according to the principle of sustainability. This is an extremely comprehensive task. From public institutions to forms of property, from the harmful ontology based on 'value' to the relentless accumulation dynamic, all structures that trigger global warming need to be redesigned.[731] Such a total transformation can only be realised in a short period of time, either by drafting new constitutions or by interpreting existing ones differently. In any case, the way forward is for a new understanding of constitutionalism to become dominant.

In fact, there is – ironically – an advantageous situation in this situation. The 'disillusionment' with global capitalism's persistent failure to limit the climate crisis and the increasing questioning of its capacity to address the

[728] Hickel, *Less is More*, p. 31.
[729] Capra – Mattei, *The Ecology of Law*, p. 12.
[730] Michael M'Gonigle – Paula Ramsay, 'Greening Environmental Law: From Sectoral Reform to Systemic Reformation', *Journal of Environmental Law and Practice*, No. 14., 2004, p. 10.
[731] Fraser, 'Climates of Capital', p. 58.

ecological crisis has already led to a strategic debate and radicalisation in different sectors of the ecology movement. We have realised that modest reforms, small-scale changes, and gradual and time-bound reductions will not stabilise the earth's climate system and prevent the ecological crisis. It is clear today that an ecological revolution, which implies a total and rapid change in humanity's relationship with nature, is the only way out of the crisis.[732] This revolution might be possible if a new social order respecting the ecosystem is democratically demanded at the grassroots and the supreme courts adopt green constitutionalism at the top.

While we should treat our one and only life-giving home with care, respect, and reverence, we are causing unimaginable damage to ecosystems and biodiversity and undermining nature's extraordinary contribution to humanity's well-being and prosperity.[733] The rapid collapse of the Earth is clear evidence that we humans are doing something terribly wrong and that our legal systems are broken.[734] By recognising and protecting the property rights of corporations to extract resources as natural rights, we have created a kind of Frankenstein.[735] For the first time since the birth of the modern state, the private sector is now even more powerful than governments.[736] Through corporations, we have tried to reduce the Earth to our human size, domesticate it, somehow fit it into our mechanistic functioning, and make it dependent on us rather than harmonise ourselves with it.[737] The problem is not just that we have developed human law or human rights; instead, it is that we have forgotten that our legal systems can only exist within the Earth's system and, therefore, do not see the need for a relationship and continuity between our legal systems and the Earth's ecosystem.[738]

Given a strong will, we have the capacity to turn capital into common assets. Still, our current laws, serving the imperatives of capitalist production, are leading us in the opposite direction. So, we need political courage and

---

732 Benlisoy, 'İklim Krizi … ', pp. 186–7.

733 Boyd, *Report of … (A/75/161)*, p. 6, § 12.

734 Cullinan, *Wild Law*, p. 35.

735 Capra – Mattei, *The Ecology of Law*, p. 31.

736 Noreena Hertz, *The Silent Takeover: Global Capitalism and the DEath of Democracy*, Harper Business, New York, 2001, cited in: Capra – Mattei, *The Ecology of Law*, p. 143.

737 Cullinan, *Wild Law*, p. 20 (foreword by Thomas Berry).

738 Cullinan, *Wild Law*, p. 72.

leadership at all levels of society to challenge the unsustainable *status quo*. The legal dimension of this political will is crucial. We must develop a set of ecologically oriented legal principles that can begin to translate a worldview in harmony with nature into institutional theory and practice.[739] We need these principles, some of which can be found in Indigenous peoples' ways of life, to replace capitalist rules rapidly.

Our current legal system cannot protect the Earth from destruction because that is not its ultimate purpose, and therefore, a paradigm shift is necessary.[740] This shift is on the horizon. Our ancestors did not create a hierarchy between nature and man. Given how short the history of modernism is compared to the history of the cosmos, one can hope that the relationship between nature and man will be very different in the future.[741] We need to hold on to this hope in the face of the threat of climate change, which scientific data now conclusively demonstrate.

3.1.1 Reflecting the paradigm shift in science to law

Science refers to an organised body of knowledge acquired through a specific method known as the scientific method.[742] Examining the relationship between science and law reveals that legal theory is an intellectual discipline with a history and conceptual structure that has surprising parallels with the natural sciences. Moreover, the interaction between science and law, like the relationship between 'laws of nature' and human laws, evolves over time.[743] As Tanuro rightly puts it, any knowledge that cannot remain in abstract form due to its connection to the world in concrete ties must actively participate alongside what is good for humanity. This use of knowledge is the only element that reflects the reality of history developed through human labour. Far from being merely concrete, any knowledge calls upon the conscious

---

739 Capra – Mattei, *The Ecology of Law*, p. 191.

740 Nathalie Rühs – Aled Jones, 'The Implementation of Earth Jurisprudence through Substantive Constitutional Rights of Nature', *Sustainability*, 8:2, pp. 174–5, cited in: Collins, *The Ecological Constitution*, p. 3.

741 Orhan, 'Modernizm ve ... ', p. 38.

742 Capra – Mattei, *The Ecology of Law*, p. 42.

743 Capra – Mattei, *The Ecology of Law*, p. 23.

producers of history.[744] Therefore, the solid scientific knowledge of climate change that we have today must be used to create the course of history in our favour.

The last thirty years have seen a fundamental paradigm shift at the forefront of science, from Descartes and Newton's mechanistic and reductionist worldview to a systemic and pervasive ecological worldview. At the core of this paradigm shift is a fundamental change of metaphor: A shift from seeing the world as a machine to understanding it as a network of ecological communities. So, science and values have changed. It is now time for our laws, institutions, cultures, economies, and behaviours to do the same.[745]

As it is well known, networks are patterns of relationships; therefore, understanding life through networks requires thinking in terms of relationships and patterns. This new scientific method is known as 'systems thinking' or 'systemic thinking'. This way of studying, which means moving forward by thinking about the relationship between sciences and ideas rather than fragmenting them and approaching problems holistically, has been excluded from dominant intellectual traditions since Bacon,[746] with reasons demonstrated in Part I,[747] in order to exploit nonhuman entities of nature. Today, however, it has been understood that nature sustains life through a set of ecological principles that are meant to produce, not exploit.[748] Indigenous peoples have always embraced this important biological reality, which modern science in the West is only now beginning to understand: Man's unity with and dependence on the rest of nature.[749]

Each part of a healthy functioning system acts in a way that contributes to the health and robustness of the whole. We can liken this to the organs of a body. Each organ has a different function, but ultimately, they all work for the health of the whole. If this were not the case, the whole system would

---

744 Ernst Bloch, *Le Principe ésperance*, Gallimard, vol. 1, Paris, 1976, p. 240, cited in: Tanuro, *L'Impossible le Capitalism vert*, p. 26.
745 Boyd, *The Rights of Nature*, p. XXXV.
746 Bennett, *Change Everything*, p. 55.
747 See 1.1.1
748 Capra – Mattei, *The Ecology of Law*, pp. 23–4.
749 John Borrows, 'With or Without You: First Nations Law (in Canada)', *McGill Law Journal*, Vol. 41, No. 3, 1996, pp. 651–2, cited in: Collins, *The Ecological Constitution*, p. 65.

begin to break down, with negative consequences for all its constituent parts, just as if one organ were to lose its function, the other organs would be affected. In this sense, self-regulation is a fundamental component of every organism or community of organisms. Any organism or community that fails to self-regulate in a way that enables its parts or members to act in the interest of the whole will eventually break down. That also means that a healthy self-regulating system must have a feedback mechanism that enables it to recognise and correct processes that harm the whole.[750] Indeed, when all parts of an ecosystem are considered parts of a larger whole, they are interconnected through a complex arrangement of self-regulating loops, feedback, and connections between different parts of the food chain.[751]

This logic inspired the British scientist James Lovelock to think about how the Earth functions. His Gaia theory emerged simultaneously with the human journey into space. That was because space travel has led to changes in our view of our planet. They provided information about the atmosphere and the Earth's surface, leading to a new understanding of the relationships between the organic and inorganic elements that inhabit it. From this, Lovelock developed the hypothesis that the Earth's organic material, the air, the oceans, and the soil form a complex system that can be perceived as a single organism and has the power to preserve the planet's vital qualities.[752] In his book, Gaia: A New Look at Life on Earth, Lovelock uses the term Gaia to refer to the biosphere as a self-organising entity with the capacity to maintain the health of our planet by controlling the chemical and physical environment.[753] Claiming that the atmosphere is not just a biological product but also a biological structure, Lovelock likened it to a cat's fur or a bird's feathers and argued that the elements that make up the biosphere function like the homeostasis found in animals, trying to keep the physical and chemical environment in optimal balance for the continuation of life on the planet.[754]

---

750 Cullinan, *Wild Law*, p. 81.
751 Ponting, *A New Green History …*, p. 14.
752 James Lovelock, *La Terre est un Être Vivant – L'Hypothèse Gaïa*, Flammarion, Paris, 1993, p. 16.
753 Lovelock, *La Terre …*, p. 19.
754 Lovelock, *La Terre …*, pp. 30–2.

Similarly, ecologists define ecosystems as communities of plants, animals, and microorganisms linked by nutritional relationships. Thus, they have developed the concept of webs of life. Food webs are networks of organisms; organisms are networks of cells, and cells are networks of molecules. So, wherever there is life, there are networks. The network has, therefore, become the key metaphor of our time, just as the machine was the key metaphor for three centuries after Descartes and Newton. However, the two are diametrically opposed because, in machine logic, it is thought that the whole can be understood when the parts are considered separately. In contrast, networks can only be understood by examining connections or relationships. This difference represents a shift from mechanistic thinking to systems thinking. In recent years, the concept of networks has become increasingly prominent in ecology, and ecosystems have begun to be seen as networks that can be understood only holistically.[755]

If we take climate science seriously and look at where the world is today, it becomes clear that this network logic of ecology must be applied to law in order to put the Earth on a path of climate stabilisation. The law must stop treating human beings, who are only a part of nature, as a separate, superior, and the only subject with rights and transform into a discipline that takes into account the other elements of the network in which humans are embedded and regulates the relations between these elements from an egalitarian perspective. If we want to stop climate change, there is no other alternative.[756]

Recent scientific discoveries, especially in ecology and climate science, show that the way to overcome the global climate crisis is to understand the ecological principles that have evolved over billions of years in ecosystems to sustain the food chain as laws that govern human behaviour.[757] Under ordinary circumstances, lawmakers should do this. The scientific data is now conclusive, and politicians must follow it if they sincerely want to protect us and the ecosystem. However, even though they admit that 'the planet is in danger', they are not showing the leadership to change the course.[758] Therefore, neither in the field of law and judicial systems nor in the public's understanding of law has there yet been a paradigm shift equivalent to that

---

755 Capra – Mattei, *The Ecology of Law*, p. 112.

756 Chomsky – Pollin, *Climate Crisis* ..., p. 180. For a critique of the application of the concept of equality to the non-human world, see Bookchin, *The Ecology of Freedom*, pp. 59–60.

757 Capra – Mattei, *The Ecology of Law*, p. 39.

758 Hansen, 'Game Over for the Climate'.

of science. Such a paradigm shift is urgently needed as the major problems of this era now permeate every corner of the globe, and the current global crisis is an ecological crisis in the broadest sense of the word.[759]

Of course, a person who does not want to give up their present way of life might argue that

> if the Earth is a natural system that is functioning in a healthy way, then we do not need to worry, because balance or 'homeostasis' will be restored over time, as our poor 'management' of the planet will lead to either our own extinction or a drastic reduction in our numbers'.

Yes, there is such an option. Still, rather than this long-term correction that will lead to our extinction along with the entire ecosystem, we are smart enough to organise our law so that it is unnecessary.[760] Instead of making up stories that we are unique on Earth or can control the ecosystem, we need to use our intellect to understand how nature works and set up constitutional rules to regulate human behaviour accordingly. In short, we must bring climate science to the very centre of our modern political and legal systems: constitutional law.[761]

The ecological legal order that will emerge when we do so will be closely tied to the science that deals with the functioning of the Earth and the complex systemic boundaries of the global ecosystem and will, therefore, organise legal principles in the light of the scientific laws of ecology. However, science alone will not determine the components of this order. Beyond science, ecological law will emerge from a normative preference for governing human behaviour to preserve ecological integrity and improve human-Earth relations in ways consistent with the conditions under which ecology, thermodynamics, and other sciences are applied.[762]

---

759 Capra – Mattei, *The Ecology of Law*, p. 10.

760 Cullinan, *Wild Law*, p. 81.

761 The first known call in this direction was made in 1936 by scientist W. P. Taylor in an article published in the journal *Ecology*. Taylor called for the drafting of an ecological constitution and suggested that the preamble 'declare the interdependence between plants, animals and their environment', cited in: Collins, *The Ecological Constitution*, p. X (foreword by David R. Boyd).

762 Geoffrey Garver, *Ecological Law and The Planetary Crisis: A Legal Guide for Harmony on Earth*, Routledge, London, 2020, p. 95, cited in: Collins, *The Ecological Constitution*, p. 7.

3.1.2 Evolution of 'environmental' sensitivity into a nature-centred demand for law

The conflicts and contradictions between environmental values and industrial and technological progress have created an awareness in societies. This situation has brought new demands to the agenda in social segments. However, the fact that the environment is polluted mainly by economic forces or public institutions reveals the difficulty of finding a solution on an individual scale. Individuals, groups, and communities can only fight for solutions with the tools they have.[763] However, these are usually far from finding lasting solutions for a problem of such magnitude as climate change.

Appropriate solutions to the problems of climate change cannot be found simply by creating a new environmental law within the current system. We need a new perspective, not more laws. If the current political structures and economic conditions remain the same, our wasteful and energy-demanding social order, which is anti-ecological and unjust, will remain as it is.[764] Therefore, if we want to stop climate change, we need to establish a legal system dominated by a nature-centred constitutional perspective and regulate current political structures and the functioning of the economy. The entire legal system, as well as our institutional structures and societies, must be based on and reflect nature-centred legal theory.[765] Any realistic hope for the future of humanity lies in rebuilding society as a whole and thus redefining the relationship between humans and the rest of the world.[766]

Even a report by the UN Environment Program states that *urgent action at an unprecedented level is necessary to arrest and reverse this situation (climate change), thereby protecting human and environmental health and maintaining the current and future integrity of global ecosystems*.[767] Likewise, the UN Food and Agriculture Organization has published a report stating that *ultimately, we need to foster a new relationship with nature*.[768]

---

[763] İbrahim Ö. Kaboğlu – Nihan Yancı Özalp, *Çevre Hakkı*, Tekin, İstanbul, 2021, pp. 37–8.

[764] Tokar, *Toward Climate Justice*, Foreword (Loc. 41).

[765] Cullinan, *Wild Law*, p. 177.

[766] Foster, *Capitalism in the Anthropocene*, p. 22.

[767] UNEP, *Global Environmental Outlook: GEO6 – Summary for Policymakers*, 2019, p. 4.

[768] FAO, *The State of the World's Forests: Forests, Biodiversity and People*, 2020, p. vii.

The clouds of uncertainty that hover over us today about climate change are not reflections of our collective ignorance of the natural world but our blindness about the human world, and they can only be dissipated by our actions. Our actions, not systems beyond our control, will determine the future climate. If we allow global warming to continue, it will be because we have chosen this outcome, knowingly and willingly walking down a path of collective suicide. If we decide to stop climate change, it will be because we have chosen to walk and exist on a different path.[769] For this, we must first create a global ecological movement that can outline an ecological society, fight for its realisation,[770] and then use it to transform our legal systems.

In order to rediscover the law of the Earth and appropriately translate it into our contemporary law, it is essential to start by looking at the fundamental laws and principles of the universe because they provide the ultimate framework within which any human legal framework must be situated. For the most practical reasons, this means understanding the functioning of nature on Earth.[771] It is important to remember that the ultimate lawgiver is the universe.[772] It is a delusion to believe that our intelligence, which we think is unique, can free us from the universal application of nature's laws. We govern ourselves as if the fundamental laws of physics that govern the planet and apply to millions of other species do not apply to *Homo Sapiens*. However, there are no loopholes in the laws of thermodynamics. Humanity cannot interrupt natural global cycles without suffering the consequences.[773]

A transformational change that begins with this reality in mind requires rethinking the goals of society, what makes us happy and what it means to live a good life, how we produce and use energy, the food we eat and how we produce it, how we produce goods, how we design our cities, and how we reduce and eliminate waste.[774] These are all subject to legal regulation and constitutional limitations. Through constitutions and supreme courts, we

---

769 Wallace-Wells, *The Uninhabitable Earth*, pp. 241–2.
770 Tokar, *Toward Climate Justice*, Foreword (Loc. 47).
771 Cullinan, *Wild Law*, p. 78.
772 Thomas Berry, *The Great Work: Our Way Into the Future*, Bell Tower, New York, 1999, cited in: Cullinan, *Wild Law*, p. 82.
773 Collins, *The Ecological Constitution*, p. X (foreword by David R. Boyd).
774 Boyd, *Report of… (A/75/161)*, p. 10, § 29.

can reorganise all of these to be in line with the laws of nature. When we do that, we can achieve sustainable societies and stop climate change.

The most critical solution to the rapid descent into ultimate disorder is to let community networks restore law and rebuild harmony between human-made laws and the laws of nature.[775] Bringing the understanding of life through systems to the social sphere means applying our knowledge of life's basic organising patterns and principles, especially our understanding of living networks, to social reality.[776] An ecological understanding of law thus has the potential to transform human behaviour by aligning legal systems with the fundamental laws of life on Earth.[777] In this framework, green constitutionalism represents an approach to harmonising human societies with nature through constitutional principles. These principles can be implemented through their incorporation into constitutional texts or through the teleological and/or dynamic reinterpretation of existing constitutional provisions.

Nature, which is usually thought of only in terms of what it 'supplies' or 'provides' to us, is now legally entitled to be thought of 'on its own'. This unique ecosystem, which existed before the emergence of *Homo Sapiens* and which enables us to exist, cannot be seen simply as a resource. Accordingly, our constitutional order must also give nature the value it deserves. However, even the mass extinction of animals and plants is almost always evaluated in terms of its negative impact on human life. This should be recognised as a catastrophe *in itself*,[778] and our legal order should be equipped with the necessary measures to prevent it.

Today, an understanding of the law that says and even dictates that only human beings are subjects of rights and everything else in nature is just an object dominates our minds. Humans can legally objectify and exploit other natural beings by exercising their rights. An ecological understanding of law requires an end to this legal exploitation within the framework of constitutional principles. Just as Rosa Parks, in her time, chose disobedience to

---

[775] Laura Nader, *The Life of the Law: Anthropological Projects*, University of California Press, Berkeley, 2005, cited in: Capra – Mattei, *The Ecology of Law*, p. 145.

[776] Capra – Mattei, *The Ecology of Law*, p. 115.

[777] Collins, *The Ecological Constitution*, p. 8.

[778] Barrau, *Le Plus Grand …*, pp. 79–80. (Emphasis is Barrau's.)

change the distinction between legal and illegal,[779] we need similar resistance to ensure that laws and practices that support the extraction and exploitation of natural resources cease to be legal and become illegal.[780] In this way, it will be possible for society to come to the conclusion that some legally protected rights are, in fact, for the benefit of neither society nor the ecosystem that sustains us, and over time, they will be recognised as crimes. This transformation must also be supported from the very top of the law. High courts should reflect this moral transformation in their decisions and apply it in the cases that come before them, evolving it into the principles of green constitutionalism. For this to happen, Supreme Court judges must become 'eco-literate' as quickly as possible.[781]

Ecological literacy or eco-literacy is the knowledge of ecological principles. The survival of humanity in the coming decades depends on politicians, business leaders, and professionals in almost every field – but especially in the judiciary – being eco-literate. A knowledge of nature-centred, not anthropocentric, ecology should be the centrepiece of education at all levels, including graduate education and professional awareness raising. Our children, students, political leaders, and corporate managers must understand the basic facts of life.[782] In this way, there will be an easier and faster social acceptance of the fact that green constitutionalism is not a means of limitation or repression than today but rather a legal way to defend all life on Earth – including ours – against the existential crisis caused by the current constitutional order.

---

[779] On 1 December 1955, a black woman, Rosa Parks, sat in a seat reserved for whites on a city bus in Montgomery, Alabama, USA, in violation of the racial segregation rules in force, and refused to give her seat to a white man. The black boycott of public transportation initiated by Martin Luther King following her arrest, which continued for over a year, severely affected the municipal public transportation system, as 70 per cent of the city's population was black. In 1956, the US Supreme Court struck down the racial segregation law on the grounds that it violated the principle of equality of citizens in the US Constitution. See '1 December 1955: Rosa Parks Ignites Bus Boycott', *History*.

[780] Ugo Mattei – Laura Nader, *Plunder: When the Rule of Law Is Illegal*, Blackwell, Malden, Massachusetts, 2008, cited in: Capra – Mattei, *The Ecology of Law*, p. 188.

[781] Ecuador is a good example in this regard. See 6.3.4

[782] Capra – Mattei, *The Ecology of Law*, p p. 188–9.

3.2 Philosophical foundations of a nature-centred legal system

Moving from an anthropocentric legal system to a nature-centred one requires, first and foremost, a paradigm shift in the relationship between humans and the Earth. Our current law focuses on a single species: the human being. However, we are not the only ones on this planet; we are only a part of it and owe our existence to it.[783] Since nothing can exist on its own, individualism, one of the dominant principles of modern thinking, is an illusion. Life on this planet is a spiral of intertwined relationships.[784] Nevertheless, in modern times, dualism and individualism have suppressed and forgotten this ancient knowledge. Due to today's dominant cultures' resilient and overwhelming progress, much of the wisdom of the Indigenous communities that organised themselves according to this and similar ancient knowledge has already been lost or is rapidly disappearing.[785] However, we are still aware of some examples to guide us. Their outlook on life, the scientific facts that climate change teaches and reminds us of, and some philosophical ideas emerging from technological advances constitute the foundations of green constitutionalism. The following is naturally open to discussion and not limited to those listed here, but they can be considered a starting point.

3.2.1 Recalling the pre-capitalist ethics of nature

Before the humanist and modern approach became dominant, we respected and lived according to the relations between humans and other natural beings, as well as between natural beings themselves. Today, when we say that we must redesign our legal system according to these natural relations, we are actually talking about recalling and adapting this old order to the present. For this reason, Passmore argues that while the call for a 'new set of moral principles' is not entirely wrong, what is needed is not so much a 'new ethic' as 'the adoption of a well-known (old) ethic'.[786]

We need a new narrative, and the roots of this narrative go back to pre-bourgeoisie legal systems. The governance systems that humanity practiced in

[783] Cullinan, *Wild Law*, p. 126.
[784] Hickel, *Less is More*, p. 280.
[785] Cullinan, *Wild Law*, p. 88.
[786] John Arthur Passmore, *Man's Responsibility for Nature: Ecological Problems and Western Traditions*, Scribner, 1974, § 186–7, cited in: DesJardins, *Environmental Ethics*, p. 206.

harmony with nature up to three centuries ago need to be recalled and used as inspiration and a basis for our new legal systems. The nature-compatible lifestyles of Indigenous peoples should guide us in this regard. We can learn important principles and techniques from their lifestyles that will be useful for developing more nature-centred governance systems for today.[787] For example, the cosmology of the Tucano Indigenous peoples of the Colombian Amazon can be considered particularly illuminating in establishing the philosophical foundations of green constitutionalism. That is because, unlike the cosmology of today's dominant cultures, the Tucano Indians see each individual as part of a universal web of relationships. Maintaining ecological balance is of paramount importance. Each individual knows that they must act in cooperation with all components of nature. According to the Tucano understanding, the Earth has finite energy that constantly flows between people, society, animals, and plants. Humans can use the energy in animals and plants (for example, by eating them), but they should only use as much as they need. Great care is taken to ensure the energy flow is not blocked or imbalanced.[788]

A study has found that Indigenous communities in the Amazon protect nature and prevent disease, saving billions of dollars in health costs simply by maintaining their existing way of life and protecting their forests from wildfires – often started by land looters and cattle ranchers. According to the study based on decades of work, protected Indigenous reserves in the Amazon rainforest absorb pollution in the air each year, preventing around 15 million respiratory and heart disease cases and saving 2 billion dollars in health care costs.[789] This reveals that, unlike modern medicine, a lifestyle that prevents diseases from the very beginning rather than treating them is a much better method for our health.

As another example of Indigenous wisdom, every year since 1854, the Menominee tribe in Wisconsin, USA, has produced around 6 million cubic metres of timber from the Menominee forest, from which it makes its living.

---

[787] Cullinan, *Wild Law*, p. 88.

[788] Cullinan, *Wild Law*, p. 91.

[789] Paula R. Prist – Florencia Sangermano – Allison Bailey et al., 'Protecting Brazilian Amazon Indigenous Territories Reduces Atmospheric Particulates and Avoids Associated Health Impacts and Costs', *Communications Earth & Environment*, Vol. 4, Paper No. 34, 2023.

Yet, although its boundaries have not changed, there are more trees in the forest now than there were a 100 years ago. Some of them are 200 years old. What enables the Menominee tribe to do this is to do the opposite of what is done in commercial forestry: putting the well-being of the forest and its people ahead of profits. They do this by cutting down sick or dying trees, harvesting trees that have naturally fallen to the ground, and leaving healthy trees to grow and reproduce. Some say this is the first sustainable forest in the US.[790]

These examples could be multiplied, showing that a social and legal order in harmony with nature is possible. Ecological orders that are in harmony with the ecosystem and do not rely on growth and exploitation are social structures that our ancestors accepted, and we can still find examples that work well today. The unsustainable system we live in today is only an anomaly that we have culturally developed at a particular time in history and can dismantle.

The laws of Indigenous communities are never 'manufactured' laws like ours; they are always 'acquired' laws. They are never the product of committees of living people; they are always the product of social evolution. They are shaped the way a bird's beak or a mole's claw is shaped; that is, in a way that works. They never reflect a tribe's concerns about what is 'right', 'good', or 'just'; they simply work for that tribe.[791] Since they work, they become rules and constitute law.

Today, we have not only forgotten how to live in harmony with the planet's rhythms, but we have also forgotten that doing so was once the primary purpose of human regulatory systems. It is likely that all human societies once organised themselves to ensure that their members lived in harmony with the requirements of the ecological community. That was seen as essential for the health of human society. Unfortunately, the traditional laws and practices of those Indigenous peoples who made it a priority to maintain a mutually enhancing relationship with their habitat have had almost no impact on the governance systems of the cultures that have become dominant today.[792]

---

790 Cara Buckley – Jamie Kelter Davis, 'The Giving Forest', *New York Times*, 22 April 2023.
791 Daniel Quinn, *The Story of B*, Bantam, 1997, p. 314, cited in: Cullinan, *Wild Law*, p. 93.
792 Cullinan, *Wild Law*, p. 68.

On the contrary, our legal systems today are built on rejecting these ancient legal systems in harmony with nature.

Since modernity created the accumulative orientation of the Industrial Age and the mentality of appropriating natural resources, and since the same mentality is at the root of today's global ecological, social, and economic crisis, both scientists and lawyers must take some responsibility for the current state of the world.[793] Mechanistic science, which creates a dichotomy between man and nature and rejects the networked structure of the ecosystem, and legal thinkers who turn this logic into a tool for exploiting natural assets are the main culprits for the existential crisis we are in today. For centuries, we have eagerly constructed an illusory 'human world' separate from the real universe. We have rejected the biosphere into which we were born and constructed a pervasive and tightly closed 'human-specific' world in our minds. We have lived in this fabricated 'homosphere' for so long and breathed in the myths of human superiority so much that the idea now seems more real to us than the Earth itself.[794] It is now time to wake up from this dream and organise ourselves appropriately to our place in the ecosystem. The reality of climate change necessitates it. We need to restructure our law not on artificial superiority but on the awareness that we are part of the ecosystem. The way to do this is by developing green constitutionalism, which limits the harmful practices of modernism and capitalism, cutting us off from nature.

Climate change is a reminder that many of the ideas cherished by Western culture are no longer viable. As Klein puts it, these are profoundly challenging moments of enlightenment for all of humanity, raised on the progressive ideals of the Age of Enlightenment, not accustomed to having their desires and ambitions constrained by natural limits.[795] If our effort is to save these ideas and industrial civilisation in its present form, there is no point and no chance of success. The goal should not be to save an already highly damaged and openly violent order.[796] The goal should be to establish a sustainable legal system that is in harmony with the ecosystem and recognises the rights of nonhuman species and natural beings. The primary role of such a theory of

---

793 Capra – Mattei, *The Ecology of Law*, pp. 9–10.
794 Cullinan, *Wild Law*, p. 51.
795 Klein, *On Fire*, p. 103.
796 Barrau, *Le Plus Grand* ..., pp. 98–9.

law is to provide a philosophical foundation to guide the development and implementation of this system of governance.[797] To do this, we must first abandon some of the fundamental beliefs and mythologies that are so dear to the cultures that dominate world society today. In particular, we must put aside our dualistic perception that separates humans and nature and recognise that every element of our well-being derives from the Earth. We will not be able to stop climate change until we design a nature-centred legal theory and a constitutional system that will enable us to once again recognise our rightful place on Earth as a component of the ecosystem.[798]

Many Indigenous tribes, such as the Tucanos, are keenly aware of the need to harmonise their social practices with the natural world rather than changing it to suit themselves. They also place great importance on respecting the other elements in their environment (especially the animals they hunt for food) and not creating waste or excess, emphasising the importance of reciprocity and the need to maintain a dynamic balance in the universe, where every give requires a take.[799] So, they have a culture but did not create it; they acquired it from nature. Rather than devising a dichotomy between themselves and nature, they have shaped their culture according to the rules of nature and thus united the two. Donna Haraway calls this 'nature–culture', stating that biophysical and social relations cannot be separated. Similarly, Val Plumwood argues that it is necessary to resist the culture–nature divide that leads us to see humans as entirely separate from all other creatures. In this sense, the 'nature–culture' approach proposes unity rather than opposition. Therefore, imagining what a 'nature–culture' might look like and focusing on the myriad interactions between humans and nature can be an essential springboard for transforming our current legal order.[800]

Remembering where we come from and who we are is necessary to reclaim our lost role in the Earth's ecosystem and develop a vision of what we can become.[801] It is not easy to abandon modern myths and look at everything from an old but new perspective. In this process, we must never forget that

---

797 Cullinan, *Wild Law*, p. 111.
798 Cullinan, *Wild Law*, p. 170.
799 Cullinan, *Wild Law*, pp. 92–3.
800 Arık, 'Bir Arada … ', p. 462.
801 Cullinan, *Wild Law*, p. 94.

we are facing a crisis of civilisation that requires a radical change.[802] Scientific research proving that man has been pushing the limits of nature too far for too long is pushing us to take measures that may seem radical today but are, in fact, natural. We cannot solve the problem of climate change with market-oriented environmentalist 'green' products or with environmental protection clauses in constitutions and environmental laws that operate on a 'polluter pays' logic. Rather than adopting the idea that humans can dominate nature, we need a new model of civilisation that allows nature to repair itself, respects the natural repair cycle, and is seriously sensitive to natural boundaries.[803] We should not even call this a 'new model of civilisation' since what needs to be done is to recall and adapt a civilisation that integrates with and respects nature. That was the reality of all societies before capitalism, and we still observe it in contemporary Indigenous peoples. For this, modernism and the capitalist economy, which have forced us out of a way of life in harmony with nature, must be overcome through green constitutional principles.

3.2.2 The telos of green constitutionalism

There is a critical issue to consider in identifying and applying the principles of green constitutionalism: What we must do is not develop and disseminate human legal theory so that it becomes a legal theory that serves all members of the ecosystem. That would mean humans philosophising and regulating on behalf of all other ecosystem members, which would be a kind of 'neo-colonialism'. Instead, we must appreciate that human legal theory and governance are part of a broader Earth self-governance and develop a better understanding of the need to limit its scope and respect other governance systems.[804] In other words, instead of trying to set rules 'for nature', we need to rebuild our legal systems in a way that respects the ecosystem and recognises that we are part of nature.

Because of what we have done and not done in the past and today, we can already accept that our civilisation based on today's philosophical assumptions is already gone. Therefore, in this process that Scranton describes as 'learning to die as a civilisation', we need to get rid of this way of life and the concepts

802 Löwy, *Ecosocialism*, What Is Ecosocialism (Loc. 175).
803 Klein, *On Fire*, p. 103.
804 Cullinan, *Wild Law*, p. 105.

such as identity, freedom, success, and progress that it imposes.[805] We do not need more laws within the current legal system; we need a 'different perspective' so that no area of the legal system is exempt. The ecological approach that brings this different perspective to law is based on nature-centredness, holism, and intergenerational and interspecies justice. According to this point of view, the law would recognise ecological interdependence and no longer take the side of humans against nature or individual rights against collective responsibilities. Fundamentally, ecological law internalises the natural conditions of human existence and makes them the basis of all law, including constitutions, human rights, property rights, corporate rights, and state sovereignty.[806]

An ecological theory of law is concerned with maintaining and strengthening relationships not only between humans but between all members of the ecosystem. In this context, it is often unhelpful to think in terms of a strict distinction between right and wrong, especially when that distinction is based on rigid standards set by humans alone. If our goal is to preserve the integrity of the Earth's ecosystem, it is more beneficial to broaden the scope to the question of 'whether an action enhances the integrity and health of the whole system and the quality or intimacy of the relationships between its components'.[807] Thus, in a legal system built from a green constitutionalist perspective, the legality of an action would be determined by whether it is beneficial for the holistic health of the ecosystem.

This approach is similar to Aldo Leopold's famous 'land ethics'. According to this approach, something is right if it aims to preserve the integrity, stability, and beauty of the biotic community. If it aims otherwise, it is wrong.[808] In a legal system consistent with this ethic, the following basic principles proposed by Thomas Berry[809] should be constitutionally and legally recognised:

---

805 Scranton, *Learning to Die*, pp. 17–18.

806 Ecological Law and Governance Association, 'Oslo Manifesto for Ecological Law and Governance', Article 5.

807 Cullinan, *Wild Law*, p. 114.

808 Aldo Leopold, *A Sand County Almanac* (Turkish version), trans. Ufuk Özdağ, Hacettepe University Press, Ankara, 2013, pp. 234–5.

809 Thomas Berry, 'Rights of the Earth: We Need a New Legal Framework Which Recognises the Rights of All Living Beings', *in* Peter Burdon (ed.), *Exploring Wild Law: The Philosophy of Earth Jurisprudence*, Wakefield Press, Kent Town, 2011, p. 229, cited in: Collins, *The Ecological Constitution*, p. 66.

1. The natural world on planet Earth has inherent rights. These rights arise from the same source from which humans derive their rights: from the universe that brought them into existence.
2. Each component of the Earth's ecosystem has three rights: the right to be, the right to habitat, and the right to fulfil its role in the ever-renewing processes of the Earth's ecosystem.
3. All rights are exclusive and limited. Rivers have river rights. Birds have bird rights. Insects have insect rights. Humans have human rights. The difference in rights is qualitative, not quantitative. The rights of an insect may have no value for a tree or a fish.

From the perspective of these principles, there is nothing necessarily immoral in taking produce from the field, cutting down trees, or even hunting and eating animals. What is immoral is when we do so without gratitude and reciprocity, taking more than we need and more than we give back.[810] Accordingly, in a legal system founded on a land ethic, exploitation, unnecessary extraction, and waste would become illegal.

Green constitutionalism takes into account the central importance of balance in the natural world. As Cullinan describes it, an ecological legal order,

> [...] must take account of the central importance of balance in the natural world. Not the stasis of the weights in each pan of the scales of justice, but the ever-changing flux and 'creative disequilibrium' of the universe: always moving, always changing, but never moving in one direction for long without swirling back to seek equilibrium or re-establish the pattern again. As the symbol of Yin and Yang graphically demonstrates, as Yin waxes, so Yang must wane, until the reverse occurs, but all the while the cycles of response and counter-response maintain the whole.[811]

However, our current legal system is shaped around a philosophy based not on the cycles of nature, but on the human ambition always to move forward. Consequently, the gap between humanity's 'ecological footprint' and the Earth's capacity to sustain life is rapidly widening. Therefore, it has become clear that understanding and living according to basic ecological principles is critical to our survival on the planet.[812] The way to build such a life following these principles is through a constitutional order built on these principles.

---

[810] Hickel, *Less is More*, p. 281.
[811] Cullinan, *Wild Law*, p. 115.
[812] Capra – Mattei, *The Ecology of Law*, p. 187.

3.2.3 Posthumanism

As emphasised earlier, the roots of climate change go back to Enlightenment philosophy and humanism. The capitalist economic order established by the bourgeoisie, which uses the humanist idea that separates man from nature and gives only him rights to commodify nature, has brought the entire ecosystem to the brink of collapse. If we want to stop this collapse, the task before us is to devise a new imagination of who we are. We must create a new humanism, a fresh humanism informed by the humanities and infused with philosophy.[813] One of these movements is the system of thought known as posthumanism. Posthumanism is a post-Enlightenment ideological move to question humanist, anthropocentric, and dualist ideas entangled with the idea of human exceptionalism.[814]

In mainstream culture, debates about posthumanism have centred on human enhancement. In academia, too, posthumanism generates both enthusiasm and anxiety about the possibility of a serious displacement of the human being who was once the measure of all things.[815] However, most of these concerns are unfounded since the 'post' in posthumanism is not only about the present and the future but also about the past, Indigenous worldviews, and traditional ecological knowledge. Therefore, Indigenous peoples' knowledge and ways of knowing should not be overlooked when considering the relationship between posthumanism and ecology.[816]

The philosopher and critic Rosi Braidotti, who has stated that humanism has a Eurocentric essence and imperialist tendencies, openly expresses her opposition to this system of thought for political and philosophical reasons.[817] Stating that the common denominator of the posthumanist position is the assumption that living matter itself is vital and self-organising, but at the same time not naturalistic, Braidotti claims that the starting point of the theory

---

813 Scranton, *Learning to Die*, p. 14.

814 Çağdaş Dedeoğlu, 'Posthümanizm: Ekoloji İlişkisinin Sürdürülebilirlik Çerçevesinde Bir Değerlendirmesi', *in* Didem Bayındır – Mine Yıldırım (ed.), *Ekoloji: Bir Arada Yaşamın Geleceği*, Tellekt, Istanbul, 2022, p. 256; Çiğdem Öztürk, 'Savaşın Yuttuğu Hayvanlar', p. 256.

815 Jürgen Habermas, *The Future of Human Nature*, Polity Press, Cambridge, 2003, cited in: Rosi Braidotti, *The Posthuman* (Turkish version), trans. Öznur Karakaş, 3rd ed., Kolektif Kitap, Istanbul, 2021, p. 12.

816 Dedeoğlu, 'Posthümanizm', p. 271.

817 Braidotti, *The Posthuman*, p. 29.

is the nature–culture continuum. According to the author, this continuum departs from the hitherto widely accepted scientific paradigm based on the categorical distinction between the given (nature) and the constructed (culture). Braidotti believes that the approach based on the opposition between nature and culture has now been replaced by a non-dualistic understanding of the interaction between nature and culture, driven by scientific and technological advances,[818] thus proposing to move beyond the humanist perspective and abandon the anthropocentric worldview. The author argues for the necessity of a new understanding of ethics in posthumanist approaches while presenting a political discourse that embraces ecological sensitivity and feminist understanding. By closely reading the processes and technology that historically construct the subject that corresponds to Anthropos and subvert nature, Braidotti criticises the humanist view that sanctifies man.[819]

In posthumanism, agency is not only attributed to the so-called privileged human subject, and nature is not considered a passive background dominated by humans. On the contrary, it is possible to speak of a layered and complex ecosystem in which human and nonhuman subjects are indispensable parts of nature. Therefore, reconstructing the standard reference for human beings, breaking the immunity attributed to the human species, and recognising that nature is a common place for everyone and every living thing is considerable that ecocriticism puts at its centre.[820] Indeed, the posthumanist perspective plays a vital role in efforts to break the monopoly of human beings as the subject of rights in modern law. Such an explicit criticism of human beings' unique, privileged, and inviolable position creates a basis for recognising the subjectivity of the rights of animals and other natural beings.

Christopher Stone similarly suggests that rather than drawing boundaries on what is and is not permissible in our relationship with what he calls 'nonhumans', we should incorporate norms into our legal system that seek to understand the essence. For example, rather than using standards such as particles per million or the transparency index for pollution spilled into

---

818 Braidotti, *The Posthuman*, pp. 12–13.
819 Gündoğan İbrişim, 'Ekolojinin Yazısı: Edebiyat', p. 435.
820 Gündoğan İbrişim, 'Ekolojinin Yazısı: Edebiyat', p. 436.

a river, the author argues that we should examine whether the 'riverness' of the river is jeopardised by the action.[821]

Surprisingly, US environmental law already contains some solutions that are close to what is needed to implement this approach. The Marine Mammal Protection Act provides that human actions, such as fishing, can intervene for conservation purposes if they threaten the 'optimum sustainable population' of an endangered marine mammal, such as the porpoise, a member of the dolphin family, in a particular habitat. That means the porpoise is protected simply because it is a porpoise and has the right to persist, not for any other reason. Indeed, the courts have interpreted this regulation to mean that once the species is no longer able to sustain its population, 'balancing the interests of the commercial fishing fleet and the pigfish is irrelevant, and the pigfish must be prioritised'.[822] This perspective can be taken as a sign that posthumanist (and postcapitalist) ideas are becoming influential, and the paradigm of rights subjectivity is changing. It seems that the transformation from a legal system in which only human beings are subjects to a nature-centred legal system has already begun. It is now time to try to identify the key criteria of green constitutionalism that will institutionalise this transformation.

---

821 Christopher Stone, *Earth and Other Ethics: The Case for Moral Pluralism*, Harper and Row, New York, 1987, p. 60, cited in: Cullinan, *Wild Law*, p. 113.

822 *Committee for Humane Legislation v Richardson*, 540 F.2d 1141, 1151, n.39 (C.A. D.C. 1976), cited in: Christopher Stone, *Earth and Other Ethics: The Case for Moral Pluralism*, Harper and Row, New York, 1987, p. 60, cited in: Cullinan, *Wild Law*, p. 113.

Key criteria of green constitutionalism

> Sometimes scientific evidence conflicts with the dominant world view of civilisation. When that happens, we have to make a choice. Either we ignore science, or we change our world view.[823]

Alternative solutions to climate change range from relatively trivial ones, such as replacing light bulbs with more energy-efficient ones, to highly dangerous technical patches, such as nuclear power or pumping particles into the atmosphere to block the sun's rays. Yet, few consider the systemic problems underlying the problem, and even fewer point to the need for a societal total ecological transformation.[824] However, due to the increasing impact of climate change, more and more people are recognising this need (and even necessity), and the ecological law is transforming from a marginal idea to a popular one.

The ecological law movement has recently emerged as an alternative to conventional environmental law, proposing a paradigm shift for a comprehensive reconstruction of the human relationship with the Earth. Similar to the legal system of Indigenous peoples, ecological law is rooted in the idea of fundamentally recognising that 'in essence, human society is a subset of the ecosphere'.[825] Therefore, ecological law is an alternative to, rather than

---

823 Hickel, *Less is More*, p. 28.

824 Tokar, *Toward Climate Justice*, Global Warming and the Struggle for Justice (Loc. 284).

825 John Borrows, 'Living between Water and Rocks: First Nations, Environmental Planning and Democracy', *UTLJ*, 47:4, 1997, p. 417, cited in: Collins, *The Ecological Constitution*, p. 4.

a reform of, existing systems.[826] That is entirely rational since it is based on fundamentally different foundations than the humanist ideas and capitalist economic system that underpin modern law.

Whereas in our current legal systems, the fundamental rights of human beings are rooted in the human-made understanding of natural law (and for some reason, in that 'world of ideas', only human beings have rights, not living or non-living beings), in ecological law the fundamental 'Earth rights' of all members of the ecosystem originate from the universe.[827] In other words, rights do not originate from an artificial theory such as natural or anthropogenic laws such as positive law.[828] Rights are rooted in the mere existence of that member of the ecosystem and the value and meaningfulness of that existence for the ecosystem.[829]

As mentioned earlier, social orders with this perspective are not new. For most of history, people have not seen a fundamental separation between themselves and the rest of the world. Rather, they recognised a deep interconnectedness with rivers, forests, animals, plants, and even the planet itself. They saw them as sentient beings, like humans, animated by the same spirit. In some cases, they even recognised them as relatives.[830] They determined their social rules inspired by nature and in accordance with it because they knew that the way to survive was to follow the rules of the Earth. As a matter of fact, for hundreds of thousands of years, they did not make any impact that would upset the balance of the ecosystem.

If we want to stop climate change and restore balance to the ecosystem, we must reshape our legal system based on nature, as ancient societies and Indigenous peoples did. This new legal perspective, called 'world system law' by

---

[826] Collins, *The Ecological Constitution*, p. 4.

[827] Cullinan, *Wild Law*, p. 118.

[828] Legal positivism rejects the idea that legal rights can exist before any form of legislation. See Ronald Dworkin, *Taking Rights Seriously* (Turkish version), trans. Ahmet Ulvi Türkbağ, Dost, Ankara, 2007, pp. 14, 40–6.

[829] At this point, ecological legal theory and green constitutionalism, as a manifestation of it, are closely related to object-oriented ontology. This ontology claims that objects exist autonomously and interact with each other in a way that is irreducible to human consciousness and opposes any kind of thought that interferes with the legitimacy of their existence. See Graham Harman, *Object-Oriented Ontology: A New Theory of Everything* (Turkish version), trans. Oğuz Karayemiş, Tellekt, Istanbul, 2020.

[830] Hickel, *Less is More*, p. 32.

Kotzé and Kim, ought to be shaped according to the principles of biomimicry.[831] Furthermore, it ought to see living things as companions and learn from the time-tested, trial-and-error knowledge and experience of companion species adapted to their environment. This alternative theoretical legal framework aims to align law (as knowledge, practice, and discipline) with a world system perspective to facilitate the design of a legal system that will keep pace with the ever-transforming world system. Kotzé and Kim seek to do this by urging lawyers and decision-makers to abandon the linearity, predictability, simplicity, and internal coherence that much of law still possesses today. They argue that we must embrace an alternative understanding of law's new role and contributions in managing the complex, non-linear, interconnected, multi-scale, and unpredictable struggles arising from the Anthropocene. They propose, first and foremost, to recognise the water, energy, and food challenges we face, which are projected to increase due to climate change, as an absolute sustainable *Grundnorm*. In other words, they argue that all national and international decisions adopted in the legal order should be based on these three interconnected problems. Thus, the authors suggest that law should be shaped according to the Earth's planetary boundaries, and its primary purpose should be to balance competing interests in a way that contributes to the planet's integrity.[832] Indeed, it is difficult to argue that a legal system that does not consider the sustainability of the water, energy, and food triad can benefit the ecosystem and people. Under the current circumstances, these three should be prioritised not only in our daily lives but also in all legal norms and texts we prepare.

Collins argues that an ecological legal order should have at least three qualities: eco-centrism, ecological priority, and ecological justice. As for their definitions, eco-centrism, according to the author, recognises and respects the value of all beings and their interconnectedness and equitably defends the interests of humans and other members of the Earth community. Ecological primacy means that social and economic behaviours and systems are ecologically constrained in a way that respects the planet's limits. Ecological justice means ensuring that present and future generations of humans and

---

831 Arık, 'Bir Birada … ', p. 452. The word biomimicry is the portmanteau of the Greek words *bios*, meaning life/living, and *mimesis*, meaning simulation/imitation. Although its plain meaning is the imitation of living things, it also encompasses an ethical stance, a way of thinking and a way of life. See Arık, 'Bir Arada … ', p. 451.

832 Kotzé – Kim, 'Towards Planetary … ', pp. 91–2.

other beings have equitable access to the Earth's capacity to continue and that environmental damage is not unfairly imposed on others.[833] These are also the core elements of a green constitutionalism perspective. Laws made within this framework, like the laws of nature, need to be understood as manifestations of an order of relations in which the individual is not seen in isolation but depends on and shares power with other inhabitants of the planet who have equal access to the global commons. This planet's inhabitants are not only human beings but also animals, plants, and, in general, all the ecosystems of the Earth.[834] The fact that our constitutions and laws only regulate the human world from a human perspective is a practice that should be left behind. We are not alone on this Earth; on the contrary, we cannot continue to exist without other ecosystem members. Therefore, our legal regulations should be drafted by taking into account other members of the ecosystem along with human beings and by observing the rules of nature. Green constitutionalism is a roadmap for realising this.

If we are to speak of an Earth democracy, as in a human democracy, constitutional principles must recognise the right to exist for all, human and nonhuman alike. This understanding of democracy is based on the idea that different cultures and communities can exist together and that we all share not only one common humanity but also one commonality with all living beings and life forms.[835] It is then legitimate to limit the interests of a particular group (people) through constitutionalism for the greater and democratically determined good of the entire ecosystem.[836] If we want to create a sustainable society, human laws must not be allowed to exploit and plunder the web of life; rather, they must serve it. A sustainable life requires that we make our different human values consistent with the course of life on Earth as a fundamental value.[837]

At this point, it must be recognised that presenting only an alternative stance consisting of some policy proposals is not enough. We need an alternative worldview to compete with the one at the root of the ecological crisis.

---

833 Carla Sbert, *The Lens of Ecological Law: A Look at Mining*, Edward Elgar, Cheltenham, 2020, pp. 78–92, cited in: Collins, *The Ecological Constitution*, p. 6.

834 Capra – Mattei, *The Ecology of Law*, pp. 48–9.

835 Shiva, *Earth Democracy*, p. 128.

836 Cullinan, *Wild Law*, p. 162.

837 Capra – Mattei, *The Ecology of Law*, p. 49.

This worldview we propose must be rooted in mutual solidarity rather than extreme individualism, reciprocity rather than domination, and cooperation rather than hierarchy.[838] What we need is a 'paradigm shift' towards a new constitutional order recognising that we are part of the Earth, not disconnected from it. Equally, we need to develop governance systems inspired by this new understanding that effectively prevent people from acting in ways that harm the Earth and, eventually, themselves.[839] That can and must be done through transformative constitutionalism. New constitutions should be written, and existing ones should be amended to bring this green system of governance to life. In countries where this has not been done, high courts should interpret existing norms in this light.

That is because law must always be a process of 'commoning', a long-term collective action of communities sharing a common purpose and culture, institutionalising their common will to maintain order and stability. Therefore, the building block of what is called ecological legal order or green constitutionalism is the community rather than the individual[840] – bearing in mind that the 'community' here includes not only human beings but also other elements of the ecosystem. The law should recognise the inherent rights of all ecosystem members, animate and inanimate, and consider their interrelationships.

The new green constitutional order should strengthen the diffusion of power and participatory democracy rather than the concentration of power and secrecy and inclusion, distributive justice, and sharing rather than exclusion, inequality, and selfishness. In such a legal system, lawyers should translate existing ecological knowledge into policy and normative interpretations of law. The core of eco-law should be the ecological community, not humans as individuals, because the most important 'law of nature' is that the whole is not the sum of its parts.[841]

In the framework of all these ideas, it can be said that green constitutionalism is based on sustainability, a new understanding of rights, and a new economic order. Their goal is a more just world and a better life for all. Let us now elaborate on these.

---

[838] Klein, *On Fire*, p. 125.

[839] Cullinan, *Wild Law*, p. 89.

[840] Capra – Mattei, *The Ecology of Law*, p. 34.

[841] Capra – Mattei, *The Ecology of Law*, p. 192.

4.1 Sustainability

Sustainability is a principle aiming to preserve ecological systems and their integrity.[842] It is generally accepted that this concept entered our lives with the Brundtland Report.[843] The term 'sustainable development' used in this report was defined as *a process of change in which the exploitation of resources, the direction of investment, the orientation of technological development; and institutional change are all in harmony and enhance both current and future potential to meet human needs and aspirations*.[844] Thus, sustainability entered our lives as an effort to preserve the existence of natural resources without giving up growth. This famous definition of the report contains two ethical elements that almost everyone recognises as the foundation of the idea of sustainable development: 1) concern for people with low incomes (intra-generational justice and equity) and 2) concern for the future (intergenerational justice and equity).[845] However, as I will discuss in more detail later under the heading 'degrowth',[846] these are not only practically impossible to achieve in a growth-based economy but also theoretically problematic.

Therefore, in the context of green constitutionalism, it is better to perceive the concept of sustainability as a principle that guides social and legal structures rather than its misleading use within the capitalist economic order. That is because it is vital for humanity's future to transform into communities that know the limits of the planet and can limit themselves for the sustainability of the ecosystem. We know enough today about the crises we face, such as climate change. What we lack knowledge about is how to transform the communities we live in.[847] Sustainability is one of the key elements that should be taken as an axis in this transformation.

Leaving a liveable world for future generations today is impossible by thinking within a short-term horizon.[848] For a society to qualify as a 'sustainable

---

842 Klaus Bosselmann, *The Principle of Sustainability – Transforming Law and Governance*, 2nd ed., Routledge, London and New York, 2017, p. 102.

843 For a detailed information on this report, see 5.1

844 Gro Harlem Brundtland, *Report of the World Commission on Environment and Development: Our Common Future*, 20 March 1987, Chapter 2, § 15.

845 Bosselmann, *The Principle of Sustainability*, p. 118.

846 See 4.3.3

847 Arık, 'Bir Arada ... ', p. 467.

848 Coşkun, *Süreklilikten Sürdürülebilirliğe*, p. 23.

society', the rules governing its lifestyles, initiatives, economy, physical structures, and technologies must be designed in such a way that they do not interfere with the way nature itself maintains its life cycle. Therefore, the first step towards building a sustainable community is understanding how nature sustains life. This perspective requires a new understanding of ecological living as 'eco-literacy' and a new kind of 'systems' thinking – in other words, rethinking society in terms of relationships, patterns, and context.[849] That is, of course, not an easy task. For example, the Ecuadorian Constitution, referred to as an example of an 'ecological constitution' below,[850] is extremely valuable because it recognises nature as a subject of constitutional rights. Still, unfortunately, it is insufficient to create an ecological society in real life because it fails to build a new system around the principle of sustainability.

It is debatable whether the term 'sustainable development' is an oxymoron. That is because development is sustainable if it can preserve the integrity and continuity of ecological systems and unsustainable if it cannot.[851] In this context, an economic growth policy of perpetually increasing GDP is intrinsically unsustainable. In contrast, sustainability is inherent in development goals that seek to protect and promote the well-being, health, and welfare of people, animals, and natural assets. Therefore, if a sustainable economy is to be achieved, it can only be an economic system in which activities directed towards enhancing the well-being of people and the ecosystem as a whole are recognised as valuable.

Sustainability means preserving and restoring the integrity of the Earth's ecological systems and is the fundamental principle that frames all other elements of green constitutionalism.[852] Moving beyond an anthropocentric perspective, the concept of sustainability encompasses not only the recognition of the human right to live in a healthy environment as a fundamental element[853] but also the survival of nonhuman species and a healthy ecosphere for future generations of humans and nonhumans.[854]

---

849 Capra – Mattei, *The Ecology of Law*, p. 48.
850 See 6.2.2
851 Bosselmann, *The Principle of Sustainability*, p. 63.
852 Collins, *The Ecological Constitution*, p. 18.
853 Boyd, *Report of… (A/75/161)* (full report).
854 Bosselmann, *The Principle of Sustainability*, pp. 118–23.

Therefore, a constitutional framework to be developed against the destructive effects of the Anthropocene needs to be built in the context of sustainability. That is how a global society must act in defining its physical environment in order to survive.[855] As is well known, constitutionalism is as much about imposing limitations and creating constraints as it is about rights and freedoms. That means if climate change is to be halted by creating a social order in harmony with nature, constitutionalism should be used to provide constitutional principles, values, and norms for sustainability.[856]

Sustainability, which has become the most fundamental principle of current environmental law, can only be guaranteed by global environmental constitutionalism through a change in legal orientation: The Earth (environment) must move from the periphery to the centre of national and international (global) law. The 'globe' should be at the centre of global constitutionalism, as it should be. That requires a significant change of perspective in the legal and institutional framework[857] because no legal system can achieve ecological sustainability when embedded in unsustainable production and consumption patterns.[858]

That is why the principle of sustainability is appearing in more and more constitutions and Supreme Court decisions today. The term 'sustainability' or 'sustainable development' can be found in twenty contemporary constitutions. However, most of the provisions containing these terms are not drafted in a way that allows for direct litigation.[859] Jurists and lawyers are also slow to use the concept as a tangible legal outcome rather than just a silent guiding principle.[860] However, even if the role of law in achieving sustainability is limited, we know that only through law can we force ourselves

---

[855] Jaria-Manzano – Borrás, 'Introduction to … ', p. 3.

[856] Louis J. Kotzé, 'Arguing Global Environmental Constitutionalism', *Transnational Environmental Law*, Vol. 1, No. 1, April 2012, p. 224.

[857] Bosselmann, *The Principle of Sustainability*, p. 166.

[858] Collins, *The Ecological Constitution*, p. 18.

[859] James R. May – Erin Daly, *Global Environmental Constitutionalism* (Turkish version), trans. Tolga Şirin – N. Umut Orcan, Ekoloji Kolektifi, Istanbul, 2018, p. 229.

[860] James R. May – Erin Daly, 'Six Trends in Global Environmental Constitutionalism', in *Environmental Constitutionalism: Impact on Legal Systems?*, Peter Lang Publishing, Oxford (in press), p. 11.

to do things.[861] Therefore, constitutions' sustainability provisions need to be used effectively by lawyers and high courts alike. That is a critical task for lawyers in creating a sustainable society.

Sustainable societies move steadily with the cycles of nature, not against them. Being in a steady state does not mean being stagnant; it involves moving and progressing on a particular trajectory. As Shiva points out, the ecological consciousness of ancient civilisations allowed them to move forward in an ecologically stable way. The Indigenous cultures of the Amazon, the Andes, and the Himalayas are examples of living cultures that have been sustainable for thousands of years.[862] The principle of sustainability in the green constitutionalism approach serves as a bridge to transfer these ancient civilisations' ecological consciousness to contemporary societies.

In sustainable communities, what will be pursued is not economic growth or competitive advantage but the entire web of life on which our long-term survival depends. In other words, a sustainable community will design its lifestyles, enterprises, economy, physical structures, and technology to support the productive power of nature rather than interfere with its inherent ability to sustain life. Of course, it could be argued that this transformation requires giving up some of the culture of individual rights that has become dominant since the Age of Enlightenment as a result of capital's appropriation of humanism.[863] That is true. However, much of what is given up will be related to using property rights at the expense of nature and people. Only then will it be possible to truly recognise the most fundamental rights, such as freedom of expression, freedom to seek happiness, the right to live in a healthy environment, and the right to live. Green constitutionalism's goal is definitely not an 'eco-fascist' society; in contrast, it aims for a just order of rights, recognising a good and healthy life for people and the ecosystem as the primary goal.

---

[861] Klaus Bosselmann, 'Property Rights and Sustainability: Can They Be Reconciled?', *in* David P. Grinlinton – Prue Taylor (ed.), *Property Rights and Sustainability: The Evolution of Property Rights to Meet Ecological Challenges*, Brill, Leiden, 2011, p. 21 and 26, cited in: Collins, *The Ecological Constitution*, p. 19.

[862] Shiva, *Earth Democracy*, p. 76.

[863] Capra – Mattei, *The Ecology of Law*, p. 188.

4.2 Reconceptualising rights

If we take existing legal systems and humanistic legal theory as a starting point for discussing the concept of rights, it is easy to get entangled in complex legal debates. These debates are difficult to resolve because they are rooted in the anthropocentric worldview itself and unresolvable within the existing legal theory and framework.[864] We ignored the diversity of life on Earth and, following the Roman Law, divided it into only two categories, namely, us and them. According to this, we are the only species with rights to the land, water, wildlife, and ecosystems of the planet.[865] We try to explain why we have rights, but we do not even try to explain why other species do not have the same rights. Our only justification is that they are not human. However, in fact, this is using an unnatural distinction of our own making as a justification. Of course, this is not at all scientific or convincing.

In the current dominant understanding, rights are devised concepts that function to protect certain human interests from being too easily sacrificed.[866] When we use the term 'human rights', we mean a special category of rights that we deem valuable enough to be protected in a special way because they relate to the fundamental qualities that define our humanity. So much so that when fundamental human rights are violated, there is a sense of solidarity that our common humanity is also being violated and that we have a collective responsibility to resist those who ignore these rights.[867]

Rights are 'barriers' owners use to prevent their interests from being sacrificed.[868] They follow an evolutionary course of development. The idea of what constitutes a right has constantly been evolving and becoming ever sharper until it finally took its current form. Some things once considered rights have ceased to be rights over time. For example, according to some philosophers in ancient civilisations, slavery was justified, and in the Middle Ages, nobles, priests, and bishops considered it their right to enslave people.[869] Similarly, some rights that did not exist before may appear at a particular

---

[864] Cullinan, *Wild Law*, p. 97.

[865] Boyd, *The Rights of Nature*, p. XXVIII.

[866] DesJardins, *Environmental Ethics*, p. 214.

[867] Cullinan, *Wild Law*, p. 104.

[868] Gary Francione, *Animals, Property and the Law*, Temple University Press, Philadelphia, 2007, p. 103.

[869] Proudhon, *Qu'est-ce que la Propriété?*, pp. 39–40.

stage in history, just as rights that previously applied only to 'someone' may later be extended to more people. An example is the emergence of the right to vote, which did not exist until the formation of representative government systems, first only for the bourgeois, then for all men, and finally for women.

Rejecting the view that rights are things waiting to be discovered in nature, Christopher Stone, at the very beginning of his famous book *Should Trees Have Standing?* refers to Charles Darwin, who argued that the history of human moral development is written in the expansion of his 'social instinct and sympathy' for things. Accordingly, every human first cares only for himself and his immediate environment. Then, he cares not only for the welfare but also for the happiness of this immediate environment. Then, his sympathy extends to other people and finally to animals. Stone thus establishes a link between the processes of evolution and the recognition of fundamental rights, starting with the bourgeoisie and spreading to the entire humanity today.[870] Indeed, the list of rights-holders has steadily lengthened. We were once told that only white men who owned land could enjoy all the rights recognised by law. Legal capacity now includes landless persons, women, black people, and Indigenous people, as well as corporations, foundations, city governments, and nations. Moreover, some actions taken against those who used to be treated as property because the law did not recognise them as having rights are now criminalised, whereas, in the past, they were legally protected. For example, we can no longer legally buy and sell a black man or a woman, although it used to be perfectly normal. That is because the rights granted to these people now protect them from harm. Today, it is time to extend this protection to other things in nature.[871] In this way, green constitutionalism proposes abandoning the human monopoly on the concept of rights and recognising nonhuman natural beings as subjects of rights.[872]

However, there is a significant obstacle: humanism. The idea that human beings are not only important but also unique and superior is so ingrained in our logic and legal systems that we have a deep-rooted understanding that rights can only be granted to human beings (or groups of human beings, such as corporations). We accept this argument almost without question.

---

870 Stone, *Should Trees Have Standing?*, p. 1.

871 DesJardins, *Environmental Ethics*, p. 221.

872 See 4.2.2

Nonetheless, this is a cultural recognition and, therefore, a human-made discourse. In nature, there is neither human-nature distinction nor something such as rights. These are stories that we have convinced ourselves are true, and it is up to us to replace them with new ones and make the existing ones more just.

However, this is still potentially confusing, even in countries where constitutions include the rights of nature so that the law can recognise the capacity of, say, a river to have rights, thereby extending the discourse of rights and responsibilities to nonhuman subjects. Terms like 'rights' and 'responsibilities' are intertwined with our experience of existing legal systems and are loaded with the implications of conflict. The language we use is shaped by the worldview we have created for the human persons alone.[873] The concepts of 'human' and 'rights' are almost intertwined. It feels as if they are inseparable because the modern fundamental rights of man were the criterion for realising the bourgeois model of society.[874] In the modern world, only man should have rights so that he can exploit other animals and natural beings. Therefore, the two concepts have almost merged.

In light of this, it must be seen that the perception that today's fundamental rights and freedoms are the result of bourgeois power and the capitalist economic order is based on a myth. On the contrary, the modern legal achievements, historically the product of bourgeois revolutions, although referring to a general and abstract idea of 'man', actually consisted of a list of rights that a very limited group of people could fully enjoy.[875] The bourgeoisie, which advocated equality in order to abolish the aristocracy's privileges by birth and class, was not willing to do so when it came to abolishing their own privileges by wealth.[876] It was not thanks to the bourgeoisie that everyone could enjoy the rights and freedoms today that are considered fundamental and protected by constitutions, but rather, it was a result of the struggle against it. The bourgeoisie, like all other economic classes, was and still is just a group of merchants pursuing their own interests. What made it grow and eventually become hegemonic was its disregard for the rights of others and

[873] Cullinan, *Wild Law*, p. 98.
[874] Dieter Grimm, *Constitutionalism: Past, Present and Future*, Oxford University Press, Oxford, 2016, p. 70, cited in: Delice, 'Karma Hükümetten … ', p. 1690.
[875] Durmaz, *Doğanın Hakları*, p. 10. (Emphasis is mine.)
[876] Proudhon, *Qu'est-ce que la Propriété?*, p. 40.

its commodification and exploitation of them. An alternative and ecological view of history reveals this in all its nakedness.

The rise of bourgeois humanist thought in the early modern era paralleled the formation of slave trade routes across the Atlantic Ocean. For three centuries, starting in the sixteenth century, Europeans enslaved 10 million Africans and transported them by ship to the Americas to work in the gold and silver mines, sugar, tobacco, and cotton plantations they established there. Slave-trading companies specially established for this purpose traded on the Amsterdam, London, and Paris stock exchanges. The European middle classes, for whom the equality and freedom of human beings was the motto, ignored their contradiction when they bought shares in these companies because it was a good investment. Most of the Africans enslaved by the 'humanist' Europeans lived short and miserable lives; millions more died in wars to capture enslaved people or on long voyages from the African interior to the shores of the Americas.[877]

The situation did not change in the nineteenth century. A concrete example of the bourgeoisie's hypocrisy on human rights is the 'non-governmental organisation' announced in 1876 by King Leopold II of Belgium to fight the slave trade, primarily around the Congo River. Founded with such a lofty goal, the organisation soon turned into a corporation that was essentially about growth and profit. The organisation quickly moved away from its original mission of developing the region and building schools and hospitals and instead became involved in mining and farming. In particular, it invested in the increasingly important rubber industry and began employing locals in rubber production. Those who did not work hard enough and 'slacked off' had their hands or arms amputated. It is estimated that between 1885 and 1908, between 6 and 10 million Congolese were killed by the Belgians. That amounted to one-fifth of the Congolese population at the time.[878] The basis for all this was the bourgeoisie's conception of human rights, which, as explained in the book's first chapter, was based on property and was nothing more than the rights of capitalist exploitation.[879] It was only as a result

---

[877] Harari, *Sapiens*, pp. 325–6.

[878] Georges Nzongoloa-Ntalaja, *The Congo from Leopold to Kabila: A People's History*, Zed Books, London, 2002, p. 22, cited in: Harari, *Sapiens*, p. 327.

[879] Paul Lafargue, *Le Droit à la Paresse* (Turkish version), trans. Ali Berktay, 6th ed., Türkiye İş Bankası Kültür Yayınları, Istanbul, September 2023, p. 36.

of a struggle against this understanding, which even led to civil war in the US, that black people were no longer treated as property and recognised as human beings subject to rights. In conclusion, the bourgeoisie did not give people their fundamental rights; people won their basic rights by fighting against the bourgeoisie.

It is no exaggeration to say that we are today engaged in a similar struggle against the bourgeoisie and its economic model, capitalism. The damage done to the biosphere, especially by the countries of the Global North and the wealthiest segments of societies, is negatively impacting a wide range of human rights, and soon, this impact will be catastrophic. Among the human rights being threatened and violated are the rights to a healthy environment, life, health, food, water, hygiene, decent living, development, and culture.[880] These are the most fundamental rights for a human being to live a dignified life. Without them, there is little point in recognising other rights in constitutions or laws. In this context, the green constitutionalist view suggests that it must be recognised that no one has the right to engage in activities that undermine the most fundamental rights of others. For example, rich people cannot have the right to fly in their private jets to watch a concert or sporting event and use fuel in such a way as to cause the death of others[881] because all other rights become secondary when the right to life is at stake.

In many cases, protecting nature leads to progress on all these rights. It is now clear that there are development pathways to meet people's rights to life, work, food, water, housing, and a dignified standard of living in an ecologically sustainable way.[882] However, the basic logic of capitalism is based on endless growth and competition, as well as a constant sense of lack. People must have a constant sense of lack so that they continue to consume. Rather than being a right or a freedom, the capitalist conception of consumption is a trap that pushes us always to want more, detaching us from our health, lives, and families. From this perspective, the opposite of capitalism, that is, freedom from want – freedom from deprivation of food, housing, and basic needs – is the most fundamental freedom. Without this foundation, other

---

880 Boyd, *Report of… (A/75/161)*, p. 10, § 31.

881 Malm, *How to Blow …*, p. 108.

882 Ashish Kothari et al., *Pluriverse: A Post-Development Dictionary*, Tulika Books, New Delhi, 2019, cited in: Collins, *The Ecological Constitution*, p. 41.

freedoms cannot be gained. It is the democratic project of our time to secure this freedom by building legal systems that respect life, consolidating civil society, empowering people rather than creating a dualism between human beings and nature, and atomising people and distancing them from the logic of solidarity.[883]

Within this project, our legal orders should take a perspective that considers not only human beings but also nature's network system of which humans are only a part. At the constitutional level, the law should regulate our behaviour and freedoms in a way that prevents us from destroying the well-being of Earth's other inhabitants and using them in ways that prevent them from fulfilling their evolutionary role.[884] These can limit and even prohibit some human actions that are today seen as rights or freedoms. Still, if this ensures that the health and integrity of people and the ecosystem are protected, how can it be argued that they are evil or oppressive?

This perspective, which Bosselman calls the 'ecological approach to human rights', establishes a link between the intrinsic value of humans and that of other species and the environment. According to this link, human rights, such as human dignity, freedom, property, development, etc., should respond to the fact that humans live not only in a social environment but also in a natural environment. Just as a person must respect the intrinsic value of other people, so must they respect the intrinsic value of other beings (animals, plants, ecosystems).[885]

The starting point for people in this approach is the recognition of the principle that each ecosystem member should be free to fulfil its role within networks of relationships. For this freedom to exist, people should not have the right to prevent them from fulfilling their role. More precisely, no one should have the right to take an action that disrupts the cycle of nature and harms sustainability. That means that we cannot build a dam across a river so that it can no longer fulfil its role in the ecosystem or destroy a habitat that a species depends on for survival.[886] In this framework, human behaviour should be evaluated and regulated according to whether it strengthens or

---

883 Shiva, *Earth Democracy*, p. 129.
884 Cullinan, *Wild Law*, p. 118.
885 Bosselmann, *The Principle of Sustainability*, pp. 148–9.
886 Cullinan, *Wild Law*, p. 105.

weakens the bonds that make up the Earth's ecosystem.[887] That is because all human rights ultimately depend on a healthy biosphere. Without a healthy and functioning ecosystem based on healthy biodiversity, there is no clean air to breathe, no clean air to drink, and no nutritious food to eat.[888] In other words, human rights are meaningless and unsustainable without the rights of nature because where the Earth cannot provide any more food or water, the 'right to life' is an empty slogan.[889]

That is why, according to green constitutionalism, actions that cause climate change or destroy the habitat of a species and drive it to extinction should not be considered a right. It can no longer be a right for people to take actions that attack the heart of the Earth's ecosystem, endangering not only themselves but also billions of other living beings. Instead, every human being has a duty to resist these attacks on the ecosystem.[890] This resistance is a struggle to defend the right to life, not only for the ecosystem but also for humanity.

Modernity claims that the Scientific Revolution awakened humanity from the 'Dark Ages', transforming the commons into capital and making it possible for people to dominate both their future and nature. However, as a result, most urban dwellers today are disconnected from the rest of the world, lack ecological literacy, and are alienated from nature.[891] Moreover, half of the world's population now lives in urban environments.[892] As Capra and Mattei describe it accurately, people stuck in the city do not know how plants grow or how food is produced, think they have the right to stay in the shower for a long time despite the drought or, even if they are aware of climate change, do not mind driving their gasoline-powered cars irresponsibly. The authors rightly point out that assuming the risks of a nuclear plant for the excessive

---

887 Cullinan, *Wild Law*, p. 118.

888 Boyd, *Report of… (A/75/161)*, p. 4, § 3.

889 Cullinan, *Wild Law*, p. 190.

890 Cullinan, *Wild Law*, p. 162.

891 For the view that urban and rural are not actually two separate parts and should be handled in a holistic manner, see Orhan, 'Farklı Ölçeklerde…'.

892 Urbanisation worldwide has increased rapidly since 1950. The urban population, which was 751 million in 1950, grew to 4.2 billion people in 2018. 55 per cent of the world's total population lives in cities as of 2018. This proportion is expected to rise to 68 per cent by 2050. See United Nations, 'World Urbanization Prospects: The 2018 Revision (Key Facts)'.

use of electricity in urban life in rich countries does not seem to be rational behaviour for a species that claims to have emerged from the Dark Ages. These behaviours do not save us from medieval superstitions; they are examples of possessive individualism that irrationally idolises egoistic rights.[893]

At this point, it is critical to remember that there is a difference between individualism and individuality. The building block of communities is individuality, not individualism. Individuality is synonymous with uniqueness. That means that each person and their characteristics are unique. An ecological community wants to see each of its members develop and function optimally. Indeed, the community can only thrive and survive when each member develops to the full potential of its purpose. It is in each community's own interest to honour and support its members.[894] Accordingly, in an ecological society, the diversity of nature is reflected in the social structure and the rule of law. For this reason, the notion that 'the bourgeoisie is the guarantor of rights and freedoms' or that 'the disappearance of capitalism will lead to the loss of rights and freedoms' is empty paranoia. On the contrary, green constitutionalism seeks a legal order in which the rights to life, health, well-being, and selfhood of every ecosystem member – human or nonhuman – are protected.

In that way, a rights-based approach would be adopted to strengthen the fight against the climate crisis. Concrete and creative use of the human rights responsibilities of states and other actors can make environmental policies fairer, more effective, and more respectful of the concerns of those most affected by environmental damage.[895] As abolitionists, women's rights defenders, civil rights activists, and Indigenous peoples have demonstrated, history shows that human rights have so far played an important role in transformative social change.[896] Yet, as we have seen, all of these struggles were

---

893 Capra – Mattei, *The Ecology of Law*, pp. 150–1.

894 Malidoma Patrice Somé, *The Healing Wisdom of Africa: Finding Life Purpose Through Nature, Ritual and Community*, Thorsons, London, 1999, p. 92, cited in: Cullinan, *Wild Law*, p. 148.

895 John H. Knox, *Report of the Independent Expert on the Issue of Human Rights Obligations Relating to the Enjoyment of a Safe, Clean, Healthy and Sustainable Environment – Compilation of Good Practices*, OHCHR, A/HRC/28/61, 3 February 2015, pp. 20–1, § 103.

896 Boyd, *Report of… (A/75/161)*, p. 21, § 82.

also fought to limit the hegemony of 'white European men'. It was through their struggles against the European bourgeoisie that enslaved people were recognised as human beings, women as equals, and Indigenous peoples as the rightful owners of their land. Today, green constitutionalism means waging this struggle against the bourgeoisie to recognise the ecosystem's rights and stop climate change.

4.2.1 Legal limitations on property rights

The commodification and private appropriation of nature are probably at the root of our current ecological crisis.[897] Applying the rules of private property to natural assets reflects the worldview that it is right and just for humans to unilaterally dominate other ecosystem elements by treating them as objects. By defining other beings as things, dominant legal philosophies legalise and facilitate exploitative relations between us and the Earth. They also prevent us from developing governance systems based on a respectful relationship with the planet and recognising that it is a reciprocal relationship between subjects with inherent rights. Thus, these laws increase our alienation from nature.[898]

Despite the systemic thinking that has gained acceptance in recent years at the forefront of science, the disciplines of law and economics continue to promote a short-term perspective, still seeing reality mechanistically. They place an atomised and abstract individual property owner at the centre of their perspective. This atom extracts value from public assets at the expense of others and acts as the owner of the planet.[899] The harm often takes the form of loss of life, habitat, or health. The law permits individuals, the subjects of rights, to use their property rights in ways that threaten and even destroy the life, health, and integrity of other human and nonhuman beings. How was this possible to accept?

People's property rights are not absolute. If ecological limits are to be placed on human rights, the most obvious and morally defensible ones,

---

[897] Klaus Bosselmann, 'Property Rights and Sustainability: Can They Be Reconciled?', *in* David Grinlinton – Prue Taylor (ed.), *Property Rights and Sustainability: The Evolution of Property Rights to Meet Ecological Challenges*, Brill, Leiden, 2011, p. 42, cited in: Collins, *The Ecological Constitution*, p. 41.

[898] Cullinan, *Wild Law*, p. 141.

[899] Capra – Mattei, *The Ecology of Law*, p. 31.

especially in developed countries, are those on property rights.[900] According to Bosselmann, property rights and sustainability can and should be reconciled, but this process requires radical changes in worldviews and the legal systems that emerge from them. In particular, he argues that the source of the 'limitations *inherent in* property rights' is the *realisation* that … *land use plays a role in controlling global climate and biodiversity and is key to a nation's or region's capacity to survive.*[901] In other words, the most essential condition for reconciling property rights and sustainability is using property in a way that does not harm the global climate and biodiversity. Therefore, in the context of green constitutionalism, private property will not be prohibited. However, it cannot be used in a way that harms the ecosystem – including humans, other living beings, and nature.

Our new knowledge about ecology requires us to remove the private property owner from the centre of the legal system and replace them with the commons. To do this, we must reanalyse and rethink the legal structure to reflect the fundamental principles of ecology and the current systemic thinking in science.[902] Climate change is forcing us to limit our traditional rights and freedoms, especially property rights, in the name of both public welfare and equity. What were correctly understood as freedoms and rights in the past can no longer be understood similarly.[903] When the traditional moral and political framework of human rights is applied to the new climate reality, it becomes necessary to reinterpret some traditional rights and create new ones.[904]

Conflict is inevitable between solidarity rights and economic rights and freedoms such as property rights, freedom of enterprise, freedom of industry and trade. Even in today's modern legal order, environmental rights limit

---

900 Collins, *The Ecological Constitution*, p. 41.

901 Klaus Bosselmann, 'Property Rights and Sustainability: Can They Be Reconciled?', *in* David P. Grinlinton – Prue Taylor (ed.), *Property Rights and Sustainability: The Evolution of Property Rights to Meet Ecological Challenges*, Brill, Leiden, 2011, p. 42, cited in: Collins, *The Ecological Constitution*, p. 42. (Emphasis is Bosselman's.)

902 Capra – Mattei, *The Ecology of Law*, p. 32.

903 William Blackstone, 'Ethics and Ecology', in *Philosophy and Environmental Crisis*, University of Georgia Press, Athens, 1974, p. 32, cited in: DesJardins, *Environmental Ethics*, p. 211.

904 DesJardins, *Environmental Ethics*, p. 211.

freedom of enterprise and property rights.[905] Today, however, any attempt to prioritise the public interest over private property is due to pay a high price. In such a case, many economists, jurists, and columnists would immediately mobilise to protect the ' sanctity' of private property and the unlimited freedom of the property owner. The legal regulation of private property has always been the exception in the Western legal tradition; the main rule is unlimited freedom.[906] However, this unlimited freedom is not about living or happiness but digging, polluting, carbonising, and exploiting. At the point climate change has reached today, we have come to realise that there should no longer be such freedom. All ecosystem-damaging investments made for capitalist rents must be withdrawn as quickly as possible. However, one of the reasons why the steady stand in the climate struggle seems such a daunting challenge is that no state is in any way ready to put this idea into practice because capitalist property is considered 'sacrosanct'. Which government would be willing to use its power to ensure that such a huge profit is cut out? Yet, this passion for property puts us at the price of losing our world.[907]

The result of continuing to maintain our current idea of property rights in this way is alienation from our deeper selves. It may seem radical to rethink property law altogether, but it is entirely justified when the benefits and harms are considered more generally. The challenge today is how to begin the process of unravelling the property relations that prevent us from establishing a healthy relationship with nature and how to build a functioning alternative in its place.[908]

According to Löwy, the first order of business is to take control of the means of production, especially investment and technological change decisions. These decision-making processes should be taken out of the hands of banks and capitalist corporations to ensure that they serve the common good of society.[909] At first sight, that may seem radical. There is no social movement on the horizon to make it happen, nor a constitutional court that would dare to do so. Yet, it is not the only way. One can also start by putting the commons back at the centre of the law. That would affect certain

[905] Kaboğlu – Yancı Özalp, *Çevre Hakkı*, p. 42.
[906] Capra – Mattei, *The Ecology of Law*, pp. 140–1.
[907] Malm, *How to Blow …*, pp. 80–1.
[908] Cullinan, *Wild Law*, p. 145.
[909] Löwy, *Ecosocialism*, What Is Ecosocialism (Loc. 227).

freedoms to extract and use natural resources. Today, these freedoms are based on unlimited property rights and the rule of law. However, given the deterioration of ecological conditions today, it is pertinent to question the extent to which freedom to extract and use resources should be protected. How can it be justified to sacrifice the rights of the unborn and the victims of climate change in favour of unlimited extraction and exploitation of natural resources?'[910] In this framework, at a minimum, the general requirement of public order also covers, with a teleological interpretation, *environmental public order*. Thus, protecting the environment can be seen as a general ground of limitation for all constitutional rights and freedoms, particularly the right to property.[911]

In addition, even today, some constitutions contain provisions that explicitly impose ecological limitations on property rights. For example, the 1991 Constitution of Romania states that the right to own property can only be exercised in conjunction with responsibilities for environmental protection.[912] The 2009 Bolivian Constitution stipulates that private property can only be used in a way that does not harm collective interests.[913] In Germany, the state's constitutional duty to protect the 'natural foundations of life' has created a legal understanding that environmental responsibilities are inherent in property ownership.[914]

On the other hand, green constitutionalism goes a step further and recognises the Earth not as a collection of objects but as a community of subjects. Accordingly, if the fundamental right of a river to flow is threatened, the legal system should prohibit the human action that threatens it.[915] That can be done through a law passed by a parliament, but in the absence of such a law, a constitutional-level Supreme Court decision would also protect this right. In this constitutionalist approach, property would not be protected if

---

910 Capra – Mattei, *The Ecology of Law*, pp. 177–8.

911 Kaboğlu – Yancı Özalp, *Çevre Hakkı*, p. 73. (Emphasis is Kaboğlu – Yancı Özalp's.)

912 Constitution of Romania, Art. 44, § 7.

913 Constitution of the Plurinational State of Bolivia, art. 56.

914 Klaus Bosselmann, 'Property Rights and Sustainability: Can They Be Reconciled?', *in* David P. Grinlinton – Prue Taylor (ed.), *Property Rights and Sustainability: The Evolution of Property Rights to Meet Ecological Challenges*, Brill, Leiden, 2011, pp. 38–9, cited in: Collins, *The Ecological Constitution*, p. 42.

915 Cullinan, *Wild Law*, p. 106.

it serves anti-social[916] purposes, such as rent accumulation, rather than public investment. Likewise, companies would not be allowed to function if they do not serve the community in which they are located.[917]

It could be claimed that this approach is 'repressive' or 'prohibitive', but this claim could only be made if the concept of freedom is seen from the perspective of the bourgeoisie. On the contrary, in a green constitutional order, the legal framework would be such that individual freedoms would be maximised, but at the same time, they would not destroy life on Earth.[918] Thus, all rights and freedoms would continue to exist and be protected but could not exercise at the expense of others since there could be no emancipatory project that does not take into account the limits and constraints of nature. Dreams of domination over nature must be abandoned in favour of a collective, well-intentioned, attentive sense of responsibility.

In this sense, we need to reconsider what freedom means to us. Accepting natural limits and respecting ecological cycles and rhythms also means accepting the limits of human freedom.[919] A legal system that regulates unlimited property rights while recognising that nature is limited is self-contradictory. It is, therefore, both logical and necessary for an ecologically literate constitution to recognise clear limits on property rights.[920] In countries where the rights of nature are not protected in the constitution, existing environmental articles should be interpreted by high courts on the basis of green constitutionalism, paving the way for limiting property rights in favour of ecosystem sustainability.

4.2.2 Recognising nonhuman beings as subjects of rights

The intentional killing of a living thing is only considered murder (and accordingly a crime) if the deceased is a subject recognised by the law. In legal terms, something that can be owned cannot be a subject but an object. Thus, for example, in Roman law, killing an enslaved person was not considered a crime. However, if someone killed an enslaved person, the owner was

---

916 Society here means not just human society, but a community that includes all members of the ecosystem.
917 Capra – Mattei, *The Ecology of Law*, p. 197.
918 Barrau, *Le Plus Grand …*, p. 88.
919 Tanuro, *L'Impossible le Capitalism vert*, pp. 20–1
920 Collins, *The Ecological Constitution*, p. 42.

entitled to compensation for the loss of property. Similarly, today, from a legal point of view, it is not legally possible to commit murder against an animal or a forest, no matter how widespread the killing or how high the degree of brutality, immorality, or violence is. At best, if it is an act of cruelty to an animal, one can be punished for violating laws prohibiting violence against animals, which are, in essence, intended to protect human sensibilities. If it is an unauthorised mining activity, the person may be penalised not for damaging the local ecosystem but for not complying with the administrative procedures for obtaining an environmental impact assessment report.[921] So, this penalty is imposed not because of the damage caused to nature but because of the failure to comply with the regulatory rules set by the state. That is because liability cannot arise directly against animals or forests in modern legal systems since they can only be objects of rights. The reason for this is the modern idea that beings other than humans do not have consciousness. According to this view, self-consciousness constitutes subjectivity; subjectivity brings about moral autonomy; moral autonomy brings about responsibility and freedom, which constitute the qualities of the subject as a person with rights and duties in the community in which they live. Therefore, from the modern point of view, plants and animals that are considered to lack these qualities are excluded from civilised life. Establishing political or economic relations with them is impossible because they are not legally recognised as subjects.[922]

However, humans are social and earthly creatures; our lives depend on both other people and nature. Therefore, it is impossible to think of human rights and the rights of nature in isolation from each other.[923] That is why green constitutionalism proposes recognising the inherent rights of nonhuman natural beings. It is well-known in history that the proposal was first found strange, frightening, or laughable in every case where a rights movement emerged. That was partly because those who had rights at the time saw this previously unredeemed element as nothing more than a 'thing' they could only dispose of.[924] For example, when the Founding Fathers of the United

---

921 Cullinan, *Wild Law*, p. 70.

922 Philippe Descola, *Beyond Nature and Culture* (Turkish version), trans. İsmail Yerguz, Istanbul Bilgi University Press, Istanbul, 2013, p. 171.

923 Giménez – Ortuño, 'An Ecological Citizenship's Triumph', p. 86.

924 Stone, *Should Trees Have Standing?*, p. 3.

States spoke of the inalienable rights of the people when they wrote the Constitution in 1787, they could imagine a society in which the millions of African Americans, Native Americans, children, and women on US soil were denied the most basic rights. They were not hypocrites; emotionally, none felt that these others were fully *people*.[925] The famous first words at the beginning of the US Constitution, *We, the people*, did not include anyone other than white men. That was because, in the legal order that was being established, only them were seen as subjects of rights, and all others were excluded from the moral community. Indigenous and black people, women, and children were objects of white men's rights, and, therefore, there could not be a direct responsibility against them.

Thanks to a civil war in which hundreds of thousands of people died, a struggle for equality that lasted for years and involved enormous sacrifices, and finally, a development in our understanding of morality, this period of legal discrimination against other people is now behind us – at least on paper. However, the hierarchical structure of the law's approach to nature has not yet changed. The idea that rights are only for human beings and that nonhuman beings are not eligible to hold rights continues to be generally accepted. On the other hand, it should be noted that this assumption has long been questioned. From the 1970s onwards, as it became clear that Western civilisation and its institutions were unable to develop an existence in harmony with nature, anthropocentrism was challenged, and an ecological critique of law emerged. Thus, the expansion of the sphere of rights beyond human beings came to the fore.[926]

As DesJardins puts it, the ecosystems in which we live and sustain us are spaces where many living beings interact with their living and non-living environments in mutually beneficial relationships. Accordingly, ecological ethics and philosophy focus on ecological communities of interdependencies rather than on individual organisms. Ecological ethics is, therefore, a holistic rather than an individualistic ethics. In other words, according to this approach, the relationships between ecological wholes and natural objects, such as ecosystems and species, non-living natural objects, are of direct moral value. Forests, wetlands, grasslands, and lakes in wild natural

---

925 Stone, *Should Trees Have Standing?*, p. 3, footnote 24. (Emphasis is Stone's.)
926 Durmaz, *Doğanın Hakları*, p. 210.

areas are valuable in their own right and deserve moral attention.[927] At the centre of ecological ethics is concern for the nonhuman natural world. From a nature-centred perspective, *justia communis*[928] includes both humans and the nonhuman world.[929] Therefore, in a legal order constructed in accordance with ecological ethics, nonhuman natural beings should also be recognised as part of the moral community and subjects of rights.

To say that natural beings should hold their own rights does not mean that they would have all the rights we can think of or the same rights as humans. Nor does it mean that everything in nature would have the same rights as everything else.[930] Each living and non-living thing would have different rights according to its qualities. However, as mentioned earlier,[931] Thomas Berry says that every ecosystem member has three common rights: the right to exist, the right to habitat, and the right to fulfil its role in the ever-renewing process of the Earth's ecosystem. To these can be added rights to complete their natural cycles, heal, interdependence and interaction, and peace.[932] Once these rights are recognised at the constitutional level, every case could be assessed in this light, and human actions could be regulated without violating these rights. If action has already taken place, whether there has been a violation of rights could again be assessed in the light of these rights.

Recognising an entity as a subject of rights requires that it be legally considerable. In other words, it must be legally recognised as having intrinsic value and not merely be seen as a means to serve 'our' interests (whoever is recognised as a rights holder at the time).[933] In the current legal system, even if a riparian complains about river pollution and wins their case, the compensation awarded is not to compensate the river for its damages. What is even worse about this shortcoming is that the most the law can do is to compensate the plaintiff river dweller for all damages. This compensation is likely to be far less than the damage done to the river and may not be enough

927 DesJardins, *Environmental Ethics*, pp. 298–9.
928 'Social justice'.
929 Bosselmann, *The Principle of Sustainability*, p. 120.
930 Stone, *Should Trees Have Standing?*, p. 3.
931 See 3.2.2
932 Giménez – Ortuño, 'An Ecological Citizenship's Triumph', p. 85.
933 Stone, *Should Trees Have Standing?*, p. 4.

to dissuade the polluter from what it has done.[934] Therefore, to prevent the pollution, poisoning, degradation, or destruction of a natural asset, it must be recognised that the responsibility lies directly with that asset. In such a case, the punishment for the perpetrator would be calculated based on the damage caused to the natural asset, not just the harm caused to humans. That would provide a deterrent in the first place and discourage most harmful actions.

It is neither inevitable nor wise that natural entities cannot be subjects of rights in such a way that they can claim compensation on their own behalf if their rights are violated. It is no excuse to say that rivers or forests cannot sue because 'they cannot speak'. Neither can companies; neither can states, children, mentally unstable people, municipalities, or universities. People or bodies authorised by law speak for them. Similarly, ordinary people with legal problems often do not speak for themselves; lawyers speak for them. Legal problems of natural beings can be solved in the same way as those of incapacitated individuals, such as persons in a vegetative state, are solved. As is well known, a court appoints a competent person to manage the affairs of an incompetent person. This guardian (or conservator or committee) represents the incapacitated person in legal matters. Similarly, we could have a legal system whereby a person could apply to the court to appoint a guardian if they felt a natural being was in danger.[935] There are no real obstacles to this. The only obstacle is the mindset we have created in our heads, which is based on human-nature dualism, which leads us to see nature as an object, not a right holder.

Of course, one could argue that *humans are different from everything else in nature and deserve different attention*. Humans are indeed different, but this applies to every species in nature. For example, lions are different from everything else in nature. However, we think that only we 'deserve different attention' and see ourselves as the rightful owners and everything else as objects. That does not make sense. Further, according to Goodpaster, neither rationality nor the ability to experience pain and pleasure (even if they are sufficient) are necessary conditions for qualifying for moral concern. It is only our own philosophical and ethical ways of thinking that prevent us from seeing this phenomenon. Being alive suffices as a reasonable and

---

[934] Stone, *Should Trees Have Standing?*, p. 7.

[935] Stone, *Should Trees Have Standing?*, p. 8.

unbiased criterion.[936] Suppose we limit the sphere of moral capacity to beings who, among all living beings, are only suffering or conscious. In that case, we are restricting the subject of moral capacity to those who are mostly like us. Without further evidence, this would be an arbitrary classification with significant environmental costs.[937] Therefore, in a green constitutional order, all living beings should be recognised as part of the moral community and treated accordingly.

It should not be ignored that the other elements of the ecosystem – soil, rivers, air, and even mountains and rocks – that keep all animals and plants alive, including humans, have a function in nature. Therefore, they, too, must be protected within the framework of their right to fulfil their functions within the ecosystem. Therefore, our responsibilities towards them must also be recognised at the constitutional level.

All this does not mean that no more animals can be killed or that river water cannot be utilised anymore. In line with green constitutionalism, we can make use of nature in a way that does not turn into exploitation and in accordance with the principles of equality, respect, and reciprocity. Otherwise, our survival would not be possible. We also have the right to fulfil our function within the ecosystem anyway. Green constitutionalism emphasises that in fulfilling this function, we should not disrupt the self-renewal cycle of nature and that human actions that disrupt this cycle should be prevented. At this point, it is imperative to recognise natural entities as subjects of rights and thus recognise that they have the capacity to sue. Suppose no one can sue against human actions that harm the ecosystem. In that case, the doors of the courts and other judicial bodies are closed, and the problem is left at the mercy of the legislature without the possibility of judicial review.[938] Given the close links of the current parliaments with capitalism and the bourgeois class, this leaves us with no solution.

Humanist thought sees nature as a single 'thing' in the human-nature dualism. However, wild nature has never been a homogeneous raw material; it has always been diverse.[939] When we look at human beings, we do not see

---

936 Kenneth Goodpaster, 'On Being Morally Considerable', *Journal of Philosophy*, Vol. 75, No. 6, 1978, p. 310.

937 DesJardins, *Environmental Ethics*, p. 244.

938 Stone, *Should Trees Have Standing?*, p. 49.

939 Leopold, *A Sand County Almanac*, p. 197.

only society; instead, we claim that each person has their characteristics and individual rights; the same is true for natural beings. Therefore, each natural being should be seen as an entity with its own rights and capacity to sue.

That, of course, implies a new understanding of ethics. According to Leopold, every kind of ethics that has developed to the present day has a single fulcrum: The individual is a member of a community of mutually interdependent parts. This 'land ethics' that we must embrace extends the boundaries of the community to embrace land, water, plants, and animals[940] and even transforms the Earth as a whole into a subject of rights.

It is essential to bear in mind that the relationship between humans and the Earth is not one between equals but between the whole and the part. Accordingly, while the needs of the part must be respected, it is inappropriate to try to weigh them against the rights of the whole. The rights of the whole cannot be compromised.[941] We must, therefore, develop tools that recognise the roles of nonhuman members of the ecosystem on Earth, prevent humans from unjustifiably impeding the fulfilment of those roles,[942] and thus protect the whole.

From a practical point of view, granting rights to nonhuman living and non-living things and preventing human actions on them through some legal instruments can be an invaluable way to protect and expand eco-communities.[943] Moreover, governance systems based on an ecological legal theory should not only recognise that nonhuman members of the ecosystem can have 'rights' but also develop a language to define these rights and legal mechanisms to fully recognise them. The challenge is to redesign and develop the philosophical basis for organising and regulating our species in a way that is more in tune with the reality of a universe of interconnected subjects.[944]

In some countries, such as Ecuador and India, nonhuman animals and, in some other countries, natural beings have been granted rights at the constitutional level. These are more symbolic than dominant at the moment, but still critical because they reflect and translate the understanding of Indigenous

---

940 Leopold, *A Sand County Almanac*, p. 213.
941 Cullinan, *Wild Law*, p. 100.
942 Cullinan, *Wild Law*, p. 118.
943 Bookchin, *The Ecology of Freedom*, p. 40.
944 Cullinan, *Wild Law*, p. 108.

people into written constitutional language when they are allowed to participate in its writing.[945]

4.2.2.1 Recognising animals as subjects of constitutional rights

As can be understood from the foregoing, it has always been at the discretion of those who have established and maintained a legal system, what constitutes a crime and what is permissible in a legal system, or who has which rights and freedoms, or under what conditions and how these rights and freedoms can be restricted. Those who hold economic, social, and political power have always decided who counts as a person and who is considered a subject of rights.[946] Black people could be sold and bought under white law, and women were considered second-class citizens under men's law. A similar discriminatory situation applies to animals in human law.

Humanist and modern Western thought, which separated humans from nature and gave them a superior position, had a negative impact on the legal position of animals. In Ancient Greece, where the roots of this thought lie, Aristotle argued that animals are inferior in the natural hierarchy because they lack reason. According to him, this natural hierarchy imposed both the right and the responsibility on those above them to use those below them. Later, the Stoics went further and argued that animals lacked the capacity to think and existed only to be used.[947] By separating mind and body, Descartes denied animals not only the faculty of reason but also a range of sensations associated with thought. As a result, he saw animals as mindless machines, far inferior to humans.[948] Immanuel Kant (1724–1804), unlike Descartes, acknowledged that animals could suffer but argued that they are not rationally self-aware and that we do not have any direct obligation towards them. According to him, since animals were not rational, they were nothing more than a 'thing'[949] and an apparatus for humans to use to achieve their ends.

---

[945] Capra – Mattei, *The Ecology of Law*, p. 195.

[946] Serkan Koybasi, 'Yeni Bir Anayasal Hak Öznesi Olarak Hayvan – I', *Journal of Constitutional Law*, Vol. 7, No. 13, 2018, p. 105.

[947] Lori Gruen, *Ethics and Animals – An Introduction* (Kindle version), Cambridge University Press, New York, 2011, p. 2.

[948] Garrard, *Ecocriticism*, p. 47.

[949] Alasdair Cochrane, *Animal Rights Without Liberation – Applied Ethics and Human Obligations*, Columbia University Press, New York, 2012, p. 26.

In this context, animals that existed only for human use had no value in themselves.[950] In line with his thoughts on nature, Locke saw animals as one of the resources God had bestowed on human beings. According to him, who thought that we should not 'destroy' and 'waste' animals because of our obligations to God and other human beings, there should be some limits to our use or treatment of them. However, these limits were no different from those on other natural resources such as land, water, or forests.[951] Our current economic and legal system, based on these ideas, has established an unimaginable system of exploitation of animals.

Nevertheless, ever since Charles Darwin proposed the theory of evolution, we have known that humans are a species of animal. Like every other species, humans have characteristics that make them different from others. However, being different does not make it 'superior' to others by itself and does not justify domination over them. As Bookchin puts it, it is fair to say that some species are more flexible than others in their ability to adapt and have more complex nervous systems. Humans can be said to be more advanced in dealing with new situations than other less flexible and less neurologically advanced species. However, in no way does it follow from this that more advanced life forms can or should dominate less advanced life forms. The notion that more advanced life forms are meant to be more dominant is a purely anthropomorphic image, reflecting elitist ideologies that justify domination, not the relationships that should exist in the natural world or, for that matter, the social world.[952] In an egalitarian and just legal system, there cannot be a relationship based on hierarchical domination between humans and other animal species. In today's legal system, however, animals are considered property[953] and are not treated equally, even when they have interests similar to those of humans. While rights protect the interests of humans, similar interests of animals do not enjoy the same protection.

It must be recognised that creatures who can feel pleasure and pain have interests. Both humans and sentient animals have certain desires to satisfy

---

[950] Francione, *Introduction to Animal Rights*, pp. 51–2.
[951] Francione, *Introduction to Animal Rights*, p. 164.
[952] Bookchin, *The Ecology of Freedom*, p. 37.
[953] For the intellectual roots of this process, which historically follows a similar process with the commodification of nature, see Koybasi, 'Yeni Bir ... – I', pp. 125–30.

their interests and thus ensure their well-being. Like humans, other animals want the conditions for a good life, such as food, shelter, access to water, and peaceful rest. The avoidance of suffering and the desire for pleasure are intuitive feelings that all animals share. Every interest – regardless of who owns it – must be pursued equally.[954] Equality is not a statement of fact but a moral idea. Therefore, as Jeremy Bentham puts forward, the question we should ask is not *Can they reason?* or *Can they speak?* but *Can they suffer?*[955] If a living being can suffer, there is no moral justification for ignoring that suffering. The principle of equality requires that this suffering be equated with similar suffering in any other living being, regardless of the nature of the suffering being.[956] Consequently, every creature with desires, pleasure, and pain – regardless of its species – must be recognised as having interests and, under this characteristic, as a member of the moral community. That means that its rights must be recognised at the constitutional level.[957]

However, the fundamental rights of nonhuman animals have not been recognised yet. Today, when we talk about 'animal rights', we actually talk about some limits on certain human actions on animals in order to improve their welfare during their exploitation. That leads to the continued comparison of the interests of humans and animals, each time prioritising the interests of humans (even the most basic ones, such as taste) over the most fundamental interests of animals (such as the interest to live). That could not be possible if animals were recognised as subjects of rights because, as Francione points out, when we say that someone has a right, it means that that person has a value that we should respect, whether or not our use of that person benefits

954 Engin Arıkan, *Hayvan Hakları İnsan Hukuku*, Ekin, Bursa, 2016, p. 16.

955 Jeremy Bentham, *Introduction to the Principles of Morals and Legislation*, chapter 17, cited in: Peter Singer, *Animal Liberation* (Turkish version), trans. Hayrullah Doğan, Ayrıntı, Istanbul, 2005, p. 44.

956 Singer, *Animal Liberation*, p. 46.

957 This perspective could be considered anthropocentric. Indeed, Goodpaster, as noted immediately earlier, argues that 'being alive' is sufficient to have moral status. See Goodpaster, 'On Being Morally Considerable', p. 316. Moreover, Goodpaster's thinking is closer to the idea that every natural being has a meaning in the ecosystem and is valuable for this reason alone. However, recognising first the rights of other sentient animals would be an important threshold for breaking the human monopoly in the concept of rights. Once this monopoly is broken, it would be easier to recognise the concept of rights for other beings of nature.

others. A right is something like a barrier between the holder and everyone else. It generally cannot be abolished simply on the grounds that it would be beneficial to someone else for the holder to lose that right.[958]

As mentioned earlier, in the past, the interests of black people or women have been ignored in favour of the interests of white men. However, thanks to those fighting for a fairer world, we now recognise these as racism and misogyny and criminalise it. However, our legal systems still emphasise whether the beneficiary is a human or animal. That is another form of discrimination, just like racism or misogyny. However, this discrimination, called speciesism,[959] is still not criminalised and even protected by our legal systems.[960]

This discriminatory approach to animals needs to be abandoned in order to establish a more just legal order respectful to rights. Every animal has a life that can be good or bad.[961] Accordingly, it must be recognised that it is the subject of its own life and has an intrinsic value. That requires its recognition as a right holder.[962] The realisation of this recognition at the constitutional level will facilitate the recognition of animals as 'beings capable of demanding the protection of their constitutional rights' by the definition of a 'legal person'.[963]

Today's legal approach, based on the distinction between 'human beings and everything else', normalises, protects, and perpetuates the incredible injustices that take place in front of our eyes every day. Chief among these injustices is our treatment of animals and the system of exploitation we have created.[964] We must abandon the notion that only humans have rights, de-monopolise the concept of rights, and protect nature's living and non-living beings, which are as important as we are, against human activities. A green

---

958 Francione, *Animals, Property and the Law*, p. 8.

959 The term was first used by Richard Ryder in *Victims of Science: The Use of Animals in Research* (Davis-Poynter, London, 1975).

960 See Koybasi, 'Yeni Bir … – I', pp. 113–18.

961 Cochrane, *Animal Rights …*, p. 40.

962 Tom Regan, *Empty Cages: Facing the Challenge of Animal Rights* (Turkish version), trans. Serpil Çağlayan, İletişim, İstanbul, 2007, p. 83.

963 Serkan Koybasi, 'Yeni Bir Anayasal Hak Öznesi Olarak Hayvan – II', *Journal of Constitutional Law*, Vol. 7, No. 14, 2018, p. 387.

964 Serkan Koybasi, 'Hayvan Hakları: Mülkiyet, Eşitlik, Hukuk', *in* Didem Bayındır – Mine Yıldırım (ed.), *Ekoloji: Bir Arada Yaşamın Geleceği*, Tellekt, Istanbul, 2022, p. 356.

constitutional order requires treating the interests of animals and humans equally and ending the current exploitation. In this way, their interests would be protected by rights, and animals would be recognised as constitutional subjects of rights.

Indeed, in countries with a high level of ecological sensitivity, decisions have begun to be seen that animals should enjoy rights protection similar to that of humans. For example, in 2018, the Uttarakhand High Court issued a decision recognising the legal personality of animals and recognising them as subjects of rights. In its ruling on a request to order that 'horses used in the border trade between India and Nepal must be vaccinated against diseases and health checks must be carried out; otherwise this traffic must be blocked',[965] the Court comprehensively evaluated the relevant scientific, philosophical, and religious sources. It also included the impact of climate change on animals in its decision.

> Many species are becoming extinct. The loss of one species causes immense damage to the entire ecosystem. Global warming has arrived and its impact can be seen in day-to-day existence. There are gaps in laws. New inventions are required to be made in law to protect the environment and ecology. The animals including avian and aquatics have a right to life and bodily integrity, honour and dignity. Animals cannot be treated merely as property.[966]

Declaring all members of the animal kingdom as legal persons, the Court said that each has a separate *persona* with the relevant rights, duties, and responsibilities of a natural person. It ruled that everyone in the State of Uttarakhand constitutes their 'human face' for the welfare and protection of animals and can protect them *in loco parentis*.[967,968]

Similarly, the Ecuadorian Constitutional Court ruled in 2021 that a chorongo[969] monkey kept in a house for years was a 'person' with *habeas corpus*

---

965 Uttarakhand High Court, *Narayan Dutt Bhatt v. Union of India and Others*, (PIL) No. 43 of 2014, 4 July 2018.

966 *Narayan Dutt Bhatt v. Union of India and Others*, § 84.

967 Latin term meaning 'in place of a parent' and describing the process by which a person or organisation takes the place of a parent and has certain rights and responsibilities following this status.

968 *Narayan Dutt Bhatt v. Union of India and Others*, § 99, A.

969 General name for woolly apes.

rights.[970] The monkey, named Estrellita, was illegally taken by Ana Beatriz Burbano Proano as a young child and lived in her home for eighteen years. When the situation became known, the Ministry of Environment took the monkey away from her and placed it in a rehabilitation centre. Estrellita died there. Ana Beatriz filed a *habeas corpus* action for the taking of the monkey. She claimed that Estrellita's seizure was an 'unlawful detention'. The first instance and appellate courts rejected this claim. Ana Beatriz then appealed to the Constitutional Court.

The question in this case was whether the concept of 'Mother Nature', recognised as a subject of rights in the Ecuadorian Constitution,[971] includes animals. The Constitutional Court ruled that animals are part of nature and should enjoy the same rights as Mother Nature. Thus, the Court recognised that Estrellita had rights deriving from the Constitution, including 'the right to the free development of her animal behaviour'. According to the Court, Estrellita's domestication amounted to a violation of her right to freedom. The Constitutional Court found that the Ministry of Environment's confinement of her in a rehabilitation centre constituted a similar violation.

As a result, the Ecuadorian Constitutional Court ruled in this historic decision[972] that Estrellita's constitutional personality rights were violated both by Ana Beatriz by confining her at home and by the state by taking her away and putting her in a rehabilitation centre. This decision is seen as revolutionary as it is the first Supreme Court ruling in the world to recognise a single animal as a subject of rights at the constitutional level. Let us hope this decision is one of the first steps towards banning speciesism.

4.2.2.2 Recognising the rights of other natural entities

The idea that other natural beings, such as animals, should also have rights is still quite radical and disturbing for many since nature as a collection of things intended for human use is one of the most universal and unquestioned concepts in contemporary society.[973] That again stems from the perception that the subject of rights in modern legal systems can only be human beings.

---

970 Constitutional Court of Ecuador, case no. 253-20-JH, judgment no. 253-20-JH/22, 27 January 2022.

971 See 6.2.2

972 'A Landmark Ruling for Animal Rights in Ecuador', *Nonhuman Rights*, 23 March 2022.

973 Boyd, *The Rights of Nature*, p. XXVI.

Those who adopt and follow the theory of human rights, which is a product of Enlightenment thought, cannot imagine any other concept of rights.[974] The reason why nature is not considered equal to humans in legal terms and why this is considered normal is that we have grown up in an anthropocentric intellectual tradition. This tradition treats the natural world as an object to be exploited and studied for human use rather than a subject to be integrated and respected.[975] Yet, this kind of treatment is not only morally wrong but also it is one of the primary reasons for climate change and must stop. We must abandon this harmful, arrogant, and unjust approach through the green constitutional movement.

The idea of nature as a subject of rights is in sharp contrast to today's anthropocentric environmental protection arrangements. Although over the last fifty years, there has been a growing recognition of the strong link between human rights and the environment in which we live, most environmental regulations have failed to prevent pollution and the extinction of species and habitats.[976] In this context, the movement towards recognising the rights of nature, a key element of green constitutionalism, can be seen as one of the most remarkable legal transformations in history since it is a movement with real potential to reorient human societies towards sustainability.[977] Boyd even calls the rights of nature 'a legal revolution that could save the world'.[978] It is not only a legal revolution but also a philosophical rupture, an economic transformation, an ecological struggle, and a collaboration with the natural sciences.[979]

Just as women's suffrage or the abolition of slavery were once unthinkable but gradually came to pass and became normalised, so the idea of the rights of nature may seem strange today. For the rights of nature to be understood and for us to make peace with the idea, just as with the end

---

974 Üskül Engin, *Ekolojik Kriz, Etik ve Hukuk*, p. 157.
975 Sigal Samuel, 'Lake Erie Now Has Legal Rights, Just Like You', *VOX*, 26 February 2019.
976 Giménez – Ortuño, 'An Ecological Citizenship's Triumph', p. 84.
977 Collins, *The Ecological Constitution*, p. 64.
978 See David R. Boyd, *The Rights of Nature: A Legal Revolution That Could Save The World*, ECW Press, Toronto, 2017.
979 Durmaz, *Doğanın Hakları*, p. 6.

of slavery, a paradigm shift is needed.[980] This transformation has already begun. As explained further, in countries ranging from New Zealand to Bangladesh, from Colombia to the United States, nonhuman natural entities, and in some cases even ecosystems, have been granted legal personality and rights. The granting of legal personality to natural assets and ecosystems prevents the unlimited exploitation of nature for the sake of maximising profits and forces governments to prioritise the sustainability of life over economic interests.[981]

Although in practice, this transformation is more visible in the countries of the Global South, where the distinction between man and nature has never been very firmly established but is only an idea brought by settlers and colonisers, intellectually, it has long been argued also in Western countries that the modern, dualistic approach to law should be abandoned and the rights of nature recognised. The struggle for their recognition consists of demands for respect for the rules governing the ecology of the Earth. Nature is a living system, indivisible, interdependent, and interconnected, with its own laws that keep the ecosystem in order and make life possible. Any fundamental change in the laws that maintain order in nature, its basic components, or ecosystems can negatively affect the health of all their components and even the existence of an entire system.[982] This idea first returned to Western legal thought in Christopher Stone's 1972 essay *Should Trees Have Standing?*[983] This work provides such strong legal arguments for why and how the concept of rights, which had been associated with human beings, could be extended to natural beings that it influenced many jurists and was cited in numerous court decisions.

Developing an entirely new perspective for his time on the ability to sue for acts harmful to nature[984] through the US Supreme Court decision *Sierra Club v. Morton*,[985] Stone seeks an answer to what it would mean for a natural

---

980 Ben Price, national director of *the Community Environmental Legal Defense Fund, in* Samuel, 'Lake Erie …'.

981 Giménez – Ortuño, 'An Ecological Citizenship's Triumph', p. 92.

982 Giménez – Ortuño, 'An Ecological Citizenship's Triumph', p. 85.

983 Collins, *The Ecological Constitution*, p. 66.

984 Tom R. Moore, 'Should Trees Have Standing? Toward Legal Rights for Natural Objects – Book Review', *Florida State University Law Review*, Vol. 2, No. 3, 1974, p. 672.

985 For more information on this decision, see 4.2.2.2 United States of America

entity to have rights. Taking a river as an example, Stone argues that in order for it to have 'its' rights, such a legal system should be conceived such that (1) a lawsuit could be brought on behalf of the river (through a guardian or agent) against the owner of the polluting factory; (2) the guardian could hold the factory liable for unjustifiably changing the river from one state to another (e.g. from one full of oxygen and fish to one without life), regardless of whether there were any economic consequences for humans; (3) the outcome of the proceedings is in the interests of the river (e.g. if the award is to make the river oxygenated and full of fish again by cleaning up the pollution – making it 'whole' again – the polluter deposits the compensation into a fund for the river and the guardian withdraws it). In other words, we can speak of the rights of the river if (1) the action is in the name of the entity itself (and not in the name of a human being), (2) the damages are calculated based on the loss suffered by the nonhuman element (and not limited to the economic losses suffered by humans), and (3) the decision is in the interest of the nonhuman element.[986]

If the rights of natural entities are recognised, it could be argued that they would be in constant conflict with the rights of human beings. While this is partly true, theoretically, any conflict between the rights of humans and those of nature can be resolved by rethinking humans as an integral part of nature since human needs and rights should also be seen as a component of the rights of nature. Indeed, when future generations are included in those who can enjoy human rights, there is a clear synergy between human rights and the rights of nature, especially at the level of ecosystems and the biosphere.[987] Therefore, it is always possible to interpret the rights of humans and nature in such a way that they do not conflict but rather nurture each other. Within this framework, some countries have recognised rights for natural assets through legislation, and others have recognised them through their supreme courts. Only New Zealand and Spain are mentioned later as examples of countries granting rights to specific natural entities through

---

986 Stone, *Should Trees Have Standing?*, p. XI.
987 Collins, *The Ecological Constitution*, p. 78.

their parliaments. However, it should be noted that Australia,[988] Bolivia,[989] Panama,[990] and Uganda[991] have also adopted similar laws, and this list is expected to grow longer. On the other hand, the fact that some natural entities have been recognised as subjects of rights through higher court decisions at national and regional levels deserves closer attention as an example of green constitutionalism in that they bind both lower courts and the legislative and executive branches. For this reason, I have tried to compile all the decisions in this direction so far.

New Zealand

Internationally, there is a general perception that New Zealand is a country with a high level of nature conservation. The fact that it is far away from industrialised and densely populated areas has indeed given it an advantage so far. New Zealand was the first place in the world where the green movement emerged as a political party, and it is a country where contact with nuclear energy is banned by law. Apart from these, the traditions of the Indigenous Māori people, who arrived on these islands 800 years before Europeans, are also an important reason why nature has been preserved as much as possible in New Zealand. Although their lifestyle, which is harmonious with nature, was largely destroyed after the arrival of European settlers, some of their cultural traits are still alive today. For example, the understanding that one cannot legally own a piece of land is an indicator of it. According to this idea, people belong to the land, but the land does not belong to people.[992]

---

988 In Australia, the State of Victoria recognised and protected the Great Ocean Road in 2020 and the Yarra River (*Birrarung* for Indigenous peoples) in 2023 as living assets. However, these natural features have not been granted legal personality.

989 With the Law on the Rights of Mother Nature (Law 300), adopted in Bolivia in 2010, nature was recognised as a subject of rights and endowed with various rights, including the right to exist, to maintain life cycles, to be in balance and not to be polluted.

990 In Panama, the Law on the Rights of Nature (Law 287) was adopted in February 2023, recognising nature as a subject of rights.

991 In Uganda, the National Environment Act adopted in 2019 recognised nature as a subject of rights. The rights granted to nature by this law include the right to exist, to continue its existence and to be reborn.

992 Klaus Bosselmann, *When Two Worlds Collide – Society and Ecology*, RSVP, Auckland, 1995, pp. 129–30. However, this understanding does not preclude full control over a certain piece of land and the structures on it, as is the case in Western law.

The Māori people's relationship with nature has gradually gained recognition in New Zealand's legislation, court judgements, government decisions, and the non-Māori population.[993]

In New Zealand, the rights of nature are enshrined in law, not in the Constitution. However, these laws are at least quasi-constitutional, as they emerge from agreements made under the Treaty of Waitangi,[994] recognised as part of the Constitution. New Zealand's intense interest in the rights of nature stems from an effort to redress historical and ongoing injustices against Māori communities. In parallel, the country has made progress in both ecological sustainability and Indigenous rights.[995]

As an indication of this, a law passed in 2014[996] granted legal rights and personality to the Te Urewera forest ecosystem, a former national park. In order to protect the intrinsic value of this ecosystem, its unique natural and cultural values, the integrity of these values, and the national significance of the forest, the law explicitly recognised Te Urewera as a legal entity. It declared that *Te Urewere is a legal entity and has all the rights, powers, duties, and liabilities of a legal person.*[997] A board was established to exercise these legal rights, powers, duties, and liabilities.[998] Its objectives include acting on Te Urewera's behalf and administering it per the law.[999] Today, the board comprises nine members, six of whom are appointed by the Indigenous Māori people[1000] and three of whom are appointed by the government.[1001]

Similarly, for more than 140 years, tribes living around the Whanganui (*Te Awa Tupua*) River had fought to have it recognised as their ancestral

---

993 Boyd, *The Rights of Nature*, p. 134.

994 The treaty signed in 1840 between Captain William Hobson, representing the British Crown, and the Māori chiefs of the North Island of New Zealand, which recognised the ownership of Māori communities over their lands, forests and other property and made Māori people British citizens.

995 Collins, *The Ecological Constitution*, p. 71.

996 *Te Urewera Act 2014 (No. 51)* (Te Urewera Act).

997 Te Urewera Act, section 11(1).

998 Te Urewera Act, chapter 16.

999 Te Urewera Act, chapter 17.

1000 *Tūhoe Te Uru Taumatau*.

1001 Te Urewera Act, section 21(2).

territory.[1002] Finally, after lengthy negotiations with Māori communities, the Te Awa Tupua Act[1003] was passed in 2017, recognising its legal personality. With this law, the river is recognised as a 'living entity' and has all the rights, powers, duties, and responsibilities of a legal entity. The law created a body called *Te Pou Tupua*, which acts as the river's trustee. As the 'human face' of the river and acting on its behalf,[1004] its central role is to promote and protect its health and well-being.[1005] Of the two people who make up *Te Pou Tupua*, one is appointed by the Māori people of Whanganui, and the other is appointed by the Kingdom of England from amongst respected Māori leaders.[1006]

This proxy body also forms part of a multi-stakeholder basin management institution. Thus, the river itself, as a legal entity, is a member of the integrated watershed management body through its trustees and can participate directly in watershed management decisions.[1007] With this guardianship body and other features, the Te Awa Tupua Law provides a model for an appropriate institutional framework for the enforcement of 'rights of nature' according to local circumstances.[1008]

Mount Taranaki, considered sacred by some Indigenous communities, is the third natural asset to be recognised as a legal entity in New Zealand. Mount Taranaki became a legal entity through a Record of Understanding[1009] agreed upon between eight Māori tribes,[1010] who regard the mountain as an ancestor and family member, and the United Kingdom. British colonists took the land around the mountain from Indigenous peoples in the nineteenth

---

1002 Eleanor Ainge Roy, 'New Zealand River Granted Same Legal Rights as Human Being', *The Guardian*, 16 March 2017.

1003 *Te Awa Tupua (Whanganui River Claims Settlement) Act 2017 (NZ), 2017/7* (Te Awa Tupua Act).

1004 Te Awa Tupua Act, section 18(2).

1005 Te Awa Tupua Act, section 19(1)(c).

1006 Te Awa Tupua Act, section 20(2).

1007 Craig M. Kauffman – Pamela L. Martin, 'How Courts Are Developing River Rights Jurisprudence: Comparing Guardianship in New Zealand, Colombia, and India', *Vermont Journal of Environmental Law*, Vol. 40, No. 4, 2019, p. 272.

1008 Bosselmann, *The Principle of Sustainability*, p. 164.

1009 *Record of Understanding for Mount Taranaki, Pouākai and the Kaitake Ranges*, 20 December 2017.

1010 Eleanor Ainge Roy, 'New Zealand Gives Mount Taranaki Same Legal Rights as a Person', *The Guardian*, 22 December 2017.

century and used it for agricultural purposes. Although the Record does not provide any compensation for Indigenous peoples for the damage done to Mount Taranaki, it does include an apology from the Crown.[1011] Recognising that the Mountain is an indivisible living entity,[1012] the Record established a body to represent and be the 'human face' of Mount Taranaki,[1013] as was the case with the other two natural entities recognised as legal entities in the country. Of this body's eight members, half are Indigenous peoples' representatives, and the Crown appoints the other half.

Colombia

Although the Colombian Constitution does not explicitly recognise the rights of nature, the Colombian Constitutional Court created a critical jurisprudence with its decision on the heavily polluted Atrato River basin.[1014] The ecosystem of the Atrato River basin, one of the most biodiverse places in the world, had been significantly damaged due to the environmental impacts of illegal mining activities that had been going on for many years. That has caused and is still causing starvation, disease, and even death among the Indigenous people living in the region, especially Afro-Colombian[1015] children. In 2014, the country's Ombudsman declared a 'humanitarian and environmental emergency' in the municipality of Chocó, 60 per cent of whose surface area is covered by this basin. Despite this fact, the region was largely 'abandoned' by the state. Infrastructure for even the most basic needs, such as drinking water or health care, was not in place.[1016]

The Colombian Constitutional Court made some crucial observations in its 2016 ruling on *an acción de tutela*[1017] filed by Indigenous communities in the Chocó region to challenge this situation. The Court said that the most

---

[1011] Memorandum of Understanding, section 4.

[1012] Memorandum of Understanding, section 3.4.

[1013] Memorandum of Understanding, section 5.14.

[1014] *Social Justice Center and Others v. Presidency and Others*, Judgment no. T-622/16, 10 November 2016 (Atrato River Judgment).

[1015] Colombians of African descent. Large numbers of Africans were enslaved and brought to Colombia in the sixteenth century, mainly to work in gold mines and sugar cane plantations. Today, the number of people of African descent is estimated to be about a quarter of the Colombian population. See 'Afro-Colombians', *Wikipedia*.

[1016] Atrato River Judgment, § 2.7.

[1017] A simplified public interest litigation process.

significant test of contemporary constitutionalism on environmental issues is to ensure the conservation and adequate protection of nature and the cultures and life forms that depend on it, as well as biodiversity. According to the Court, they should be recognised as subjects of rights not because of the material, genetic, or productive function they provide to human beings but because they are living units composed of many life forms and cultural representations. That requires comprehensive protection and respect for the rights of all living elements of nature by states and societies. In sum, the Colombian Constitutional Court has set aside a purely utilitarian, economic, or efficiency-limited conceptual approach to nature, its members, and their cultures and has stated that it is only through an attitude of deep respect and humility towards them that we can enter into a just and equitable relationship with them. Noting the interconnectedness of all living beings on Earth, the Court pointed out that rather than defining ourselves in terms of normative categories of domination, exploitation, or self-interest, we should see ourselves as one of the parts that make up the whole of the global ecosystem – the biosphere – and based this on the principle of cultural and ethnic pluralism in the Colombian Constitution.[1018]

Thus, the Court developed a nature-centred approach that acknowledges nature as a subject of rights, which the state must recognise, and that these rights are realised through the representatives of the communities that live in the area or have developed a special relationship with it. That resulted in a holistic assessment of the critical link between human ecological rights and the rights of nature.[1019]

Thanks to this perspective, the Court held that the respondent state organs were responsible for the violation of the applicant ethnic communities' fundamental rights to water and food security, the pollution of the Atrato River basin as a result of illegal mining activities in the area, and the failure to find an appropriate, effective and institutionalised solution to this problem.[1020] In addition, the Court decided that, although there is no provision in the Constitution that nature is a subject of rights, the Atrato River itself, its basin, and its tributaries should be recognised as a subject of rights to be

[1018] Atrato River Judgment, § 5.10.
[1019] Collins, *The Ecological Constitution*, p. 75.
[1020] Atrato River Judgment, § 9.34.

protected, preserved, cared for and restored by the State and local communities, under the heading 'orders' of its judgement. Additionally, the Colombian Constitutional Court ordered the national government to establish an institution to protect and represent the rights of the Atrato River, similar to the trusteeship institutions established in New Zealand, with the representation of the applicant Indigenous communities living in the area.[1021]

These legal developments in New Zealand and Colombia are considered globally revolutionary and pioneering examples of the recognition and codification by national legal systems of an Indigenous worldview that accepts humans and the rest of the natural world as inextricably linked. As can be seen, these decisions stand in stark opposition to the dominant Western legal paradigm that sees the natural world as a 'commodity' to be used or exploited by humans[1022] and force its transformation.

As these decisions by the Constitutional Courts of New Zealand and Colombia highlight, the most effective way to implement rights of nature legislation is to ensure that an institution of agency represents the natural asset and participates in integrated governance systems.[1023] This approach not only improves ecological outcomes but also supports a more widespread ecological democracy. That is because, as part of the legal realisation of these rights, governments are forced to grant legal mandates to local citizens, who have often historically been deprived of control over their own essential ecological resources.[1024] That suggests a direct link between recognising the rights of nature and strengthening democracy. These decisions make it even more apparent that the claim arguing that a liberal economic order is the *sine qua non* of democracy is not justified and that, in essence, the opposite is true.

India

Like in New Zealand and Colombia, the Indian Constitution does not include any article on the rights of nature. It does not even include a human right to a healthy environment. In the world's most populous country, these rights

---

[1021] Atrato River Judgment, § 10.2 (1)

[1022] 'Rights of Nature Case Study – Mount Taranaki / Taranaki Maunga ', *Anima Mundi Law Initiative*, p. 3.

[1023] Kauffman – Martin, 'How Courts … ', p. 289.

[1024] David Takacs, 'We Are the River', *University of Illinois Law Review*, No. 2, 2012, p. 550, cited in: Collins, *The Ecological Constitution*, p. 73.

have been incorporated into the legal system through court decisions. In 2017, the Uttarakhand High Court recognised the Ganges and Yamuna rivers and their tributaries as 'juristic/legal persons/living entities having the status of a legal person with all corresponding rights'[1025] due to the fact that mining activities had created an extraordinary situation that threatened the existence of them, which necessitated extraordinary measures.[1026]

Noting that the Ganges and Yamuna rivers are sacred to Hindus,[1027] the Court referred to previous judgements[1028] pointing out that the concept of 'legal personality' is a concept that is determined according to need within the framework of human and social development and that anything, whether living or object, can be designated as a legal person by law.[1029] Although the Court continued its anthropocentric perspective by emphasising at the beginning of paragraph 17 of its judgement how sacred these two rivers are to half of Indian society and how closely linked to their health and well-being, it also stated in the last sentence of the same paragraph that the Ganges and Yamuna 'breathe' and 'live'. Consequently, the Uttarakhand High Court said that it was imperative to establish a body called the Ganga Management Board[1030] to protect and preserve these two rivers, declaring them 'legal persons with rights, duties, and responsibilities just like a natural person' and designating certain officials to represent them as the human face of these rivers.[1031]

In the subsequent 'Glaciers' case,[1032] the same Court went further and issued a *parens patriae*[1033] decision on the grounds that the Gangotri and Yamunotri glaciers, located within the borders of the State of Uttarakhand, where the Ganges and Yamuna rivers originate, have been melting rapidly due to pollution and climate change, especially since the 1970s. Referring to

---

1025 Uttarakhand High Court, *Mohd. Salim v. State of Uttarakhand*, (PIL) No. 126 of 2014, 20 March 2017, § 19.

1026 *Mohd. Salim v. State of Uttarakhand*, § 10.

1027 *Mohd. Salim v. State of Uttarakhand*, § 11.

1028 *Mohd. Salim v. State of Uttarakhand*, § 12.

1029 *Mohd. Salim v. State of Uttarakhand*, § 16.

1030 *Mohd. Salim v. State of Uttarakhand*, § 18.

1031 *Mohd. Salim v. State of Uttarakhand*, § 19.

1032 Uttarakhand High Court, *Lalit Miglani v. State of Uttarakhand*, (PIL) No. 140 of 2015, 30 March 2017.

1033 Latin for 'parent of the country'. In legal terms, it indicates a type of judgment issued by a state or court to protect those within its jurisdiction.

the Stockholm Declaration and the reports prepared by the IPCC, the resolution pointed out that the loss of natural resources threatens all of humanity. The Court referred to a part of the book of Vikram Soni and Sanjay Parikh where they highlight that *We must understand that the fundamental human rights on which human survival depends are Nature's rights*,[1034] thus establishing the part-whole relationship between human beings and nature in line with green constitutionalism.

Although it did not reject anthropocentrism outright by referring to the Stockholm Declaration of the UN on page 18 of the judgement stating, *Of all things in the world, people are the most precious*, the Uttarakhand High Court, throughout the judgement, demonstrated the importance of nature, both in general and in its individual elements, by describing in detail the ecosystems around these two glaciers. Consequently, the Court declared that the glaciers, rivers, streams, creeks, lakes, air, pastures, valleys, dense forests, forest wetlands, meadows, springs, and waterfalls, including Gangotri and Yamunotri, are *legal entity/legal person/juristic person/juridical person/moral person/artificial person having the status of a legal person, with all corresponding rights, duties and liabilities of a living in order to conserve and preserve them*.[1035] Noting that these elements of nature are endowed with rights close to fundamental rights/ legal rights, the Court said that the rights of these legal entities are equal to the rights of human beings and, consequently, any harm to them must be considered as harm to human beings.[1036] The Uttarakhand High Court, which has set up a committee of guardians comprising independent jurists and government officials to exercise the status of these natural entities and look after their health and well-being, has banned mining on rivers originating from glaciers and ordered the immediate sealing of industrial enterprises, hotels, ashrams,[1037] and other businesses that discharge effluents into the rivers.[1038]

The Uttarakhand High Court was not the only court in India that ruled in favour of natural beings. The joint high court of the northern states of Punjab and Haryana also ruled in March 2020 that Sukhna Lake in Chandigarh

[1034] *Lalit Miglani v. State of Uttarakhand*, p. 7.

[1035] *Lalit Miglani v. State of Uttarakhand*, p. 70.

[1036] *Lalit Miglani v. State of Uttarakhand*, p. 66, § 2 and 5.

[1037] In India, the name given to a place in the forest or mountains where sages live in peace, away from the bustle of the world.

[1038] *Lalit Miglani v. State of Uttarakhand*, p. 66, § 6.

district is a legal person and ordered the demolition of illegal and unauthorised structures in its catchment area.[1039] The Court fined the state governments for condoning illegal construction and ordered them to declare Sukhna Lake a protected wetland under the relevant environmental legislation.

Bangladesh

Three major rivers originating in the Himalayas converge in Bangladesh, creating the largest delta in the world. Eighty per cent of the densely populated country of 165 million is floodplain. As a result, millions of fishermen and farmers inevitably live in the riverbed.[1040] In 2016, one of Bangladesh's national newspapers published an article about filling the Turag River bed, which flows through the capital, Dhaka, the occupation of land, and the construction of illegal structures in this area.[1041] The article claimed that the Turag River was 'dying' due to the construction around it. The article, supported by photographs, revealed the illegal construction on the river bed. The article mentioned that several lawsuits had been filed against it and that the courts had ordered the demolition of these structures but that these decisions had not been implemented.

Following the publicity of this story, in a case brought in the public interest by an organisation called Human Rights and Peace for Bangladesh against the Ministry of Transport and some other state bodies, the Bangladesh High Court, relying on the public trust doctrine[1042] and following the terminology of local high courts in India,[1043] declared the Turag River a legal person/legal entity/living entity.[1044] The Court then extended this legal status and

---

[1039] Saurabh Malik, 'HC: Sukhna Lake of Chandigarh Is Legal Entity, Raze Buildings in Catchment Area', *The Tribune India*, 3 March 2020.

[1040] Rina Chandran, 'Fears of Eviction as Bangladesh Gives Rivers Legal Rights', *Reuters*, 4 July 2019.

[1041] Tawfique Ali, 'Time to Declare Turag Dead', *The Daily Star*, 6 November 2016.

[1042] A legal principle, originated in the United States, whereby the government secures certain natural resources for public use without regard to private ownership.

[1043] Mohammad Sohidul Islam – Erin O'Donnell, 'Legal Rights for the Turag: Rivers as Living Entities in Bangladesh', *Asia Pacific Journal of Environmental Law*, Vol. 23, No. 2, 2020, p. 161.

[1044] Supreme Court of Bangladesh, *Human Rights and Peace for Bangladesh and Others v. Ministry of Transport Secretariat and Others*, WP no. 13989 of 2016, 30 January and 3 February 2019.

protection to all rivers in Bangladesh and issued numerous orders to the state and other respondents, saying that the rivers are shrinking every day due to illegal development in the riverbeds.[1045] Declaring several important international environmental principles, including the precautionary and polluter pays principles, to be part of the country's legal system from now on, and citing similar legal developments around the world where natural assets are recognised as legal entities, the Court established a body called the National River Conservation Commission and designated it as the legal guardian (*in loco parentis*) of all rivers in the country. Thus, it followed the decision on the Atrato River in Colombia.[1046] However, unlike the Atrato River judgement, it declared the body established according to the judgement to be the guardian of all rivers in the country, not just a single river.

The commission established by this decision is an advisory body. As such, it has no legal authority to take action against river occupation or pollution.[1047] However, it has a legal responsibility to protect and preserve rivers. With this decision, the commission has been recognised as having a say in any project involving any river, canal, or body of water in the country. Henceforth, government agencies will have to obtain a 'no objection' certificate from the commission in order to move forward with projects involving these natural assets.

In addition, the Supreme Court of Bangladesh has issued several orders to address damage to the Turag River and land encroachment that must be implemented immediately. These include demolishing illegal structures in the basin within thirty days and punishing those who cause encroachment and pollution through various means, including exposure, future bank loans, or ineligibility to run in elections.

Therefore, although the decision was favourable in terms of making natural assets the subjects of rights and establishing a commission to defend their rights, it was also the target of criticism. The implementation of the decision has chiefly affected people experiencing poverty who rely on fishing and agriculture in the river. In the wake of the decision, the government began demolishing illegal structures on the riverbed in Dhaka, threatening to evict

---

[1045] 'Turag River Case', Human Rights and Peace for Bangladesh.
[1046] Islam – O'Donnell, 'Legal Rights … ', p. 161.
[1047] Islam – O'Donnell, 'Legal Rights … ', p. 174.

millions of people from their homes, where they had lived for years, and built them to be close to their workplaces.[1048] Although Muzibur Rahman Howlader, the chairman of the National River Conservation Commission established with the decision, said that the policy would also look after local communities and that protecting the river would also mean protecting the entire ecosystem, including the fishermen and farmers who make their living from the river,[1049] the fact that the Commission, unlike similar bodies established in New Zealand, does not include representatives of local communities is seen as a significant shortcoming.[1050] Unlike other river cases in Colombia and New Zealand, this case is not based on the values of local peoples, and in fact, unlike the other cases, it is against those who live around the river and make their living from it. Indeed, as Collins points out, this case shows how important it is to develop an integrated approach to the rights of nature and the environmental rights of humans. It must be acknowledged that to reach a just and fair outcome through these decisions, those who live closest to nature need to be considered and empowered in the processes of protecting and restoring ecological systems.[1051]

United States of America

One might think that in a country like the United States, which is considered a bastion of capitalism, it is not possible to recognise nature as a subject of rights. After all explained earlier, there is, of course, a grain of truth in this thought. As a matter of fact, neither an animal nor a natural being has ever been recognised as a subject of rights by any Supreme Court at the state or federal level so far. However, since the legal developments in this country have reverberated worldwide, special attention should be paid to this country.

The struggle to recognise the rights of natural assets in the United States began long ago. In 1965, the United States Forest Service put out a tender for constructing a recreational facility in the Mineral King Valley in the Sequoia National Park in Tulare County, California. The Walt Disney Company won the bid with a $35 million ski resort project that would be visited by

---

[1048] Chandran, 'Fears of Eviction … '.
[1049] Chandran, 'Fears of Eviction … '.
[1050] Islam – O'Donnell, 'Legal Rights … ', p. 177.
[1051] Collins, *The Ecological Constitution*, p. 78.

1.7 million people a year. The Sierra Club, an environmental organisation opposed to this massive project, filed a lawsuit under the Administrative Procedure Act to stop the project. According to the organisation, Disney's ski resort would cause 'irreversible harm to the public interest'. The case, which went all the way to the US Supreme Court on appeal, centred on whether the Mineral King Valley had standing to sue. The Supreme Court dismissed the case on the grounds that the Sierra Club would not be directly harmed by the project in the valley.[1052] Under this jurisprudence, those not directly harmed by actions that harm a natural asset in the United States are barred from suing on its behalf.[1053]

However, the famous dissenting opinion in this decision written by Supreme Court Justice William O. Douglas sparked an important debate in the United States and around the world about the rights of nature. *Contemporary public concern for protecting nature's ecological equilibrium should lead to the conferral of standing upon environmental objects to sue for their own protection*, Justice Douglas wrote, noting that the case would be more properly labelled as *Mineral King v. Morton* rather than *Sierra Club v. Morton*.[1054] Reminding that even corporations are recognised as 'persons', Douglas argued that *so it should be as respects valleys, alpine meadows, rivers, lakes, estuaries, beaches, ridges, groves of trees, swampland, or even the air, that feels the destructive pressures of modern technology and modern life*.[1055]

In 1972, the year of the judgement, Prof Christopher Stone was inspired by the case to write *Should Trees Have Standing?*, a seminal book for those fighting for the recognition of the rights of nature. This book has catalysed numerous articles and books on whether natural beings should have rights

---

[1052] US Supreme Court, *Sierra Club v. Morton*, 405 U.S. 727, 19 April 1972.

[1053] After this case, environmental organisations have developed a method of filing lawsuits through any of their members who are directly affected by projects affecting the environment. The Sierra Club filed a new lawsuit against Mineral King, claiming that their trips to the area would be harmed if the project went ahead. The court ordered a survey of the area. Meanwhile, the Forest Service received thousands of complaints about the proposed ski resort, and eventually Governor Reagan withdrew his support for the project, citing costs. Today, the valley is protected as a wilderness area under a law signed by Obama in 2009. See 'Sierra Club v. Morton', *Wikipedia*.

[1054] *Sierra Club v. Morton*, dissenting opinion of Justice Douglas, § 2.

[1055] *Sierra Club v. Morton*, dissenting opinion of Justice Douglas, § 4.

embedded in the legal system.[1056] While the corpus and the struggle for the recognition of the rights of animals[1057] and nature have grown in the United States over the years, there has yet to be a development reflected in Supreme Court decisions at either the federal or state level.

However, the water crisis that erupted in Toledo, Ohio, in 2014 had an interesting legal outcome. The pollution in Lake Erie, which supplies water to the region, had started to have a negative impact on the lives of people in Toledo. In response, a referendum on 26 February 2019,[1058] granted Lake Erie rights that normally only belong to humans. According to the Lake Erie Bill of Rights, all citizens can now take any significant environmental damage to the lake to court. The Declaration protects the lake, its tributaries, and many of its inhabitants. That is the first document in the United States to protect an entire ecosystem.

Spain

Since the 1960s, the Mar Menor Lagoon and its basin in the Autonomous Region of Murcia in southeastern Spain have experienced significant human impacts. These include urbanisation, fishing, the construction of two canals and marinas linking the lagoon to the Mediterranean Sea, irrigation for legal and illegal agriculture and the drilling of illegal wells, increased use of pesticides and fertilisers, livestock residues, leaks containing heavy metals from current and past mining activities, and increased tourism activities. All these have caused the lagoon's water to become polluted and toxic.[1059] Conservation organisations and scientists have raised the lagoon's ecosystem's dangerous, worsening, and catastrophic state for over thirty years. However, existing administrative and legal mechanisms have been insufficient to stop

---

[1056] Samuel, 'Lake Erie … '.

[1057] *Nonhuman Rights Project* is a non-governmental organisation that has been lobbying strongly for the recognition of animal rights in the US for many years and has been trying to make progress through strategic litigation. For more information, see <https://www.nonhumanrights.org/>.

[1058] Turnout was 8.9 per cent and 61 per cent of the votes were in favour. See Ryan Prior, 'An Ohia City Has Voted to Grant Lake Erie the Same Right as a Person', *CNN*, 27 February 2019.

[1059] Ludwig Krämer, 'Rights of Nature in Europe: The Spanish Lagoon Mar Moner Becomes a Legal Person', *Journal for European Environmental & Planning Law*, No. 20 (2023), p. 6.

the ecological deterioration. The conservation statutes adopted over the last twenty-five years to protect the Mar Menor have emphasised the lagoon's ecological importance but have failed to protect it effectively. In fact, despite the Mar Menor Lagoon having the highest international recognition for biodiversity conservation, ecological decline has not been prevented.[1060] That has been compounded by a lack of coordination between national and local authorities, which are in the hands of different parties.[1061]

As a result, tons of fish and other marine life living in the lagoon died en masse and washed ashore in 2016, 2019, 2021 and 2022. In response, local people, concerned that timely and adequate measures had not been taken to protect the lagoon,[1062] organised a social movement and began to think about how to repair the damage to the lagoon. The Legal Clinic of the Faculty of Law of Murcia University has launched a study on the possibility of granting Mar Menor legal personality and specific rights. The outcome of this study was published in the press in May 2020.

Maria Teresa Vicente Giménez, a law professor at the University of Murcia, then launched a 'people's legislative initiative' on the issue.[1063] The primary reason for the initiative was that the area had recently suffered severe ecological destruction. Secondly, the existing legal regulations for protecting the Mar Menor had been ineffective. The inaction of the public authorities that caused this situation was another grounds for the initiative. Lastly, the need to strengthen civil society in order to enable effective participation in environmental issues was put forth.[1064]

The 500,000 signatures needed for the procedure to move forward were physically collected on the streets, in shops, and in other places accessible to people, as electronic signatures were not accepted. The process was complicated because of the lockdowns due to the COVID-19 pandemic.[1065] Despite this fact, 639,826 signatures were quickly collected, and the draft proposal

[1060] Giménez – Ortuño, 'An Ecological Citizenship's Triumph', pp. 90–1.
[1061] Krämer, 'Rights of Nature in Europe', pp. 7–8.
[1062] Krämer, 'Rights of Nature in Europe', p. 6.
[1063] The people's bill is recognised as a right under Article 87 (3) of the Spanish Constitution of 1987.
[1064] Giménez – Ortuño, 'An Ecological Citizenship's Triumph', pp. 88–9.
[1065] Giménez – Ortuño, 'An Ecological Citizenship's Triumph', p. 92.

was submitted to the Spanish Parliament. Although the Parliamentary bodies finalised the draft, no significant changes were made to its content.[1066]

The Spanish Parliament has overwhelmingly[1067] passed the law recognising the Mar Menor Lagoon and its basin as a legal entity.[1068] The rights of the Mar Menor recognised under the law include the right to exist, evolve naturally, recover, heal, be protected, preserved, maintained, cared for, and restored. Restoring and re-naturalising the basin in the law means restoring the natural qualities of rural Cartagena. In this context, with the transition to organic agriculture and animal husbandry, thirty-four cattle-run trails are envisaged to be protected. The movement of livestock and animals used in this context, which has shaped the natural environment for centuries, is considered to ensure the sustainable use of the natural environment.[1069]

The law transformed the lagoon from a mere object to be protected, rehabilitated, and developed into a biological, environmental, cultural, and spiritual subject.[1070] The Mar Menor legal entity exercises the rights granted to it through *the Tutoría del Mar Menor*, a body of representation, governance, and public participation regulated by the same law. Within this guardianship body, there are three different committees. These are the Representatives Committee, the Monitoring Committee, and the Scientific Committee. Three members of the Committee of Representatives are appointed by the central government, three by the local government of Murcia, and seven by civil society, which initiated the process of public proposal of the law.[1071] The Committee has no decision-making powers. Its main task is to propose the necessary measures for protecting, conserving, maintaining, and restoring the lagoon and observing its rights.[1072] In addition, it was agreed

---

[1066] Krämer, 'Rights of Nature in Europe', p. 7.

[1067] Only members of the far-right Vox Party voted against the proposal.

[1068] Law No. 19/2022, which was finally adopted on 21 September 2022, entered into force after being published in the Official Gazette dated 30 September 2022.

[1069] Giménez – Ortuño, 'An Ecological Citizenship's Triumph', p. 92.

[1070] Krämer, 'Rights of Nature in Europe', p. 9.

[1071] Law No. 19/2022, Art. 3. For the English translation, see <https://www.um.es/documents/23559040/35080450/LEY+19_2022+IN+ENGLISH.pdf>.

[1072] Krämer, 'Rights of Nature in Europe', pp. 9–10.

that everyone[1073] has the right to submit requests to the administration and the courts to defend the rights of the Mar Menor ecosystem.[1074]

The law provides criminal, judicial, environmental, and administrative penalties for Mar Menor's rights violations.[1075] If the infringing action is carried out by public authorities, the law states that the action is void and must be reviewed by the administration or the courts.[1076] As can be seen, regardless of whether the criminalised acts harm other people or not, it is considered sufficient if they harm the Mar Menor Lagoon. That means a direct, rather than indirect, responsibility for a natural asset is created. Thus, this law is the first legal step towards a nature-centred understanding of law on the European continent.[1077]

4.2.3 Recognising ecocide as a crime

Although the history of capitalism is often identified with 'progress' and 'prosperity', it is, in fact, a history of destruction and death. Contemporary nation-states and constitutional systems that emerged as a result of this economic order are also based on this history. For example, in the late 1700s, after the British captain James Cook seized many of the islands he had 'discovered', particularly Australia and New Zealand, for Britain, 90 per cent of the Indigenous population was killed by European settlers. The survivors were forced to live under strict racial discrimination. The natives of Tasmania, who had lived in complete isolation for 10,000 years before these discoveries, were exterminated entirely down to the last man, woman, and child. European settlers first drove the natives away from the resource-rich areas of the island, then seized even the remaining wilderness and systematically

1073 Krämer points out that the fact that the law grants the right to sue to 'everyone', not just those living around the Mar Menor or in the region of Murcia, or to Spanish citizens is a new element in the system of conferring rights to nature. See Krämer, 'Rights of Nature in Europe', p. 17.

1074 Law No. 19/2022, art. 6. According to this article, if the application is found to be justified, the applicant does not have to bear any costs, including expenses for lawyers and courts.

1075 Law No. 19/2022, Art. 4.

1076 Law No. 19/2022, Art. 5.

1077 Giménez – Ortuño, 'An Ecological Citizenship's Triumph', p. 84.

hunted and killed them.[1078] Similar examples occurred in Africa, North and South America, and the rest of the colonised world.

Therefore, it is crucial to examine the links between the plunder of nature and the appropriation of Indigenous peoples' lands. Contrary to European claims of *terra nullius*,[1079] the pieces of nature appropriated by capital have almost always constituted the living conditions of particular groups of people. Whether the African steppes or the Amazonian rainforest, these landscapes constituted the habitat where various peoples lived and the space for meaningful social interaction, livelihoods, and the material basis for social reproduction. That shows that ecological issues cannot be separated from issues of political power on the one hand and racial oppression, imperial domination, and the dispossession and genocide of Indigenous peoples on the other.[1080]

In other words, the long legacy of colonialism, the denial of rights to Indigenous peoples, and ongoing injustices follow similar processes to the exploitation of nature and nonhuman animals. Ecologically destructive actions often jeopardise the lives, existence, and resilience of Indigenous peoples, even if they are not directly targeted. This link between ecocide and genocide is inextricable for them.[1081] Defined as *unlawful or wanton acts committed with knowledge that there is substantial likelihood of severe and either widespread or long-term damage to environment being caused by those acts*,[1082] ecocide almost always results in the physical and cultural harm and destruction of Indigenous peoples living in the area. Like genocide, ecocide can be direct or indirect; it can take the form of the destruction of land or the destruction of a way of life.[1083] Often, natural resource extraction activities, with their massive destruction of soil and water resources, bring about the end of a way of life in an area and the slow death of cultures that have become an

[1078] Harari, *Sapiens*, pp. 276–7.
[1079] Latin for 'unclaimed/empty land'.
[1080] Fraser, 'Climates of Capital', p. 84.
[1081] Gene Ray, 'Writing the Ecocide-Genocide Knot: Indigenous Knowledge and Critical Theory in the Endgame, *Documenta14*, No. 3, p. 120.
[1082] The definition of ecocide proposed by the Stop Ecocide Foundation, an international committee of legal experts from various countries, for inclusion in the Rome Statute, the founding document of the International Criminal Court.
[1083] Polly Higgins – Damien Short – Nigel South, 'Protecting the Planet: A Proposal for a Law of Ecocide', *Crime, Law and Social Change*, No. 59, April 2013, p. 11.

integral part of the landscape.[1084] Consequently, the appropriation of nature, the overexploitation of land and water, and the lack of respect for a people's ties to their culture and land have both ecocidal and genocidal consequences for vulnerable Indigenous peoples who depend materially and spiritually on their endangered environment.[1085]

There are, of course, various differences between the two. For example, genocide and ecocide are about different kinds of harm: one is directed against social groups, the other against humanity's dependence on the ecosystem. However, both cause death and destruction on a large scale, and the possible prosecution for both is based on criminal and human rights law.[1086] At this intersection, ecocide must be recognised as a crime, too, and that action must be taken to turn the processes that result from it into law.[1087]

In this respect, the criminalisation of ecocide is also instrumental for global green constitutionalism aimed at tackling climate change. After the information in the IPCC's assessment reports had been shared with the world, no politician (or corporate executive) could say, *I did not know that.* These reports contain scientific scenarios that a 2°C temperature increase in the Earth's atmosphere would lead to disasters like wildfires, droughts, sudden weather events, diseases, and, eventually, the displacement of millions of people. Further, a 3.5°C temperature increase would reduce agricultural production at all latitudes, including all cereals, and lead to a global famine. No one can claim not to be aware of them today.[1088] For example, it is already known that the capital of the Kiribati Islands in the Pacific Ocean will soon become uninhabitable due to climate change, that the fresh water on the islands is salinised due to sea level rise, and that fishing, the primary source

---

1084 Klein, *On Fire*, p. 190.

1085 A. Dunlap, 'The "solution" is now the "problem": Wind energy, colonisation and the "genocide-ecocide nexus" in the Isthmus of Tehuantepec, Oaxaca', *International Journal of Human Rights*, Vol. 22, No. 4, 2018, p. 557, cited in: Martin Crook – Damien Short – Nigel South, 'Ecocide, genocide, capitalism and colonialism: Consequences for indigenous peoples and glocal ecosystems environements', *Theoretical Criminology*, Vol. 22, No. 3, 2018, pp. 299–300.

1086 Bronwyn Lay – Laurent Neyret – Damien Short – Michael Urs – Antonio A. Oposa Jr, 'Timely and Necessary: Ecocide Law as Urgent and Emerging', *The Journal Jurisprudence*, Vol. 28, 2015, p. 437.

1087 Lay – Neyret – Short – Urs – Oposa Jr, 'Timely and Necessary', p. 437.

1088 Tanuro, *L'Impossible le Capitalism vert*, p. 38.

of livelihood, is no longer productive due to the migration of fish as the ocean warms. A similar situation applies to the Eskimos living in Greenland, where the ice melts due to global warming. Unable to hunt enough due to the late freezing and early thawing of the sea, the Inuit people cannot feed themselves or the dogs they live with. They are forced to abandon or kill them.[1089] Despite having these pieces of information, it is unacceptable to legally protect the continuation of activities that cause global warming. Moreover, research has recently revealed that oil companies had this information much earlier than us.

In 1982, researchers at Exxon[1090] estimated that burning oil, coal, and natural gas would raise the planet's average temperature by about 2°C by 2060. According to their report, that would cause significant and severe climate disruptions. Researchers at Shell came to similar conclusions in 1988. Yet, these two companies kept this information from the public. Thus, they paid no heed to the warming of the Earth for the sake of profits. From this perspective, the attitude of oil companies towards climate change presents a dramatic case study of neoliberalism in practice.[1091] For the sake of short-term economic interests, the lives of millions of people, natural assets, and the ecosystem as a whole have been, and are still being, knowingly and willingly jeopardised. Moreover, governments provide legal and economic support to oil companies in this process. Despite publicly promising to reduce state subsidies to fossil fuel companies, G20 countries gave 1.4 trillion dollars to the coal, oil, and natural gas industry in 2022.[1092]

Therefore, it should urgently be recognised as a legal duty to prevent the activities of both the giant fossil fuel companies and the state administrations that support them, which put the climate in danger of collapse. In particular, criminalising economic activities based on fossil fuel production and consumption at both the international and national levels would be one of green constitutionalism's most fundamental and urgent functions. In countries where the judiciary – especially the high courts – remain independent, including a prohibition of ecocide in constitutions at the national

---

[1089] Üskül Engin, *Ekolojik Kriz, Etik ve Hukuk*, pp. 27–8.
[1090] The company's current name is '*ExxonMobil*'.
[1091] Chomsky – Pollin, *Climate Crisis …*, p. 41.
[1092] Ajit Niranjan, 'G20 Poured More Than $1tn into Fossil Fuel Subsidies Despite COP26 Pledges – Report', *The Guardian*, 23 August 2023.

level would be a supportive element in individual applications for violations of the right to a healthy environment or in administrative lawsuits to protect nature. Moreover, since ecocide is a nature-centred crime type rather than a human-centred one, those who are not directly harmed by the activity that weakens the ecosystem could also be applicants or plaintiffs. That would broaden the scope of action of the national judicial body in nature protection[1093] and provide a strong justification against fossil fuel companies, especially in climate cases.[1094]

If recognised as a crime at the international level, ecocide would be the first 'nonhuman-centred' international crime.[1095] That is highly important because, in many countries, national jurisdictions, including the high courts, are incapable of prosecuting crimes against nature for various reasons, including a lack of independence from the executive and legislative organs. By recognising ecocide as a crime, victims would be able to contribute to the prosecution and inform the public about the risks of corporate activities. Individuals and even national judicial bodies suing multinational corporations, such as oil companies, who know about the harmful effects of their activities but hide it, cannot access today the information held by these companies on various grounds such as 'trade secrets'. If ecocide is included in the Rome Statute, the International Criminal Court would be able to request this information judicially. Thus, the 'information imbalance' between corporations and the individuals harmed could be eliminated. Finally, it is more likely that an international tribunal, rather than national courts, would be able to

---

1093 Serkan Koybasi, 'Ekokırım Suçunun Tanınması', *Bahçeşehir University Law Faculty Review*, Vol. 17, No. 210, September to October 2022, p. 1066. Although the recognition of ecocide as a crime is accepted as a principle in some constitutions, it would be more appropriate to address the elements of the crime and the penalties prescribed in the criminal code of the country or in a separate law. On the elements of the crime of ecocide, see Koybasi, 'Ekokırım Suçunun Tanınması', pp. 1067–78.

1094 In Italy, where crime of ecocide is not legally recognised, the country's first climate lawsuit against the oil company Eni has been filed based on the elements of it. The plaintiffs demand that the company be punished for its lobbying and greenwashing activities despite being aware of climate change since the 1970s. The case is pending. See Stella Levantesi, 'Italian Oil Firm Eni Faces Lawsuit Alleging Early Knowledge of Climate Crisis', *The Guardian*, 9 May 2023.

1095 Romina Pezzot – Jan-Phillip Graf, 'Ecocide – Legal Revolution pf Symbolism?', *Völkerrechtsblog*, 3 February 2022.

impose a binding and effective sanction on a company guilty of ecocide.[1096] Therefore, ecocide should not only be banned at the constitutional level but also recognised as an international crime by adding it to the Rome Statute.

The recognition of a crime that would have such a significant impact on the protection of nature in the legal world is certainly not desirable for some, like oil companies. For this reason, they have been actively resisting such a development for a long time. Especially in the US, the counter-propaganda efforts of coal and oil companies, which started by covering up the results of their own research, turned into an organised campaign in the 1990s to create doubt about climate change.[1097] Despite all the data, reports, and concrete events available to us today, the source of the idea that[1098] climate change is not accurate, or even if it is accurate, that capitalist economic activities do not cause it, is, in fact, the lobbying activities of oil companies, which have had the information of climate change since the 1970s and have poured incredible amounts of money into hiding it.

For years, oil companies have not only tried to deny climate change or at least create uncertainty about it, but they have also tried to block the transition to a sustainable energy infrastructure. Several alternative technological methods of energy production have been blocked by pressure from the powerful companies of the fossil energy sector, despite – or even because of – the fact that they are effective solutions.[1099] While less polluting alternative energies were kept out of sight, the adverse effects of fossil fuels were concealed through lobbying. Since the 1980s, business circles in the

[1096] Marco Colacurci, 'The Draft Convention Ecocide and the Role for Corporate Mediation. Some Insights from the International Monsanto Tribunal and a Recent Research Proposal', *International Criminal Law Review*, 2021, p. 5. Although currently only individuals can be prosecuted for the crimes enumerated in the Rome Statute, after the inclusion of the crime of ecocide, it could be possible for companies to be held liable since they are 'legal persons'.

[1097] Neela Naberjee – John H. Cushman Jr – David Jasemyer – Lisa Song, *Exxon: The Roas Not Taken*, Inside Climate News, 2005, cited in: Şahin, 'İklim Krizine … ', p. 21.

[1098] In the 22 August 2023 debate on *FOX* TV, none of the candidates vying to be the Republican Party's nominee in the 2024 US Presidential Election saw climate change as an urgent problem. One of them, Vivek Ramaswamy, even claimed that climate change is not real. See Maanvi Singh, 'Republican Hopefuls Shrug When Asked About Climate Crisis During Debate', *The Guardian*, 24 August 2023.

[1099] Tanuro, *L'Impossible le Capitalism vert*, p. 62.

United States with close ties to fossil fuels have poured large sums of money into lobbies to buy scientists, journalists, and politicians. Their goal was to prevent the emerging consensus among climate scientists from influencing decision-makers and public opinion.[1100] One of the factors that enabled them to lobby so strongly to prevent politicians from taking action was the non-binding nature of international climate agreements. They also developed incredibly successful disinformation campaigns to erode public support for action against climate change. They did this in the United States because if not, it was a country that could lead a global transformation.[1101]

As a result, companies and the US administration have been able to continue ecosystem-damaging activities as if climate change did not exist. For example, despite the fact that plastic, a petroleum product that takes hundreds of years to biodegrade, is known to harm nature, biodiversity, and the climate, and therefore, its production should be reduced, the fossil fuel company Shell could open a massive facility in Ohio, USA in 2022 to produce non-biodegradable plastic. This facility, which employs 9,500 people in its construction alone, produces 1.6 million tons of plastic annually.[1102] As it is known, plastic in the world is constantly accumulating, and its long-term impact on nature is unpredictable. Due to the ever-increasing plastic production, *we are trapped in an experiment that we cannot unplug.*[1103]

This reckless attitude is replicated in other parts of the ruling class. One example is members of the executive board of JP Morgan Chase, the largest bank in the US, who undoubtedly understand the threat of global warming as well as other educated people. The bank continues to pour enormous resources into fossil fuel development, including the most dangerous of them all – Canadian tar sands.[1104] A leaked report by JP Morgan to alert its clients to the economic challenges posed by climate change acknowledges that humanity is in danger of extinction and that the *status quo* is unsustainable. The report implicitly blames the investment strategy of US banks, stating

---

[1100] Tanuro, *L'Impossible le Capitalism vert*, p. 62.

[1101] Hickel, *Less is More*, p. 19.

[1102] 'Shell Molymers Monaca', *Shell.*

[1103] Quoted by Roland Geyer, professor of industrial ecology at the University of California *in* Michael Corkery, 'A Giant Factory Rises to Make a Product Filling Up The World: Plastic', *New York Times*, 12 August 2019.

[1104] Chomsky – Pollin, *Climate Crisis …*, p. 78.

that continued investment in fossil-intensive industries such as oil and gas carries financial and reputational risks. However, from the adoption of the Paris Agreement until 2020, when the report was published, the same bank provided $75 billion in financing to companies aggressively investing in the fossil fuel production sector.[1105]

At this point, we should recall Greta Thunberg's question:

> If burning fossil fuels was so bad that it threatened our very existence, how could we just continue like before? Why were there no restrictions? Why wasn't it made illegal?[1106]

It is a very pertinent question and one that needs to be answered. The people who need to answer it are fossil fuel company executives and politicians. The problem is that they are largely responsible for our current predicament.[1107] So, instead of answering the question, they deny or ignore climate change. It is important to remember that not only the management of these companies but even the most extreme deniers are well aware of the impending climate change catastrophe.[1108] They know that they are burning the world and killing millions of people, yet they continue to operate. It is unacceptable that this is protected by law. However, the law is currently structured in such a way that those who invest in and manage these companies can escape all criminal, financial, social, and moral responsibility for their actions. These transactions are (at least theoretically) deemed to be carried out by the companies, not the managers. Courts recognise the right of shareholders to hide behind the 'corporate veil' and rarely set aside the presumption that the company is a legal entity in order to hold those pulling the strings accountable for actions taken on its behalf.[1109] However, the decision-makers in these companies are real people, and they should be prosecuted for knowingly causing climate change and endangering the lives of others and the ecosystem.

Not only corporations but also politicians collaborating with them are responsible for the current ecological collapse. For example, in the US, the country most responsible for climate change and with the power to slow or

---

1105 Patrick Greenfield – Jonathan Watts, 'JP Morgan Economists Warn Climate Crisis Is Threat to Human Race', *The Guardian*, 21 February 2020.

1106 Greta Thunberg, TED Talk (12 December 2018) Transcript: School Strike for Climate.

1107 Hickel, *Less is More*, p. 19.

1108 Chomsky – Pollin, *Climate Crisis …*, p. 79.

1109 Cullinan, *Wild Law*, p. 66.

even stop it, President Joe Biden has not only failed for years to declare a climate emergency despite all calls for one, but he also has authorised more oil pipelines and drilling than even under his predecessor Donald Trump, a climate denier. That is contrary to science, common sense, and life on Earth.[1110] In a legal order that adopts a green constitutionalism approach, national and international courts will not only be able to severely restrict fossil fuel production and consumption but also to prosecute and punish those who continue and authorise these activities.

4.3 Devising an economic model in harmony with nature

> We live in capitalism. Its power seems inescapable.
> But then, so did the divine right of kings.[1111]

The science of ecology tells us that we must learn to think of the economy not in isolation from ecology but together with it. That is a radical challenge to today's dominant worldview and capitalism[1112] because the rules governing the Earth's ecosystem and the growth-based rules of capitalism are diametrically opposed. Growth has now become an existential threat. Our survival now depends on whether we can change our economic model.[1113] In other words, when we think about these two issues together, it becomes clear that we need to abandon the rules of capitalism and harmonise the economy with nature.

Even though the necessity to change the current economic system because of climate change is a fact, many powerful interest groups are happy for things to continue business as usual. Moreover, these are not just the fossil fuel giants who have funded decades of misinformation, confusion, and obfuscation campaigns about the reality of global warming.[1114] Hand in hand with energy companies, decision-makers insist on promoting various false solutions as the answer to climate change. Rather than implementing necessary

---

1110 Peter Kalmus, 'Joe Biden Must Declare A Climate Emergency. And He Must Do So Now', *The Guardian*, 27 July 2023.

1111 Ursula K. LeGuin, *in* the speech in acceptance of the National Book Foundation Medal for Distinguished Contribution to American Letters, 19 November 2014.

1112 Hickel, *Less is More*, p. 125.

1113 Parrique, *Ralentir ou Périr*, p. 15.

1114 Klein, *On Fire*, p. 30.

changes in energy production and the structure of the economic system, they prefer to create in-system solutions such as carbon markets or large-scale experiments in geoengineering[1115] the atmosphere. Environmentally destructive and uncertain energy technologies, including nuclear power, carbon sequestration from coal plants, and the widespread burning of biomass for energy, are promoted as if they are part of the solution and will do nothing but perpetuate existing problems.[1116]

The geoengineering perspective promises to take the human-nature dichotomy to new, irrational heights, unimagined even by Bacon and Descartes. In this way, it is argued that the planet will bend to human will, and capitalist growth can continue indefinitely. The main problem with geoengineering is that it is ecologically incoherent, trying to solve the ecological crisis with the same perspective that caused it. Because of its continued adherence to the growth logic, even if (and this is a big if) they can reduce carbon emissions, these proposed solutions cannot be expected to address ocean acidification, deforestation, soil degradation, or mass extinction.[1117]

Neither growth nor the capitalist economic order is a necessity. We are easily capable of preparing ourselves for any kind of social order, including those with much longer planning horizons and much greater respect for natural life-support systems. As noted earlier, humans have lived in harmony with nature for most of their historical past. Many Indigenous cultures have kept earth-centred cosmologies alive to this day. Capitalism is but a tiny interruption in the collective story of the human species.[1118] This interruption, created by the bourgeoisie, emerged as an economic order through the incessant growth of capital. The logic of growth has become an attack on nature and life. For this reason, defending nature and life today necessitates waging war on capital[1119] and its central growth logic because it contradicts how nature works.

The central logic of nature is reciprocity. According to it, one must give at least as much as they take. This logic, which has an inherent ecological value,

---

[1115] Also called 'climate engineering', an umbrella term for initiatives that aim to capture carbon dioxide from the air or manage radiation from the sun at a global level through technological products.
[1116] Tokar, *Toward Climate Justice*, Preface to the Revised Edition (Loc. 184).
[1117] Hickel, *Less is More*, p. 145.
[1118] Klein, *On Fire*, p. 296.
[1119] Benlisoy, 'İklim Krizi … ', p. 175.

is directly opposed to capitalism's fundamental growth logic, which requires taking more than it gives back. That is the basic mechanism of growth.[1120] Accordingly, if left unbridled, both ideological and institutional fundamental elements of capitalism lead directly to the destruction of the foundations of organised social life.[1121] Any new alternative that promises to halt this destruction must contend with the entrenched interests of corporations and the *status quo* attitude of consumers who are relatively content with their present lives.[1122] It can be rightly argued that this cannot be done through law; therefore, a green logic of constitutionalism is insufficient to bring about this transformation. Indeed, the emergence of an economic model in harmony with nature is more likely possible through strengthening green and ecological political and social movements and, thus, through a grassroots democratic effort.

However, it should not be overlooked that the law can also be instrumental in two ways. First, the transformation in infrastructure would need to be adequately reflected in superstructural institutions. At this point, the principles of green constitutionalism would guide the proper establishment of this superstructure. Secondly, the legitimising and thus socially transformative effect of legal rules and principles could accelerate the transition to an ecological economy. Given that it is unexpected for these rules to emerge from parliaments dominated by the bourgeoisie, the nature-centred rulings of courts, especially high courts, that adopt a green constitutionalist approach would become extremely important.

Realistic solutions to the climate crisis require establishing a much more equitable and advanced economic system. At the same time, this new system must close inequalities, strengthen and transform the public sphere, create a large number of decent jobs, and largely rein in corporate power.[1123] These transformations are only possible if legal regulations and court decisions back them.

Replacing the current economic system with a more equitable one is no longer a mere ideological preference but has become an existential necessity for all living beings.[1124] Of course, the transformation of the relations of production, the means of production, and today's dominant consumption

---

1120 Hickel, *Less is More*, p. 32.
1121 Chomsky – Pollin, *Climate Crisis …*, p. 76.
1122 Wallace-Wells, *The Uninhabitable Earth*, p. 198.
1123 Klein, *On Fire*, p. 101.
1124 Klein, *On Fire*, p. 141.

patterns can only make sense by adopting a new way of life and a break from modern Western capitalist/industrial civilisation.[1125] Therefore, while determining the rules of this new economic infrastructure, steps must also be taken to support social transformation through legal instruments.

However, it should be emphasised that establishing an economic infrastructure in harmony with nature cannot be the work of law alone. Still, it must also be recognised that economics and law are not independent fields. I think I have made this sufficiently clear in the work so far. Therefore, the present section, which includes proposals and alternatives for a postcapitalist economy to be transitioned to in the context of climate change, may not be seen as directly linked to green constitutionalism. However, if I claim that the root cause of today's climate change is the capitalist economic infrastructure and the current constitutional structure as its protector, then I need to put forward a view on how the economic infrastructure should also look in a legal order where the green constitutionalism view is dominant. I believe the current economic order and constitutional structures are inseparable. Therefore, how the economy should be regulated, what should be permitted and encouraged, and what should be prohibited are essential areas of regulation in green constitutionalism. That also reflects my rejection of the modern mechanistic worldview that separates the sciences and transfers the scientific systemic perspective that emphasises networks to the field of law.

4.3.1 Key elements of an economic infrastructure in harmony with nature

It is easier to imagine the end of the world than the end of capitalism.[1126]

During the 1970s, 660 disasters were reported, including droughts, floods, extreme temperatures, major wildfires, and storms. In the 2000s, this number increased fivefold to 3,322. That is a shocking increase in just thirty

---

[1125] Löwy, *Ecosocialism*, Preface: Before the Flood: The Political Challenge (Loc. 73).

[1126] Mark Fisher, in his 2009 book *Capitalist Realism: Is There No Alternative?*, he says that the phrase originally belongs to Frederic Jameson and Slovaj Žižek. William Wallace-Wells, on the other hand, states that Frederic Jameson used the phrase in his article 'Future City' in the May-June 2003 issue of *New Left* Review, stating that 'someone once said it'. See Wallace-Wells, *The Uninhabitable Earth*, p. 177. Saito also thinks that it belongs to Jameson. See Saito, *Slow Down*, p. 191.

years. Obviously, not all of this increase was caused by global warming. Yet, it is also clear that the climate is issuing a warning. However, over the same thirty-year period, governments in almost every country in the world have gradually eroded the health and resilience of the public sphere due to neoliberal policies.[1127] Whereas the threat of climate change required breaking the power of corporations and putting them under strict public control, the opposite has happened. Over the last thirty years, any control over the market has been vilified, and neoliberal policies have become dominant. While responding to the climate crisis required planning, more effective and stronger public services, and reining in the market, the wind has been blowing in the opposite direction; deregulation, financialisation, and the absolute dominance of the market have prevailed with the neoliberal counter-revolution.[1128]

Today, it seems more likely and realistic to some to spew sulphur into the air and paint the sky red to cool the planet by a degree or two than to stop capitalism from extracting fossil fuels. To many, it seems more feasible to install technologies to capture carbon from the air all over the Earth than to cut the trillions poured into fossil fuel subsidies.[1129] That is because we do not know how to get rid of capitalism, and we cannot even imagine it because the bourgeoisie has established a cultural hegemony[1130] in our minds. Today, we are experiencing a sharp rupture in our daily lives and social sensitivities caused by the contrast with pre-industrial cultures. We live so embedded in our present that it limits all our sensibilities and, thus, our capacity to think of alternative social forms.[1131] Any anti-capitalist idea is perceived as a radical orientation and is considered 'unimaginable' by

---

1127 Klein, *That Changes Everything*, p. 154.

1128 Benlisoy, 'İklim Krizi … ', p. 187.

1129 Wallace-Wells, *The Uninhabitable Earth*, p. 177.

1130 Cultural hegemony is a concept coined by the Marxist writer Antonio Gramsci and is defined as 'the momentary approval by large sections of society of the general direction given to social life by the dominant basic group'. See T. J. Jackson Lears, 'The Concept of Cultural Hegemony: Problems and Possibilities', *The American History Review*, Vol. 90, No. 3, June 1985, p. 568.

1131 Bookchin, *The Ecology of Freedom*, p. 83.

most people. The more people say this, the less possible these orientations become.[1132]

However, if we want to stop climate change, we must imagine and even achieve the end of capitalism because it treats our planet like a mine and a dumping ground, creating miserable, precarious, and unhealthy societies.[1133] According to Marx, capitalism as a mode of production has two distinctive features: First, it produces its products as commodities. It is not the fact that it produces commodities but that being a commodity is the dominant and determining characteristic of its products that distinguishes it from other modes of production. The second characteristic is producing surplus value as the immediate aim and determining the motive of production.[1134] Capitalism's transformation of all human relations into 'things' in order to realise these two aims and generation of economic activities as ends rather than means to meet human needs is both the cause of the current ecological crisis and the reason why this crisis cannot be solved within capitalism.[1135]

The basic principle that the 'environment' can be adequately protected without touching capitalist society's institutional framework and structural dynamics has always been a major problem.[1136] Capitalism, of course, stubbornly and blindly resists the changes we need to make. The ruling class, which continues to follow Locke's praise of greed, opposes any effective anti-growth transformation. Virtually all circles of power and influence impose a false realism, as if all alternatives are impossible and the only option is still 'growth'.[1137] Yet, this is not realism, and it is not even a fact. Economy models that are in harmony with nature existed before capitalism; they exist now and will continue to exist. Sustainable economy models that do not treat nature as a mere raw material and give it its actual value are on the agenda today more than ever, even by international organisations such as the UN.[1138]

1132 Malm, *How to Blow …*, p. 158.

1133 Bennett, *Change Everything*, p. 99.

1134 Karl Marx, *Capital*, Volume 3, 2nd ed., trans. Alaattin Bilgi, Sol, Ankara, 1990, p. 771, cited in: Balta – Mısır, 'Bir Politik … ', p. 21.

1135 Balta – Mısır, 'Bir Politik … ', p. 21.

1136 Fraser, 'Climates of Capital', p. 86.

1137 Löwy, *Ecosocialism*, Preface: Before the Flood: The Political Challenge (Loc. 37–8).

1138 IPBES, *Summary for Policymakers of the Methodological Assessment Regarding the Diverse Conceptualization of Multiple Values of Nature and its Benefits, Including Biodiversity and Ecosystem Functions and Services*, July 2022, IPBES/9/L.13, pp. 25–6.

The current oligarchic structure leading us to destruction must be legally limited without wasting any more time, and an alternative green economic order must be established in its place.

Capitalism represents climate change's social and historical driver and the central institutionalised dynamic that must be dismantled to stop it. Therefore, the dominant organising theme underlying a new nature-centred economic order can only be 'anti-capitalism'. In other words, whatever the economic system in the new green constitutional order against climate change, it must be anti-capitalist. In this respect, anti-capitalism represents a key element in developing a powerful counter-hegemonic project of eco-social transformation by exposing the links between the many different branches of injustice and irrationality.[1139] There is still time to prevent catastrophic warming, but we cannot do so within the already-established rules of capitalism. Ironically, climate change may be the best argument we have so far for changing these rules.[1140]

Claiming that an anti-capitalist economic infrastructure needs to be established does not directly imply claiming the necessity to move to a communist or socialist economy. It is impossible to say that the few socialist countries today are behaving more responsibly regarding carbon emissions, nor were they in the past.[1141] The twentieth-century balance sheet of the Soviet Union and Eastern European countries ruled by communist regimes showed that a society based on collective ownership of the means of production can be as damaging to nature as a society based on private property, if not more so. Before the fall of the Berlin Wall, Czechoslovakia emitted 20.7 tons of carbon dioxide per capita per year, and East Germany 22 tons. In the United States, Canada, and Australia, the major emitters of carbon dioxide in the developed capitalist world and countries with higher GDP per capita, the figures for the same period were 18.9, 16.2, and 15 tons, respectively.[1142]

In the Soviet Union, the once crystal-clear Lake Baikal was polluted by industrial waste, and Lake Aral dried up as its water was used for cotton plantations. The air in the cities of the Soviet Union was among the most polluted

---

[1139] Fraser, 'Climates of Capital', p. 51.
[1140] Klein, *On Fire*, p. 144.
[1141] Wallace-Wells, *The Uninhabitable Earth*, p. 163.
[1142] Tanuro, *L'Impossible le Capitalism vert*, p. 175.

in the world. Not forgetting, of course, the explosion at the Chernobyl nuclear plant in 1986.[1143] Similarly, in China, smoke from steel mills left a grey coating on fields used for food production, rivers ran black from industrial pollution, and Beijing residents had to wear masks when riding their bicycles to work to avoid filling their lungs with soot. For thirty-five years, the new growth-oriented economic model has made this situation worse, not better.[1144]

Therefore, when thinking about a postcapitalist economic order, it is necessary to learn from past mistakes and create new sustainable alternative models. There is an intense debate around the world on which model is right. Some common points of these alternatives are mentioned later as an introduction to these debates.

4.3.1.1 Expanding public space

It has been recurring structural neglect that has turned natural disasters into unnatural ones. Floods have burst neglected levees, heavy rains have collapsed sewage systems and caused sewers to overflow. In recent years, a growing number of large forest fires have raged out of control due to a lack of workers and equipment to extinguish them.[1145] For example, during the wildfires in southern Türkiye in 2021, it was revealed that there were no night-vision firefighting planes and that unmaintained planes were rotting in hangars.[1146] In the August 2023 forest fire on the US island of Maui that killed hundreds of people, the alarm system did not work.[1147] From all corners of the world, there are constant reports of bridges collapsing because there is not enough budget allocated for their maintenance, heat waves causing deaths because the necessary precautions are not taken, and people losing their lives and property in floods because there is no early warning system.

We can actually immediately have all the tools we need to stop this destruction and extinction. With a political body and a carbon tax to effectively put an end to dirty energy, a new approach to agricultural practices, a shift away from meat and dairy in the global diet, and increased government

---

1143 Marks, *The Origins of …*, p. 196.
1144 Marks, *The Origins of …*, p. 196.
1145 Klein, *That Changes Everything*, pp. 154–5.
1146 'THK Uçakları Uçmasın, Yeşil Yansın Diye Her Şey Yapıldı', *Cumhuriyet*, 30 June 2021.
1147 Ray Sanchez, 'Hawaii Has a Robust Emergency Siren Warning System. It Sat Silent During the Deadly Wildfires', *CNN*, 13 August 2023.

investment in green energy and carbon capture technologies, we can stop climate change and the disasters it brings with it.[1148] However, doing so and building a successful global climate stabilisation project requires much more potent forms of state intervention in the normal functioning of capitalist markets than intra-system solutions such as carbon trade. In addition, we need public investment in critical economic sectors, strong regulations, as well as public subsidies for private green investments. This policy mix will move us away from fossil fuels much faster than a carbon tax on its own.[1149]

New economic policies enabling large-scale public investment into reconstructing cities and even nations are indispensable to tackling climate change.[1150] A significant portion of the public money to be spent on mitigating the impacts of climate change will have to go to ambitious emission reduction projects such as solar energy, smart grids, electric vehicles, light rail systems, bike lanes, city-wide composting systems, building renovations, integrated public transportation systems, and new urban planning. The private sector would not undertake these large infrastructure investments as they are not rent-generating.[1151] Therefore, public bodies need to fund these adaptation projects against climate change.

High-cost investments designed to reduce carbon emissions on a mass scale are needed. That means the ubiquity of subway networks, trams, and light rail systems alone is not enough; they must also be affordable (even free).[1152] There should also be energy-efficient housing along these public transport lines that people can afford, smart electric grids that can provide renewable energy, and extensive research to ensure we use the best possible methods. These services need to be planned and implemented by the public sector,

---

1148 Wallace-Wells, *The Uninhabitable Earth*, p. 249.

1149 Chomsky – Pollin, *Climate Crisis …*, pp. 91–2.

1150 Saito, *Slow Down*, p. 56.

1151 Klein, *That Changes Everything*, p. 156.

1152 In Luxembourg, the small and wealthy member of the European Union, the entire public transport system became free in 2019 and remains free. Thanks to this initiative, which low taxpayers pay little or nothing for and high taxpayers pay more, private car use, noise and air pollution and emissions have decreased. This has improved the quality of life through traffic relief, reduced the income gap between social classes and taken an effective measure against climate change. See Daniel Bellamy, 'The Richest Country in Europe Is Celebrating Three Years of Free Public Transport', *Euronews*, 22 March 2023.

which the private sector would be reluctant to do because they would not be profitable, even if they were in the public interest.

Nevertheless, the governments that have pursued growth so far have privatised public services, cut social spending, reduced wages and worker protections, granted tax breaks to the rich, and thus increased inequality, all under the influence of neoliberal policies. In this age of climate collapse, we need to do precisely the opposite.[1153] That is because a truly prosperous society requires the provision of natural environmental goods such as water and land, social infrastructure such as electricity and public transportation, and social systems such as health and education to ensure people's well-being. These should be considered common goods for the entire society and, therefore, excluded from the market economy.[1154] Even the nationalisation of large corporations, which are sure to resist any new rules that reduce their profits, should not be left out of the discussion.[1155] The transition to a green economic order will be easier if constitutions facilitate the nationalisation of some companies in order to combat climate change and if a certain budget of the state is allocated to adaptation and emission reduction policies.

In the capitalist economic order, public services such as health, education, or public transportation can only be included in the calculation of GDP to the extent of their calculable costs. Most of this contribution comes from wages paid. However, if companies provide these services, the payments made by citizens and the profits made by companies can also be included in GDP. Therefore, providing a service by a private company rather than a public institution boosts growth.[1156] That is why, especially since the 1980s, many institutions and services have been privatised around the world under neoliberal policies. However, this has been reflected in a decline in both the income and welfare of the people. While the economy grew, people's welfare declined. In a growth economy that reverses this policy, simultaneously increasing people's incomes and welfare is possible by facilitating access to public services and other commons. That could be done by re-nationalising previously privatised essential services such as health, education, and

---

[1153] Hickel, *Less is More*, p. 186.
[1154] Saito, *Slow Down*, p. 89.
[1155] Klein, *On Fire*, p. 115.
[1156] Parrique, *Ralentir ou Périr*, p. 29.

transport and providing them free of charge. In this case, even if GDP shrinks, everyone's lives would improve. Therefore, in a postcapitalist era, the economy must be reorganised, but this time around the needs of people and ecology, not those of corporations.[1157] A collective and democratic reorganisation of the production system would simultaneously meet real social needs, reduce working hours, suppress unnecessary and/or dangerous production, and replace fossil fuels with renewable energy sources. All this requires an intense repression of capitalist rules and a radical expansion of the public sector.[1158]

4.3.1.2 Planning

Acting on climate would create many jobs and reorganise people's collective lives. However, all this requires a government that is not afraid to boldly plan for the long term and, therefore, a social movement that would ensure that the population wants to realise such a concept.[1159] Furthermore, serious consideration should be given to giving a constitutional basis to planning for the well-being of society and the ecosystem, especially in light of the transience of governments and the possibility that society may abandon ecological concerns in favour of short-term interests. A planned economic order that takes climate change into account should be included in the constitution, not as an article of wishful thinking but as a binding article that can provide the high courts with a basis for their decisions.

Thus, in addition to reversing the thirty-year privatisation trend, planning activities would be resurrected as one of the key responses to the climate threat. In a green constitutional order, there will be as much planning as possible in all areas of the economy. In addition to industrial and land-use planning, there should be cooperation planning at the national and international levels, and each society should show in these plans how it will transition from fossil fuels to renewable energy.[1160] The plans of the countries of the Global North to phase out fossil fuels should envisage a sharper and faster transition because of their historical responsibilities. Countries of the Global South, which so far have not caused much climate change but

---

[1157] Hickel, *Less is More*, pp. 185–6.
[1158] Löwy, *Ecosocialism*, Preface: Before the Flood: The Political Challenge (Loc. 64).
[1159] Klein, *That Changes Everything*, p. 178.
[1160] Klein, *On Fire*, p. 106.

are more severely affected by the consequences of global warming, should prepare plans that focus primarily on adaptation policies and thus reduce the loss of life and property. As mentioned earlier, strengthening the public sphere should be prioritised to reach this goal.

4.3.1.3 Limiting corporate activities

The sheer size, financial resources, and influence of corporations in today's world have led us to give them an almost mythological status in our minds, like the giants of ancient times. Yet, they have only been around for a few centuries, and their very existence depends on whether our legal systems will continue to sustain them.[1161] That is clear from history. Corporations were created by the bourgeoisie through law at a certain stage in history. We must again use law but this time to constrain and transform them. For example, if an effective legal mechanism ensures that if a company causes ecological damage, both the managers and the company are obliged to fully compensate for the damage to people and nature – whatever the cost – then companies are likely to significantly reduce their environmental damage.[1162]

We must re-emphasise the law's core purpose of preventing directly dangerous and destructive behaviour. That means using legal means to prevent corporations from engaging in environmentally destructive activities. Legal measures could include strict caps on the amount of carbon companies are allowed to emit into the atmosphere, banning new coal-fired power plants, limiting industrial animal husbandry through strict measures, and phasing out projects that use or produce dirty energy.[1163] A 2019 paper argued that achieving the Paris Agreement's goal of limiting global warming to 1.5°C above pre-industrial levels is still technically possible. Still, one of the conditions for this is a total global ban on new production of carbon dioxide-emitting devices.[1164] However, even though billions of people would suffer and the planet would become a greenhouse, the likelihood that the ruling classes would consider a proposal for a global ban on such devices would be,

---

[1161] Cullinan, *Wild Law*, p. 64.

[1162] Cullinan, *Wild Law*, p. 66.

[1163] Klein, *On Fire*, pp. 108–9.

[1164] Dan Tong and others, 'Committed Emissions From Existing Energy Infrastructure Jeopardise 1.5°C Climate Target', *Nature*, Vol. 572, p. 376, cited in: Malm, *How to Blow …*, pp. 78–9.

in Malm's words, *about the same as the likelihood that they would line up on the summit of one of the steepest mountains and gently throw themselves off the cliff.*[1165] For this reason, Malm argues that the people themselves should declare the ban and damage, burn, and destroy the vehicles emitting carbon dioxide. While recognising that violence has an important place in history and has, in some cases, been transformative, I am not suggesting this. If the higher courts care about the lives of billions of humans and other living beings and the planet's ecosystem and recognise these as 'primary considerations' in their rulings, then we could also use the binding force of law to prevent the reckless actions of the ruling classes in pursuit of their economic interests.

To do this, constitutional and legal rules should require companies to reduce their actions, subsidiaries, and suppliers that negatively impact ecosystems and biodiversity, reduce the damage to nature caused by using their products and services, and disclose the resulting damage honestly to the public. In addition, companies should be required to support, rather than oppose, laws and policies to conserve, protect, restore, and ensure the sustainable use of ecosystems and biodiversity.[1166] This mandatory legal support could be through companies transforming their own activities in this direction, as well as by financially supporting nature-centred projects of public institutions. The logic that all companies benefit from a presumption of philanthropy in the name of 'freedom of enterprise' should be reversed. A company's survival should depend on having a mission (and a plan to achieve it) that is aligned with the needs of the country and its people. There should be a dual democratic selectivity in production regarding ends (what do we want to produce?) and means (how do we want to produce it?). That would not only prevent using precious resources to meet trivial needs but also encourage abandoning socially and ecologically harmful production techniques.[1167]

In parallel, a new approach to taxation on climate change must be adopted. The only way to meaningfully manage the financial dimensions of the ecological crisis is to go where the money is. That means taxing carbon emissions and financial speculation. It means raising taxes on corporations and the wealthy, cutting bloated military budgets, and eliminating subsidies to the

---

1165 Malm, *How to Blow ...*, p. 79.
1166 Boyd, *Report of ... (A/75/161)*, p. 20, § 77.
1167 Parrique, *Ralentir ou Périr*, p. 228.

fossil fuel industry.[1168] Since taxation is directly related to state sovereignty, these proposed measures should be the subject of constitutional provisions. In particular, the prohibition of subsidies to the fossil fuel industry from the state budget should be enshrined in a constitutional provision, both as a limitation on the executive branch and as a matter of property rights. Once enacted, such a regulation would be highly effective in stopping climate change, as it would lead to the rapid downsizing of the industry in question.

4.3.1.4 Separation of economy and politics

Today, one of the main reasons why climate change cannot be stopped despite the knowledge of its economic causes is the close relationship between those who carry out these economic activities and the rule-makers – if they are not the same people. Contrary to what is usually said, politics is not independent of the economy; it is subordinate to it.[1169] This relationship is often manifested in lobbying between corporate executives and parliamentarians. Once elected, those elected by popular vote may tend to prioritise their short-term interests over campaign promises. Therefore, they do not take measures to combat climate change that are in favour of communities but against corporations. That is why relations between politicians and business people, whether elected or not, should be regulated by law.

For example, politicians should be banned from accepting donations or bribes from the industries they regulate, and political donations should be both fully disclosed and strictly regulated. In addition, the public should have broad access to election campaigns, which should be publicly funded.[1170] Of course, the share allocated to parties should be based on objective criteria and needs, and waste should be avoided.

Beyond election campaigns, there must be an immediate end to the close relationship between states and fossil fuel companies in particular. As the UN climate change rapporteur has demanded, sectors that harm ecosystems and biodiversity, including fossil fuel, mining, and industrial agriculture, should not benefit from state subsidies.[1171] It should be enshrined in the constitutions

---

[1168] Klein, *On Fire*, p. 113.
[1169] Saito, *Slow Down*, p. 230.
[1170] Klein, *That Changes Everything*, pp. 216–17.
[1171] Boyd, *Report of… (A/75/161)*, p. 22, § 84.

that these sectors cannot be subsidised. If such a ban is not adopted, high courts should strike down subsidy laws based on the constitutional right to life and a healthy environment.

All industries and industrial agriculture must be controlled, limited, and restructured to avoid global warming and other threats to human and natural existence. Instead, local, small, and medium-sized enterprises and subsistence economies should be promoted. That should provide jobs for all. For such changes to take place, there must be arrangements for the control of the means of production in accordance with the needs of society and for democratic planning of production and change. Democratic decisions on investments and technological developments must replace the control of capitalist corporations, investors, and banks in order to serve society's and nature's common good in the long term.[1172]

In addition to clean air and water, access to fertile land should also be recognised as a fundamental right, as well as enjoying chemical-free food and renewable energy sources. Far from being 'despotic', collective decision-making at local, regional, national, and international levels should also be recognised as a right of society in the exercise of shared freedom and responsibility.[1173] In other words, decision-making should no longer be a process between a group of politicians and business people, as it is today. It should be given back to the people, as is the origin of the concept of 'democracy'.[1174] To this end, it is necessary to bring the administrative units as close to the people as possible and to strengthen and prioritise local governments in the administrative structure. Once this is done, it will be possible for decisions to be made by people's assemblies that will be formed with the direct participation of the people, which is in line with true democracy.[1175] Going even one step further, in nature-centred governance, *demos* should be understood to include flora and fauna as well as humans, and it should be ensured that the rights of animals and nature are taken into account in decision-making processes and not violated.[1176] The first way coming to mind to do this would

---

[1172] Löwy, *Ecosocialism*, The Belém Declaration (Loc. 1171).

[1173] Löwy, *Ecosocialism*, The Belém Declaration (Loc. 1167).

[1174] The word democracy is the portmanteau of the Greek words *demos*, meaning people, and *kratia*, meaning power.

[1175] For a realistic proposal in this regard, see Bookchin, *The Next Revolution*, pp. 129–45.

[1176] Kaboğlu – Yancı Özalp, *Çevre Hakkı*, pp. 167–8.

be to involve civil society organisations fighting for animal and nature rights in decision-making processes as their guardians or to appoint officials within the administrative organisation to defend animal and nature rights at the local and regional level.

4.3.1.5 The precautionary principle

The precautionary principle, also referred to as *in dubio pro natura*[1177] in some texts, means that if it is scientifically claimed that an economic activity is likely to cause irreversible damage to nature, it must be proven otherwise to proceed. If this cannot be done, the activity must be terminated. This principle, which is not based on a precise prediction of the effects of actions but aims to reduce the risk of a systemic collapse by reducing our pressure on the natural world, requires broad precautionary measures in economic activities. Of course, for such an approach to be effective, it requires legal controls that operate at the macro level of policymaking.[1178] For this, it is crucial that the precautionary principle is enshrined in constitutions and implemented through laws. Various steps have already been taken around the world in this regard.

For example, according to the Constitution of Zambia, *where there is a risk of serious or irreversible damage to the environment, lack of scientific certainty cannot be used to justify delaying cost-effective measures to prevent environmental degradation.*[1179] Thus, by adopting a general definition of the precautionary principle, the Constitution recognises it as one of the country's fundamental environmental management principles.

The Constitution of Côte d'Ivoire has a stronger version of this principle: *When there is a risk of serious and irreversible damage to the environment, the State and communities must assess the potential harm and take preventive measures using the precautionary principle.*[1180]

1177 Latin, meaning 'interpretation in favour of nature in case of doubt'.

1178 Olivia Woolley, *Ecological Governance: Reappraising Law's Role in Protecting Ecosystem Functionality*, Cambridge University Press, Cambridge, 2014, p. 38, cited in: Collins, *The Ecological Constitution*, p. 94.

1179 Constitution of Zambia 1991 as amended in 2016, art. 255 (c).

1180 2016 Constitution of Côte d'Ivoire, Art. 40.

Similarly, the Environmental Charter,[1181] which is considered part of the French Constitution, stipulates that

> as soon as there is a threat of serious and irreversible environmental damage, despite scientific uncertainty, public authorities are obliged to follow, in their respective fields, the application of risk assessment procedures and the adoption of proportionate and provisional measures to prevent the occurrence of damage by applying the precautionary principle.[1182]

Ecuador is one of the countries with the most vigorous regulation and implementation of the precautionary principle. According to the Constitution,

> In order to guarantee, individually and collectively, the right to live in a healthy and ecologically balanced environment, the State guarantees to everyone the right to resort to judicial and administrative authorities to seek effective guardianship in environmental matters, including the possibility to take legal action even if their interests are not directly affected and to request precautionary measures that would make it possible to put an end to the environmental damage or threat thereof. The burden of proof for the absence of potential or actual danger is on the actor or defendant.[1183]

The principle appears in different guises in other articles of the Ecuadorian Constitution. For example, according to the Constitution, *when there is doubt about the scope of legal regulations on environmental matters, the interpretation of these regulations that is more effective for the protection of nature shall be considered appropriate.*[1184]

The most crucial advantage of constitutional articles regulating the precautionary principle is that they enable authorised institutions and citizens to step in and question the project before any harm is done to nature. Once a scientific claim is made, the burden of proof shifts to the company and/or the state that would realise the project. One of the best examples of this is the Canal Istanbul project. The project, which scientists insistently say

[1181] *Charte de l'Environnement*, adopted on 1 March 2005 by Constitutional Amendment Law No. 2005–205.

[1182] Environmental Charter, Art. 5.

[1183] 2008 Constitution of Ecuador, art. 397.

[1184] Constitution of Ecuador of 2008, art. 395 (4).

would cause an ecological disaster,[1185] is still moving forward, albeit slowly, without a satisfactory response to these claims. If there was a provision in the Turkish Constitution or laws on the precautionary principle, the project could not proceed unless the state and the companies undertaking the project proved otherwise.

It is essential to recognise that the precautionary principle often comes into play concerning local projects. The principle is often used to stop or cancel a particular project affecting a particular region. However, it has now become clear that assessing each environmental development on a case-by-case basis, as if it operates in isolation from others, is a highly inappropriate approach to ensuring the well-being of individual ecosystems and the Earth's ecosystem as a whole.[1186] The precautionary principle should, therefore, also be considered for general economic activities that harm the Earth's ecosystem. For example, while there is strong scientific evidence that the production and consumption of fossil fuels are causing global climate change, the burden should be on oil companies to prove that this is not the case. When they fail to do so, they should be obliged to stop these activities according to the precautionary principle.

4.3.1.6 Producing and consuming locally

Statistics on material production show that high-income countries are most responsible for ecological collapse. However, there is another side to this equation: We also need to ask where in the world this collapse is taking place. High-income countries are heavily dependent on excavations in the countries of the Global South. Research shows that half of the material they consume comes from excavation in developing countries, often under conditions of injustice and exploitation.[1187] That is enabled by the economic system of exploitation that began with Grotius' idea of the open sea and continues today with neoliberalism's praise of the 'global economy'. The wealthy countries of the Global North have achieved their economic development

---

[1185] See Istanbul Metropolitan Municipality, *Kanal Istanbul Çalıştay Raporu*, 10 January 2020.

[1186] Rakhyun E. Kim – Brendon Mackey, 'International Environmental Law as a Complex Adaptive System', *International Environmental Agreements*, No. 14, 2014, p. 5, cited in: Collins, *The Ecological Constitution*, p. 93.

[1187] Hickel, *Less is More*, p. 110.

by exploiting the human and natural resources of developing countries for years, and today, they continue this exploitation through the rules of the free-market economy.

The devastating damage free trade has done to production, local businesses, and farming in Global South countries is now well known. In addition, the atmosphere has been one of the hardest hit by unrestricted international trade. Cargo ships, airplanes, and heavy trucks carrying raw resources and products around the world are heavy consumers of fossil fuels and emit vast amounts of greenhouse gases. Moreover, the cheap products they produce, which are rarely repaired and replaced almost immediately, not only lead to the massive consumption of many other non-renewable resources but also create waste that cannot be disposed of properly.[1188] An economy that respects ecological limits should limit energy-intensive intercontinental transport, reserving such transport only for cases where local production is impossible or is more carbon-intensive.[1189] Therefore, localising production and consumption through legal means and, most importantly, international constitutional norms would play an essential role in combating climate change. That could be achieved through high taxation on imported products with domestic equivalents, subsidising domestic producers that respect nature, and intensive state incentives for research and development. However, the most effective policy would, of course, be to abandon the growth logic and reduce consumption.

4.3.1.7 Regulating consumption

> O, reason not the need! Our basest beggars
> Are in the poorest thing superfluous.
> Allow not nature more than nature needs,
> Man's life is cheap as beast's.[1190]

[1188] Klein, *On Fire*, p. 109.

[1189] However, given that this situation is related to international trade and that the World Trade Organization can make binding decisions on this issue, it is necessary either to sever relations with this organisation or to make agreements that encourage local production in international law. For this, it is crucial that green constitutionalism moves from the local to the global dimension.

[1190] William Shakespeare, *King Lear*, Act 2, Scene 4.

When looking at anthropology's history, it is seen that all societies have always splurged, spent, and consumed beyond the necessary expenditures. Baudrillard argues that this is because societies, like individuals, depend on excessive consumption to feel they are living beyond existence.[1191] As a matter of fact, people today live thinking that it is their most natural right to consume as many resources as they can in their lifetime.[1192] However, as Shiva points out, turning to production and consumption models that take more than we need means resorting to violence. Unsustainable production and consumption establish a violent economic order because taking more than what is needed means not leaving enough resources for other species in the ecosystem and not maintaining the ecological processes needed to ensure sustainability.[1193]

The narrative that consumption is a sign of existence has dominated our cultural world since the Industrial Revolution. However, a new narrative is needed in the Anthropocene to reconceptualise social networks. At the centre of it should be the shift from quantity to quality and the lesson from nature that well-being does not depend on overconsumption.[1194] Well-being and prosperity are not dependent on consumption but rather are lost by working beyond human limits to increase it. The legal order should focus on promoting human well-being and prosperity, not consumption, for the sake of growth.

Trapped in a capitalist economic system, humans are consuming and destroying the elements that keep the Earth's ecosystem alive at such a rate that they have no time to replenish themselves. Moreover, our rate of consumption continues to increase. While economists proudly point to the sevenfold growth of the world economy between 1950 and 2000, today, world trade is growing even faster. Ecologists see this as a wasteful use of the Earth's 'natural capital'.[1195]

Our current consumption habits are often blamed on 'human nature', which always craves more and acts selfishly to increase its well-being.

[1191] Baudrillard, *La Société de Consommation*, p. 41.
[1192] Üsköl Engin, *Ekolojik Kriz, Etik ve Hukuk*, p. 51.
[1193] Shiva, *Earth Democracy*, pp. 164–5.
[1194] Capra – Mattei, *The Ecology of Law*, p. 191.
[1195] Lester Brown, *Eco-Economy: Building an Economy for the Earth*, W. W. Norton & Co., New York, 2001, pp. 7–8, cited in: Cullinan, *Wild Law*, p. 37.

Yet, none of us are born with this urge to shop so much. Moreover, not long ago, we were happier by consuming significantly less than we do today. The real issue is the exaggerated role assigned to consumption in our age.[1196] For many years, we have been subjected to propaganda that we must 'have' something to fulfil our needs. Within the framework of this propaganda, our perception of 'need' has been distorted. For example, if my clothes are dirty, I need not buy a washing machine but to have my clothes cleaned. If I had access to a washing machine that would clean my clothes, I could fulfil my needs without buying one.[1197] This way, I would not have to work harder to earn the money to buy the machine and could spend more time with myself and my family. Additionally, I would not have to find space in my house for a big machine that would be mostly idle, so that a smaller house would be enough for me, and the production of the machine would be reduced, using less raw materials and energy and increasing the efficiency of the machine. Also, during my time in the laundromat, I would have more opportunities to meet and socialise with my neighbours and create a sense of community. Therefore, the shared use of washing machines has many advantages and is highly efficient in every respect.

Nevertheless, having a washing machine to wash dirty clothes has become so normalised today that laundromats are seen as a symbol of deprivation. If I wash my clothes in a laundromat, I would probably be considered either a homeless person, a tourist, or, in the best case, a student. Obviously, not every item we own would fit this example; we cannot exchange our sofa at home for a bench in the park. So, there are some things we need to have exclusively. Nonetheless, examples of unnecessary and/or inefficient consumption can be multiplied. For example, the social assumptions that one must have a car to go somewhere, buy a book to be knowledgeable, and have a fancy big house for a good life are culturally produced perceptions within the capitalist growth logic. However, what is needed in a productive society is the provision of quality public transportation infrastructure, the establishment of libraries that are accessible and free to all, and the construction of solid social housing and healthy public spaces compatible with human dignity.

[1196] Klein, *On Fire*, p. 150.

[1197] Parrique, *Ralentir our Périr*, p. 148.

So, it is not more consuming power that we should demand to meet our needs, but more public service provision.

However, a closer look at this propaganda for our needs shows that, especially in the countries of the Global North, the glorified biographies of heroes of production have been replaced by biographies of heroes of consumption. In Baudrillard's view, the exemplary lives of 'the man who started from scratch' and the founders, pioneers, explorers, and colonial Europeans who followed the lives of saints and historical figures have given way to the lives of movie, sports, and gaming stars, gilded princes or international feudals, in short, the 'great spendthrifts'. They are always glorified for their extravagant lives and ability to spend outrageously.[1198] Today, with the influence of the internet and social media applications, consumption is triggered by some influencers[1199] praising products we do not need and luxurious lives, turning consumption into a desire rather than a compulsory action to fulfil a need. Thus, regardless of their needs, people are led to unnecessary consumption by putting them into a psychology that the things they own are always insufficient and that they are poor and deprived.

The luxurious lifestyle highlighted by the mass media is culturally nothing but a reflection of a much deeper and systematic extravagance integrated into capitalist economic processes. It is produced at the same time as the production of material goods, embedded in these goods, and necessarily consumed as one of the qualities and dimensions of the object of consumption. As everyone knows, most products today are unnecessarily fragile and put on the market with planned obsolescence[1200] and, therefore, doomed to impermanence. Everything that is produced today is produced not according

---

[1198] Baudrillard, *La Sociéte de Consommation*, p. 44.

[1199] This word refers to people who influence people's consumption habits on social media platforms. It has been seen that these people are almost always happy, wealthy, trouble-free and 'glittering' thanks to the goods, houses, yachts or services they own.

[1200] That means that a product is artificially designed by its makers to have a shorter lifespan. Thus, when the product reaches the end of its predetermined lifespan, it either works worse or doesn't work at all. That forces consumers to buy the latest version of the product once again. This has become so widespread today that Lafargue claims that our age will be called 'the age of adulteration, falsification, counterfeiting', inspired by the fact that the early ages of humanity were called the Stone Age or the Bronze Age because of the nature of production. See Lafargue, *Le Droit à la Paresse*, p. 26.

to its use value or its possible lifespan but, on the contrary, according to its destruction.[1201]

In the rush to increase sales, companies seek to create products that will break down/wear out and be replaced after a relatively short period. Today, planned obsolescence is a form of deliberate inefficiency widely used in capitalist production. Inefficiency makes (interestingly) sense in terms of maximising profits. Still, from the perspective of human needs and ecology, wasting resources and unnecessary energy consumption is entirely irrational.[1202] The main reason for this irrationality is that in the current economic order, products are produced to increase companies' profits rather than to meet the needs of people. Indeed, it can be said that the vast majority of the 'products' have no purpose or function other than to make more profit for big corporations. The problem here is not 'overconsumption' in the abstract but the current pervasive consumption mode based on an incredible amount of waste, commercial alienation, obsessive hoarding of products, and the compulsory acquisition of fabricated innovations imposed as 'fashion'.[1203]

It must also be noted that capitalism is a system organised around the exchange value of products, not their use value. Much of the goods production is geared towards accumulating profit rather than satisfying human needs. In fact, in a growth-oriented system, the aim is to avoid satisfying human needs and to ensure the continuity of needs. Because if a person could satisfy their needs with a product, they would no longer consume. However, for growth to continue, they must continue to consume. Therefore, capitalism does not produce abundance but rather scarcity.[1204] Once this is understood, it becomes clear that much of today's economy is actively and wilfully wasteful and serves no meaningful human purpose.[1205] The fundamental problem of contemporary capitalism is no longer the contradiction between 'maximisation of profit' and 'rationalisation of production' but the contradiction between potentially unlimited productivity and the necessity of getting products to market and selling them. Therefore, in the current economic order, not only

---

[1201] Baudrillard, *La Sociéte de Consommation*, p. 45.
[1202] Hickel, *Less is More*, pp. 207–8.
[1203] Löwy, *Ecosocialism*, Ecosocialism and Democratic Planning (Loc. 517).
[1204] Saito, *Slow Down*, p. 148.
[1205] Hickel, *Less is More*, p. 206.

the product but also the demand for its consumption must be produced.[1206] That is what advertising and influencers are for.

Establishing a harmless and mutually reinforcing presence is not easy since we have internalised the false beliefs and attitudes on which most cultures are founded. As we have been taught, we think in dichotomies and, for example, sincerely believe that increased consumption would increase our happiness. Ralph Metzner, a leading figure in eco-psychology, puts it this way:

> Several different diagnostic metaphors have been proposed to explain the ecologically disastrous split – pathological alienation – between human consciousness and the rest of the biosphere. The standard psychological categories such as addiction, dissociation, autism, and amnesia may provide useful diagnostic metaphors to explain our determination to distance ourselves from our habitat and context.[1207]

In other words, capitalist consumerism has disconnected us from reality and distorted our psychology. Products and needs are created endlessly around the growth logic, causing an increasing dissatisfaction.[1208] In our search for the happiness promised by the economic order, we are caught in a spiral of consumption, and we do not want to see how harmful it is to the Earth and other people.

Most of us are aware of the danger facing the Earth. However, we are not doing much to change the system and our daily lives, which is the primary cause. Behavioural surveys show that a significant proportion of the public sees global warming as a threat, but few are willing to change their lives in any significant way. Social psychologists call that 'future discounting', whereby people do not approach the future with the same level of realism as they do the present. Accordingly, a small reward today is preferred to a larger reward in the future. The same principle applies to risks. One of the best examples of this is smoking cigarettes.[1209] Smokers prefer the fleeting pleasure of the moment to the diminished quality of life due to future health problems. Since people have sovereignty over their own bodies, this can be seen as their choice. However, our current consumption habits affect the

---

[1206] Baudrillard, *La Sociéte de Consommation*, p. 81.
[1207] Cited in: Cullinan, *Wild Law*, p. 49.
[1208] Latouche, *Vers une Société d'Abondance frugale*, p. 26; Saito, *Slow Down*, p. 164.
[1209] Gidden, *The Politics of Climate Change*, p. 13.

lives of others and violate their most basic rights. So, there is a considerable difference regarding the outcomes of these two future discountings. While the law might allow the former, it should not allow the latter.

The wealthiest 10 per cent of the world's population is responsible for half of all emissions, and the top 1 per cent emit half as much carbon as all people on the planet. They often do this by consuming luxuries, taking non-essential trips, travelling in private jets[1210] or boats, and producing unnecessary products that increase the consumption of others. That means that a significant limit on the purchasing power of the wealthiest and a crackdown on their waste would significantly impact reducing carbon emissions at the global level.[1211] Moreover, a person who owns, for example, a super yacht could easily abandon it if they wanted to, without giving up a vital need or right. In stark contrast to a low-income family burning wood for cooking, there can be no excuse for emissions from luxury living.[1212] For this reason, Latouche suggests that additional complementary taxes on luxury goods should continue to exist, and if they do not exist, they should be introduced. The author also argues that taxation should be raised up to 100 per cent on income that exceeds a legal upper limit.[1213] After all, in order to make progress towards the zero emissions target, we first need to get rid of the most unnecessary emissions.[1214]

That would have to be done through legal regulations and even constitutional norms because these would be regulations related to property, which today is considered a fundamental right. Private jets and boats that can no longer be used due to these new norms can be converted into ambulances or otherwise made available to the public. That would reduce the incentive for people to consume unnecessarily in the name of 'living like them' since a wasteful life would no longer be an incentive, improving their economic situation. As a result, a policy that reduces the incomes of the

---

1210 According to calculations, a passenger on a private jet emits up to fourteen times more carbon than a passenger on a scheduled flight. Yet, private aviation is taxed at a remarkably lower rate than commercial aviation. See Edward J. Markey, 'Private Jets Are Awful for the Climate. It's Time to Tax the Rich Who Fly in Them', *The Guardian*, 10 August 2023.

1211 Thomas Piketty, 'The Illusion of Centrist Ecology', *Le Monde*, 11 June 2019.

1212 Malm, *How to Blow …*, p. 102.

1213 Latouche, *Vers une Société d'Abondance frugale*, p. 30.

1214 Malm, *How to Blow …*, p. 107.

extremely wealthy would yield positive gains in both ecological and social terms. Moreover, the excessive income of the rich does not contribute to their well-being. Therefore, preventing their income from becoming excessive can be done without any social cost.[1215] No one should have either too much or not enough of anything. The happy awareness arising from the 'voluntary simplicity' concept practiced by those who follow this principle depends on collective organisation.[1216] One of the most effective ways to do this is through constitutional regulation of consumption.

Within the scope of these regulations, marketing, advertising, and packaging that cause people to unnecessarily desire things they do not need could be banned.[1217] Mandatory extension of product warranties is another thing that comes to mind when considering measures to prevent planned obsolescence. Likewise, consumers could be granted a legal 'right to repair', making it illegal for companies to produce products that cannot be repaired with spare parts cheaply available to ordinary consumers or independent repairers. For large and complex products that citizens cannot repair themselves, manufacturers could be required to undertake their repair free of charge wherever it is possible to improve efficiency.[1218]

Reducing the power of advertising is another way to reduce unnecessary consumption. We would already know what we really need and somehow acquire it. In contrast, advertising artificially creates the feeling that something is missing.[1219] To satisfy this false sense of deprivation, we feel a necessity to buy the product we do not actually need. That becomes a never-ending cycle, and so we never achieve the feeling of satisfaction. One solution to eliminate this cycle would be to determine a maximum advertising budget that could be customised for each company and product according to objective criteria set by law. Likewise, advertising that is psychologically manipulative or creates a false perception in people could be prohibited by law. In addition, billboards and other means used for advertisements could be removed from public spaces where people have no chance to decide what they see.[1220]

1215 Hickel, *Less is More*, p. 183.

1216 Parrique, *Ralentir ou Périr*, p. 238.

1217 Saito, *Slow Down*, p. 196.

1218 Hickel, *Less is More*, p. 209.

1219 Hickel, *Less is More*, p. 231.

1220 Hickel, *Less is More*, p. 213.

To those who would argue that this would be an 'oppressive' proposal, the advertising bans on tobacco and alcohol products that are already in place in many countries should be reminded. The freedom to advertise these products, which are scientifically proven to harm the health of individuals and their environment, might be restricted to protect personal and public health, and these restrictions are generally considered reasonable. Similarly, in order to protect the ecosystem and the global right to health and life, if not all ads, at least ads for products that cause climate change, could be banned.[1221] A good example of this has already taken effect in the Hague, the Netherlands, as of the beginning of 2025. Fossil fuel products and climate-damaging services can no longer be advertised in the city. Under the ban, advertisements for petrol and diesel fuels or aviation and cruises – regardless of whether the public sector or private companies make them – will no longer be allowed on billboards or at bus stops.[1222]

All this does not mean that the world economy will stop or that no one will consume anything anymore. Almost everything produced today will continue to be produced, but the frequency and volume will decrease while the quality[1223] and, consequently, duration of use will increase. The focus here should be on curbing and controlling wasteful consumption, especially in rich countries. Because, at this stage, nothing will be as beneficial as a bit of contempt for material blessings.[1224] However, consumption in the Global South countries can and should increase. Yet, of course, this should be an increase in consumption that meets basic needs and must not turn into a wasteful economy.

In addition, in every country, the share of the public sector, cooperatives, local businesses, and non-profit organisations in overall economic activity should be expanded. The same opportunity should be given to sectors such as education, caring professions, and leisure activities that significantly

---

1221 UN Secretary General Antonio Guterres made a similar call. See Oliver Milman, '"Godfathers of Climate Chaos": UN Chief Urges Global Fossil-fuel Advertising Ban', *The Guardian*, 5 June 2024.

1222 Isabella Kaminski, 'The Hague Becomes World's First City to Pass Law Banning Fossil Fuel-related Ads', *The Guardian*, 13 September 2024.

1223 Parrique, *Ralentir ou Périr*, p. 190.

1224 Leopold, *A Sand County Almanac*, p. XXVII.

contribute to society's well-being while having minimal impact on the ecology. That would both be meaningful consumption and create jobs.[1225]

In short, the new green society would be one that produces to meet people's real needs. These should include essential services such as water, food, clothing, and shelter, as well as health, education, transportation, and culture.[1226] Although the relations of production and consumption seem to be outside the realm of law and more the domain of economics and politics, the essential services needed by individuals and society are essentially related to fundamental rights and freedoms, many of which are already enshrined in the constitution. There is, therefore, ample legal justification for higher courts to step in and make decisions that protect these rights rather than economic interests. When judges of these courts are convinced to implement green constitutionalism in their decisions, the conditions for a postcapitalist economic order are more likely to emerge and develop. Once these conditions have matured, various economic order alternatives will emerge automatically according to the principles of this new constitutionalism. Here, I would like to focus on two of them: The Green New Deal and degrowth. The former tries to find a solution while continuing business as usual, while the latter is a genuine solution compatible with green constitutionalism.

4.3.2 Green New Deal

The Green New Deal, which proposes a rapid decarbonisation of the existing economic order rather than a revolutionary break with it, is a concept introduced into the political literature by green parties in Europe and is now mostly associated with the European Union. The key element of this proposal can be summarised as an urgent decarbonisation, a transition to efficient and renewable energy production, and the creation of millions of jobs.[1227] That would be achieved by promoting renewable energy and electric vehicles through large-scale public investment. Creating stable and high-paying jobs in these areas would strengthen and stimulate the economy.[1228] Therefore,

[1225] Klein, *On Fire*, pp. 112–13.

[1226] Löwy, *Ecosocialism*, Ecosocialism and Democratic Planning (Loc. 517–23).

[1227] The Greens in the European Parliament, 'Yeşil Yeni Düzene Neden İhtiyaç Duyuyoruz?', trans. İnan Mayıs Aru, *in* Ahmet Atıl Aşıcı – Ümit Şahin (ed.), *Yeşil Ekonomi*, Yeni İnsan, Istanbul, (year not mentioned), p. 136.

[1228] Saito, *Slow Down*, p. 32.

the Green New Deal does not directly criticise the concept of growth and claims that a sustainable and green growth is possible.

According to this view, ecological sustainability can be achieved in a way that is reconcilable with economic growth and social goals. In a market-dominated economy, the most obvious way to achieve this is through the pricing of goods and services by ecosystems. According to this approach, also called 'market environmentalism'[1229] or ' green Keynesianism',[1230] if climate change results from a 'small but significant market failure', the market can be improved by setting prices for atmospheric damages and making them tradable. The Green New Deal sees 'green growth' as a path to poverty reduction, ecosystem recovery, and climate stabilisation.[1231] In other ways, climate change is a golden opportunity to boost economic growth like never before.[1232]

Proponents of a Green New Deal aim to turn the multiple crises made visible by climate change into an opportunity to create a more just economic and social order. Accordingly, the fight against the factors that are destroying the planet and those that harm people's quality of life offers the opportunity to solve many intertwined crises simultaneously.[1233] That requires using public resources in areas that promote real human well-being. Green investments will ensure sustainability if governments have to pour money into the economy to get out of economic and ecological crises.[1234] The widespread use of not only solar panels but also electric vehicles and quick-charge batteries, coupled with the development of biomass energy, will require large-scale transformations in the economy that will create new jobs. Moreover, the need for a complete transformation of the existing social infrastructure due to climate change requires large-scale investments.[1235]

Indeed, as it has become clear that current market mechanisms cannot solve the climate crisis, there is a need for large-scale, coordinated government

---

1229 Hulme, *Why We Disagree …*, p. 268.
1230 Saito, *Slow Down*, p. 32.
1231 Hulme, *Why We Disagree …*, p. 268.
1232 Saito, *Slow Down*, p. 33.
1233 Klein, *On Fire*, p. 43.
1234 Ahmet Atıl Aşıcı, 'Sayılarla Dünyada ve Türkiye'de Yeşil Yeni Düzen', *in* Ahmet Atıl Aşıcı – Ümit Şahin (ed.), *Yeşil Ekonomi*, Yeni İnsan, İstanbul, (year not mentioned), p. 216.
1235 Saito, *Slow Down*, p. 33.

action. Therefore, proponents of the Green New Deal argue for an unprecedented public investment in renewable energy infrastructure.[1236] Accordingly, a viable Green New Deal must involve significant public investment, public ownership, and numerous regulations. These investments and regulations should be used to radically reduce fossil fuel consumption and transition to an economy based entirely on renewable energy. This transition should include fair working conditions, full employment, and broadly improved living conditions for all, especially marginalised communities.[1237]

One of the most important elements on which the Green New Deal is based is decoupling. In the framework of this proposal, decoupling means breaking the link between economic growth and the increase in environmental problems through new technologies. In other words, it is an effort to ensure that the economy grows without the negative impacts of growth on the environment.[1238] The transition from oil-powered cars to electric vehicles in transportation and from coal-fired power plants to solar panels and wind turbines in electricity generation are the most well-known examples of decoupling. That avoids emitting carbon dioxide into the atmosphere and helps the economy grow by producing new technological products.[1239]

As an example of the arrangements that need to be made under the Green New Deal, Chomsky and Pollin point to the future management of electricity companies. According to the authors, if some electricity companies are to remain privately owned, they should be required to reduce their carbon dioxide emissions annually by amounts calculated to achieve net-zero emissions by 2050. Failure to meet the requirements could result in jail time for the companies' chief executive officers.[1240] Of course, following the principle

---

[1236] Hickel, *Less is More*, p. 137.

[1237] Schmelzer – Vetter – Vansintjan, *The Future is Degrowth*, p. 8.

[1238] Saito, *Slow Down*, p. 36; Parrique, *Ralentir ou Périr*, p. 54.

[1239] The debate in this area involves three issues: 1) Relative decoupling, whereby the material and carbon intensity of GDP is reduced so that GDP increases by more than material use and emissions, 2) Absolute decoupling where material use and emissions decrease while GDP increases and 3) Sufficient absolute decoupling, or genuine green growth, where GDP continues to grow while material use and emissions decline enough to keep the economy within planetary boundaries. For details, see Kallis – Hickel – O'Neill – Jackson – Victor – Raworth – Schor – Steinberger – Ürge-Vorsatz, 'Post-growth', p. e65-e66.

[1240] Chomsky – Pollin, *Climate Crisis …*, p. 92.

of legality in crime and punishment, this offence must already be defined in the law. Therefore, in order to establish the Green New Deal, some legal arrangements must first be made.

The Green New Deal could create important new opportunities for alternative forms of ownership, including various smaller-scale combinations of public, private, and cooperative ownership. Large private companies would also be included in this mix, but not in the same unrestricted freedom as before. These companies would need to be heavily regulated and controlled.[1241]

The Green New Deal is also closely related to repair and compensation. It calls for creating living-wage jobs, 'restoring and protecting fragile ecosystems threatened by danger and extinction', and 'cleaning up existing hazardous waste as well as abandoned land and securing economic development and sustainability in these areas'.[1242] Proponents of the Green New Deal argue that decarbonising the economy would also create many jobs. Nevertheless, these jobs must be in ecologically sustainable sectors. Indeed, for example, in 2023 alone, 142,000 jobs were created in the renewable energy sector, in line with US President Biden's plan to transition to 100 per cent clean energy by 2035. That accounted for 56 per cent of all jobs in the energy sector.[1243]

As a result, the Green New Deal supporters argue that this new approach to the economy can become a vehicle for defeating both the aggressively pro-corporate neoliberal variant of capitalism that has dominated the global economy for two generations and the rise of neofascism that has emerged in the last decade as a twisted deceptively populist response to neoliberalism.[1244] Moreover, it is seen as an initiative that can raise living standards for the masses in the Global South, expand job opportunities, and ensure clean air, land, and water. In this respect, the Green New Deal is presented as a viable framework for preventing the coming decades from being characterised by steadily rising average global temperatures, as well as neoliberalism that leads to severe economic crises and lower living standards.[1245]

However, there is also criticism that the Green New Deal, which some governments and international organisations also support, is a version of

---

[1241] Chomsky – Pollin, *Climate Crisis …*, p. 99.

[1242] Klein, *On Fire*, pp. 316–17.

[1243] Department of Energy, *2024 U.S. Energy & Employment Jobs Report (USEER)*, p. 6.

[1244] Chomsky – Pollin, *Climate Crisis …*, p. 120.

[1245] Chomsky – Pollin, *Climate Crisis …*, pp. 157–8.

capitalism ecologically adapted to the present day and, therefore, cannot be sustainable, even if implemented temporarily.[1246] It is strongly argued that if economic growth continues, greenhouse gas emissions cannot be reduced at a sufficient pace despite all efforts to transition to sustainable energy. Hence, decoupling is only possible on a small scale and can only happen in anomalous and exceptional circumstances. In fact, according to Jason Hickel, it is a fantasy. He argues that 835 empirical studies show that green growth and decoupling are inadequate for achieving climate goals,[1247] noting that it seemed possible for a while in the 1990s when GDP grew slightly faster than material use, but then things went in the opposite direction.[1248] Indeed, according to a very recent study published by a group of expert economists, it is very difficult, if not impossible, to decouple economic activity from emissions and achieve a net-zero target while GDP continues to grow. Necessary reductions in energy and material use, which can never be zero and can only be reduced, are much easier to achieve in a post-growth economic order to prevent climate change.[1249] Taking a harder line, Timothée Parrique argues that decoupling is impossible within the capitalist economic order and that green growth is nothing more than a piece of fake news.[1250]

Many economists believe that an economic order that should be seen as the primary source of climate change cannot offer a solution under any circumstances, which is why the concept of 'degrowth' has increasingly come to the fore in recent years. This concept, which directly criticises capitalism's dependence on growth, differs from the Green New Deal in this respect.

4.3.3 Degrowth

The knowledge and experience needed for a good life are currently available in our societies. However, due to the fragmented and reductionist education system of modernism, the complex wholeness of the Earth and the interconnectedness of everything is not comprehended. The mainstreaming of *growth for growth's sake*, despite resilient communities in every corner of our planet,

---

[1246] Schmelzer – Vetter – Vansintjan, *The Future is Degrowth*, pp. 7–9.
[1247] Hickel, *Less is More*, p. 23.
[1248] Hickel, *Less is More*, p. 102.
[1249] Kallis – Hickel – O'Neill – Jackson – Victor – Raworth – Schor – Steinberger – Ürge-Vorsatz, 'Post-growth', p. e66.
[1250] Parrique, *Ralentir ou Périr*, pp. 53–90.

prevents the realisation of holism and interconnectedness.[1251] The quantitative perspective of economic reason based on GDP has colonised our imagination in a totalitarian spirit.[1252] Any measure of economic success other than growth is unfathomable under the dominant contemporary culture. This metric has captured our world of ideas so that we are more concerned about the effects of climate change on GDP than we are about the consequences of our economic model on our planet.[1253]

However, the results of recent empirical research suggest two points. First, even though they use far fewer resources and emit far less carbon, some middle-income countries can achieve better social outcomes than high-income countries. For example, despite being the world's largest economy, education and health outcomes in the United States are much worse than in Finland, which has a much smaller economy. The second point is that there is no country today that can stay within planetary boundaries and still achieve good social outcomes. In other words, all the countries in the world today that are able to provide a good life for their citizens are contributing to climate change and ecological collapse. So, at this point, we face an important dilemma. On the one hand, there are high-income countries that have succeeded in ensuring the well-being of their citizens, but in doing so have far exceeded their share of planetary limits. In this respect, they should not be a model for other countries. If other countries want to grow in a similar way and become high-income countries, we will not be able to stop climate change. On the other side, there is the fact that achieving the desired level of human development while staying within planetary boundaries is almost impossible in today's dominant economic order.[1254] Is there a solution to this dilemma?

Yes, there is. It is important to realise that GDP is just a numerical measure of the volume of monetary flows in a given economy, and its growth is not always good news, as it tells us nothing about the positive and negative impacts of the goods and services produced.[1255] Indeed, the policies shielding the phenomenal growth of the global economy today are the same policies

---

1251 Arık, 'Bir arada … ', p. 452. (Emphasis is Arık's.)

1252 Latouche, *Vers une Société d'Abondance frugale*, pp. 12–13 (foreword by Tahir Karakaş).

1253 Parrique, *Ralentir ou Périr*, p. 13.

1254 Kallis – Hickel – O'Neill – Jackson – Victor – Raworth – Schor – Steinberger – Ürge-Vorsatz, 'Post-growth', p. e72.

1255 Parrique, *Ralentir ou Périr*, p. 30.

destroying the Earth's support systems. By every conceivable ecological criterion, these are failed policies.[1256] If GDP is one-eyed about the economy's well-being, it is totally blind to human well-being, deaf to social misery, and mute to the state of the planet.[1257] Moreover, there is no adequate justification for the belief that growth is necessary. Those who call for perpetual growth at the expense of ecological stability are literally risking everything for things we do not even really need.[1258] Moreover, anyone who believes that unlimited exponential growth can go on forever in a finite world is, in the words of Kenneth E. Boulding, either crazy or an economist.[1259]

As mentioned in the first chapter, pro-growth advocates claim that when an economy grows, everyone benefits and gets richer. However, several economic crises, the coronavirus pandemic, the wildfires in the Amazon forest, and the genocide of Indigenous peoples in the past and present show that growth-based capitalism is already a disaster.[1260] The pitiful state of nature in the Anthropocene shows us that economic growth itself destroys the very basis of what humans need to thrive.[1261] In addition, social inequalities are on the rise in growth-based economies. According to what Lafargue described as 'one of the inexorable laws of capitalist production', in this economic order, as social wealth grows, so does workers' misery.[1262] One of the reasons for this is that when growth falters – and it often happens all over the world – governments are at the mercy of the financial markets, which force them into harsh austerity. Cutting wages, reducing or selling off public services, and privatising everything possible are often proposed solutions. By implementing them, governments risk creating deflation and entering the terrible cycle of a depressive spiral.[1263]

Growing inequalities are not the only problem with economic growth. Another major problem is that growth is increasingly destroying the integrity

---

[1256] Lester Brown, *Eco-Economy: Building an Economy for the Earth*, W. W. Norton & Co., New York, 2001, pp. 7–8, cited in: Cullinan, *Wild Law*, p. 37.

[1257] Éloi Laurent, *Sortir de la Croissance: Mode d'Emploi*, Actes Sud, Arles, 2019, p. 61, cited in: Parrique, *Ralentir ou Périr*, p. 31.

[1258] Hickel, *Less is More*, p. 199.

[1259] Cited in: Saito, *Slow Down*, p. 17.

[1260] Schmelzer – Vetter – Vansintjan, *The Future is Degrowth*, p. 21.

[1261] Saito, *Slow Down*, p. 1.

[1262] Lafargue, *Le Droit à la Paresse*, p. 13.

[1263] Latouche, *Vers une Société d'Abondance frugale*, p. 32.

of ecosystems. Almost everyone today agrees that economic growth that does not harm nature is an illusion[1264] because the relationship between economic growth and ecological collapse has been empirically demonstrated.[1265] As Hickel points out,

> As onshore oil reserves run dry we can switch to offshore reserves, but both sources contribute to climate breakdown. We might be able to substitute one metal for another, but ramping up the mining of any metal is going to poison rivers and ruin habitats. And we might be able to intensify our extraction from the land by pumping it full of chemicals, but not without triggering soil depletion and pollinator collapse. The process of substitution and intensification might get us around resource limits for a while, but it still drives ecological breakdown. That's the problem.[1266]

That is because economic growth in a market economy relies on three elements: consumers who always need to buy more things, companies that always need to sell more things, and a government that supports the whole process. Each of these three elements has its own indicator: individuals want to maximise their income, companies want to maximise their profits, and governments want to maximise their GDP.[1267] The way to do this is almost always through commodifying the resources of nature's economy for the market. Thus, as capital grows, nature shrinks.[1268] Indeed, the market economy, based on the logic of 'grow or die', is ruthlessly destroying the natural basis of complex life forms,[1269] and the pursuit of 'growth' is leading us in the short term to an unprecedented catastrophe such as global warming.[1270] So, while 'grow or die' may be a proper logic for companies to survive in the market, actual death is a growing risk for us if we continue to pursue growth policies.

From a biological point of view, nonhuman species and ecosystems seem to strike a balance between energy consumption and material use. That is because energy spent on excessive growth can damage a creature's survival

---

1264 Schmelzer – Vetter – Vansintjan, *The Future is Degrowth*, p. 17.
1265 Hickel, 'What Does Degrowth Mean?', p. 1105.
1266 Hickel, *Less is More*, pp. 120–1.
1267 Parrique, *Ralentir ou Périr*, p. 45.
1268 Shiva, *Earth Democracy*, p. 52.
1269 Bookchin, *The Next Revolution*, p. 66.
1270 Löwy, *Ecosocialism*, Preface: Before the Flood: The Political Challenge (Loc. 24).

ability. Therefore, living things have checks and balances that have evolved over thousands, if not millions, of years. In nature, maximisation is rejected and balanced, while optimisation is encouraged. An example of this principle is bones. Bones can be loaded with calcium in some places to provide strength against stress. However, this also means that the bones become heavier, which has an energy cost to the body. Therefore, calcium is removed from body parts where the bone does not need strength. Thus, weight is optimised.[1271] That is true for everything in nature. Nothing in nature grows forever. If it does, it eventually collapses. Nevertheless, our current dominant economic model's 'grow to grow' logic is in denial of this principle. In other words, capitalism is an economic model that goes against nature's fundamental principles.

This unnatural process of production and consumption, which has been going on since the Industrial Revolution, has finally brought the climate system to the brink. To prevent climate change from intensifying and threatening the lives of hundreds of millions of people, we must radically reduce greenhouse gas emissions and the consumption of fossil fuels needed to transform nature's resources and, thus, material production.[1272] Reducing material use would reduce energy demand, facilitating a rapid transition to renewable resources. This approach is also ecologically sound. By reducing the use of materials, we would not only take action against climate change but also reduce pressure on planetary boundaries.[1273] That would mean moving to an economic model that aligns with ecological principles.

Of course, we should try to produce as much renewable energy as possible. However, this alone cannot solve the crisis if the global economy continues to grow. Although it is possible that we can eventually move to 100 per cent renewable energy production, if we continue to grow the global economy at current rates, we cannot do it at a rate that will allow us to stay below 1.5°C or 2°C. More growth means more energy demand, which makes it very difficult to meet all of this demand from renewables in the short time remaining.[1274] That will likely happen in the future, but we need this transformation now

---

[1271] Arık, 'Bir Arada ... ', p. 457.
[1272] Tanuro, *L'Impossible le Capitalism vert*, pp. 17–18.
[1273] Hickel, 'What Does Degrowth Mean?', p. 1106.
[1274] Hickel, 'What Does Degrowth Mean?', p. 1105.

because otherwise, it will be too late. That is why growth-based economic policy needs to be abandoned immediately.

Even when we fully transition to clean energy, we will continue to put pressure on the living world if we use that energy to dig and produce more and more, as capitalism demands. Clean energy can solve our problem with emissions, but it alone cannot reverse deforestation, marine overfishing, land degradation, and mass extinction. A growth-obsessed economy, even one powered by clean energy, would again lead us to ecological catastrophe.[1275] Therefore, the primary measure to stabilise the climate should not only be to turn to green technologies but also to reduce energy consumption, that is, the production and transportation of materials.[1276] Put in another way, to save the climate, production needs to happen less and closer to consumers.[1277]

Relatedly, degrowth is a model that emphasises that further growth, especially in industrialised countries, is unsustainable. Even if this growth is 'green' or 'inclusive' or part of a progressive programme of massive investment in renewable energy production and sustainable transition, industrialised countries cannot reduce their environmental impact quickly and effectively enough as long as they continue to grow.[1278] The transformation needed in industrialised countries requires the economies of the Global North to shrink if they are to allow the countries of the Global South to develop by rapidly reducing their emissions and environmental damage.[1279]

One of the familiar narratives of those who resist changing our current production and consumption approach and growth-oriented economic system is that technological progress can reverse climate change. However, we do not yet have such technology, and it is doubtful that there ever will be. Technology companies continue to spend vast sums of money on research and development and the production of new technologies, not to reverse climate change but to increase their profits by creating new markets. One of the best examples is the air purifiers that have become popular recently. Companies that have been polluting the air and violating people's right to clean air with their production for years are now trying to sell us air purifiers

---

1275 Hickel, *Less is More*, p. 22.
1276 Tanuro, *L'Impossible le Capitalism vert*, p. 185.
1277 Tanuro, *L'Impossible le Capitalism vert*, p. 87.
1278 Saito, *Slow Down*, p. 39.
1279 Schmelzer – Vetter – Vansintjan, *The Future is Degrowth*, p. 3.

so that we are not affected. Those who can afford these high-priced devices believe they are protecting themselves – at least in their homes – from industrial air pollution. For those who cannot afford it, the idea is that 'if I work harder and earn more money, I can buy it too; if I cannot breathe clean air, it is because of my failure'. Therefore, the tendency to solve the climate crisis based on technological progress, such as biofuels, genetically modified crops, or nuclear energy, cannot create a solution because it ignores the injustice it creates and ignores the fundamental problems of capitalism as a system that supports inequality.[1280] As is well known, the solution to a problem cannot be found in the source that created it. Therefore, finding a solution to climate change without harming the growth-based capitalist economic order is nothing but a waste of precious time.

If we lived in an economic order that was not organised around growth, our technological inventions might function according to our expectations of them. In a post-growth economy, productivity advances could reduce our impact on the planet. Once we are freed from the growth imperative, we are free to focus on different inventions. These inventions would be designed to improve the well-being of people and the ecology rather than to accelerate the rate of extraction and production.[1281] So what we need to do is to abandon the current logic of growth as a whole, whose historical background is much shorter than we think and which is essentially the fruit of a Western enterprise in some specific circumstances, and replace it with an alternative society united around new values.[1282] This new society's economic health should be measured by ecological sustainability, human well-being, and prosperity, not by a number invented for profit maximisation.

GDP calculation is limited to goods and services with a market value. Nothing other than visible and measurable factors according to the criteria of economic rationality can be included in this calculation.[1283] GDP is, therefore, insufficient as a comprehensive indicator of human and ecological well-being. Using GDP as the sole measure of economic growth and social

---

[1280] 'Climate Change New Opportunity to Renew Old Orders', *Down to Earth*, 15 April 2008.

[1281] Hickel, *Less is More*, p. 155.

[1282] Latouche, *Vers une Société d'Abondance frugale*, pp. 16–17 (foreword by Tahir Karakaş).

[1283] Baudrillard, *La Sociéte de Consommation*, p. 38.

'progress' leads to disruptions in public order.[1284] For example, seemingly negative things such as wars, deforestation, hospitals overflowing with patients, or the construction of coal-powered power plants increase GDP. Since GDP is not concerned with the human body and psyche damage caused by overwork and pollution, these can be sacrificed in the name of the economy.[1285] This perspective creates a systemic blindness to the actual cost of economic growth.[1286] Moreover, this measurement method does not include domestic labour, scientific research, or most cultural activities. Instead, some things are included in this calculation only because they are measurable,[1287] like a car accident or prescription of anti-depressant drugs. Thus, in the logic of growth measured by GDP, everything produced is sacralised simply because it could be produced and sold. Accordingly, anything produced and measurable is positive. Production thus becomes a collective obsession.[1288]

The important thing should not be to increase accumulated production but what we produce. In a properly functioning economic system, the main thing to consider is whether people have access to what they need to live a decent life and how income is distributed.[1289] What is necessary for a person's well-being is not purchasing power but living power,[1290] in other words, whether they are living a quality and happy life. For that, we need to get rid of the tyranny of GDP. Only then will it be possible to imagine a different kind of economy and think more rationally about how to respond to the climate emergency.[1291] Degrowth, proposed as a product of such thinking, means moving from quantity (growth) to quality (prosperity). It is a broad transformation plan that aims to reduce the economic gap between social classes, expand social security, and increase leisure time, all while respecting

---

[1284] Hulme, *Why We Disagree ...*, p. 134.

[1285] Chomsky – Pollin, *Climate Crisis ...*, pp. 144–5.

[1286] David Bollier – Burns Weston, 'The Rise of Ecological Stewardship Responsibility with the Commons and the Perception of Human Rights', *in* Lisa Mastny (ed.), *State of the World 2014*, trans. Gülru Hotinli, İş Bankası Yayınları, Istanbul, 2014, p. 125, cited in: Üskül Engin, *Ekolojik Kriz, Etik ve Hukuk*, p. 41.

[1287] Baudrillard, *La Sociéte de Consommation*, p. 38.

[1288] Baudrillard, *La Sociéte de Consommation*, pp. 38–9.

[1289] Hickel, *Less is More*, p. 29.

[1290] Parrique, *Ralentir ou Périr*, p. 214.

[1291] Hickel, *Less is More*, pp. 202–3.

planetary boundaries.[1292] In this regard, it is a term increasingly used by academics and activists critical of the hegemony of the concept of growth in our minds, suggesting a reorganisation of society in ways that significantly reduce the use of energy and resources. In addition, degrowth proponents are also working to ensure that societies see this economic system transformation as necessary, possible, and desirable.[1293]

Degrowth is not about a decline in GDP but in the volume of jobs.[1294] Therefore, it does not mean the collapse of the economy. On the contrary, it means that the downsizing and slowdown in the volume of work required to prevent climate change is planned, socially just, and democratic.[1295] Nor does degrowth mean economic stagnation. Instead, it has the opposite meaning. Economic stagnation is undesirable, whereas degrowth is planned and desirable. Recessions make inequalities worse, whereas degrowth seeks to reduce them. Recessions often involve reductions in public spending, whereas degrowth is about decommodifying essential goods and services. During recessions, governments rush to increase environmentally damaging actions to restart growth. However, degrowth is part of a plan for a rapid transition to renewable energy, restoring soil fertility, and reversing ecological collapse.[1296]

Degrowth, in the words of the UN IPBES, emphasises strategies to reduce material flows in society by protecting human well-being through the equitable distribution of material wealth and by limiting energy and resource consumption in order to achieve inter- and intra-generational equity and a decent standard of living for all in the most industrialised countries.[1297] Thus, it is not simply against consumption but against today's culture in which consumption dominates social and political life. Degrowth criticises policies promoting GDP growth, which does not distinguish between the useful and the harmful or between the essential and the superfluous. Instead, degrowth distinguishes between certain economic activities and modes of production and consumption and proposes policies that reduce some and increase others, depending on how well they meet social needs, justice,

---

[1292] Saito, *Slow Down*, p. 84.
[1293] Schmelzer – Vetter – Vansintjan, *The Future is Degrowth*, p. 3.
[1294] Hickel, 'What Does Degrowth Mean?', p. 1106.
[1295] Parrique, *Ralentir ou Périr*, p. 14.
[1296] Hickel, 'What Does Degrowth Mean?', p. 1108.
[1297] IPBES/9/L.13, p. 26.

care, and sustainability.[1298] In short, degrowth is the democratically planned reduction of production and consumption in order to alleviate our pressure on the ecological system in a spirit of social justice and with the goal of personal well-being.[1299]

Degrowth is a proposal for an economic model that prioritises human health, well-being, and nature. A good life could be lived without growth, and society could be more just, democratic, and truly prosperous. When pondered, most actions that are important for our well-being have a minimal ecological footprint and cannot be bought with money: spending time with friends, hiking in nature, reading, making art, or participating in political debates. Less production would reduce working time, so we could spend more time on all these activities that make us happy but do not count towards GDP.[1300] In order to realise this again, the basic political and economic structure of society needs to be reorganised in a way that aims to overcome the various structural growth dependencies inherent in the capitalist economy.[1301] In this context, degrowth is envisioned as an economic order in which useful goods and services are produced, people make rational and informed decisions about what to buy, are fairly compensated for their labour, people's real needs are met while waste is minimised, money is returned to those who need it, inventions make products better and last longer, ecological pressure is reduced, working hours are reduced, human well-being is increased, and ultimately, the ecosystem's health on which we all depend is cared for rather than ignored.[1302] In this model, economic activities that are inherently unsustainable, have little use value or lead to unnecessary consumption would be downsized or eliminated in a planned manner. Examples of these activities include advertisements, planned obsolescence, unnecessary jobs, private planes, and the fossil fuel and defence industries.[1303]

According to this model, the weekly working week and the pace of work should be reduced without reducing wages, and equalising employment measures should be introduced to produce less. It also calls for redistribution

[1298] Schmelzer – Vetter – Vansintjan, *The Future is Degrowth*, p. 24.
[1299] Parrique, *Ralentir ou Périr*, p. 15.
[1300] Parrique, *Ralentir ou Périr*, p. 216.
[1301] Schmelzer – Vetter – Vansintjan, *The Future is Degrowth*, p. 4.
[1302] Hickel, *Less is More*, p. 241.
[1303] Schmelzer – Vetter – Vansintjan, *The Future is Degrowth*, p. 9.

of wealth through reform of the tax system, expansion of the public sector, and free essential services. A fight against social inequalities must accompany that. Otherwise, there would be a danger that large parts of society would be unable to find work, lose their jobs, and be left without essential goods and services. To affirm less production and consumption also means to demand more leisure time and a better life. This demand means reawakening the collective desire for a peaceful world with a basic social consensus on what is needed, for whom, why, and how much, where conditions for welfare, public health, education, and democratic participation are improved, and where we work less and differently. A world where co-producers learn to 'dialogue' collectively with nature again would not be poorer than today's world; it would be more meaningful, less stressful, less oppressive, and simply more prosperous.[1304] Thus, in a degrowth economy, people's well-being would not be negatively affected; on the contrary, degrowth is a proposal for an economic model to improve people's lives.[1305]

In other words, degrowth means redefining happiness as 'abstemious abundance in a society based on solidarity'.[1306] In this model, excessive use of energy and resources would be reduced in a planned way to rebalance the economy towards a secure, just, and equitable world.[1307] Degrowth's goals are to reduce material and energy consumption while distributing income and resources more equitably, freeing people from unnecessary work and investing in the public goods they really need.[1308] In short, degrowth can be defined as a democratic transition to a society that relies on using less energy and materials to achieve global ecological justice, deepening democracy, and securing a good life and social justice for all.[1309] This proposal envisages an economic model that does not need growth and is oriented towards the growth of well-being[1310] organised around human happiness and ecological stability[1311] rather than the continuous accumulation of capital.

[1304] Tanuro, *L'Impossible le Capitalism vert*, pp. 98–9.
[1305] Hickel, *Less is More*, p. 206.
[1306] Latouche, *Vers une Société d'Abondance frugale*, p.25.
[1307] Hickel, *Less is More*, p. 29.
[1308] Hickel, *Less is More*, p. 204.
[1309] Schmelzer – Vetter – Vansintjan, *The Future is Degrowth*, p. 4.
[1310] Latouche, *Vers une Société d'Abondance frugale*, p. 36.
[1311] Hickel, *Less is More*, p. 204.

Although realising such an economic model is more a matter for the political and social sphere, constitutions and law can also play a leading and catalytic role in transitioning to this model. Especially when the connection between the current economic infrastructure and the legal superstructure is taken into account, it becomes clear that this is entirely possible and even necessary. That is because states' primary duty is to ensure their citizens live well and prosper. That can only be achieved through a cooperative, non-profit, and democratic management of the health, education, transportation, energy, food, and housing sectors[1312] and an economic model in harmony with nature. Consequently, constitutions could include provisions limiting weekly working hours, recognising longer leisure time (and perhaps even laziness) as a right, ensuring a minimum level of income for all, requiring production to be organised in a way that does not exceed planetary limits, and facilitating the active fight against social inequalities. Where this is not the case, the higher courts could interpret existing constitutional norms in a way that is fairer and more in harmony with nature, and that favours a better and more prosperous life for people rather than growth.

4.3.4 Transition to renewable energy

> If the emissions have to stop, then we must stop the emissions. To me, that is black or white. There are no gray areas when it comes to survival. Either we go on as a civilization, or we don't. We have to change.[1313]

There is only one sure way to stop global warming from accelerating out of control: stop emitting carbon dioxide immediately.[1314] That is a necessity based on scientific reality. The IPCC's 2014 report is clear: *Climate change can only be mitigated and global temperature be stabilised when the total amount of CO2 emitted is limited and emissions eventually approach zero.*[1315] Therefore, whatever economic model we adopt, for it to be in harmony with nature, it must be based on an energy that does not need to emit carbon emissions.

1312 Parrique, *Ralentir ou Périr*, p. 239.
1313 Thunberg, TED Talk.
1314 Scranton, *Learning to Die*, p. 35.
1315 IPCC, *Climate Change 2014 – Mitigation of Climate Change*, 2014, p. 527.

As scientists led by James Hansen have shown, carbon dioxide in the atmosphere must be reduced to 350 ppm as soon as possible. This number should be the target to change the nature of the energy policy debate and make fundamental changes. Achieving this goal requires a plan that spans decades, considering changes in the climate and the subsequent response of the oceans to warming. The plan should include a global cap on carbon dioxide emissions and a phase out of coal. The only exception should be if the carbon dioxide emitted can be captured and sequestered. Current policies, including the continued construction of coal-fired power plants that do not capture the carbon dioxide they emit, show that decision-makers do not understand how serious the situation is.[1316]

To prevent climate collapse, we must rapidly transition to renewable energy to halve emissions worldwide by 2030 and reduce them to zero by 2050. Nevertheless, we must keep in mind that this is a 'global average target'. Therefore, because of their historical responsibility for emissions, high-income countries need to move faster and reach net zero by 2030.[1317] In this context, the closure of the last coal-fired power plant in the United Kingdom on 30 September 2024, marking the first time a G7 country has completely transitioned away from coal in power generation,[1318] is important, but unfortunately, not enough. The UK has set 2050 as its net-zero target.[1319] By 2030, it aims to reduce greenhouse gas emissions by only 68 per cent compared to 1990.[1320] However, suppose it is accepted that the emission reduction targets of the Global South countries, which historically cannot be held responsible for climate change, may be more lenient. In that case, the way to reach net zero globally by 2050 is for the Global North countries, historically responsible for climate change, to make much more drastic reductions. That is a responsibility they have to bear as part of climate justice.

Respecting these deadlines given by climate science can only be realised by planning the inevitable investments in a new and efficient energy system based

1316 Hansen et al., 'Target Atmospheric CO_2', p. 229.

1317 Hickel, *Less is More*, p. 21.

1318 Jillian Ambrose, 'The Deep History of British Coal – From the Romans to the Ratcliff Shutdown', *The Guardian*.

1319 House of Commons, *The UK's Plans and Progress to Reach Net Zero by 2050*, 26 September 2024, p. 7.

1320 House of Commons, *The UK's Plans …*, p. 9.

on renewable energy, regardless of its costs. The potential of renewable energy has the capacity to meet humanity's needs ten times over,[1321] and, in fact, we have already developed solutions in the form of green energy. Theoretically, it is possible to dispense with fossil fuels altogether without resorting to nuclear power[1322] and using the sun as the primary energy source.[1323] According to a 2008 study, half of the American states could get all their energy from renewable sources. As much as 81 per cent of New York's energy needs could be met by wind and solar panels alone.[1324] Moreover, wind and solar energy do not require exclusive ownership to be realised. Both forms of energy are ubiquitous in radical abundance. They are truly limitless and free. And they can be deployed relatively cheaply and used by anyone, anywhere.[1325]

However, this transition does not occur because such attributes are fatal to capitalism. Therefore, one of the biggest obstacles to this transition has been resistance from fossil fuel companies. Ed Legge of the Edison Electric Institute, one of the leading lobbyists for the power companies, summarises the general policy of these companies as follows: *We would never approve anything that would shrink our business.*[1326] In other words, it is more important for fossil fuel companies not to downsize their business than the future of the Earth. Therefore, the problem is not a lack of technology or physical impossibilities but the absence of legal obligations to prevent these companies from emitting carbon.

Such legal obligations have not been accepted because economic concerns prevent limits from being imposed on these companies. Today, the total

---

[1321] Tanuro, *L'Impossible le Capitalism vert*, pp. 18–19.

[1322] It is important to underline that nuclear energy is not only dirty, dangerous, and expensive but also subject to a completely opposite operating logic to renewable energy systems. Renewable energy production is decentralised and maximally efficient, while nuclear energy is produced according to principles of extreme centralisation and wastefulness. According to Tanuro, choosing to use solar and atomic energies together, even for a transitional period, means combining fire and water. In the end, this only complicates the necessary and inevitable energy revolution. See Tanuro, *L'Impossible le Capitalism vert*, p. 145.

[1323] Tanuro, *L'Impossible le Capitalism vert*, p. 81.

[1324] The Institute for Local Self-Sufficiency report, cited in: McKibben, *Eaarth*, p. 190.

[1325] Saito, *Slow Down*, p. 165.

[1326] Anya Kamenetz, 'Why the Microgrid Could BE the Answer to Our Energy Crisis', *Fast Company*, 1 July 2009, cited in: McKibben, *Eaarth*, p. 191.

carbon in reserves worldwide is estimated to be worth roughly $27 trillion. That is more than ten times the annual GDP of the United Kingdom. If we are serious about keeping warming below 2°C, 80 per cent of these reserves should not be turned into profit. With such incredible figures in mind, it is no mystery why fossil fuel companies fight fiercely to block any legislation that would limit emissions and why some of them give vast amounts of financial support to the climate change denial movement.[1327]

Today, it is more evident than ever that a revolutionary approach is necessary to reduce climate destabilising emissions and take meaningful steps towards a fossil fuel-free economy. Modern capitalism is a product of fossil fuels and the myth of unlimited 'cheap energy'. The resolute resistance against the expansion of fossil fuel infrastructure would not be enough to oppose this system strongly. We also need to rethink the underlying assumptions and beliefs of our society.[1328] That means rebuilding the world's energy, transportation, infrastructure, industry, and agriculture systems.[1329] All this can only be possible through the enabling role of law because today's commercial legislation does not allow for important measures to be taken to deal with climate change. Under the current conditions, it does not seem possible to have a sustainable economy and keep the rules of international trade as they are at the same time.[1330] Therefore, international trade rules, in particular, need to be rewritten in the context of climate change.

The fight against the fossil fuel industry, which today seems so daunting, is actually not such an 'impossible' struggle. That is because giant fossil fuel companies, like all capitalist companies, operate within a 'grow or die' system. Accordingly, they have to constantly reassure investors that their products will be in high demand not only today but also in the future. Therefore, legal regulations that draw a clear line between fossil fuel companies and the state would quickly rein in this industry. As soon as governments stop issuing new licenses for exploration and drilling on the grounds that we need

---

[1327] John Fullerton, 'The Big Choice', *Capital Institute*, 19 July 2011, cited in: Klein, *That Changes Everything*, pp. 212–13.

[1328] Tokar, *Toward Climate Justice*, False Solutions in the US Congress (Loc. 1380–90).

[1329] Wallace-Wells, *The Uninhabitable Earth*, p. 196.

[1330] Quoted from a personal interview with Steven Shyrbman, Klein, *That Changes Everything*, pp. 106–7.

to move to 100 per cent renewable energy due to climate change, investors will immediately abandon fossil fuel companies.[1331]

In summary, it is clear that the only way to reduce the negative impacts of fossil fuels on climate, the environment, and public health is to limit their use.[1332] Under normal circumstances, that should be done by governments and/or through legislation. However, if that is not done for obvious reasons, the high courts in climate lawsuits that have already been filed could decide not to encourage, expand, or even stop these companies' fossil fuel production. Moreover, in principle, this would not violate the freedom of enterprise or property rights. Companies could continue their activities. However, in the face of these decisions prioritising the right to life against climate change, they must inevitably redirect their investments to renewable energy production in order to continue to exist. That would create a win-win situation.

4.4 Climate justice

There are many situations where climate change and inequality interact. Therefore, it is necessary to start examining the question of climate justice with the following question: Who is responsible for climate change? More specifically, who releases greenhouse gases into the atmosphere that cause climate change?[1333]

Climate change is not only a threat to our societies in general but also to our sense of social justice. It is profoundly unfair that those who suffer the most from climate change are those who cause it the least. This simple understanding lies at the heart of climate justice[1334] because human-induced climate change is mainly about the rich people creating risks, costs, and harms for ordinary people.[1335] In a legal order guided by basic human rights principles and dominated by morality, justice should be owed to the victims of this crisis caused by the actions of others.[1336] The concept of justice is, therefore, central to the struggle against climate change. Rather than understanding

---

[1331] Klein, *On Fire*, pp. 72–3.
[1332] Tokar, *Toward Climate Justice*, Which Energy Choices (Loc. 1141).
[1333] Chomsky – Pollin, *Climate Crisis …*, p. 117.
[1334] Tokar, *Toward Climate Justice*, Foreword (Loc. 28).
[1335] Jaria-Manzano – Borrás, 'Introduction to … ', p. 10.
[1336] Klein, *On Fire*, p. 65.

climate change primarily within a scientific or economic framework, climate justice discourse raises profound questions about the injustice caused by climate change.[1337]

Today, even the slightest concern for justice and equity leads us to conclude that a complete social and economic transformation is irrevocably necessary to avoid the worst consequences of an increasingly unstable and warming climate.[1338] A sound global warming policy must also be a policy of economic and social justice.[1339] We must find a set of complementary, complete solutions. We must create solutions that tackle structural inequalities while drastically reducing emissions and tangibly improving most people's lives.[1340]

Therefore, any constitutional framework to respond to climate change must start with environmental justice. This justice should consist of a fair distribution of the burdens and profits of the global social metabolism (distributive justice) and respect for the pluralism of modes of social reproduction (recognitional justice).[1341] The core message underlying the demand for climate justice is that those who contribute the least to greenhouse gas emissions are most affected by climate change. This reality has been recognised by many different but complementary popular movements around the world. Of course, the loudest voices belong to Indigenous and other land-dependent peoples in the Global South, as these communities are already seeing the effects of climate disruption threatening their lands and their entire way of life.[1342]

The costs of climate change impacts cannot be measured in monetary terms alone. They also have profound equity and justice implications for vulnerable groups of people and nonhuman species. Climate justice in the Anthropocene requires promoting a just transition to a sustainable future. This transition must protect the most vulnerable people and countries from the impacts of human-induced climate change. Constitutionalism has a

---

[1337] Dehm, *Reconsidering REDD+*, p. 30.

[1338] Tokar, *Toward Climate Justice*, Global Warming and the Struggle for Justice (Loc. 315).

[1339] J. Andrew Hoerner – Nia Robinson, *A Climate of Change: African Americans, Global Warming, and A Just Policy in the U.S.*, Environmental Justice and Climate Change Initiative, Oakland, California, 2008, p. 1.

[1340] Klein, *On Fire*, p. 158.

[1341] Jaria-Manzano – Borrás, 'Introduction to … ', p. 3.

[1342] Tokar, *Toward Climate Justice*, Preface to the Revised Edition (Loc. 166).

lot to do with this.[1343] Within the logic of green constitutionalism, both at the national and international level, vulnerable groups' fundamental rights and freedoms must take precedence over efforts to maintain the current economic order. The groups most affected by climate change they did not cause should be the first to access public resources through constitutional norms and principles. That should enable them to own and control their green energy projects and benefit from all the employment opportunities, benefits, and skills that will remain in society. In this context, climate justice means transferring the public resources owed to these communities in compensation for damages.[1344]

Climate justice also requires workers in high-carbon producing sectors, many of whom have lost their health in coal mines and oil refineries, to be fully engaged and democratic stakeholders in this justice-driven transformation. The guiding principle should be that no worker should be forgotten and left behind.[1345]

Measures to ensure climate justice should be adopted at the constitutional level and implemented in a way binding on governments. Free public transport services as part of the right to transportation and low-cost renewable energy systems as part of the right to energy access should be subsidised. Low-income countries should have access to renewable energy sources as part of a global climate justice approach. People who are forced to migrate because they lose their habitats due to drought and the worsening effects of climate change or because mining companies owned by rich countries pollute the land they live on should be protected under constitutional rules.[1346] Constitutions should make special provisions for climate migrants and, in particular, prevent countries of the Global North from refusing to accept them. For this, international and national judicial bodies should recognise the refusal of climate migrants as a human rights violation.

The struggle for climate justice around the world is not only a struggle against the greatest ecological crisis of all time; it is also a struggle for land, water, and food sovereignty, for Indigenous rights, human rights, and the

---

[1343] Jaria-Manzano – Borrás, 'Introduction to … ', p. 16.
[1344] Klein, *On Fire*, p. 237.
[1345] Klein, *On Fire*, p. 237.
[1346] Klein, *On Fire*, pp. 238–9.

well-being of all people, for a new economy, a new energy system, a new democracy, a new relationship with the planet and each other.[1347] In this struggle, those who must first be defended and constitutionally protected are those who are not the cause of climate change but who will be most affected by it. These include children and future generations, countries of the Global South, and Indigenous peoples. Of course, even stronger measures are needed for those who are and will be intersectionally affected by climate change.

4.4.1 Intergenerational climate justice

Climate change is unlike any other challenge we have ever faced as humanity, both because of its scale and because it is not only about the present but also the future.[1348] Scientists say that unless we make transformational changes in all areas of life over the next ten years, the Earth's biodiversity will take millions of years to recover, meaning that future generations will live in a biodiversity-poor world.[1349] That is why today's children and those to be born in the future, whether rich or poor, are demanding climate justice within their own countries as well as between states.[1350]

Current increasingly erratic weather patterns are not a product of the present. Global warming is the result of actions and inactions of the recent past.[1351] The lifestyles and decisions of today and the last two generations are also irreversibly changing the life prospects of future generations for centuries to come.[1352] In the lifetimes of children and young people, this change will be manifested in the desertification of more forests, flooding of cities, loss of animal species and biodiversity, and increased destruction, violence, and conflict between people. Children who are aware of this are suffering from

---

[1347] Miya Yoshitani, 'Confessions of a Climate Denier in Tunisia', *Asian Pacific Environment Network*, 8 May 2013, cited in: Klein, *That Changes Everything*, p. 222.

[1348] Gidden, *The Politics of Climate Change*, p. 12.

[1349] Eric Dinestein et al., 'A Global Deal for Nature: Guiding Principles, Milestones and Targets', *Science Advances*, Vol. 5, No. 4, April 2019, cited in: Boyd, *Report of… (A/75/161)*, p. 10, § 30.

[1350] Elizabeth Gibbons, 'Climate Change, Children's Rights, and the Pursuit of Intergenerational Climate Justice', *Health and Human Rights Journal*, Vol. 16, No. 1, June 2014, p. 20.

[1351] Andreas Malm's *The Progress of This Storm*, cited in: Wallace-Wells, *The Uninhabitable Earth*, p. 222.

[1352] Gibbons, 'Climate Change … ', p. 20.

a psychological problem called 'climate anxiety'. This intense anxiety stems from children's fear, anguish, and feelings of powerlessness about their own and their loved ones' well-being.[1353]

In addition to the psychological impact on them, according to the World Health Organisation, children and young people will be affected by 80 per cent of illnesses, injuries, and deaths caused by climate change.[1354] Similarly, it is estimated that this will have negative psycho-social impacts on parents' physical, emotional, and social well-being, family functioning, and economic situation, as young children, in particular, will become more dependent on their parents due to extreme weather events related to climate change.[1355]

The consequences of climate change affect poor children disproportionately. As will be analysed in the next section, the most significant impacts of climate change occur in low- and middle-income countries. Eighty-five per cent of the world's children live in these countries. These children, along with the disadvantaged in developed countries, face more risk factors but benefit from fewer protections. Given that children are already at higher risk of the impacts of climate change than adults, children growing up in conditions where the most substantial impacts of climate change are experienced face double jeopardy arising from intersectionality.[1356] In other words, children in impoverished countries face not only psychological but also physical challenges. Problems such as displacement due to climate change, loss of home, lack of access to clean and healthy food and water, migration, and social upheaval are consequences that are added to factors such as heat waves, droughts, and floods due to extreme weather events.

Globally, climate emergency, biodiversity decline, and pollution violate children's most fundamental rights. That is why the UN Committee on the Rights of the Child, in a General Comment published in August 2023, stated that states have a responsibility not only to immediately fulfil their environmental responsibilities under the Convention on the Rights of the

---

1353 Natasa Mavronicola, 'The future is a foreign country: Understanding state (in)action on climate change as ill-treatment', *Strasbourg Observer*, 19 October 2021.

1354 Cited in: Ann V. Sanson – Susie E. L. Burke, 'Climate Change and Children: An Issue of Intergenerational Justice', *in* Nikola Balvin – Daniel J. Christie (ed.), *Children and Peace – From Research to Action*, Springer Open, 2020, p. 345.

1355 Sanson – Burke, 'Climate Change and Children', p. 345.

1356 Sanson – Burke, 'Climate Change and Childern', p. 346.

Child but also to take measures against foreseeable threats to the environment arising from their actions and inactions.[1357] Noting that children's right to life is endangered by environmental degradation, including climate change, and that children face serious violations of their rights due to migration, hunger, and increased violence, which prevent them from realising their full potential,[1358] the Committee stated that climate change is 'structural violence directed against children'[1359] and that states must protect children not only from harm to the environment caused by their actions but also from harm caused by corporations through the regulation of their activities.[1360]

According to the UN Convention on the Rights of the Child, member states have an obligation to make decisions in the child's best interests.[1361] However, they have so far failed to fulfil this obligation on climate change, both through their actions in continuing to emit greenhouse gases and their inaction in taking the necessary measures. Member states of the UN Framework Convention on Climate Change also violate their responsibility to 'protect the climate system for the benefit of present and future generations'.[1362,1363] Unfortunately, these violations have not resulted in any concrete sanctions on states. Therefore, governments' obligations towards children in the context of climate change must be recognised as binding at the national level. That can only be achieved by revising the constitutional provisions on children's rights in line with the current crisis and reflecting this in the decisions of the high courts.

Incorporating the concept of intergenerational justice into constitutions can play an important role against political short-termism, which is seen as the leading sustainability challenge in democratic societies. The need to satisfy voters every five years or similar cycles means that politicians shape their

---

1357 UN Committee on the Rights of the Child, *General Comment No. 26 on Children's Rights and the Environment, with a special focus on climate change*, CRC/C/GC/26, 2023, p. 2, § 11.

1358 UN Committee on the Rights of the Child, *General Comment* ..., p. 4, § 20–23.

1359 UN Committee on the Rights of the Child, *General Comment* ..., p. 6, § 35.

1360 UN Committee on the Rights of the Child, *General Comment* ..., p. 12, § 68, 78–81.

1361 Convention on the Rights of the Child, Article 3.

1362 UN Framework Convention on Climate Change, Article 3.1.

1363 Gibbons, 'Climate Change ... ', p. 27.

actions according to voters' short-term needs and desires.[1364] Consequently, the environmental rights of future generations who cannot vote in today's elections are mostly ignored. Only if constitutional amendments prevent this or supreme courts expand the right to life to the next generations will it be possible to anticipate the long-term consequences of government policies and plan them in a way that respects the rights of future generations.

Today, about twenty countries have already taken steps in this direction. Their constitutions include the concept of 'future generations'. For example, Article 20(a) of the German Constitution states that the state is responsible for future generations. Article 225 of the Brazilian Constitution stipulates that the government and society have an obligation to defend and protect the environment for present and future generations. The Constitution of Armenia also states in Article 48(10) that the state's duty in the economic, social, and cultural spheres is to pursue a policy of environmental security for present and future generations.[1365] The 2011 Constitution of Hungary mentions future generations in different provisions and states that 'protecting the interests of future generations' is among the duties of the members of the Fundamental Rights Commission.[1366] Moreover, in Germany, the relevant article was the basis for a critical decision on both intergenerational justice and the responsibilities of states to prevent climate change. The *Neubauer* decision[1367] of the Federal Constitutional Court of Germany is revolutionary for the climate struggle.

The idea of protecting future generations requires transforming the classical harm-victim relationship in current law.[1368] Children who have to grow up with all kinds of positive and negative conditions of the environment they are born into are already affected by inequalities due to the conditions they experience as children today. However, these inequalities also

---

[1364] Jörg C. Tremmel – Martin Viehöver, 'The Dilemma of Short-Term Politics', Vol. 3, No. 12, p. 12, cited in: Collins, *The Ecological Constitution*, p. 53.

[1365] For full translations of these articles and related provisions in other constitutions, see May – Daly, *Global Environmental Constitutionalism*, pp. 280–2.

[1366] Constitution of Hungary, Art. 30(3).

[1367] See 6.3.9

[1368] Kaboğlu – Yancı Özalp, *Çevre Hakkı*, p. 89.

determine their future adulthood, that is, their future.[1369] Unless we develop a rights-based approach to protecting the biosphere, future generations will have to live in an ecologically impoverished world. That means they will be deprived of nature's important contributions to human well-being, struggle with increasingly frequent pandemics, and be torn apart by deepening environmental injustice.[1370] For this reason, actions that today have no direct impact on anyone in the short term and are therefore not prohibited should be criminalised and prevented in line with green constitutionalism due to their cumulative future consequences.

Climate change is also negatively affecting the education of today's and future generations of children. When schools are destroyed or closed due to a flood or other weather event, children are not only deprived of education for months and sometimes years, but they also lose the routine of going to class that is good for their psyches. Reports show that school attendance, especially among girls, dropped dramatically after floods and droughts in India, Indonesia, Pakistan, Uganda, Nicaragua, Mongolia, Indonesia, Pakistan, Uganda, Nicaragua, and Mongolia, with the impact lasting up to ten years.[1371] Climate change robs children of their right to education and the lifelong opportunities it can provide. In addition, climate change affects children and young people's right to education even when schools are not closed. New generations are forced to put aside their individual and institutional education and socialisation opportunities, such as playing, having fun, and meeting new friends, to create political movements to save their future and try to convey their voices to decision-makers through various actions[1372] interrupting their education.

Education and information provide children with the opportunity to participate effectively and sustainably in decision-making, build their capacity for

---

[1369] Gizem Kıygı, 'Çocuklarla Kentsel Ekoloji: Bir Çınarın Gölgesinde Adaleti Aramak', *in* Didem Bayındır – Mine Yıldırım (ed.), *Ekoloji: Bir Arada Yaşamın Geleceği*, Tellekt, Istanbul, 2022, pp. 472–3.

[1370] Boyd, *Report of… (A/75/161)*, p. 26, § 94.

[1371] J. Lawler, *Children's Vulnerability to Climate Change and Disaster Impacts in East Asia and Pacific*, UNICEF – East Asia and Pacific Regional Office, 2011, p. 12, cited in: Gibbons, 'Climate Change … ', p. 22.

[1372] The most well-known of these are the school strikes around the world, initiated by Swedish climate activist Greta Thunberg, followed by other students not going to school on Friday. For more information, see Fridays for Future, <https://fridaysforfuture.org>.

creativity, and adapt to the drastic changes envisioned. When children and youth receive a strong education that builds their environmental awareness and resilience from an early age, they become 'potential disaster management experts of the future and teachers of domestic disaster management today'.[1373] Therefore, violating young people's right to education for climate change-related reasons not only deprives them of the chance to participate in decision-making processes in the future but also reduces our chance of living in more resilient societies to climate change.

When their right to information is recognised, children can meaningfully participate in risk mitigation, community climate adaptation, and climate change policymaking at local and national levels. Children are better positioned to recognise the risks specific to their age group and circumstances and develop proposals to address them in child-friendly ways. As climate change is irreversibly transforming more and more of their world, it is their right and obligation to support the participation of children and young people in decision-making processes to develop creative solutions. Given the necessary support to claim their right to participate in decisions affecting them, children in both wealthy and impoverished countries can mainstream the climate crisis into national policy processes and ensure that intergenerational climate justice becomes a priority in global climate negotiations, both domestically and beyond.[1374]

An immediate and extremely dangerous dimension of climate change for children is the sudden loss of family support in the aftermath of natural disasters. Millions of children displaced by sudden disasters are at increased risk of being separated from their families, orphaned, and deprived of the protection of an adult. That dramatically increases their risk of exploitation, sexual abuse, and trafficking.[1375] Therefore, special protective measures for children who lose their families and become vulnerable due to natural disasters need to be enshrined in constitutions and laws. The capacity, authority, and budget of state institutions that take care of children in need of protection should be expanded accordingly.

[1373] UNICEF – Innocenti Research Center, *Climate Change and Children: A Human Security Challenge*, UNICEF, 2008, p. 25, cited in: Gibbons, 'Climate Change … ', p. 24.

[1374] Gibbons, 'Climate Change … ', p. 25.

[1375] Gibbons, 'Climate Change … ', p. 22.

The concept of responsibility towards future generations has already found its way into some high court decisions. For example, in one of the most detailed environmental decisions in history, the Supreme Court of the Philippines[1376] ordered relevant government agencies to clean up and restore Manila Bay. The Court, which created a body called the Manila Bay Advisory Board to facilitate the cleanup process and appointed the judge who authored the decision as its chairperson, stated in its ruling that government agencies *cannot shirk their responsibility to future generations of Filipinos to keep the waters of Manila Bay as clean and clear as humanly possible*. Anything less, the Court said, would be a betrayal of their trust.

In a 2014 decision, the Supreme Court of Canada recognised the right of future generations of Indigenous peoples to enjoy their lands.[1377] Although there is no reference to future generations in the Canadian Constitution, the Court included the concept of intergenerational justice in the case decision regarding the constitutionally recognised land rights of Indigenous peoples.[1378] The case took place in the Canadian province of British Columbia. Unlike the rest of the country, this is a place where land agreements with Indigenous peoples after the European occupation remained tenuous. The Tsilhqot people are among the hundreds of Indigenous peoples in the province where land disputes still exist.[1379] In a dispute over logging on land that the Tsilhqot have historically claimed as theirs, the Supreme Court held that

> the government must act in a way that respects the fact that Aboriginal title is a group interest that inheres in present and future generations. The beneficial interest in the land held by the Aboriginal group vests communally in the title-holding group. This means that incursions on Aboriginal title cannot be justified if they would substantially deprive future generations of the benefit of the land'.[1380]

[1376] *Metropolitan Manila Bay Development Authority v. Concerned Residents of Manila Bay*, GR Nos. 171947–48, 18 December 2008.

[1377] *Tsilhqot'in Nation v. British Columbia*, SCC 44, 26 June 2014.

[1378] Constitution of Canada, art. 35, § 3.

[1379] *Tsilhqot'in Milleti v. British Columbia*, § 4.

[1380] *Tsilhqot'in Milleti v. British Columbia*, § 86.

In addition, the Supreme Court ruled that these territories cannot be used in a way that would 'destroy the ability of (Indigenous) peoples to sustain future generations'.[1381]

The case *Juliana v. United States*[1382] also offered the promise of a comprehensive conceptualisation of the law regarding the right of future generations to have the atmosphere recognised as a public commons.[1383] In the case brought by the non-governmental organisation Our Children's Trust on behalf of two teenagers living in the state of Oregon, it was argued that the atmosphere should be protected by the government as a 'common asset' under the Public Trust Doctrine in order to protect the public interest of present and future generations. This doctrine, developed by US judges, indicates that the government should protect certain natural and cultural resources in the public interest. However, at the end of the proceedings, the Oregon Supreme Court rejected the plaintiffs' claim, stating that the Public Trust Doctrine is primarily concerned with waters and cannot be extended to the atmosphere.[1384]

By contrast, there was a promising decision for intergenerational climate justice in the US state of Montana. Unlike the *Juliana* case, young people in Montana took to court the climate policy of their home state of Montana, not the US federal government.[1385] A district court judge ruled in favour of sixteen young people who argued that a provision in Montana's Environmental Policy Act prohibiting consideration of the climate impact of energy projects violated their constitutional right to a clean and healthy environment. The court's decision is considered the first major climate victory in the US.[1386] The decision is not yet final. There will be an appeals process, and the Montana Supreme Court's decision will be what matters, but it does show that there is some progress on climate justice in the US.

[1381] *Tsilhqot'in Milleti v. British Columbia*, § 121.

[1382] Oregon Federal Court, *Juliana v. United States*, 6:15-cv-01517.

[1383] Tom Jr Zeller, 'Why Teenagers Are Suing States over Climate Change', *Forbes*, 8 April 2015.

[1384] For detailed information, see Terry Lodge, 'Building Our Children's Trust Needs to Start with Reality', *CELDF*, 11 May 2022.

[1385] Montana District Court, *Held v. Montana*, CDV-2020-307.

[1386] Ahmet Soysal, 'ABD'de Gençler Küresel İklim Değişikliğine Karşı Hukuk Mücadelesini Kazandı', *Yeşil Gazete*, 26 August 2023.

4.4.2 Climate justice for the Global South

Just because global warming is caused by human activity does not mean we are all equally to blame. That is because the increase in the Earth's average temperature is the result of cumulative emissions since the invention of the steam engine.[1387] Until now, the industrialised countries of the Global North have emitted disproportionately more greenhouse gases and continue to do so. It is certainly not easy to determine the historical responsibility of these countries for the greenhouse gases they emit. Nevertheless, reliable estimates of carbon dioxide emissions from the energy and cement sectors can be made. Information on these dirtiest sectors as far back as the distant past can be obtained by utilising the archives of companies and governments. The carbon dioxide released can be calculated thanks to these sources, which show the amount of fuel used. In this context, experts say that historically, developed countries have been responsible for 70 per cent to 80 per cent of climate change.[1388]

Regarding carbon dioxide in the atmosphere, it is better to look at the historical contribution rather than annual emissions. Once in the atmosphere, carbon dioxide stays there for 300–1,000 years. That means that when humans change the atmosphere by emitting carbon dioxide, this change affects other people for generations.[1389] Suppose we trace the burning of fossil fuels back to the beginning of the Industrial Age. In that case, it becomes clear that the highly industrialised countries of the Global North, and in particular the United States and Western Europe, are responsible for much of the problem.[1390] These countries are responsible for around 70 per cent of all cumulative emissions on Earth up to 1980. The discrepancy in contributions to emissions is even more extreme when looking at per capita emissions. For example, by 1980, average annual emissions in the United States were 21 tons per capita, fourteen times that of China, which had emissions of 1.5 tons per capita that year, and forty-two times that of India, which had

[1387] Malm, *How to Blow ...*, p. 104.
[1388] Tanuro, *L'Impossible le Capitalism vert*, p. 75.
[1389] Alan Buis, 'The Atmosphere: Getting a Handle on Carbon Dioxide', *NASA*, 9 October 2019.
[1390] Hickel, *Less is More*, p. 111.

emissions of 0.5 tons per capita.[1391] This gap has relatively closed today, but the Global North countries, which account for around 20 per cent of the world's population, still use two-thirds of all energy produced – the vast majority of which comes from fossil fuels.[1392]

As a contemporary example, the total amount of carbon dioxide emitted by the East African country of Somalia since 1950 is equal to what the Unites States emits in an average of three days.[1393] It is incredibly unfair to equate and compare the greenhouse gases emitted by European or North American countries with those emitted by developing countries because this would mean equating the carbon emitted by the SUV that a family in Los Angeles buys for their 18-year-old child with the methane emitted by subsistence farmers in Thailand as they work in paddy fields or herd cattle. One comes from luxury and wasteful consumption, the other from the struggle for survival.[1394] Moreover, the Global North countries owe their current wealth, technological products, and global hegemony largely to centuries of exploitation of the Global South[1395] and their excessive use of fossil fuels. Ironically, however, it is the impoverished and underdeveloped peoples of the South who are suffering the most devastating effects of the increasingly severe climate crisis.[1396]

The 'underdevelopment' of the countries now being referred to as the Global South, especially in discussions on climate change, is not the result of insufficient contact with capitalism but the result of the uneven incorporation of various regions of the world into global capitalism throughout history. In other words, lowering the living standards of those living in the Global South is a prerequisite for capitalism to function. Therefore, the power imbalance between North and South is not an anomaly but rather a consequence of

---

1391 Hannah Ritchie – Max Roser, 'CO_2 and Greenhouse Gas Emissions', *ourworldindata.org*, cited in: Chomsky – Pollin, *Climate Crisis …*, p. 117.

1392 Marks, *The Origins of …*, p. 217.

1393 Justin Rowlatt, 'Climate Change is Turbo-Charging Somalia's Problems – But There's Still Hope', *BBC*, 18 September 2024.

1394 Anil Agarwal – Sunita Narain, 'Global Warming in an Unequal World: A Case of Environmental Colonialism', *in* Navroz K. Dubash (ed.), *India in a Warming World*, Oxford University Press, 2019, p. 82.

1395 Bennett, *Change Everything*, p. 221.

1396 Tokar, *Toward Climate Justice*, Foreword (Loc. 23).

the proper functioning of the system.[1397] South's 'underdevelopment' results from a violent process of deindustrialisation and redesign of local economies in favour of imperial metropolises.[1398] Similarly, the ecological devastation in the countries of the South often reflects the extent of colonialism understood only after independence was achieved.[1399]

As mentioned earlier, Watt's invention of the steam engine tremendously accelerated the Industrial Revolution, and the steamships developed from it later opened up sub-Saharan Africa and India to colonial plunder. Before the eighteenth century, for example, textiles in England were produced by individual entrepreneurs. In the early eighteenth century, the invention of steam engines made mass production possible, although Bengal already had a robust textile industry. In 1750, India was indeed producing 25 per cent of the world's textiles. In order to put an end to this dominance, the import of finished textile products to England was banned first through law.[1400] Then, the East India Company, mentioned in the first part of the book as the first company in the world, started to operate in these lands and began to transfer unprocessed cotton to England. Thus, while Britain's share in world textile production increased, India's began to decline. By 1800, it had fallen to 20 per cent, then to 10 per cent in 1860. Twenty years later, it was only 3 per cent. It is, therefore, safe to say that Britain's industrial rise was based mainly on the forced deindustrialisation of India.[1401] So, while enriching Europe, Watt inadvertently contributed to the impoverishment of other parts of the world and the perpetuation of coal-burning inequalities to this day. From this perspective, coal was the black ink on which the story of modern capitalism was written.[1402]

Another negative consequence of the Industrial Revolution was the deterioration of the land quality in Europe. That was due to the fact that the nutrients produced on rural land were transported to the city and consumed

---

[1397] Saito, *Slow Down*, p. 3.

[1398] Tzouvala, *Capitalism as Civilization*, p. 4.

[1399] Radkau, *Nature and Power*, p. 259.

[1400] The Calico Laws in 1700 and 1721.

[1401] Alexander Anievas – Kerem Nişancıoğlu, *How the West Came to Rule: The Geopolitical Origins of Capitalism*, Pluto Press, London, p. 262, cited in: Tzouvala, *Capitalism as Civilization*, p. 4.

[1402] Klein, *That Changes Everything*, p. 248.

there. Thus, the soil in rural areas steadily lost important minerals, and the nutrient cycle was massively disrupted. This 'rift' in the metabolic cycle of the soil has led to its depletion and is still happening.[1403] The solutions tried to correct the crisis of land impoverishment in Europe only served to shift it to other countries. One of these solutions was the import of bird manure, a highly profitable venture. Bird droppings scraped from the steep cliffs off the coast of Peru by Chinese workers in semi-slavery conditions were transported by ship to Europe and sold as agricultural fertiliser. Of course, the European bourgeoisie, mostly British investors, made the biggest profit from this trade.[1404]

This bird manure initiative revealed that the appearance of independence from land and animal power was an illusion. Coal-based industrialisation in Europe, North America, and Japan was based on hidden resource exploitation based on solar energy in the periphery. In other words, it was the vast quantities of 'cheap nature' forcibly imported from the masses of disenfranchised and dependent labour in colonised lands that kept the factories in Manchester ticking over.[1405] Industrialisation thrived on cheap cotton to feed the looms, cheap sugar, tobacco, coffee, and tea to mobilise the workers, and cheap bird droppings to feed the soil that provided the food for the workers. Thus, what outwardly appeared to be a saving of labour and land was, in fact,

---

[1403] Saito, *Slow Down*, p. 21. Marx was the first to use the term 'rift' to refer to this situation that contradicts the interdependence between social and natural metabolisms. See Saito, *Slow Down*, pp. 100–1.

[1404] John Bellamy Foster – Brett Clark – Richard York, *The Ecological Constitution Rift: Capitalism's War on the Earth*, Monthly Review Press, New York, 2011, cited in: Fraser, 'Climates of Capital', pp. 71–2. When the reserves accumulated over hundreds of years were exhausted in a few decades, a new attempt was made, and chemical fertilisers were invented and put into use. This resulted in soil acidification, groundwater contamination, dead zones in the oceans, and an increase in nitrous oxide gas in the atmosphere, all of which are extremely harmful to humans and other animals. See Fraser, 'Climates of Capital', p. 72.

[1405] Fraser states that he borrowed this expression from Jason Moore, 'The Rise of Cheap Nature', *Anthropocene or Capitalocene? Nature, History and the Crisis of Capitalism*, PM Press, Oakland, 2016, pp. 78–115.

a kind of 'peripheral load shifting'; in other words, the demand for biomass was shifted from the centre to the periphery.[1406]

The colonial powers reinforced this process through deliberate moves to eradicate productive activity in their colonies. By deliberately destroying textile production in Egypt and India, Britain turned these countries into 'captive markets' that supplied cotton to its factories and to which it could sell its products.[1407] This inequality between countries, created through colonialism, increased as growth-based capitalism became the international economic order, causing the current gap between state economies. This gap cannot be closed if the current economic order is maintained. Indeed, economists looking at environmental input and output data have shown that growth in high-income countries is largely based on the appropriation of materials, energy, land, and labour from countries in the Global South. This unequal exchange is made possible by the ability of rich countries to use their financial and geopolitical power to suppress the price of labour and resources in the Global South, while at the same time channelling production there into the global commodity chain. This process reduces the productive capacity of countries in the Global South to meet the needs of local populations and more directly pursue development goals.[1408]

Additionally, the fossil fuels that the countries of the Global North have been using as a source of energy since the period of colonialism and rapid industrialisation affect the most exploited countries today. These situations constitute the most important areas of the struggle for climate justice. Within the scope of international green constitutionalism, the historical responsibilities of the Global North countries should be recognised, and within this framework, the Global South countries should be provided with substantial

---

[1406] Alf Hornborg, 'Footprints in the Cotton Fields: The Industrial Revolution as Time-Space Appropriation and Environmental Load Displacement', *Ecological Economics*, 59(1), 2006, pp. 74–81, cited in: Fraser, 'Climates of Capital', pp. 72–3. The similarity of this situation with the 'carbon markets' that are currently being proposed as a solution to climate change is astonishing.

[1407] Aaron Jakes, *Egypt's Occupation: Colonial Economism and the Crises of Capitalism*, Stanford University Press, Stanford, 2020, cited in: Fraser, 'Climates of Capital', p. 73.

[1408] Kallis – Hickel – O'Neill – Jackson – Victor – Raworth – Schor – Steinberger – Ürge-Vorsatz, 'Post-growth', p. e73.

compensation, solidarity in the adaptation process, and free technology transfer.

Indeed, China is now the largest emitter of carbon dioxide, having experienced a historically unprecedented economic growth rate since the early 1980s. In 2022, China emitted 12.1 giga tons of carbon dioxide in energy production, compared to 4.7 giga tons in the US.[1409] However, in terms of per capita emissions, China emitted 10.3 tons of carbon dioxide per capita in the same year, compared to 18.6 tons in the US, almost twice as much. In India, which, according to the latest statistics, has become the world's most populous country, annual carbon emissions per capita were only 2.8 tons in 2022.[1410] Thus, an Indian's contribution to climate change is almost one-eighth that of a US citizen. As can be seen, per capita footprints[1411] vary significantly between people in different parts of the world.

Looking at statistics such as the average footprint or carbon emissions per person worldwide, it is clear that we have exceeded the earth's carrying capacity and that our current way of life is not sustainable. World Overshoot Day in 2023 took place on 2 August; in other words, we have exhausted the biological resources that enable the earth to renew itself in just seven months.[1412] Our footprint is only 1.5 planets despite our current lifestyle because many people around the world live far below the one-planet footprint standard due to material poverty. By contrast, the footprint of North Americans is more than three planets. If everyone in the world lived as they do in the United States, the 'land of the free', we would need five planets to survive in the future.[1413] This lifestyle of people in the Global North that is based on a waster consumption through the extraction of energy and natural resources from the Global South has been called the 'Imperial Mode of Living' by German sociologists Ulrich Brand and Markus Wissen.[1414]

1409 IEA, *CO_2 Emissions in 2022*, March 2023.

1410 For continuously updated figures, see World Emissions, <www.worldemissions.io>.

1411 The personal footprint mentioned here does not refer to the average greenhouse gas emissions that each individual in those countries emits in their daily lives. This number is arrived at for each country by dividing the total emissions by government agencies and companies by the population.

1412 See <https://www.overshootday.org/>.

1413 Capra – Mattei, *The Ecology of Law*, pp. 186–7.

1414 Cited in: Saito, *Slow Down*, p. 9.

These figures reveal how destructive the capitalist understanding of freedom is for the Earth, the Global South, and all of us. The current production and consumption model in industrialised countries, based on the logic of unlimited accumulation of capital, profit and goods, waste of resources, conspicuous consumption, and increasing destruction of the environment, cannot be extended to the rest of the world without causing a massive ecological crisis. That means this system necessarily operates through the maintenance and increase of the glaring inequality between North and South.[1415] The subject of capitalism's exploitation is not only human labour but also natural resources, energy, and food, plundered from the Global South through an 'unequal exchange'.[1416] Therefore, it is imperative to replace it, which perceives freedom as unlimited production and consumption, with a different understanding of freedom that is in harmony with nature and the ecosystem in our legal and social order, both to stop climate change and to eliminate the injustice between the Global North and South.

While much of the ecological destruction is caused by overconsumption in the Global North, the consequences disproportionately hit the Global South. We see this both in the case of emissions and in the context of resource extraction. On the one hand, Northern countries are responsible for 92 per cent of global carbon dioxide emissions that exceed the safe planetary limit.[1417] However, the South bears the brunt of the damage from climate change, both in terms of monetary cost and loss of life. On the other hand, central to the functioning of high-income countries is the massive appropriation of resources from the rest of the world. In other words, resource consumption in the North leads to an ecological impact whose consequences are felt mainly in the South.[1418] One of the main reasons for this is that natural resources are

---

[1415] Löwy, *Ecosocialism*, What Is Ecosocialism (Loc. 207).

[1416] Saito, *Slow Down*, p. 12. (Emphasis is Saito's.)

[1417] Jason Hickel, 'Quantifying national responsibility for climate breakdown: An equality-based attribution approach to carbon dioxide emission in excess of planetary boundaries', *Lancet Planetary Healt*, 2020, cited in: Hickel, 'What Does Degrowth Mean?', p. 1109.

[1418] Dorninger – Alf Hornborg – David J. Abson – Henrik von Wehrden – Anke Schaffartzik – Stefan Giljum – John-Oliver Engler – Robert L. Feller – Klaus Hubacek – Hanspeter Wieland, 'Global patterns of ecologically unequal exchange: Implications for sustainability in the 21st century', *Ecological Economics*, 2020, cited in: Hickel, 'What Does Degrowth Mean?', p. 1109.

mostly located in Southern countries. Another reason is that Northern companies have shifted many activities that damage ecosystems and biodiversity from high-income to low-income countries. Thus, they benefit from lower or non-existent environmental standards there.[1419] Therefore, a more accurate picture of national responsibility for greenhouse gas emissions needs to look not only at emissions stemming from production within borders but also at consumption-based emissions.[1420]

For these two reasons, almost all deforestation in recent decades has occurred in the tropics of Africa, Asia, and Latin America, where some of the world's poorest people live. With the loss of thousands of animal and plant species, their natural ecosystems have become radically less biodiverse and, consequently, less resilient.[1421] This weakening of ecosystems will exacerbate the impacts of climate change. Indeed, it is estimated that by 2030, 92 per cent of the damage from climate change will occur in Southern countries. The total damage in these countries is estimated at $954 billion. It is also projected that by 2030, 530,000 people will die annually due to climate change-related problems, and almost all of these deaths will occur in Southern countries. Climate change deaths in wealthy countries will constitute only 1 per cent of the total.[1422]

The world's poorest people live in the tropics and subtropics. They are already struggling to survive in a world of increasingly uncertain rainfall, prolonged droughts, coastal flooding, loss of wetlands and fisheries, and dwindling freshwater. As the IPCC points out, a severe increase in flooding will likely adversely affect the inhabitants of large river deltas in Asia and Africa. One-sixth of the world's population that depends on water from glaciers will see freshwater lakes grow for a short time as glaciers melt. However, then the loss of glaciers will become a life-threatening reality.[1423]

The report, prepared by the UK-based International Alert, emphasises that those who will suffer the most from climate change are those living in poverty and under poor governments in underdeveloped and unstable countries. According to the report, the physical consequences of climate

---

1419 Boyd, *Report of… (A/75/161)*, p. 20, § 75.
1420 Hickel, *Less is More*, p. 111.
1421 Marks, *The Origins of…*, p. 228.
1422 Hickel, *Less is More*, pp. 114–15.
1423 IPCC, *Climate Change 2007 – Synthesis Report*, 2007, p. 49.

change, such as extreme weather events, melting glaciers, and shorter agricultural seasons, will add to the authoritarian environment in which these populations already live. Backgrounds of poverty and poor governance mean that many of these people have a low capacity to adapt to climate change and face a higher risk of violence.[1424]

The Global South people face not just this physical violence but what Rob Nixon calls 'slow violence'. According to Nixon, unlike instantaneous, sudden, and spectacular violence, the destruction caused by environmental violence is cumulative. Moreover, it is either recognised late because it is spread over time and space over a very long period or not even recognised as violence.[1425] This kind of indifference to the deaths that have occurred and will occur due to climate change cannot be functionally displayed without an entrenched racist attitude, even if it seems invisible to the eye. That would be impossible if there were not such a phenomenon called Orientalism and all the effective tools (including legal ones) at the disposal of the powerful that allow the lives of the less powerful to be disregarded.[1426]

To summarise, low-income countries and most countries in the Global South operate within planetary boundaries. In many cases, they even need to increase their use of energy and resources to meet the essential needs of their citizens. The region to focus on in terms of climate change is the wealthy Global North. In these countries, the consumption of energy and goods has become completely divorced from any notion of necessity and far exceeds what is needed for human well-being. Accordingly, the global ecological collapse is almost entirely due to excessive growth in high-income countries and, in particular, excessive accumulation by the richest. However, the consequences of this collapse are disproportionately impacting the Global South and people with low incomes. In addition, these people are less able to invest in climates, sea walls, and other adaptation methods. Climate models show that the regions that will be hit hardest by global warming – including drought-prone parts of sub-Saharan Africa and typhoon-prone South

---

1424 Smith – Vivekananda, *A Climate of Conflict…*, p. 3.

1425 Rob Nixon, *Slow Violence and the Environmentalism of the Poor*, Harvard University Press, Cambridge, 2011, pp. 2–3, cited in: Gündoğan İbrişim, 'Ekolojinin Yazısı: Edebiyat', p. 437.

1426 Klein, *On Fire*, pp. 187–8.

and South East Asia – are where some of the world's poorest people live.[1427] Therefore, for the sake of global justice, serious consideration should be given to the need for specific provisions in the constitutions of the Global North countries to address this unequal and inequitable situation and for their high courts to rule on national responsibilities in the context of climate justice. International judicial bodies should also take into account the historical responsibilities of Global North countries for climate change and place the burden of implementing adaptation policies largely on industrialised countries.

The fight against climatic upheaval is everyone's business. However, a sense of justice and goodwill demands that everyone's responsibilities, capacity for action, and technological and financial means be considered. It is inescapable that climate justice is necessary, albeit of a different nature than physical limitations. The global consensus needed to save the climate can only be built on this basis. The UN's first agreement on climate change[1428] has already adopted the principle of 'common but differentiated responsibilities' for wealthy and impoverished countries.[1429] Accordingly, the struggle against climate change should be fought first and foremost in the Global North countries. Sharp carbon emission reductions, zero emissions by 2030, large grants to the Global South countries for a green transformation, technology and investment transfer in renewable energy, opening the doors to climate migrants, and many other obligations fall within their responsibilities. Nevertheless, they are unwilling to do these things, often for economic reasons. So, we need national and international legal principles and instruments to compel the industrialised states to implement them. Due to the softness of international law, the most effective instruments are constitutions and supreme courts in the Global North.

Demands for climate justice in the Global South bring together an impressive diversity of Indigenous and land-dependent peoples' movements. These include rainforest dwellers opposing giant dams and oil palm plantations, African communities resisting land grabs for industrial agriculture and

---

1427 James K. Boyce, *Economics for People and the Planet*, Anthem Press, 2019, p. 7, cited in: Chomsky – Pollin, *Climate Crisis …*, pp. 118–19.

1428 The Rio Agreement of 1992.

1429 Tanuro, *L'Impossible le Capitalism vert*, p. 76.

agro-fuel production, Pacific islanders facing the loss of their homes to rising sea levels, and peasant farmers fighting for food security and fundamental land rights.[1430] The impact of these movements is already being seen at international gatherings.

At the 27th Conference of the Parties (COP27) in Egypt in 2022, more than 200 countries agreed to establish a 'loss and damage fund' to be financed by developed countries historically responsible for climate change. It was agreed that the money collected here would be used to compensate developing states for losses and damages due to climate change, to transition from a carbon economy to one based on sustainable energy, and to help them adapt to the increasingly negative consequences of climate change.[1431] However, the details of how the money in this fund, which was announced as one of the most important achievements of the conference, will be paid by rich countries and how it will be distributed to impoverished countries have not been clarified. Moreover, just before the 28th Conference of the Parties (COP28) in Dubai in 2023, US Climate Envoy John Kerry, in response to a question, stated that 'under no circumstances' would they pay compensation to countries that had suffered climate change-related disasters.[1432] Nevertheless, in line with the principle of 'common but differentiated responsibilities' enshrined in the Rio Agreement, the Convention on Biological Diversity requires rich countries to contribute substantially to the costs of maintaining, protecting, and restoring healthy ecosystems and biodiversity in low-income countries.[1433] However, since international environmental conventions do not have binding judicial mechanisms and there is no constitutionalism yet in place to force the acceptance of the concept of climate justice by the Global North, the United States and other wealthy ones can ignore their responsibilities towards other countries.

Climate justice, a core element of green constitutionalism, requires that we protect the way of life in the Global South, which has not developed due to its colonial past, by returning their natural resources to their rightful owners,

---

[1430] Tokar, *Toward Climate Justice*, Origins of Climate Justice (Loc. 900–910).

[1431] Esme Stallard, 'What is Loss and Damage and Will Rich Nations Pay for Climate Change?', *BBC*, 20 November 2022.

[1432] Oliver Slow, 'US Refuses Climate Reparations for Developing Nations', *BBC*, 14 July 2023.

[1433] Convention on Biological Diversity, Articles 8(m) and 9(e).

enabling their communities to defend themselves against extreme weather conditions and to escape poverty through clean technology.[1434] Forcing impoverished countries to pay the costs of protecting their nature when the problem lies in the high production, consumption, and emissions rates in rich countries violates basic principles of justice.[1435] The fact that billions of people in the Global South are suffering and will suffer even more because of the excessive emissions of a few rich countries for the sake of productivist policies following their growth obsession is a crime against humanity, and we must be clear to call it like it is.[1436]

4.4.3 Respect for Indigenous peoples' rights

It is a fact that, in some cases, Indigenous peoples have caused significant damage to wildlife, interfered with nature as much as they could, and changed it significantly. As a result of their actions, wildlife was overhunted, forests were cut down or burned, mountainous areas were terraced, and large cities were built. The differences surrounding these facts are less about the reality of a significant intervention than the details or scale of the intervention.[1437] However, Indigenous peoples have learned through experience that the harm they inflict on nature is ultimately the harm they inflict on themselves. Those who survived to this day are communities that have built social and economic systems in harmony with their natural environment and have recognised the importance of natural balance and biodiversity.

As a result, today, Indigenous peoples around the world have to face the challenges of climate change more than anyone else.[1438] Although Indigenous peoples are not monolithic and cannot be perceived as uniform ecological actors, they all have a unique relationship with their traditional lands.[1439]

1434 Klein, *On Fire*, pp. 65–6.

1435 Boyd, *Report of… (A/75/161)*, p. 20, § 74.

1436 Hickel, *Less is More*, p. 115.

1437 Bookchin, *The Ecology of Freedom*, p. 48.

1438 James Anaya, *Report of the Special Rapporteur on the Rights of Indigenous People – Extractive Industries and Indigenous People*, Human Rights Council, A/HRC/24/41, 1 July 2013, p. 3, § 1–2.

1439 Benjamin J. Richardson, 'The Ties That Bind: Indigenous Peoples and Environmental Governance', *in* Benjamin J. Richardson – Shin Imai – Kent MecNeil (ed.), *Indigenous Peoples and the Law: Comparative and Critical Perspectives*, Hart Publishing, Oxford, 2009, p. 337, cited in: Collins, *The Ecological Constitution*, p. 40.

Therefore, states have special responsibilities towards Indigenous peoples, as well as local communities and peasants with similar relationships with the Earth. The most important of these is recognising their rights over their lands and acknowledging their distinct traditions and systems. These include collective property and governance models.[1440]

The UN Human Rights Committee clearly states that states cannot pursue their economic development in violation of the rights of minorities protected under Article 27 of the UN Covenant on Civil and Political Rights. According to the Committee, whether measures that substantially interfere with the culturally significant economic activities of a minority community are acceptable depends on whether community members participated in the decision-making processes by which these measures were adopted and whether they can continue to benefit from their traditional economy. The Committee has also set conditions for participation in decision-making. Participation must be effective and based on community members' free, prior, and informed consent, not just consultation. In addition, economic measures taken by the state must respect the principle of proportionality so that they do not jeopardise the survival of the community and its members.[1441]

The Inter-American Court of Human Rights also stated that states have an obligation to ensure the effective participation of Indigenous peoples and access to their traditional lands when creating new protected areas. According to the Court, in principle, the protection of natural areas and the right of Indigenous peoples and tribes to protect the natural resources on their lands are compatible. In fact, Indigenous peoples contribute significantly to nature conservation through their way of life. Thus, they should be able to hunt, fish, gather, farm, and access their traditional lands for cultural purposes in a manner consistent with sustainable use, even in protected areas. In addition, Indigenous peoples should be able to share the benefits arising from conservation initiatives equitably. Thus, in connection with the conservation of natural resources found on the territories of Indigenous peoples and tribes, states need to have appropriate mechanisms in place to ensure their

---

[1440] Boyd, *Report of… (A/75/161)*, p. 19, § 72.

[1441] John H. Knox, *Report of the Special Rapporteur on the Issue of Human Rights Obligations Relating to the Enjoyment of a Safe, Clean, Healthy and Sustainable Environment*, UN Human Rights Council, A/HRC/34/49, 19 January 2017, p. 17, § 54.

rights to a dignified life and cultural identity.[1442] Indeed, the UN Declaration on the Rights of Indigenous Peoples states that states should recognise and incorporate into their law the rights of Indigenous peoples to their territories, boundaries, and resources.[1443] The Declaration also stipulates that *Indigenous peoples have the right to the conservation and protection of the environment and the productive capacity of their lands or territories and resources*.[1444]

Compounding the injustice against Indigenous peoples and local communities, who are materially, culturally, and spiritually dependent on their traditional lands, is the fact that they are often not receiving a fair share of the economic benefits despite being heavily affected by the adverse conditions created by actions that harm the environment. On the contrary, the profits from the occupation of Indigenous peoples' lands often undermine their traditional economies. For example, following the clearing of natural forests for palm oil production, Indigenous peoples in Indonesia have seen their income from forest honey drastically reduced. Moreover, the decline in biodiversity in this region has triggered the erosion of cultural diversity, and many Indigenous languages have disappeared.[1445]

Another injustice faced by Indigenous peoples and local communities who lack a formal right to land and property is forced migration. These people are forced to leave their lands due to land confiscation, industrial mining, and agricultural activities. Constructing parks or protected areas as part of some nature conservation activities without Indigenous peoples' and local community members' free, prior, and informed consent violates their rights.[1446] Indigenous peoples' cultural rights and access to livelihoods are undermined when they are evicted from their traditional lands and homes as part of nature conservation policies. States often blame this on overgrazing and overexploitation of natural resources by them, but this approach ignores the complexity of Indigenous peoples' ecological and social relationships with

1442 Inter-American Court of Human Rights, *Kaliña and Lokono Peoples v. Suriname*, Judgment, 25 November 2015, § 181.

1443 *UN Declaration on the Rights of Indigenous People*, 13 September 2007, Art. 27.

1444 *UN Declaration on the Rights of Indigenous People*, 13 September 2007, art. 29, § 1.

1445 Boyd, *Report of… (A/75/161)*, p. 14, § 52.

1446 Boyd, *Report of… (A/75/161)*, p. 14, § 54–55.

their ecosystems.[1447] States must, therefore, recognise the right of Indigenous peoples to their lands and prevent human rights violations such as evictions, displacement, violence, torture, and killing for conservation purposes.[1448] When recognised, Indigenous peoples, local communities, and peasants significantly contribute to the conservation, protection, restoration, and sustainable use of ecosystems and biodiversity. Contrary to state claims, evidence shows they protect nature through their traditional knowledge, legal systems, and culture.[1449]

Indigenous communities have become central in the fight for environmental and climate protection in recent years, especially in Latin America. That is not only because of their local actions to protect their rivers and forests against international oil and mining companies but also because they offer an alternative way of life to globalised neoliberal capitalism.[1450] Indigenous cultures are known to have developed rules and other tools to regulate human behaviour that have successfully kept people alive as part of a larger community of living and non-living beings for a very long time. In other words, unlike what we do, they have managed not to destroy their environment. So they know some things we have forgotten and would be helpful for us to remember.[1451] So, it is clear that we have a lot to learn from the approaches of past and present Indigenous peoples to environmental protection.[1452] There is no contradiction in combining their ecological sensitivity with our analytical sensitivity, provided we transcend both sensibilities with a new way of thinking and experiencing.[1453] In particular, Indigenous legal systems should be taken as a guide for governments and courts to achieve sustainability at all levels, as they crystallise a worldview in harmony with nature within effective governance systems.[1454]

[1447] Victoria Tauli-Corpuz, *in* 'Indigenous People's Rights Are Violated in the Name of Conservation', *OHCHR*, 26 August 2016.

[1448] Boyd, *Report of… (A/75/161)*, p. 19, § 72.

[1449] See Stephen T. Garnett et al., 'A Spatial Overview of the Global Importance of Indigenous Lands for Conservation', *Nature Sustainability*, vol. 1, No. 7, July 2018.

[1450] Löwy, *Ecosocialism*, Ecosocial Struggles of Indigenous Peoples (Loc. 828).

[1451] Cullinan, *Wild Law*, p. 88.

[1452] Garnett et al., 'A Spatial Overview of…', p. 369.

[1453] Bookchin, *The Ecology of Freedom*, p. 84.

[1454] Collins, *The Ecological Constitution*, p. 40.

Central to the Indigenous peoples' concept of 'community' is the idea of having certain rights and responsibilities for a common purpose and exercising them as a community.[1455] Just as in Roman law, where *res communis omnius* is seen as the *commons*, Indigenous peoples use forests, rivers, and other natural assets in a common and sustainable way. However, as explained in the book's first part, the emergence of today's capitalist order was influenced by the transformation of *res communis omnius* into *res nullius*, meaning 'what no one owns,' and the enclosure and seizure of natural entities that everyone once used in common. Therefore, one could say there is a kind of 'negative correspondence' between Indigenous ethics and the spirit of capitalism.[1456] Although the two are similar regarding the appropriation of land and other natural assets, Indigenous peoples give the use to the whole community. However, the capitalist logic grants this authority to only one person in the form of a right to deny it to others.

As mentioned earlier, important principles and techniques that will be useful for transforming the dominant cultures of the twenty-first century into more nature-centred governance systems for today can be learned from Indigenous peoples. Much of the wisdom of these communities has already been lost or is rapidly disappearing due to the resilient and overwhelming advance of capitalist culture today. That is why preserving and learning from these societies is so important. Not to do so would be extremely arrogant, foolish, and irresponsible.[1457]

Therefore, states should respect the rights of Indigenous peoples, local communities, and peasants in all their actions to conserve, protect, restore, sustainably use, and equitably share the benefits of healthy ecosystems and biodiversity. That should include respect for traditional knowledge and practices and Indigenous peoples' right to free, prior, and informed consent.[1458] Where governments fail to do so, higher courts, mobilised through litigation, should take into account the situation of Indigenous peoples, who are more vulnerable to climate change. In addition, the relationship between them and land-dependent peasants, such as villagers, and their relationship with their

---

1455 Cullinan, *Wild Law*, p. 149.

1456 Löwy, *Ecosocialism*, Ecosocial Struggles of Indigenous Peoples (Loc. 840).

1457 Cullinan, *Wild Law*, p. 88.

1458 Boyd, *Report of… (A/75/161)*, p. 18, § 69 (g).

ecosystems and the governance systems among them should also be used to guide the courts' decisions. Particularly in climate cases, courts should use the traditional rules and principles of Indigenous communities in their relationship with nature as a substitute for today's dominant capitalist ethics.

4.4.4 Protecting groups intersectionally affected by climate change

The regions projected to be significantly adversely affected by global changes in the Earth's climate, biodiversity, and ecosystem functioning are also those with the highest concentrations of Indigenous peoples and some of the world's poorest communities. Since their existence, livelihoods, and health are highly dependent on nature and what it provides, they are also disproportionately more vulnerable to adverse changes.[1459] Therefore, looking closely at the social groups that will be intersectionally affected by climate change and their rights that will be violated is important for establishing climate justice.

Over the last few centuries, our dependence on dirty energy sources has caused the most significant harm to the most pauper and vulnerable people of colour, many of them with Indigenous roots. They are the people whose land has been usurped and whose land has been poisoned by mining activities. Their poor cities are also where the most polluting refineries and power plants are built.[1460] These social groups are more intersectionally affected by both the dirty forms of production that cause climate change and its devastating impacts. A young person living in the Global North is probably concerned about the future due to the changing climate, but a young person in the South is also threatened with unemployment and loss of life due to natural disasters. Additionally, if this young person is a woman, she is even more exposed to these threats because of gender inequality. When she can no longer withstand these threats and is forced to migrate, she faces the threat of rape, human trafficking and slavery. That is also the case for other underprivileged groups. The risks posed by climate change pose a greater threat to women, children, Indigenous and African people, LGBTIQ+ persons, persons with disabilities, refugees, and those living in rural, remote, conflict-prone, and natural disaster-prone areas.

[1459] IPBES/7/10/Add.1, p. 7.

[1460] Klein, *On Fire*, p. 237.

Therefore, it is important to take constitutional measures to address those more intersectionally affected by the threats posed by climate change. Their rights are more threatened than others, which places a responsibility on states and courts to take measures and decisions with this in mind. The focus here will be on approaching the three groups of people more intersectionally affected by the climate crisis. However, what follows can and should also be applied to other social groups, both those listed here and those not listed.

4.4.4.1 People with little to no income

While the concept of the Anthropocene helps point to humanity's impact on the Earth's ecosystem, it also masks some deep inequalities. Yes, we are all of the same species, but we are not equal when it comes to responsibility for and exposure to present and future ecological disasters.[1461] It is the rich who are mainly responsible for the overconsumption and pressure on nature that is causing climate change.[1462] In contrast, the harmful consequences of declining ecosystem functioning are disproportionately borne by poorer and marginalised people, as they depend more on ecosystems for survival. That means globally, the weakening of ecosystems contributes to increasing inequality and discrimination between groups of people and is sometimes even a key driver of poverty and social conflict.[1463]

While climate change will eventually pose an existential threat to all humanity, we are all well aware that in the short term, it discriminates and hits the poor first and worst. Sometimes, this is in the form of people abandoned to their fate on rooftops in New Orleans during Hurricane Katrina, and sometimes in the form of the 36 million people threatened with starvation due to drought in southern and eastern Africa.[1464] Since the atmosphere is already chock-full of greenhouse gases, every unnecessary emission by those living luxurious lifestyles has a bullet-like effect on poor people.[1465] In other words, environmental destruction and climate change is an act of collective violence by the rich against the poor.[1466]

[1461] Parrique, *Ralentir ou Périr*, p. 10.
[1462] Boyd, *Report of… (A/75/161)*, p. 7, § 16.
[1463] Cullinan, *Wild Law*, p. 41.
[1464] Klein, *On Fire*, p. 199.
[1465] Malm, *How to Blow …*, pp. 104–5.
[1466] Löwy, *Ecosocialism*, The Belém Declaration (Loc. 1117).

The numbers prove that global warming is a crisis caused by the wealthiest segments of society. According to a report by the Oxford Famine Relief Organisation, almost half of global carbon is emitted by the wealthiest 10 per cent of the world's population. The poorest 50 per cent are responsible for only 10 per cent of emissions.[1467] While the rich benefit from the use of fossil fuels, the poor suffer the negative impacts of both extraction and emissions. It is always people with low incomes and peasants who lose their health by working in the mines or their land when mining companies take over. The situation is no different in cities. It is people experiencing poverty who are forced to live in urban areas near power plants and refineries because of job opportunities, whose fields in their villages have been taken over, or who have been forced to migrate to the city because they can no longer grow crops efficiently due to thermal power plants. For example, an official study in the United States shows that people of different skin colours, black people, and Latinos live in dense concentrations around power plants.[1468] These are the so-called no-go areas, where respiratory illnesses and cancers occur at high rates, forced to bear the toxic burden of our collective dependence on fossil fuels.[1469]

The governments that impose the costs of economic crises on people with low incomes by cutting education, health, and social security budgets are also trying to make them pay for the climate crisis created by fossil fuel companies.[1470] People experiencing poverty in developed countries are not exempt from the structural disadvantages in the countries of the Global South. For example, Hurricane Katrina, which hit the US city of New Orleans in 2005, hit almost entirely black neighbourhoods. Three-quarters of the people living in flooded neighbourhoods were black.[1471]

As a matter of fact, the California-based Environmental Justice and Climate Change Initiative published a report in 2008, which revealed that African Americans living in the United States are the social group that will be most affected by climate change, even though they have contributed less to it than other citizens. Noting that all six states with the highest number of African

[1467] OXFAM, *Extreme Carbon Inequality* (press release).
[1468] EPA, 'Power Plants and Neighboring Communities'.
[1469] Klein, *On Fire*, pp. 188–9.
[1470] Klein, *That Changes Everything*, p. 169.
[1471] PNUD, *Rapport sur le développement humain – 2011*, pp. 67–8.

Americans are located in the Atlantic hurricane zone, the report also revealed that historically, African Americans have a higher risk of heat-related mortality than other social groups.[1472] According to another study, one reason for this is that black and Hispanic people in the United States mostly live in the inner cities where heat islands form and work in outdoor jobs such as agriculture and construction. Another reason is that they are less likely than whites to own private cars, making it more difficult for them to access cool places and hospitals during heat waves.[1473]

As can be seen, in the countries of the Global North, non-white people, in general, are more affected by climate change because they have been historically impoverished. However, this does not mean that white people experiencing poverty are not affected by the negative consequences of the climate crisis. For example, according to another study, 1.6 million people in Great Britain today live in areas at high risk of flooding. Most of these people are British working families. This number is projected to rise to 2.3 to 3.6 million by 2080.[1474] This figure refers only to those who will be affected by rising ocean levels and increased rainfall. The impact of short but heavy rains, which the report characterises as urban flooding, where sewage systems will be inadequate, should be added. The report emphasises that these floods will pose a risk to public health as rainwater mixes with sewage.[1475] The poorer segments of society, referred to as the 'disadvantaged', will be even more affected, as they are generally less able than the rest of society to insure their homes and businesses against flooding, compensate for damages, and pay for expensive repairs.[1476] That is, of course, the case for all coastal countries. Therefore, the governments of these countries need to provide additional support to people in poverty in adapting to climate change.

As mentioned earlier, the Global North countries should take more responsibility for halting climate change. Accordingly, some European governments are trying to reduce carbon emissions by various means. However,

---

[1472] Hoerner – Robinson, *A Climate of Change*, p. 2.

[1473] Rachel Morello-Frosch – Manuel Pastor – James Sadd – Seth B. Shonkoff, *The Climate Gap: Inequalities in How Climate Change Hurts Americans & How to Close the Gap*, University of Southern California, Los Angeles, 2009, pp. 7–12.

[1474] UK Government Office of Science, *Future Flooding*, Executive Summary, p. 18.

[1475] UK Government Office of Science, *Future Flooding*, p. 19.

[1476] UK Government Office of Science, *Future Flooding*, p. 20.

the problem is that these methods put additional economic pressure on low-income people. That is because, within the existing balance of power between classes, a capitalist state tends to start by intervening in emissions from the other side, that is, from the struggle for livelihoods.[1477] That has the potential to lead to some social explosions. The political crises caused by austerity in Europe can be taken as an indication of what we might experience in the future when we reduce carbon emissions without social policies.[1478] If a powerful government imposes a high carbon price to curb climate change, uprisings by small entrepreneurs such as farmers, fishermen, or truckers, whose economic activities rely heavily on oil, could paralyse or at least put the brakes on environmental policies.

As it will be remembered, the Macron government's policy of shifting the economic burden on ordinary people arising from its goal of both maintaining economic growth and reducing carbon emissions in 2018 turned into months-long demonstrations with violent street clashes. The movement started with car owners demonstrating against the additional tax on oil. It became known as the 'yellow vests'[1479] because they wore the reflective vests mandatory on vehicles during demonstrations, bringing the country to a standstill.[1480] The immediate cause of the uprising was a proposed increase in fuel taxes, allegedly designed to address environmental concerns, which would hit the impoverished and rural workers particularly hard. However, the backdrop to the protests was more generally a host of Macron 'reforms' that benefited the rich at the expense of the poor and working people. *You talk about the 'end of the world', but we are interested in the 'end of the month', how are we going to survive with your 'reforms'?* said one of the protesters.[1481] After months of demonstrations against the €30 carbon tax, it was first reduced to €17 and then cancelled by the Constitutional Council.[1482] This example clearly shows that the burden of measures against climate change should fall

---

[1477] Malm, *How to Blow …*, p. 107.
[1478] Scranton, *Learning to Die*, p. 37.
[1479] Originally called '*gilets jaunes*'.
[1480] See Angelique Chrisafis, 'Who Are the Gilets Jaunes and What Do They Want?', *The Guardian*, 7 December 2018.
[1481] Chomsky – Pollin, *Climate Crisis …*, pp. 67–8.
[1482] Tanuro, *L'Impossible le Capitalism vert*, p. 91.

on the rich who caused this crisis, not on the poor, who are already more affected by it.

The reason why even a relatively small tax increase has caused such a massive backlash in a Global North country like France is that ordinary people smashed under neoliberal policies for years lack the resources to adapt to climatic changes. Rather than putting the burden of adapting to climate change on the public, governments should provide material support to them. Obviously, that should not be done through a price reduction that would increase the use of oil but through public services such as better quality and free public transportation or free courses to fill the employment gap in the renewable energy sector. The budget to finance these services should come from higher taxes on the top 10 per cent.

The situation for people in poverty in countries of the Global South in the face of climate change is even more dire. High rents or homelessness drive them to settle, sometimes illegally, in the most dangerous parts of cities, on flood-prone land or steep hills designated as areas prone to landslides or mudflows in the event of heavy downpours. People with low incomes, who have no means of escaping during a disaster, live in fear of being unable to return and losing their only property even if they can escape.[1483] Farmers in arid regions rely on rain for irrigation and forests for protection from flooding. So, as droughts and floods increase in frequency and severity, they are the most affected. When prices skyrocket after a drought or flood, people in poverty in the South are in danger of being unable to access even basic foodstuffs. These countries also lack water drainage systems and the dykes and dams needed to prevent flooding in poor neighbourhoods.[1484] In addition, the weak health system in impoverished countries reduces access to health care for the population in general, especially for poor people and children, and increases the risk of death.[1485]

For these reasons, in order to finance social programmes that will enable a just transition, taxes should be raised for everyone except people experiencing poverty. Public attitudes towards taxation would change significantly if the money collected is redirected to social programmes and services that reduce

---

[1483] Tanuro, *L'Impossible le Capitalism vert*, pp. 40–1.
[1484] Chomsky – Pollin, *Climate Crisis …*, p. 123.
[1485] Gibbons, 'Climate Change … ', p. 21

inequality and make people's lives more secure and stable.[1486] In constitutions, various provisions could be included to prevent the current inequitable situation for poorer segments of society from worsening due to climate change-related challenges. These provisions could range from new tax regulations to imposing new obligations on the state to help them adapt to climate change. Even in the absence of these, high courts should consider that people with little or no income are intersectionally affected by climate change in cases of rights violations arising from incidents such as forest fires or floods.

In addition to other forms of additional physical and legal protection, it should be recognised as a right for people and communities to access adequate and affordable financial insurance against climate change damage. Since the cost of relevant private insurance that protects against property or crop damage is too high for many of the most vulnerable people, such insurance should take the form of public programmes in almost all cases. Premiums for public climate insurance should be applied on an economy-wide basis, perhaps linked to existing social insurance programmes such as social security or unemployment insurance.[1487] Laying the legal foundations of this public insurance system that will protect people with little or no income against climate change through constitutional arrangements would protect it from the policies of parties that come to power with short-term programmes and become a state policy.

4.4.4.2 Women

For many years, our legal and social systems have made a distinction between men and women similar to the dualism between man and nature. Accordingly, women are associated with nature, the material, the emotional, and the private, while men are associated with culture, the immaterial, the rational, and the abstract.[1488] Thus, as a reflection of the European colonialist perspective, men are thought to have a superiority over women. Thanks to their rational way of thinking, men found in themselves the right to possess women physically and intellectually. Within the scope of this right,

---

[1486] Klein, *That Changes Everything*, p. 171.

[1487] Chomsky – Pollin, *Climate Crisis …*, p. 125.

[1488] Victoria Davion, 'Is Ecofeminism Feminist?', *in* Karen J. Warren, *Ecological Feminsim*, Routledge, London, 1994, cited in: Garrard, *Ecocriticism*, p. 45.

women, like the Indigenous people in the colonies, were not recognised as humans equal to men and were considered part of nature.[1489] Accordingly, women had value and meaning only within the boundaries set by men. Of course, this view has been left behind – at least on paper – but centuries of social inequalities still negatively affect the situation of women today. That is known scientifically and socially in many areas, from the school enrolment rate of girls to the number of women in parliaments, from employment rates to wage inequalities. This history of discrimination is still a burden on women's shoulders.

The impact of climate change on gender inequality exacerbates this problem. It is one of the most pressing challenges of our time, posing a threat to the lives, health, and safety of women and girls around the world. In this sense, the climate crisis is a gendered problem because women around the world are more dependent on natural resources yet have less access to them than men.[1490]

Of the 1.3 billion people in the world living below the poverty line, 80 per cent are women. Moreover, women are subjected to deplorable living conditions because of the oppression they face. In the least developed countries, they face worsening conditions for collecting wood for heating and reduced income from agricultural labour.[1491] In many regions, women are disproportionately responsible for obtaining food, water, and fuel. In low- and lower-middle-income countries, agriculture is the sector where women work the most. During periods of drought and excessive rainfall, women work even harder to secure their families' income and livelihoods as producers of agricultural products. That puts pressure on girls to drop out of school to help their mothers, who are overwhelmed by the increased workload.[1492] Even in developed countries, women are more vulnerable to disasters caused by climate change. Unemployment, part-time work, and low wages have a greater impact on women, who are increasingly less able to protect themselves

[1489] The fact that women's right to vote was not recognised in some European countries until the middle of the twentieth century indicates this misogynistic view.

[1490] UN Women, *Explainer: How Gender Inequality and Climate Change are Interconnected*, 28 February 2022.

[1491] Tanuro, *L'Impossible le Capitalism vert*, p. 42.

[1492] UN Women, *Explainer: How Gender Inequality and Climate Change are Interconnected*, 28 February 2022.

against the effects of global warming. As an example, more women than men died in the heat wave that hit Europe in 2003.[1493]

Consequently, women are at the forefront of the fight against climate change, biodiversity loss, and the destruction of nature. From India to Uganda, from Ecuador to Türkiye, women worldwide are defending trees, standing up to coal mines, and fighting for their future.[1494] States must join this struggle and integrate gender equality into all their actions to conserve, protect, restore, use, and fairly share the benefits of nature.[1495] Measures to be taken against climate change should take into account gender equality provisions in constitutions and be based on the principle of substantive equality. That should be done in a participatory manner and in cooperation with women's organisations.

4.4.4.3 Refugees

The reason why refugees, whose numbers continue to grow to the point where they constitute an important part of humanity today, are such an uncomfortable element for the nation-state order is, first and foremost, that they put the original fiction of modern sovereignty into crisis by breaking the continuity between human and citizen, between *birth* and *nationality*.[1496] For this reason, refugees who do not fit into the logic of the nation-state as a superstructural institution of capitalism are always seen as a problem. Nevertheless, these people are dying at the borders of states and sea, suffering at the hands of human traffickers, imprisoned, and kept in squalor in removal centres. Everyone must acknowledge that no one would willingly put up with this. No one leaves their home unless they have to.

Two parameters stand out in international migration due to climate change. Firstly, the income level of the countries of migration. Those who leave their homelands tend to migrate to countries in the Global North, where the economy is strong and job opportunities are more abundant, hoping for a better life. The second parameter is how much the destination country will be affected by climate change. Most Global North countries are

---

[1493] PNUD, *Rapport sur le développement humain – 2011*, p. 68.

[1494] See Elif Şafak, 'In the Battle to Save the World's Forests, Women are Leading the Resistance', *The Guardian*, 26 August 2023.

[1495] Boyd, *Report of… (A/75/161)*, p. 18, § 69 (f).

[1496] Agamben, *Homo Sacer*, p. 172. (Emphasis is Agamben's.)

both geographically less likely to be affected by global warming and have more opportunities for adaptation, making them a centre of attraction.[1497]

However, refugees are not actually fleeing *somewhere*; they are fleeing *from* somewhere. They would probably prefer to live in their homeland.[1498] The first thing to do, then, is to make this possible. It is the rich countries that are responsible for the climatic conditions that force people to flee their homes. Therefore, they must not only end their destructive mining and fossil fuel activities in the countries of the South but also compensate them for the damage they have already caused to nature. Where this is impossible, they should increase employment and prosperity through the investments necessary for a sustainable economic order.

Another measure should be to establish humane asylum procedures. They should open their doors to migration caused by the sharing of natural resources or the consequences of climate change, such as drought. It would be incompatible with their historical and moral responsibility to block refugees on the grounds of 'undermining the economy' or 'disrupting demographics'. They have achieved the prosperity they enjoy today by plundering nature in the refugees' countries, enslaving people, forcing them to work, exploiting their labour, and impoverishing them in a planned way.

The impacts of emissions, caused mainly by wealthy nations, hurt the world's poorest first and worst, forcing more and more people to flee their countries. Moreover, instead of taking steps towards climate justice, the countries of the North are, on the contrary, closing their doors even more tightly to migrants and falling further and further into a nationalist right-wing populism. Especially after 2010, there has been a rapid and dramatic change in the political landscape and a resurgence of far-right views. It has gained strength worldwide by inciting hatred against ethnic, religious, and racial minorities. It has often expressed xenophobia and hatred against the growing number of people who have been forced to flee their homes. This political trend appears to be in a deadly dialogue with climate change.[1499] The number of climate refugees grows every day, and the countries of the

[1497] For a detailed study on this issue, see Albano Rikani – Katja Frieler – Jacob Schewe, 'Climate Change and International Migration: Exploring the Macroeconomic Channel', *PLoS One*, 17(11), 16 November 2022.

[1498] Chomsky – Pollin, *Climate Crisis* ..., p. 161. (Emphasis is Chomsky – Pollin's.)

[1499] Klein, *On Fire*, p. 34.

North seek only to suppress the symptoms they have caused rather than take responsibility and treat the disease.

Climate change is causing not only international migration but also internal migration. According to a study commissioned by the World Bank, by 2050, more than 216 million people worldwide will leave their home regions and migrate within their own countries due to climate stress. In the sub-Saharan region alone, this number will reach 85.7 million. In Eastern Europe and Central Asia, 5.1 million people are projected to move to safer places in their country.[1500] However, according to the same report, these numbers would drop by 60 to 80 per cent if there is a sharp reduction in carbon emissions and inclusive and resilient development in these countries.[1501]

The idea of justice requires us to recognise at a legal and constitutional level that people who have lost their habitat due to drought and rising sea levels have the right to seek a place of safety. That should be recognised as a legal responsibility at both the national and international levels, especially in the Global North countries. States that have so far failed to act on climate change, despite all scientific warnings, owe it to people to offer them the right to asylum and social status in the new cities and countries they arrive in. In fact, amid all their losses and suffering, we as a society owe them much more than that: They have already earned compassion, mercy, and a sincere apology.[1502]

4.5 The principle of *buen vivir*

For most of the history of capitalism, characterised by European enclosure, genocides of Indigenous peoples, the Atlantic slave trade, the expansion of European colonialism, and famine, growth has not increased the well-being of ordinary people; on the contrary, it has reduced it. It is important to remember that the spread of capitalism depends on the artificial deprivation and scarcity created.[1503] Capitalists have fenced off the commons – the

---

1500 Viviane Clement – Kanta Kumari Rigaud – Alex de Sherbinin – Bryan Jones – Susana Adamo – Jacob Schewe – Nian Sadiq – Elham Shahabat, *Groundswell: Acting on Internal Climate Migration – Part II – Overview*, World Bank Group, 2021, p. 4.

1501 Clement et al., *Groundswell*, p. 9.

1502 Klein, *On Fire*, p. 66.

1503 Saito, *Slow Down*, p. 148.

land, forests, pastures, and other resources on which people depend for their livelihoods – and destroyed subsistence economies, forcing them to 'fall' into labour markets. The threat of hunger was used as a weapon to strengthen competitive efficiency. Even as GDP grew, artificial deprivation often caused ordinary people's living conditions and well-being to collapse[1504] because economic growth was conceived as a driver of political, social, and cultural progress, measured in numbers of production, exchange, and consumption. However, it would be a mistake to think that proponents of growth and capitalism are uncomfortable with this. In this respect, climate change presents unique opportunities for them. Due to global warming, water, agricultural land, and housing are becoming scarce. This increase in scarcity means an increase in demand. Thus, rising prices enable capitalists to make high profits.[1505]

Today, the drive for growth leads to stress and depression due to overwork and lack of sleep, and disease, diabetes, and heart disease due to pollution.[1506] In general, criteria such as hygiene or life expectancy have indeed improved compared to previous centuries. At the same time, however, the gap between the rich and the poor has widened, and many people, including the middle class, are no longer living in prosperity. Working under extreme and stressful working conditions, burdened by credit card debts, afraid of getting sick due to inadequate public health care, cut off from nature, and with very limited recreational opportunities, the majority of society lives a life that is definitely not good. That, of course, affects people's mental health, and they look for solutions either in the form of anti-depressants with sedative effects or in new spiritual and metaphysical movements.

To date, productivity gains in the workplace have not improved the well-being of workers because they have been appropriated by capital. Rather than reducing working hours and raising wages, companies have pocketed the extra profits and asked workers to work as much as before. In other words, productivity gains were used to fuel perpetual growth, not to liberate people. In this way, capitalism betrayed the very Enlightenment thought it claimed to defend. By creating endless needs, capitalism has made human emancipation

---

[1504] Hickel, *Less is More*, p. 171.
[1505] Saito, *Slow Down*, p. 160.
[1506] Hickel, *Less is More*, p. 177.

forever impossible.[1507] However, 'development', which means creating social conditions that allow human personality and resources to flourish in all their possibilities and dimensions, is not only liberation from underdevelopment but also from the degradation caused by bad events.[1508] Therefore, it must also include the deterioration of people's living and working conditions.

Even in these circumstances, those who advocate the continuation of the present order are fear-mongering, claiming that what is proposed in a green constitutional order is a harsh and uncomfortable future of constant deprivation and state controls. It is true that if we move to an alternative green order, there will be some 'negative' changes in the way of life of a small group of the most affluent. They will have to cut back on some consumption habits, including air travel, meat consumption, and wasteful energy use. However, this will also create abundance and prosperity, new pleasures, and new public spaces for many people.[1509] In a postcapitalist economic and legal order, the main goal will be the 'good life' of humans, animals, and the ecosystem as a whole.

The principle of the *buen vivir*, inherited from the cultures of Latin American Indigenous peoples and enshrined in the constitutions of Ecuador and Bolivia, is centred on justice for present and future generations, for both human and nonhuman beings. These two constitutions have thus developed a unique approach to sustainability guided by the Indigenous idea of the good life.[1510] According to this principle, what matters is not living a long

---

[1507] Hickel, *Less is More*, p. 224.

[1508] Kaboğlu – Yancı Özalp, *Çevre Hakkı*, p. 40.

[1509] Klein, *On Fire*, p. 312.

[1510] According to Carla Sbert, it is a loose translation of the Quechua *sumak kawsay* and Aymara *suma qamaña*. She argues that the true meaning of these terms and other related concepts of the Indigenous peoples of the Andes is closer to the idea of 'living well together/coexistence' and reflects the relationship between humans and nature as well as between humans. See Carla Sbert, *The Lens of Ecological Law: A Look at Mining*, Edward Elgar, Cheltenham, 2020, pp. 170–1, cited in: Collins, *The Ecological Constitution*, p. 23. Boyd also argues that 'good living' would be a rough translation of the term and he thinks that the more accurate translation would be 'harmonious coexistence', referring to relations between people, nature, and society. See Boyd, *The Rights of Nature*, p. 171.

life but living a life worth living every day and every moment.[1511] Individuals have rights and obligations towards others, and recognising diversity as part of self-realisation and working for the unity of political society in order to coexist with this diversity and build a common future are all components of the principle of the good life.[1512] The principle of *buen vivir* means opposing the extraction of natural resources for commodification in markets. Instead, social and ecological well-being is the primary goal of this principle.[1513]

Buen vivir is an expression that envisions the coexistence of different human communities, nonhumans and humans, and living and non-living beings. In line with the thoughts of Aldo Leopold, who characterises human actions as *right when they preserve the integrity, balance, and beauty of the biotic community, and wrong otherwise, buen vivir* is a way of living that preserves the integrity, balance, and beauty of the biotic community.[1514] Therefore, the path to social transformation to achieve a high quality and good life for all in harmony with nature is through biodiversity conservation, large-scale restoration of degraded ecosystems, rapid transition to clean energy and a circular economy, reduced material consumption by wealthy individuals, and restructuring of supply chains to reduce their environmental impact.[1515]

In this context, there are many lessons to be learned from the actions led by Indigenous peoples in Bolivia and Ecuador, whose calls for ecological transformation centre on the concept of *buen vivir*, as opposed to the strategies based on consumption and planned obsolescence that have captured our lives.[1516] The principle of *buen vivir* is based on meeting real social needs and respecting nature. It, therefore, starkly contrasts capitalism's cults of growth,

---

1511 On the contrary, for the concept of 'a life not worth living', see Agamben, *Homo Sacer*, pp. 180–7.

1512 René Ramírez Gallegos, 'Uchronia for Living Well', *in* Henry Veltmeyer – Edgar Záyago Lau (ed.), *Buen Vivir and the Challenges to Capitalism in Latin America*, Routledge, London and New York, 2021, p. 176.

1513 Natasha Cahassagne, *Buen Vivir as an Alternative to Sustainable Development: Lessons from Ecuador*, Taylor & Francis, 2020, p. 31 and 33, cited in: Durmaz, *Doğanın Hakları*, pp. 307–8.

1514 Ufuk Özdağ, *Edebiyat ve Toprak Etiği: Amerikan Yazınında Leopold'cu Düşünce*, Ürün Yayınları, Ankara, 2017, p. 36, cited in: Arık, 'Bir Arada … ', p. 451.

1515 Boyd, *Report of … (A/75/161)*, p. 21, § 82.

1516 Klein, *On Fire*, p. 312.

expansion, and 'development', accompanied by a consumer obsession with 'always more'.[1517]

The concepts of 'Mother Nature's rights' and *buen vivir* are spreading rapidly in Indigenous and ecological movements as well as all global justice movements. That is to be expected, given that true justice is only possible if it takes everyone into account. The principle of *buen vivir* must be incorporated into constitutions not only in Latin America but worldwide, and related laws must be approved by parliaments to accelerate the transformation towards a social and economic structure harmonious with nature.

[1517] Löwy, *Ecosocialism*, Ecosocial Struggles of Indigenous Peoples (Loc. 954).

Green constitutionalism in courts

If we do not do the impossible, we shall be faced with the unthinkable![1518]

As described in previous chapters, the environmental crises in the Anthropocene are closely linked to the legal rules, policies, and institutions that enable a tiny fraction of humanity to plunder nature, with economic and ecological consequences for the planet's most marginalised communities.[1519] In other words, it is about the very existence and interests of these few but powerful people. For this very reason, expecting the ruling class to act against its own interests to stop the climate crisis and prevent ecological destruction is wishful thinking that deserves the adjective 'dangerous'.[1520] It is necessary to accept that today's corporations and the bourgeois state, which is their protector and supporter, will not act to tackle climate change, even though they know that they are leading us all to extinction. At this point, as Benlisoy quotes, Marx's statement that Louis XV's famous 'After me, the deluge'[1521] is 'the motto of every capitalist and every capitalist state' becomes more meaningful. This motto shows that the insensitivity shown in the face of climate catastrophe is a requirement of the laws of capital accumulation, regardless of individual capitalists' good or bad intentions. Marx goes on to say: 'In the absence of coercion from society, capital is indifferent to the

1518 Bookchin, *The Ecology of Freedom*, p. 114.
1519 Gonzalez, 'Foreword: Deconstructing … ', p. ix.
1520 Benlisoy, 'İklim Krizi … ', p. 169.
1521 The original sentence is '*après moi, le déluge*'.

health of the worker and the length or shortness of his life'.[1522] Marx wrote these lines about Victorian England's prevailing working conditions and long working hours. Similarly, today, the ruling classes do not seem to care much about the imminent death of the planet and its billions of inhabitants, including humans, due to climate change. Their short-term economic interests trump long-term rational behaviour. Unless there is an external pressure, a compulsion against the capitalist class, capital will continue to turn the world upside down for fossil fuels.[1523] It is desirable that this external pressure comes from mass society and that the economic system is changed from the grassroots. However, there seems to be no time left for this mass organisation at the current level of global warming. Therefore, limiting the economic and political elites through the judiciary imposes itself as a solution. Ideally, given the current circumstances, of course, these two forces, the people and the judiciary, should exert pressure simultaneously from the bottom and the top to break the resistance to inaction.

Scientists warned us in the 1970s and 80 s while we were still having the chance to find fairly simple solutions to climate change. For example, in 1988, the Conference on the Changing Atmosphere in Toronto recommended that emissions be 20 per cent below the 1988 level by 2005. One of the scientists attending the conference said:

> If we choose to face this challenge, we can significantly slow the rate of change, giving us time to develop mechanisms to minimise the cost to society and damage to ecosystems. If, on the other hand, we close our eyes and hope for the best, we will have no choice but to pay the high cost when the bill is presented.[1524]

We did not listen to this warning that day; today, it is time to pay that cost.

If politicians had listened to what scientists were saying back then and implemented policies that would have started to reduce carbon emissions fifty years ago, the measures we would have taken might not have had to be so contrary to the capitalist economic model. We could have proceeded calmly and slowly: We could have gradually eliminated our carbon footprint,

---

[1522] Karl Marx, *Capital, Critique of Political Economy*, vol. 1, trans. Mehmet Selik and Nail Satlıgan, Yordam, Istanbul, 2010, pp. 263–4, cited in Benlisoy, 'İklim Krizi … ', p. 170.

[1523] Benlisoy, 'İklim Krizi … ', p. 170.

[1524] Spencer Weart, *The Discovery of Global Warming*, Harvard University Press, Cambridge, 2008, p. 149, cited in: Klein, *That Changes Everything*, pp. 80–1.

managing to reduce it by a few percentage points a year. We could have taken a very measured, gradual, and moderate path and stopped climate change without resorting to methods that are seen as radical today.

However, not only has this not been done, but since then, the world population has almost tripled, our demands have multiplied, and the capitalist economy has grown. Having lost so much precious time, we are today closer than ever to running out of resources and drowning in our own waste, and we need to act fast.[1525] That is why the measures that must be taken today are no longer radical but imperative. The problem worsens every day as we continue to increase carbon emissions. We must slam on the brakes and make significant cuts to get back to safe levels.[1526] It may not be a pleasant example, but we need to stop the world – as it functions today – as we did when the COVID-19 pandemic was at its most frightening. Because for the first time in this period, when transportation was limited and people cut back on consumption beyond essential needs, we were very close to the carbon emission reductions we needed to stop climate change.

Five years before COVID-19, the Paris Agreement was signed, and almost everyone pledged to reduce emissions. However, global emissions continued to rise in the following period until that terrible pandemic. We stayed indoors, and in 2020, global carbon emissions fell by 2.6 gigatons. That was a 7 per cent reduction from 2009 levels. We had inadvertently set ourselves on the path to avert a climate change catastrophe, and we should have taken measures to continue this decline similarly after COVID-19.[1527] However, with the end of the pandemic, we returned to the old 'normal', as if we had no climate change problem at all. This normalcy we have returned to is not normal; it is causing climate change and is more dangerous than COVID-19 because there is no solution like the invention of a simple vaccine. Nevertheless, we can tackle this problem not with tedious measures that lock us in our homes

1525 Rob Hengeveld, *Wasted World: How Our Consumption Challenges the Planet* (Turkish version), trans. Nafiz Güder, Türkiye İş Bankası, Istanbul, 2019, p. 106.

1526 Klein, *On Fire*, pp. 212–13.

1527 Corinne Le Quéré – Glen P. Peters – Pierre Friedlingstein – Robbie M. Andrew – Josep G. Canadell – Steven J. Davis – Robert B. Jackson – Matthew W. Jones, 'Fossil CO_2 Emissions in the Post-COVID-19 Era', *Nature Climate Change*, Vol. 11, March 2021, p. 197.

but by adopting a happier and more abundant lifestyle in a new economic and legal system harmonious with nature.

While people in the Global South and Indigenous and land-dependent societies around the world grapple daily with life-and-death issues arising from rampant resource extraction and exploitation, people in developed countries are reluctant to recognise that a global crisis is already underway. Unfortunately, many activists who acknowledge this crisis limit their struggle to grapple with the details of energy and climate policy. These detailed, scientific, and political debates are important, but due to them, we have so far been unable to find the time to launch a full-scale struggle against the climate-based problems we face.[1528] What we need is to redesign the entire economic system and the legal order around the principle of sustainability in a nature-centred way. This new green constitutional order needs to be firmly rooted in science and the laws of nature, starting with a clear recognition of the Earth's biological and physical limits.[1529] In other words, the current legal system needs to be replaced by an 'Earth system law'. This law should provide a framework to manage the questioning of environmental law's obstacles to *thinking with the world system*. It should thus ultimately provide a roadmap for environmental law to become more sensitive to and reflective of the workings of the world system.[1530]

As the climate descends into chaos, this transformation in law is no longer optional. Our survival depends on rejecting the global *status quo* and embracing a more humanly and ecologically balanced way of life.[1531] In order to find the right and just legal rules to establish such a way of life and to eliminate the dangers posed by the ecological crisis, a new ideological infrastructure of law and the relationship between nature and human beings must be designed and devised. When the relationship between nature and humans is transformed

---

[1528] Tokar, *Toward Climate Justice*, Social Ecology and the Future of Ecological Movements (Loc. 1649–54).

[1529] David R. Boyd, 'Sustainability Law: (R)Evolutionary Directions for the Future of Environmental Law', *Journal of Environmental Law and Practice*, No. 14, 2004, pp. 357–67, cited in: Collins, *The Ecological Constitution*, p. 18.

[1530] Kotzé – Kim, 'Towards Planetary … ', p. 87. (Emphasis is Kotzé – Kim's.) In their article, the authors consider 'Earth system law' as a law that should replace international environmental law. However, there is no obstacle to applying it to national law, too.

[1531] Tokar, *Toward Climate Justice*, Climate Justice and the Future (Loc. 1069).

from one of exploitation to a different one, this will require a different legal system.[1532] This new legal system should centre not on humans but on the Earth's ecosystem, of which humans are a part. Thus, even though it would not be anthropocentric in today's sense, since it would centre on nature, the emerging legal order, in the long run, would actually look out for the welfare of human beings as well. So, the most important difference between this legal system and the current one is that it would look out not only for the welfare of human beings but also for the ecosystem's other members' welfare.

Business as usual is no longer possible. Some activities destroying the climate and driving us all towards extinction must be curbed. Car companies producing SUV-type vehicles, the top 1 per cent flying everywhere in private planes, encouraging excessive meat consumption, fishing vessels catching all kinds of fish – no matter what the season,[1533] taking private cars to places that can easily be reached by public transportation, producing products that are planned to become obsolete or are perishable, and many other activities that increase unnecessary fossil fuel use and consumption should be legally prevented. These may seem 'freedom-limiting' today. That is because the understanding of freedom based on the capitalist value system for the realisation of a certain way of life is dominant throughout the world. This understanding causes us to drive ourselves to extinction by destroying the sources of life.[1534] Considered from this perspective, these limitations will, in fact, mean fewer children dying in traffic accidents, less warming of the planet, less animal exploitation, protection of vulnerable marine life, quieter cities, and happier people in the long run.

The proposal for a green constitutional order turns today's exception into a rule by putting the commons back in focus. In effect, it brings into the present the law of people who have lived in harmony with nature for hundreds of thousands of years. Ecologically literate lawyers, politicians, and people would find it entirely plausible to reverse the relationship between rule and exception. A reasonable person would not perceive the restriction on using private airplanes as a restriction on the 'freedom of property' of the 1 per cent. On the contrary, owning such an airplane should be considered

---

[1532] Üskül Engin, *Ekolojik Kriz, Etik ve Hukuk*, p. 6.
[1533] Capra – Mattei, *The Ecology of Law*, p. 196.
[1534] Saito, *Slow Down*, p. 174.

an unacceptable restriction on the freedom to survive happily on this planet. After all, when the United States was founded, enslaving people was as natural as owning a private jet today if one can afford it.[1535] Just as nobody has the right to enslave people today, no one should have the right to own private airplanes tomorrow. Just as there are rules for producing and buying weapons today, the production and selling of certain goods and services should be restricted tomorrow since they must be regarded as a type of weapon aimed at vulnerable people worldwide.

Courts around the world are already being flooded with lawsuits for climate damages. The most striking are those against oil companies. These are lawsuits brought by the public, or at least on behalf of the public, claiming to protect public health against companies known to engage in disinformation or political influence campaigns. That is very appropriate since the first authority to be held to account for climate change should be the companies that profit from the production and consumption of fossil fuels[1536] and the states that provide suitable conditions.

In this sense, one of the most important accusations related to climate change was made in the United States in the case of *Juliana v. United States*.[1537] This case, including allegations about burdening today's young people with decades of environmental costs due to the federal government's failure to take action against global warming, is pending and has not yet reached the Federal Supreme Court. Nevertheless, that does not change the fact that this is an inspiring accountability case brought by a group of children on behalf of their entire generation and generations to come against the governments their parents and their parents' parents voted into office.[1538] By rightly making climate change their priority, young people are holding past policies to account through the law and, in doing so, forcing the law to change.

The law has also been used as a tool against climate change in different ways other than cases. For instance, in Italy, the Rodotà Commission,[1539]

[1535] Capra – Mattei, *The Ecology of Law*, p. 196.

[1536] Wallace-Wells, *The Uninhabitable Earth*, p. 183.

[1537] See 4.4.1

[1538] Wallace-Wells, *The Uninhabitable Earth*, pp. 183–4.

[1539] A commission established by the Italian Ministry of Justice in 2007, chaired by Stefano Rodotà, professor of civil law, with the main objective of reforming the articles on public property in the Civil Code of 1942.

established to reform property law, first distinguished between structures that could never be owned by private individuals, such as railroads or historic waterways, and property that is currently dedicated to the public, but may, in fact, be privately owned, such as parks and art collections. It then proposed that those in the first category, that is, what is today considered state property or unsalable property, should be recognised as 'common property'.[1540] The Commission has taken the initiative to introduce the 'collective capacity to sue' as a rule for the protection of the commons, thus giving birth to a popular movement for it in Italy. That will enable us to fulfil our duty to give animals, plants, and future generations access to ecological justice.[1541]

The IPCC report published in 2018 clearly laid out what needs to be done to keep global warming below 1.5°C compared to the pre-industrial period. In order to achieve this goal, it is stated that mitigation measures should be taken in different areas, and a balance should be established between the rate of decarbonisation and the rate of freedom from carbon dioxide dependence by reducing the intensity of energy and resource use. In other words, we are recommended to move away from fossil fuels and towards sustainable resources in many fields, from energy to agriculture and industry to urbanism.[1542] As scientists point out, there is a solution. The problem is the lack of political will to bring us to it. The way to create this political will is both through democratic organisations at the grassroots level and by transforming the law through lawsuits and decisions. In this section, I will focus on good examples of green constitutionalism, first at the international and then at the national level. Ultimately, I argue that these examples demonstrate that the national level is more suitable and adequate for tackling climate change than the international one.

[1540] Mario Pagano, 'Urban Commons, From Italy to Europe', *Transformative Private Law Blog*, 21 July 2023.

[1541] S. Bailey – G. Farrell – Ugo Mattei, *Protecting Future Generations through Commons*, Trends in Social Cohesion 26, Council of Europe, Strasbourg, 2014, cited in: Capra – Mattei, *The Ecology of Law*, p. 198.

[1542] IPCC, *Global Warming of 1.5°C – Summary for Policymakers*, 2018, pp. 12–16.

International law in the face of climate change

International environmental law has been developing since the 1970s, when damage to nature became a cause for concern, and has now become a branch of law in its own right. Its scope is beyond the scope of this book. However, there is a close link between international environmental law and the problem of climate change. Therefore, within the scope of this study, it is necessary to address the developments and structural problems in international environmental law regarding climate change.

At present, rather than preventing the human exploitation and destruction of the Earth, the governance systems of the international community facilitate and legalise it.[1543] The reason for this, as has been emphasised throughout this study, is the capitalist patterns of production and consumption based on private property, the bourgeois understanding of the nation-state that emerged as a result of these patterns, and an international legal order that has developed through the sovereignty of nation-states. Therefore, by virtue of its raison d'être, today's international law is unsuitable for establishing a new order in harmony with nature.

The concept of 'thinking like a planet' is so alien to modern perspectives and so far removed from thinking as a neoliberal subject in a system of ruthless competition that initially sounds childish and naïve. However, when it comes to climate change, reasoning from first principles seems plausible and even necessary.[1544] What we need to do is to go back to that first perspective of

[1543] Cullinan, *Wild Law*, p. 29.
[1544] Wallace-Wells, *The Uninhabitable Earth*, p. 248.

humans acting harmoniously with nature at the national and international legal levels. We must put aside the arrogance and greed that humans have acquired through their 'growth' and re-establish a reciprocal relationship with nature.

By embedding interdependence and interrelationships in the new global governance structure, the international system could become more stable, and cooperative action could be encouraged. In such a governance pattern, it would become even more irrational to fight other societies for resources or to destroy nature irreversibly simply because it is in another country. In a global green constitutional order, it would be clear that the healthy functioning of the whole and the well-being of individuals depends on each society taking care of its 'own' part of the Earth and contributing to the health of the Earth's ecosystem in that place.[1545]

If climate change can unite us and we can establish such a new international legal order, it would be the result of the developments so far. So, let us look first at the development of international environmental law concerning climate change, then at the inadequacies of current international law in the face of this significant challenge, and finally at efforts to address these inadequacies through litigation.

5.1 Development of international environmental law on climate change

Environmental law, in general, was born as a result of the realisation that the Earth's resources are not infinite and that the aim should be to limit damage to the planet. Since the 1970s, protective mechanisms and texts in environmental law at the national and international levels have diversified, and environmental protection discourse has become mainstream. However, these failed to make a real difference.[1546] If these things had been implemented since then, and if we had started to reduce carbon dioxide in the atmosphere even by as little as 3 per cent per year, we might not have a

---

[1545] Cullinan, *Wild Law*, p. 153.

[1546] Sumudu A. Atapattu, *Emerging Principles of International Environmental Law*, Transnational Publishers, New York, 2007, p. 2, cited in: Durmaz, *Doğanın Hakları*, p. 3.

problem like climate change today. Instead, after the fall of the Berlin Wall, capitalism expanded into new markets and spread across the world in the form of neoliberalism. In addition to expanding human exploitation, that has led to increased pressure on the ecosystem.[1547]

International environmental law has evolved through numerous regional and global conferences and summits, at which countless instruments have been adopted. It is neither necessary nor possible to list them all here. However, some important events and documents need to be mentioned to understand this process. The UN Conference on the Environment in Stockholm in 1972 raised widespread awareness of the extent of human impact on the environment and climate, which is now recognised as the birthplace of international environmental law.[1548] Subsequently, concern was heightened by the Limits to Growth report published by the Club of Rome in the same year and the oil crisis in 1973.[1549] The main message of this report was that the global economy could not grow unlimitedly due to limited natural resources. Early in the study, the first conclusion was that *if present growth trends in world population, industrialisation, pollution, food production, and resource depletion continue unchanged, the limits to growth on this planet will be reached sometime within the next one hundred years.*[1550]

In March 1987, the Brundtland Commission, established under the umbrella of the UN in response to growing environmental concerns, prepared a report entitled Our Common Future. The underlying idea was a sustainable development framework in which environmental policy and development strategies could be brought together. The report focused on almost every dilemma related to climate change: sustainable development, the relationship between the environmental, economic, and social dimensions of global change, the well-being of future generations, the responsibilities of the present generation, and institutional inadequacies in a globalising world.[1551]

[1547] Saito, *Slow Down*, pp. 17–18.

[1548] Usha Natarajan – Julia Dehm, 'Introduction: Where is the Environment? Locating Nature in International Law', *in* Usha Natarajan – Julia Dehm (ed.), *Locating Nature: Making and Unmaking International Law*, Cambridge University Press, Cambridge, 2022, p. 3.

[1549] Hulme, *Why We Disagree …*, pp. 86–7.

[1550] Meadows – Meadows – Randers – Behrens III, *Limits to Degrowth*, p. 23.

[1551] Hulme, *Why We Disagree …*, pp. 260–1.

Nevertheless, until James Hansen, then director of NASA's Goddard Institute for Space Studies, made a presentation to the US Congress in 1988, a concept such as climate change had not existed in people's minds.[1552]

The year 1988 began with reverberations of a report by the University of East Anglia in the United Kingdom, based on the records of the global temperature series, showing that 1987 had been the warmest year in the last thirty years and according to the records, the five warmest years had been recorded in the 80s. In May 1988, the first major intergovernmental conference on climate change took place in Toronto. The final document of the Changing Atmosphere: Implications for Global Security called for a 20 per cent reduction in carbon emissions in industrialised countries by 2005 compared to 1988.[1553]

1988 was also the year the UN IPCC was founded. Established by the World Meteorological Organisation and the UN Environment Programme, it was tasked with reviewing and compiling international scientific data on climate change and writing reports. However, to ensure that its work served governmental and policy needs, its governance was entrusted to an official body of elected government representatives. That, in effect, conservatised the Panel and gave the impression that it was not an autonomous body.[1554]

Since the 1970s, when climate change was first demonstrated with scientific data, numerous international summits and regulations have been convened and organised on the environment. One of the most important of these was the 'Earth Summit' organised in 1992 in honour of the twentieth anniversary of the first UN Conference on the Environment. Delegates from 179 countries attended this event, called the Conference on Environment and Development, held in Rio De Janeiro, Brazil.[1555] The UN Framework Convention on Climate Change (UNFCCC) was adopted at this summit. The Convention imposed various non-binding limits on greenhouse gas emissions. It was decided to organise a Conference of the Parties (COP) every year to monitor compliance

---

[1552] Foster, *Capitalism in the Anthropocene*, p. 19.

[1553] Hulme, *Why We Disagree ...*, p. 88.

[1554] Hulme, *Why We Disagree ...*, pp. 117–18.

[1555] For details and documents adopted at the Conference, see 'United Nations Conference on Environment and Development, Rio de Janeiro, Brazil, 3–14 June 1992', *United Nations*.

with these emission limitations.[1556] However, as the name of the Conference suggests, rather than abandoning growth in the face of the ecological crisis, this summit sought to combine environmental protection and growth around the new concept of 'sustainable development'. As a result, an agreement was reached that, in order to sustain corporate profits, care must be taken to ensure that nature remains a means of production for a certain period.[1557]

The initial UN framework on greenhouse gas emissions, established in 1992, was expanded in 1997 with the Kyoto Protocol. Although hailed as a political and diplomatic success,[1558] the Protocol has not been characterised in the same way by scientists.[1559] The Kyoto Protocol was an international agreement between sovereign states, with targets and programmes set by countries to control greenhouse gas emissions. The Protocol was an important milestone in the UNFCCC process in that, for the first time, it set binding targets for countries to reduce their greenhouse gas emissions and prescribed the means to achieve these targets. The greatest responsibility for emissions reductions was rightly placed on the wealthiest states, while other states recognised their 'common but differentiated responsibilities' to mitigate the potential climate crisis, using the terms of the 1992 climate agreement.[1560]

On 22 April 2009, the UN General Assembly adopted a resolution submitted by Bolivia to declare 22 April as 'International Mother Nature Day'. In his address to the General Assembly, Bolivian President Evo Morales Ayma said that while the twentieth century was known as the 'century of human rights', the twenty-first century will be known as the 'century of Mother Nature rights'. Morales called on member states to draft a 'Universal Declaration of the Rights of Mother Nature', including the right to life for all living beings, the right of Mother Nature to live unpolluted, and the right to harmony and balance within and among all things. A few months later, on 17 October 2009, the nine countries that make up the Bolivarian Alliance for the Peoples of the Americas issued a declaration expressing their support

---

[1556] These conferences have been held every year since 1995, except for one that could not be held due to the COVID-19 pandemic.

[1557] Balta – Mısır, 'Bir Politik … ', p. 22.

[1558] See Hulme, *Why We Disagree* …, p. 303. However, Hulme also says two pages later that the failure of Kyoto is clear.

[1559] Jaria-Manzano – Borrás, 'Introduction to … ', p. 11.

[1560] Tokar, *Toward Climate Justice*, Beyond Kyoto? (Loc. 597).

for this call and laying out the basic principles of a legal order harmonious with nature. Likening climate change to the humanitarian crisis of World War II, they emphasised that human beings are only part of a system called Mother Nature, in which plants, animals, hills, forests, oceans, and air are interconnected.[1561]

COP15 in Copenhagen in December 2009 was pivotal in developing grassroots movements for climate justice. Although observers warned of too much corporate influence in the preparations for the Conference, the hope that people from all over the world felt in the run-up to the Conference was immense. Climate campaigners had long hoped the world's elites would finally reach a meaningful, long-term agreement. Just before the Conference, the United States elected Barack Obama to replace George W. Bush, and the European Union (EU) decided to cut carbon dioxide and other greenhouse gas emissions more rapidly. Hopes were that Copenhagen would be the turning point. However, it did not. On the contrary, the Conference created a deadlock that will last many years, accelerating our transition to an unstable and chaotic climate.[1562]

The cause of this deadlock was the legal climate regime that emerged with the Copenhagen Accord. The initial draft of a comprehensive global climate agreement, especially as a result of the efforts of the US, was eventually turned into a patchwork of individual state commitments. With the Copenhagen Accord, the concept of 'voluntary commitments by states' became the new global norm for implementing climate policies. Under the agreement, nothing was binding on states or companies, and commitments were to be 'assessed' only every five years.[1563] These assessments had no legal consequences, regardless of their outcome.

Indeed, in a paper published in *Nature* in 2010 by Germany's most prestigious climate researchers, an analysis of the emission reduction pledges of the signatories to the Copenhagen Accord and their possible consequences revealed that the states had prepared their emission reduction plans for 2020 based on a scenario in which everything would proceed almost precisely as

---

[1561] Cullinan, *Wild Law*, p. 186.

[1562] Tokar, *Toward Climate Justice*, The UN Climate Negotiations and Beyond (Loc. 541-546-556).

[1563] Tokar, *Toward Climate Justice*, Coercive Diplomacy (Loc. 703).

it did on that day. In the absence of a legally binding agreement, the authors said, states will only try to meet the lower limit of their pledges, making it impossible to meet the then-target of 2°C and possibly causing the world to warm by 3°C. The paper's scientists described the lack of short-term emission reduction targets as *speeding towards a cliff and hoping to stop just before it.*[1564] That hope is about to be dashed today, in part because of the failure of the Copenhagen Accord.

Following the failure in Copenhagen to agree on an international institution with binding legal powers to monitor states on climate change, Bolivian President Morales called for a World Peoples' Conference on Climate Change and the Rights of Mother Nature to be convened in his country in April 2010. The Conference was to draft a Universal Declaration on the Rights of Mother Nature, establish an International Tribunal for Climate Justice, and work on strategies for action and mobilisation to defend Mother Nature's rights. A total of 15,000 people were expected to attend the conference, but the eruption of the Eyjafjallajökull volcano in Iceland just before the conference made air travel from Europe and Asia impossible. Nevertheless, 35,000 people attended the Conference in Cochabamba, Bolivia. After working in seventeen working groups, the participants finally adopted the Peoples' Agreement on Mother Nature Day on 22 April 2010, declaring the Universal Declaration on the Rights of Mother Nature.

The issuance of this declaration by the people participating in the Conference is central to the process that is hoped to bring about fundamental changes in today's dominant legal, political, and economic systems. The Declaration recognises that the Earth is an indivisible and living community of interrelationships and interdependencies of beings with inherent rights. It recognises all natural elements that are part of Mother Nature – including plants, animals, rivers, and ecosystems – as subjects with inherent and inalienable rights to exist and to play their role in the community of beings.[1565] In this sense, the Declaration has become a manifesto to bring together a broad coalition of peoples and organisations that share the conviction that we cannot tackle humanity's fundamental challenges without transforming

---

1564 Joeri Rogelj et al., 'Copenhagen Accord Pledges Are Paltry', *Nature*, Vol. 464, 2010, pp. 1126–8, cited in: Tokar, *Toward Climate Justice*, Beyond Copenhagen (Loc. 735–745).

1565 Cullinan, *Wild Law*, p. 188.

industrial civilisation's core values and governance systems.[1566] That means replacing the current anthropocentric international environmental law of the North with the nature-centred constitutionalism of the South. This change will not happen immediately, but the fact that this document was adopted at such a well-attended meeting shows that the transformation has at least begun.

One of the most important developments in international law on climate change took place at the COP21 in Paris in 2015. One hundred and ninety-five countries and the EU participated in this conference, which resulted in a binding agreement on climate change for the first time in twenty years of UN negotiations.[1567] According to this agreement, global warming will be kept below 2°C, but if possible below 1.5°C compared to pre-industrial times, and human-induced greenhouse gas emissions will be net zero[1568] by 2050. The agreement requires signatory states to report on how they will reduce their emissions through their 'Nationally Determined Contributions' to be submitted every five years starting in 2020. However, although the Paris Agreement is recognised as 'the first binding international climate agreement', no sanction mechanism is envisaged in case states fail to comply with the promises in these contribution declarations.

Moreover, when the promises of the signatories to the Paris Agreement by 2020 are listed one after the other, an interesting situation emerges. Combined, these pledges do not even come close to keeping global warming below 1.5°C. On top of that, even the goal of keeping it below 2°C cannot be reached. Even if all countries fulfil their pledges – and it should be noted that they are not binding – global emissions will continue to rise. According to calculations, even if the pledges are fulfilled, global warming will reach 3.3°C by the end of the century. Therefore, a disaster awaits us even if the Paris Agreement is fully implemented.[1569]

As a result, the work taking place under the auspices of the UN, while very important, has so far been little more than a forum for the discussion of corporate-friendly pseudo-solutions, ranging from carbon trading and

---

1566 Cullinan, *Wild Law*, p. 189.

1567 'The Paris Agreement', *UNFCCC*.

1568 The term used to refer to the absorption of all emitted greenhouse gases by nature or other means.

1569 Hickel, *Less is More*, p. 127; Saito, *Slow Down*, p. 3.

offsetting to the myth of 'clean coal', from nuclear energy to industrial-scale agro-fuel plantation attacks. In the face of the growing influence of corporate interests in UN processes, one of the participants at the 2007 climate conference in Bali described it as *a giant shopping extravaganza, marketing the earth, the sky, and the rights of the poor.*[1570]

In Löwy's words, 'beyond a cosmetic veneer', the reforms of the last thirty-five years have been a monstrous failure. There have been some minor successes, but even these are dwarfed by the unregulated expansion of the current economic system and the chaotic nature of production.[1571] One reason is that Western environmentalism has turned nature into an object to be cherished and protected. Although all these developments are generally welcomed as a global paradigm shift, this kind of environmentalism is, in fact, nothing more than a product of Western history and culture.[1572] Therefore, it is not a break with it but a continuation. Today's international environmental law is nothing but a greenwash over a rotten capitalist international legal order.

Consequently, we must acknowledge that international environmental law has generally failed to halt and reverse the rapid deterioration of the planet's life-support systems. While the number of multilateral, regional, and bilateral environmental agreements grows daily, so does the rate of environmental degradation.[1573] Carbon dioxide emissions that cause climate change continue to rise every year, causing global temperatures to rise at an accelerating rate. The fact that number of parts per million (ppm), which was around 325 in 1979, when the first global climate conference was held, has exceeded the safe number of 350 over the years despite so many conferences, protocols, and agreements on the subject, exceeded 400 in 2015, when the Paris Agreement was held, and was measured as 423.85 in November 2024[1574] clearly shows how dysfunctional the efforts to stop climate change within the framework of current international law are.

[1570] Personal conversation with Rachel Smolker, cited in: Tokar, *Toward Climate Justice*, Beyond Kyoto? (Loc. 672).

[1571] Löwy, *Ecosocialism*, The Belém Declaration (Loc. 1137).

[1572] Natarajan – Dehm, 'Introduction: Where … ', p. 4.

[1573] Gonzalez, 'Foreword: Deconstructing … ', p. ix.

[1574] For regular monitoring of the number of parts per million in the atmosphere, see <www.co2.earth>.

To understand why international law is still far from being the solution to climate change, despite the existential threat we face, we must look at its structural problems. The most prominent of these is that it is soft law, and the second is that it is still trying to maintain the capitalist economic order.

5.2 Structural problems of international law in the face of climate change

> I have participated in several meetings, and many times they talk, talk, talk, approve a document, and nothing happens.[1575]

At first glance, international law seems to be the most appropriate tool for dealing with environmental problems since their impact is not confined to national borders. For example, the problem of allocating water resources transcends national borders; the effects of climate change are felt everywhere from the Equator to the poles; minerals and other natural resources are valued on international markets; and some places, such as the Amazon riverbeds and the Great Barrier Reef, are of economic and environmental importance not only to local communities but to the entire planet.[1576] Climate change, mass extinction, deforestation, desertification, and the increasing pollution and toxicity of air, water, and soil are problems that transcend national borders. These are global concerns that people look to international law to address.[1577]

However, two general characteristics of international legal orders significantly reduce their effectiveness. The first is that they are reductionist. In other words, they are content with setting common standards on a particular issue without considering the networked nature of the ecosystem. In this sense, they still follow a mechanistic perspective. The second quality that reduces their effectiveness is that they are considered soft law. Therefore, on important issues such as environmental protection, global warming, and animal rights, international legal standards are either set very low and vague or are set out in documents that are not formally binding. Thus, it is impossible to

[1575] Lula Da Silva, *in* 'Carbon Credits – Land Grab or the Amazon's Future', *BBC*, 8 August 2023.
[1576] May – Daly, *Global Environmental Constitutionalism*, p. 27.
[1577] Natarajan – Dehm, 'Introduction: Where ... ', p. 1.

say that any existing international environmental legal regime envisages an enforceable environmental right.[1578]

Underpinned by the human-nature distinction that Enlightenment philosophers inherited from Christianity, today's international environmental law essentially regulates human interventions that either facilitate domination and extraction or protect and manage nature. Either way, it creates human supremacy over nature by mapping, monitoring, or managing it. That turns nature into an 'other' beneath humanity and allows it to be regulated and controlled to serve multinational corporations.[1579]

Even though the impact of climate change is increasing every day, not much has changed in the environmental policies that have been familiar for many years. Too many environmental policy advocates continue to accept inadequate and short-term approaches to tackling climate-related pollution in the name of a misguided political 'realism'. At the UN level, international representatives continue to argue that the most viable way to reduce greenhouse gas emissions is through 'voluntary' national pledges, and policymakers insist that proposed reductions be implemented through market-based trading of carbon emission permits.[1580]

Numerous reports, recommendations, resolutions, and observations, especially those prepared by UN agencies on various occasions, have and are still being prepared on how economic activities trigger climate change and environmental degradation and how they violate the rights of women, children, and Indigenous peoples in particular.[1581] However, it is debatable to what extent these non-binding documents can stop and limit the activities of states that harm the environment. Indeed, there has been no significant improvement in climate change indicators since the adoption of these decisions.

As a result, international lawyers have so far failed to find solutions to environmental problems. Numerous treaties, principles, jurisprudence, institutions, research, and training have been put in place, and a growing specialisation in international environmental law has been created. Despite all this, environmental crises are worsening. In the case of climate change

---

1578 May – Daly, *Global Environmental Constitutionalism*, p. 28.

1579 Gonzalez, 'Foreword: Deconstructing … ', p. x.

1580 Tokar, *Toward Climate Justice*, Preface to the Revised Edition (Loc. 177).

1581 For a short list of these, see Boyd, *Report of … (A/75/161)*, pp. 16–17, § 62–65.

and biodiversity loss, although the two have been the focus of international environmental law since the 1990s, half of the greenhouse gases in the atmosphere today have been emitted in the last thirty years,[1582] and a million species are now threatened with extinction.[1583] Nevertheless, the path to a more just world, where the balance of the ecosystem is prioritised over short-term interests, is still not on the horizon. That is because international jurists are still unable to extricate themselves from the orbit of global capitalism and to find viable solutions to growing inequalities and environmental destruction.[1584]

Given the state of international politics today, the idea of a global, comprehensive, and enforceable carbon dioxide emission ban, which is urgently needed today, seems nothing short of absurd.[1585] One of the main reasons for this is that states are still recognised as sovereign entities. The second reason is the refusal to question and limit the global capitalist order.

5.2.1 International legal system based on the sovereignty of States

The concept of sovereignty, which has in its past the memory of the Roman Imperial period, the feudal institution of seigneurialism, the theory of property, the theoretical teachings of the thirteenth century, the theories of the Protestant thinkers of the sixteenth century, and the teachings of the encyclopedists and philosophers of the eighteenth century,[1586] is classically defined as 'the supreme will over a territory'. The internal sovereignty of the modern state, which means the sole possession of all power and administrative authority within its territory, can be considered the most striking feature of the nineteenth-century rule of law.[1587] External sovereignty, on the other hand, ensures the equality of states, at least before international law. In this sense, sovereignty is defined as a will with the unique characteristic of not being determined by anything other than itself. The only reason that can

---

[1582] Adam Vaughan, 'Global Carbon Emissions From Energy Hit a Record High', *New Scientist*, 26 March 2019.

[1583] IPBES, *Global Assessment ...*, p. XVI.

[1584] Natarajan – Dehm, 'Introduction: Where ... ', p. 2.

[1585] Scranton, *Learning to Die*, p. 36.

[1586] Léon Duguit, 'Egemenlik ve Özgürlük', *in* Cemal Bâli Akal, *Devlet Kuramı*, 2nd ed., Dost, Ankara, 2005, pp. 380–1.

[1587] Poggi, *The Development of the Modern State*, p. 113.

mobilise the sovereign's will can only be a reason that it finds in itself.[1588] That is also true when it comes to the protection of nature and the climate. As contemporary modern states are considered sovereign, they are not *obliged* to enter into cooperative regimes to protect the environment, and if they do, they are free to implement and manage regimes in ways that protect their own strategic 'interests'.[1589]

In a system of sovereign states, each is a self-sovereign and self-powered unit that pursues only its interests. However, the interests of each state are constantly redefined according to changes in the internal and external demographic, military, economic, and political environment. That means that the balance of the system is very delicate and needs recalibration.[1590] In an international order based on growth and competition, this understanding of state sovereignty, which is still mostly accepted and valid today, is an obstacle to cooperation against climate change.

Climate change is a global threat of such magnitude that everyone would accept genuine international cooperation. Nevertheless, at a time when such cooperation is most needed, we are retreating into nationalistic corners, away from collective responsibility and away from each other.[1591] In contrast, since climate change is a global problem, states must cooperate to achieve a low-carbon, climate-resilient, and sustainable future. That means rich countries must share knowledge with less rich countries and build capacity by transferring zero- or low-carbon and high-efficiency technologies.[1592] In contrast, they neither recognise their historical responsibilities and pay compensation to impoverished countries suffering from climate change, provide the necessary material support for adaptation investments, nor transfer renewable energy. Moreover, they are demanding repayment of the loans they have made to the Global South countries within the historically unequal and unjust capitalist order of international law. That is a new form of colonialism that traps the

[1588] Duguit, 'Egemenlik ve Özgürlük', p. 383.
[1589] Robyn Eckersley, *The Green State: Rethinking Democracy and Sovereignty* (Kindle edition), MIT Press Academic, Cambridge, Massachusetts, 2004, p. 22. (Emphasis is Eckersley's)
[1590] Poggi, *The Development of the Modern State*, p. 109.
[1591] Wallace-Wells, *The Uninhabitable Earth*, p. 28.
[1592] Collins, *The Ecological Constitution*, p. 112.

Global South in a growth trap that makes them even more dependent on fossil fuels[1593] and exacerbates climate change.

Given the evidence of increasing biosphere degradation, even the classic principles of traditional international law are being jeopardised. For example, the traditional rule of 'do no harm' is being violated by corporations from the Global North through the transformation and overuse of the Global South's lands, climate change, pollution, and invasive species.[1594] Today, the natural resources and the labour of the people of countries at the periphery of the capitalist economic order continue to be exploited by corporations from the centre for profit maximisation. That means controlling the world's economies through commercial globalisation and destroying the world's resources and ecosystems for the industrialised global economy. The oil wars in the Middle East, Central Asia, and Africa, as well as the new food and land wars, are part of this dynamic.[1595] Due to what can be called 'ecological imperialism', life in the countries of the South is becoming unsustainable in terms of both ecological balance and agricultural resources, and these countries are becoming poorer.[1596] That forces people to migrate to the Global North countries for a better and more dignified life, which is exploited by populist nationalist far-right parties to gain power.[1597] Thus, a vicious cycle is born.

Consequently, wealthy countries are now closing their doors to climate migrants based on their sovereign powers and the rules of international law on migration. They are able to keep people outside their borders by defining them as 'illegal migrants/refugees', although they had to leave their homelands due to problems these countries caused. When it comes to real solidarity, the countries of the Global North, who speak of 'humanity' at international conferences, unfortunately, retreat into their own corners under the pretext of protecting their economies and cultural structures. Therefore, new green constitutionalism is based on a transnational and post-nation-state understanding. That can be achieved by establishing a judicial body with the

---

[1593] Kaamil Ahmed, 'Rich Countries "Trap" Poor Countries into Relying on Fossil Fuels', *The Guardian*, 21 August 2023.

[1594] Boyd, *Report of … (A/75/161)*, p. 19, § 73.

[1595] Vandana Shiva, *Soil Not Oil: Environmental Justice in an Age of Climate Crisis* (Turkish version), 2nd ed., Sinek Sekiz, Istanbul, 2014, p. 25.

[1596] Reyhan, *Ekolojik Emperyalizm*, p. 142.

[1597] Saito, *Slow Down*, p. 29.

power to limit and make binding decisions on the activities of nation-states and multinational corporations.

The judicial mechanism established by the European Convention on Human Rights (ECHR) is an example of such an understanding. A version of The European Court of Human Rights (ECtHR), the court with the power to adjudicate member states established by this Convention, should be established. It should be equipped with the authority to judge both states and corporations globally on climate change issues. The problem is that under the current international legal system, establishing such a court could only be possible through an international convention signed by current nation-states. However, in a competitive environment based on the growth of their economies, sovereign states would refrain from signing such a convention. That puts us in another vicious circle.

There are three ways out of it. The first is for insistent social demands to become strong enough to force governments to stop competing and start cooperating on climate change. While it can be acknowledged that there is growing democratic pressure in this direction, it would be overly optimistic to think that it will become strong enough in the short term. The second way would be to engage existing international human rights mechanisms, which is one of the goals of green constitutionalism. Due to the weak enforcement mechanisms of international environmental law, states and corporations that have never been held accountable for missed targets may be forced to act in solidarity if they are held accountable before international human rights courts and judicial bodies such as the International Criminal Court over the right to life, the right to live in a healthy environment, the right to respect for sovereignty and even – ironically – the property right. Finally, there is the possibility that the ecological disasters associated with climate change could become so devastating that states would be forced to cooperate. In this last case, however, it will already be too late.

The best that countries of the Global South can do in the short term under the current international law seems to be to insist that international environmental law holds countries of the Global North responsible for climate change and that they should, therefore, do most of the work in protecting nature globally. Indeed, legal principles such as sustainable development and 'common but differentiated responsibility' for global warming make this case. However, it must also be acknowledged that international environmental law has so far failed to put these principles into practice and change the behaviour of wealthy countries.[1598] The main reason is that the dominant capitalist economic order at the root of the problem and its ties with the current international legal system have not yet been confronted.

5.2.2 The dominion of capitalism over the international law

In the name of growth and economic development, the wealthy countries of the Global North have plundered the resources of Africa, Asia, the Caribbean, Latin America, and the Pacific over the years and continue to do so, sometimes by force, but more often through international trade law, international investment law, trade agreements and the lending practices of international financial institutions. These rules and institutions have allowed multinational corporations headquartered in the Global North to seize land, water, energy, minerals, and food and create unimaginable levels of pollution to the detriment of the poor, Indigenous peoples, and other marginalised groups.[1599]

In the 1990s, a period of rapid change in every respect, negotiations in the areas of climate and international trade ran quite parallel to each other. Within a few years, groundbreaking agreements were reached in both areas. As mentioned earlier, in 1992, governments adopted the UNFCCC in Rio. The same year, the North American Free Trade Agreement (NAFTA) was signed and entered into force two years later. In 1994, an agreement was reached in negotiations to establish the World Trade Organization (WTO), and this new trade body was launched the following year. The Kyoto Protocol was adopted in 1997, setting the first binding emission reduction targets. In 2001, China became a full member of the WTO. The most interesting aspect of these simultaneous climate-related and trade-related processes is that they operate on entirely separate planes. Indeed, these two processes have been carried out by ignoring the most obvious signs of how they affect each other and pretending that the other area does not exist.[1600]

For example, the contradiction between the promises made in Rio to reduce carbon emissions and the rule on the 'elimination of trade restrictions', which directly contradicted this, was ignored. However, there was a

---

[1598] Natarajan – Dehm, 'Introduction: Where … ', p. 5.
[1599] Gonzalez, 'Deconstructing the … ', p. ix.
[1600] Klein, *That Changes Everything*, pp. 111–12.

fundamental difference between the two schemes: The commitments made in the climate negotiations operated *de facto* on a system of honour. In other words, a weak and non-threatening mechanism existed for countries that failed to keep their promises. Meanwhile, in trade agreements, commitments were enforced by a sanctioned dispute settlement mechanism, and non-compliance meant that governments were hauled before trade tribunals, often with severe penalties.[1601] So, for all these years, governments have preferred sticking to their promises in trade agreements rather than their pledges to prevent climate change.

As a reflection of this, international climate change law has been constructed by ignoring three essential elements crucial to climate constitutionalism and climate governance: justice/equity, rights, and responsibilities. That has led to a highly contradictory outcome. After years of climate debate, climate governance has moved in the opposite direction to the goals of climate justice. The failure of governments to take meaningful, urgent, and coordinated political measures to tackle climate change, combined with the praise of neoliberalism and free-market logic as the only way to solve the climate crisis, has become the dominant trend.[1602]

As Australian political scientist Robyn Eckersley puts it, this was the decisive link that determined the relationship between the climate and trade regimes because it ensured that the global economy, expanding through liberalised trade, was protected against trade-restrictive climate policies. In practice, this meant ensuring that the negotiations at all those climate conferences and summits did not take into account bold and 'trade-restrictive' political preferences that could be coordinated internationally. Therefore, implementing renewable energy programmes based on local resources or restricting trade in goods produced with high-carbon compounds was impossible because they restricted free trade.[1603] Indeed, for example, strong green energy transition programmes, seen as necessary to rapidly reduce emissions

[1601] Klein, *That Changes Everything*, pp. 112–13.

[1602] Jaria-Manzano – Borrás, 'Introduction to … ', p. 10.

[1603] Robyn Eckersley, 'Understanding the Interplay Between the Climate and Trade Regimes', in *Climate and Trade Policies in a Post-2012 World*, United Nations Environment Programme, p. 17, cited in: Klein, *That Changes Everything*, p. 113.

globally, are increasingly being nullified by international trade agreements, particularly the rules of the WTO.[1604]

One of the consequences of trade liberalisation under neoliberalism is that investments can now be shifted to countries with cheap labour and more lax environmental regulations. When companies based in the Global North shifted their factories to the South, much of the pollution generated also did so. In this way, the price per labour unit fell, and environmental damage in their own countries was reduced; thus, public environmental concerns were alleviated, although revenues continued to flow. Countries in the Global South welcomed this situation because, on the one hand, it would reduce unemployment by creating jobs. On the other hand, it would increase production and GDP through investments coming into the country. Therefore, they deliberately and wilfully tended not to increase environmental regulations or to ignore the neglect of existing ones because otherwise, companies planning to invest in their countries might be put off by the suspicion that their profits would be reduced. Of course, the companies' purpose in shifting factories to Southern countries was not to increase emissions; they were looking for cheap labour to maximise their profits. However, the result was that the countries of the South were trapped in growth policies based on fossil fuels and the exploitation of their people and nature. The climate has thus become even more unstable, an inevitable consequence of global capitalism with relaxed rules.[1605]

Within the framework of these hypocritical policies, states have so far broken their promises and failed to meet their targets for protecting and conserving ecosystems and biodiversity. For example, none of the countries that signed the Convention on Biological Diversity in 2002, promising a significant reduction in the rate of biodiversity loss at global, regional, and national levels by 2010, have been able to deliver. Likewise, on 25 September 2015, a UN summit adopted the document Transforming Our World: The Sustainable Development Agenda for 2030. By 2022, although some progress had been made, none of the seventeen targets had been met.[1606]

[1604] For various examples on this subject, see Klein, *That Changes Everything*, pp. 94–101.

[1605] Andreas Malm, 'China as Chimney of the World: The Fossil Capital Hypothesis', *Organization & Environment*, 25 (2012), pp. 147–62, cited in: Klein, *That Changes Everything*, pp. 119–20.

[1606] UN, *The Sustainable Development Goals Report 2022.*

In 1997, when US Vice President Al Gore took the floor at the UN climate conference in Kyoto, he said that the United States would sign the agreement under two conditions. The first was that the targets for emission reductions would be much lower than the original ones. The second condition was that the emission reductions would be implemented through a market-based 'right to pollute' trade between various companies and states. In the 'cap-and-trade' model in the Protocol, which was prepared following these conditions, companies would act within an 'upper limit' for their emissions within the framework of regulatory programmes to be made by the states. Thus, the total amount of emissions of chemicals such as carbon dioxide from industrial activities would be limited. If companies failed to meet their cap, they could buy the difference from another company that had managed to reduce its emissions faster and cheaper. That would – theoretically – reduce climate damage without a carbon tax and in a way that would not be too damaging to industrialists. While economists say that this system would steer companies towards the most cost-effective changes as quickly as possible, the practice has shown that the carbon market is just as open to fraud and manipulation as any other financial market.[1607]

The Protocol's compliance mechanisms were so weak that states could opt for more flexible mechanisms that allowed them to reject their mitigation obligations without penalty and receive 'mitigation credits'. Indeed, Canada exceeded its Kyoto emissions target by 45 per cent in 2010 yet faced no sanctions.[1608] The US, one of the largest producers of carbon dioxide, signed the Protocol but never ratified it. George W. Bush withdrew the United States from the Kyoto Protocol not because the science of climate change was uncertain and incomplete but because he thought it would harm the US economy and prosperity.[1609] The rest of the world was then left with consequences such as an inconvenient but corporate-friendly carbon trading system. That has meant that the necessary carbon reductions have so far failed to materialise.[1610]

At the COP15 meeting in Copenhagen in 2009, the situation, as mentioned earlier, did not improve. Much of the talk at this Conference was about the

---

[1607] Tokar, *Toward Climate Justice*, Trading Pollution (Loc. 1164–1175).

[1608] S. Barret, *Climate Change Negotiations Reconsidered*, Briefing Paper for Policy Network, London, 2008, p. 3, cited in: Hulme, *Why We Disagree …*, p. 305.

[1609] Hulme, *Why We Disagree …*, p. 130.

[1610] Tokar, *Toward Climate Justice*, Beyond Kyoto? (Loc. 608).

technicalities of how much of the atmosphere could be exploited without causing climate change and how much of a 'carbon budget' powerful states would have. On the other hand, the meeting was also marked by negotiations on how little 'adaptation funds' should be paid to countries that contribute the least to the problem but are most severely affected by its consequences. National interests, power, and money, rather than climate, were the main concerns of those at the meeting. Perhaps fittingly, the Conference ended with a small group of states agreeing behind closed doors to the Copenhagen Accord, which, if implemented, would result in the disappearance of most island states.[1611]

When the 2020 Paris Climate Conference's goal of keeping global warming below 2°C was announced, many African delegates described it as a 'death sentence' because it meant nothing but more desertification and deforestation on the continent. When low-altitude island nations also reacted with the slogan '1.5°C for Survival', a last-minute addition to the agreement's text changed the target to a pledge that countries would 'strive to keep the temperature rise at 1.5°C'. However, the governments that made this pledge in Paris are investing in extracting the world's most carbon-intensive fossil fuels through much more intensive fracking and mining today. Norway, for example, encouraged its companies to explore new oil deposits in the North Sea despite UN IPCC calls to the contrary. In a lawsuit against it, Norwegian courts rejected the claim that this violated peoples' right to live in a healthy environment and allowed oil exploration.[1612] Similarly, the Australian government approved a request to increase the capacity of three coal mines in the country. The coal from this approval means another 1.3 billion tons of carbon dioxide will soon be released into the atmosphere.[1613] These activities are blatantly incompatible with the 2°C target, let alone keeping warming to the upper limit of 1.5°C.[1614]

On the other hand, Russia's invasion of Ukraine in 2022 and the subsequent energy crisis have further militarised the international system, making it even

---

1611 Cullinan, *Wild Law*, p. 187.

1612 Alister Doyle – Terje Solsvik, 'Norway's Government Wins Arctic Oil Lawsuit, Greens Lose', *Reuters*, 4 January 2018.

1613 Graham Redfearn, 'Tanya Plibersek Approves Three Coalmine Expansions in Move Criticised as "the Opposite of Climate Action"', *The Guardian*, 24 September 2024.

1614 Klein, *On Fire*, p. 199.

more competitive. That has further weakened the prospects for international coordination in the face of the climate crisis. Moreover, the escalation of geopolitical competition has further increased the appetite for fossil fuel resources.[1615] For example, although his first act after his election was to return to the Paris Agreement, US President Biden approved the Willow Project in Alaska in March 2023, which is planned to extract 600 million barrels of oil.[1616] Similarly, the UK government aims to increase oil and gas exploration and extraction activities in the North Sea.[1617]

In 2018, 33.2 billion tons of carbon dioxide were emitted globally, according to the 2019 edition of the World Energy Outlook prepared by the International Energy Agency (IEA). According to what the IEA calls the 'Current Policies Scenario',[1618] which is based not on speculation but on emission reduction policies and measures that states have pledged to implement in international documents such as the Paris Agreement, this figure will rise to 35.5 billion tons by 2040. As the IEA underlines, this is far from the emission reductions needed to reach the targets set in the Paris Agreement.[1619] The IEA's projections are in stark contrast to the IPCC's target of reducing global carbon dioxide emissions by 45 per cent by 2030 and achieving net-zero emissions by 2050.[1620]

We must face unpleasant realities. The modern conception of economic development transforms nature into natural resources through unlimited commodification and forces international law to believe in endless economic growth. That is why the current international legal system is one of the causes of ecological degradation rather than a tool to correct the damage done to nature.[1621] Scientists have demonstrated climate change with data and warned us of what is coming. For years, we have been wasting time with UN negotiations, actions promoted by the Kyoto Protocol, and G8

1615 Benlisoy, 'İklim Krizi … ', p. 167.

1616 Ella Nilsen, 'Biden administration approves controversial Willow oil drill project in Alaska, which has galvanized online activism', *CNN*, 14 March 2023.

1617 Fiona Harvey, 'UK to defy net zero targets with more oil and gas drilling', *The Guardian*, 6 April 2022.

1618 IEA, *Global Energy Outlook 2019*, 2019, p. 751.

1619 IEA, *Global Energy Outlook 2019*, p. 47.

1620 Chomsky – Pollin, *Climate Crisis …*, pp. 165–6.

1621 Usha Natarajan – Kishan Khoday, 'Making and Unmaking International Law', *in* Usha Natarajan – Julia Dehm (ed.), *Locating Nature: Making and Unmaking International Law*, Cambridge University Press, Cambridge, 2022, pp. 24–5.

summits with climate on the agenda. None of the economics, international relations, diplomacy, and political platforms on climate change have lived up to expectations[1622] and have done what needed to be done. That is because they have sought a solution without touching the source of the problem, namely the capitalist economic infrastructure, and without harming the almost sacralised concepts such as growth. We must now acknowledge that that was an impossible mission.

Therefore, higher judicial bodies and courts, which have binding decision-making powers, need to step in with the awareness of protecting the right to life today and in the future without being bound by the interests of economic and political elites. As a matter of fact, various global and regional courts and committees have begun to issue promising decisions in cases brought before them for climate change-related reasons. In the following, I will focus first on the rulings on climate change at the UN and the ECtHR and then on green constitutionalism in national jurisdictions. Reasonable people, especially young people, in every corner of the world are calling on the courts to defend their right to life through national and international environmental law. It is now up to judges at all levels to heed this call for a just and liveable world.

5.3 Prominent decisions of international judicial bodies on climate change

Climate change is a global problem, and it is caused by states and companies operating under their legal systems. States are obliged to take measures to ensure that actions that take place in their jurisdiction or under their control do not harm the environment or people in other states or places and people beyond their national jurisdiction.[1623] Although a critical factor in the global climate crisis is that despite repeated failures to deliver on their promises, states and corporations have not been held accountable by the weak enforcement mechanisms of international environmental law, international and national human rights law has treaty bodies, courts, commissions, and processes to

[1622] Hulme, *Why We Disagree …*, pp. 338–9.

[1623] International Court of Justice, *Pulp Mills on the Uruguay River (Argentina v. Uruguay)*, Decision, 20 April 2010.

ensure accountability.[1624] For this reason, much of the legal struggle against the climate crisis so far has been based on human rights violations.

5.3.1 Applications to the United Nations

The UN, founded in 1945 after the Second World War to maintain world peace and promote international economic, social, and cultural cooperation, is today an international organisation with 193 members with the potential to deal with problems stemming from climate change. Applications on this issue are made to the Committee on the Rights of the Child and the Human Rights Committee, two committees tasked with implementing international agreements adopted within the UN. While there is no coercive mechanism to enforce the decisions of these committees, they are usually implemented by states due to the prestige of the decisions and the pressure of international public opinion. These two UN committees have received many submissions on climate change but have issued only two decisions so far.

5.3.1.1 Sacchi and Others vs. Argentina and Others (UN Committee on the Rights of the Child)

The decision on the application of sixteen children from twelve different countries to the United Nations Committee on the Rights of the Child against Argentina, Brazil, Germany, France, and Türkiye was announced on 11 October 2021.[1625] The Committee found the application inadmissible for failure to exhaust domestic remedies. However, the Committee also opened the door to a transformation in international environmental law by stating in the decision that a member state may be responsible for all children living within or outside its borders who suffer from the harmful effects of carbon emitted under its control. In this respect, the decision reflects a perspective that significantly advances the understanding of international human rights law on the scope of state responsibility in the context of climate change.[1626]

[1624] Boyd, *Report of… (A/75/161)*, p. 17, § 67.

[1625] UN Committee on the Rights of the Child, *Sacchi and Others vs. Argentina and Others*, CRC/C/88/D/105/2019.

[1626] Aoife Nolan, 'Children's Rights and Climate Change at the UN Committee on the Rights of the Child: Pragmatism and Principle in Sacchi v Argentina', *EJIL: Talk*, 20 October 2021.

The applicants demanded a determination of the responsibility of the respondent states whose reckless actions caused the climate change that threatened their lives and who, to this day, have failed to take adequate measures to avert the crisis. The children argued that the states failed to take the necessary preventive and precautionary measures to respect, protect, and fulfil the right to life under Article 6, the right to health under Article 24, and the right to enjoy culture under Article 30 of the UN Convention on the Rights of the Child. The applicants argued that climate change was increasing due to these states' extraction and use of fossil fuels and their inaction to reduce emissions. Noting that the global average temperature had increased by 1.1º C compared to pre-industrial times, devastating heat waves were occurring, infectious diseases were spreading rapidly, forest fires, extreme weather events, and floods were occurring, and seawater levels were rising, the children claimed that they were more mentally and physically affected by climate change than adults due to these events that directly threatened their lives.

When asked why the complaint was filed against these five countries, it is clear that the reason was that they are both historically the largest emitters among the parties to the UNFCCC and influential countries in the G20. In other words, these states are directly responsible for the threat of climate change. In addition, these five states have the capacity to mobilise other G20 countries that are significant carbon emitters but are not parties to the Optional Protocol to the Convention on the Rights of the Child on the Communications Procedure to take the necessary measures for decarbonisation 'through legal, diplomatic and economic means'.[1627]

In this context, the children requested the Committee not only to determine the responsibility of states for climate change but also to recommend that these five States initiate an international cooperative movement to mitigate the climate crisis, prevent further harm to the petitioners and other children, and protect their rights. Children also requested the Committee to call on states to ensure children's right to be heard and to express their views freely in all international, national, and sub-national efforts to mitigate and adapt to climate change.

The Committee's decision of inadmissibility was influenced by the fact that none of the applicants had recourse to any judicial remedy in their home

[1627] Nolan, 'Children's Rights ... '.

country. As a justification for not resorting to domestic judicial remedies, the children argued that judicial mechanisms in a country's domestic law *cannot rule on other countries' climate policies or states' failure to cooperate internationally.* At this very moment, however, the German Federal Constitutional Court ruled in March 2021 in an individual application decision[1628] that it was 'conceivable in principle' that the protection obligations arising from fundamental rights compelled the German state to take action against applicants living outside the country for damages caused by global climate change. Likewise, the Federal Court stated that the German Constitution obliges the state to take international action at the global level to combat climate change and that the state must act for the climate in an international framework. Of course, these developments weakened the applicants' ability to 'bypass' domestic judicial remedies through Article 7(e) of the Optional Protocol.[1629] As a result, the Committee found the application inadmissible.

However, the Committee on the Rights of the Child's resolution also made some critical observations on climate change, future generations' rights, and climate litigation's impact on states. First of all, the Committee recognised that the transboundary responsibility of states may arise due to climate change. According to the Committee,

> [...] when transboundary harm occurs, children are under the jurisdiction of the State on whose territory the emissions originated for the purposes of article 5 (1) of the Optional Protocol if there is a causal link between the acts or omissions of the State in question and the negative impact on the rights of children located outside its territory, when the State of origin exercises effective control over the sources of the emissions in question.[1630]

According to this approach, if the carbon emission takes place on the state's territory, if the state has effective control over the sources of the emission, and if a causal link can be established between the emission and the violation

---

[1628] Federal Constitutional Court of Germany, *Neubauer and Others vs. Germany*, 1 BvR 2656/18, 1 BvR 288/20, 1 BvR 96/20, 1 BvR 78/20, 24 March 2021. See 6.3.9

[1629] Article 7(e) of the Optional Protocol to the Convention on the Rights of the Child on the Communications Procedure provides that the principle of exhaustion of domestic remedies shall not apply to remedies that are unreasonably long and unlikely to produce an effective result.

[1630] *Sacchi and Others*, § 10.7.

of the rights of children outside its borders, the state is also responsible for the children outside its borders whose rights are violated.

The Committee, which also included the principle of 'common but differentiated responsibility', as reflected in the Paris Agreement, in its resolution, stated that the fact that climate change is a global problem does not absolve individual states of responsibility for the harm caused to all children, wherever they are in the world, by gases emitted from sources within their borders.[1631]

One of the most important aspects of the decision is that the Committee found that the link between the emissions and the harm suffered by the applicants is *prima facie*[1632] established. Thus, the Committee recognised that children have victim status because of the real and substantial harm they have suffered without seeking full proof. If the respondent State claims that the harm suffered by children was caused by an emission not under its sovereign jurisdiction, it must prove it. Hence, the burden of proof has shifted. The UN Committee on the Rights of the Child placed the status, distinctive characteristics, and experiences of the applicants at the centre of its reasoning:[1633]

> The Committee considers that, as children, the authors are particularly affected by climate change, both in terms of the manner in which they experience its effects and the potential of climate change to have an impact on them throughout their lifetimes, particularly if immediate action is not taken. Due to the particular impact on children, and the recognition by States parties to the Convention that children are entitled to special safeguards, including appropriate legal protection, States have heightened obligations to protect children from foreseeable harm.[1634]

Moreover, in a very candidly written statement sent to the applicants,[1635] the Committee almost apologised to the children for not finding a violation:

> We want you to know that the Committee spent many hours discussing your case, and we struggled with the fact that although we entirely understood the significance and urgency of your complaint, we had to work within the limits of the legal powers given to us under the Optional Protocol on a Communications Procedure (OPIC).

[1631] *Sacchi and Others*, § 10.10.
[1632] Latin legal term meaning 'at first sight'.
[1633] Nolan, 'Children's Rights … '.
[1634] *Sacchi and Others*, § 10.13.
[1635] UN Committee on the Rights of the Child, 'Open Letter to the Authors'.

In other words, the Committee would have found the complaint admissible and perhaps even held States responsible if the applicants had resorted to domestic remedies in their home countries or had been able to justify why they had not with concrete evidence.

Thus, the UN Committee on the Rights of the Child has sent the message that it is keeping the door open for possible new applications in the future. The Committee acknowledged that climate change violates children's rights but conditioned its finding of violation on the fulfilment of the admissibility criteria as a requirement of the principle of subsidiarity. However, it is clear from the text of the Sacchi decision and the statement sent to the children that the Committee tends to apply the admissibility criteria flexibly, rather than with excessive rigidity, in applications on an issue as complex and important as climate change.

5.3.1.2 Daniel Billy and Others vs. Australia (UN Human Rights Committee)

In the first UN Human Rights Committee decision on climate change,[1636] the applicants were eight Australian nationals and their six children. Living on four low-altitude islands in the Torres Strait region, they brought a complaint against the Australian government on the grounds that changing weather patterns directly impacted their lives, culture, and traditional ways of life. The Torres people consider the preservation of their ancestral graves, visiting them, and communicating with the dead an important part of their culture. However, severe flooding due to rising sea levels has damaged family cemeteries in recent years. In addition, the most important ceremonies for the Torres people, such as coming of age and initiation, must take place on the community's own land in order to be meaningful. The applicants also alleged that changes in the climate have caused extreme rainfall and storms, which have damaged their land and trees, resulting in a decline in food from traditional fishing and farming.

[1636] UN Human Rights Committee, CCPR/D/135/D/3624/2019.

The applicants alleged that the Australian state had failed to adapt to climate change[1637] for various reasons, including raising sea walls around the islands and reducing greenhouse gas emissions, in violation of their fundamental rights under the UN Covenant on Civil and Political Rights.[1638] That is the first UN complaint from a low-altitude island against a national government for its inaction on climate change.[1639]

On 23 September 2022, in a historic decision, the UN Human Rights Committee ruled that Australia had failed to adequately protect Indigenous Torres Strait inhabitants from the harmful effects of climate change by failing to take timely and adequate measures. Accordingly, it found the applicants' claims of violations of the right to enjoy their culture and the right to be free from arbitrary interference with their private lives, families, and dwellings justified. The Committee's decision emphasised that the islands' inhabitants' spiritual connection to their traditional lands and cultural integrity depend on the health of the surrounding ecosystem. The Committee urged Australia to compensate Indigenous people for the harm they have suffered, to engage in meaningful consultations with communities to assess their needs, and to take measures to ensure their continued safe presence on the islands.

The decision is significant as it is the first case in which an international body has looked at the merits of climate change and found that national states are obligated under human rights law to reduce carbon emissions. Although there is no coercive mechanism to enforce the Human Rights Committee's judgements, they do put international pressure on states. Accordingly, states have generally acted in accordance with the judgements. In this context, it can be assumed that Australia will comply with the Committee's decision,

[1637] Indeed, there is no policy adopted by the Australian government to fulfil its very low commitment to reduce carbon emissions by 26–28 per cent by 2030. The government continues to support the fossil fuel industry. Australia is the 14th biggest carbon emitter in the world. It is the largest fossil fuel exporter among OECD countries. See Tom Swann, *High Carbon from a Land Down Under: Quantifying CO_2 from Australia's Fossil Fuel Mining and Exports*, The Australia Institute, July 2009.

[1638] The rights that the applicants claim to have been violated are the right to culture under Article 27 of the Convention, the right not to be subjected to arbitrary interference with private life, family and home under Article 17, and the right to life under Article 6.

[1639] 'Daniel Billy and others v Australia (Torres Strait Islanders Petition)', *Climate Case Chart.*

compensate the Torres Strait residents for material damages, and quickly complete the raising of the sea walls that have already begun. However, one should be more sceptical about whether the Australian government, which has one of the world's worst per capita carbon emission records,[1640] will adopt a more aggressive policy on emission reductions. Indeed, as mentioned earlier, this decision did not prevent the government from approving the capacity expansion of three coal mines.

5.3.2 Verein KlimaSeniorinnen Schweiz and Others vs. Switzerland Judgement of the ECtHR

As is well known, the ECtHR, established to ensure the implementation of the ECHR, is an international court operating within the Council of Europe, which can issue binding judgements on member states. The execution of judgements is overseen by a body called the Committee of Ministers. A member state that fails to comply with a final judgement faces various sanctions, the most severe of which is expulsion from the Council. In this respect, the ECHR is seen as an exception to the classical international legal order as it is a supranational judicial mechanism with sanctioning powers. In addition, the Court, to which anyone under the jurisdiction of a member state can appeal on the grounds of a violation of one or more of the human rights enumerated in the Convention, is generally recognised as the most effective international court in the world.[1641] That begs the question of whether it can be transformed into an effective mechanism in cases related to climate change.

Accordingly, climate change applications to the Court have increased in recent years. So far, only three of them have been decided,[1642] and the ECtHR has found a violation of rights only in the application against Switzerland,

---

[1640] Australia ranks 11th out of 209 countries in per capita carbon emissions. See 'CO_2 Emissions Per Capita', *Worldometer.*

[1641] As an example among many other different sources, see L aurence R. Helfer, 'Redesigning the European Court of Human Rights: Embeddedness as a Deep Structural Principle of the European Human Rights Regime', *The European Journal of International Law*, Vol. 19, No. 1, p. 125.

[1642] These judgements, delivered on 9 April 2024, are *Claudia Duarte Agostinho and Others v. Portugal and 32 Other States*, No. 39371/20, *Câreme vs. France*, No. 7189/21, and *Verein KlimaSeniorinnen Schweiz vs. Switzerland*, No. 53600/20.

Verein KlimaSeniorinnen Schweiz and Others.[1643] Therefore, although the others are also important for the development of climate law,[1644] only this application will be mentioned here.[1645] With this decision, the ECtHR both recognised climate change as a human rights issue and ruled that states have a positive obligation to adopt and effectively implement in practice regulations and measures to mitigate the actual and potential irreversible impacts of climate change.[1646] This landmark decision establishes a strong link between international climate change law and human rights law.[1647]

The applicant, the *KlimaSeniorinnen* Association, was founded as part of the efforts to bring a case against the Swiss Federal Government, similar to the lawsuit brought and won by the *Urgenda* Foundation in the Netherlands. This goal of strategic litigation is clearly stated in the association's statute.

[1643] The ECtHR declared inadmissible the application of six Portuguese youths against thirty-three Council of Europe Member States (*Duarte Agostinho and Others v. Portugal and thirty-two Other States*) for failure to exhaust domestic remedies, and the application of Daniel Carême, the former mayor of Grande-Synthe Municipality, one of the places to be affected by climate change, against France (*Carême v. France*) because Carême no longer resides within the boundaries of the municipality in question and therefore, lost his victim status

[1644] These applications shed light both on the negative impacts of climate change on human rights under the ECHR and on the direction in which the ECtHR's future jurisprudence will proceed. The climate applications have led to a rethinking of victim status, the capacity of non-governmental organisations, the causal link between the act and the harm, transboundary and shared responsibility, the balancing of environmental and economic interests, and the doctrines of subsidiarity and margin of appreciation. See Corina Heri, 'Climate Change Before the European Court of Human Rights: Capturing Risk, Ill-Treatment and Vulnerability', *The European Journal of International Law*, Vol. 33(3), 2022, pp. 925, 926–7.

[1645] Although their outcomes and specific conditions are different, the three applications share common features. For example, all three petitions targeted government regulation of climate change mitigation and the inadequacy of state efforts to reduce greenhouse gases. Although inspired by the *Urgenda* case in the Netherlands, these applications do not only seek to raise the greenhouse gas reduction target but also allege violations of a broad bundle of rights. From this perspective, all three applications allege violations of human rights through the inadequacy of states' emission reduction targets and practices. See Maxim Bönnemann – Maria Antonia Tigre, 'The Transformation of European Climate Change Litigation' *Verfassungsblog*, 9 April 2024.

[1646] For the same opinion, see Bönnemann – Tigre, 'The Transformation … '.

[1647] Johannes Reich – Flora Hausammann – Nina Victoria Boss, 'Climate Change Litigation Before the ECtHR', *Verfassungsblog*, 16 May 2022.

Founded by older women, as they are one of the social groups most affected by climate change, the association 'pursues its purpose in particular through the provision of information, including educational activities, and by taking legal action in the interests of its members with regard to the effects of climate change'.[1648]

Four members of the association, as well as the association itself, first claimed in domestic law that their rights had been violated by the inaction of the Swiss federal institutions in the face of climate change. After losing at the first instance courts, the Swiss Federal Supreme Court (FSC), the last stage exhausted under domestic law, dismissed the case without going into its merits, stating that the rights of the applicants had not yet been violated and that it was still possible to limit global warming to the 2°C target set by the Paris Agreement. The Court advised the association and the other plaintiffs to use direct democracy in Switzerland to amend the Federal Constitution in line with their demands, implicitly reminding them of the separation of powers and sending the message that regulation and policy on climate change is a matter for the legislature and the executive, not the judiciary.

The association and the women then applied to the ECtHR, arguing that the inadequacy of Swiss legislation on climate protection, the inaction to revise the Federal CO2 Act, and the government's unwillingness to enforce even its weak provisions should be considered a breach of the state's positive obligations. They argued that the association members, whose average age was seventy-three at the time of its founding, are significantly and adversely affected by climate change-induced heat waves, which are becoming stronger and more frequent due to Switzerland's failure to reduce its greenhouse gas emissions to the required extent.

5.3.2.1 The new causal link between (in)action and breach

The applicants alleged three main violations. The first was the alleged violation of the rights to life and respect for private life under Articles 2 and 8 of the ECHR, respectively, due to Switzerland's climate policies that were incompatible with the Paris Agreement. The applicants also claimed that their right to a fair trial under Article 6 of the Convention had been violated by the FSC's decision, which they characterised as arbitrary. Finally, according

[1648] *KlimaSeniorinnen*, § 10.

to the applicants, the Swiss authorities' failure to respond to their complaints amounted to a violation of their right to an effective remedy under Article 13 of the ECHR.

The Grand Chamber of the ECtHR first rejected the argument invoked by the Swiss State, according to which it is impossible to prove that the situation of individual petitioners is aggravated by the state's conduct and thus establish a link between the obligation to mitigate climate change and human rights.[1649] Noting that the specific characteristics of climate change require a different interpretation of the causal link, the ECtHR stated that if there is a possibility that reasonable measures not taken by local authorities could have led to a different outcome or lesser harm, this alone is sufficient to give rise to state responsibility.[1650] Thus, by rejecting this argument, which has been raised in almost all climate cases worldwide, the Court has created an important jurisprudence that should be considered in all future cases and applications before national and international judicial bodies.

5.3.2.2 Recognition of the standing of associations in applications regarding climate change

One of the most important and controversial aspects of the case was the novelty of the victim status. That is because, in general, individual application mechanisms are only designed to compensate individuals who have suffered a specific, measurable, and unlawful injury under the jurisdiction of the party legally responsible for the violation.[1651] In the Court's own words,

> the Convention does not provide for the institution of an 'actio popularis' and that its task is not normally to review the relevant law and practice 'in abstracto', but to determine whether the manner in which they were applied to, or affected, the applicant gave rise to a violation of the Convention.[1652]

One of the main issues in *KlimaSeniorinnen* was, therefore, whether the alleged inadequacy (or inadequate application) of a law on global warming,

---

[1649] Pranav Ganesan, 'Not Just Another ECtHR Judgement: Analysis of KlimaSeniorinnen Schweiz v Switzerland (Part 1 of 3)', *Climate Rights Database*, 18 April 2024.

[1650] *KlimaSeniorinnen*, § 444.

[1651] Reich – Hausammann – Boss, 'Climate Change … '.

[1652] *Roman Zakharov vs. Russia*, application no. 47143/06 (Grand Chamber 4 December 2015) § 164.

which affected everyone, not just the applicants, was sufficient to establish the applicants' capacity to sue, as it might in the future violate their individual rights.

The ECtHR found the applications of four women who applied on their own behalf inadmissible on the grounds that they did not have victim status. In its reasoning, the Court stated that two basic criteria must be met for this status to be recognised in applications relating to climate change: First, that the applicant had been subjected to the adverse effects of climate change with a high degree of intensity and, second, that there was an overriding need for the protection of the applicant as an individual, based on the absence or inadequacy of reasonable measures to mitigate the harm.[1653] According to the Court, these four applicants failed to meet these two criteria. Since, according to the Court, they have not yet been directly affected by the adverse effects of climate change, they do not have victim status. Moreover, if their applications were accepted, this would violate the prohibition of *actio popularis*.[1654]

However, in finding that the Association, which was founded by the applicants with other women of the same status and aimed at protecting their rights in the face of climate change, has standing under Article 8, the ECtHR significantly broadened its position on the capacity to apply in favour of non-governmental organisations. The Court underlined, among other reasons, the unique situation of climate change, which is a common concern of humanity, and the need to promote the sharing of the burden of climate change between generations.[1655]

The Court's recognition of the standing for the association established by women to protect their rights in the face of climate change, rather than women who have a high potential to be directly affected by climate change, and finding this part of the application admissible, of course, raises questions and has been criticised. For example, Justice Tim Eicke, in his dissenting opinion, argued that by doing so, the Court paved the way for *actio popularis* applications, which it had previously banned.[1656] Interestingly, the majority of

---

[1653] *KlimaSeniorinnen*, § 487.

[1654] *KlimaSeniorinnen*, § 483–484. However, this approach has been criticized as incompatible with the Court's decision in *Modinos vs. Cyprus*. See George Letsas, 'Did the Court in Klimaseniorinnen Create an Actio Popularis?', *EJIL:Talk!*, 13 May 2024.

[1655] Bönnemann – Tigre, 'The Transformation … '.

[1656] *KlimaSeniorinnen*, partial dissenting opinion by Tim Eicke, § 45.

the Court rejected this criticism on the grounds that this application by an association of older women should be accepted in the name of protecting the rights of future generations from climate change. At this stage of its decision, obviously inspired[1657] by the *Neubauer* judgement of the German Federal Constitutional Court (GFFC),[1658] the ECtHR stated that future generations, who are at a representational disadvantage today, will be more affected by the effects of climate change, which is a common concern of humanity, than current generations, and that it is, therefore, a requirement of the Convention that an intergenerational burden-sharing should take place.[1659]

In this context, according to the Court, in order for an association to bring an application on climate change, it must a) be lawfully established in the country concerned, b) be able to demonstrate that it aims to protect the rights of its members or other affected individuals against threats arising from climate change, and c) be able to demonstrate that it is recognised as the representative of its members or other affected individuals whose rights to life, health or welfare protected by the Convention are being harmed or threatened by the adverse consequences of climate change.[1660] As a result, in the interest of the 'proper administration of justice', the ECtHR accepted the capacity of the *KlimaSeniorinnen* Association, which it found to meet these criteria, and extended its previous jurisprudence on the victim status of non-governmental organisations.

5.3.2.3 Judicial review of compliance with the Paris Agreement

The ECtHR did not accept the Swiss State's objection based on the principle of separation of powers that *combating climate change is a matter for the legislative and executive branches, not the judiciary*,[1661] which the Swiss national courts also used as a justification for their rejecting decisions. Although recognising that the primary responsibility for dealing with the complex

---

[1657] In the same direction, see Aoife Nolan, 'Inter-generational Equity, Future Generations and Democracy in the European Court of Human Rights' Klimaseniorinnen Decision', *EJIL: Talk!*, 15 April 2024.

[1658] See 6.3.9

[1659] *KlimaSeniorinnen*, § 489.

[1660] Ganesan, 'Not Just … '.

[1661] 'Comments of the Swiss Government on Admissibility and the Merits, I. Preliminary Comments', *Climate Case Chart*, §4.

scientific, political, and economic problems arising from climate change lies with the legislative and executive branches,[1662] the ECtHR, following in the footsteps of the GFFC, took into account that future generations, in particular, will be placed under a more significant burden due to climate change as a result of the short-term policies of today's governments and that the countries that signed the Paris Agreement have various responsibilities in this regard. Accordingly, the Strasbourg Court ruled that the judiciary can review whether these responsibilities have been fulfilled and whether a sustainable policy has been pursued.[1663]

Therefore, what the Court did is a judicial review to determine whether states are protecting the rights of present and future generations by taking the necessary measures to address climate change and whether the obligations undertaken by signing international agreements are being fulfilled. In this respect, contrary to Switzerland's argument, the principle of separation of powers would be violated if the legislature and the executive were to prevent the judicial branch from conducting such a review.[1664] Accordingly, the Court recalled that when a case comes before it in which the conventional rights of an individual or group are affected by the policies of a member state, it is no longer merely a matter of policy but also a matter of law, requiring the interpretation and application of the Convention.[1665] While recognising that states have a margin of appreciation for measures to take, the ECtHR stated that this margin narrows when it comes to the obligation to combat climate change and its adverse effects and to set the necessary targets. According to the Court, once the state has set net zero carbon targets, it is free to determine the policies on how to achieve these targets.[1666] However, it is the duty and right of the judiciary to monitor whether these policies will achieve the net-zero target since failure to achieve these targets would lead to violations of conventional rights and freedoms.

[1662] *KlimaSeniorinnen*, § 413.
[1663] *KlimaSeniorinnen*, § 420.
[1664] Charlotte Blattner, 'Separation of Powers and KlimaSeniorinnen', *Verfassungsblog*, 30 April 2024.
[1665] *KlimaSeniorinnen*, § 450.
[1666] *KlimaSeniorinnen*, § 543.

5.3.2.4 State obligations under the Convention due to climate change

In *KlimaSeniorinnen*, the ECtHR stated that the primary obligation of states is to adopt regulations and measures appropriate to mitigate the present and future and potentially irreversible effects of climate change and to implement them effectively in real life.[1667] The Court ruled that

> the Contracting States need to put in place the necessary regulations and measures aimed at preventing an increase in GHG concentrations in the Earth's atmosphere and a rise in global average temperature beyond levels capable of producing serious and irreversible adverse effects on human rights, notably the right to private and family life and home under Article 8 of the Convention.[1668]

According to the Court, states must take measures to substantially and progressively reduce greenhouse gas emissions and achieve a net-zero emissions target within thirty years.[1669] In paragraph 550 of the judgement, the ECtHR listed the criteria for legal responsibility arising from this target. According to these five criteria, national authorities must a) adopt general measures detailing a timetable for achieving net-zero carbon, b) set interim GHG reduction targets and roadmaps on the road to net zero, c) provide evidence that these targets have been or will be achieved in a timely manner, d) update these GHG reduction targets as necessary in light of new data emerging, and finally d) adopt measures by making relevant regulations and act in a timely, appropriate and consistent manner in implementing them. In addition, in order to effectively protect individuals' rights to life, health, well-being, and quality of life, these measures must be complemented by adaptation measures aimed at mitigating the most serious and imminent consequences of climate change, the Court said, noting that procedural safeguards must also be in place to monitor whether these measures are being taken.[1670] Two of the most important of these safeguards are providing accurate information on climate regulations and measures to all, especially to the most vulnerable groups most

---

[1667] *KlimaSeniorinnen*, § 545.

[1668] *KlimaSeniorinnen*, § 546.

[1669] According to Ganesan, it is unclear how this thirty-year period referred to by the ECtHR was determined, and therefore, it is controversial. The author also states that the Court's 'substantial and progressive greenhouse gas emission reduction' order has no legal basis. See Ganesan, 'Not Just … '.

[1670] *KlimaSeniorinnen*, § 552–553.

affected, and adopting procedures to ensure that citizens' views on regulations and measures are taken into account in decision-making processes.[1671]

Accordingly, the Court found that Switzerland had violated the right to respect for private and family life under Article 8 of the ECHR by failing to adopt a regulatory framework to mitigate climate change.[1672] In its judgement, the ECtHR stated that in the context of climate change, Article 8 imposes an obligation not only on Switzerland but also on *each Contracting State undertake measures for the substantial and progressive reduction of their respective GHG emission levels, with a view to reaching net neutrality within, in principle, the next three decades.*[1673]

This decision is already recognised as a landmark regarding climate change and human rights protection. It not only imposes positive responsibilities on the member states of the Council of Europe on climate protection but also recognises that climate change is a human rights issue and has important implications for the defence of human rights that are violated or likely to be violated due to the climate crisis by non-governmental organisations.[1674]

The five substantive criteria and two procedural safeguards cited earlier represent the minimum level for states to respect conventional rights in the context of climate change.[1675] It should be noted that the substantive and procedural criteria listed by the Court are binding on all Contracting States. While Switzerland was convicted of a violation due to the shortcomings of its existing climate law and its failure to meet its previous net-zero carbon emission targets, some Council of Europe countries and many countries around the world have yet to adopt an overarching climate law. Given the regional and global impact of the *KlimaSeniorinnen* judgement, states that have yet to adopt legislation to address climate change should adopt a law as soon as possible that includes necessary and sufficient measures and that sets out in detail the final and intermediate targets for a net-zero policy that the ECtHR found necessary. Failure to do so would mean that that climate change policy is inadequate and, thus, in breach of the Convention.

[1671] *KlimaSeniorinnen*, § 554.

[1672] *In KlimaSeniorinnen's* application, the ECtHR also found a violation of Article 6 of the ECHR on the right to a fair trial. However, this part of the judgement is not quoted as it is not directly relevant to the book's topic.

[1673] *KlimaSeniorinnen*, § 548.

[1674] Bönnemann – Tigre, 'The Transformation … '.

[1675] Blattner, 'Separation of … '.

Constitutional law in the Anthropocene

The basic claim is that law is supra-interest and thus brings peace and order to a society torn apart by conflicting interests. However, this claim does not focus on how, for what purpose, and by whom the law is created and executed. In short, the source of law and the social order on which it is shaped are ignored.[1676] However, law cannot be separated from the social and economic structures it regulates. These emerge from and nourish each other.

As shown in the book's first part, the current legal orders are intertwined with the bourgeois nation-state and its capitalist economic order based on fossil fuels. Therefore, the necessity to phase out fossil fuels due to climate change requires us to consider abandoning the current anthropocentric legal order alongside the growth-based economic system. A similar transformation took place in the United States at the time of the abolition of slavery. Through a paradigm shift in human rights, a particular form of property was eliminated by force. That is an apt analogy for the challenge we face today. The anti-slavery struggle, like the struggle for climate justice, was confronted with the need to dispossess at least part of the ruling class. The way to avert climate catastrophe is by eliminating fossil capital through constitutional prohibitions, just as in the case of the slave capital.[1677] In other words, a constitutional order that looks at rights and nonhuman beings from a different perspective needs to be established.

[1676] Özenç, *Hukuk Devleti*, p. 48.
[1677] Benlisoy, 'İklim Krizi … ', p. 173.

Any illusion that fossil fuels could be phased out through a smooth, evolutionary, prudent transition must be quickly dispelled.[1678] All over the world, the energy sector operates as state-owned or privately owned property. In the oil and gas industry alone, state-owned national companies control around 90 per cent of the world's reserves and 75 per cent of production. The companies controlling oil and gas infrastructure systems include Saudi Aramco, Russian Gazprom, China's National Petroleum Corporation, Iran's National Iranian Oil Company, Venezuela's Petroleos de Venezuela, Brazil's Petrobras and Malaysia's Petronas. None of these state-owned companies operate with the same profit imperatives as large private energy companies such as ExxonMobil, British Petroleum, and Royal Dutch Shell. Nevertheless, that does not mean they are prepared to tackle climate change simply because we face a global environmental emergency. National development projects, lucrative careers, and political power depend on this vast ongoing flow of fossil fuel revenues. So, we should not expect state-owned energy companies to provide themselves with a more favourable framework for moving towards more effective industrial clean energy policies.[1679] In the race for growth and competition between states, governments seek to maximise profits from these companies. Regardless of the financial consequences of shutting down privately owned and state-owned fossil fuel companies, the only body that can stop these activities seems to be the higher courts, such as the Supreme or Constitutional Court. That is because rights are too precious to be measured in money, and the supreme judiciary's raison d'être should be to protect fundamental rights, no matter what the cost. Indeed, as will be explained shortly, such decisions have already been taken in various countries.

It is true that the inherent characteristics of capitalism lead to unavoidable environmental destruction and that putting an end to capitalism should be the main priority of the environmental movement, so let social movements bring about this transformation. The main problem with this argument is the time scale. It is almost impossible to achieve a national and international mobilisation to dismantle capitalism in the time we have left to avert this vital

[1678] Benlisoy, 'İklim Krizi … ', p. 190.
[1679] Chomsky – Pollin, *Climate Crisis* …, p. 95.

crisis.[1680] That is why the higher courts must step in and make bold decisions based on the legitimacy gained by the lawsuits brought by the people as part of this mobilisation. In doing so, all national and international supreme judicial bodies should communicate and coordinate with each other.

We must take immediate action and radical measures in all countries. There is no time left to wait for governments intertwined with fossil fuel companies or their subsidiary industries, such as construction, to take these measures. That is a transformation that everyone, but above all lawyers, must now embrace as a civilisational duty, both in their own countries and in each of the world's major economies.[1681] In this context, the relationship between property and the right to life must be reconsidered, and economic activities that violate the right to life must be recognised as outside the scope of rights and prevented by law. In addition, the concept of rights in the constitutional sense should be considered with a posthumanist and nature-centred approach beyond the anthropocentric perspective, which is the main problem that creates the threat of climate change. Under this heading, I will first examine whether existing environmental regulations in constitutions can be interpreted from this new green perspective. Then, I will discuss nature-centred constitutional regulations and high court decisions.

6.1 Constitutionalisation of the environment

The constitution is the basic regulation that determines how public authority should be exercised.[1682] In this sense, the constitution is defined by its superiority over state functions.[1683] Protecting rights in constitutions is important because it is the highest order in a national legal system. Moreover, the constitution has a crucial cultural role in that it reflects the values and

---

[1680] Chomsky – Pollin, *Climate Crisis …*, p. 174.

[1681] Klein, *On Fire*, p. 213.

[1682] Emer de Vattel, *Le Droit des Gens ou Principes de la Loi naturelle appliquée à la Conduite et aux Affaires des Nations et de Souverains*, Volume 1, 1758, Book 1, Chapter 3, p. 31, cited in: Boyar, *Anayasal Yoruma Giriş*, p. 79.

[1683] Boyar, *Anayasal Yoruma Giriş*, pp. 79–80.

goals of a society.[1684] Therefore, societies that care about protecting[1685] nature, albeit from an anthropocentric perspective, should welcome the inclusion of provisions with this purpose in their constitutions. Since constitutions are hierarchically above other legal provisions in domestic law, including environmental protection provisions in the constitution makes them more effective. It can also positively shape society's view of nature.[1686] Evidently, many contemporary constitutions include provisions for environmental protection. Of course, at this point, what should be understood from the concept of environment gains importance.

Although it is extremely difficult to say that there is a consensus on the definition of the environment, according to the Lugano Convention[1687] prepared by the Council of Europe, which is the only convention in which this concept is defined, the environment includes the following elements: 1) living and non-living natural resources such as air, water, soil, fauna and flora and the interaction between the same factors; 2) Assets that constitute cultural heritage; 3) Views with landscape characteristics. Therefore, the natural and cultural assets humans interact with constitute their environment.

With the realisation of the degradation of nature, protecting the human environment became a matter of interest for constitutional law in the last quarter of the twentieth century. As the damage caused by human activities became visible, societies felt the need to include provisions for protecting the environment in their social contracts. As a legacy of this, recognising environmental human rights, environmental rights, or rights of nature is

---

[1684] UN General Assembly, *Right to a Healthy Environment: Good Practices*, A/HRC/43/53, 30 December 2019, p. 4, § 10.

[1685] Kaboğlu and Yancı Özalp argue that the right to the environment should be understood not only as a human right but also as the right of all living beings, especially animals. See Kaboğlu – Yancı Özalp, *Çevre Hakkı*, p. 85. However, this approach contrasts with the concept of 'environment' itself. This is because this concept is the product of an understanding that puts human beings at the centre and places everything else on the periphery. If animals, for example, were to have 'environmental rights', then humans would have to be in the periphery. However, it is not logically possible to be both in the centre and in the periphery.

[1686] Durmaz, *Doğanın Hakları*, p. 271.

[1687] Full title: 'Convention on Civil Liability for Damage Caused by Activities Hazardous to the Environment', 21 June 1993.

a common trend in twenty-first-century constitutions.[1688] Rachel Carson's book, Silent Spring, about the effects of pesticides and other toxic substances used in agriculture on the human body, and the widespread awareness of the dangers of nuclear energy through the green movement, have led people to accept certain constitutional limitations on the protection of nature, albeit mostly at the expense of their own health. These have indirectly contributed to the protection of nature.

Without a safe, healthy, and habitable environment, we cannot enjoy any other fundamental human rights that flow from our nature as free and rational creatures. It is clear, then, that the right to a habitable environment is essential to ensure a humane life.[1689] In this framework, protecting the environment is understood as a right-duty based on 'collective solidarity' that encompasses all public and private entities.[1690]

Regarding the time element, the right to a healthy environment differs from other rights because it has an intergenerational character. Present generations are responsible for protecting not only their own environment but also that of future generations. This right emphasises the relationship between the actions and behaviours of present-day people and the quality of the future environment, the responsibility of present-day people towards their children and grandchildren, and a solidarity that connects present-day humanity with future humanity.[1691] In this sense, the right to a healthy environment has a positive aspect in terms of fulfilling the concept of intergenerational justice. However, within the current economic order, realising this function at a level that can stop climate change is impossible. I will try to explain why this is so below.

1688 Kaboğlu – Yancı Özalp, *Çevre Hakkı*, p. 57.

1689 William Blackstone, 'Ethics and Ecology', in *Philosophy and Environmental Crisis*, University of Georgia Press, Athens, 1974, p. 32, cited in: DesJardins, *Environmental Ethics*, pp. 210–11.

1690 Kaboğlu – Yancı Özalp, *Çevre Hakkı*, p. 57.

1691 Kaboğlu – Yancı Özalp, *Çevre Hakkı*, pp. 87–8.

6.1.1 The status of constitutional provisions on the environment in the face of climate change

As mentioned earlier,[1692] today's environmental law stems from modern Western law, rooted in religious anthropocentrism, Cartesian dualism, philosophical individualism, and ethical utilitarianism.[1693] In this respect, the ecological inadequacy of current environmental law is in its DNA because it is embedded in an unsustainable and 'growth-insistent' economic system.[1694]

Consequently, the most fundamental weaknesses of environmental law around the world are that it is anthropocentric, fragmented, and reductionist in origin. It is not only blind to ecological interdependence but also politically weak relative to other, more powerful areas of law, such as individual property and corporate rights.[1695] Indeed, the purpose of the vast majority of environmental law today is to facilitate the exploitation of commodified natural resources rather than to protect the stability and resilience of natural systems.[1696] In general, environmental provisions in constitutions serve no different purpose. These constitutional provisions are either mere words with no real function because they are just wishful thinking, or they have an anthropocentric perspective that sets limits on the conditions under which nature can be exploited.

Thus, even in environmental law, whether or not a person should be punished for damaging a natural feature is determined by interpreting texts that set standards for human behaviour. Human – and therefore corporate – rights emerge independently of the context of the damaged Earth ecosystem. For example, a company is only penalised if it discharges into a river a liquid containing more pollutants than the law allows to be released into rivers. Pollution below the level the law permits is not subject to penalties. However, that amount of pollution also harms the river, nature, and people. Taken as

---

1692 See 1.2.5.4

1693 Ecological Law and Governance Association, 'Oslo Manifesto', Article 3.

1694 Geoffrey Garver, *Ecological Law and the Planetary Crisis: A Legal Guide for Harmony on Earth*, Routledge, London, 2020, p. 4, footnote 14, cited in: Collins, *The Ecological Constitution*, p. 3.

1695 Ecological Law and Governance Association, 'Oslo Manifesto ', Article 4.

1696 Christina Wood, *Nature's Trust: Environmental Law for a New Ecological Age*, Cambridge University Press, Cambridge, 2013, citing the entire book: Collins, *The Ecological Constitution*, p. 3.

a whole, our management systems are not sophisticated enough to address the situation from an ecological perspective and investigate the impact of the discharge on the functioning of the river and the ecosystem – including people.[1697]

However, within the hierarchy of law, it makes perfect sense to include any important public interest in constitutions. That is because constitutions are the supreme documents capable of neutralising all conflicting legislation, limiting the actions of power, and ensuring stability over time.[1698] Constitutions are, therefore, one of the tools that can be used to achieve the goal of a sustainable planet through the coordinated accumulation of local action.[1699] The constitutional recognition and codification of environmental value as a 'right' of individuals and citizens implies the explicit provision of remedies and, ultimately, sanctions for failure to fulfil environmental duties and responsibilities. Emphasising the positive aspects of constitutional recognition, whether in the form of a directive provision or a binding legal norm as a human right, should be considered important and functional in terms of accelerating the judicialisation process of the right to a healthy environment.[1700] As will be seen shortly, this function can be highly instrumental in preventing climate change and establishing green constitutionalism.

From a green perspective, the duty-rights dichotomy not only strengthens the individual's position in preventing environmental pollution, protecting the country's natural fabric, and improving the environment but also provides a firm constitutional basis for the initiatives of non-governmental organisations. Such a constitutional basis theoretically gives citizens and non-governmental organisations the right to intervene directly in activities that destroy nature. In the face of this intervention, law enforcement cannot use force in the name of 'public order'.[1701] That is because what citizens guard is the 'environmental public order' and the unity and integrity of the country. In conclusion, the obligation imposed on the state by the environmental regulations in the constitution constitutes a constitutional basis for

---

[1697] Cullinan, *Wild Law*, p. 113.

[1698] Collins, *The Ecological Constitution*, p. 19.

[1699] Collins, *The Ecological Constitution*, p. 1.

[1700] Kaboğlu – Yancı Özalp, *Çevre Hakkı*, p. 59.

[1701] The concept of 'country' here is used by Kaboğlu and Yancı Özalp not in the sense of a political unit with sovereignty but an ecosystem within borders.

effectively implementing the right to live in a healthy environment and the precautionary principle.[1702] In addition, the constitutional recognition of 'environmental crimes', such as ecocide,[1703] would ensure a more effective realisation of the right to a healthy environment.[1704]

An example of ecological measures that can be taken within the framework of existing constitutional provisions is the criminalisation of industrial fishing in Venezuela, which significantly harms marine life, and its prohibition to protect small-scale fisheries. Thus, both the natural balance and the economic livelihoods of Indigenous and local people were protected.[1705] Thus, on the one hand, people's right to live in a healthy and balanced environment and their right to self-development and a life worthy of human dignity have been guaranteed, while on the other hand, contributing to the preservation of the ocean ecosystem. Adopting a similar approach is possible for other countries as well.

6.1.2 Whether existing environmental provisions in constitutions can serve as a basis for a green constitutional order

Constitutions are important because these texts, at the top of the legal system, set the rules that society must follow, including human rights and the responsibilities of power. Constitutions also express who we are as a society and who we aspire to be. However, on climate change, our current constitutions are failing us. To date, constitutions worldwide have reflected our grand human conceit that we are somehow separate from and even superior to the rest of the natural world.[1706] Nevertheless, reinterpreting existing constitutions in the light of green constitutionalism principles with climate change in mind – especially given that politicians are unlikely to change them under the current circumstances – is one practical way to prevent the problem from deepening.

Understandably, the first written constitutions focused not on protecting nature but on limiting political power since rights and freedoms were proclaimed through declarations. The United States and France are typical

[1702] Kaboğlu – Yancı Özalp, *Çevre Hakkı*, pp. 71–2.
[1703] See 4.2.3
[1704] Kaboğlu – Yancı Özalp, *Çevre Hakkı*, p. 59. (Emphasis is mine.)
[1705] Löwy, *Ecosocialism*, Ecosocial Struggles of Indigenous Peoples (Loc. 985).
[1706] Collins, *The Ecological Constitution*, p. IX (foreword by David R. Boyd).

examples of this. Article 16 of the 1789 Declaration of the Rights of Man and Citizen states that *in a society where the separation of powers is not ensured and liberties are not secured, there is no constitution*, providing the classic definition of a constitution. The inclusion of rights and freedoms in constitutional texts was generally secondary until the twentieth century.[1707] Until then, the focus of constitutions was usually on the organs of the state and the balance between them. The conception of constitutionalism as a general guarantee of rights and freedoms for all and of a life of dignity for all came later, mainly after World War II. Still, nature was not a concern for the constituent powers for centuries.

However, the last three decades have seen an explosion of states globally seeking to protect the environment through rights-based provisions enshrined in constitutions. Boyd rightly calls this the 'environmental rights revolution'.[1708] Besides, other rights already enshrined in constitutions can also be violated by states and corporations, either directly harming nature or indirectly failing to prevent harm. From this perspective, the rights to equality, life, liberty, security of person, water, and health, as well as the concept of human dignity, can serve as a valuable guide for taking the necessary measures against climate protection.[1709] Of course, for this to happen, human rights must be considered a nonhuman-centred concept, which in itself is a revolutionary approach.[1710]

In this framework, Kaboğlu and Yancı Özalp argue that in constitutions that first regulate the state and power, and then rights and freedoms, thanks to that the territorial element of the state as a part of the Earth is now more visibly present, a kind of constitutionalisation of the country or, conversely, a process of territorialisation of the constitution has been observed. That is because humans exist thanks to nature, and the state exists thanks to humans. Therefore, humans and the state owe their existence to the environment and nature.[1711] Moreover, the anachronism that occurs today when we talk about the sovereignty of states and the protection of territories within borders is

---

1707 Kaboğlu – Yancı Özalp, *Çevre Hakkı*, p. 48.

1708 See David R. Boyd, *The Environmental Rights Revolution: A Global Study of Constitutions, Human Rights, and the Environment*, UBC Press, Vancouver, 2012.

1709 Collins, *The Ecological Constitution*, p. 112.

1710 Bosselmann, *The Principle of Sustainability*, p. 151.

1711 Kaboğlu – Yancı Özalp, *Çevre Hakkı*, pp. 48–9.

most evident in environmental policies. That is because at the centre of the concept of state sovereignty is the protection of territorial integrity against external threats. However, harmful substances crossing borders and reaching the territory violate this integrity daily. At the current level of the industrial age, states are unable to fulfil even their most basic duties, namely, to protect the territory of their citizens against foreign invasions.[1712] Accordingly, many constitutions, despite their shortcomings and problematic provisions, should now be recognised as texts open to reading from the perspective of an environmental state.[1713]

Some of the states that include provisions on environmental protection in their constitutions guarantee the right to a healthy and balanced environment, while others impose an obligation, and sometimes a duty, on governments to protect the environment. Some constitutions also impose similar duties on citizens.[1714] For example, Article 45 of the Spanish Constitution sets out the main rule with the sentence, *Everyone has the right to enjoy an environment favourable to the development of his personality and is under an obligation to protect it.* Similarly, Article 66 of the Portuguese Constitution states, *Everyone has the right to a healthy and ecologically balanced environment and is also under a duty to defend it.* Thus, these two constitutions impose a duty on public authorities, based on the need for collective solidarity, to protect and improve the quality of life, to take measures to protect the environment, to rationally use all natural resources to defend and restore the environment and to protect and enhance environmental values.[1715] Similarly, Article 56 of the Constitution of the Republic of Türkiye states that *Everyone has the right to live in a healthy and balanced environment. It is the duty of the State and the citizen to improve the environment, to protect environmental health, and to prevent environmental pollution*, thus placing the duty to improve, protect, and prevent environmental pollution on both the state and the citizen.

1712 Bosselmann, *When Two Worlds Collide*, p. 92.

1713 Kaboğlu – Yancı Özalp, *Çevre Hakkı*, p. 78.

1714 P. Kromerk, 'Quel Droit à l'Environnement? Historique et Développements', in *Enviorennement et Droits de l'Homme*, UNESCO, 1986, p. 113 et seq., cited in: Kaboğlu – Yancı Özalp, *Çevre Hakkı*, p. 50.

1715 Kaboğlu – Yancı Özalp, *Çevre Hakkı*, p. 57. For some other examples, see Kaboğlu – Yancı Özalp, *Çevre Hakkı*, pp. 58–9.

Harm to nature has a present and foreseeable negative impact on exercising a wide range of rights. Therefore, eliminating these harms should be recognised as primarily the responsibility of states.[1716] In this context, states should develop a rights-based approach to conserving, protecting, restoring, using, and enjoying healthy ecosystems and biodiversity. Developing a rights-based approach would clarify the responsibilities of states and corporations, trigger ambitious action, highlight the plight of people experiencing poverty and the most vulnerable, and engage people in generating and implementing solutions.[1717]

Within the scope of the green constitutionalism approach, activities that have a detrimental impact on the environment should be subjected to a proportionality test since they limit the right to a healthy and balanced environment, and it should be examined whether they touch the essence of the right. It should be noted that the concepts of 'balance and health' go beyond human beings and include animals (fauna) and plants (flora).[1718] When the balance between flora, fauna, and humans, all the ecosystem's components, is disrupted, the essence of the right to a healthy environment is violated. For example, suppose mining in a forested area disrupts this triple relation balance as 'components of life' in that forest, in other words, the ecosystem. In that case, it means that the essence of the right to the environment is violated.[1719]

Accordingly, even in today's capitalist economic order, environmental provisions in constitutions and environmental law require public authorities to use their existing powers to limit the freedom of trade and industry. Concerns that such a restriction would be unlawful are unfounded, as the social and public function of the right to property justifies restrictions on this right. As a matter of fact, property rights, which can be restricted for the purpose of public interest, cannot be exercised contrary to them.[1720] Therefore, in light of climate change, it is necessary to re-evaluate which economic activities can

---

1716 For a comprehensive report on various court decisions on environmental damages, the link between these damages and human rights, and the human rights obligations of states arising from this link, see OHCHR, A/HRC/28/61.

1717 Boyd, *Report of… (A/75/161)*, p. 17, § 66.

1718 Kaboğlu – Yancı Özalp, *Çevre Hakkı*, p. 73.

1719 Kaboğlu – Yancı Özalp, *Çevre Hakkı*, p. 77.

1720 Kaboğlu – Yancı Özalp, *Çevre Hakkı*, pp. 42–3.

be restricted for public interest purposes and which can be halted because they are contrary to the public interest.

In countries where rights violations can be brought before higher judicial authorities through mechanisms such as individual application, the rights to life and health and the right to live in a healthy environment stand out as the rights on which courts base their decisions. These rights can become obstacles to climate change worsening through the teleological and/or dynamic interpretation method used by the high courts. In the teleological interpretation method, the *ratio legis*[1721] of the regulations comes to the forefront rather than their text. What is meant by this is the 'basic understanding' on which the regulation is based. In particular, objective-teleological interpretation aims to reveal the objective purpose of the norm by ignoring or overriding the meaning and purpose attributed to the norm by the historical rule-maker.[1722]

Dynamic interpretation, on the other hand, assumes that the rule-maker cannot determine the meanings of norms in a single and unchangeable way and that meanings can change, especially over time. In this framework, the judge's task is to reflect the change over time in the norm and to adapt the meaning of the norm to the change.[1723] Whether through teleological or dynamic interpretation, the rights to life, a healthy environment, and health, found in almost all constitutions today, can be transformed into tools to stop climate change within the framework of green constitutionalism. Nevertheless, that is only possible if the high courts develop a perspective and will in this direction.

6.1.2.1 Right to life

The right to life, considered the most fundamental human right, has long been violated by the current economic order. For example, it has long been known that chemicals used as insecticides or to prevent wild plants from damaging crops can cause significant health problems and even death. As early as 1962, Carson wrote that,

---

1721 Latin for 'legal meaning and purpose'.

1722 Bertil Emrah Oder, *Anayasa Yargısında Yorum Yöntemleri*, Beta, İstanbul, 2010, pp. 102–4.

1723 Oder, *Anayasa Yargısında Yorum Yöntemleri*, p. 225.

> If the Bill of Rights contains no guarantee that a citizen shall be secure against lethal poisons distributed either by private individuals or by public officials, it is surely only because our forefathers, despite their considerable wisdom and foresight, could conceive of no such problem.[1724]

Despite being so toxic, these chemicals were allowed to be used by people unaware of the danger. Industrial agricultural practices have brought many people into contact with these toxic substances without their consent, causing cancer and their eventual death.

For many years, activities that damage ecosystems and the decline in biodiversity have violated and threatened the right to life.[1725] *Environmental degradation, climate change, and unsustainable development constitute some of the most pressing and serious threats to the ability of present and future generations to enjoy the right to life*, the UN Human Rights Committee stated in its 2018 general comment.[1726] As an example of this perspective being reflected in national high court decisions, the Supreme Court of Pakistan, in its judgement on the construction of an electricity grid,[1727] recognised the concept of life as a free, convenient, comfortable, and clean life and stated that any action likely to harm life would violate the citizen's right to enjoy life in accordance with the law. Thus, it rightly put the right to life ahead of economic activity.

The Supreme Court of India took a similar approach. In a case brought by a person who claimed that his field and drinking water were contaminated due to the dumping of waste in the Bokaro River by an iron and steel company, the Supreme Court ruled that the right to life includes the right to enjoy unpolluted water and air for the full enjoyment of life.[1728] Thus, it ruled that the right to life guarantees not only 'not to be killed' but also protection against pollution that would prevent the enjoyment of life.

[1724] Carson, *Silent Spring*, p. 19.

[1725] Boyd, *Report of… (A/75/161)*, p. 11, § 37.

[1726] UN Human Rights Committee, *General Comment No. 36 on Article 6: Right to Life*, CCPR/C/GC/36, 2018, p. 13, § 62.

[1727] *Shehla Zia and Others vs. WAPDA*, PLD SC 693, 1994.

[1728] *Subhash Kumar v. States of Bihar and Ors*, AIR 420, 1991 SCR (1) 5, 9 January 1991. However, it has been criticised that the Court did a cursory reading of the right to a healthy environment by rejecting the applicant's request for a *Public Interest Litigation* and not deciding not to delve deep into the crucks of the matter. See Surbhi Pareek, *Case Analysis – Subhash Kumar V. State of Bihar, 1991*, p. 6.

These two decisions are examples of how the right to life, which is enshrined in almost all constitutions worldwide, could be used effectively against environmental degradation and the destruction of nature. In this respect, the right to life can also be instrumental in limiting the economic order based on fossil fuels that cause climate change since it is now a scientifically proven fact that fossil fuels cause global warming, which is driving us towards the sixth extinction, as presented at the book's first part. Today, despite this fact, explorations of new oil deposits, natural gas agreements, coal mine operations, and openings of new fossil fuel-fired thermal power plants constitute a direct interference with the right to life of people and the ecosystem. For the judiciary to allow this to happen is contrary to the very purpose of law: to keep all of us safe and sound. International courts and higher judicial bodies should take this into account and actively use the right to life in climate cases to prevent further damage to the ecosystem that sustains us.

6.1.2.2 Right to a healthy environment

As seen earlier, environmental interests can be protected through judicial interpretation of other rights. However, the best practice in this area is the recognition of an autonomous right to the environment that goes beyond the scope of existing rights, such as the right to life.[1729] The right to a clean, healthy, and sustainable environment is constitutionally guaranteed in 110 countries around the world.[1730] Data also reveal that environmental rights recognised in constitutions are effective: Countries that recognise constitutional environmental rights rank higher in environmental performance, have smaller carbon footprints, and are better at preventing dangerous air pollutants, including greenhouse gases, than countries that do not.[1731]

[1729] Collins, *The Ecological Constitution*, p. 35. At this point in her work, Collins refers to the *Compilation of Good Practices* report prepared by John H. Knox for the UN as '*best practice*'. However, Knox emphasises in paragraph 4 of his report that it should be called 'good practices' rather than 'best practice' because in many cases there is no single 'best' practice. See OHCHR, A/HRC/28/61, p. 3, § 4.

[1730] UN General Assembly, *A/HRC/43/53*, p. 4, § 10.

[1731] David R. Boyd, *The Right to a Healthy Environment: Revitalizing Canada's Constitution*, UBC Press, Vancouver, 2015, pp. 107–21, cited in: Collins, *The Ecological Constitution*, p. 36.

Despite this empirical evidence of their effectiveness, there is also criticism of the constitutional right to a healthy environment. It is claimed that human rights-based environmental rights are anthropocentric, Eurocentric, neo-colonialist, ineffective, misunderstood, and even counterproductive.[1732] At the core of these criticisms is the anthropocentric legal order and the judicial rights structures articulated to it. As a matter of fact, the right to live in a healthy environment has become a tool that creates, justifies, and legitimises the legal powers of humans over nature. This anthropocentric law and structuring reinforces these powers by treating (in most cases constitutional) claims about the environment and its benefits for human development as a right. Such an unwavering anthropocentric ideological orientation towards rights seems to endorse, legitimise, and reinforce the type of unrestrained anthropocentric behaviour many today consider to have ushered the Earth into the Anthropocene.[1733]

There are points where these criticisms are justified. However, it should be reiterated that the right to live in a healthy environment can be interpreted in a nature-centred way through various methods of interpretation. Therefore, this right is also one of our best tools in the fight against climate change. We should, therefore, focus and build on examples of good practice. Although the protection of the natural environment is actually a humanist imperative,[1734] even this anthropocentric perception makes a significant contribution to sustainability. That is because the needs of humans and other natural beings, such as clean air, clean water, and biodiversity, overlap to a great extent. Empirical evidence shows that such rights make a difference on the ground and improve ecological health for all species. So, whether or not environmental human rights form a core element of a nature-centred law, they undoubtedly serve the struggle for ecological sustainability.[1735]

From a nature-centred perspective, the fundamental element of the right to live in a healthy environment is the existence of healthy ecosystems and

---

[1732] For sources on these claims, see Collins, *The Ecological Constitution*, p. 36.

[1733] Louis J. Kotzé – Paola V. Calzadilla, 'Somewhere between Rhetoric and Reality: Environmental Constitutionalism and the Rights of Nature in Ecuador', *Transnational Environmental Law*, Vol. 6, No. 3, November 2017, pp. 401–3, cited in: Collins, *The Ecological Constitution*, p. 37.

[1734] Löwy, *Ecosocialism*, What Is Ecosocialism (Loc. 213).

[1735] Collins, *The Ecological Constitution*, p. 39.

the preservation of biodiversity. Following an application by Colombia, the Inter-American Court of Human Rights (IACtHR) stated that the right to a healthy environment as an autonomous right, unlike other rights, protects not only human beings but also the other components of nature, such as forests, rivers, and seas. According to the Court, the legal interests inherent in the components of nature should be protected through this right, even if there is no certainty or evidence of a risk to humans. That means that the right to a healthy environment protects nature and the environment not only because of its benefits to humanity or the negative impact of its degradation on other human rights, such as health, life, or personal integrity but also because of its importance for other living organisms with which we share the planet and which deserve protection in their own right.[1736] The Court's approach is truly an example of green constitutionalism and is highly illuminating on how existing constitutional norms can be effectively used to protect ecosystems.

In another case brought against Argentina by an association representing Indigenous communities, the IACtHR ruled that the right of Indigenous communities to live in a healthy environment was violated due to damage to forests and biodiversity in their territories,[1737] continuing the nature-centred human rights perspective of considering human and natural rights together.

In order to realise the right to live in a healthy and balanced environment, it is important to fulfil various preconditions. These conditions, which have become an international legal document through the 1998 Aarhus Convention,[1738] are known as the rights to information, participation, and access to justice. In the context of climate change, it should be recognised that states have an obligation to provide the public with accessible, affordable, and understandable information on the causes and consequences of the global climate crisis. That includes incorporating the importance of healthy biodiversity into education curricula at all levels.[1739]

[1736] Inter-American Court of Human Rights, Recommendation OC-23/17, date: 15.11.2017, § 62.

[1737] Inter-American Court of Human Rights, *Association of Indigenous Communities of Lhaka Honhat (Our Land) vs. Argentina*, Judgment, date: 06.02.202.

[1738] Original title '*Convention on Access to Information, Public Participation in Decision-Making and Access to Justice in Environmental Matters*'.

[1739] Boyd, *Report of… (A/75/161)*, p. 18, § 69 (a).

States should also develop an inclusive, equitable, and gender-based approach to public participation in all actions related to the conservation, protection, restoration, and sustainable use of nature. That should prioritise the empowerment of the most directly affected segments of society.[1740]

Finally, states must recognise and realise the right of all those affected by climate change to access justice and other effective remedies at low cost and without delay. That would hold accountable states and corporations that fail to fulfil their responsibilities in preserving, protecting, and restoring nature.[1741]

6.1.2.3 Right to health

Healthy ecosystems act as a buffer against the emergence of epidemics. In contrast, damage to nature, such as deforestation, contributes to the emergence of diseases in wildlife, domestic animals, and humans. For example, research shows that the fragmentation of North American forests increases the risk of Lyme disease spread by ticks. The emergence of the Nipah virus has also been linked to the intensification of pig farms in Malaysia. Similarly, deforestation in West Africa has contributed to the emergence and spread of the Ebola outbreak.[1742] In addition, scientists have long recognised the link between the degradation of ecosystems and the emergence of zoonotic diseases. It is even claimed that the spread of COVID-19, which recently turned into a global pandemic, is also linked to ecosystem degradation.[1743] Therefore, climate change and biodiversity loss also violate the right to health.

Moreover, local and Indigenous communities often rely on traditional medicines, especially in developing countries. These medicines rely on a wide variety of wild plant and animal species. The illegal collection and trade of these species and the loss of their habitats adversely affect the health systems of millions of people, thus jeopardising their right to health.[1744] From this perspective, the right to health is a right that can be used by high courts to protect ecosystems if they establish a link between it and biodiversity.

[1740] Boyd, *Report of… (A/75/161)*, p. 18, § 69 (b).
[1741] Boyd, *Report of… (A/75/161)*, p. 18, § 69 (c).
[1742] Boyd, *Report of… (A/75/161)*, p. 12, § 40.
[1743] See Chiara Castelli – Marta Castelli – Nicola Comincioli – Maria Laura Parisi – Nicola Pontarollo – Sergio Vergalli, 'Ecosytem Degradation and the Spread of COVID-19', *Environmental Monitoring and Assessment*, No. 195, paper 836, 2023.
[1744] Boyd, *Report of… (A/75/161)*, p. 12, § 42.

Similarly, the link between the right to a healthy life and the right to access healthy food, clean water, and hygienic conditions must be considered. The right to a healthy life cannot be protected in an environment where food, water, and hygienic conditions are unhealthy. In this context, courts can limit and prevent state and corporate activities that violate access to healthy food, water, and hygienic conditions through the right to health.

The ecological approach to the right to health is reflected in court decisions in Germany, where, in an increasing number of cases, courts are ruling that the use of land and resources under property rights is limited according to the 'public welfare'. That includes, for example, limiting the use of chemical fertilisers and insecticides in fields, protecting livestock from overgrazing, and banning certain harmful ingredients. That is one of the results of the GFCC's *Naßauskiesung* ruling many years ago, which can be seen as green constitutionalism.[1745] In this case, the Court held that private land use can be limited by the rights and interests of the general public to access certain elements, such as water, which are essential for human well-being. The Court found that the legislature's regulation excluding groundwater from the scope of the property right did not contravene the German Constitution, as water is one of the most important essential elements for humans, animals, and plants.[1746] However, it should not be overlooked that the overriding concern in the judgement was not ecological but public health in the context of the social state principle under Article 20 of the German Constitution. Respect for the intrinsic value of the life of nonhuman beings cannot be observed in this decision, as this would have required the adoption of much harsher restrictions on human access to water.[1747] Today, however, it is clear that it is no longer possible to consider human and public health in isolation and that the health of humans, animals, and nature must be considered together within the framework of the 'one-health' approach.[1748]

[1745] Decision of 15 July 1981, BVerfGE 58, 300.

[1746] BVerfGE 58, 300, § 341

[1747] Bosselmann, *The Principle of Sustainability*, p. 153.

[1748] See 'One Health', *United Nations*, 21 September 2017.

6.2 Climate change's impact on constitutions

Green constitutionalism is a more inclusive approach that transcends constitutional texts and emerges to transform anthropocentric legal orders into nature-centred legal orders within the climate change framework. As seen under the preceding headings, constitutional norms can be interpreted within the scope of green constitutionalism and used to protect the ecosystem. However, ideally, constitutions should first and foremost be drafted with an ecological logic and establish a nature-centred social and legal structure.

A constitution can turn into an ecological one through amendments, judicial interpretation, or a combination of both. For an ecosystemic democracy, explicit amendment is preferable because it opens space for dialogue and debate and increases the legitimacy of outcomes. However, even without explicit amendment, ecological principles can be incorporated into the constitutional bloc through judicial interpretation. In the current ecological crisis, as Collins points out, many judges in many countries see the logic of measuring the legitimacy of state action by the extent to which it comports with the non-derogable ecological laws.[1749]

Just as one cannot fight an atomic bomb with wooden swords, one cannot fight a planet-wide crisis with simple regulatory measures.[1750] In this context, the ecological transformation of national constitutions aims to harmonise these supreme texts of domestic law with the non-negotiable laws of nature. Such harmonisation is urgently needed in the Anthropocene and amid climate change.[1751]

As the impact of climate change has become more keenly felt by people, many countries have sought to enshrine climate protection provisions in their constitutions. For example, the 1998 amendment to the Constitution of the Dominican Republic established that it is a priority of the State to legally prepare and implement a nationwide regulatory plan to ensure the efficient and sustainable use of the Nation's natural resources, in line with the need to adapt to climate change.[1752] As amended in 2013, the Vietnamese Constitution includes an article stating that it is a state policy to take initiatives to prevent

---

[1749] Collins, *The Ecological Constitution*, pp. 24–5.
[1750] Barrau, *Le Plus Grand …*, pp. 126–7.
[1751] Collins, *The Ecological Constitution*, p. 2.
[1752] 2015 Constitution of the Dominican Republic, art. 194.

and build resilience to natural disasters and climate change.[1753] Thailand's new 2017 constitution also states that national change should aim for effective, equitable, and sustainable water resources management that addresses all aspects of water demand as well as environmental and climatic changes.[1754]

The new Cuban Constitution, adopted as recently as 2019, also felt the need to address climate change under the heading 'International Relations'. According to the Constitution, in its international relations, the Cuban State promotes the protection and conservation of the environment, as well as the prevention of climate change, which threatens the existence of the human species, through the recognition of common but differentiated responsibilities; the establishment of a more just and equitable international economic order; and the elimination of irrational patterns of production and consumption.[1755] Following a 2016 amendment, the Zambian Constitution is more direct, stating that the state shall establish and implement mechanisms to prevent climate change.[1756]

The democratic uprising in Tunisia in December 2010 against corruption and economic stagnation is considered the start of the Arab Spring. Most countries in the region have yet to stabilise after their leaders fled the country or, as in Libya, were assassinated. Tunisia was the only country to emerge from the uprisings with a successful new constitution.[1757] Even though Tunisia has embarked on an anti-democratic path again due to the repressive practices of President Qais Said, the new constitution adopted in 2016 makes Tunisia – at least at the constitutional level – a pioneer in the world on climate change. The new Constitution guarantees the right to a healthy and balanced environment and the right to participate in climate protection.[1758] Thanks to this article, Tunisia is currently the only country in the world that constitutionally grants its citizens procedural rights on climate change.[1759]

[1753] 1992 Constitution of Vietnam, art. 63, § 1.
[1754] Constitution of the Kingdom of Thailand of 2017, art. 258, (g), § 1.
[1755] Cuban Constitution of 2019, art. 16, (f).
[1756] 1991 Constitution of Zambia, art. 257 (g).
[1757] See Serkan Koybasi, 'Yeni Tunus Anayasası'nın Yazım Süreci ve Sürecin Sonuca Yansıması', *Prof Dr Feridun Yenisey'e Armağan*, Vol. II, Beta, İstanbul, 2014, pp. 2297–362.
[1758] 2016 Constitution of Tunisia, Art. 45.
[1759] Colling, *The Ecological Constitution*, p. 107.

These examples that explicitly address climate change are promising. However, unless there is a change in the economic infrastructure, we should not expect these regulations to create miracles. Unfortunately, It is impossible to say that they have been fully implemented and that these states are no longer contributing to and combating climate change. Tunisia's exceptional procedural rights aside, the most glaring gap in climate constitutionalism around the world today is the lack of clear and substantive constitutional rights to a safe climate.[1760] However, it is also evident that the humanist dualist approach is being questioned at the constitutional level, mainly due to the struggles for animal and nature rights, and that some current constitutions are even written with a more nature-centred approach. If this situation spreads across the world, it could be predicted that constitutional law will play an important role in tackling climate change. Therefore, it is worth taking a closer look at such constitutions.

6.2.1 Basic principles of nature-centred constitutions

Like all other life forms, humans need a healthy biosphere to survive, prosper, and reproduce. Recognising this scientific reality, today's ecological constitutions represent one of humanity's best remaining hopes for overcoming our own destructive hubris and building a sustainable future. That is because nature-centred constitutions see nature not merely as an asset humans can exploit but as an extraordinary community we are fortunate to be a part of.[1761] The regulations in constitutions that recognise nature as a subject of rights establish a non-Western interpretation of the human-nature relationship and make Indigenous peoples' view of nature the basis of social rules. From this perspective, green constitutionalism does not establish a hierarchical government but one that takes into account the rights of all members of the ecosystem, including humans, and regulates all forms of this governance in accordance with basic ecological principles.[1762] It also ensures that human rights, such as the right to live in a healthy environment and the related rights to health, culture, and social rights, are more secure.[1763]

1760 Collins, *The Ecological Constitution*, p. 107.
1761 Collins, *The Ecological Constitution*, p. XI (foreword by David R. Boyd).
1762 Bosselmann, *The Principle of Sustainability*, p. 171.
1763 Durmaz, *Doğanın Hakları*, p. 270.

Accordingly, constitutions that take climate change into account recognise not just people but all members of the ecosystem and the ecosystem as a whole as subjects of rights. Adopting such a rights-based approach would clarify the obligations of states and corporations, foster strong social movements, make the plight of the poorest and most vulnerable more visible, and empower people to find and implement solutions.[1764] Similarly, constitutional recognition of the rights of nature and human environmental rights paves the way for large-scale public participation in climate change decision-making. This participation makes it possible to recognise and respect Indigenous peoples' traditional knowledge as part of the climate science corpus and Indigenous legal systems as an important source of climate law.[1765]

In addition, the adoption of a nature-centred approach by constitutions not only increases the ecological literacy of citizens and encourages them to mobilise legal remedies for nature protection but also provides a democratic and constitutional basis for the decisions of local and national courts, especially the higher judicial bodies. Thus, it facilitates law to function as a tool and even take a leading role in protecting nature and ecosystems and preventing climate change.

A nature-centred constitution recognises humanity's fundamental dependence on nature for our survival and well-being, replaces the anthropocentric perspective with a nature-centred one, ensures that nature's supreme laws shape all human actions, articulates that everyone has environmental rights and responsibilities, holds governments accountable for ensuring that the environmental rights of both people and nature are not violated, and are protected and fulfilled, and defines key guiding principles, including polluter pays, precaution, public trust, *in dubio pro natura* and do not worsen.[1766]

Since green constitutionalism is about making meaningful changes in the real world, nature-centred constitutions and constitutional articles must be understood as binding, not wishful thinking.[1767] First, therefore,

---

[1764] Boyd, *Report of… (A/74/161)*, p. 17, § 62.

[1765] Cuthbert Casey Makondo – David S. G. Thomas, 'Climate Change Adaptation: Linking Indigenous Traditional Knowledge with Western Science for Effective Adaptation', *Environmental Science & Policy*, vol. 88, November 2018, p. 83, cited in: Collins, *The Ecological Constitution*, p. 111.

[1766] Collins, *The Ecological Constitution*, p. IX-X (foreword by David R. Boyd).

[1767] Boyd, *The Environmental Rights Revolution*, pp. 71–7.

constitution-makers should place ecological clauses in the litigable sections of constitutions, and judges should recognise them as enforceable in appeals. Second, to facilitate their implementation, ecological constitutions should establish state authorities tasked with advising the executive and legislature and ensuring that constitutional rights and duties relating to the environment are upheld in the courts.[1768] These could take the form of an ombudsman or boards of civil society and scientists. Their independence from the legislative and executive branches must be constitutionally guaranteed.

Given climate change, states must find ways to constitutionalise ecological sustainability in order to serve their citizens and ensure their own survival.[1769] The best way to do this is to enshrine this principle at the very top of national law. The principle of sustainability should be seen as the underlying foundation of constitutions; in other words, sustainability should not only be enshrined in constitutions but also accepted as a *Grundnorm*. Only in this way would building an 'eco-constitutional' state be possible.[1770]

There are many ways to incorporate the logic of sustainability into constitutions. For example, if a new constitution is being drafted, it would be right to explicitly acknowledge in the opening sentences of its preamble that human existence and health depend on the Earth's ecosystem from which we are born and which ensures our survival. That could be followed by a statement that caring for the ecosystem is one of the primary responsibilities of the new country.[1771] In the case of an existing constitution, it could be amended so that the state recognises the principle of ecological sustainability and observes it in all its actions. It could be enshrined in related articles of constitutions or placed in the 'general principles' section, where it would be recognised that all articles should be understood and interpreted within this framework.

Green constitutionalism inevitably requires international cooperation because the world, in an ecological sense, is globally interconnected. Therefore, the constitutionalisation of sustainability should take place not only at the local level but across the globe. At the heart of global constitutionalism should be a sustainability goal that provides the framework for the

---

1768 Collins, *The Ecological Constitution*, p. 8.
1769 Collins, *The Ecological Constitution*, p. 26.
1770 Bosselmann, *The Principle of Sustainability*, p. 166.
1771 Cullinan, *Wild Law*, p. 19 (foreword by Thomas Berry).

entire transformation. In addition to the important efforts to optimise international environmental law and prepare a global environmental constitution, economic international solidarity seems inevitable. Developing countries need help to break out of unsustainable development models and implement ecological constitutionalist approaches.[1772] The climate funds agreed upon at the last UN climate summits, but never fully realised, should be effectively implemented, and the money collected there should be transferred to the countries of the Global South in a supervised and controlled manner, with the vulnerable countries that will be affected by climate change in the short term first. In addition, the Global North countries should actively assist the countries of the South both materially and physically in their efforts to reduce greenhouse gases and adapt to climate change. All these processes should be supported by a supranational judicial mechanism with sanctioning authority to be established under the umbrella of the UN.

Under green constitutionalism, states are responsible for ensuring that their actions do not violate the right to a healthy environment or other human rights linked to healthy ecosystems and biodiversity. States also have a responsibility to ensure that third parties, especially corporations, do not violate these rights. In addition, states are obliged to create, implement, and enforce the laws, policies, and programmes necessary to realise these rights.[1773]

The Convention on Biological Diversity provides a practical guide to the substantive state responsibilities necessary for green constitutionalism. The list of responsibilities from Articles 5 to 14 of the Convention can be summarised as follows:[1774]

(a) Monitoring and reporting of biodiversity status and threats to biodiversity;
(b) Adoption and implementation of national biodiversity plans;
(c) Prioritising biodiversity in other policy areas, such as health and finance;
(d) Creation of protected areas and other protection measures;
(e) Adopting rules to ensure the sustainable use of biodiversity;
(f) Preparation of legal regulations to protect endangered species;
(g) Restoring degraded ecosystems;

[1772] Collins, *The Ecological Constitution*, p. 9.
[1773] Boyd, *Report of… (A/75/161)*, p. 18, § 70.
[1774] Boyd, *Report of…*, pp. 18–19, § 70.

(h) Preventing the spread of invasive species;
(i) Providing incentives for nature conservation and sustainable use.

This list should be recognised as a core principle of green constitutionalism and actively used by both national and international judicial bodies to monitor the biggest emitter states.

6.2.2 The Constitution of Ecuador as an example of a nature-centred constitution

Many constitutions have already taken a holistic approach to rights-based protection of nature, thus blurring the modern boundaries between humans and nature. The constitutions of Bhutan, Brazil, East Timor, Dominican Republic, Ecuador, Costa Rica, Maldives, Paraguay, Portugal, Venezuela, and Cape Verde include provisions on substantive environmental rights, including an element of ecological balance.[1775]

Some other constitutions set the right to the environment as a limit to other rights, although they cannot yet be defined as nature-centred. Article 37 of the Constitution of Madagascar stipulates that limitations may be imposed on freedom of enterprise in the interest of respect for the environment. In the Estonian Constitution, Article 34 stipulates that freedom of movement and settlement may be limited in order to protect the environment. Article 19 of the Chilean Constitution makes a general provision that certain rights and freedoms may be limited on grounds of environmental protection.[1776]

Today, only two constitutions in the world can be considered to be genuinely nature-centred. These belong to Ecuador and Bolivia. The most important feature of these constitutions, which see ecological diversity as equal to the protection of multiculturalism and extend the tendency to strengthen democracy and participation to environmental democracy, is that they are texts that recognise human beings as part of nature and grant rights to all living beings.[1777]

When we look at the process of the emergence of these constitutions, we see that they are part of the intensive constitution-writing process that has

---

[1775] Collins, *The Ecological Constitution*, p. 38.

[1776] Kaboğlu – Yancı Özalp, *Çevre Hakkı*, p. 62.

[1777] Nihan Yancı Özalp, 'Türkiye Ekolojik Anayasacılığın Neresinde?', *in* Nihan Yancı Özalp – Sinem Şirin (ed.), *1982 Anayasası'nın 30. Yıl Bilançosu*, On İki Levha Yayınları, 2014, Istanbul, p. 109.

been taking place worldwide since the mid-1980s. One reason for this process was the emergence of new states following the collapse of the Soviet Union. The independence of former colonial states such as South Africa also contributed to this wave of constitution writing. Other countries either rewrote or substantially amended their constitutions for various reasons. In most constitutions written during this period, the rising social sensitivity against the destruction of nature and ecosystems found its reflection, and various environmental regulations were incorporated into them. In this context, the coming to power of leftist governments in Latin America in the early 2000s enabled an anti-capitalist ecological tendency to be reflected in constitutions. In this respect, it can be said that the developments in Latin America opened a breach in the dominant ideology worldwide and accordingly created a unique constitutional category.[1778]

In the 2009 Bolivian Constitution, the right to live in a healthy environment is enshrined as a human and natural right, while at the same time, the protection of environmental values is imposed on both the Bolivian people and the state. While the Constitution places environmental sustainability as a duty on the state, Bolivians are also tasked with protecting and defending environmental values.[1779] Article 8 of the Constitution defines the good life as one of the ethical and moral principles of a plural society. Article 34 states that everyone has standing in the case of an attack against the environment. Furthermore, the Bolivian Constitution regulates natural resources, energy, and water separately, and Article 371 prohibits the transfer of nationalised mines to the private sector. In this context, the Bolivian Constitution pushes the boundaries of classical state models, including environmental regulations.[1780]

[1778] Tolga Şirin, 'Yeni Bolivya Anayasası Üzerine Bazı Notlar', *in* Mahmut Fevzi Özlüer – Ilgın Özkaya Özlüer – Tolga Şirin – Nazım Sinan Odabaşı (ed.), *Bolivya Anayasası: Hukuk, Demokrasi, Özerklik*, Phoenix, Ankara, 2012, p. 12.

[1779] Kaboğlu – Yancı Özalp, *Çevre Hakkı*, p. 60.

[1780] Şirin, 'Yeni Bolivya…', p. 34.

A precursor to the Bolivian Constitution that deserves a more detailed examination is the Ecuadorian Constitution,[1781] adopted in 2008.[1782] Indigenous peoples actively participated in drafting this constitution, one of the most important developments to date in the transition from an anthropocentric constitutional order to green constitutionalism. In this way, Mother Nature, a part of Latin American culture, was transformed into a constitutional subject by recognising her rights in this Constitution. Thus, the anthropocentric approach was abandoned in favour of a nature-centred approach, which is considered by Boyd a īme-changing cultural and legal shift that reflects the interdependence of all species and the ecosystems that make life on Earth possible.[1783]

For this reason, it is worth taking a closer look at the Ecuadorian Constitution, the normative pioneer of green constitutionalism. This supreme law, which stipulates that the welfare of the state and citizens should be sought in harmony with nature, is considered the first constitution to recognise the rights of nature.[1784] Thus, by recognising the rights of *Pachamama*, focusing on having a good life in harmony with nature, and including a comprehensive array of environmental rights and responsibilities, the Ecuadorian Constitution became the world's first ecological constitution.[1785] While the Ecuadorian Constitution is generally recognised for these features, it has also taken important steps to realise a complete social transformation[1786] by recognising the principle of *buen vivir* in many of its articles, including the Preamble, which speaks of the intention of the Ecuadorian people to *build a new form of coexistence, in diversity and harmony with nature, to achieve* buen vivir, *the* sumak kawsay. As seen, the principle of the good life is mentioned in the Constitution as both *el buen vivir* in Spanish and *el sumak kawsay*, the term used by the Indigenous Quichwa people.

1781 For the English translation of the Ecuadorian Constitution, see 'Constitution of the Republic of Ecuador', *Political Database of the Americas (Georgetown University)*.

1782 For the developments in Ecuador that formed the historical basis for the adoption of a nature-centred constitution until 2008, see Durmaz, *Doğanın Hakları*, pp. 274–79.

1783 Boyd, *The Rights of Nature*, p. 174.

1784 Cullinan, *Wild Law*, p. 184.

1785 Collins, *The Ecological Constitution*, p. X (foreword by David R. Boyd).

1786 Collins, *The Ecological Constitution*, p. 23.

In addition, the seventh chapter of the second part of the Constitution, Rights to *Buen Vivir*, is entitled Rights of Nature and regulates the rights to water, food, a healthy environment, and nature. Article 71 of this chapter speaks of the right to the integral protection of nature and provides that all persons, communities, peoples, and nations may demand that administrative authorities fulfil their rights to nature. Thus, this article is more comprehensive than the 'right to live in a healthy environment' found in other countries' constitutions. That is because this provision, drafted from a nature-centred perspective, emphasises that nature has its own intrinsic value, separate from humans and that in the event of damage, not only the damage to humans but also to nature should be remedied.[1787]

The article's first paragraph states, *Nature (or* Pachamama*), where life is reproduced and occurs, has the right to integral respect for its existence and for the maintenance and regeneration of its life cycles, structure, functions and evolutionary processes.* Thus, the right of nature to regenerate itself is regulated. In this sense, specific responsibilities are imposed on natural and legal persons and the state to respect and protect this process. That means that any activity that interrupts nature's life cycles and prevents ecological sustainability, even if it does not reach the level of ecocide, has become a violation of the Constitution.

Similarly, the Constitution speaks of collective ownership of the country, territories, as well as natural and cultural assets. The need to protect and develop the qualitative characteristics of the country's territory is also interspersed in various articles.[1788]

Article 275 of the Constitution states that in exercising their rights and fulfilling their responsibilities, individuals, communities, peoples, and nationalities must remain within the framework of interculturality, respect for pluralism, and coexistence in harmony with nature, in accordance with the principle of *buen vivir.* Thus, it is seen that the diversity and pluralism in nature are tried to be reflected in social life. That is a successful application of biomimicry at the constitutional level. That is an obvious reflection of the Indigenous people's contribution to the constitution-writing process.

Article 277 of the Constitution obliges the state to actively safeguard the principle of *buen vivir*, including by guaranteeing the rights of nature.

[1787] Durmaz, *Doğanın Hakları*, p. 282.

[1788] Kaboğlu – Yancı Özalp, *Çevre Hakkı*, p. 60.

Article 319 is also relevant to realising this principle, as it calls for promoting forms of production that improve citizens' quality of life and avoiding the ones that threaten the rights of citizens and nature.

In addition, the second part of the seventh chapter of the Constitution is devoted to biodiversity and natural resources. Articles 395 to 415 enumerate various environmental principles and set out the responsibilities of the state and the rights of individuals to protect nature, biodiversity, and ecosystems. Under this heading, Article 395(1) of the Constitution guarantees a model of sustainable development 'to meet the needs of present and future generations' that preserves biodiversity and the capacity of ecosystems to regenerate themselves naturally, is environmentally balanced, and respects cultural pluralism. Thus, intergenerational justice and sustainability become constitutional regulation, and it is seen that the economic infrastructure is attempted to be transformed through the constitution.

Article 398 requires competent and timely consultation with local communities on any government decision or permit likely to harm the environment and states that public opinion will be considered following criteria established by law and international human rights mechanisms. Thus, the principle of public participation in decision-making, also enshrined in the Aarhus Convention, has been transformed into a constitutional right.

Article 400 of the Constitution, which recognises biodiversity and the country's genetic assets, particularly in agriculture and wildlife, as a public good, is followed by Article 401, which prohibits genetically modified crops and seeds. According to this article, the state must set strict biosafety standards for modern biotechnology products, their experimentation, use, and marketing. The Constitution completely bans risky and experimental biotechnologies. That is a perfect example of how constitutional prohibitions can effectively be used to prevent the right to life from being jeopardised.

Article 406 states that the state should regulate the protection, management, sustainable use, restoration, and boundaries of sensitive and endangered ecosystems and lists some of these ecosystems one by one. High Andes steppes, wetlands, cloud forests, dry and wet tropical forests, mangroves, and marine and coastal ecosystems are the natural assets that the Constitution highlights. In the remainder of this section, natural resources, soil, water, and the biosphere are regulated in detail under separate headings. This section concludes with articles on urban ecology and alternative energy sources.

In addition to these constitutional provisions, Ecuador has also adopted a law that gives nature standing rights and everyone, including the national ombudsman, the right to represent the interests of nature in court. Thus, Christopher Stone's question in the 1970s, 'Should trees have standing? ' has been answered in the affirmative in Ecuador. Since 2008, in this Latin American country, not only trees have standing, but all nature holds full ecological rights.[1789]

All these legal regulations distinguish Ecuador from other countries that pursue economic growth and transform it into a country that seeks the well-being of people in a way that does not threaten the rights of nature.[1790] This approach is a decisive contribution to the green constitutionalism movement that we need in the fight against climate change. That is why the 2008 Ecuadorian Constitution is a milestone in this struggle.

However, there was an intense debate in Ecuador after the entry into force of the Constitution on the realisation of Mother Nature's rights and their effectiveness. Doubts were immediately expressed as to whether the amendments to the Constitution would be implemented.[1791] Indeed, it was not easy to recognise nature as a subject of rights to be integrated into the legal system and applied in complex cases. That is because, traditionally, people have tended to see nature as an *object* or, more precisely, as a *resource*. For this reason, lower courts were initially hesitant to give nature a voice.

However, the government's strong political stance on the rights of Mother Nature has encouraged the judiciary to rule in accordance with the new, changing law. For example, after the government took action against an illegal gold mine, a court[1792] ordered an immediate halt to mining activities in order to protect the rights of nature and people and ordered that the Ecuadorian armed forces and the national police cooperate to control the illegal mining activities in the area, which pose a significant danger to nature and the immediate environment, and to destroy all objects, vehicles, and other tools used in the mining activity. Indeed, a few days later, nearly 120 machines used

---

[1789] See also Hugo Echevarría, 'When Courts Meet Nature: A Real Case on Rights of Nature', *Vermont Journal of Environmental Law (blog)*, 18 August 2018.

[1790] Cullinan, *Wild Law*, p. 185.

[1791] For one of these, see Levent Korkut, *in* Mahmut Boynudelik (ed.), *Ecological Constitution*, Yeni İnsan Publishing House, Istanbul, 2011, p. 96.

[1792] The Second Pichincha Criminal Guarantees Tribunal.

in illegal mining were destroyed with explosives dropped from helicopters. In response to the miners' claim that this violated their property rights, the government held meetings to emphasise that the economic interests of the owners of the destroyed machinery were secondary to the rights to life and health of the local population.[1793]

In the case of a legal mining operation, in September 2020, the Cotacachi Court issued a ruling halting the operations of a copper mine in a highly biodiverse cloud forest in Llurimagua. Stating that the rights of nature trumped the economic rights of mining companies, the court ordered the Ministry of the Environment, under the supervision of non-governmental organisations, including universities, to take steps to remedy the situation within three months and decided on the revocation of the relevant permits if the government failed to prove that mining in the area could be carried out without threatening the extinction of endangered species.[1794] Thus, in this case, the Court not only recognised nature as an autonomous subject of constitutional rights but also used the precautionary principle precisely as it should.

What completed this revolutionary transformation was the Constitutional Court's incorporation of articles recognising nature as a subject of constitutional rights into its decisions.[1795] Two of these decisions will be discussed in detail later.[1796] Thanks to these decisions, it was confirmed that the constitutional provisions would not remain on paper and that they were, in the words of the Court, *(…) not mere rhetorical lyricism, but a transcendental statement and a historical commitment.*[1797]

6.2.3 Are nature-centred constitutions practically transformative?

Without changing the economic infrastructure, changing constitutions, which are merely superstructure institutions, would not yield the expected and hoped-for results against climate change. In an environment where the international political and economic order is based on capitalism, there is

---

1793 May – Daly, *Global Environmental Constitutionalism*, pp. 225–6.

1794 'Court Decision on Llurimagua – Rights of Nature Case – Ecuador', *Global Alliance for the Rights of Nature*, 12 November 2020.

1795 Echevarría, 'When Courts Meet Nature'.

1796 See 6.3.4

1797 Case no. 1149-19-JP/20, § 31.

always the possibility that the transformation seen in the constitutions of Ecuador and Bolivia, which also continue to be part of the capitalist world, would remain on paper. Nobody realistically expected these countries to change overnight. These experiences show that even when a society recognises the rights of nature, there will still be tremendous challenges when these rights confront entrenched interests.[1798] Indeed, the governments of Bolivia's Evo Morales and Ecuador's Rafael Correa, who continued to engage in high risk and ecologically harmful extractive activities for economic reasons, have disappointed those who expected a social and legal green transformation from these countries.

These promises depended on genuine respect for Indigenous cultures, which have strong political bases in both countries, have resisted marginalisation, and have survived centuries of oppression. Accordingly, the Indigenous understanding of *buen vivir*, aiming to build societies in harmony with nature, became the official discourse of governments and was even recognised by law. In both cases, however, the escalation of industrial-scale development and mineral extraction replaced this promising discourse.[1799]

In the context of class contradictions, it has become evident every day that the development of Mother Nature as an entity could only be possible through the development of social conditions for a 'good life', both material and spiritual.[1800] Evo Morales' rhetoric on combating climate change and defending Mother Nature has not always been in line with his government's concrete practices. Oil production and mining have remained central to the Bolivian government's development strategy since the adoption of the Constitution. Moreover, expansionist policies have pitted Morales against Indigenous peoples. A highway project through a pristine forest led to protests and a temporary halt. Like a right-wing populist politician, Morales' deputy Álvaro García Linera, who was once imprisoned as a youth for his involvement in the Indigenous Tupa Katari guerrilla movement, accused the protesting communities of being 'enemies of national development' and of

[1798] Boyd, *The Rights of Nature*, p. 183.

[1799] Klein, *That Changes Everything*, p. 256.

[1800] Fevzi Özlüer, 'Pachamama'nın Gücü ya da Bolivya Anayasası'nın Uluslararası Hukuka ve Siyasete Etkisi', *in* Mahmut Fevzi Özlüer – Ilgın Özkaya Özlüer – Tolga Şirin – Nazım Sinan Odabaşı (ed.), *Bolivya Anayasası: Hukuk, Demokrasi, Özerklik*, Phoenix, Ankara, 2012, p. 73.

being 'manipulated by non-governmental organisations that serve foreign interests'.[1801]

Similarly, implementing nature's rights has become a formidable challenge in Ecuador due to the state's plan to promote economic growth through increased extraction, including in sensitive and protected ecological areas. Constitutionalising nature's rights has not prevented the spread of unsustainable mining. In fact, in the few years immediately after the new constitution came into force in 2008, the Ecuadorian government arrested hundreds of Indigenous and civil society leaders protesting its aggressive plans to expand mining.[1802] Ecological Action,[1803] a long-standing organisation founded by ecofeminists, and the Pachamama Foundation,[1804] another well-established organisation that had worked to enshrine the rights of Indigenous peoples and nature in the Constitution, were shut down for their involvement in acts of violence.[1805]

Therefore, after the recognition of the rights of nature in the Constitution, an uphill struggle for protecting these rights continued. The main reason for this was that capitalist practices could not be abandoned.[1806] In Ecuador, where oil revenues constitute one of the most important items in the state treasury, the government of Rafael Correa, who can be considered the architect of the ecological constitution, made an agreement with the international community in 2007, just before the adoption of this constitution, to leave 1 billion barrels of oil under the ground in Yasuní National Park,[1807] the extraction of which had been a matter of debate since the mid-1980s. This region is one of

---

1801 Löwy, *Ecosocialism*, Ecosocial Struggles of Indigenous Peoples (Loc. 989).

1802 Craig M. Kauffman – Pamela L. Martin, 'Can Rights of Nature Make Development More Sustainable? Why Some Ecuadorian Lawsuits Succeed and Others Fail', *World Development*, Vol. 92, April 2017, pp. 132–3, cited in: Collins, *The Ecological Constitution*, p. 68.

1803 Original name: '*Acción Ecológica*'.

1804 Original name: '*Fundación Pachamama*'.

1805 Durmaz, *Doğanın Hakları*, pp. 286–7.

1806 On how the struggle for nature protection in Ecuador progressed after 2008, see Durmaz, *Doğanın Hakları*, pp. 285–9.

1807 See Laura Rival, 'The Yasuní-ITT Initiative: Oil Development and Alternative Forms of Wealth Making in the Ecuadorian Amazon', *in* A. Bebbington (ed.), *Extractive Economies, Socio-Environmental Conflicts and Territorial Transformations in the Andean Region* (in press).

the most biodiverse areas in the world and home to many Indigenous peoples. The decision would significantly contribute to the fight against climate change by not extracting the oil from the area, and in return, would receive $3.6 billion from the international community, half of the revenue that would be generated if the oil were extracted – at 2007 prices. However, when support from other countries only amounted to $200 million,[1808] Correa's government shelved the decision and opened the region to multinational fossil fuel companies. That shows how even seemingly progressive and green governments can easily sacrifice nature for oil revenues.[1809]

Nevertheless, the issue was then put to a national referendum after resistance from the Indigenous population. On 20 August 2023, nearly 60 per cent of the population voted to end oil exploration in Yasuní National Park. The result means that the state oil company will cease all activities in this region, home to two tribes without contact with modern civilisation and an incredible biodiversity.[1810]

However, even though this outcome was in favour of protecting nature, the danger of putting such issues to referendum should not be underestimated. Just as it is unacceptable to put human rights to a referendum on reasonable and logical grounds, the same should be valid for the rights of nature. A nature-centred perspective requires that the referendum ban on rights should continue regardless of who owns them. Otherwise, the rights of nature would be sacrificed for the sake of the daily and personal interests of people within the capitalist economic order, in which case the fact that these rights are written in the constitution would be meaningless. Therefore, it should be recognised that the constitutional rights of nature – just like human rights – are protected by supreme courts, not protean majorities, and issues concerning the rights of nature should not be put to referendum.

At this point, the importance of constitutional articles that can form the basis for green constitutionalism emerges once again. That is because they provide the basis for the legal review of the decisions taken – or forced to be taken – by governments in the name of economic interests in the current

---

[1808] 'Yasuní-ITT', *Wikipedia*.

[1809] Löwy, *Ecosocialism*, Ecosocial Struggles of Indigenous Peoples (Loc. 989).

[1810] 'Ecuadorians Reject Oil Drilling in the Amazon, Ending Operations in Protected Area', *Associated Press*, 21 August 2023.

international order in the context of the rights of nature and climate change and can directly affect the outcome of the proceedings. In Ecuador, for example, courts actively use the *in dubio pro natura* principle enshrined in the Constitution. The 2011 ruling of the Loja Regional Court of Justice on the pollution of the Vilcabamba River[1811] was the first in the country on the rights of nature. The case concerned dumping rocks, soil, gravel, and trees into the riverbed while widening a road between Vilcabamba and Quinara. The project continued for three years without any environmental impact assessment. The narrowing of the riverbed by the dumped material not only accelerated the river's flow but also made flooding more likely, especially in winter. In response, Richard Frederick Wheeler and Eleanor Geer Huddle, whose homes lie in the riverbed, brought a lawsuit directly on behalf of the river in the District Court of Justice, raising the responsibility of the administrators. In this first case won based on the constitutional rights of Mother Nature, the Court relied on the precautionary principle, stating in its judgement that,

> based on the precautionary principle, until it is objectively demonstrated that the probability of certain danger that a project undertaken in an established area does not produce contamination or lead to environmental damage, it is the responsibility of the constitutional judges to incline towards the immediate protection and the legal tutelage of the rights of nature, doing what is necessary to prevent contamination or call for remedy. Note that we consider in relation to the environment that one acts not only under the certainty of damage but (also) its probability.[1812]

In the following years, similar rulings became more frequent in Ecuador. Likewise, court decisions in various countries now signal the establishment of a nature-centred green constitutional order. Unfortunately, it is not possible to compile all of these decisions here. However, in this final part of the book, it is helpful to look at the decisions of supreme courts worldwide that have contributed to the fight against climate change by adopting a nature-centred approach to see that green constitutionalism is moving from utopia to reality.

[1811] *Richard Frederick Wheeler y Eleanor Geer Huddle c. Director de la Procuraduria General Del Estado de Loja*, decision no. 11121-2011-0010, 30 March 2011.

[1812] Natalie Greene, 'The First Successful Case of the Rights of Nature Implementation in Ecuador', *GARN*, 21 May 2011.

6.3 National supreme courts' decisions on climate change

The number of people applying to the courts claiming their rights have been violated due to inadequate measures taken by states in the fight against climate change is increasing daily. This is a highly positive situation because these cases, known as climate litigation, demonstrate the increase in eco-literacy in society and constitute the democratic base of green constitutionalism. Therefore, it is necessary to take a closer look at the decisions of national and federal courts at the highest level of the legal hierarchy that can be considered examples of green constitutionalism, either because they are directly related to climate change or because they recognise nature as a subject of rights.

I have chosen to cite these decisions in chronological order rather than by region or topic because I believe that there is an interaction and influence between the highest national courts on this issue. In line with this gradually progressive context, it seems that the decision of one supreme court on climate change or the rights of nature encourages or puts pressure on others. In this sense, a kind of global case law logic is at work on climate change.

Constitutions are often considered a barrier against the arbitrary rule of power. However, a closer look reveals that they are merely paper barriers. In legal language, they constitute a formal and normative barrier to the restraint of the executive. Political practice usually goes in the opposite direction, and the practical restriction of the executive organ is rare. Especially in countries without a tradition of constitutionalism, the gap between political reality and the constitution's text widens.[1813] Nevertheless, climate change is such a grave and vital danger that the supreme courts, through their decisions interpreting what is written in the constitution within the logic of green constitutionalism and incorporating principles that are not written into the legal order, must bridge this gap and help us turn away from the path of destruction that irresponsible governments have put us on.

For many years, the dangers posed by global warming were not tangible, urgent, or visible in everyday life. Therefore, neither the governments nor ordinary people, even if they were aware of climate change, lifted a finger and did anything concrete about the problem. Today, such dangers have become more visible, but not yet of a grave nature. However, if we wait until

---

[1813] Pactet, *Institutions Politiques*, p. 66.

the consequences of climate change are undeniably collapsing, it will be too late to take serious action. There is currently no known way to eliminate the greenhouse gases that have been released into the atmosphere for hundreds of years and will continue to pollute it in the future.[1814] That is why we need to take up the long-standing call of scientists and immediately ban the extraction and use of fossil fuels. If parliaments do not do it, the courts with the power to bind them must. Against this backdrop, the decisions listed below force modern law to accept a more nature-centred perspective, paving the way for the emergence of a new postmodern and posthumanist legal paradigm – in other words, a green constitutional order that would enable us to stop climate change.

Today's fossil fuel capital is not simply a group of capitalists or an economic sector that, like enslavers of the past, is only concerned with its own interests; it is a group whose profits and power are inseparable from the ruling class as a whole. To suggest that this group can be persuaded to voluntarily dismantle its economic interests, in other words, to commit a kind of suicide, is contrary to both our historical knowledge and the current reality of political power relations. In this respect, the fossil fuel industry can only be defeated by the long and arduous struggle of a collective 'dispossession movement', just like slavery.[1815] However, the problem is that it was President Abraham Lincoln and the counterforce of the Northern states standing up to the Southern states of the United States that led to the abolition of slavery. There is no such counterforce in the political arena to confront the fossil fuel industry today. As shown in the book's first part, the bourgeoisie has captured both the legislature and the executive organ. Therefore, only the judicial branch remains to lead this movement. Our advantage is that – at least where the rule of law prevails – the highest courts, which form the apex of the judicial branch, are still relatively independent of the legislature and the executive and vested with the power to make binding decisions. This power should be used to stop climate change. Indeed, some supreme courts are already doing so, and their number is growing daily.

[1814] Giddens, *The Politics of Climate Change*, p. 12. Giddens describes this situation as 'Giddens' paradox'.

[1815] Benlisoy, 'İklim Krizi ... ', p. 174.

6.3.1 Philippines

As early as 1992, 43 children in the Philippines, representing future generations, filed a lawsuit in the Federal Supreme Court[1816] against the government for failing to protect the country's rainforests.[1817] In this case, now known as *Minors Oposa*, the children demanded intergenerational climate justice in relation to the management of environmental resources by adults and the impact of these actions on their future.

First, the Supreme Court had to resolve the question of the children's standing in this application, which was different from the ones made until then. That was because the applicants did not have a direct and concrete victimisation in the classical sense. Moreover, they were applying for future generations yet to be born. Following its assessment, the Court accepted that the children had the capacity to represent their own and future generations:

> We find no difficulty in ruling that they can, for themselves, for others of their generation and for the succeeding generations, file a class suit. Their personality to sue on behalf of the succeeding generations can only be based on the concept of intergenerational responsibility insofar as the right to a balanced and healthful ecology is concerned. Such a right, as hereinafter expounded, considers the 'rhythm and harmony of nature'. [...] Needless to say, every generation has a responsibility to the next to preserve that rhythm and harmony for the full enjoyment of a balanced and healthful ecology. Put a little differently, the minors' assertion of their right to a sound environment constitutes, at the same time, the performance of their obligation to ensure the protection of that right for the generations to come.

Thus, the Court recognised and put into practice the concept of intergenerational justice at that very moment. Later in the case, the government enacted a law stating that the remaining forests are national protected areas permanently protected for the benefit of present and future generations yet to be born.[1818] That positively impacted nature and climate protection even before the case was concluded.

[1816] The court, known in official correspondence and colloquially as the *Corte Suprema*, was established in 1901 and is the highest court in the Philippines' legal system.

[1817] *Minors Oposa v. Secretary of the Department of Environment and Natural Resources*, 33 I. L. M. 173 (1994), 30 July 1993.

[1818] L. Stone – K. Lofts, *Climate Change, Child Rights and Intergenerational Climate Justice IDS In Focus Policy Briefing*, Issue 13, November 2009: (Oposa v. Factoran, 224 SCRa 792, 808 – 1993), cited in: Gibbons, 'Climate Change ... ', p. 28.

Although ecological principles are not explicitly written in the Constitution of the Philippines, the Supreme Court applied principles written in other texts to the facts of the case. It stated the following in its ruling:

> While the right to a balanced and healthful ecology is to be found under the Declaration of Principles and State Policies and not under the Bill of Rights, it does not follow that it is less important than any of the civil and political rights enumerated in the latter. Such a right belongs to a different category of rights altogether for it concerns nothing less than self-preservation and self-perpetuation – aptly and fittingly stressed by the petitioners – the advancement of which may even be said to predate all governments and constitutions. As a matter of fact, these basic rights need not even be written in the Constitution for they are assumed to exist from the inception of humankind.

As can be seen, in this application, considered the first climate case in history, the Supreme Court of the Philippines realised a genuine application of green constitutionalism for protecting nature and the ecosystem as early as 1992. However, for many years, this decision remained an exceptional judgement in international environmental law and did not affect the judgements of other countries. Probably, the fact that the Philippines is considered a Global South country played an important role in this.

6.3.2 Nigeria

A 2005 Federal High Court of Nigeria ruling is another important example of green constitutionalism. The case, brought by Jonah Gbemre on behalf of himself and the Iwherekan community in the Niger Delta, was brought against the state and the fossil fuel company Shell. Gbemre alleged that Shell had failed to consider the environmental impact of its activities on the living conditions of the local community during decades of gas flaring.[1819] The state also bears responsibility for Shell's failure to stop these activities, Gbemre said, adding that gas flaring contributes to climate change, potentially threatening lives. He claimed that such gas flaring violates the right to life and human dignity of the community he is a member of, as enshrined in the Nigerian Constitution and enshrined in the African Charter on Human and Peoples' Rights.

[1819] A dirty and wasteful practice that has been used for 160 years to remove other gases produced during oil and gas production.

The Federal High Court of Nigeria upheld the plaintiff Gbemre's claims.[1820] The ruling stated that the constitutional right to life 'inevitably includes the right to a "clean, non-toxic, healthy environment"'.[1821] The Court ruled that Shell's gas flaring while exploring for and extracting oil in the region where the Iwherekan community lives and the state's authorisation of the flaring were a 'significant violation' of the community's fundamental right to live in a clean and healthy environment and of human dignity and that the flaring must cease immediately.[1822] An important detail was that Judge Nworokie wrote 'including a healthy environment' in parentheses next to the right to life. Thus, the Judge emphasised the link between the right to a healthy environment and the right to life.

In addition, the Court ordered the Attorney General of Nigeria to act swiftly to amend the law that provides the legal basis for this ecosystem-damaging activity and to bring it in line with the rights enshrined in the Constitution and the African Charter.[1823] As a result, not only was the extraction of climate change-causing fossil fuels recognised as a violation of fundamental rights and freedoms in a supreme court ruling and the economic activity halted, but also national legislation was amended to protect nature and not violate fundamental rights and freedoms.

6.3.3 The United States

In 2007, a United States Supreme Court case[1824] pitted eleven states, including Massachusetts, against the US Environmental Protection Agency (EPA). The case centred on whether the EPA could control carbon dioxide emissions. The states argued that the EPA should regulate carbon dioxide emissions and other greenhouse gases that pollute the environment and cause climate change. Their argument was based on the Clean Air Act,[1825] which governs EPA's responsibilities to protect and enhance the nation's air quality and stratospheric ozone layer. Under this law, the EPA has the authority to set

[1820] *Gbemre v. Shell Petroleum Development Co Nigeria Ltd*, FHC/B/CS/53/05, 14 November 2005.

[1821] *Gbemre v. Shell Petroleum Development Co Nigeria Ltd*, § 5(3).

[1822] *Gbemre v. Shell Petroleum Development Co Nigeria Ltd*, § 5(4).

[1823] *Gbemre v. Shell Petroleum Development Co Nigeria Ltd*, § 6(6).

[1824] *Massachusetts v. EPA*, 549 U.S. 497, 2 April 2007.

[1825] Paragraph (a)(1) of section 202 of the Act.

emission standards for any air pollutant that, in its judgement, causes or contributes to air pollution from motor vehicles or motor vehicle machinery that may reasonably be expected to endanger the public health or welfare. Based on this authority, the states requested that the EPA also regulate greenhouse gas emissions.

In 2003, the EPA rejected the application made by the states on two grounds. The first was lack of authority, as the Clean Air Act does not give it the authority to regulate carbon dioxide and other greenhouse gases in relation to climate change. The second reason was that even if EPA had such authority, it could refuse to set greenhouse gas emission standards for vehicles. In other words, even if it had such authority, it preferred not to use it.

After the Court of Appeals of the District of Columbia found the EPA's decision to be lawful in 2005, the case went to the Supreme Court. One of the main arguments the plaintiff states presented to the Supreme Court was that the Clean Air Act's definition of 'air pollutant' was too broad. Claiming that carbon dioxide should be considered an air pollutant because its high concentration makes it toxic and causes global warming, the states argued that the EPA violated the Act by failing to regulate carbon dioxide and other greenhouse gas emissions.

The EPA argued before the Supreme Court that the Clean Air Act also gives it the authority not to regulate. It also suggested that it was unclear whether anthropic carbon dioxide emissions were causing global warming. The case suddenly attracted attention, with the expectation that the Supreme Court would rule on the truth or falsity of theories about global warming. Indeed, in the decision written by Justice Stevens, the majority of the Supreme Court recognised that the harms associated with climate change are serious. In addition, the Court emphasised that EPA has not disputed the existence of a causal link between human emissions and global warming. That allowed the Court to draw important public attention to the weight of scientific knowledge.[1826]

However, the questions before the Court were narrower and more legal than the public expectation. The Court only examined whether the EPA had a valid justification under the Clean Air Act for rejecting the request before it. Ultimately, in a five-to-four decision, the Supreme Court held that

---

[1826] Stone, *Should Trees Have Standing?*, p. 56.

greenhouse gases fall within the Clean Air Act's definition of 'air pollutant' and that the Act authorises EPA to regulate greenhouse gas emissions from vehicle tailpipes. The court required the agency to issue and periodically renew a regulation on emissions from motor vehicles. Beyond that, the ruling did not explicitly rule on whether anthropic carbon dioxide emissions were causing global warming.

Although the decision is disappointing in this respect, the fact that these debates are even taking place in a country like the US, which has the potential to affect global legal systems, is significant. Moreover, by not deciding in favour of the EPA in this case, the Supreme Court has shown that it does not approve inaction on climate change.

6.3.4 Ecuador

As mentioned earlier,[1827] Ecuador is one of the two countries with a nature-centred constitution. From the beginning, it was a question of whether this 2008 constitution would remain on paper and have any concrete impact. It was the Ecuadorian Constitutional Court that brought it to life. In a 2015 ruling,[1828] the Court stated that the right to *buen vivir* and the rights of nature are at the heart of the Constitution and affect other rights, including property-related ones. It thus upheld the executive branch's intervention in companies' unsustainable use of resources.[1829]

The case originated in the Ministry of Environment's decision to close a shrimp farm established in the mangrove ecosystem of the Cayapas-Mataje Ecological Reserve. In the farm's appeal against this decision, the Esmeraldas District Court abstained from enforcing the rights of Mother Nature enshrined in the Constitution and overruled the Ministry's closure decision, citing property rights. The Ministry of Environment appealed this decision to the Constitutional Court. The government defended its closure order on the grounds that the rights of nature are constitutionally recognised and that it is an obligation for public authorities to protect these rights. According to the government, the Constitutional Court should have

---

[1827] See 6.2.2

[1828] Decision no. 166-15-SEP-CC.

[1829] Collins, *The Ecological Constitution*, p. 24.

upheld the decision to shut down the enterprise based on the supremacy of the constitution.

In reaching its decision, the Constitutional Court took into account the fact that mangrove ecosystems are given special constitutional protection in the Ecuadorian Constitution. The Constitution had indeed enshrined this provision due to the people's thirty-year struggle to protect these ecosystems from shrimp farms.[1830] In its reasoning, the Constitutional Court said that it was unusual for a lower court to ignore the significant environmental impacts caused by a shrimp farm in a sensitive ecosystem:

> This Constitutional Court has been emphatic in pointing out the importance of the rights of nature; rights derived from the obligation of the State and its officials to encourage and promote respect for all the elements that are part of a system [...] This aspect has obviously not been observed by the judges [...] who did not analyze the existence or non-existence of violations of the rights of nature despite their obvious relevance. The central issue was a shrimp farm operating within the Cayapas-Mataje Ecological Reserve, an area that possesses a mangrove system with great diversity of fauna and flora.[1831]

In this judgement, the Constitutional Court stated that the principle of *buen vivir* and the rights of nature are 'transversal' to each other and affect all other constitutional rights, including property rights. In addition, the Court stated that the Constitution adopts *a biocentric approach that prioritises Nature in contrast to classic anthropocentric conception in which the human being is the centre and measure of all things.*[1832] From this sentence, it is clear how deeply constitutional norms that take ecological balance into account can influence the decisions of high courts. Therefore, transforming constitutions with a nature-centred approach is of utmost importance. However, as this decision shows, in order to ensure that these norms do not remain on paper, high courts should also interpret these articles within the framework of green constitutionalism and actively use them in their decisions.

[1830] Echevarría, 'When Courts Meet Nature'.

[1831] For this part of the judgement, I used Hugo Echevarría's English translation. See Hugo Echevarría, 'Rights of Nature: The Ecuadorian Case', *Revista Esmat*, Y. 9, No. 13, July-December 2017, p. 83.

[1832] Cited in: Collins, *The Ecological Constitution*, p. 68.

A subsequent ruling by Ecuador's Constitutional Court was even more resounding than this one. Known as the Los Cedros decision,[1833] it concerned a mining operation in a fog forest. In 2017, the government granted a state-owned company, ENAMI EP, two mining concessions in Los Cedros, a protected cloud forest. The state-owned company then entered into agreements with several private companies to prepare for mining. In response, local organisations in the area affected by the mining activity went to court, claiming that both the rights of nature and their right to be informed and consulted beforehand had been violated. The district court hearing the case ruled that the local authorities' right to be consulted had been violated. However, according to the court, a deeper investigation was needed to determine whether the rights of nature had been violated. The plaintiffs then appealed to the Constitutional Court on the rights of nature part of their application.

On 10 November 2021, the Ecuadorian Constitutional Court ruled that mining concessions and environmental permits granted by the government violated both the rights of nature, the rights of the inhabitants to water and a healthy environment, and – as the local court noted – the right of local communities to be consulted. In the section on the rights of nature, the Court's transformation of the 'rights of Mother Nature' recognised in the Constitution from simple and general words of wishful thinking into substantial rights of a natural being is considered revolutionary. Thus, just as the fundamental rights and freedoms enshrined in constitutions can be used as shields to protect each individual human being, so too can the elements of nature be protected individually. In this case, the Court went beyond saying that nature in general holds rights; it said that a particular forest is a rights holder, thereby recognising it as a subject of constitutional rights. In other words, the human monopoly on characterising the subject of rights, at least in the case of Ecuador, has been broken.[1834]

[1833] Decision no. 1149-19-JP/21. The text of the decision is based on Gustavo Prieto's English translation: Gustavo Prieto, 'The Los Cedros Forest Has Rights', *Verfassungsblog*, 10 December 2021.

[1834] Serkan Koybasi, 'Ekvator Anayasası'nda Doğa Ana'nın Haklarının Tanınmasının Anayasa Yargısına Etkisi', *in* Asos Congress, *Tam Metin Kitabı*, Asos Yayınevi, Elazığ, 2022, p. 399.

It is important to take a closer look at the methodology applied in this case by the Ecuadorian Constitutional Court to determine whether Mother Nature's rights have been violated, as it has the potential to shed light on nature-centred decisions that other constitutional courts may make in the future. This method followed a two-stage course after determining that the natural entity is the subject of rights. In the first stage, the Court examined whether there was a risk of serious and irreversible damage to nature by the proposed activity. In the second stage, the Court looked at whether there was complete scientific certainty about the adverse effects of this action.[1835] Under these two tests, according to the Court, if the company cannot prove that its economic activity will not have an irreversible impact on nature, this means that the activity violates the rights of nature. Applying this logic, clearly reflecting the precautionary principle, to the case, any mining activity in the Los Cedros Forest would destroy the ecosystem and biodiversity there forever, leaving the Court with no choice but to revoke the permits. As a result of this decision, which prioritises the rights of nature over economic interests, any excavation activity in the Los Cedros Forest is banned permanently.

In this decision, it is of utmost importance to note that the forest ecosystem itself is protected, independently of the rights of local people whom the mining activity will harm. The court ruled that Los Cedros Forest has an intrinsic value independent of the value people place on it and is, therefore, protected by its right to exist on its own.[1836] Although this decision does not seem directly related to climate change, it is crucial for the climate struggle as it stands in stark opposition to the view that 'nothing other than human beings can be the subject of constitutional rights', which lies at the root of this problem. Moreover, the two-stage test conducted by the Constitutional Court provides a tool that can be used both in nature protection struggles and climate lawsuits regarding damages to the atmosphere.

6.3.5 South Africa

Although there is no direct regulation on climate change in the Constitution, the Constitutional Court of South Africa 'challenged' positive law in an

---

[1835] Prieto, 'The Los Cedros …'.

[1836] Koybasi, 'Ekvator Anayasası'nda … ', p. 400.

important case brought by Earth Life Johannesburg.[1837] In 2017, this non-governmental organisation asked the Court to rule on whether climate change should be considered in the environmental impact assessment of a new coal-fired power plant expected to be operational by 2060. Asked for its opinion on whether the environmental review of the plans for the 1,200 MW Thabametsi Power Project under the National Environmental Management Act of 1998 included the project's impact on climate change and climate change's impact on the project, the Court answered in the affirmative. Although the Court acknowledged that the relevant law does not explicitly include climate change among the 'issues to be assessed', it ruled that this issue is 'an assessment of environmental impact'. Accordingly, the Court ruled in 2018 that the Ministry of Environment's decision to approve the project's environmental impact assessment was unlawful as this assessment had not been carried out.

In a lengthy, highly detailed, and comprehensive judgement, the Court relied on many grounds, including the climate commitments made by the Republic of South Africa in signing the Paris Agreement, and pointed out that the Department's approval clearly ignored climate change.[1838] Although this important decision was primarily based on the interpretation of the law, the provision in Article 24 of the Constitution, which includes both a substantive right to the environment and the state's responsibility to ensure ecologically sustainable development and resource utilisation so that present and future generations can live in a protected environment, seems to have influenced the decision in this direction.[1839] That constituted a good example of how existing constitutional provisions can be instrumentalised in climate change cases within the framework of green constitutionalism.

[1837] *EarthLife Africa Johannesburg v. Ministry of Environmental Affairs and Others*, Case no. 65662/16.

[1838] Following the decision, the Ministry of Environment, after conducting a climate change impact assessment, re-approved the facility on the grounds that 'although the facility will emit greenhouse gases intensively, the benefits from energy production are greater'. A lawsuit was filed against this approval. However, before the case was concluded, the Constitutional Court, in accordance with a compromise between the parties, issued an order cancelling all governmental authorisations for the power plant and imposing court costs on the state.

[1839] Louis J. Kotzé – Anél du Plessis, 'Putting Africa on the Stand: A Bird's Eye View of Climate Change Litigation on the Continent', *University of Oregon Journal of Environmental Law and Litigation*, Vol. 50, No. 3, 2019, p. 20.

6.3.6 Colombia

In another 2018 ruling in a climate case, perfectly in line with green constitutionalism, Colombia's Supreme Court of Justice[1840] recognised the legal personality of the Amazon forest and imposed responsibilities on the government to reduce deforestation and take other measures to respect both environmental human rights and the rights of nature. In a lawsuit brought by twenty-five young people aged between 7 and 26, arguing they live in cities that will be most affected by climate change[1841] against the Colombian government, some municipalities, and some companies, using the Constitution's mechanism for the protection of fundamental rights and freedoms,[1842] the applicants claimed that deforestation in the Amazon[1843] violated their and future generations' rights to life, health, and a healthy environment. They demanded that the state stop deforestation and establish an intergenerational plan to achieve this goal and that public participation be ensured in this process.

In the first instance, the lower court rejected the application, stating that the constitutional remedy could only be used for individual rights, not collective ones. On appeal, the Supreme Court of Justice annulled the lower court's interpretation, ruling that the mechanism can be used if the violation of collective rights also violates individual rights.

The Supreme Court of Justice then stated that the fundamental rights to life, health, minimum living conditions, liberty, and respect for human dignity are fundamentally interconnected and determined by the environment and ecosystem and that without a healthy environment, subjects of rights and sentient beings in general cannot survive. Observing that without the protection of the environment, neither the family, society, nor the state itself can exist,[1844] the Court ruled that by causing deforestation, the government violated the rights and interests of animals and plants, as well as the rights

---

1840 *Future Generations v. Ministry for the Environment and Others*, Decision no. STC4360-2018.

1841 'Climate Change and Future Generations Lawsuit in Colombia: Key Excerpts from the Supreme Court's Decision', *Dejusticia*, 13 April 2018, in translation of key parts of the judgment, p. 1, § 2.1.

1842 *Acción de tutela*, Colombian Political Constitution of 1991, art. 86.

1843 Despite international commitments by the Colombian state to reduce deforestation, it increased by 44 per cent between 2015 and 2016. See 'Climate Change … ', *Dejusticia*, judgment translation, p. 1, § 2.3.

1844 'Climate Change … ', *Dejusticia*, judgment translation, p. 13.

and interests of future generations yet to be born. The following phrase used by the Court in its judgement – even though it contains very optimistic predictions – is a good example of how scientific data should be used in the higher judiciary in climate change cases:

> In terms of intergenerational equity, the transgression is obvious, as the forecast of temperature increase is 1.6 degrees in 2041 and 2.14 in 2071; future generations, including children who brought this action, will be directly affected, unless we presently reduce the deforestation rate to zero.[1845]

Underlining that the increasing degradation of the environment is a serious attack on the right to life and other rights, present and future, the Court said that Colombians are sickened by the denial of the fundamental rights to water, to breathe clean air, and to enjoy a healthy environment. According to the Court, this also increases the lack of clean water and reduces the possibility of enjoying a dignified life.[1846]

Stating that the idea of 'protection of fundamental rights' does not only concern a particular individual but also implies the 'other', the Supreme Court of Justice said that the other consists of not only all humans on Earth but also other animal and plant species. Therefore, they should be taken into account when exercising rights. In addition, the other also includes future generations yet to be born who deserve to enjoy the same environmental conditions as us.[1847]

Drawing attention to the adverse effects of climate change, the Court cited the extreme rise in temperatures, the melting of the poles, the massive extinction of animal and plant species, and the increase in the frequency of meteorological events and disasters outside the ranges considered normal as evidence of imminent dangers.[1848] The Court pointed to humanity, which has assumed a hegemonic position on a global scale by adopting an anthropocentric and selfish model whose fundamental characteristics are detrimental to environmental stability, and listed the main characteristics of this model as (1) overpopulation, (2) acceptance of a system of rapid growth guided by

---

[1845] 'Climate Change … ', *Dejusticia*, judgment translation, p. 34, § 11.2.
[1846] 'Climate Change … ', *Dejusticia*, judgment translation, p. 13.
[1847] 'Climate Change … ', *Dejusticia*, judgment translation, p. 18, § 5.2.
[1848] 'Climate Change … ', *Dejusticia*, judgment translation, p. 15.

consumerism and existing political-economic systems, and (3) overexploitation of natural resources.[1849]

We are all obligated to stop exclusively thinking about our self-interest, the Court said, calling on us to *consider the way in which our daily actions and behaviours affect society and nature*. The Supreme Court of Justice said that we must move from 'private ethics', which focuses on private favours, to 'public ethics', which is the acceptance of moral values that aim to achieve a different concept of social justice.[1850] Thus, albeit implicitly, it rejected Lockean thinking that atomised society by following Newton's path. Moreover, given that the Court sees society as a whole, including not only humans but also animals and plants, the 'public ethic' in this decision is an ethic that is in line with green constitutionalism, which takes into account the 'Earth's ecosystemic network'.

The Court identified the two foundations on which the environmental rights of future generations rest as (1) the ethical duty of species solidarity and (2) the intrinsic value of nature, noting that, with respect to the first of these, failure to adopt a fair and prudent approach to consumption would result in the depletion of essential living resources, making it impossible for humanity to continue as a species. With regard to the second ground, the Court stated that it was necessary to go beyond the anthropocentric perspective and focus on the 'ecocentric-anthropic' criterion that would prevent humans from arrogant, disrespectful, and irresponsible consumption of natural resources.[1851] The Court's use of this criterion inevitably reminds us of Donna Haraway's 'nature–culture' approach mentioned earlier.[1852] It is seen that the Court has developed a similar perspective, rejecting the nature–culture dualism and focusing on the fact that human beings are also a part of nature in its decision.

As a result, in this case, the Colombian Supreme Court of Justice not only accepted the applicants' claims but also recognised the Colombian Amazon as a 'subject of rights',[1853] just as the Colombian Constitutional Court did in

---

[1849] 'Climate Change … ', *Dejusticia*, judgment translation, p. 16.
[1850] 'Climate Change … ', *Dejusticia*, judgment translation, p. 18.
[1851] 'Climate Change … ', *Dejusticia*, judgment translation, p. 20.
[1852] See 3.2.1
[1853] 'Climate Change … ', *Dejusticia*, judgment translation, p. 45, § 14.

the aforementioned Atrato River decision.[1854] It ruled that 'protecting the Amazon, the so-called 'lung of the world', is a national and global imperative'.[1855] However, the Colombian State has failed to effectively combat the problem of deforestation in the Amazon despite all its international commitments, laws, and case law on the subject.[1856] The Court said that the country faced imminent and serious harm since deforestation causes carbon dioxide emission into the atmosphere, which has a greenhouse effect, leading to the transformation and fragmentation of ecosystems and the alteration of water resources.[1857]

It, therefore, ordered the Presidency of the State and the Ministries of Environment and Agriculture to establish an 'Intergenerational Pact for the Life of the Colombian Amazon', in which the petitioners, affected communities, and research and scientific institutions would be represented, to reduce deforestation and limit the greenhouse gas emissions.[1858]

As César Rodríquez Garavito, the applicants' lawyer, rightly puts it, the Colombian Supreme Court of Justice's decision is historic at both the national and international levels since, at the national level, it recognises future generations as subjects of rights and orders the government to take concrete measures to protect the country and the planet where they will live. Also, at the international level, this decision sets a precedent for courts worldwide to force governments to fulfil and increase their commitments to fight climate change.[1859]

6.3.7 The Netherlands

A process that started in 2012 when the *Urgenda* Foundation, a non-governmental organisation that develops plans and measures against climate change, wrote a letter to the Prime Minister of the Netherlands, demanding that the state take all mandatory measures to reduce emissions that cause climate change, ended in 2019 with a decision that made a global impact. After lower courts ruled that the Dutch government's inadequate climate

---

[1854] See 4.2.2.2 Colombia
[1855] 'Climate Change … ', *Dejusticia*, judgment translation, p. 30.
[1856] 'Climate Change … ', *Dejusticia*, judgment translation, p. 34, § 13.
[1857] 'Climate Change … ', *Dejusticia*, judgment translation, p. 34.
[1858] 'Climate Change … ', *Dejusticia*, judgment translation, p. 45, § 14.
[1859] 'Climate Change … ', *Dejusticia*, § 9.

targets were unlawful and that the commitment to tackle climate change needed to be stepped up, the Supreme Court followed suit.[1860]

The government's response to the *Urgenda* Foundation's request at the beginning of the process stated that there was not enough international action on climate change and that the Netherlands had set a target to reduce its emissions in 2020 by 17 per cent compared to 1990. Claiming that this target was insufficient to keep global warming below 2°C, which UN bodies have set as the goal for preventing climate change, the Foundation filed a lawsuit against the government in 2013, claiming that by knowingly endangering its citizens, the government violated Article 2 of the ECHR, considered part of domestic law, which regulates the right to life and Article 8 of the ICCPR, which regulates the right to respect for private and family life. The Foundation demanded that the promised reduction rate be increased to 25–40 per cent.[1861]

The Foundation won the case on its own behalf and on behalf of 886 people at the first instance court in 2015 and the appeal in 2018. The case was brought to the Supreme Court, which upheld the lower courts' decisions. It ruled that the state has an obligation to take measures to mitigate climate change due to 'the gravity of the consequences and the great risk of the occurrence of climate change'. Although the Court did not directly rely on Article 21 of the Constitution, which imposes a responsibility on the state to keep the country habitable and to protect and improve the environment, it based its decision more on Articles 2 and 8 of the ECHR. In addition, the reasoning also referred to EU emission reduction targets, the principles of the ECHR, the principle of 'do no harm' in international law, the hazardous negligence doctrine, the principle of fairness, the precautionary principle, and the principle of sustainability in the UN FCCC.

According to the Court,

> [...] (N)o other conclusion can be drawn but that the State is required pursuant to Articles 2 and 8 ECHR to take measures to counter the genuine threat of dangerous climate change if this were merely a national problem. [...] (A)fter all, this constitutes a 'real and immediate risk' [...] and it entails the risk that the lives and welfare of Dutch residents could be seriously jeopardised. The same applies to,

---

[1860] *Urgenda Foundation v. State of the Netherlands*, Case no. 19/00135, 20 December 2019.

[1861] According to the Foundation, this range of rates is both mandatory and the most cost-effective economically.

> inter alia, the possible sharp rise in the sea level, which could render part of the Netherlands uninhabitable. The fact that this risk will only be able to materialise a few decades from now and that it will not impact specific persons or a specific group of persons but large parts of the population does not mean – contrary to the State's assertions – that Articles 2 and 8 ECHR offer no protection from this threat [...]. This is consistent with the precautionary principle [...]. The mere existence of a sufficiently genuine possibility that this risk will materialise means that suitable measures must be taken.[1862]

Thus, in a breakthrough in human rights jurisprudence up to that time, the Court ruled that Articles 2 and 8 of the ECHR could be used to prevent the threat of climate change. In this framework, it was ruled that the mitigation target should be set at least 25 per cent as a positive obligation of the state. Stating that this is the 'absolute minimum', the Supreme Court assessed that achieving this reduction by 2020 is an obligation against dangerous climate change risks that will seriously impact Dutch citizens' lives and well-being.[1863] Although climate change is a global problem, the Supreme Court clearly stated that the state could not escape its individual responsibility and had to do its part.[1864] The Supreme Court did not give a definite to-do list on how to achieve the 25 per cent emission reduction target stated in its decision; it merely stated that this is an issue that remains in the political sphere and that the government and parliament should deal with it by using their broad discretionary power.[1865] In other words, the Court's message was, 'I am telling you what to do about climate change; how you do it is up to you'.

This decision is another example of green constitutionalism. In addition, what makes the decision important for climate law is that courts at all levels rejected the state's argument that judicial interference in climate change policy is an impermissible violation of the separation of powers. Transferable to other climate cases around the world, the Supreme Court said the lower court's decision reflected the fundamental rule of constitutional democracy, which is that courts can order governments to fulfil their legal obligations.[1866]

1862 *Urgenda Foundation v. State of the Netherlands*, § 5.6.2.

1863 *Urgenda Foundation v. State of the Netherlands*, § 7.5.1.

1864 Client Earth, '10 Landmark Climate Change Cases', July 2022, pp. 5–6.

1865 *Urgenda Foundation v. State of the Netherlands*, § 8.3.2, 8.3.4.

1866 Collins, *The Ecological Constitution*, p. 110.

This decision is also revolutionary as it is the first time in history that a court has ruled that a state has a national obligation to increase its climate targets. Another important aspect of the *Urgenda* case is that the state did not deny climate change, which is at the heart of the case. Therefore, the debate was not about whether to reduce emissions but how much to reduce them. The Court's violation decision concerns the state's failure to reduce emissions sufficiently and its efforts to postpone them in a situation that is seen as an emergency in the light of scientific data. According to the judges, every time the necessary measures are not taken, the most important rights of Dutch citizens are violated. Following the ruling, the Dutch government revised its greenhouse gas reduction targets and adopted a more aggressive climate policy. Today, the Netherlands aims to reduce greenhouse gas emissions by 49 per cent in 2030 and 95 per cent in 2050 compared to 1990.[1867]

6.3.8 Ireland

The Urgenda judgement in the Netherlands quickly became both a guiding light for non-governmental organisations and a jurisprudence used by high courts around the world. Ireland was one of the countries that transposed this decision into its national judicial system. Friends of the Irish Environment (FIE) filed a case in the High Court[1868] claiming that the insufficiently strong measures in the government's 2017 National (Climate Change) Mitigation Plan violated the Constitution and the ECHR, as well as the Climate Action and Low Carbon Development Act 2015.

According to the organisation, the plan to transition to a low-carbon economy by 2050 not only violated the law but also human rights as it did not target carbon reductions in the short term. In other words, the FIE believed that the plan should also include how much reduction would be achieved in which year in the period until 2050. Because 2050 is a distant date, the government that drafted this plan would likely not be around at that time, and no one would be found responsible for its shortcomings if, by 2050, sufficient emission reductions had not been achieved. Therefore, FIE asked

---

1867 'Climate Policy', *Government of Netherlands*.

1868 According to the Irish judicial system, there are three supreme courts established by the Constitution: *High Court*, *Court of Appeal* and *Supreme Court*. The first one deals with civil and criminal law cases. The latter is the highest and final court of appeal in the country.

the Court to annul the government's decision to adopt this plan, which did not show what would be done in the short term.

The High Court rejected the organisation's demands in its September 2019 ruling. Thus, the government's decision was not annulled. According to the Court, the law did not require setting interim reduction targets until 2050. Moreover, the adopted plan was only a first step towards a low-carbon, climate-resilient, and sustainable economy, which could be reviewed and modified according to the circumstances of the day. Nevertheless, in the framework of this decision, the Court recognised the right to live in an environment compatible with human dignity, even though it is not enshrined in the Irish Constitution, and recognised that the organisation had the right to bring a claim for violation of these rights.

At this point, departing from the traditional appeals system, which should have gone in order, FIE simultaneously appealed the decision to both the Court of Appeal and the Supreme Court. Despite this procedural problem, the Supreme Court agreed to hear the case, recognising the urgency of climate change in light of the scientific evidence. Then, in July 2020, it announced its decision to cancel the plan.[1869] Referring to the devastating effects of climate change on Ireland[1870] for scientific reasons based on carbon emissions[1871] and citing the *Urgenda* case by name,[1872] the Court stated that the National Mitigation Plan adopted in response to climate change did not have the certainty required by the relevant law, because anyone reading the plan could not understand how Ireland would meet the targets set by 2050.[1873] The Court indicated that a lawful plan must set out the entire process in sufficient detail up to that target date.[1874] However, the Court also annulled the High Court-level win, ruling that the Friends of the Irish Environment organisation lacked standing because, as a legal entity, it could not bring a claim for a violation of the right to life or bodily integrity protected under the Constitution or the ECHR.[1875] Consequently, the recognition of the right

---

1869 *Friends of the Irish Environment v. Government of Ireland*, Case No. 793 JR, 31 July 2020.
1870 *Friends of the Irish Environment v. Government of Ireland*, § 3.2.
1871 *Friends of the Irish Environment v. Government of Ireland*, § 3.3.
1872 *Friends of the Irish Environment v. Government of Ireland*, § 3.4.
1873 *Friends of the Irish Environment v. Government of Ireland*, § 6.20.
1874 *Friends of the Irish Environment v. Government of Ireland*, § 9.2.
1875 *Friends of the Irish Environment v. Government of Ireland*, § 9.4.

to live in an environment compatible with human dignity, which the lower court had recognised, was also lost.

However, the Court left the door open to the possibility that the state's stance on the environment could lead to a violation of existing constitutional provisions.[1876] As a result, Ireland has joined the ranks of countries that have used the high courts to force their governments to take concrete and decisive action on climate change.

6.3.9 Germany

One of the most vigorous national high court decisions on climate change so far, and the one most in line with the logic of green constitutionalism, was taken in Germany. Moreover, the fact that Germany is a Global North country and the largest economy in the European Union increases the importance of the decision. For this reason, this one, known as the *Neubauer* decision,[1877] needs to be discussed in more detail. This decision, which is partly inspired by the previous decisions of *Urgenda* in the Netherlands and Friends of the Irish Environment in Ireland, is of such high quality that its influence on subsequent climate change decisions is evident. So much so that even the ECHR, famous for its lack of academic references in its judgements, explicitly cited *Neubauer* in *KlimaSeniorinnen*. At the centre of the decision is the Federal Climate Protection Act[1878] (*KlimaSchutzGesetz* – KSG), which the German Parliament adopted in 2019 within the framework of climate change mitigation and adaptation efforts. The law envisaged a 55 per cent reduction in greenhouse gas emissions by 2030 compared to 1990. Germany's net-zero carbon target was set for 2050.

With the support of Greenpeace, a group of young people led by Luisa Neubauer, including citizens of Bangladesh and Nepal, filed a constitutional complaint against the law. They argued that the 55 per cent reduction target for 2030 was incompatible with the Paris Agreement, to which Germany is a party, to limit global warming to 2°C below pre-industrial levels in any case and 1.5°C if possible. According to the applicants, the reduction target

[1876] Collins, *The Ecological Constitution*, p. 111.

[1877] *Neubauer and Others v. Germany*, 1 BvR 2656/18, 1 BvR 288/20, 1 BvR 96/20, 1 BvR 78/20, 24 March 2021.

[1878] Originally called '*Bundesklimaschutzgesetz*'.

for 2030 should be at least 70 per cent, and as such, the law violates the fundamental rights to a future compatible with human dignity enshrined in Article 1(1) of the Federal Constitution of Germany, the rights to life and physical integrity in Article 2(2), and the related provision for the 'protection of the natural foundations of life' in Article 20a, which creates a responsibility for future generations. They also claimed that the law violated their property rights and right to a minimum ecological standard of living. They asked the GFCC both to find these violations and issue a ruling ordering Parliament to set new mitigation rates against climate change and to respect the principle of proportionality in doing so.

6.3.9.1 Legal justification based on science

In the application before it, firstly interpreting the obligation to 'protect the fundamentals of life' in Article 20a of the Constitution as meaning that *the legislature also has an obligation to take measures against climate change*,[1879] the GFCC referred to the scientific data on climate change. Among these, the Court stated that, in particular, when the Nationally Determined Contributions (NDCs) submitted by the states within the framework of the Paris Agreement are analysed, it is understood that even the 2°C warming target set as an upper limit in the Agreement will not be met,[1880] and then, based on IPCC data, pointed out that global warming is human-induced and is primarily caused by CO2 emissions based on fossil fuel use. Stating that how much the global average temperature will rise depends on the amount of these human-induced emissions,[1881] The GFCC has thus given the message at the very beginning of its decision that climate change is a problem that can be prevented with the convenient policies and that the decisions to be taken by states in this regard will be decisive.

The Court then gave some examples of the negative impacts of climate change on human life, again based on IPCC reports.[1882] Listing heat waves,

---

[1879] Agnes Hellner – Yaffa Epstein, 'Allocation of Institutional Responsibility for Climate Change Mitigation: Judicial Applications of Constitutional Environmental Provisions in the European Climate Cases *Arctic Oil, Neubauer,* and *l'Affaire du Siècle*', *Journal of Environmental Law*, Vol. 35, No. 2, July 2023, p. 220.

[1880] *Neubauer,* § 10.

[1881] *Neubauer,* § 18–19.

[1882] *Neubauer,* § 23.

droughts, extreme rainfall, floods, storms, and forest fires among the consequences of climate-related extreme weather events, the GFCC also made a strong link between climate change and individual rights and freedoms, pointing to disruptions in the food and water supply chain, damage to infrastructure and housing, illness and death, and mental health and well-being. In addition, noting that climate change has already caused displacement and migration due to droughts and rising sea levels, the GFCC noted that social inequalities and competition for water, food, and agricultural land, exacerbated by climate change, also increase the risk of violent conflict.[1883] In this way, the Court laid the groundwork for its view, which it conveyed later in its judgement, that failure to stop climate change today will mean a world in more challenging conditions for future generations.

Moreover, at this point, the judges addressed the issue from the perspective of global climate justice, pointing out that half of the human-induced greenhouse gas emissions in the atmosphere originate from industrialised countries, including Germany, and that per capita carbon emissions in Germany are twice the world average.[1884] Thus, the Court signalled that it does not view state responsibility for climate change from a nationalist perspective but from the perspective of rights and freedoms and recognised a broader view of interconnected planetary system processes that cannot be confined to national borders and national judicial systems.[1885]

This point of view showed its first result on the standing issue, and the GFCC recognised that young people living in Bangladesh and Nepal also have standing. According to the Court, the fundamental rights and freedoms enshrined in the German Constitution imposed an obligation on the German state to protect young people even outside its borders from climate change.[1886]

[1883] *Neubauer*, § 28.

[1884] *Neubauer*, § 29.

[1885] Louis J. Kotzé, '*Neubauer et al. versus Germany*: Planetary Climate Litigation for the Anthropocene?', *German Law Journal*, Vol. 22, No. 8, December 2021, p. 1434.

[1886] *Neubauer*, § 90. Although not cited in the judgement, this view is in line with the UN Committee on the Rights of the Child's consideration of 'extraterritorial responsibility' in *Sacchi and Others v. Argentina and Others*. Accordingly, a state is responsible for the violation of the rights of a child outside its borders by a carbon emission occurring within its borders and under its control (§ 9.7–9.9). The fact that all countries contribute to climate change does not absolve individual states of their responsibility to reduce greenhouse gas emissions (§ 9.10).

6.3.9.2 The emergence of the concept of 'advance interference-like effect'

In the section dealing with the alleged violation of the applicants' right to life and physical integrity, the GFCC judges held that Article 2(2) of the Constitution includes 'protection against risks to life and health arising from climate change'.[1887] In this context, noting that the applicants, who are minors, are likely to face violations of their rights to life, physical integrity, and property in the coming years due to the level of climate change, the GFCC highlighted that the claim that they have not yet been violated today simply because these violations will occur in the future is not acceptable. According to the Court, regulations that pose significant risks to fundamental rights during their future implementation may also violate the Constitution. That is particularly the case for a chain of events that can no longer be corrected once started.[1888] In other words, the GFCC concluded that when climate change is likely to become irreversible due to inadequate regulation, the regulation in question already constitutes a violation of rights, even if adverse effects have not yet been observed, as they are certain to occur in the future.

Having rejected the administration's *actio popularis* objection by stating that the fact that a large number of people will be affected by climate change does not change the fact that the rights of the young applicants will also be violated,[1889] the Court then came to the part that made this decision one of the turning points in the history of climate law: From that point on, the GFCC began to examine whether the KSG unacceptably shifted the burden of greenhouse gas emission reductions beyond 2030.

First, the Court indicated that the only rational solution to climate change is reducing CO_2 emissions. Stating that this reduction can only be achieved as a result of a change in people's behaviour and that one of the most effective ways to get people to change their behaviour is through legal regulations,[1890] the GFCC created the concept of 'advance interference-like effect'[1891] and introduced it to climate law. In this framework, considering that if the mitigation target until 2030 is insufficient, those who will live and govern in the years

[1887] *Neubauer*, § 99.
[1888] *Neubauer*, § 108.
[1889] *Neubauer*, § 110.
[1890] Kotzé, '*Neubauer et al. versus Germany*', p. 1435.
[1891] Original name: '*Eingriffsänliche Vorwirkung*'.

after 2030 will have to mitigate more rapidly in a very short time to reach the 2050 targets, the Court pointed out that this would mean disproportionately limiting their freedoms. The judgement stated:

> (U)nder these provisions (of the KSG), they may be faced with substantial burdens to reduce greenhouse gas emissions from the year 2031 onwards. The scale of the ensuing restrictions on fundamental rights is already partially determined by the aforementioned provisions. This advance effect on future freedom might have violated the fundamental rights of the complainants.[1892]

Thus, noting that the greenhouse gas emissions permitted under the KSG until 2030 have an impact on mitigation efforts after that date, the GFCC pointed out that one of the important factors affecting the extent of future loss of freedom is the time remaining for the social and economic transition towards a net-zero carbon target.[1893] Noting that Germany has a limited carbon budget in line with the Paris Agreement target of 'no more than 2°C and, if possible, 1.5°C' and that as this budget decreases, rights protecting carbon-emitting activities will have to be increasingly restricted, the Court pointed out that[1894] therefore, the limitations on freedoms that will be mandatory in the future stem from the generosity of the current climate change legislation.[1895]

In forming its opinion, the Court relied on numerous scientific references and placed it in a comprehensive and creative context. The pages and pages of scientific data cited by the GFCC show a deep respect for credible climate science.[1896] Based on this data, the high judges in Karlsruhe could confidently make the following striking statement without being scared of being stigmatised as 'fearmonger: '

> Climate action measures that are presently being avoided out of respect for current freedom will have to be taken in future – under possibly even more unfavourable conditions – and would then curtail the exact same needs and freedoms but with far greater severity.[1897]

[1892] *Neubauer*, § 116.
[1893] *Neubauer*, § 118.
[1894] *Neubauer*, § 247.
[1895] *Neubauer*, § 120.
[1896] Kotzé, '*Neubauer et al. versus Germany*', p. 1432.
[1897] *Neubauer*, § 120.

Accordingly, noting that the applicants' fundamental rights[1898] would be violated today because the risk of future rights limitations arises from existing regulations, the GFCC stated that it cannot be argued that the constitutional complaint should be lodged after 2030, when freedoms will have already been severely restricted. That is because by then, the carbon that will cause the irreversible effects of climate change will have already been emitted, and it will, therefore, be too late.[1899]

The Court, which also imposed an obligation on the State to take preventive measures to mitigate the adverse effects of climate change should it reach an unavoidable stage or materialise,[1900] emphasised that these measures are crucial to keep the adverse effects of climate change 'at a level acceptable to constitutional law'.[1901] Recognising that the power and responsibility to determine and implement such measures rests with the legislature, the GFCC nevertheless stated that it is competent to check whether these measures have been taken and, if so, whether they are adequate and appropriate to protect fundamental rights in the face of climate change.[1902]

[1898] It should be noted that the GFCC distinguished between the rights of the applicants and the rights of the generations yet to be born, giving more importance to the former. This was influenced by the fact that the applicants, as the young generation that will experience the consequences of climate change more in the future, are real persons with rights and freedoms, whereas the generations yet to be born are not yet recognised as subjects of rights due to their unborn status. Thus, the Court was able to bypass the problem of temporality in rights violations through the precautionary principle and the concept of intergenerational justice. See Beudart, Manon, *Right to a Healthy Environment: Shortcomings in Rights-Based Climate Litigation and Possible Advancements in Europe* (Master's thesis, Department of Public Law and Governance – Tilburg Law School, Tilburg University), Tilburg, 2023, pp. 30–1.

[1899] *Neubauer*, § 130.

[1900] *Neubauer*, § 150.

[1901] *Neubauer*, § 150.

[1902] *Neubauer*, § 152. It should be recalled that this jurisprudence emerged in the Dutch *Urgenda* judgement against the separation of powers-based objection of state authorities to measures to be taken against climate change. The GFCC applied this logic to its own case. Later, the same point of view appeared in the *KlimaSeniorinnen* application at the ECtHR. Thus, there seems to be an implicit communication and continuity between these higher judicial bodies.

Thus, applying climate science to constitutional law in a very striking way, the GFCC concluded that the applicants' fundamental rights[1903] were violated because the emissions permitted by the KSG until 2030 were planned in such a way as to cause a substantial burden for emission reductions in the following years.[1904] Calling this new doctrine 'advance interference-like effect',[1905] which links the emission permits in the current law with the emission reductions that will be mandatory after 2030,[1906] the Court stated that the Constitution imposes an obligation on the administration to protect fundamental freedoms over time and to spread the possibilities attached to that freedom proportionately between generations. This new concept is regarded as a creative legal justification that goes beyond a nuance regarding the limits of the supervisory jurisdiction of the GFCC set out in the Constitution and takes into account the country's remaining carbon budget.[1907]

6.3.9.3 The principle of equitable sharing of the burden between generations

According to the judges hearing the *Neubauer* application, 'inter-temporal guarantees of liberty' require that the applicants be protected against the unilateral imposition of the burden of greenhouse gas emission reductions on them in the future.[1908] Accordingly, the Court asked the legislature to amend the KSG to improve the targets therein and tighten the roadmap for future emission reductions, particularly through specific regulations specifying emission targets beyond 2030.[1909] In this framework, the GFCC ruled

---

[1903] It has been criticised that the Court's decision did not concretise which rights of future generations would be violated and that the imposition of the mitigation burden arising from the carbon budget on future generations would violate their rights in general. See Kirsty Fairhurst, *Our Obligation to Future Generations – A Human Rights Approach in the Case of Neubauer et al. v Germany* (Master's Thesis, Universitat Pompeu Fabra, European and Global Law), 2022, Barcelona, p. 26.

[1904] *Neubauer*, § 142.

[1905] *Neubauer*, § 183.

[1906] Petra Minnerop, 'The "Advance Interference-Like Effect" of Climate Targets: Fundamental Rights, Intergenerational Equity and the German Federal Consitutional Court', *Journal of Environmental Law*, Vol. 34, No. 1, March 2022, p. 146.

[1907] Minnerop, 'The "Advance Interference-Like Effect" … ', p. 137.

[1908] *Neubauer*, § 183.

[1909] Kotzé, '*Neubauer et al. versus Germany*', p. 1424.

that the state must limit private, professional, and economic activities that emit carbon dioxide and that the legislator cannot remain inactive on the emission of gases that cause climate change.[1910] Pointing out that all activities that cause carbon emissions, which are currently recognised as rights, will eventually be banned altogether,[1911] the Court stated that this limitation and prohibition activity should be spread over time and shared proportionally over generations.[1912]

With the *Neubauer* judgement, the Court examined the content of the legislature's regulation to implement the directive principle to protect the foundations of life in the Basic Law and conducted a constitutionality review on the basis of whether the principle was fulfilled.[1913] Based on scientific evidence, the Court found that it was not possible to fulfil the constitutional mandate with the current legislation and, in addition to ruling that the KSG is unconstitutional in its current form, ordered the German Parliament, the Bundestag, to amend the law in line with its decision by 31 December 2022. In line with this order, the amendment adopted by the Bundestag in June 2022, which entered into force in August 2022, raised the carbon emission reduction target for 2030 from 55 per cent compared to 1990 to 65 per cent. In addition, an emission reduction target of 88 per cent was set for 2040, and the country's net-zero carbon emission target was moved from 2050 to 2045.[1914]

As a result, the GFCC took an important legal stance against those who take refuge in denialism in the face of the reality of climate change and against politicians who refuse to take the necessary measures for short-term interests. This decision, which is a response to the fragility of the ecosystem and the human rights violations and injustices caused by climate change, has given a strong signal that a legal regulation supported by scientific data can be established.[1915] By transforming the IPCC's emission reduction targets

---

[1910] *Neubauer*, § 184–185.
[1911] *Neubauer*, § 186.
[1912] *Neubauer*, § 192.
[1913] Hellner – Epstein, 'Allocation of Institutional Responsibility … ', p. 220.
[1914] In response, another constitutional complaint was filed, claiming that the new targets are also incompatible with the Paris Agreement. This new complaint, *Steinmetz and Others v. Germany*, was filed this time by young people from Germany alone and is pending as of January 2025.
[1915] Kotzé, '*Neubauer et al. versus Germany*', p. 1440.

into a national carbon budget open to judicial review, the Court extended classical constitutional limits, thus demonstrating how constitutional courts can strengthen their role in protecting constitutional rights and freedoms in a scientifically and legally complex issue.[1916] With this decision, the Karlsruhe Court ruled that climate change is a constitutional and human rights issue and that, while adaptation measures are important, there is no alternative but to reduce greenhouse gas emissions to avoid violating constitutional rights.[1917]

Thus, the GFCC has transformed from just another national court into a global climate leader.[1918] Developing a holistic view of climate science, the impacts of climate change, planetary justice, the fragility of the Earth system, and global climate law on a highly complex issue such as climate change,[1919] the GFCC has become a decisive actor in Germany's national climate policies with this decision[1920] and has developed a new approach to the concept of 'interference' with rights in constitutional doctrine.[1921] This decision, which is seen as a landmark in terms of a national supreme court's explanation of the national and international responsibilities of the state in the face of climate change from the perspective of the protection of rights and freedoms, is a decision that protects the rights of future generations in the emerging field of climate law and sheds light on how these rights can be developed and strengthened. In this respect, *Neubauer* is a 'prototypical decision' for all high courts worldwide.[1922]

1916 Minnerop, 'The "Advance Interference-Like Effect" … ', p. 148.
1917 Minnerop, 'The "Advance Interference-Like Effect" … ', p. 148.
1918 Kotzé, '*Neubauer et al. versus Germany*', p. 1442.
1919 Kotzé, '*Neubauer et al. versus Germany*', p. 1425.
1920 Another decision that demonstrates the extent to which this decision affects national climate policies was handed down by the Berlin-Brandenburg Higher Administrative Court on 30 November 2023. The court ruled that the federal government must adopt an urgent action programme (*Sofortprogramm*) for the implementation of the KSG in order to meet the annual carbon emission reduction targets for 2024 and 2030 in the construction and transport sectors. This decision is a domestic echo of the *Neubauer* judgement, but unlike it, it does not focus on fundamental rights, but on administrative issues for climate management and implementation. See Maxim Bönnemann, 'Litigating Enforcement: Germany's Contested Climate Governance and the New Wave of Climate Litigation', *Climate Law – A Sabin Center Blog*, 12 December 2023.
1921 Minnerop, 'The "Advance Interference-Like Effect" … ', p. 136.
1922 The term is Ran Hirschl's. See Fairhurst, *Our Obligation* …, p. 17.

6.3.10 France

Last but not least, the lawsuit filed against the government in the Paris Administrative Court in 2019 for failing to take decisive action on climate change, following the collection of 2 million signatures in the 'Trial of the Century' campaign launched by four civil society organisations[1923] in France, is worth mentioning. On 3 February 2021, the Administrative Court ruled that the state is liable for failing to fulfil its obligations to reduce greenhouse gas emissions. In reaching this conclusion, the Court referred to France's obligations under international law, as well as the obligation to reduce and limit the environmental impact under the Environmental Charter,[1924] which was affixed to the Constitution in 2005.[1925] That is the first time a French court has ruled that ecological damage has been caused by non-compliance with recognised climate obligations. In the second phase of the ruling, on 14 October 2021, the French state was sentenced to keep its promises to reduce greenhouse gas emissions due to climate change and to compensate for the damages caused by its inaction. Subsequently, the non-governmental organisations that filed the lawsuit petitioned the Court on 14 June 2023, demanding the state to pay €1.1 billion in compensation in line with their calculations.[1926]

According to the applicant organisations, the cost of six months of inaction was €122 million. Calculated from the start of the campaign in 2018 until the filing of the petition, the cost amounted to €1.102 billion. The lawsuit is pending, and the cost continues to rise. The main reason why the demand is so high is political. Non-governmental organisations want to show government officials who think that investments to stop climate change are expensive that the cost of not making those investments is even higher. Indeed, according to Cécile Duflot, director general of Oxfam France, *what they want to tell the government that says they do not have the financial means is that the cost of inaction is much higher than action.*[1927]

[1923] These organisations are OXFAM France, Greenpeace France, *La Fondation Nicolas Hulot pour la Nature et l'Homme* and *Notre Affaire à Tous*.

[1924] *Charte de l'Environnement*, Law No. 2005–205 of 1 March 2005.

[1925] Collins, *The Ecological Constitution*, p. 111.

[1926] For a chronology of the course of the case, see 'L'Affaire du Siècle: L'État Poursuivi Pour Inaction Climatique', *Oxfam France*.

[1927] Marie Astier, 'Les ONG Climat Réclament Plus d'Un Milliard d'Euro à l'État', *Reporterre*.

Another important case in France is the Carême case, which runs almost parallel to the Trial of the Century and is supported scientifically and legally by the same non-governmental organisations.[1928] The Council of State found the lawsuit brought by Damien Carême, Mayor of Grande-Synthe, admissible on behalf of his town, which will be severely affected by climate change. The case demanded an end to state inaction and the fulfilment of the promises made in the Paris Agreement. On 19 November 2020, the Council of State issued a decision considered a historic advance for climate justice. Pointing out that the goals set in laws are not just empty words or beautiful ambitions, the high court ruled that they are binding and, therefore, the state has an obligation to take the necessary measures to achieve them. Accordingly, it gave the state three months to demonstrate that the measures taken today are sufficient to reduce greenhouse gas emissions by 40 per cent by 2030 compared to 1990. Thus, in France, such 'reduction by a certain percentage by a certain date' rules, which were previously considered 'soft law', have been transformed into legally mandatory obligations, hence 'hard law'.[1929]

Another feature of the decision is that it will prevent government officials who think they may not be re-elected from shirking responsibility for future problems. That is because the fact that the effects of inaction on climate change are not seen immediately, but in ten to twenty years, can lead politicians to use their already limited budgets to meet short-term demands rather than climate investments whose results will be seen in the future and, therefore, will benefit subsequent governments. In other words, politicians may tend to favour investments that will solve citizens' immediate problems over long-term investments that will, in layman's terms, 'skim the cream off the top'. However, that constantly delays the adoption of vital climate change measures. The Council of State's decision is critical in this sense because it places the responsibility for future climate change-related problems on today's politicians by demanding that they reveal whether the necessary measures have been taken or planned to meet the carbon dioxide reduction rates in the threshold years of 2030 and 2050.

[1928] The part of this case brought before the ECtHR was declared inadmissible on 9 April 2024. See *Carême v. France* (Grand Chamber), application no. 7189/21.

[1929] 'Une Décision Historique du Conseil d'État pour la Justice Climatique', *Oxfam France*.

After the expiration of the three-month deadline and following correspondence with the government, on 11 July 2021, the Council of State ruled in Carême's favour, finding that the emission reductions in 2019 and 2020 were minimal and would be ineffective unless new measures were taken urgently. It thus annulled the implied refusals to respond to Carême's petitions to the President, the Prime Minister, and the Minister of Ecological Transition and Solidarity. According to the Court, a 12 per cent reduction between 2024 and 2028 alone is required to meet the emission reduction targets. In parallel, in the long term, the Council of State ordered the government to take additional measures by 31 March 2022, and reduce greenhouse gas emissions by 40 per cent by 2030 to meet the Paris Agreement targets.

Conclusion

> We are now so abusing the Earth that it may rise and move back to the hot state it was in fifty-five million years ago, and if it does most of us, and our descendants, will die.[1930]

The historical record shows that *Homo Sapiens* is an ecological serial killer.[1931] We have already caused the extinction of many species, and more than a million species are in danger of extinction due to our activities. Moreover, this situation has become such that not only species are disappearing, but the ecosystem that sustains us has also come to the point of collapse. In other words, we are about to become the killers of our own species.

It has already been proven that the unrestrained movement of capital to increase its profits is fundamentally incompatible with the cycles of nature. This incompatibility is the root cause of the climate change we are facing.[1932] If current policies and practices continue on their current course, organised social life will collapse.[1933]

Only through a more sustainable relationship with the Earth and an ecological and social revolution that will create the conditions for material equality in society as a whole can humanity survive the Anthropocene rather than reaching the critical threshold in its long developmental process and

---

1930 Lovelock, *The Revenge of Gaia*, p. 1.
1931 Harari, *Sapiens*, p. 78.
1932 Saito, *Slow Down*, p. 100.
1933 Chomsky – Pollin, *Climate Crisis …*, p. 163.

disappear at the end of it.[1934] That requires rethinking and re-establishing our relationship with each other and with other living and non-living beings in nature; in other words, an economic and legal paradigm shift. That does not mean we should cut off our humanity or past. On the contrary, if we are to succeed in creating an ecological society in the future, it will be possible with the insights, knowledge, and data we have gained throughout our history thanks to our philosophy, science, technology, and rationality. We must assimilate what is ethically and intellectually valuable in our history and abandon what is harmful.[1935]

However, we have neither easy solutions to the global climate crisis nor instant policy changes to stop the impending climate chaos.[1936] Proposals without a reconstructive vision and global opposition without real impact lead to exhaustion and burnout. Alternative institutions with no ties to vital, anti-systemic social movements are persuaded or coerced by market forces to become 'green' businesses that pose no danger. They are thus transformed into so-called 'socially responsible' products that serve only an elite class of consumers.[1937] However, we need to change the system, not the products.

That is why *change the system, not the climate!* is not just a simple slogan but the very essence of what needs to happen. In order to achieve such a radical change, we first need to discuss capitalism, the corporate system motivated by nothing but profit, the governments that they guide, and the legal systems that protect them. As I have tried to show throughout this book, the bourgeoisie's transformation into a hegemonic power through the burning of fossil fuels, the capitalist economic order it established, and the legal orders that cause inequality and injustice everywhere today are processes that emerged from and intertwined with each other. The climate crisis cannot be solved without changing the capitalist system, without breaking the domination of corporations, without eliminating the massive inequalities and injustices on which the system is built, and without creating a system based on democratic

---

[1934] Foster, *Capitalism in the Anthropocene*, pp. 21–2.

[1935] Bookchin, *The Ecology of Freedom*, p. 65.

[1936] Tokar, *Toward Climate Justice*, Social Ecology and the Future of Ecological Movements (Loc. 1654).

[1937] Tokar, *Toward Climate Justice*, Social Ecology and the Future of Ecological Movements (Loc. 1939).

participation and under the control of ordinary people, not power holders.[1938] In other words, if we want to stop climate change and prevent extinction, we must replace the capitalist economic system with an ecological economic order, limit corporations, and establish a new legal order that will enable us to achieve a more equal and just world. Constitutional law can be transformed into a useful, valid, and practical tool to achieve this goal.

These steps to save life on Earth will also lead to significant changes in the public's consciousness.[1939] The most important of these changes must be to create a consciousness and a movement that will remove human domination over humans and nature from our daily lives. As Bookchin points out, to allow the poison of domination and the dominationist understanding to continue to prevail is to ignore the most fundamental roots and sources of our social and ecological problems today.[1940] New rules and decisions in line with green constitutionalism, which will replace the current structure based on the exploitation of human beings and nature with a nature-centred structure, will increase the eco-literacy of societies. After all, is it possible to achieve harmony between man and nature without creating a human society that lives in permanent balance with its natural environment?[1941] Green constitutionalism, which aims to create this society, is an idea that suggests harmonising law with the ecosystem and prioritising life.

The ecological crisis requires a radical policy shift. We must cut high-income countries' excessive use of energy and materials, phase out fossil fuels, and move swiftly to renewable energies. We also need to adopt a postcapitalist economic model focusing on human well-being and ecological stability rather than perpetual growth. However, we cannot stop there. We also need a new way of thinking about our relationship with the living world.[1942] We need to internalise and integrate into our economic and legal systems an understanding that nature is not a blessing but that we are but a part of its complex web.

The first thing we need to do with the economic order is to set aside the rules of the bourgeoisie. A rational way out of this crisis is possible if we can

---

[1938] Şahin, 'İklim Krizine … ', p. 35.
[1939] Chomsky – Pollin, *Climate Crisis …*, p. 163.
[1940] Bookchin, *The Next Revolution*, p. 66.
[1941] Murray Bookchin, 'Ecology and Revolutionary Thought', *The Anarchist Library*.
[1942] Hickel, *Less is More*, p. 287.

simultaneously put together four initiatives: (1) meet the demand of real social needs; (2) reduce global material production by reducing labour time and eliminating unnecessary, harmful production and much of transportation; (3) radically increase energy efficiency and switch to fully renewable energies, regardless of their cost; (4) create the political and cultural conditions for collective responsibility for what is produced, and consumed, so that the transformation takes place democratically. These initiatives are not possible without a series of interventions in private property[1943] and property rights on which our legal systems are based. In this context, the entire legal order needs to be reshaped with social and ecosystemic interests in mind rather than individual ones. Therefore, the current understanding of the unlimited use of individual property rights should be abandoned, and all sectors, from transportation to health and banking to agriculture, should be regulated by law following green constitutionalism. The goal of these regulations should not be the GDP growth or the capital's salvation but the well-being of people and other living beings and the sustainability of the ecosystem.

Until now, there has always been a state of dynamic equilibrium on our planet. All species have adapted to the limits of the planet over long periods of time. Contrary to popular belief, they have done so not by emphasising competition but rather by cooperating. While competition and predation between species may exist on an individual level, from a systems perspective, we live on a planet where one life allows other lives to flourish. In other words, nature sustains life not by consuming it but by producing and deriving it. As one of the species on this planet, we, too, should set the rules by which we govern ourselves within this framework. In other words, we must learn how to weave the good life together with the earth through biomimicry.[1944]

Is this a utopia? Etymologically, it definitely is because utopia means 'something that does not exist anywhere'. A global society organised through the principles of green constitutionalism does not exist for the moment. However, any movement that wants to change an established order must have an alternative vision of the future, a utopia.[1945] Theories have significant practical value, especially when they can guide action. For humanity to bring about

---

[1943] Tanuro, *L'Impossible le Capitalism vert*, pp. 169–70.
[1944] Arık, 'Bir Arada … ', p. 467.
[1945] Löwy, *Ecosocialism*, Ecosocialism and Democratic Planning (Loc. 570).

a coherent and consistent transformation in how we regulate our behaviour, we need to have a coherent idea of why we need to do it, what the overall purpose behind our governance systems is, and how we should go about doing it.[1946] In this sense, green constitutionalism is an idea that suggests that in order to tackle climate change, we should abandon our hierarchical form of governance between humans and humans and nature and establish a new one together with other elements of the ecosystem, abandon the anthropocentric approach stemming from humanism and adopt a nature-centred approach. We must abandon the dualistic and divisive perspective of modernism and make humans and nature 'one' again. We can do this through constitutional law and supreme courts.

Supreme courts must step in effectively to protect the rights and freedoms of the ecosystem, nature, and people, both because of their historical responsibility for the contribution of the legal orders they preside over to climate change so far and because they have the power to make binding decisions on the main actors of the capitalist order: corporations and their protector state bodies. These courts, as we have seen previously, can significantly contribute to stopping climate change by ruling on appeals from young people, Indigenous peoples, and social movements around the world who apply to them in search of a legal solution for a more just world. As a fitting analogy, the strategic doctrine of the African National Congress (ANC), which fought against the *apartheid* regime in the Republic of South Africa in the 1980s, was 'the hammer of armed struggle on the anvil of mass action'.[1947] Today, in the fight against climate change, the high courts can similarly use the law as a hammer on the anvil of mass action and appeal to bring down the causes of climate change, particularly the capitalist economic order.

One could argue that national supreme courts are 'part of the existing system' and that 'the solution cannot be sought within the problem itself'. This is true. Indeed, the supreme courts' judges have mostly voted in favour of preserving the *status quo* so far, reflecting their raison d'être. However, until relatively recently, we were unaware that we had a vital problem like climate change. Today, circumstances have changed. Judges need to take these new

---

[1946] Cullinan, *Wild Law*, p. 54.
[1947] Malm, *How to Blow …*, p. 64.

circumstances into account and be brave enough to protect life by voting to change the existing order, not to preserve it.

However, if they do so, it is not difficult to foresee that they will be accused by the bourgeoisie of violating the separation of powers, defying democracy, and establishing a 'juristocratic order'. In essence, it is only when this is done that the bourgeoisie's hegemony will be counterbalanced, and an order that respects the rights of societies will be established. Therefore, an ecological movement organised at the grassroots level should support the supreme courts against the bourgeoisie and encourage them to adopt a green constitutional approach by interpreting constitutional norms or invoking supra-constitutional principles, thereby creating a source of legitimacy for their nature-centred decisions.

Today, liberal individualism, market hegemony, and the undisputed supremacy of liberal democratic ideology – embraced by much of the Western world – have combined to prevent nations from implementing the political, economic, and social reforms necessary to tackle climate change.[1948] Given this, some might argue that 'civil liberties and ecological survival compete with each other; ' therefore, individual liberties should be limited, and authority should be increased on climate change.[1949] They may even justify these claims with concrete examples. Indeed, China, which has long had an authoritarian government, has become the world's number one state in electric vehicles, renewable energy production, and energy storage with its investments in renewable energy after 2010.[1950] Of the three countries responsible for more than 50 per cent of global emissions, China, India, and the US, only China and India – which has also surrendered to right-wing populist rhetoric in recent years under Modi – comply with the emission reduction targets in the Paris Agreement.[1951]

Nevertheless, one thing needs to be clear: Defending authoritarian governments in the face of climate change means that we have not learned

---

[1948] Hulme, *Why We Disagree …*, p. 316.

[1949] For an example, see David Shearman, 'Democracy and Climate Change: A Story of Failure', *Open Democracy*, 7 November 2007.

[1950] Scott Malcomson, 'How China Became the World's Leader in Green Energy', *Foreign Affairs*, 28 February 2020.

[1951] 'China and India Lead Global Renewable Energy Transition', *United Nations Climate Change*, 21 April 2017.

any lessons from the problems we have experienced. All these disasters are caused by legal orders based on the hierarchy some people have established for their own interests. Just as the exploitation of human beings and nature are inseparable patterns in the capitalist economic order, the imposition of one group's ideology on others is born out of the same logic as the imposition of man's rules on nature. Nature does not function with one voice but with pluralistic networks. What we need are not strong authoritarian regimes but constitutional orders that establish equality and justice at all levels.

Green constitutionalism indeed suggests limitations on certain rights and freedoms, but only on those protecting activities causing climate change. What needs to be changed through green constitutionalism is the consideration of overproduction, excessive consumption, exploitation of humans, animals, and nature, and the reckless pursuit of economic growth, which the capitalist system feeds and glorifies right. These harmful and destructive activities for people and nature should no longer be categorised as rights or freedoms. Current rights and freedoms other than these should not be restricted but instead protected and strengthened, taking the diversity and pluralism of nature as an example, which is in line with biomimicry. When everyone can express themselves freely, find free time to spend with themselves or their friends, easily access healthy food and water at affordable prices, meet their basic needs such as quality health care and education free of charge, meet with others on issues of their choice and succeed in changing thoughts democratically, in short, when everyone can live a dignified life freely and as themselves, we will genuinely transfer the logic of nature's functioning to our law. To put it more directly, a social order in harmony with nature can be established not by authority but by respect for rights and freedoms, and any order that is not in harmony with nature is doomed to fail in tackling climate change. Therefore, green constitutionalism is based on the idea that rights and freedoms other than harmful and destructive ones are not suppressed but empowered.

Consequently, green constitutionalism is not a search for an oppressive order but rather an order in which pluralism is preserved. Preserving pluralism means, above all, allowing alternatives to flourish in nature and society, in ecosystems and information systems. Nurturing and protecting pluralism is not a luxury today but a necessity for survival. In pluralism, even the smallest things have value and function. Allowing small things to flourish is the accurate measure of freedom.[1952]

Nor does the green constitutionalism approach suggest 'going backward' or, to use a more exaggerated expression, 'going back to the cave'. The transformation in law should, of course, be realised by considering today's conditions. Advances in technology, transportation, and communication cannot be ignored. However, their use in an ecosystem-destroying way must be prevented. For this, as Aldo Leopold suggests, in order to sustain each other, the places where we live, and 'fellow travellers on the path of evolution', humanity must create a new ethics, an ethics in which humans see themselves as part of the larger community of life.[1953]

The way to establish such an ethic is for humanity, first and foremost, to acknowledge the damage it is doing to nature and the Earth, to recognise that this damage endangers the ecological balance and future generations, and then to transform law, as in so many other areas.[1954] As life's complex and delicate fabric is rapidly disintegrating before our eyes and slipping through our fingers, the world urgently needs an entirely new paradigm of social governance. However, we need not only to understand the new ways but also to act on them. A truly global approach to this issue must develop a critical perspective on the Eurocentric human rights and constitutionalism phenomena. Global environmental constitutionalism must aim to move nature from the periphery to the centre of constitutions.[1955] Indeed, the *Pachamama* constitutions in Latin America, the eco-constitutional debates in Europe, and the growing nature-centred jurisprudence movement are steps in the right direction that have begun to fundamentally challenge and transform Western anthropocentrism. These examples need to be replicated, strengthened, and globally harmonised in the fight against climate change. Ultimately, we need to explore new ways of building societies and reorienting human behaviour to be friendly to the Earth, not hostile to it.[1956] The legal approach to meet this imperative is what I call green constitutionalism.

[1952] Shiva, *Earth Democracy*, p. 135.
[1953] Leopold, *A Sand County Almanac*, p. X (foreword by Curt Meine).
[1954] Üskül Engin, *Ekolojik Kriz, Etik ve Hukuk*, p. 5.
[1955] Bosselmann, *The Principle of Sustainability*, p. 175.
[1956] Cullinan, *Wild Law*, p. 60.

Bibliography

Books

Agamben, Giorgio, *Homo Sacer: Sovereign Power and Bare Life* (Turkish version), trans. İsmail Türkmen, Ayrıntı, Istanbul, 2001.

Akal, Cemal Bâli, *Hukuk Nedir?*, Dost, Ankara, 2017.

Arıkan, Engin, *Hayvan Hakları İnsan Hukuku*, Ekin, Bursa, 2016.

Barrau, Aurélien, *Le Plus Grand Défi de l'Histoire de l'Humanité: Face à la Catastrophe Ecologique et Sociale*, Michel Lafon, Neuilly-sur-Seine, 2019.

Baudrillard, Jean, *La Société de Consommation* (Turkish version), trans. Hazal Deliceçay – Ferda Keskin, 3rd ed., Ayrıntı, Istanbul, 2008.

Bennett, Natalie, *Change Everything*, Unbound, London, 2024.

Beudart, Manon, *Right to a Healthy Environment: Shortcomings in Rights-Based Climate Litigation and Possible Advancements in Europe* (Master's thesis, Department of Public Law and Governance – Tilburg Law School, Tilburg University), Tilburg, 2023.

Bookchin, Murray, *The Next Revolution: Popular Assemblies and the Promise of Direct Democracy* (Turkish version), trans. İbrahim Yıldız – Soner Torlak, Dipnot Yayınları, Ankara, 2015.

Bookchin, Murray, *The Ecology of Freedom: The Emergence and Dissolution of Hierarchy* (Turkish version), trans. Mustafa Kemal Coşkun, Sümer Yayıncılık, İstanbul, 2013.

Bookchin, Murray, *Social Ecology and Communalism* (Turkish version), trans. Fuat Dara Elhüseyni, Sümer Yayıncılık, Istanbul, 2013.

Bosselmann, Klaus, *The Principle of Sustainability: Transforming Law and Governance*, 2nd ed., Routledge, London & New York, 2017.

Bosselmann, Klaus, *When Two Worlds Collide: Society and Ecology*, RSVP, Auckland, 1995.

Boyar, Oya, *Anayasal Yoruma Giriş*, On İki Levha, Istanbul, 2021.

Boyd, David R., *The Environmental Rights Revolution: A Global Study of Constitutions, Human Rights, and the Environment*, UBC Press, Vancouver, 2012.

Boyd, David R., *The Rights of Nature: A Legal Revolution That Could Save The World* (Kindle edition), ECW Press, Toronto, 2017.

Braidotti, Rosi, *The Posthuman* (Turkish version), trans. Öznur Karakaş, 3rd ed., Kolektif Kitap, Istanbul, 2021.

Capra, Fritjof – Mattei, Ugo, *The Ecology of Law: Toward a Legal System in Tune with Nature and Community* (Turkish version), trans. Ebru Kılıç, Koç University Press, Istanbul, 2017.

Carson, Rachel, *Silent Spring* (Kindle edition), Tingle Books, Hapur, 2021.

Chomsky, Noam – Pollin, Robert, *Climate Crisis and the Global Green New Deal* (Turkish version), trans. Onur Orhangazi, Ütopya, Ankara, 2021.

Cochrane, Alasdair, *Animal Rights Without Liberation: Applied Ethics and Human Obligations*, Columbia University Press, New York, 2012.

Collins, Lynda, *The Ecological Constitution: Reframing Environmental Law*, Routledge, London & New York, 2021.

Coşkun, İzel Levi, *Süreklilikten Sürdürülebilirliğe: Bir Kurumsal Sürdürülebilirlik Yolculuğu*, 3rd ed., Artisan, Istanbul, 2022.

Cullinan, Cormac, *Wild Law: A Manifesto for Earth Justice* (Kindle edition), 2nd ed., Green Books, Totnes, 2011.

Davis, Margaret, *EcoLaw: Legality, Life, and the Normativity of Nature*, Routledge, Abingdon & New York, 2022.

Dehm, Julia, *Reconsidering REDD+: Authority, Power and Law in the Green Economy*, Cambridge University Press, Cambridge, 2021.

DesJardins, Joseph R., *Environmental Ethics: An Introduction to Environmental Philosophy* (Turkish version), trans. Ruşen Keleş, İmge, Ankara, 2006.

Descola, Philippe, *Beyond Nature and Culture* (Turkish version), trans. İsmail Yerguz, Istanbul Bilgi University Press, Istanbul, 2013.

Durmaz, Evrim, *Doğanın Hakları: Çevre Hukukuna Alternatif Bir Kuram*, On İki Levha, Istanbul, 2023.

Dworkin, Ronald, *Taking Rights Seriously* (Turkish version), trans. Ahmet Ulvi Türkbağ, Dost, Ankara, 2007.

Eckersley, Robyn, *The Green State: Rethinking Democracy and Sovereignty* (Kindle edition), MIT Press Academic, Cambridge, Massachusetts, 2004.

Fairhurst, Kirsty, *Our Obligation to Future Generations: A Human Rights Approach in the Case of Neubauer et al. v Germany* (Master's thesis, Universitat Pompeu Fabra, European and Global Law), Barcelona, 2022.

Fowles, John, *The Tree* (Turkish version), trans. Süha Sertabiboğlu, Ayrıntı, Istanbul, 2020.

Freund, Peter – George Martin, *The Ecology of the Automobile* (Turkish version), trans. Gürol Koca, Ayrıntı Yayınları, Istanbul, 1996.

Foster, John Bellamy, *Capitalism in the Anthropocene: Ecological Ruin or Ecological Revolution*, Monthly Review Press, New York, 2022.

Fotopoulos, Takis, *Towards an Inclusive Democracy: The Crisis of the Growth Economy and the Need for a New Liberatory Project*, Cassel, London & New York, 1997.

Francione, Gary, *Animals as Persons: Essays on the Abolition of Animal Exploitation*, Columbia University Press, New York, 2008.

Francione, Gary, *Animals, Property and the Law*, Temple University Press, Philadelphia, 2007.

Francione, Gary, *Introduction to Animal Rights: Your Child or the Dog?* (Turkish version), trans. Renan Akman – Elçin Gen, İletişim, Istanbul, 2008.

Garrard, Greg, *Ecocriticism* (Turkish version), trans. Ertuğrul Genç, Kolektif Kitap, Istanbul, 2016.

Gimpel, Jean, *La Révolution industrielle au Moyen Age* (Turkish version), trans. Nazım Özüaydın, 6th ed., TÜBİTAK, Ankara, 2004.

Gruen, Lori, *Ethics and Animals: An Introduction* (Kindle version), Cambridge University Press, New York, 2011.

Harari, Yuval Noah, *Sapiens: A Brief History of Humankind* (Turkish version), 11th ed., Kolektif Kitap, Istanbul, 2016.

Harman, Chris, *A People's History of the World: From the Stone Age to the New Millenium* (Turkish version), trans. Uygur Kocabaşoğlu, 3rd ed., Yordam Kitap, Istanbul, 2013.

Harman, Graham, *Object-Oriented Ontology: A New Theory of Everything* (Turkish version), trans. Oğuz Karayemiş, Tellekt, Istanbul, 2020.

Hengeveld, Rob, *Wasted World: How Our Consumption Challenges the Planet* (Turkish version), trans. Nafiz Güder, Türkiye İş Bankası, Istanbul, 2019.

Hickel, Jason, *Less is More: How Degrowth Will Save the World* (Kindle edition), Windmill Books, London, 2021.

Hulme, Mike, *Why We Disagree about Climate Change: Understanding Controversy, Inaction and Opportunity* (Turkish version), trans. Merve Özenç, Alfa, Istanbul, 2016.

Jackson, Tim, *Post Growth: Life after Capitalism* (Turkish version), trans. Akın Emre Pilgir, Ayrıntı, Istanbul, 2023.

Kaboğlu, İbrahim Ö., *Anayasa Hukuku Dersleri (Genel Esaslar)*, 16th ed., Legal, İstanbul, 2021.

Kaboğlu, İbrahim Ö. – Nihan Yancı Özalp, *Çevre Hakkı*, Tekin, İstanbul, 2021.

Keleş, Ruşen – Can Hamamcı – Aykut Çoban, *Çevre Politikası*, 7th ed., İmge, Ankara, 2012.

Klein, Naomi, *This Changes Everything: Capitalism vs. the Climate* (Turkish version), trans. Osman Akınhay, Agora Kitaplığı, Istanbul, 2015.

Klein, Naomi, *On Fire: The Burning Case for a Green New Deal* (Turkish version), trans. Elif Sema Mutlu, Doğan Kitap, Istanbul, 2021.

Kolbert, Elizabeth, *Sixth Extinction: An Unnatural History* (Turkish version), trans. Nalan Tümay, 7th ed., Okuyan Us, Istanbul, 2022.

Kurnaz, Levent, *Son Buzul Erimeden: İklim Değişikliği Hakkında Merak Ettiğiniz Her Şey*, 3rd ed., Doğan Kitap, Istanbul, 2022.

Lafargue, Paul, *Le Droit à la Paresse* (Turkish version), trans. Ali Berktay, 6th ed., Türkiye İş Bankası Kültür Yayınları, Istanbul, September 2023.

Latouche, Serge, *Vers une Société d'Abondance frugale* (Turkish version), trans. Tahir Karakaş, İletişim, Istanbul, 2018.

Leopold, Aldo, *A Sand County Almanac* (Turkish version), trans. Ufuk Özdağ, Hacettepe Üniversitesi Yayınları, Ankara, 2013.

Lovelock, James, *La Terre est un Être Vivant: L'Hypothèse Gaïa*, Flammarion, Paris, 1993.

Lovelock, James, *The Revenge of Gaia: Earth's Climate Crisis & The Fate of Humanity*, Hachette UK, London, August 2007.

Löwy, Michael, *Ecosocialism: A Radical Alternative to Capitalist Catastrophe* (Kindle edition), Haymarket Books, Chicago, 2015.

Malm, Andreas, *How to Blow Up a Pipeline: Learning to Fight in a World on Fire* (Turkish version), trans. Kurtay Kağan Işıtan, Ayrıntı, Istanbul, 2022.

Marks, Robert B., *The Origins of the Modern World: A Global and Environmental Narrative from the Fifteenth to the Twenty-First Century* (Kindle edition), 4th ed, Rowman & Littlefield, Lanham, 2020.

May, James R. – Erin Daly, *Global Environmental Constitutionalism* (Turkish version), trans. Tolga Şirin – N. Umut Orcan, Ekoloji Kolektifi, Istanbul, 2018.

Mbembe, Achille, *Brutalism* (Turkish version), trans. P. Burcu Yalım, İletişim, Istanbul, 2022.

McKibben, Bill, *Eaarth: Making a Life on a Tough New Planet* (Turkish version), trans. Emel Anıl, Türkiye İş Bankası Kültür Yayınları, Istanbul, 2011.

Meadows, Donella H. – Meadows, Dennis L. – Randers, Jørgen – Behrens III, William W., *Limits to Degrowth: A Report for the Club of Rome's Project on the Predicament of Mankind*, Universe Books, New York, 1972.

Morton, Timothy, *Hyperobjects: Philosophy and Ecology after the End of the World* (Turkish version), trans. Bilge Demirtaş, Tellekt, Istanbul, 2020.

Oder, Bertil Emrah, *Anayasa Yargısında Yorum Yöntemleri*, Beta, Istanbul, 2010.

Özenç, Berke, *Hukuk Devleti: Kökenleri ve Küreselleşme Çağındaki İşlevi*, İletişim, Istanbul, 2014.

Pactet, Pierre, *Institutions Politiques – Droit Constitutionnel*, 16th ed., Armand Colin, Paris, 1997.

Parrique, Timothée, *Ralentir ou Périr: L'Économie de la Décroissance*, Seuil, Paris, 2022.

Poggi, Gianfranco, *The Development of the Modern State: A Sociological Introduction* (Turkish version), trans. Şule Kut – Binnaz Toprak, 4th ed., Istanbul Bilgi University Press, Istanbul, 2007.

Ponting, Clive, *A New Green History of the World: The Environment and the Collapse of Great Civilisations* (Turkish version), trans. Ayşe Başcı-Sander, Sabancı University Press, Istanbul, 2000.

Proudhon, Pierre-Joseph, *Qu'est-ce que la Propriété?* (Turkish version), trans. Devrim Çetinkasap, 12th ed., Türkiye İş Bankası Kültür Yayınları, Istanbul, June 2023.

Radkau, Joachim, *Nature and Power: A Global History of the Environment* (Turkish version), trans. Nafiz Güder, Türkiye İş Bankası Kültür Yayınları, Istanbul, 2017.

Regan, Tom, *Empty Cages: Facing the Challenge of Animal Rights* (Turkish version), trans. Serpil Çağlayan, İletişim, İstanbul, 2007.

Regan, Tom, *The Case for Animal Rights*, University of California Press, California, 1983.

Reyhan, Hakan, *Ekolojik Emperyalizm: Gıdaya Tahakkümün Biyopolitiği*, Alter, Ankara, 2012.

Saito, Kohei, *Slow Down: How Degrowth Communism Can Save The Earth* (Kindle edition), trans. Brian Bergstrom, Weidenfeld & Nicolson, London, Ocak 2024.

Schmelzer, Matthias – Vetter, Andrea – Vansintjan, Aaron, *The Future is Degrowth: A Guide to a World Beyond Capitalism*, Verso, London & New York, 2022.

Scranton, Roy, *Learning to Die in the Anthropocene: Reflections on the End of a Civilization* (Turkish version), trans. Deniz Tordum, Edebi Şeyler, Istanbul, 2019.

Serres, Michel, *Le Contrat Naturel* (Turkish version), trans. Turhan Ilgaz, Yapı Kredi Yayınları, Istanbul, 1994.

Shiva, Vandana, *Soil Not Oil: Environmental Justice in an Age of Climate Crisis* (Turkish version), trans. Özge Olcay, 2nd ed., Sinek Sekiz, Istanbul, 2014.

Shiva, Vandana, *Earth Democracy: Justice, Sustainability, and Peace* (Turkish version), trans. Ali K. Saysel – Elçin Gen – Onur Günay, BGST Yayınları, Istanbul, 2010.

Singer, Peter, *Animal Liberation* (Turkish version), trans. Hayrullah Doğan, Ayrıntı Yayınları, Istanbul, 2005.

Smith, Adam, *An Inquiry into the Nature and Causes of the Wealth of Nations*, Liberty Classics, Indianapolis, 1979.

Stone, Christopher D., *Should Trees Have Standing? Law, Morality, and the Environment* (Kindle edition), 3rd ed., Oxford University Press, New York, 2010.

Tanuro, Daniel, *L'Impossible Capitalisme vert* (Turkish version), trans. Volkan Yalçıntoklu, Habitus, Istanbul, 2011.

Tokar, Brian, *Toward Climate Justice: Perspectives on the Climate Crisis and Social Change* (Kindle edition), New Compass Press, Porsgrunn, 2014.

Touchard, Jean, *Histoire des Idées Politiques* (Turkish version), trans. İsmail Yerguz, Islık Yayınları, Istanbul, 2015.

Tzouvala, Ntina, *Capitalism as Civilisation: A History of International Law*, Cambridge University Press, Cambridge, 2020.

Üskül Engin, Zeynep Özlem, *Ekolojik Kriz, Etik ve Hukuk*, Filiz Kitabevi, Istanbul, 2017.

Yılmaz, Gaye, *Suyun Metalaştırılması: Kıtlığın Nedeni Kıtlığa Çare Olabilir mi?*, Evrensel Basım Yayın, Istanbul, 2013.

Van Caenegem, R. C., *An Historical Introduction to Private Law* (Turkish version), trans. Ali Acar – Caner Birdal – İbrahim Doğan Takavut – O. Vahdet İşsevenler – Zeynep Arslan, Pinhan Yayıncılık, Istanbul, 2022.

Vile, Maurice John Crawley, *Constitutionalism and the Separation of Powers*, 2nd ed., Liberty Fund, Indianapolis, 1998.

Wallace-Wells, David, *The Uninhabitable Earth: A Story of the Future* (Turkish version), trans. Ebru Kılıç, Domingo, İstanbul, 2020.

Wood, Ellen Meiksins, *Liberty and Property: A Social History of Western Political Thought from the Renaissance to Enlightenment* (Turkish version), trans. Oya Köymen, 2nd ed., Yordam Kitap, Istanbul, 2016.

Articles and book chapters

Agarwal, Anil – Narain, Sunita, 'Global Warming in an Unequal World: A Case of Environmental Colonialism', *in* Navroz K. Dubash (ed.), *India in a Warming World*, Oxford University Press, 2019, pp. 81–91.

Akgül, Onur, 'Adil Dönüşüm: İklim Krizinden Sağ Çıkmanın Politikası', *in* Didem Bayındır – Mine Yıldırım (ed.), *Ekoloji: Bir Arada Yaşamın Geleceği*, Tellekt, Istanbul, 2022, pp. 91–107.

Aşıcı, Ahmet Atıl, 'Sayılarla Dünyada ve Türkiye'de Yeşil Yeni Düzen', *in* Ahmet Atıl Aşıcı – Ümit Şahin (ed.), *Yeşil Ekonomi*, Yeni İnsan, Istanbul, (year not mentioned), pp. 206–17.

Arık, Burcu Meltem, 'Bir Arada İyi Yaşamı Yeryüzüyle (Birlikte) Öğrenerek Örmek: Biyomimikri', *in* Didem Bayındır – Mine Yıldırım (ed.), *Ekoloji: Bir Arada Yaşamın Geleceği*, Tellekt, Istanbul, 2022, pp. 449–67.

Balta, Ecehan – Mısır, Mustafa Bayram, 'Bir Politik Hareket Olarak Ekososyalizmin Ayırd Ediciliği ve Birleştiriciliği', *Praksis*, No. 25, 2011/11, pp. 11–29.

Barnosky, Anthony D. – Matzke, Nicolas – Tomiya, Susumu – Wogan, Guinevere O. U. – Swartz, Biran – Quental, Tiago B. – Marshall, Charles – MacGuire, Jenny L. – Lindsey, Emily L. – Maguire, Kaitlin C. – Mersey, Ben – Ferrer, Elizabeth A., 'Has the Earth's sixth mass extinction already arrived?', *Nature*, 471(7336), 2011.

Bayındır, Didem, 'Şimdinin Tarihini' Okumak', *in* Didem Bayındır – Mine Yıldırım (ed.), *Ekoloji – Bir Arada Yaşamın Geleceği*, Tellekt, Istanbul, 2022, pp. 7–14.

Bedford, Richard – Bedford, Charlotte, 'International Migration and Climate Change: A Post-Copenhagen Perspective on Options for Kiribati and Tuvalu', *in* Bruce Burson, *Climate Change and Migration – South Pacific Perspectives*, Institute for Policy Studies, 2010, pp. 89–134.

Benlisoy, Foti, 'İklim Krizi ve Yaklaşan İç Savaş', *in* Didem Bayındır – Mine Yıldırım (ed.), *Ekoloji – Bir Arada Yaşamın Geleceği*, Tellekt, İstanbul, 2022, pp. 161–91.

Bookchin, Murray, 'Ecology and Revolutionary Thought', *The Anarchist Library*, <https://theanarchistlibrary.org/library/lewis-herber-murray-bookchin-ecology-and-revolutionary-thought> (visited on 02.08.2023)

Castelli, Chiara – Castelli, Marta– Comincioli, Nicola – Parisi, Maria Laura – Pontarollo, Nicola – Vergalli, Sergio, 'Ecosytem Degradation and the Spread of COVID-19', *Environmental Monitoring and Assessment*, No. 195, paper no. 836, 2023.

Christie, Gordon, 'A Colonial Reading of Recent Jurisprudence: Sparrow, Delgamuukw, and Haida Nation', *Windsor Yearbook of Access to Justice*, Vol. 23, Allard Faculty Publications, 2005, pp. 17–53.

Colacurci, Marco, 'The Draft Convention Ecocide and the Role for Corporate Mediation. Some Insights from the International Monsanto Tribunal and a Recent Research Proposal', *International Criminal Law Review*, 2021, pp. 1–27.

Corina Heri, 'Climate Change Before the European Court of Human Rights: Capturing Risk, Ill-Treatment and Vulnerability', *The European Journal of International Law*, No. 33(3), 2022, pp. 925–51.

Crook, Martin – Short, Damien – South, Nigel,'Ecocide, genocide, capitalism and colonialism: Consequences for indigenous peoples and glocal ecosystems environements', *Theoretical Criminology*, Vol. 22, No. 3, 2018, pp. 298–317.

Çebi, Sezgin Seymen, 'Ekoloji, İdeoloji, Özneleşme ve Hukuk', *Doğu Batı*, No. 95, November-December-January 2020–21, pp. 11–44.

Çoraman, Emrah, 'Altıncı Büyük Yok Oluşu Durdurmak', *in* Didem Bayındır – Mine Yıldırım (ed.), *Ekoloji: Bir Arada Yaşamın Geleceği*, Tellekt, Istanbul, 2022, pp. 207–28.

Dedeoğlu, Çağdaş, 'Posthümanizm: Ekoloji İlişkisinin Sürdürülebilirlik Çerçevesinde Bir Değerlendirmesi', *in* Didem Bayındır – Mine Yıldırım (ed.), *Ekoloji: Bir Arada Yaşamın Geleceği*, Tellekt, Istanbul, 2022, s. 253–72.

Delice, Aslan, 'Karma Hükümetten Denetim ve Dengeye Erkler Ayrılığı İlkesi', *Selçuk University Faculty of Law Review*, Vol. 30, No. 3, 2022, pp. 1667–704.

Duguit, Léon, 'Egemenlik ve Özgürlük', *in* Cemal Bâli Akal, *Devlet Kuramı*, 2nd ed., Dost, Ankara, 2005, pp. 379–400.

Echeverría, Hugo, 'Rights of Nature: The Ecuadorian Case', *Revista Esmat*, Y. 9, No. 13, July-December 2017, pp. 77–86.

Easterbrook, Don. J., 'Geologic Evidence of Recurring Climate Cycles and Their Implications for the Cause of Global Climate Changes – The Past is the Key for the Future', *in Evidence-Based Climate Science*, Elsevier, 2011.

Fraser, Nancy, 'Climates of Capital' (Turkish version), trans. Deniz Keskin, *in* Didem Bayındır – Mine Yıldırım (ed.), *Ekoloji: Bir Arada Yaşamın Geleceği*, Tellekt, Istanbul, 2022, pp. 47–89.

Garnett, Stephen T. et al., 'A Spatial Overview of the Global Importance of Indigenous Lands for Conservation', *Nature Sustainability*, Vol. 1, No. 7, 2018, pp. 369–74, <https://www.nature.com/articles/s41893-018-0100-6> (visited on 05.06.2023.) <https://doi.org/10.1038/s41893-018-0100-6>

Gibbons, Elizabeth, 'Climate Change, Children's Rights, and the Pursuit of Intergenerational Climate Justice', *Health and Human Rights Journal*, Vol. 16, No. 1, June 2014, pp. 19–31.

Giménez, Teresa Vicente – Ortuño, Eduardo Salazar, 'An Ecological Citizenship's Triumph: From the Popular Legislative Initiative to the Rights Granted for the Mar Menor', *in* Jenny García Ruales – Katarina Hovden – Helen Kopnina – Colin D. Robertson – Hendrik Schoukens (ed.), *Rights of Nature in Europe: Encounters and Visions*, Routledge, Abingdon & New York, 2024, pp. 83–101.

Gonzalez, Carmen G., 'Foreword: Deconstructing the Legal Architecture of the Anthropocene', *in* Usha Natarajan – Julia Dehm (ed.), *Locating Nature – Making and Unmaking International Law*, Cambridge University Press, Cambridge, 2022, p. ix–xi.

Goodpaster, Kenneth, 'On Being Morally Considerable', *Journal of Philosophy*, Vol. 75, No. 6, 1978, pp. 308–25.

Gündoğan İbrişim, Deniz, 'Ekolojinin Yazısı: Edebiyat', *in* Didem Bayındır – Mine Yıldırım (ed.), *Ekoloji: Bir Arada Yaşamın Geleceği*, Tellekt, Istanbul, 2022, pp. 427–48.

Gürcan, Efe Can, 'Guerre et Crise Agraire en Syrie: Revisiter le Conflit Syrien au Prisme de la Justice Écologique', *Possibles*, Vol. 41, No. 2, Spring 2017, pp. 63–74.

Hansen, James – Sato, Makiko – Kharecha, Pushker – Beerling, David – Berner, Robert – Masson-Delmotte, Valerie – Pagani, Mark – Raymo, Maureen – Royer, Dana L. – Zachos, James C., 'Target Atmospheric CO_2: Where Should Humanity Aim', *The Open Atmospheric Science Journal*, No. 2, 2008, pp. 217–31.

Haraway, Donna, 'Anthropocene, Capitalocene, Plantationocene, Chthulucene: Making Kin', *Environmental Humanities*, Vol. 6, 2015, pp. 159–65.

Helfer, Laurence R., 'Redesigning the European Court of Human Rights: Embeddedness as a Deep Structural Principle of the European Human Rights Regime', *The European Journal of International Law*, Vol. 19, No. 1, pp. 125–59.

Hellner, Agnes – Epstein, Yaffa, 'Allocation of Institutional Responsibility for Climate Change Mitigation: Judicial Applications of Constitutional Environmental Provisions in the European Climate Cases *Arctic Oil, Neubauer*, and *l'Affaire du Siècle*', *Journal of Environmental Law*, Vol. 35, No. 2, July 2023, pp. 207–27.

Hickel, Jason, 'What Does Degrowth Mean? A Few Points of Clarification', *Globalizations*, Vol. 18, No. 7, 2021, pp. 1105–11.

Higgins, Polly – Short, Damien – South, Nigel, 'Protecting the Planet: a Proposal for a Law of Ecocide', *Crime, Law and Social Change*, No. 59, April 2013, doi: <10.1007/s10611-013-9413-6>, pp. 251–66.

Hsiang, Solomon – Burke, Marshall – Miguel, Edward, 'Quantifying the Influence of Climate on Human Conflict', *Science* 341, 1235367

(Summary through Stanford University: <https://web.stanford.edu/~mburke/papers/Hsiang_Burke_Miguel_2013_summary.pdf> [visited on 16.01.2025])

Islam, Mohammad Sohidul – O'Donnell, Erin, 'Legal Rights for the Turag: Rivers as Living Entities in Bangladesh', *Asia Pacific Journal of Environmental Law*, Vol. 23, No. 2, 2020, pp. 160–77.

Jaria-Manzano, Jordi – Borrás, Susana, 'Introduction to the Research Handbook on Global Climate Constitutionalism' *in* Jordi Jaria-Manzano – Susana Borrás (ed.), *Research Handbook on Global Climate Constitutionalism*, Edward Elgar, 2019, pp. 1–16.

Kallis, Giorgos – Hickel, Jason – O'Neill, Daniel W. – Jackson, Tim – Victor, Peter A. – Raworth, Kate – Schor, Juliet B. – Steinberger, Julia K. – Ürge-Vorsatz, Diana, 'Post-growth: The Science of Wellbeing within Planetary Boundaries', *Lancet Planet Health*, No. 9, 2025, pp. e62–e78.

Kelley, Colin P. – Mohtadi, Shahrzad – Cane, Mark A. – Seager, Richard – Kushnir, Yochanan, 'Climate Change in the Fertile Crescent and Implications of the Recent Syrian Drought', *PNAS*, Vol. 112, No. 11, 17 March 2015, pp. 3241–6, <https://www.pnas.org/doi/epdf/10.1073/pnas.1421533112> (visited on 14.08.2023)

Kauffman, Craig M. – Martin, Pamela L., 'How Courts Are Developing River Rights Jurisprudence: Comparing Guardianship in New Zealand, Colombia, and India', *Vermont Journal of Environmental Law*, Vol. 40, No. 4, 2019, pp. 260–89.

Kıygı, Gizem, 'Çocuklarla Kentsel Ekoloji: Bir Çınarın Gölgesinde Adaleti Aramak', *in* Didem Bayındır – Mine Yıldırım (ed.), *Ekoloji: Bir Arada Yaşamın Geleceği*, Tellekt, Istanbul, 2022, pp. 469–85.

Kotzé, Louis J., 'Arguing Global Environmental Constitutionalism', *Transnational Environmental Law*, Vol. 1, No. 1, April 2012, pp. 199–233.

Kotzé, Louis J., '*Neubauer et al. versus Germany*: Planetary Climate Litigation for the Anthropocene?', *German Law Journal*, Vol. 22, No. 8, December 2021, pp. 1423–44.

Kotzé, Louis J. – du Plessis, Anél, 'Putting Africa on the Stand: A Bird's Eye View of Climate Change Litigation on the Continent', *University of Oregon Journal of Environmental Law and Litigation*, Vol. 50, No. 3, 2019. (Through the archive of Lincoln University: <http://eprints.lincoln.ac.uk/id/eprint/36688/> [visited on 06.07.2023]),

Kotzé, Louis J. – Kim, Rakhyun E., 'Towards Planetary Nexus Governance in the Anthropocene: En Earth System Law Perspective', *Global Policy*, No. 13 (Suppl. 3), 2022, pp. 86–97.

Koybasi, Serkan, 'Ekokırım Suçunun Tanınması', *Bahçeşehir University Law Faculty Review*, Vol. 17, No. 210, September-October 2022, pp. 1047–85.

Koybasi, Serkan, 'Ekvator Anayasası'nda Doğa Ana'nın Haklarının Tanınmasının Anayasa Yargısına Etkisi', *in* Asos Congress, *Tam Metin Kitabı*, Asos Yayınevi, Elazığ, 2022, pp. 384–402.

Koybasi, Serkan, 'Hayvan Hakları: Mülkiyet, Eşitlik, Hukuk', *in* Didem Bayındır – Mine Yıldırım (ed.), *Ekoloji – Bir Arada Yaşamın Geleceği*, Tellekt, Istanbul, 2022, pp. 337–57.

Koybasi, Serkan, 'Yeni Bir Anayasal Hak Öznesi Olarak Hayvan – I', *Journal of Constitutional Law*, Vol. 7, No. 13, 2018, pp. 103–56.

Koybasi, Serkan, 'Yeni Bir Anayasal Hak Öznesi Olarak Hayvan – II', *Journal of Constitutional Law*, Vol 7, No. 14, 2018, pp. 357–422.

Koybasi, Serkan, 'Yeni Tunus Anayasası'nın Yazım Süreci ve Sürecin Sonuca Yansıması', *Prof Dr Feridun Yenisey'e Armağan*, Vol. II, Beta, İstanbul, 2014, pp. 2297–362.

Krämer, Ludwig, 'Rights of Nature in Europe: The Spanish Lagoon Mar Moner Becomes a Legal Person', *Journal for European Environmental & Planning Law*, No. 20 (2023), pp. 5–23.

Küçük, Mustafa Emir – Onur İnal, 'Antroposentrizmin Ötesinde: Türkiye Modernleşme ve Kent Tarihinde Çalışan Hayvanlar', *in* Didem Bayındır – Mine Yıldırım (ed.), *Ekoloji: Bir Arada Yaşamın Geleceği*, Tellekt, Istanbul, 2022, pp. 399–425.

Lay, Bronwyn – Neyret, Laurent – Short, Damien – Urs, Michael – Oposa Jr, Antonio A., 'Timely and Necessary: Ecocide Law as Urgent and Emerging', *The Journal Jurisprudence*, Vol. 28, December 2015, pp. 431–52.

Le Quéré, Corinne – Peters, Glen P. – Friedlingstein, Pierre – Andrew, Robbie M. – Canadell, Josep G. – Davis, Steven J. – Jackson, Robert B. – Jones, Matthew W., 'Fossil CO_2 Emissions in the Post-COVID-19 Era', *Nature Climate Change*, No. 11, March 2021, pp. 197–99.

Lears, T. J. Jackson, 'The Concept of Cultural Hegemony: Problems and Possibilities', *The American History Review*, Vol. 90, No. 3, June 1985, pp. 567–93.

Lenton, Timothy M. – Rockström, Johan – Gaffney, Owen – Rahmstorf, Stefan – Richardson, Katherine – Steffen, Will – Schellnuber, Hans Joachim, 'Climate Tipping Points Too Risky to Bet Against', *Nature*, 575(7784), 2020, pp. 592–95, <https://doi.org/10.1038/d41586-019-03595-0>.

M'Gonigle, Michael – Ramsay, Paula, 'Greening Environmental Law: From Sectoral Reform to Systemic Reformation', *Journal of Environmental Law and Practice*, S. 14, 2004. (Accessed through Polis Project: <https://polisproject.org/polis-research-publication/greening-environmental-law-from-sectoral-reform-to-systemic-re-formation/> [visited on 23.05.2023])

May, James R. – Daly, Erin, 'Six Trends in Global Environmental Constitutionalism', in *Environmental Constitutionalism: Impact on Legal Systems?*, Peter Lang Publishing, Oxford (in press). (Accessed through SSRN: <https://papers.ssrn.com/sol3/papers.cfm?abstract_id=3252636> [visited on 24.05.2023])

Mavronicola, Natasa, 'The future is a foreign country: Understanding state (in)action on climate change as ill-treatment', *Strasbourg Observer*, 19 October 2021, <https://strasbourgobservers.com/2021/10/19/the-future-is-a-foreign-country-understanding-state-inaction-on-climate-change-as-ill-treatment/> (visited on 30.08.2023)

Minnerop, Petra, 'The 'Advance Interference-Like Effect' of Climate Targets: Fundamental Rights, Intergenerational Equity and the German Federal Constitutional Court', *Journal of Environmental Law*, Vol. 34, No. 1, March 2022, pp. 135–62.

Moore, Tom R., 'Should Trees Have Standing? Toward Legal Rights for Natural Objects – Book Review', *Florisa State University Law Review*, Vol. 2, No. 3, 1974, pp. 672–75.

Natarajan, Usha – Dehm, Julia, 'Introduction: Where is the Environment? Locating Nature in International Law', *in* Usha Natarajan – Julia Dehm (ed.), *Locating Nature: Making and Unmaking International Law*, Cambridge University Press, Cambridge, 2022, pp. 1–18.

Natarajan, Usha – Khoday, Kishan, 'Making and Unmaking International Law', *in* Usha Natarajan – Julia Dehm (ed.), *Locating Nature: Making and Unmaking International Law*, Cambridge University Press, Cambridge, 2022, pp. 21–44.

Neef, Andreas – Benge, Lucy, 'Shifting Responsibility and Denying Justice: New Zealand's Contentious Approach to Pacific Climate Mobilities', *Regional Environmental Change*, No. 22, paper no. 94, 2022, <https://doi.org/10.1007/s10113-022-01951-x>.

Nolan, Aoife, 'Children's Rights and Climate Change at the UN Committee on the Rights of the Child: Pragmatism and Principle in Sacchi v Argentina', *EJIL: Talk*, 20 October 2021, <https://www.ejiltalk.org/childrens-rights-and-climate-change-at-the-un-committee-on-the-rights-of-the-child-pragmatism-and-principle-in-sacchi-v-argentina/?utm_source=pocket_saves> (visited on 12.12.2022)

Orhan, Gözde, 'Farklı Ölçeklerde Yerleşme, Tahribat ve Adalet Sorunları: Kent ve Kır Ekolojileri', *in* Didem Bayındır – Mine Yıldırım (ed.), *Ekoloji: Bir Arada Yaşamın Geleceği*, Tellekt, Istanbul, 2022, pp. 381–97.

Orhan, Gözde, 'Modernizm ve Kapitalizm Sarmalında Ekoloji: Devlet, Sermaye, Sivil Toplum', *Praksis*, No. 25, 2011/1, pp. 31–47.

Özer, Sanem, 'İklim Değişikliği ve Çatışmalar', *Doğu Batı*, No. 95, November-December-January 2020–21, pp. 45–73.

Özlüer, Fevzi, 'Ekososyalist Bir Kır Hareketine Doğru', *Ecotopianetwork*, 14 December 2009, <https://ecotopianetwork.wordpress.com/2009/12/14/ekososyalist-bir-kir-kent-hareketine-dogru-fevzi-ozluer/> (visited on 26.07.2023)

Özlüer, Fevzi, 'Pachamama'nın Gücü ya da Bolivya Anayasası'nın Uluslararası Hukuka ve Siyasete Etkisi', Mahmut Fevzi Özlüer – Ilgın Özkaya Özlüer – Tolga Şirin – Nazım Sinan Odabaşı (ed.), *Bolivya Anayasası: Hukuk, Demokrasi, Özerklik*, Phoenix, Ankara, 2012, pp. 63–83.

Öztürk, Çiğdem, 'Savaşın Yuttuğu Hayvanlar', *in* Didem Bayındır – Mine Yıldırım (ed.), *Ekoloji: Bir Arada Yaşamın Geleceği*, Tellekt, Istanbul, 2022, pp. 273–92.

Pezzot, Romina – Graf, Jan-Phillip, 'Ecocide – Legal Revolution pf Symbolism?', *Völkerrechtsblog*, 3 February 2022, doi: 10.17176/20220203-120935-0, <https://voelkerrechtsblog.org/ecocide-legal-revolution-or-symbolism/> (visited on 28.08.2023)

Prior, Stephen A. – Runion, G. Brett – Marble, S. Christopher – Rogers, Hugo H. – Gilliam, Charles H. – Torbert, H. Allen, 'A Review of Elevated Atmospheric CO_2 Effects on Plant Growth and Water

Relations: Implications for Horticulture', *Horticulture Science*, Vol. 46, No. 2, February 2011, pp. 158–62.

Prist, Paula R. – Sangermano, Florencia – Bailey, Allison et al., 'Protecting Brazilian Amazon Indigenous Territories Reduces Atmospheric Particulates and Avoids Associated Health Impacts and Costs', *Communications Earth & Environment*, Vol. 4, paper 34, 2023, <https://doi.org/10.1038/s43247-023-00704-w>.

Ray, Gene, 'Writing the Ecocide-Genocide Knot: Indigenous Knowledge and Critical Theory in the Endgame', *Documenta14*, No. 3, pp. 118–36.

Rikani, Albano – Frieler, Katja – Schewe, Jacob, 'Climate Change and International Migration: Exploring the Macroeconomic Channel', *PLoS One*, Vol. 17, No. 11, 16 November 2022.

Rival, Laura, 'The Yasuní-ITT Initiative: Oil Development and Alternative Forms of Wealth Making in the Ecuadorian Amazon', *in* A. Bebbington (ed.), *Extractive Economies, Socio-Environmental Conflicts and Territorial Transformations in the Andean Region* (in press). (Accessed through Research Gate: <https://www.researchgate.net/publication/46475250_The_Yasuni-ITT_Initiative_Oil_Development_and_Alternative_Forms_of_Wealth_Making_in_the_Ecuadorian_Amazon> [visited on 03.08.2023])

Sanson, Ann V. – Burke, Susie E. L., 'Climate Change and Children: An Issue of Intergenerational Justice', *in* Balvin, Nikola – Christie, Daniel J. (ed.), *Children and Peace – From Research to Action*, Springer Open, 2020, pp. 343–62.

Schweickart, David, 'Is Sustainable Capitalism an Oxymoron?', *Perspectives on Global Development and Technology*, Vol. 8, No. 2–3, 2009, pp. 557–78 (Accessed through Research Gate: <https://www.researchgate.net/publication/315339512_Is_Sustainable_Capitalism_An_Oxymoron> [visited on 02.08.2023])

Şahin, Ümit, 'İklim Krizine Kavramsal Bir Giriş', *in* Didem Bayındır – Mine Yıldırım (ed.), *Ekoloji: Bir Arada Yaşamın Geleceği*, Tellekt, Istanbul, 2022, pp. 17–45.

Şirin, Tolga, 'Yeni Bolivya Anayasası Üzerine Bazı Notlar', *in* Mahmut Fevzi Özlüer – Ilgın Özkaya Özlüer – Tolga Şirin – Nazım Sinan Odabaşı (ed.), *Bolivya Anayasası – Hukuk, Demokrasi, Özerklik*, Phoenix, Ankara, 2012, pp. 7–40.

The Greens in the European Parliament, 'Yeşil Yeni Düzene Neden İhtiyaç Duyuyoruz?', çev. İnan Mayıs Aru, *in* Ahmet Atıl Aşıcı – Ümit Şahin (ed.), *Yeşil Ekonomi*, Yeni İnsan, İstanbul, (year not mentioned), pp. 133–49.

Yancı Özalp, Nihan, 'Türkiye Ekolojik Anayasacılığın Neresinde?', *in* Nihan Yancı Özalp – Sinem Şirin (ed.), *1982 Anayasası'nın 30. Yıl Bilançosu*, On İki Levha Yayınları, 2014, Istanbul, pp. 105–23.

Yurtcanlı Duymaz, Seda, 'Bir İnsan Hakları Sorunu Olarak İklim Değişikliği', *Journal of Constitutional Law*, Vol. 8, No. 16, 2019, pp. 491–532.

White Jr, Lynn, 'The Historical Roots of Our Ecological Crisis', *Science*, Vol. 155, No. 3767, 10 March 1967, pp. 1203–7.

Reports

Aid, Christian, *Climate Breakdown 2024 – 6 Months of Climate Chaos Since COP 28*, June 2024.

Anaya, James, *Report of the Special Rapporteur on the Rights of Indigenous People – Extractive Industries and Indigenous People*, Human Rights Council, A/HRC/24/41, 1 July 2013, <https://undocs.org/Home/Mobile?FinalSymbol=A%2FHRC%2F24%2F41&Language=E&DeviceType=Desktop&LangRequested=False> (visited on 05.06.2023)

Asian Development Bank, *Addressing Climate Change and Migration in Asia and the Pacific – Final Report*, 2012, <https://www.adb.org/sites/default/files/publication/29662/addressing-climate-change-migration.pdf> (visited on 31.07.2023)

Boyd, David R., *Report of the Special Rapporteur on the Issue of Human Rights Obligations Relating to the Enjoyment of a Safe, Clean, Healthy and Sustainable Environment*, BM General Assembly, UN DOC A/74/161, 15 July 2019, <https://undocs.org/Home/Mobile?FinalSymbol=A%2F74%2F161&Language=E&DeviceType=Desktop&LangRequested=False> (visited on 05.07.2023)

Boyd, David R., *Report of the Special Rapporteur on the Issue of Human Rights Obligations Relating to the Enjoyment of a Safe, Clean, Healthy and Sustainable Environment*, BM General Assembly, UN DOC A/75/161, 15 July 2020, <https://documents-dds-ny.un.org/doc/UNDOC/GEN/N20/184/48/PDF/N2018448.pdf?OpenElement> (visited on 11.05.2023)

Brundtland, Gro Harlem, *Report of the World Commission on Environment and Development: Our Common Future*, 20 March 1987, <https://sustainabledevelopment.un.org/content/documents/5987our-common-future.pdf> (visited on 25.07.2023)

Clement, Viviane – Rigaud, Kanta Kumari – de Sherbinin, Alex – Jones, Bryan – Adamo, Susana – Schewe, Jacob – Sadiq, Nian – Shahabat, Elham, *Groundswell: Acting on Internal Climate Migration – Part II – Overview*, World Bank Group, 2021, <https://openknowledge.worldbank.org/entities/publication/2c9150df-52c3-58ed-9075-d78ea56c3267> (visited on 31.08.2023)

CNA, *National Security and the Threat of Climate Change*, 2007, <https://www.cna.org/archive/CNA_Files/pdf/national%20security%20and%20the%20threat%20of%20climate%20change.pdf> (visited on 14.08.2023)

Department of Energy, *2024 US Energy & Employment Jobs Report (USEER)*, <https://www.energy.gov/policy/us-energy-employment-jobs-report-useer> (visited on 01.10.2024)

FAO, *The State of the World's Forests: Forests, Biodiversity and People*, 2020, <https://www.fao.org/documents/card/en/c/ca8642en> (visited on 12.05.2023)

Hoerner, J. Andrew – Robinson, Nia, *A Climate of Change: African Americans, Global Warming, and A Just Policy in the U.S.*, Environmental Justice and Climate Change Initiative, Oakland, California, 2008, <https://climateaccess.org/resource/climate-change-african-americans-global-warming-and-just-climate-policy-us> (visited on 01.08.2023)

House of Commons, *The UK's Plans and Progress to Reach Net Zero by 2050*, 26 September 2024, <https://researchbriefings.files.parliament.uk/documents/CBP-9888/CBP-9888.pdf> (visited on 01.10.2024)

Human Rights Watch, *'The Sea Is Eating The Land Below Our Homes' – Indigenous Community Facing Lack of Space and Rising Seas Plans Relocation*, 2023, <https://www.hrw.org/report/2023/07/31/sea-eating-land-below-our-homes/indigenous-community-facing-lack-space-and-rising> (visited on 31.07.2023)

IEA, *CO_2 Emissions in 2022*, March 2023, <https://www.iea.org/reports/co2-emissions-in-2022> (visited on 30.08.2023)

IEA, *Global Energy Outlook 2019*, 2019, <https://iea.blob.core.windows.net/assets/98909c1b-aabc-4797-9926-35307b418cdb/WEO2019-free.pdf> (visited on 29.03.2023)

IPBES, *Global assessment report on biodiversity and ecosystem services of the Intergovernmental Science-Policy Platform on Biodiversity and Ecosystem Services*, 2019, E. S. Brondizio, J. Settele, S. Díaz, and H. T. Ngo (ed.), IPBES secretariat, Bonn, Germany, <https://doi.org/10.5281/zenodo.3831673> (visited on 20.03.2023)

IPBES, *Report of the Plenary of the Intergovernmental Science-Policy Platform on Biodiversity and Ecosystem Services on the work of its seventh session*, Sandra Díaz – Josef Settele – Eduardo Brondízio et al., 2019, IPBES/7/10/Add.1, <https://www.ipbes.net/ipbes710add1arpdf> (visited on 11.05.2023)

IPBES, *Summary for Policymakers of the Methodological Assessment Regarding the Diverse Conceptualization of Multiple Values of Nature and its Benefits, Including Biodiversity and Ecosystem Functions and Services*, July 2022, IPBES/9/L.13, <https://vert.eco/wp-content/uploads/2022/07/IPBES_SPM_ValuesAssessment_11Jul2022.pdf> (visited on 08.11.2024)

IPCC, *Climate Change 2007 – Synthesis Report*, 2007, <https://www.ipcc.ch/site/assets/uploads/2018/02/ar4_syr_full_report.pdf> (visited on 31.07.2023)

IPCC, *Climate Change 2014 – Mitigation of Climate Change*, 2014, <https://www.ipcc.ch/report/ar5/wg3/> (visited on 21.07.2023)

IPCC, *Global Warming of 1.5°C – Summary for Policymakers*, 2018, <https://www.ipcc.ch/site/assets/uploads/sites/2/2022/06/SPM_version_report_LR.pdf> (visited on 16.03.2023)

Istanbul Metropolitan Municipality, *Kanal İstanbul Çalıştay Raporu*, 10 January 2020, <https://kanal.istanbul/wp-content/uploads/2021/12/kanal_istanbul_calistay_raporu.pdf> (visited on 29.08.2023)

Knox, John H., *Report of the Independent Expert on the Issue of Human Rights Obligations Relating to the Enjoyment of a Safe, Clean, Healthy and Sustainable Environment – Compilation of Good Practices*, OHCHR, A/HRC/28/61, 3 February 2015, <https://documents-dds-ny.un.org/doc/UNDOC/GEN/G15/017/26/PDF/G1501726.pdf?OpenElement> (visited on 26.05.2023)

Knox, John H., *Report of the Special Rapporteur on the Issue of Human Rights Obligations Relating to the Enjoyment of a Safe, Clean, Healthy and Sustainable Environment*, UN Human Rights Council, A/HRC/34/49, 19 January 2017, <https://undocs.org/Home/Mobile?FinalSymbol=A%2

FHRC%2F34%2F49&Language=E&DeviceType=Desktop&Lang Requested=False> (visited on 16.05.2023)

Morello-Frosch, Rachel – Pastor, Manuel – Sadd, James – Shonkoff, Seth B., *The Climate Gap: Inequalities in How Climate Change Hurts Americans & How to Close the Gap*, University of Southern California, Los Angeles, 2009, <https://dornsife.usc.edu/assets/sites/242/docs/The_Climate_Gap_Full_Report_FINAL.pdf> (visited on 01.08.2023)

OXFAM, *Extreme Carbon Inequality*, (press release), <https://oxfamilibrary.openrepository.com/bitstream/10546/582545/9/mb-extreme-carbon-inequality-021215-en.pdf> (visited on 20.03.2023)

PNUD, *Rapport sur le développement humain – 2011*, <https://ise.unige.ch/isdd/IMG/pdf/HDR_2011_FR_Complete.pdf> (visited on 02.10.2024)

Smith, Dan – Vivekananda, Janani, *A Climate of Conflict: The Links Between Climate Change, Peace and War*, International Alert, November 2007, <https://www.international-alert.org/publications/climate-conflict/> (visited on 31.07.2023)

Tom Swann, *High Carbon from a Land Down Under: Quantifying CO_2 from Australia's Fossil Fuel Mining and Exports*, The Australia Institute, July 2009, <https://australiainstitute.org.au/wp-content/uploads/2020/12/P667-High-Carbon-from-a-Land-Down-Under-WEB_0_0.pdf> (visited on 02.09.2023)

UK Government Office of Science, *Future Flooding*, Executive Summary, <https://assets.publishing.service.gov.uk/government/uploads/system/uploads/attachment_data/file/300332/04-947-flooding-summary.pdf> (visited on 31.08.2023)

UN, *The Sustainable Development Goals Report 2022*, <https://unstats.un.org/sdgs/report/2022/> (visited on 11.05.2023)

UN Committee on the Rights of the Child, *General Comment No. 26 on Children's Rights and the Environment, with a special focus on climate change*, CRC/C/GC/26, 2023, <https://www.ohchr.org/en/documents/general-comments-and-recommendations/general-comment-no-26-2023-childrens-rights-and> (visited on 30.08.2023)

UN General Assembly, *Right to a Healthy Environment: Good Practices*, A/HRC/43/53, 30 December 2019, <https://undocs.org/Home/Mobile?FinalSymbol=A%2FHRC%2F43%2F53&Language=E&DeviceType=Desktop&LangRequested=False> (visited on 12.05.2023)

UN Human Rights Committee, *General Comment No. 36 on Article 6: Right to Life*, CCPR/C/GC/36, 2018, <https://www.ohchr.org/en/calls-for-input/general-comment-no-36-article-6-right-life> (visited on 16.05.2023)

UNEP, *Global Environment Outlook – 4*, 2007, <https://www.unep.org/geo/geo-resources/geo-4> (visited on 19.04.2023)

UNEP, *Global Environmental Outlook: GEO6 – Summary for Policymakers*, 2019, <https://www.unep.org/resources/assessment/global-environment-outlook-6-summary-policymakers> (visited on 12.05.2023)

Union of Concerned Scientists, 'World Scientists' Warning to Humanity', 1992, <https://www.ucsusa.org/resources/1992-world-scientists-warning-humanity#:~:text=We%20the%20undersigned%2C%20senior%20members,not%20to%20be%20irretrievably%20mutilated>. (visited on 20.03.2023)

WWF, *Living Planet Report 2022 – Building a Nature Positive Society*, R. E. A. Almond – M. Grooten – D. Juffe Bignoli – T. Petersen (ed.), Gland, Switzerland, 2022, <https://wwfint.awsassets.panda.org/downloads/embargo_13_10_2022_lpr_2022_full_report_single_page_1.pdf> (visited on 07.08.2023)

Decisions

Bangladesh

Supreme Court, *Human Rights and Peace for Bangladesh and Others v. Secretary of the Ministry of Shipping and Others*, WP no. 13989 of 2016, 30 January and 3 February 2019, <http://files.harmonywithnatureun.org/uploads/upload1130.pdf> (visited on 21.06.2023)

Canada

Supreme Court, *Tsilhqot'in Nation v. British Columbia*, SCC 44, 26 June 2014, <https://scc-csc.lexum.com/scc-csc/scc-csc/en/item/14246/index.do> (visited on 14.01.2025)

Colombia

Supreme Court, *Future Generation v. Ministry of Environment and Others*, Decision no. STC4360-2018, Radicación no. 11001-22-03-000-2018-00319-01,

5 April 2018, <https://www.elaw.org/CO_Amazon> and <https://cortesuprema.gov.co/corte/wp-content/uploads/2018/04/STC4360-2018-2018-00319-011.pdf> (visited on 07.06.2023)

Constitutional Court, *Center for Social Justice Studies and Others v. Presidency of the Republic and Others*, Decision no. T-622/16, 10 November 2016, <http://files.harmonywithnatureun.org/uploads/upload838.pdf> (visited on 14.01.2025)

Ecuador

Constitutional Court, decision no. 166-15-SEP-CC, case no. 0507-12-EP, 20 May 2015, <https://www.derechosdelanaturaleza.org.ec/wp-content/uploads/casos/Ecuador/Jurisprudencia/Sentencia%20166-15-SEP-CC.pdf> (visited on 24.05.2023)

Constitutional Court, decision no. 253-20-JH/22, case no. 253-20-JH, 27 January 2022, <https://animal.law.harvard.edu/wp-content/uploads/Final-Judgment-Estrellita-w-Translation-Certification.pdf> (English translation by Carolina Aguilera Marinovic) (visited on 27.08.2023)

Loja District Court of Justice, *Richard Frederick Wheeler y Eleanor Geer Huddle v. Director de la Procuraduria General Del Estado de Loja*, decision no. 11121-2011-0010, 30 March 2011, <https://www.elaw.org/content/juicio%2011121-2011-0010> (visited on 14.01.2025)

European Court of Human Rights

Carême v. France, application no. 7189/21 (Grand Chamber, 9 April 2024)

Claudia Duarte Agostinho and Others v. Portugal and 32 Other States, application no. 39371/20 (Grand Chamber, 9 April 2024)

Roman Zakharov v. Russia, application no. 47143/06 (Grand Chamber, 4 December 2015)

Verein KlimaSeniorinnen Verein and Others v. Switzerland, application no. 53600/20 (Grand Chamber, 9 April 2024)

Germany

Federal Constitutional Court, *Neubauer and Others v. Germany*, 1 BvR 2656/18, 1 BvR 288/20, 1 BvR 96/20, 1 BvR 78/20, 24 March 2021, <https://www.bundesverfassungsgericht.de/SharedDocs/Entscheidungen/EN/2021/03/rs20210324_1bvr265618en.html> (visited on 10.01.2025)

Federal Constitutional Court, BVerfGE 58, 300, 15 July 1981, <https://www.servat.unibe.ch/dfr/bv058300.html> (visited on 07.10.2024)

India

Supreme Court, *Subhash Kumar v. State of Bihar and Ors*, AIR 420, 1991 SCR (1) 5, 9 January 1991, <https://indiankanoon.org/doc/1646284/> (visited on 25.05.2023)

Uttarakhand Supreme Court, *Lalit Miglani v. State of Uttarakhand*, (PIL) No. 140 of 2015, 30 March 2017, <https://indiankanoon.org/doc/92201770/> (visited on 20.06.2023)

Uttarakhand Supreme Court, *Mohd. Salim v. State of Uttarakhand*, (PIL) No. 126 of 2014, 20 March 2017, <https://www.ielrc.org/content/e1704.pdf> (visited on 19.06.2023)

Uttarakhand Supreme Court, *Narayan Dutt Bhatt v. Union of India and Others*, (PIL) No. 43 of 2014, 4 July 2018, <https://indiankanoon.org/doc/157891019/> (visited on 20.06.2023)

Inter-American Court of Human Rights

Kaliña and Lokono Peoples v. Suriname, Decision, 25 November 2015, <https://www.corteidh.or.cr/docs/casos/articulos/seriec_309_ing.pdf> (visited on 22.05.2023)

Indigenous Communities of Lhaka Honhat (Our Land) v. Argentina, Decision, 6 February 2020, <https://www.corteidh.or.cr/docs/casos/articulos/seriec_400_ing.pdf> (visited on 22.05.2023)

Advisory Opinion OC-23/17, 15 November 2017, <https://www.corteidh.or.cr/docs/opiniones/seriea_23_ing.pdf> (visited on 22.05.2023)

International Court of Justice

Pulp Mills on the River Uruguay (Argentina v. Uruguay), Decision, 20 April 2010, <https://www.icj-cij.org/case/135/judgments> (visited on 14.01.2025)

Ireland

Supreme Court, *Friends of the Irish Environment v. Ireland*, Decision no. 793 JR, 31 July 2020, <http://climatecasechart.com/non-us-case/friends-of-the-irish-environment-v-ireland/> (visited on 10.07.2023)

Nigeria

Gbemre v. Shell Petroleum Development Co Nigeria Ltd, FHC/B/CS/53/05, 14 November 2005, <https://www.globalhealthrights.org/wp-content/uploads/2013/02/HC-2005-Gbemre-v.-Shell-Petroleum-Development-Company-and-Ors..pdf> (visited on 04.09.2023)

Pakistan

Lahor Supreme Court, *Ashgar Leghari v. Federation of Pakistan*, W. P. No. 25501/201, <http://climatecasechart.com/non-us-case/ashgar-leghari-v-federation-of-pakistan/> (visited on 05.07.2023)

Supreme Court, *Shehla Zia and Others v. WAPDA*, PLD SC 693, 1994, <https://elaw.org/pk.shehla.zia.1994> (visited on 25.05.2023)

South Africa

Constitutional Court, *EarthLife Africa Johannesburg v. Minister of Environmental Affairs and Others*, Decision no. 65662/16, <http://climatecasechart.com/non-us-case/4463/> (visited on 06.07.2023)

The Netherlands

Supreme Court, *Urgenda Foundation v. The Netherlands*, Decision no. 19/00135, 20 December 2019, <http://climatecasechart.com/non-us-case/urgenda-foundation-v-kingdom-of-the-netherlands/> (visited on 06.07.2023)

The Philippines

Supreme Court, *Metropolitan Manila Bay Development Authority v. Concerned Residents of Manila Bay*, G. R. Nos. 171947-48, 18 December 2008, <https://leap.unep.org/countries/ph/national-case-law/metropolitan-manila-bay-development-authority-v-concerned-residents> (visited on 07.06.2023)

Supreme Court, *Minors Oposa v. Secretary of the Department of Environment and Natural Resources*, 33 I. L. M. 173 (1994), 30 July 1993, <http://hrlibrary.umn.edu/research/Philippines/Oposa%20v%20Factoran,%20GR%20No.%20101083,%20July%2030,%201993,%20on%20the%20State's%20Responsibility%20To%20Protect%20the%20Right%20To%20Live%20in%20a%20Healthy%20Environment.pdf> (visited on 25.05.2023)

The United States

US Supreme Court, *Sierra Club v. Morton*, 405 U.S. 727, 19 April 1972, <https://caselaw.findlaw.com/court/us-supreme-court/405/727.html> (visited on 22.06.2023)

US Supreme Court, *Massachusetts v. EPA*, 549 U.S. 497, 2 April 2007, <https://supreme.justia.com/cases/federal/us/549/497/> (visited on 02.08.2023)

Montana District Court, *Held v. Montana*, CDV-2020-307, <https://climatecasechart.com/case/11091/> (visited on 01.09.2023)

Oregon Federal Court, *Juliana v. United States*, 6:15-cv-01517, <https://climatecasechart.com/case/juliana-v-united-states/> (visited on 01.09.2023)

Türkiye

Constitutional Court, E. 2006/99, K. 2009/9, 15 January 2009, <https://normkararlarbilgibankasi.anayasa.gov.tr/ND/2009/9?EsasNo=2006%2F99> (visited on 21.01.2025)

United Nations

Committee on the Rights of the Child, *Sacchi and Others v. Argentina and Others*, CRC/C/88/D/105/2019, <https://tbinternet.ohchr.org/_layouts/15/treatybodyexternal/SessionDetails1.aspx?SessionID=1351&Lang=en> (visited on 12.12.2022)

Committee on the Rights of the Child, 'Open Letter to the Authors', <https://www.ohchr.org/sites/default/files/2021-12/Open_letter_on_climate_change.pdf> (visited on 02.09.2023)

Human Rights Committee, *Daniel Billy and Others v. Australia*, CCPR/D/135/D/3624/2019, <https://tbinternet.ohchr.org/_layouts/15/treatybodyexternal/Download.aspx?symbolno=CCPR%2FC%2F135%2FD%2F3624%2F2019&Lang=en> (visited on 14.01.2025)

Internet

'1 December 1955: Rosa Parks Ignites Bus Boycott', *History*, <https://www.history.com/this-day-in-history/rosa-parks-ignites-bus-boycot> (visited on 23.08.2023)

'10 Landmark Climate Change Cases', *Client Earth*, July 2022, pp. 5–6, <https://www.clientearth.org/latest/documents/10-landmark-climate-change-cases/> (visited on 04.02.2023)

'2013 State of the Climate: Record-Breaking Super Typhoon Haiyan', *Climate.gov*, 13 July 2014, <https://www.climate.gov/news-features/understanding-climate/2013-state-climate-record-breaking-super-typhoon-haiyan> (visited on 20.09.2024)

'A Landmark Ruling for Animal Rights in Ecuador', *Nonhuman Rights*, 23 March 2022, <https://www.nonhumanrights.org/blog/landmark-ruling-animal-rights-ecuador/> (visited on 27.08.2023)

'Aarhus Convention', *UNFCCC*, <https://unfccc.int/documents/45192?gclid=CjwKCAjw3dCnBhBCEiwAVvLcu2R76KcpexATC7QqIQFeOfD9wQDV-7wlDlCg8W0M2KXN1Q-y0wiJFxoCWMoQAvD_BwE> (visited on 03.09.2023)

'Afro-Colombians', *Wikipedia*, <https://en.wikipedia.org/wiki/Afro-Colombians> (visited on 15.06.2023)

Ahmed, Kaamil, 'Rich Countries 'Trap' Poor Countries into Relying on Fossil Fuels', *The Guardian*, 21 August 2023, <https://www.theguardian.com/global-development/2023/aug/21/rich-countries-trap-poor-nations-into-relying-on-fossil-fuels?CMP=Share_AndroidApp_Other&utm_source=pocket_saves> (visited on 02.09.2023)

Ali, Tawfique, 'Time to Declare Turag Dead', *The Daily Star*, 6 November 2016, <https://www.thedailystar.net/frontpage/time-declare-turag-dead-1310182> (visited on 15.08.2023)

Ambrose, Jillian, 'The Deep History of British Coal – From the Romans to the Ratcliff Shutdown', *The Guardian*, 30 September 2024, <https://www.theguardian.com/business/2024/sep/30/the-deep-history-of-british-coal-from-the-romans-to-the-ratcliffe-shutdown> (visited on 01.10.2024)

'Anthropocene', *National Geographic*, <https://education.nationalgeographic.org/resource/anthropocene/> (visited on 21.03.2023)

Anthropocene Working Group, 'Results of Binding Vote by AWG, Released 21 May 2019', <http://quaternary.stratigraphy.org/working-groups/anthropocene/> (visited on 13.07.2023)

Astier, Marie, 'Les ONG Climat Réclament Plus d'Un Milliard d'Euro à l'État', *Reporterre*, 14 June 2023, <https://reporterre.net/Les-ONG-climat-reclament-plus-d-un-milliard-d-euros-a-l-Etat#:~:text=Trois%20ONG%20

ont%20demand%C3%A9%20le,mesures%20n%C3%A9cessaires%20pour%20le%20climat>. (visited on 11.07.2023)

Badshah, Nadeem, 'July Was World's Hottest Month on Record, Climate Scientists Confirm', *The Guardian*, 8 August 2023, <https://www.theguardian.com/environment/2023/aug/08/july-2023-worlds-hottest-month-climate-crisis-scientists-confirm?utm_source=pocket_saves> (visited on 14.08.2023)

'Bakan Özhaseki: Türkiye'nin Yeni Sıcaklık Rekoru 49.5°C ile Eskişehir'de Kırıldı', *Yeşil Gazete*, 16 August 2023, <https://yesilgazete.org/bakan-ozhaseki-turkiyenin-yeni-sicaklik-rekoru-495c-ile-eskisehirde-kirildi/> (visited on 21.08.2023)

Bellamy, Daniel, 'The Richest Country in Europe Is Celebrating Three Years of Free Public Transport', *Euronews*, 22 March 2023, <https://www.euronews.com/green/2023/03/22/richest-country-in-europe-marks-third-year-of-free-public-transport> (visited on 31.03.2023)

Blattner, Charlotte, 'Separation of Powers and KlimaSeniorinnen', *Verfassungsblog*, 30 April 2024, <https://verfassungsblog.de/separation-of-powers-and-klimaseniorinnen/> (visited on 23.09.2024)

Bönnemann, Maxim, 'Litigating Enforcement: Germany's Contested Climate Governance and the New Wave of Climate Litigation', *Climate Law – A Sabin Center Blog*, 12 December 2023, <https://blogs.law.columbia.edu/climatechange/2023/12/12/litigating-enforcement-germanys-contested-climate-governance-and-the-new-wave-of-climate-litigation/> (visited on 09.10.2024)

Bönnemann, Maxim – Tigre, Maria Antonia, 'The Transformation of European Climate Change Litigation' *Verfassungsblog*, 9 April 2024, <https://verfassungsblog.de/the-transformation-of-european-climate-change-litigation/> (visited on 14.06.2024)

'Brazil, Rio Grande de Sul – Floods – Emergencey Appeal No: MDRBR011', *ReliefWeb*, 13 May 2024, <https://reliefweb.int/report/brazil/brazil-rio-grande-do-sul-floods-emergency-appeal-no-mdrbr011> (visited on 20.09.2024)

Buckley, Cara – Kelter Davis, Jamie, 'The Giving Forest', *New York Times*, 22 April 2023, <https://www.nytimes.com/2023/04/22/climate/menominee-forest-sustainable-earth-day.html?utm_source=pocket_saves> (visited on 25.04.2023)

Buis, Alan, 'The Atmosphere: Getting a Handle on Carbon Dioxide', *NASA*, 9 October 2019, <https://climate.nasa.gov/news/2915/the-atmosphere-getting-a-handle-on-carbon-dioxide/#:~:text=Once%20it's%20added%20to%20the,timescale%20of%20many%20human%20lives>. (visited on 10.08.2023)

'Call for Emergency Action to Limit Global Temperature Increases, Restore Biodiversity, and Protect Health', *The BMJ*, 2021: 374, <https://www.bmj.com/content/374/bmj.n1734> (visited on 04.05.2023)

Carbonaro, Giulia, 'Seven new oil and gas projects approved since IPCC report called for an end to fossil fuels', *Euronews*, 15 April 2022, <https://www.euronews.com/green/2022/04/10/seven-new-oil-and-gas-projects-approved-since-ipcc-report-called-for-an-end-to-fossil-fuel> (visited on 17.03.2023)

Carpenter, Scott, 'After Abandoned 'Beyond Petroleum' Re-Brand, BP's New Renewables Push Has Teeth', *Forbes*, 4 August 2020, <https://www.forbes.com/sites/scottcarpenter/2020/08/04/bps-new-renewables-push-redolent-of-abandoned-beyond-petroleum-rebrand/?sh=116f49c11ceb> (visited on 17.03.2023)

Chandran, Rina, 'Fears of Eviction as Bangladesh Gives Rivers Legal Rights', *Reuters*, 4 July 2019, <https://www.reuters.com/article/us-bangladesh-landrights-rivers-idUSKCN1TZ1ZR> (visited on 22.06.2023)

'China and India Lead Global Renewable Energy Transition', *United Nations Climate Change*, 21 April 2017, <https://unfccc.int/news/china-and-india-lead-global-renewable-energy-transition?gclid=Cj0KCQjwzdOlBhCNARIsAPMwjbwac5YLC2C-w6kJR5BCdnmg2GO-63GhpckJxR_78FPSYUoduTfGwrwaAhPSEALw_wcB> (visited on 18.07.2023)

Chrisafis, Angelique, 'Who Are the Gilets Jaunes and What Do They Want?', *The Guardian*, 7 December 2018, <https://www.theguardian.com/world/2018/dec/03/who-are-the-gilets-jaunes-and-what-do-they-want> (visited on 31.08.2023)

'Clean Air Act Text', *EPA*, <https://www.epa.gov/clean-air-act-overview/clean-air-act-text> (visited on 02.08.2023)

'Climate Change and Future Generations Lawsuit in Colombia: Key Excerpts from the Supreme Court's Decision', *Dejusticia*, 13 April 2018, <https://www.dejusticia.org/en/climate-change-and-future-generations-lawsuit-in-colombia-key-excerpts-from-the-supreme-courts-decision/> (visited on 16.06.2023)

'Climate Change and Health', *UN World Health Organization*, 30 October 2021, <https://www.who.int/news-room/fact-sheets/detail/climate-change-and-health> (visited on 21.08.2023)

'Climate Change New Opportunity to Renew Old Orders', *Down to Earth*, 15 April 2008, <https://www.downtoearth.org.in/news/climate-change-new-opportunity-to-renew-old-orders-4400> (visited on 18.07.2023)

'Climate Change Widespread, Rapid and Intensifying – IPCC', *IPCC*, 9 August 2021, <https://www.ipcc.ch/2021/08/09/ar6-wg1-20210809-pr/> (visited on 04.08.2023)

'Climate Indicators Explorer', *US Environmental Protection Agency*, <https://edap.epa.gov/public/extensions/CCIDataViewer/CCIDataViewer.html#greenhouse-gases&atm-conc-ghg> (visited on 19.07.2023)

'Climate Policy', *Government of Netherlands*, <https://www.government.nl/topics/climate-change/climate-policy#:~:text=Judgment%20in%20the%20climate%20case,Foundation%20against%20the%20Dutch%20State> (visited on 04.09.2023)

'CO_2 Emissions Per Capita', *Worldometer*, <https://www.worldometers.info/co2-emissions/co2-emissions-per-capita/> (visited on 03.02.2023)

'Comments of the Swiss Government on Admissibility and the Merits, I. Preliminary Comments', *Climate Case Chart*, <https://climatecasechart.com/non-us-case/union-of-swiss-senior-women-for-climate-protection-v-swiss-federal-council-and-others/> (visited on 04.10.2024)

'Constitution of the Republic of Ecuador', *Political Database of the Americas (Georgetown University)*, <https://pdba.georgetown.edu/Constitutions/Ecuador/english08.html> (visited on 13.06.2023)

Corkery, Michael, 'A Giant Factory Rises to Make a Product Filling Up The World: Plastic', *New York Times*, 12 August 2019, <https://www.nytimes.com/2019/08/12/business/energy-environment/plastics-shell-pennsylvania-plant.html> (visited on 28.08.2023)

'Court Decision on Llurimagua – Rights of Nature Case – Ecuador', *Global Alliance for the Rights of Nature*, 12 November 2020, <https://www.garn.org/court-decision-on-llurimagua-rights-of-nature-case-ecuador/> (visited on 13.06.2023)

Cusick, Daniel, 'Phoenix Roast in Record Breaking 110-Plus-Degree Heat, With No End in Sight', *Scientific American*, 17 July 2023, <https://www.

scientificamerican.com/article/phoenix-roasts-in-record-breaking-110-plus-degree-heat-with-no-end-in-sight/?utm_source=pocket_saves> (visited on 14.08.2023)

'Daniel Billy and others v Australia (Torres Strait Islanders Petition)', *Climate Case Chart*, <http://climatecasechart.com/non-us-case/petition-of-torres-strait-islanders-to-the-united-nations-human-rights-committee-alleging-violations-stemming-from-australias-inaction-on-climate--change/> (visited on 03.02.2023)

Doherty, Ben – Roy, Eleanor Ainge, 'World Bank: Let Climate-Threatened Pacific Islanders Migrate to Australia or NZ', *The Guardian*, 8 May 2017, <https://www.theguardian.com/environment/2017/may/08/australia-and-nz-should-allow-open-migration-for-pacific-islanders-threatened-by-climate-says-report> (visited on 31.07.2023)

Doyle, Alister – Solsvik, Terje, 'Norway's Government Wins Arctic Oil Lawsuit, Greens Lose', *Reuters*, 4 January 2018, <https://www.reuters.com/article/us-climatechange-norway/norways-government-wins-arctic-oil-lawsuit-greens-lose-idUSKBN1ET1KW?utm_source=pocket_saves> (visited on 02.09.2023)

Echevarría, Hugo, 'When Courts Meet Nature: A Real Case on Rights of Nature', *Vermont Journal of Environmental Law (blog)*, 18 August 2018, <https://vjel.vermontlaw.edu/courts-meet-nature-real-case-rights-nature> (visited on 13.06.2023 – not accessible as of 08.01.2025)

'Ecuadorians Reject Oil Drilling in the Amazon, Ending Operations in Protected Area', *Associated Press*, 21 August 2023, <https://apnews.com/article/amazon-ecuador-oil-drilling-referendum-yasuni-5c72a325755976c47a3ec138bdab8537> (visited on 21.08.2023)

'Erdoğan İklim Sözlerinden Çark Etti: Türkiye'nin Kömür Gerçekleri', *Yeşil Gazete*, 8 August 2023, <https://yesilgazete.org/erdoganin-soylediginin-aksine-komur-gercekleri/> (visited on 19.08.2023)

Frost, Rosie, 'Fossil fuel firms set to spend more than €800 bn on new oil and gas fields by 2030', *Euronews*, 13 April 2023, <https://www.euronews.com/green/2022/04/12/world-s-biggest-oil-and-gas-companies-projected-to-spend-more-than-800bn-on-new-fields-by-#:~:text=in%20the%20City-,Fossil%20fuel%20firms%20set%20to%20spend%20more%20than%20%E2%82%AC800bn,and%20gas%20fields%20by%202030&text=The%20world's%20biggest%20oil%20and,and%20gas%20fields%20by%202030>. (visited on 17.03.2023)

Ganesan, Pranav, 'Not Just Another ECtHR Judgement: Analysis of KlimaSeniorinnen Schweiz v Switzerland (Part 1 of 3)', *Climate Rights Database*, 18 April 2024, <https://climaterightsdatabase.com/2024/04/18/not-just-another-ecthr-judgment-analysis-of-klimaseniorinnen-schweiz-v-switzerland-part-1-of-3/> (visited on 23.082024)

Gebru, Girmay – Juma, Mercy, 'Ethiopia's Tigray Crisis: Deaths From Starvation After Aid Halted – Official', *BBC*, 18 August 2023, <https://www.bbc.com/news/world-africa-66540039> (visited on 21.08.2023)

Greene, Natalie, 'The First Successful Case of the Rights of Nature Implementation in Ecuador', *GARN*, 21 May 2011, <https://www.garn.org/first-ron-case-ecuador/> (visited on 03.07.2023)

Greenfield, Patrick – Watts, Jonathan, 'JP Morgan Economists Warn Climate Crisis Is Threat to Human Race', *The Guardian*, 21 February 2020, <https://www.theguardian.com/environment/2020/feb/21/jp-morgan-economists-warn-climate-crisis-threat-human-race#:~:text=JP%20Morgan%20economists%20warn%20climate%20crisis%20is%20threat%20to%20human%20race,-This%20article%20is&text=The%20world's%20largest%20financier%20of,according%20to%20a%20leaked%20document> (visited on 29.03.2023)

Income Per Capita, Atlas Method (current US$), 2022, <https://data.worldbank.org/indicator/NY.GNP.PCAP.CD> (visited on 11.04.2023)

Haiven, Max, 'Our Age of Uprisings: We Are a Remaking Itself', *ROAR*, Issue 11, <https://roarmag.org/magazine/our-age-of-uprisings/> (visited on 21.01.2025)

Hansen, James, 'Game Over for the Climate', *The New York Times*, 9 May 2012, <https://www.nytimes.com/2012/05/10/opinion/game-over-for-the-climate.html?auth=login-google1tap&login=google1tap> (visited on 19.07.2023)

Harvey, Fiona, 'IPCC issues 'bleakest warning yet' on impacts of climate breakdown', *The Guardian*, 28 February 2022, <https://www.theguardian.com/environment/2022/feb/28/ipcc-issues-bleakest-warning-yet-impacts-climate-breakdown#:~:text=IPCC%20issues%20'bleakest%20warning%20yet'%20on%20impacts%20of%20climate%20breakdown,-This%20article%20is&text=Climate%20breakdown%20is%20accelerating%20rapidly,Change%20(IPCC)%20has%20said> (visited on 17.03.2023)

Harvey, Fiona, 'UK to defy net zero targets with more oil and gas drilling', *The Guardian*, 6 April 2022, <https://www.theguardian.com/environment/2022/apr/06/uk-more-oil-gas-drilling-north-sea-energy-security-strategy-kwasi-kwarteng-net-zero-targets#:~:text=The%20UK%20government%20is%20set,emissions%20instead%20of%20raising%20them> (visited on 17.03.2023)

Henley, Jon, 'Death Toll Exceeds 180 as Germany and Belgium Hit by Devastating Floods', *The Guardian*, 18 July 2021, <https://www.theguardian.com/world/2021/jul/16/western-germany-floods-angela-merkel-horror-catastrophe-deaths-missing-search-flooding-belgium> (visited on 19.08.2023)

Henley, Jon, 'Spain and southern France hit by second extreme heat event this year', *The Guardian*, 13 June 2022, <https://www.theguardian.com/world/2022/jun/13/spain-and-southern-france-hit-by-second-extreme-heat-event-of-year> (visited on 17.03.2023)

'Indigenous People's Rights Are Violated in the Name of Conservation', *OHCHR*, 26 August 2016, <https://www.ohchr.org/en/stories/2016/08/indigenous-peoples-rights-violated-name-conservation> (visited on 31.08.2023)

IUGS, 'The Anthropocene', <https://www.iugs.org/_files/ugd/f1fc07_40d1a7ed58de458c9f8f24de5e739663.pdf?index=true> (visited on 17.09.2024.)

Jensen, Derrick, 'Forget Shorter Showers', *Orion*, 7 July 2009, <https://orionmagazine.org/article/forget-shorter-showers/> (visited on 21.01.2025)

Kalmus, Peter, 'Joe Biden Must Declare A Climate Emergency. And He Must Do So Now', *The Guardian*, 27 July 2023, <https://www.theguardian.com/commentisfree/2023/jul/27/joe-biden-climate-emergency-peter-kalmus> (visited on 27.07.2023)

Kaminski, Isabella, 'The Hague Becomes World's First City to Pass Law Banning Fossil Fuel-related Ads', *The Guardian*, 13 September 2024, <https://www.theguardian.com/world/2024/sep/13/the-hague-becomes-worlds-first-city-to-ban-fossil-fuel-related-ads> (visited on 08.11.2024)

Keeling, Ralph, *in* 'Atmosferde İklim Tarihinin En Yoğun Karbondioksiti Birikti: 415,5 ppm', *Yeşil Gazete*, 16 May 2019, <https://yesilgazete.org/atmosferde-insanlik-tarihinin-en-yogun-karbondioksiti-birikti-4155-ppm/> (visited on 18.08.2023)

Kingsnorth, Paul – Hine, Dougald, *Uncivilisation – The Dark Mountain Manifesto*, The Dark Mountain Project, <https://dark-mountain.net/about/manifesto/> (visited on 06.04.2023)

Kusnetz, Nicholas, 'Canada's Tar Sands: Destruction So Vast and Deep It Challenges the Existence of Land and People', *Inside Climate News*, 21 November 2021, <https://insideclimatenews.org/news/21112021/tar-sands-canada-oil/> (visited on 19.07.2023)

'L'Affaire du Siècle: L'État Poursuivi Pour Inaction Climatique', *Oxfam France*, <https://www.oxfamfrance.org/laffairedusiecle/> (visited on 11.07.2023)

'Latest CO_2 Daily', *CO_2-Earth*, <https://www.co2.earth/daily-co2#:~:text=417.04%20ppm&text=This%20table%20presents%20the%20most,Source%20%3D%20NOAA%20GML>. (04.08.2023 visited on)

Lawson, Alex, 'BP criticised over plan to spend billions more on fossil fuels than green energy', *The Guardian*, 27 December 2022, <https://www.theguardian.com/business/2022/dec/27/bp-plan-spend-billions-fossil-fuels-green-energy-oil-gas-renewables> (visited on 17.03.2023)

Letsas, George, 'Did the Court in Klimaseniorinnen Create an Actio Popularis?', *EJIL:Talk!*, 13 May 2024, <https://www.ejiltalk.org/did-the-court-in-klimaseniorinnen-create-an-actio-popularis/> (visited on 23.08.2024)

Levantesi, Stella, 'Italian Oil Firm Eni Faces Lawsuit Alleging Early Knowledge of Climate Crisis', *The Guardian*, 9 May 2023, <https://www.theguardian.com/environment/2023/may/09/italian-oil-firm-eni-lawsuit-alleging-early-knowledge-climate-crisis?utm_source=pocket_saves> (visited on 28.08.2023)

Lindsey, Rebecca, 'Climate Change: Atmospheric Carbon Dioxide', *Climate.gov*, 12 May 2023, <https://www.climate.gov/news-features/understanding-climate/climate-change-atmospheric-carbon-dioxide#:~:text=In%20May%202023%2C%20carbon%20dioxide,people%20are%20burning%20for%20energy> (visited on 19.07.2023)

Lodge, Terry, 'Building Our Children's Trust Needs to Start with Reality', *CELDF*, 11 May 2022, <https://celdf.org/2022/05/building-our-childrens-trust-needs-to-start-with-reality/> (visited on 08.03.2023)

Lula Da Silva, *in* 'Carbon Credits – Land Grab or the Amazon's Future', *BBC*, 8 August 2023, <https://www.bbc.com/news/world-latin-america-66435166> (visited on 08.08.2023)

Maden, Tuğba Evrim, 'Suriye'de İç Savaş ve Değişen Su Güvenliği', *ORSAM*, 27 November 2014, <https://www.orsam.org.tr/tr/suriye-de-ic-savas-ve-degisen-su-guvenligi/> (visited on 31.08.2023)

Malcomson, Scott, 'How China Became the World's Leader in Green Energy', *Foreign Affairs*, 28 February 2020, <https://www.foreignaffairs.com/articles/china/2020-02-28/how-china-became-worlds-leader-green-energy?gad=1&gclid=Cj0KCQjwzdOlBhCNARIsAPMwjbyztEAdTezFC2RCyE4cNpa0tgm51ILPx0f5l9CrHbC970oEx7PcjlEaAlVCEALw_wcB> (visited on 18.07.2023)

Malik, Saurabh, 'HC: Sukhna Lake of Chandigarh Is Legal Entity, Raze Buildings in Catchment Area', *The Tribune India*, 3 March 2020, <https://www.tribuneindia.com/news/chandigarh/hc-sukhna-lake-of-chandigarh-is-legal-entity-raze-buildings-in-catchment-area-50017#google_vignette> (visited on 21.06.2023)

Markey, Edward J., 'Private Jets Are Awful for the Climate. It's Time to Tax the Rich Who Fly in Them', *The Guardian*, 10 August 2023, <https://www.theguardian.com/commentisfree/2023/aug/10/private-jets-are-awful-for-the-climate-its-time-to-tax-the-rich-who-fly-in-them?CMP=twt_a-environment_b-gdneco> (visited on 10.08.2023)

'Massachusetts v. EPA', *Wikipedia*, <https://en.wikipedia.org/wiki/Massachusetts_v._EPA> (visited on 02.08.2023)

Milman, Oliver, ''Godfathers of Climate Chaos': UN Chief Urges Global Fossil-fuel Advertising Ban', *The Guardian*, 5 June 2024, <https://www.theguardian.com/environment/article/2024/jun/05/antonio-guterres-un-chief-fossil-fuels-advertising> (visited on 08.11.2024)

Mogul, Rhea – Mitra, Esha – Suri, Manveena – Saifi, Sophia 'India and Pakistan Heatwave is 'testing the limits of human survivability' experts say', *CNN*, 2 May 2022, <https://edition.cnn.com/2022/05/02/asia/india-pakistan-heatwave-climate-intl-hnk/index.html> (visited on 17.03.2023)

Mulvaney, Kieran, 'Climate change already worse than expected, says new UN report', *National Geographic*, 28 February 2022, <https://www.nationalgeographic.com/environment/article/climate-change-already-worse-than-expected-un-report> (visited on 17.03.2023)

Nilsen, Ella, 'Biden administration approves controversial Willow oil drill project in Alaska, which has galvanized online activism', *CNN*, 14 March 2023, <https://edition.cnn.com/2023/03/13/

politics/willow-project-alaska-oil-biden-approval-climate/index.html#:~:text=The%20Biden%20administration%20has%20approved,owned%20by%20the%20federal%20government>. (visited on 17.03.2023)

Niranjan, Ajit, 'G20 Poured More Than $1tn into Fossil Fuel Subsidies Despite COP26 Pledges – Report', *The Guardian*, 23 August 2023, <https://www.theguardian.com/environment/2023/aug/23/g20-poured-more-than-1tn-on-fossil-fuel-subsidies-despite-cop26-pledges-report> (visited on 23.08.2023)

Nolan, Aoife, 'Inter-generational Equity, Future Generations and Democracy in the European Court of Human Rights' Klimaseniorinnen Decision', *EJIL:Talk!*, 15 April 2024, <https://www.ejiltalk.org/inter-generational-equity-future-generations-and-democracy-in-the-european-court-of-human-rights-klimaseniorinnen-decision/> (visited on 23.09.2024)

'One Health', *United Nations*, 21 September 2017, <https://www.who.int/news-room/questions-and-answers/item/one-health> (visited on 07.10.2024)

'Oslo Manifesto for Ecological Law and Governance', *Ecological Law and Governance Association*, June 2016, <https://elgaworld.org/oslo-manifesto> (visited on 08.05.2023)

Pagano, Mario, 'Urban Commons, From Italy to Europe', *Transformative Private Law Blog*, 21 July 2023, <https://transformativeprivatelaw.com/urban-commons-from-italy-to-europe/> (visited on 01.09.2023)

Pareek, Surbhi, *Case Analysis – Subhash Kumar v. State of Bihar, 1991*, <https://judicateme.com/wp-content/uploads/2021/11/Subhash-Kumar-v.-State-of-Bihar_JudicateMe.pdf> (visited on 25.05.2023)

Piketty, Thomas, 'The Illusion of Centrist Ecology', *Le Monde*, 11 June 2019, <https://www.lemonde.fr/blog/piketty/2019/06/11/the-illusion-of-centrist-ecology/> (visited on 10.08.2023)

Poynting, Mark – Rivault, Erwan – Dale, Becky, '2024 First Year to Pass 1.5C Global Warming Limit', *BBC*, 10 January 2025, <https://www.bbc.com/news/articles/cd7575x8yq5o?utm_source=pocket_reader> (visited on 12.01.2025)

Pressly, Linda, 'The Island People With a Climate Change Escape Plan', *BBC*, 21 September 2017, <https://www.bbc.com/news/magazine-41337815> (visited on 21.08.2023)

Prietro, Gustavo, 'The Los Cedros Forest Has Rights', *Verfassungsblog*, 10 December 2021, <https://verfassungsblog.de/the-los-cedros-forest-has-rights/> (visited on 04.09.2023)

Prior, Ryan, 'An Ohia City Has Voted to Grant Lake Erie the Same Right as a Person', *CNN*, 27 February 2019, <https://edition.cnn.com/2019/02/21/us/ohio-city-lake-erie-rights-trnd/index.html> (visited on 23.06.2023)

'Power Plants and Neighboring Communities', *EPA*, <https://www.epa.gov/power-sector/power-plants-and-neighboring-communities#:~:text=On%20January%2027%2C%202021%2C%20Climate,Over%20age%2064>. (visited on 02.04.2024)

'Rights of Nature Case Study – Mount Taranaki / Taranaki Maunga', *Anima Mundi Law Initiative*, <http://files.harmonywithnatureun.org/uploads/upload1136.pdf> (visited on 14.06.2023)

Record of Understanding for Mount Taranaki, Pouākai and the Kaitake Ranges, 20 December 2017, <https://www.govt.nz/assets/Documents/OTS/Taranaki-Maunga/Taranaki-Maunga-Te-Anga-Putakerongo-Record-of-Understanding-20-December-2017.pdf> (visited on 14.06.2023)

Redfearn, Graham, 'Tanya Plibersek Approves Three Coalmine Expansions in Move Criticised as 'the Opposite of Climate Action'', *The Guardian*, 24 September 2024, <https://www.theguardian.com/australia-news/2024/sep/24/tanya-plibersek-approves-three-coal-mine-expansions-in-move-criticised-as-the-opposite-of-climate-action> (visited on 03.10.2024)

Reich, Johannes – Hausammann, Flora – Boss, Nina Victoria, 'Climate Change Litigation Before the ECtHR', *Verfassungsblog*, 16 May 2022, <https://verfassungsblog.de/climate-change-litigation-before-the-ecthr/> (visited on 12.06.2024)

Roy, Eleanor Ainge, 'New Zealand Gives Mount Taranaki Same Legal Rights as a Person', *The Guardian*, 22 December 2017, <https://www.theguardian.com/world/2017/dec/22/new-zealand-gives-mount-taranaki-same-legal-rights-as-a-person> (visited on 14.06.2023)

Rowlatt, Justin, 'Climate Change is Turbo-Charging Somalia's Problems – But There's Still Hope', *BBC*, 18 September 2024, <https://www.bbc.com/news/articles/c62rr5qe602o?utm_source=pocket_shared> (visited on 20.09.2024)

Roy, Eleanor Ainge, 'New Zealand River Granted Same Legal Rights as Human Being', *The Guardian*, 16 March 2017, <https://www.theguardian.com/world/2017/mar/16/new-zealand-river-granted-same-legal-rights-as-human-being> (visited on 15.06.2023)

Samuel, Sigal, 'Lake Erie Now Has Legal Rights, Just Like You', *VOX*, 26 February 2019, <https://www.vox.com/future-perfect/2019/2/26/18241904/lake-erie-legal-rights-personhood-nature-environment-toledo-ohio> (visited on 22.06.2023)

Sanchez, Ray, 'Hawaii Has a Robust Emergency Siren Warning System. It Sat Silent During the Deadly Wildfires', *CNN*, 13 August 2023, <https://edition.cnn.com/2023/08/12/us/hawaii-emergency-warning-system-maui-wildfires/index.html> (visited on 28.08.2023)

Shabecoff, Philip, 'Global Warming Has Begun, Expert Tells Senate', *The New York Times*, 24 June 1988, <https://www.nytimes.com/1988/06/24/us/global-warming-has-begun-expert-tells-senate.html> (visited on 21.07.2023)

Shearman, David, 'Democracy and Climate Change: A Story of Failure', *Open Democracy*, 7 November 2007, <https://www.opendemocracy.net/en/democracy_and_climate_change_a_story_of_failure/> (visited on 18.07.2023)

'Shell Molymers Monaca', *Shell*, <https://www.shell.us/about-us/projects-and-locations/shell-polymers.html> (visited on 28.08.2023)

'Sierra Club v. Morton', *Wikipedia*, <https://en.wikipedia.org/wiki/Sierra_Club_v._Morton#cite_note-Sierra_Club_v._Hickel-8> (visited on 22.06.2023)

Singh, Maanvi, 'Republican Hopefuls Shrug When Asked About Climate Crisis During Debate', *The Guardian*, 24 August 2023, <https://www.theguardian.com/us-news/2023/aug/24/republican-hopefuls-shrug-when-asked-about-climate-crisis-during-debate> (visited on 28.08.2023)

Slow, Oliver, 'US Refuses Climate Reparations for Developing Nations', *BBC*, 14 July 2023, <https://www.bbc.com/news/world-us-canada-66197366> (visited on 14.07.2023)

Soloski, Alexis, 'Los Angeles Is Starring in an All-Too-Real Disaster Story', *The New York Times*, 11 January 2025, <https://www.nytimes.com/2025/01/11/arts/television/los-angeles-fires-disaster.html> (visited on 12.01.2025)

Solnit, Rebecca, 'Big Oil Coined 'Carbon Footprint' to Blame Us for Their Greed. Keep Them on the Hook', *The Guardian*, 23 August 2021, <https://www.theguardian.com/commentisfree/2021/aug/23/big-oil-coined-carbon-footprints-to-blame-us-for-their-greed-keep-them-on-the-hook> (visited on 18.08.2023)

Soysal, Ahmet, 'ABD'de Gençler Küresel İklim Değişikliğine Karşı Hukuk Mücadelesini Kazandı', *Yeşil Gazete*, 26 August 2023, <https://yesilgazete.org/abdde-gencler-kuresel-iklim-degisikligine-karsi-hukuk-mucadelesini-kazandi/?utm_source=pocket_saves> (visited on 01.09.2023)

Stallard, Esme, 'What is Loss and Damage and Will Rich Nations Pay for Climate Change?', *BBC*, 20 November 2022, <https://www.bbc.com/news/science-environment-63478446> (visited on 14.07.2023)

Şafak, Elif, 'In the Battle to Save the World's Forests, Women are Leading the Resistance', *The Guardian*, 26 August 2023, <https://www.theguardian.com/commentisfree/2023/aug/26/world-forests-women-akbelen-turkey-india-brazil-developers?CMP=Share_AndroidApp_Other&utm_source=pocket_saves> (visited on 31.08.2023)

Tanuro, Daniel, 'Impacts of warming faster and more severe than expected says IPCC', *International View Point*, 3 March 2022, <https://internationalviewpoint.org/spip.php?article7546> (visited on 17.03.2023)

Te Awa Tupua (Whanganui River Claims Settlement) Act 2017 (NZ), 2017/7, *ILO*, <https://www.ilo.org/dyn/natlex/natlex4.detail?p_lang=en&p_isn=108218&p_country=NZL&p_count=502> (visited on 14.06.2023)

Te Urewera Act 2014 (No. 51), *FAO*, <https://www.fao.org/faolex/results/details/en/c/LEX-FAOC159972/> (visited on 14.06.2023)

'The Carbon Market', *UNFCCC*, <https://unfccc.int/process/conferences/pastconferences/bali-climate-change-conference-december-2007/statements-and-resources/the-carbon-market?gclid=Cj0KCQjw84anBhCtARIsAISI-xf0M2OuMIVRkcH2JC1mbvyPCgIY57fzG5Mgc-D1F-PF67HGKV-TJz4aAtY5EALw_wcB> (visited on 20.08.2023)

'The Charter of the Forest', *The Canadian Encyclopedia*, <https://www.thecanadianencyclopedia.ca/en/article/the-charter-of-the-forest#:~:text=Carta%20of%201215.-,The%201217%20Charter%20of%20the%20Forest%20(Carta%20de%20Foresta)%20is,continue%20to%20the%20present%20day>. (visited on 14.08.2023)

'The Glorious Revolution', *House of Commons Information Office*, Factsheet G4 – General Series, August 2010, <https://www.parliament.uk/globalassets/documents/commons-information-office/g04.pdf> (visited on 17.08.2023)

'The Paris Agreement', *UNFCCC*, <https://unfccc.int/process-and-meetings/the-paris-agreement> (visited on 01.09.2023)

'THK Uçakları Uçmasın, Yeşil Yansın Diye Her Şey Yapıldı', *Cumhuriyet*, 30 June 2021, <https://www.cumhuriyet.com.tr/haber/thk-ucaklari-ucmasin-yesil-yansin-diye-her-sey-yapildi-1848534> (visited on 28.08.2023)

'Turag River Case', *Human Rights and Peace for Bangladesh*, <http://hrpb.org.bd/upload/judgement/Writ-Petition-No.-13989-of-2016-only-17-directions--River-Turag-Case.pdf> (visited on 22.06.2023)

UN Women, *Explainer: How Gender Inequality and Climate Change are Interconnected*, 28 February 2022, <https://www.unwomen.org/en/news-stories/explainer/2022/02/explainer-how-gender-inequality-and-climate-change-are-interconnected?gclid=Cj0KCQjw9MCnBhCYARIsAB1WQVVaL7t5Be1bix8jiuDxKCvkoiTjYFV3_k3jLy5S4eqIL7of_BXO3uwaAg4bEALw_wcB> (visited on 31.08.2023)

'Une Décision Historique du Conseil d'État pour la Justice Climatique', *Oxfam France*, 27 November 2020, <https://www.oxfamfrance.org/climat-et-energie/une-decision-historique-du-conseil-detat-pour-la-justice-climatique/> (visited on 11.07.2023)

Union of Concerned Scientists, 'World Scientists' Warning to Humanity', 1992, <https://www.ucsusa.org/resources/1992-world-scientists-warning-humanity#:~:text=We%20the%20undersigned%2C%20senior%20members,not%20to%20be%20irretrievably%20mutilated>. (visited on 20.03.2023)

'United Nations Conference on Environment and Development, Rio de Janeiro, Brazil, 3–14 June 1992', *United Nations*, <https://www.un.org/en/conferences/environment/rio1992> (visited on 26.07.2023)

United Nations, 'World Urbanization Prospects: The 2018 Revision (Key Facts)', <https://population.un.org/wup/Publications/Files/WUP2018-KeyFacts.pdf> (visited on 08.03.2023)

Ursula K. LeGuin, the speech in acceptance of the National Book Foundation Medal for Distinguished Contribution to American Letters,

19 November 2014, <https://www.ursulakleguin.com/nbf-medal> (visited on 28.01.2025)

Vaughan, Adam, 'Global Carbon Emissions From Energy Hit a Record High', *New Scientist*, 26 March 2019, <https://www.newscientist.com/article/2197643-global-carbon-emissions-from-energy-hit-a-record-high-in-2018/> (visited on 01.09.2023)

'Water: At the Center of Climate Crisis', *UN*, <https://www.un.org/en/climatechange/science/climate-issues/water?gclid=CjwKCAjwloynBhBbEiwAGY25dEFIsDsrWvT4nMtM3yoJeYLtS_fWFMRwFhRUWwVprAvC8w_ijPkawRoCS0sQAvD_BwE> (visited on 21.08.2023)

'Western North American extreme heat virtually impossible without human-caused climate change', *World Weather Attribution*, 7 July 2021, <https://www.worldweatherattribution.org/western-north-american-extreme-heat-virtually-impossible-without-human-caused-climate-change/> (visited on 17.03.2023)

Willson, Edward O., 'The 8 Million Species We Don't Know', *The New York Times*, 3 March 2018, <https://www.nytimes.com/2018/03/03/opinion/sunday/species-conservation-extinction.html> (visited on 05.04.2023)

World Emissions, <www.worldemission.io> (visited on 30.08.2023)

'Yasuní – ITT', *Wikipedia*, <https://en.wikipedia.org/wiki/Yasun%C3%AD-ITT_Initiative> (visited on 03.08.2023)

Zeller, Tom Jr, 'Why Teenagers Are Suing States over Climate Change', *Forbes*, 8 April 2015, <https://www.forbes.com/sites/tomzeller/2015/04/08/why-teenagers-are-suing-states-over-climate-change/?sh=3d3482d71704> (visited on 08.03.2023)

Index

www.ingramcontent.com/pod-product-compliance
Ingram Content Group UK Ltd.
Pitfield, Milton Keynes, MK11 3LW, UK
UKHW041822031026
15587UKWH00002B/501

9 783631 936634